School Dropout and Completion

Stephen Lamb · Eifred Markussen
Richard Teese · Nina Sandberg · John Polesel
Editors

School Dropout
and Completion

International Comparative Studies in Theory and Policy

 Springer

Editors
Prof Stephen Lamb
University of Melbourne
Centre for Post-Compulsory Education
and Lifelong Learning
Melbourne Graduate School of Education
Parkville Victoria
Australia 3010
lamb@unimelb.edu.au

Eifred Markussen
NIFU
Wergelandsveien 7
0167 Oslo
Norway
eifred.markussen@nifu.no

Prof Richard Teese
University of Melbourne
Centre for Post-Compulsory
Education and Lifelong Learning
Melbourne Graduate School of Education
Parkville Victoria
Australia 3010
rvteese@unimelb.edu.au.

Nina Sandberg
NIFU
Wergelandsveien 7
0167 Oslo
Norway
nina.sandberg@nifu.no

John Polesel
University of Melbourne
Parkville Victoria
Australia 3010

ISBN 978-90-481-9762-0   e-ISBN 978-90-481-9763-7
DOI 10.1007/978-90-481-9763-7
Springer Dordrecht Heidelberg London New York

Printed on acid-free paper

Springer is part of Springer Science+Business Media (www.springer.com)

Acknowledgements

The preparation of this book was made possible through the generous support of the research and administrative staff of the Centre for Post-Compulsory Education and Lifelong Learning (CPELL) in the Melbourne Graduate School of Education at the University of Melbourne. We particularly wish to thank Robyn Klepetko, Tim Jones, Lyn Robinson, Sue Helme and Genevieve Bunyan for their valuable and generous assistance.

Special thanks go to Beverly Bavaro, Editor and Web Manager for the California Dropout Research Project, for her expert editorial work with various parts of the manuscript.

An earlier version of Chapter 2 was prepared as a report for the California Dropout Research Project. The support from the project and its director, Russell Rumberger, is gratefully acknowledged.

The project was also supported by the Albert and Elaine Borchard Foundation, Pasadena, California, which provided a generous grant allowing contributing authors to meet, discuss and advance the work at a colloquium held in France. We want to thank Kristen Beling for her hospitality while hosting the colloquium.

We would also like to thank the publishing staff at Springer Publishing, in particular Yoka Janssen, Astrid Noordermeer and Harmen van Paradijs.

Contents

List of Tables

List of Figures

Contributors

Sherri L. Bisset
Postdoctoral Fellow, School Environment Research Group, University of Montreal, Canada

Marianne Blanchard
Researcher, Centre Maurice Halbwachs, École Normale Supérieure, France

Kristjana Stella Blondal
University of Iceland, Iceland

Jorunn Spord Borgen
Research Professor, NIFU Nordic Institute for Studies in Innovation, Research and Education, Norway

Mari Wigum Frøseth
Researcher, NIFU Nordic Institute for Studies in Innovation, Research and Education, Norway

Maribel Garcia
Assistant Lecturer, Department of Sociology, Autonomous University of Barcelona, Spain

Michel Janosz
Professor and Director, School Environment Research Group, University of Montreal, Canada

Tero Järvinen
Senior Researcher, Centre for Research on Lifelong Learning and Education, University of Turku, Finland

Jón Torfi Jónasson
Professor and Dean, Department of Education, University of Iceland, Iceland

Ewa Kurantowicz
Professor of Education, University of Lower Silesia, Poland

Stephen Lamb
Professor and Deputy Director, Centre for Post-Compulsory Education and
Lifelong Learning, University of Melbourne, Australia

Ben Levin
Professor and Canada Research Chair in Education Leadership and Policy,
Ontario Institute for Studies in Education, University of Toronto, Canada

Berit Lødding
Senior Researcher, NIFU Nordic Institute for Studies in Innovation,
Research and Education, Norway

Eifred Markussen
Head of Research in Primary and Secondary Education, NIFU Nordic Institute for
Studies in Innovation, Research and Education, Norway

Rafael Merino
Lecturer, Education and Work Research Group (GRET), Autonomous University
of Barcelona, Spain

Piotr Mikiewicz
Assistant Professor, International Institute for the Study of Culture and Education,
University of Lower Silesia, Poland

Adrianna Nizińska
Researcher, University of Lower Silesia, Poland

Linda S. Pagani
Professor, School Environment Research Group, University of Montreal, Canada

Elisabetta Pagnossin
Research Associate, Institut de Recherche et de Documentation pédagogique (IRDP),
Switzerland

John Polesel
Associate Professor, Melbourne Graduate School of Education,
University of Melbourne, Australia

David Raffe
Professor of Sociology of Education, Centre for Educational Sociology,
University of Edinburgh, United Kingdom

Andrea Reupold
Lecturer, Institute of Pedagogy and Educational Research,
Ludwig-Maximilians-University Munich, Germany

Risto Rinne
Professor and Director, Centre for Research on Lifelong Learning and Education,
University of Turku, Finland

Russell W. Rumberger
Professor of Education, Gevirtz Graduate School of Education,
University of California, Santa Barbara, United States

Nina Sandberg
Head of Research in Primary and Secondary Education, NIFU Nordic Institute for
Studies in Innovation, Research and Education, Norway

Rémi Sinthon
Centre Maurice Halbwachs, École Normale Supérieure, France

Alice Sullivan
Senior Lecturer, Institute of Education, University of London, United Kingdom

Anne-Christin Tannhäuser
Researcher, School of Education, University of Iceland, Iceland

Richard Teese
Professor and Director, Centre for Post-Compulsory Education and Lifelong
Learning, University of Melbourne, Australia

Rudolf Tippelt
Professor and Director, Institute of Pedagogy and Educational Research,
Ludwig-Maximilians-University Munich, Germany

Lorna Unwin
Professor of Vocational Education, Institute of Education, University of London,
United Kingdom

Role of Editors

The editorial work for this book has been shared with the order of editors reflecting the relative contributions. The ideas for this comparative work on dropout and completion had their origins in a study undertaken by Stephen Lamb for the California Dropout Research Project, and the current book was developed as part of the ongoing program of work of the International Research Network on Youth Education and Training (IRNYET). The research members of IRNYET, covering a range of OECD nations, share a common interest in research on education systems and student outcomes and are working currently on a major program of collaborative research on schools and youth transitions.

Stephen Lamb, who took the lead in overseeing and coordinating the various stages of work for this book, would like to thank his co-editors for their various contributions. He, along with the co-editors, express thanks to all of the authors in the book for their important and valued contributions.

Chapter 1
School Dropout and Completion: An International Perspective

Stephen Lamb and Eifred Markussen

Introduction

In most OECD countries, graduation from secondary school is now viewed as the minimum level of educational attainment needed for successful participation of young people in further study and work. This is because in most nations, secondary education serves as the foundation for entry to university and other education and training opportunities as well as preparation for entry into the labour market. Over time, it has become more and more important in deciding how economic and other life benefits, such as good health and well-being, are distributed. Despite this, in some countries, the numbers of young people leaving school without completing a relevant upper secondary qualification can be quite large. Even in nations where the numbers appear small, this does not guarantee that education systems have met all of the challenges in adequately equipping every graduate with the basic skills and knowledge necessary to take advantage of the full range of education and labour market opportunities. When it comes to rates of school completion and promoting universal attainment of upper secondary qualifications, all school systems display patterns of success and failure, which are more or less marked Every system has 'failure' – varying numbers of young people who fail to gain an upper secondary qualification – though the level of failure may be concealed or debated depending on the measures that are used. The social patterns of dropout suggest that in all countries, the opportunities and benefits associated with successful completion are difficult to penetrate for 'non-traditional' users. Yet, some systems have been more successful than others in promoting high rates of completion and providing programs that accommodate the majority of young people. This book offers a systematic analysis of how different school systems work and the impact of differences in institutional and program arrangements on patterns of student dropout and completion.

S. Lamb (✉)
Centre for Post-Compulsory Education and Lifelong Learning, University of Melbourne, Australia

E. Markussen
NIFU Nordic Institute for Studies in Innovation, Research and Education, Norway

S. Lamb et al. (Eds.), *School Dropout and Completion: International Comparative Studies in Theory and Policy*, DOI 10.1007/978-90-481-9763-7_1,
© Springer Science+Business Media B.V. 2011

There has been ongoing interest across all nations in the issue of secondary school dropout and completion and part of the reason for this has to do with the consequences. While rates of school dropout and completion vary across western nations, one thing that does not vary much is the finding that, for individuals, not completing school and failing to gain equivalent education and training qualifications is associated with poorer labour market outcomes. Consistently, research in different countries shows that dropouts are more likely to become unemployed, stay unemployed for longer, have lower earnings and over their life course accumulate less wealth (e.g., see Rumberger & Lamb, 2003; OECD, 2001; Barro, 1997; Shavit & Mueller, 1998). Dropouts also more often experience poorer physical and mental health, have higher rates of crime and less often engage in active citizenship (Owens, 2004; Rumberger, 1987). In addition to the costs for individuals, there are also social costs associated with increased welfare needs and reduced taxation revenue (Owens, 2004).

In response to these issues, governments have been seeking policies to increase rates of secondary school completion and reduce dropout. Addressing the problem of dropout, however, presents a major test for education and training systems. For any system, the challenge in encouraging more young people to remain at school is finding ways to deal with pupil diversity. In all countries, young people who leave school before obtaining an upper secondary qualification tend to come from disadvantaged social and racial backgrounds, they tend more often to have become disengaged from school, are less motivated scholastically and more often experience personal difficulties and behavioural issues that place them at risk. They also tend to have histories of school failure and low academic achievement during the compulsory years. In the past, many systems have not needed or attempted to provide for all young people in an inclusive way within the school system at upper secondary level. Encouraging more low achievers and other young people at risk of dropout to remain at school and complete an upper secondary qualification exerts great pressure on the flexibility of institutional arrangements and qualification structures.

Responses to these issues vary across nations, depending on the organisation and structure of upper secondary education. One type of response is to diversify the range of opportunities available at upper secondary level within the school sector in order to encourage young people to remain in school and graduate. This sort of approach, with a focus on accommodating young people within the school sector, involves what might be termed 'internal differentiation strategies', that is, strategies internal to school systems, which seek to reduce the problem of dropout by changing or expanding the sorts of opportunities available in post-compulsory programs and the requirements for entry and successful completion. Two broad types are evident:

1. Some countries have attempted to expand opportunities by offering alternative qualifications in the senior school years. This can be done in separate single-purpose schools as in China or Germany. However, even where students attend a single school type, different courses may be offered according to the students' ability or interest, such as in Australia or New Zealand. These courses may lead to different levels of qualification and therefore, grant access to different educational

and employment opportunities. Some European and other OECD countries have made serious efforts to encourage more students to remain in secondary school and to improve qualification rates by diversifying the sorts of programs and qualifications provided in the post-compulsory years. For example, in the 1980s and 1990s, Finland, Sweden and Norway implemented a number of educational reforms focusing largely on expanding vocational education options as a means of encouraging students to participate in and complete upper secondary. All three nations saw growth in upper secondary graduation rates (OECD, 2001).

2. Other countries provide alternative options within the same qualification to address pupil diversity. Within a school type, the students may be directed towards different tracks leading to a similar qualification. Some countries offer upper secondary diplomas based on satisfactory achievement in a core of common subjects, a block of subjects specific to the chosen area of study and a range of elective subjects. The requirements for qualification can vary substantially across systems. Sweden and the United States offer credit-based models, in which each course provides a set number of points that may be accumulated over the course of the program towards high school graduation and the attainment of a high school diploma. Other systems, such as those in England and many jurisdictions in Australia, require students to successfully complete a set minimum number of subjects to qualify for a school certificate, even if the specific subjects can vary substantially across types and fields of study.

In terms of the different approaches to the provision of senior school programs and qualifications, there can be substantial variation within as well as across countries. Federated systems, such as those in the United States and Australia can have different approaches, qualifications and completion requirements across jurisdictions. For example, the recent introduction of exit exams in California as a hurdle requirement to graduation sets this state apart from others in the United States. Similarly, in Australia, the state of Victoria provides an alternative senior school certificate to the mainstream diploma, while other states and territories do not.

School-based diversification strategies are not the only focus of efforts to respond to non-completion. Some countries provide alternative pathways to work and adult life for young people who are no longer at school and who left without gaining a qualification. This reflects more of a focus on 'external diversification strategies' to provide alternative opportunities for young people, particularly dropouts. These strategies can include extended opportunities for school graduation through recovery programs or study in alternative settings, provision of a breadth and depth of alternative qualifications and study opportunities through further education colleges, provision of work-based indentured training contracts such as apprenticeships, and alternative routes involving combinations of work, training and study.

It is possible for countries to employ both types of approaches – to encourage young people to remain in school and gain a qualification through the provision of more diversified senior school offerings and to strengthen the range of post-school pathways available to those who leave without at first gaining a qualification from school. Such approaches are evident in several systems and reflect the continuing tension between effort to prevent school dropout and strategies to assist those who have already dropped out. One facet of this tension is the potential for successful alternative pathways outside of the school system to act to encourage larger numbers of young people to leave school before completing a qualification. This sort of counter-effect needs to be considered in assessing the value, impact and importance of alternative pathways.

Countries differ in the upper secondary school programs that they offer and how these are provided. The aim of this book is to compare and evaluate various approaches by evaluating their impact on rates of dropout and completion. It involves an examination of different approaches to provision and how well they work in delivering mass completion rates while maintaining high and even standards. Case studies of national systems will be used to highlight the different approaches including institutional arrangements and the various alternative secondary school programs and their outcomes. The evaluation will be based around several key questions: What are the main approaches? How do they work? For whom do they work? And, how successful are they in promoting high rates of completion and equivalent outcomes for all?

Defining and Measuring Completion and Dropout

Central to this book is a comparative analysis of school dropout and completion across nations. In some respects, this is a difficult and challenging task. The very terms present major issues when comparing national systems. For example, the term 'dropout' is used mainly in the United States and Canada to refer to young people who leave school without gaining a high school diploma. It is a term used rarely by the statistical agencies, education authorities and research centres of other countries. Other nations have similar concepts, such as 'early school leaving' and 'not in education, employment or training' (NEET), but these are measured differently. This also applies when looking at the notion of 'school completion.' This is referred to as 'graduation' in some contexts, while other systems tend to employ measures such as 'retention to the final year' and 'obtaining an upper secondary certificate or equivalent.' In some systems, such as in England and Scotland, there is no concept of school completion or graduation. After a young person reaches the end of compulsory schooling, usually at the age of 16, the level, duration, mode and content of learning vary widely and until recently, there has not been a standard or benchmark by which to judge whether an individual completes secondary education or not (Raffe, 2010).

Despite these differences, there is consensus around the need to measure educational productivity based on completion and there is shared understanding of some of the principal concepts, such as dropout or early school leaver. To illustrate this point, Table 1.1 shows how a dropout is defined by researchers from different countries who wrote case study chapters for this book and were asked to use

Table 1.1 Definitions of a dropout used by researchers in 13 different countries

Country	A dropout is defined as someone who
Australia	leaves school before Year 12 (the final year of secondary school) or begins Year 12 but leaves without obtaining an upper secondary qualification
Canada	has not successfully completed high school and is not enrolled in education or in a work study program
England	does not hold an upper secondary qualification and is no longer in education, employment or training
Finland	does not hold an upper secondary qualification and is no longer in education, employment or training
France	is no longer in school and did not reach the recognised standard of achievement in the final year of their academic or vocational study
Germany	leaves school without gaining any official upper secondary qualification or certificate
Iceland	by the age of 24 has not completed an upper secondary qualification
Norway	left upper secondary education before the final year or who remained to the end, but failed to fulfil the graduation requirements
Poland	has not completed an upper secondary qualification in the 'regular' or specified period
Scotland	does not hold an upper secondary qualification and is no longer in education, employment or training
Spain	enrols in the *baccalaureate* or in vocational training but does not complete it
Switzerland	as an 18- to 24-year-old has not successfully completed post-compulsory education and does not enter another type of training
USA	does not complete a high school diploma or equivalent credential

national data to reflect national circumstances and institutional arrangements When looking at the table, it is quite clear that all of the definitions actually share a similar understanding of a dropout and that is of a person who is no longer at school and does not hold an upper secondary qualification. While there may be classificatory distinctions based on current activity at the time of being measured (whether being in further education, employment or training), there is a broadly comparable view on who a dropout is.

However, shared understandings tend to fall away when it comes to measuring how many dropouts there are. There are few common measures. While systems may have a similar view about what dropout is, they do not share a similar way of measuring it. Even within countries, there is sometimes little consensus on how to measure dropout and completion. In the United States, for example, different agencies and jurisdictions often use different definitions of dropout. There are three different measures that tend to be used: the event dropout rate, the status dropout rate and the cohort dropout rate (Laird et al., 2006). The event rate measures the percentage of a specified or given group (such as students of a particular age enrolled in high school) who drop out of school in a particular time period, such as a single year. The status dropout rate measures the percentage in a population or sub-population (such as 16- to 24-year-olds) who are not enrolled in a high school program and do not hold a high school diploma. The cohort rate refers to the rate of dropping out within an age or grade cohort over a specified period of time, such as the percentage of students in Grade 8 who had not attained a high school diploma by the age of 20. Each measure can produce different estimates and lead to different conclusions about the dimensions of dropout and completion.

Measuring dropout and completion across nations is also made complex by the levels of diversification involving programs (certificates and qualifications) and institutions. In some systems, such as the United States, Canada and Sweden, students who fulfil the graduation requirements for upper secondary education receive a diploma that permits them, theoretically at least, to continue their studies in higher education in both academic and vocational programs. However, this is not the case in a range of other countries where only a proportion of those who complete upper secondary education will receive qualifications enabling access to higher level academic programs. In the Netherlands, for example, the majority of students complete upper secondary education, but only a minority (about one third or less of all students) become qualified to enter university study. The reason is that upper secondary education is divided into separate tracks, often located in different types of schools, leading to different qualifications: academic (*voorbereidend wetenschappelijk onderwijs* or VWO), vocational (*voorbereidend middelbaar beroepsonderwijs* or VMBO) and technical (*hoger algemeen voortgezet onderwijs* or HAVO). The diversity of programs and qualifications raises issues of equivalence in cross-national comparisons, of whether graduation or completion in one system provides the same foundation, and means the same, as in another.

This issue is often a source of debate within, let alone across, systems. For example, there is considerable debate within the United States about the role of the General Education Development (GED) certificate as an equivalent to the high school diploma, because research suggests that the earnings and employment returns to those with the GED certificate are significantly less than the returns to those with the regular high school diploma (e.g., Cameron & Heckman, 1993; Heckman & LaFontaine, 2006). Therefore, should dropouts who attain the GED be counted as high school graduates or not? The same issue applies in comparative analyses of systems that offer vastly different types of upper secondary qualifications. Should shorter cycle upper secondary vocational qualifications available in some systems be treated as equivalent (in terms of the quality of learning and levels of skills acquisition) to longer cycle upper secondary programs provided in the same system, as well as to those in other systems? Students who complete vocational programs in upper secondary education in some systems are often qualified to enter higher-level vocational programs or seek entry to the labour market but not to pursue academic higher education leading to the professions. These differences need to be considered in making cross-national comparisons.

It is also the case in comparisons of dropout and completion rates that these terms are not necessarily complementary or equal opposites. It is possible for young people who drop out of school to later 'complete' by either returning to school or finishing their study in another setting. It is also possible for some young people to remain at school until the end of their school program and in some systems, therefore, be counted as completers, yet they fail to complete the requirements for graduation. In some systems there is also a level of flexibility allowing young people to change programs or undertake their study in alternative settings without age restrictions. Graduation and dropout rates will then vary depending on the point or age at which they are measured.

The point or age at which dropout and completion are measured is important when comparing systems. The modal age at which young people complete upper secondary programs varies across systems, but in most systems, it is between 17 and 20 years of age. However, some systems provide flexibility in study options, in length of time to complete and in provision for study in alternative adult settings outside of secondary school systems. Therefore, if a modal completion age, such as 19 years, is used as the point at which to count those who have completed an upper secondary qualification or not, this might underestimate real completion levels and overestimate dropout rates in those systems. It is possible to make a distinction between 'initial' or 'modal time' estimates of dropout and completion based on measurements using modal ages and grade cohorts (notwithstanding differences in grade repeating) and 'later point' estimates, which are based on a delayed or older age for measurement (such as age 24 or more), in order to take account of varying arrangements (as illustrated in Fig. 1.1). In systems that have more flexible arrangements, later point estimates are likely to reveal lower dropout rates and higher completion rates than those obtained as initial estimates. The differences between initial and later point estimates are themselves likely to reveal important cross-national differences in the organisation and arrangements of programs and institutions and in opportunities.

There is also a need to consider starting points in making cross-national comparisons. Some countries only measure dropout and completion in the upper secondary years. In Norway, for example, official dropout and completion rates are often based on the cohort of students entering upper secondary education (Statistics Norway, 2009). Therefore, students who dropped out between the end of compulsory education and the beginning of upper secondary education are not counted. In other systems, the rates can reflect status and activities across all stages of schooling. In some systems, such as in the United States and Canada, concepts such as 'compulsory' and 'post-compulsory' education, 'lower secondary,' and 'upper

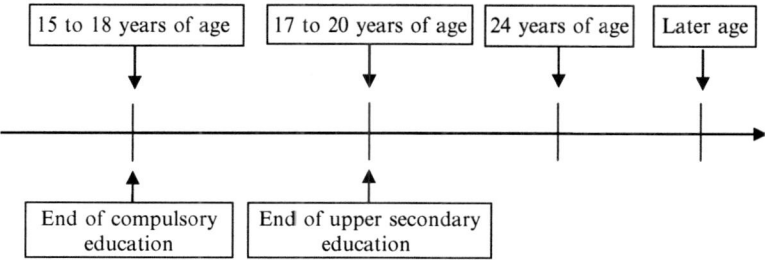

Fig. 1.1 When to measure dropout and completion?

secondary' do not have much meaning. Generally, high school covers Grades 9–12 and bridges the phases of lower and upper secondary defined in some other systems. Cohort estimates using longitudinal data often relate to those entering high school, which would be lower secondary or compulsory education in many European systems. The distinctions become an issue if in those systems where it is relevant, there are varying numbers of students who drop out of school before or at the end of compulsory schooling and who are not included when estimating the rates of dropout and completion.

While comparing dropout and completion across countries, it is, therefore, important to recognise that countries use different measures and classifications of dropout and completion. This is partly due to differences in the sorts of data that different countries employ. There are few commonly designed data sets with which to calculate comparable estimates. Some countries use administrative records while others use longitudinal survey data, data from school census returns, school leaver surveys or national population census surveys. Measures, classifications and sources of data vary. There is no common base or denominator: some use birth cohorts, others use age cohorts and some grade cohorts. Similarly, there is no common end or estimation point at which to count the numbers of completers and dropouts: sometimes it is at age 19, sometimes in the age range 20–24, and sometimes in the final school year.

Despite these differences, all systems recognise the importance of school attainment and report in a similar way on attainment levels, and most have measures of discontinuation ('early school leaving,' 'dropout,' 'NEET'). Even if there is variation in the classifications and methods of calculation, behind these differences there are commonalities making it possible to arrive at some shared and consistent understandings for comparing levels of dropout and completion across systems. Nearly all OECD nations can report on the proportion of an age group (such as 20- to 24-year-olds or a specific age, such as 20-year-olds) no longer in education or training and without an upper secondary qualification. This is often used by the European Union countries to define and report rates of early school leaving (e.g., see Van Es, 2008). It is very similar to the status dropout rate reported in the United States (see Laird et al., 2006) and age attainment rates reported in other countries such as Australia (see Lamb & Mason, 2008). Completion or graduation rates are often obtained using the same method, but not counting as completers those who are still enrolled in education or training and who have not yet attained an upper secondary qualification means that dropout and completion rates are not complementary. Of course, comparisons using such rates do not take into account equivalence of programs. Upper secondary qualifications and graduation requirements can vary in terms of quality, inclusiveness and criteria for attainment.

In this book, the aim is to use such measures to evaluate the scale and dimensions of school dropout and completion across different OECD countries. The indicator that is most frequently used in international comparisons of school completion is the upper secondary graduation rate reported annually in OECD's *Education at a Glance* (e.g., see OECD, 2008a). The rate is derived by dividing the number of upper secondary graduates in each country by the total population at the typical age of graduation (multiplied by 100). One problem with using this measure is that it tends to inflate estimates in systems where upper secondary courses are of varying durations and can span different ages, such as in Germany, Greece and Norway. For example, the reported upper secondary graduation rate for Norway in 2004 was 100% – 86% for males and 114% for females (OECD, 2006). The rates reported by national sources in Norway place upper secondary completion at closer to 70% (Markussen et al., 2008; Statistics Norway, 2009). The preference in this book is to use published and reported estimates from recognised sources within each country rather than estimates based on international comparisons using the OECD indicator. Where available, cohort rates will be used in order to capture the number of young people of a given age or entering grade who, at a given point of measurement, have either attained an upper secondary qualification (completion) or who have not (dropout). As the focus of the book is on how different school systems work and the impact of differences in institutional and program arrangements on patterns of student dropout and completion, it will be important to obtain not only single national estimates, but also estimates for different programs and different groups. This will permit comparison of the roles of alternative programs and qualifications operating in different systems.

Social Inequality and School Completion

Despite international variations in dropout and completion rates, research undertaken in various countries reveals similar profiles of the characteristics of those who complete and those who drop out (e.g., see Rumberger & Lim, 2008, on the United States; Lamb et al., 2004, on Australia; Markussen et al., 2008, on Norway; the Applied Research Branch of Human Resources Development Council Canada, 2001, on Canada; and Traag & van de Velden, 2008, on the Netherlands). Most point to features of family background (such as socioeconomic status, family structure and parental education), demographic factors (such as gender, race, ethnicity, location), individual attributes (such as disability, health, self-esteem) and experiences in school (such as academic achievement, attitudes towards school, grade repetition or retention) as important. They also point to the impact of school context as well as community and economic settings.

The persistence of social patterns in dropout and completion remains a pressing issue because the costs of failure generated within systems continue to remain concentrated within the same social groups. This is despite the formal goals of governments to open up schooling to all. Social theories on reproduction point to the varying relations between family background and the structures of educational systems in which social power becomes embedded (e.g., see Bourdieu, 1984; Collins, 1979). To understand why inequality continues, as one study notes, there is a need to study 'societal differences in the structure of educational systems and in the processes of educational stratification' (Blossfeld & Shavit, 1993, p. 5).

It remains a major challenge facing all school systems in the provision of secondary education to construct and deliver programs that cater to diverse populations of students. However, it is not only about providing space, it is also important to ensure evenness of quality so that all places generated within the structure of upper secondary opportunities deliver similar value or benefits from both a learning and outcomes perspective. Recent international comparisons of upper secondary graduation rates are revealing, both in terms of what they disclose about the success of some countries in building mass systems of secondary education capable of delivering programs to a whole cohort, and in what they conceal about differences in access and effectiveness in terms of quality of outcomes (e.g., see OECD, 2008a). In such comparisons, systems that are the most segmented in terms of provision can appear to provide the highest levels of completion, while school systems that are formally comprehensive and have advanced further down the road of democratisation can display higher levels of dropout. However, segmented systems tend to display marked patterns of social stratification across programs, while more comprehensive systems can provide greater opportunity for children from lower socioeconomic status backgrounds to qualify for university entry.

According to recent comparative studies on achievement, some nations have been more successful than others in reducing social gaps. In his work on cross-country differences in PISA achievement, Willms (2004) reports that while social differences in achievement are quite strong in some nations, others achieve both above-average levels of student achievement and weaker effects of socioeconomic status on educational success. To what extent does this apply to dropout and completion rates and what arrangements and features support outcomes leading to greater equality of educational opportunity?

Modern Growth in School Completion

There has been a marked increase in most countries in the proportion of the population that completes upper secondary education. This is evident in looking at generational differences in attainment profiles. Figure 1.2 reports the percentages of populations with upper secondary education qualifications broken out by age group: 25- to 34-year-olds, 35- to 44-year-olds, 45- to 54-year-olds and 55- to 64-year-olds. It shows that, apart from the United States, educational attainment levels are greater in younger age groups, highlighting recent growth in the numbers completing upper secondary education. The difference in attainment is quite marked in several countries, in some cases almost doubling across generations. For example, in France, about 49% of 55- to 64-year-olds attained an upper secondary qualification compared with 80% of 25- to 34-year-olds. Similar intergenerational growth is evident for Canada, Italy, Japan and the United Kingdom. Generational change has seen major increases in access to upper secondary education.

Such growth is not as evident in the United States. The proportion of younger adults (25–34 years of age) who had completed upper secondary education was about the same as the proportion of the oldest adults (55–64 years of age). This reflects the fact that the United States had already achieved a mass system of upper

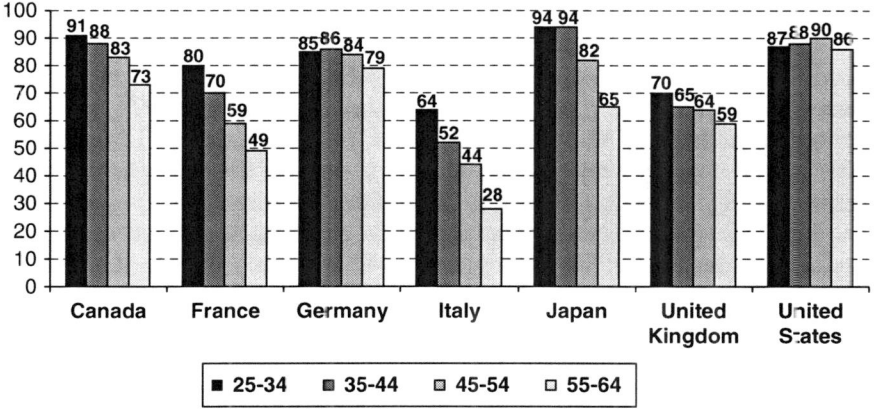

Fig. 1.2 Percentage of the population that has completed at least an upper secondary education, by age group and country: 1999 (Source: OECD, 2006)

secondary education many decades ago. Its relatively high and stable levels of access to senior schooling across generations suggests a much longer history of inclusive secondary education, at least in terms of overall levels of participation. The evident success in achieving mass participation almost two generations before many European countries, according to Goldin (2001) and Benavot (2006), has been based in part on strong public funding of education, the removal of a selective or elite model of institutional organisation and a comprehensive model of provision with a common general curriculum supplemented by a broad range of subject and course offerings. Recent concern has been expressed about the lack of further increases in graduation rates in the United States (e.g., see National Center on Education and the Economy, 2007), but history suggests stable longer term patterns of upper secondary participation when compared with other nations.

The recent expansion in upper secondary education in European as well as other OECD countries (see Lamb et al., 2004, for an outline of developments in Australia and OECD, 2006, for recent figures on other countries), representing large reductions in the levels of dropout, reflects several influences including labour market factors as well as changes in the provision and structure of upper secondary education.

Changing patterns of employment and the demands of employers for a better educated labour force have affected the demand for upper secondary education. In some countries, measured over the long term, there is a relationship between participation in upper secondary education and the state of labour markets. As Furlong (2007) has observed in the United Kingdom, as recently as 25 years ago, the majority of young people left school at the end of the compulsory phase to enter full-time jobs. However, opportunities for unqualified teenagers declined, due to both deterioration in the youth labour market, and long-term structural changes in industry and the demand for labour, which reduced full-time job opportunities for young people and led to rises in youth unemployment. Studies in several countries show long-term falls in full-time teenage job opportunities (e.g., Lamb et al., 2004, in Australia; Furlong, 2006, in the United Kingdom). Structural changes to economies over the last 30 years have gradually, but dramatically, changed the number and types of jobs available to young people. In Norway, 31% of all young people aged 16–19 were working in 1975, while this proportion had fallen to 8% in 1990 (Grøgaard, 1992). The teenage labour market vanished and upper secondary education had to open its doors to whole cohorts. Accompanying the fall in full-time work has been the substantial growth in part-time jobs. These have been focused largely in areas (such as retail and related services) that tend to employ young people still in the education system, in jobs that are more often short-term. Such jobs are not those sought by young people wanting full-time work and careers.

As labour markets have changed and full-time jobs for young people have dried up, students have tended to remain longer at school and gain qualifications to facilitate labour market entry and career growth. In this sense, school has acted as a refuge from deteriorating teenage labour markets, leading to higher levels of upper secondary participation. One consequence of this is a decline in the value of upper secondary qualifications (qualification deflation). However, the corollary to this is that upper secondary qualifications have become, increasingly, a minimum requirement for labour market entry. Increased competitiveness for job opportunities makes dropouts and nonqualified school leavers less attractive to employers, placing pressure on students to stay on and complete school qualifications or enter alternative forms of upper secondary education and training. Upper secondary education has become the main educational point of entry into the full-time labour force across OECD countries and young people without upper secondary or equivalent qualifications increasingly struggle to find full-time work.

This point becomes apparent when looking at patterns of employment linked to educational attainment. Figure 1.3 presents the employment rates for young people 5 years after leaving initial education, by level of educational qualification, for eight OECD countries. It shows that in nearly all cases, the rates of employment are

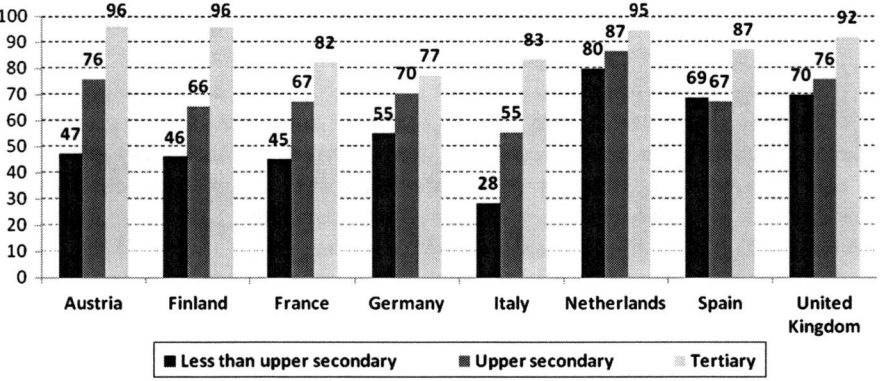

Fig. 1.3 Employment rates 5 years after leaving initial education, by educational attainment (%) (Source: OECD, 2008b)

markedly lower among those without upper secondary qualifications compared with those who either gain an upper secondary qualification or a tertiary education credential. The exception is Spain, where the rates are similar for those with and without upper secondary qualifications, though the rates are higher for those with tertiary qualifications. The pattern is consistent across nations even though the level of qualification gained varies. In the United Kingdom, for example, there was a 6 percentage point gap between dropouts (those with less than upper secondary attainment) and graduates (those with an upper secondary qualification). The gap in Austria was 29 points and in Italy, 27 points. The employment gains are even stronger for those with tertiary qualifications.

Similar patterns of returns are evident for spells of unemployment, types of occupations and earnings (OECD, 2008b).

Other works show that the returns to higher levels of upper secondary graduation relate not only to individuals. There are social and broad economic gains. The social returns to education include the monetary and non-monetary costs and benefits associated with improvements in health, family structure, fertility and child welfare, crime and environment. A range of studies suggest that higher levels of educational attainment are likely to lead to improvements in health and a reduction in poverty and associated problems (Behrman & Stacey, 1997; Levin et al., 2007). For example, while there may be debate about the exact amounts, increases in educational attainment are likely to lead to improvements in the quality of health for individuals leading to reductions in public expenditure on healthcare. There are also likely to be cost savings in other areas, such as from reduced criminal activity. Additionally, for communities, there are the broad economic gains associated with increased lifetime income and tax payments that accrue from higher levels of upper secondary graduation (see Levin et al., 2007; Hanushek, 2005).

Despite the economic and labour market pressures promoting growth in upper secondary education, the capacity for national systems of education to respond has varied depending on the structure of upper secondary provision. Growth has occurred in most systems, but not evenly. Some countries are doing better than others in promoting mass systems of upper secondary education. This is largely due to the institutional and certification arrangements that some nations have in place at upper secondary level to support broad participation.

However, even across countries that appear to have achieved mass systems, providing places for the vast majority of students and virtually eliminating dropout, it is not the case that all positions have equal value. Rather, the positions occupied within upper secondary education are not equal either across or within countries, reflecting differences in access and variations in quality of courses of study. Upper secondary programs are diverse and can include general, vocational and technical programs, with variations in entry requirements and in pathways to post-school opportunities. These variations are important to consider in order to gain a sense of which structures of provision operate to benefit the largest number and range of students. Which systems provide options that deliver not only quantity (making places available), but also quality (good outcomes for all) in terms of learning and outcomes?

Plan of the Book

This book is organised in three parts. Part One provides a comparative study of alternative pathways to upper secondary qualifications across OECD nations. The comparative study documents and evaluates some of the programs that different nations offer in upper secondary education. It examines both the range of different opportunities provided within schools and the alternative pathways provided for young people outside of school. It identifies and documents the main pathways, how they work, for whom they work and whether or not they are of equivalent value. Evidence collected from various national sources is used to examine the benefits and costs of alternatives provided in different systems. This includes a comparison of the pathways in terms of differentiation (content, rigor and graduation requirements), inclusiveness and outcomes. The comparative study notes that over recent decades many western nations have stepped up their efforts to reduce the numbers of dropouts by providing alternative pathways in upper secondary education. How systems have approached this, and how successful they are, varies. There is considerable diversification in upper secondary education.

Part Two of the book presents case studies of different educational systems. The case studies were prepared and written by educational researchers from 13 different OECD nations. The researchers have met regularly since 2005 as part of a collabouration called the *International Research Network for Youth Education and Training* (IRNYET). In preparing their chapters, the researchers agreed to address a set of common questions about dropout and completion in their country:

1. What are the main features of secondary education and training provision?
2. What are the main rates of dropout and completion, past and present?
3. Do dropout and completion vary by social background?
4. How have dropout and completion been studied and explained?
5. What alternative means are there for obtaining upper secondary qualifications for those who drop out of school?
6. What programs, policies and practices have been developed to reduce dropout and improve completion rates?

Authors were encouraged to focus on the features of their system which were most relevant to the theme of the book. The aim was to highlight the various options that nations offer students to complete an upper secondary certificate or diploma. Part of this involves a comparison of the different pathways in terms of content, rigor and completion requirements as well as how effectively they work to reduce dropout rates and deliver real benefits for those who participate. This means also considering the extent to which alternative pathways are inclusive and deliver quality learning and outcomes.

The countries are banded into three broad groups. The first group comprises countries of Western and Central Europe, namely England, Scotland, France, Germany, Switzerland, Spain and Poland. The systems in these countries represent some of the older or more traditional models of secondary education provision, often based originally on preparing an academic elite for university study and others for a technically and vocationally skilled workforce through alternative vocational programs (see Müller et al., 1987). There is, though, considerable diversity across these systems. The second group is based on the Nordic countries and includes Finland, Iceland and Norway. The systems of these countries are sometimes viewed as forming a more egalitarian model because of the adoption of a comprehensive upper secondary school catering more broadly across the population, even if programs remain diversified. The third group of countries is loosely termed the 'new world' and includes the United States, Canada and Australia. The more recently developed systems in these countries, particularly in the United States and Canada, have promoted the comprehensive school ideal as a part of creating mass systems (Trow, 1977).

The secondary school systems examined in Part Two represent a range of different models of programs and institutions. The range is marked by several dimensions including (1) comprehensive or stratified schooling, (2) academic and vocational elements, (3) differences in graduation requirements and (4) early or delayed academic selection.

Part Three presents some key reflections based on the material presented in the national case studies. These are in the form of syntheses of findings on key topics, which are presented in separate chapters. The first, Chapter 16, reflects on the role of vocational education programs and their importance to understanding differences in rates of dropout and completion. Vocational education is delivered in different ways across countries. It is the main alternative pathway in upper secondary education in some systems and yet negligible in others. To what extent is vocational education important in the way systems work, in which systems is it important and with what outcomes? The chapter examines the various approaches from primarily employment-based systems (e.g., Germany) or systems in which employment-based provision plays a large role (e.g., Norway) to systems where vocational education, if offered, is mainly school-based and weakly structured. The focus is on the role of vocational education, how it works in different systems and its importance to understanding differences in rates of dropout and completion.

School-based pathways are not the only opportunities for young people to gain upper secondary qualifications Some countries provide alternative pathways to work and adult life for young people who are no longer at school and who dropped out without gaining a qualification. This reflects more of a focus on 'external pathways' to provide alternative opportunities for young people, particularly dropouts. Such external pathways can include extended opportunities for school graduation through recovery programs or study in alternative settings including adult education, provision of a breadth and depth of alternative qualifications and study opportunities through further education colleges, provision of work-based indentured training contracts such as apprenticeships, and alternative routes involving combinations of work, training and study. Chapter 17 compares these opportunities and pathways across various countries and their relevance to dropout and completion.

Chapter 18 takes up the issue of school completion and social inequality. Rates of school dropout and completion vary by social background in every nation, suggesting that there are commonalities of process that wealthy nations share. Yet, the extent of inequality and its impact can be stronger or weaker depending on the form and architecture of institutional and program arrangements. In some nations, the social gaps in dropout and completion are weaker and the chances of success for the poor are stronger. This chapter explores this issue. It draws on the national case studies to examine patterns of inequality in relation to dropout and completion. It begins by looking at research from each country on the patterns of dropout and completion and the factors that influence them. Attention then turns to an examination of the effects of social background and how this varies across nations. The final section develops a framework for examining international differences in dropout and completion and in the levels of inequality.

Chapter 19, the final chapter, examines the important issue of policy and what systems are doing to reduce dropout and improve completion rates. The case studies reveal that rates of dropout and completion vary, but also that raising school completion rates is a major policy objective in all of the countries. There is an ongoing concern to reduce dropout and increase completion rates. Some systems have even set up ambitious goals or targets aiming to achieve completion rates in excess of 90%. To attempt to achieve these goals, some systems have transformed their programs or implemented large-scale interventions to address dropout. The case studies reveal that across countries, various types of policy measures have been or are being, implemented, some of which are similar and some which are more specific and unique. This chapter draws together and compares the array of policy interventions to improve completion and reduce dropout, particularly for at-risk students. What strategies are systems employing to address the issue of dropout? With what success?

References

Applied Research Branch, Human Development Council Canada. (2001). *Dropping out of high school: Definitions and costs.* Quebec, Canada: Human Resources Development Council Canada.
Barro, R. J. (1997). *Determinants of economic growth: A cross-country empirical study.* Cambridge, MA: MIT Press.
Behrman, J., & Stacey, N. (Eds.). (1997). *The social benefits of education.* Ann Arbor, MI: University of Michigan Press.
Benavot, A. (2006). The diversification of secondary education: School curricula in comparative perspective. *Revista de Currículum y Formación del Profesorado, 10*(1), 1–26.
Blossfeld, H.-P., & Shavit, Y. (1993). Persisting barriers: Changes in educational opportunities in thirteen countries. In Y. Shavit & H.-P. Blossfeld (Eds.), *Persistent inequalities: A comparative study of educational attainment in thirteen countries* (pp. 1–24). Boulder, CO: Westview Press.
Bourdieu, P. (1984). *Distinction. A social critique of the judgement of taste.* Cambridge, MA: Harvard University Press.
Cameron, S. V., & Heckman, J. (1993, January). The nonequivalence of high school equivalents. *Journal of Labour Economics, 11*(1), 1–47.
Collins, R. (1979). Functional and conflict theories of educational stratification. In J. Karabel & A. H. Halsey (Eds.), *Power and ideology in education* (pp. 118–136). New York: Oxford University Press.

Furlong, A. (2007). Supporting the transitions of vulnerable youth: UK perspectives (The Japan Institute for Labour Policy Training Report No. 5). *Transition support policy for young people with low educational background* (pp. 77–90). Tokyo: The Japan Institute for Labour Policy and Training.

Goldin, C. (2001). The human capital century and American leadership: Virtues of the past. *Journal of Economic History, 61*(2), 263–292.

Grøgaard, J. B. (1992). *Skomaker, bli ved din lest* [Shoemaker, tick to your last]. Oslo, Norway: Fafo.

Hanushek, E. (2005, August). The economics of school quality. *German Economic Review, 6*(3), 269–286.

Heckman, J., & LaFontaine, P. (2006). *Bias corrected estimates of GED returns* (NBER Working Paper No. 12018). Cambridge, MA: National Bureau of Economics Research.

Laird, J., DeBell, M., & Chapman, C. (2006). *Dropout rates in the United States: 2004* (NCES 2007–024). Washington, DC: National Center for Education Statistics, U.S. Department of Education. Retrieved February 2, 2009, from http://nces.ed.gov/pubsearch

Lamb, S., & Mason, K.. (2008). *How young people are faring, 2008*. Melbourne, Austra ia: Foundation for Young Australians.

Lamb, S., Walstab, A., Teese, R., Vickers, M., & Rumberger, R. (2004). *Staying on at school: Improving student retention in Australia*. Brisbane, Australia: Ministerial Council on Employment, Education and Training and Queensland Department of Education. Retrieved from www.mceetya.edu.au/verve/_resources/studentretention_main_file.pdf

Levin, H., Belfield, C., Muennig, P., & Rouse, C. (2007). *The costs and benefits of an excellent education for all of America's children*. New York: Center for Benefit-Cost Studies of Education, Teachers College, Columbia University. Retrieved from www.cbcse.org/media/download_gallery/ Leeds_Report_Final_Jan2007.pdf

Markussen, E., Frøseth, M. W., Lødding, B., & Sandberg, N. (2008). *Bortvalg og kompetanse. Gjennomføring, bortvalg og kompetanseoppnåelse i videregående opplæring blant 9749 ung-dommer som gikk ut av grunnskolen på østlandet våren 2002: hovedfunn, konklusjoner og implikasjoner fem år etter* [Early leaving, non-completion or completion? On completion, drop-out and achievement of qualification in upper secondary education among 9749 young people that left lower secondary in the spring of 2002] (Report 13). Oslo, Norway: NIFU STEP.

Müller, D. K., Ringer, F., & Simon, B. (1987). *The rise of the modern educational system: Structural change and social reproduction, 1870–1920*. Cambridge, UK/Paris: Cambridge University Press/Maison des Sciences de l'Homme.

National Center on Education and the Economy (NCEE). (2007). *Tough choices, tough times. The report of the new commission on the skills of the American workforce*. Washington, DC: NCEE. Retrieved from www.skillscommission.org/pdf/exec_sum/ToughChoices_EXECSUM.pdf

Organisation for Economic Co-operation and Development (OECD). (2001). *Transition from initial education to working life*. Paris: OECD.

Organisation for Economic Co-operation and Development (OECD). (2006). *Education at a glance: OECD indicators 2006*. Paris: OECD.

Organisation for Economic Co-operation and Development (OECD). (2008a). *Education at a glance: OECD indicators 2008*. Paris: OECD.

Organisation for Economic Co-operation and Development (OECD). (2008b). *Employment out-look 2008*. Paris: OECD.

Owens, J. (2004). *A review of the social and non-market returns to education*. Wales, UK: Education and Learning Network

Raffe, D. (2010). Participation in post-compulsory learning in Scotland. In S. Lamb, E. Markussen, R. Teese, N. Sandberg, & J. Polesel (Eds.), *School dropout and completion: International comparative studies in theory and policy*. Dordrecht, The Netherlands: Springer.

Rumberger, R., & Lim, S. (2008). *Why students drop out of school: A review of 25 years of research* (Report No. 15, California Dropout Research Project). Santa Barbara, CA: UCSB. Retrieved from http://cdrp.ucsb.edu/dropouts/pubs_reports.htm

Rumberger, R. W. (1987). High school dropouts: A review of issues and evidence. *Review of Educational Research, 57,* 101–121.

Rumberger, R. W., & Lamb, S. (2003). The early employment and further education experiences of high school dropouts: A comparative study of the United States and Australia. *Economics of Education Review, 22*(4), 353–366.

Shavit, Y., & Muller, W. (1998). *From school to work: A comparative study of educational qualifications and occupational destinations.* Oxford, UK: Clarendon Press.

Statistics Norway. (2009). *Starts in vocational studies, general education completion.* Kongsvinger, Norway: SSB. Retrieved from http://www.ssb.no/english/subjects/04/02/30/vgogjen_en/

Traag, T., & van de Velden, R. (2008). *Early school-leaving in the Netherlands.* Netherlands: Maastricht University, Research Centre for Education and the Labour Market. Retrieved from http://www.roa.unimaas.nl/pdf_publications/2008/ROA_RM_2008_3.pdf

Trow, M. (1977). The second transformation of the American school system. In J. Karabel & A. H. Halsey (Eds.), *Power and ideology in education* (pp. 105–118). New York: Oxford University Press.

Van Es, W. (2008). Unqualified school leavers in nine European cities: A short analysis of measures. Paper prepared for Sardes, The Netherlands.

Willms, J. D. (2004). What can we say about the quality and equality of educational systems from the first cycle of PISA? *Education Journal, 32*(1), 161–175.

Part I
Structures and Pathways

Chapter 2
Pathways to School Completion: An International Comparison

Stephen Lamb

Over recent decades, many western nations have stepped up their efforts to increase secondary school completion rates while maintaining high standards. How systems have approached this, and how successful they are, varies. One of the key differences is in the range of programs that are offered and the different pathways to completion. In some systems there is a menu of separate certificates and qualifications, each tied to a different strand of learning, and each representing a different pathway. In other systems there is a single certificate or qualification, but with structured options producing academic, general, and vocational tracks that work as pathways to different post-school options. This chapter compares some of the different pathways to completion of upper secondary qualifications offered by different countries. What are the main qualifications and pathways? How do they work? For whom do they work? Are they of equal value? Answers to these questions require an evaluation of the various options nations offer students to complete secondary school qualifications. The evaluation needs to consider criteria such as content, rigor and graduation requirements as well as how effectively the different options work to reduce dropout rates and deliver real benefits to those who participate. There is little use providing alternatives to deal with pupil diversity if the alternatives simply function to promote stratification by working as sources of relegation and offering only weak returns. For this reason, it is important to consider the extent to which different pathways are inclusive (who gets included) and promote equivalent standards of learning and outcomes. The discussion begins by comparing school-based pathways across countries, and then moves on to look in more detail first at academic pathways, then at alternatives such as vocational education. Finally, the discussion turns to alternative pathways to completion specifically available to dropouts.

S. Lamb (✉)
Centre for Post-Compulsory Education and Lifelong Learning,
The University of Melbourne, Australia

S. Lamb et al. (Eds.), *School Dropout and Completion: International Comparative Studies in Theory and Policy*, DOI 10.1007/978-90-481-9763-7_2,

School-Based Pathways

Differences in Provision

The provision of upper secondary education tends to vary across two main dimensions. The first is the level of *program diversification* or the variety of programs that are offered. This can include differently focused strands or streams such as academic programs, professional and technical courses, vocational education, and in some countries, subject-based strands such as specialist art, music, humanities and science programs (as in Italy, for example). The different programs orient students toward different post-school outcomes. The second main dimension is the extent of *institutional segregation* (or integration), which refers to the extent to which young people are separated into different schools or streams and tracks on the basis of the programs or qualifications in which they enrol.[1] In some systems this can occur early and extends well back into lower secondary or even primary school. In Germany, for example, it is common at the end of the primary school years for many students to be separated into different schools based on interests and aptitudes. Schools tend to be divided into those offering a more academic, university-preparatory curriculum (*Gymnasium*), those offering specialist technical training (*Realschule*) and those with a more vocational focus (*Hauptschule*). Alternatively, in other systems, such as in Sweden, Canada and the United States, students tend to remain in the same type of school through both the lower and upper secondary years, able to pursue a variety of programs or courses within one institution.

Institutional segregation and *program diversification* are mutually linked. Both are driven by curriculum requirements, and the demands of the academic curriculum are central to this. All systems give pre-eminence to academic knowledge. Some call it *general education*, while others refer to it more directly as *academic*. Even when alternative programs and curricula are developed, the academic curriculum enjoys the highest prestige. This is in part because of its role in preparing and selecting students for highly valued and sought after places in university. This function has worked against the development of truly democratic, inclusive and universal programs of teaching and learning built around a common curriculum. The stratifying effect of providing academic programs geared to university preparation operates in all countries, with the extent varying by the structure and number of alternative programs and the organisation of schools.

Table 2.1 presents information for a number of OECD countries on features of school organisation. It reports on school settings including the ages at which

---

[1]This is different to the process of residential segregation which produces marked divisions in some systems, separating students on the basis of where they live and their racial and social backgrounds. Regional or residential segregation can create sharp divisions between schools in terms of intake, separating students almost as effectively as selective schooling. It also has a marked impact on student progress and outcomes, at least according to a range of school effectiveness studies (see, for example, Willms, 2006).

Table 2.1 Comparisons of pathways to completion: features of school organisation

	Compulsory Years	Features of upper secondary schooling (organisational setting)		
	Age range	Age of entry	Level of segregation	Admission to type of upper secondary school
Australia	5–16	16	Mixed: largely comprehensive, some selective-entry schools	Partly selective: some schools use ability testing for entry
Austria	5–15	14	High: academic, technical, vocational, specialist schools	Selective: entry is dependent on type of school attended and academic achievement
Denmark	4–16	16	Mixed: some integration, though largely separate: general (gymnasium), technical, vocational	Partly selective: entry is dependent on completion of formal exams at the end of compulsory education and teacher recommendation
England	4–16	16	Low: largely comprehensive	Non-selective
Finland	6–16	16	Mixed: general (gymnasium) and vocational schools	Non-selective
France	3–16	15	Mixed: general (general and technological *lycées*) and vocational schools (*lycées professionnels*)	Partly selective: entry is dependent on completion of formal exams at the end of compulsory education
Germany	6–18	15	High: academic (gymnasium), technical, vocational, specialist schools	Selective: entry is dependent on type of school attended and academic achievement
Iceland	3–16	16	Mixed: some integration, though largely separate: general (gymnasium), comprehensives, vocational	Partly selective: Varied admission based on results at end of compulsory education
Italy	3–15	14	Mixed: general (*liceo*) and vocational schools (*istituti*)	Non-selective
Japan	4–15	15	High: academic senior high school and vocational and technical schools	Selective: highly competitive entrance exams
Netherlands	5–18	12	High: academic (VWO), general (HAVO), vocational (VMBO) schools	Selective: entry is dependent on type of school attended and academic achievement, selection at end of primary school

(continued)

Table 2.1 (continued)

	Compulsory Years	Features of upper secondary schooling (organisational setting)		
	Age range	Age of entry	Level of segregation	Admission to type of upper secondary school
Norway	6–16	16	Low: largely comprehensive	Non-selective
Scotland	4–16	16	Low: largely comprehensive	Non-selective
Spain	3–16	16	Mixed: largely comprehensive (Institutes for Secondary Education), though some specialist vocational schools	Non-selective
Sweden	6–16	16	Low: largely comprehensive	Non-selective
United States	6–16	16	Low: largely comprehensive	Non-selective

Sources: OECD (2006); Qualifications and Curriculum Authority, International Review of Curriculum and Assessment Frameworks Archive; Eurydice: Eurybase – the information database on education systems in Europe.

young people enter secondary school and the level of institutional differentiation or segregation. High levels of segregation operate where young people attend different schools either because of the streams or courses that they enter, or because they are divided across schools on academic ability lines. Low levels of segregation occur in systems that more often operate comprehensive schools, catering for a range of student skills and interests within one type of school. There are also countries that have mixed arrangements in which there is some separation across schools on the basis of academic skills or program choices, though there also are integrated or comprehensive schools that cater to a wide variety of students. Admission requirements vary depending on the types of schools and their level of differentiation.

Table 2.2 presents features of secondary school programs and qualifications. It provides details on the various programs and qualifications that are offered in each country. This includes information on the typical duration of courses, program-specific entry requirements (what criteria are set to enter each type of program and qualification), broad course content (in terms of core subjects and electives and associated arrangements) and the main form of assessment (whether exams, school-based assessment or other forms). To compare differences in qualifications standards, which can vary both within and across national systems, it is important to consider the formal completion criteria – what the requirements are to graduate and obtain a qualification. These can affect both the post-school opportunities, such as entry to university, and the rates of completion. Details on these are provided together with completion rates expressed in terms of the typical age cohort, revealing the proportions of young people in each country who are likely to graduate with each type of qualification.

Table 2.3 presents some broad outcome indicators. These are provided at a system level rather than at a qualification level, since qualification-specific outcomes are not available either widely or consistently in an appropriate form for valid comparison. The broad indicators that are presented give some insight into the overall function and performance of system arrangements. Measures include *achievement levels* (mathematics achievement measured through the Programme for International Student Assessment [PISA]), *access indicators* (how inclusive are the qualifications and programs for the whole student population) and *transition outcomes* (what the upper secondary arrangements deliver in terms of labour market experience). The levels of PISA achievement relate to 15-year-olds and, therefore, achievement prior to upper secondary schooling in many systems. However, they provide a measure of the impact of school organisation and differentiation. The measures selected for inclusion are those that relate to between-school differences in achievement (percentage of variation in student achievement that is linked to differences between schools rather than students, all else equal). The second PISA measure is the percentage of between-school differences accounted for by the SES backgrounds of students and schools. This gives us an indication of the extent to which school arrangements and diversification work to stratify or separate students along social lines. The *access indicators* include measures of the percentages of young people who have left school without obtaining a qualification. They provide an assessment of the capacity of secondary school programs to accommodate and retain students. The *transition indicators* assess returns to study. They report rates of unemployment for dropouts and for graduates. Also included is the university entry rate, expressed as a percentage difference from the OECD average.

Academic Pathways to Graduation

Every system provides programs and courses that work to prepare or select students for university, and this influences school and program organisation. Even so, there is considerable variation in the requirements for graduation and access to higher education.

In some systems, neither the number of subjects nor the disciplines to be studied for accreditation are prescribed. For example, students in England and Scotland may achieve accreditation in a single subject of their own choosing. In these systems, there are no compulsory subjects at upper secondary level – only electives, with the breadth of subject offerings dependent on school size and student demand. Students choose from a range of subjects available at *General Certificate of Education (GCE) Advanced Level ('A level')* and *GCE Advanced Subsidiary Level ('AS level')*. Assessment is academic and competitive, involving external examinations controlled

Table 2.2 Comparisons of pathways to completion: features of qualifications

	Structure	Qualification	Duration (Years)	Entry requirements	Content	Form of assessment	Minimum completion requirements	Provides access to:	Cohort grad. rate %
					Features of upper secondary qualifications (program setting)				
Australia	Varies by state	Senior school certificate (varies by state)	2	Open	Elective-based system, English compulsory in some states	External and school-based	Pass grades in at least four subjects	University, work, further education	68.0*
		VET certificates, school-based apprenticeships (single or dual)	1–2	Open	Module-based, industry specific	School/module-based assessment	Successfully completed course work	Work, further education	14.0*
		Certificate of Applied Learning (Victoria only)	1–2	Open	Elective-based system, VET focus	School-based assessment	Successfully completed course work	Work, further education	4.8
Austria	Separate	Certificate of Secondary Education (*Reifeprüfung* certificate)	4	Dependent on type of school attended and academic achievement	Core subjects (mathematics, German, foreign language) and small number of electives	School-based written and oral exams with examination panel including at least one external panel member	Passing grades in compulsory subjects and electives (matriculation)	University and professional schools	12.8

CSE and TVE Diploma (*Reifeprüfung* and TVE Diploma)	4	Dependent on type of school attended and academic achievement	Core subjects (mathematics, German, foreign language) and electives	School-based written, practical and oral exams with examination panel	Passing grades in compulsory subjects and electives (matriculation)	University and professional schools	8.6
Professional matriculation certificate (*Berufsreife prüfung*)	4	Training certificate completion	Core subjects (mathematics, German, foreign language) and professionally relevant subject	External examination	Passing grades in compulsory subjects and electives (matriculation)	University and professional schools	20.5
Apprenticeship certificate (dual system)	3–4	Open	Core subjects (mathematics, German, foreign language) and professionally relevant subjects	Examination	Passing grades in compulsory subjects	Trades, occupations, higher education	30.2
Vocational certificates	2–4	Open	Core subjects (mathematics, German, foreign language) and professionally relevant subjects	School-based written, practical and oral exams with examination panel	Passing grades in compulsory and practical subjects	Trades, occupations, *Berufsreife prüfung*	17.9

(continued)

Table 2.2 (continued)

	Structure	Qualification	Duration (Years)	Entry requirements	Content	Form of assessment	Minimum completion requirements	Provides access to:	Cohort grad. rate %
					Features of upper secondary qualifications (program setting)				
Denmark	Separate	Gymnasium upper secondary certificate (STX)	3	Dependent on successful completion of formal exams at the end of compulsory education and teacher recommendation	Two main programs (languages, mathematics). Core subjects common to both programs (Danish, history, biology, music, geography, visual arts, religious education, classical studies, physical education), core subjects unique to each program and specialist electives Some options can be taken at different levels (intermediate or high)	External written and oral exams in ten subjects	Successfully completed examinations and program work with a minimum grade point average	University	22.7

| Higher preparatory upper secondary certificate (HF) | 2 | Dependent on successful completion of formal exams at the end of compulsory education and teacher recommendation | Common core subjects, three optional subjects and a major written assignment. Some options can be taken at different levels (intermediate or high) | External written and/or oral exams in every subject studied | Successfully completed examinations and program work with a minimum grade point average | University | 4.0 |
| Higher commercial upper secondary certificate (HHX) | 3 | Dependent on successful completion of formal exams at the end of compulsory education and teacher recommendation | Business and commercial studies focus. Core subjects, optional subjects and a major written assignment. Subjects are offered at different skill levels (A, B, C) | External written and oral exams in ten subjects | Successfully completed examinations and program work with a minimum grade point average. At least two of the subjects must be at 'A' (highest skill) Level | University | 7.9 |

(continued)

Table 2.2 (continued)

Structure	Qualification	Duration (Years)	Entry requirements	Content	Form of assessment	Minimum completion requirements	Provides access to:	Cohort grad. rate %
	Higher technical upper secondary certificate (HTX)	3	Dependent on successful completion of formal exams at the end of compulsory education and teacher recommendation	Technical studies focus. Core subjects, optional subjects and a major written assignment. Subjects are offered at different skill levels (A, B, C)	External written and oral exams in ten subjects	Successfully completed examinations and program work with a minimum grade point average. At least two of the subjects must be at 'A' (highest skill) Level	University	2.8
	Vocational education and training (EUD)	1–4	Open	Seven programs comprising basic and main courses	School-based assessment with tests and an exam to measure proficiency	Successfully completed exam and program work with a final exam/proficiency mark	Trades and occupations	42.8
	Vocational education and training (EUD)	1–4	Open	Seven programs comprising basic and main courses	School-based assessment with tests and an exam to measure proficiency	Successfully completed exam and program work with a final exam/proficiency mark	Trades and occupations	42.8

Features of upper secondary qualifications (program setting)

England	Separate								
		2	General Certificate of Education (GCE) Advanced Level (A Levels). Single subject qualifications	GCE AS Levels	Range of elective subjects, commonly between two and four taken by a student	External examination	Pass grade in exam	University	42.4
		1	GCE Advanced Subsidiary Level (AS Levels). Single subject qualifications	No official criteria, though General Certificate of Secondary Education (GCSE) results can be considered	Range of elective subjects, cover half of the content of 'full' A Levels. Commonly four or more subjects selected	External examination	Pass grade in exam	University and further education	
		2	General Certificate of Education A Levels in Applied Subjects. Four qualifications available.	No official criteria, though GCSE results can be considered	Courses are available in ten vocational subject areas and are organised on the lines of the GCE AS and A format	External tests and internal assessment	Pass grade in requisite subjects	Work and further education	8.2

(continued)

Table 2.2 (continued)

	Structure	Qualification	Duration (Years)	Entry requirements	Content	Form of assessment	Minimum completion requirements	Provides access to:	Cohort grad. rate %
					Features of upper secondary qualifications (program setting)				
Finland	Separate	Matriculation examination certificate	3	Dependent on successful completion of the compulsory education syllabus	Mother tongue (Finnish or Swedish) and three other core subjects from the second national language, other language, mathematics, general studies (science and humanities subjects) and at least one elective. Subjects in some core areas are offered at different levels of difficulty	National written examinations	Passing grades in all compulsory subjects with at least one subject taken at the advanced level (matriculation)	University	27.6
		Certificate in general upper secondary education	3	Dependent on successful completion of the compulsory education syllabus	Core subjects and electives. Subjects in some core areas are offered at different levels of difficulty	School-based	Passing grades in program syllabus	Polytechnics (professional higher education)	3.8

		Credential	Duration	Entry requirement	Curriculum	Assessment	Certification	Destination	%
		Certification in Vocational Upper Secondary Education and Training	3	Dependent on successful completion of the compulsory education syllabus	Mixture of core general studies (same as national core curriculum), electives and workplace learning. 52 qualifications, 113 study programs across eight broad industry sectors	School work, theory and competence-based assessments	Successful completion of studies	Work and polytechnics	36.5
		Apprenticeship qualification certificate	1–4	Dependent on successful completion of the compulsory education syllabus	Mixture of core general studies (same as national core curriculum), electives and workplace learning	School work, theory and competence-based assessments	Successful completion of studies	Work and polytechnics	11.5
France	Separate	General Baccalaureate	3	Completion of lower secondary education	Three types of programs (literary, economic and social sciences, scientific). Minimum of eight or nine compulsory subjects plus a maximum of two optional subjects in each program	National written and/or oral examinations in core and elective subjects	Passing grades in examinations	University	34.6

(continued)

Table 2.2 (continued)

Structure	Qualification	Duration (Years)	Entry requirements	Content	Form of assessment	Minimum completion requirements	Provides access to:	Cohort grad. rate %
				Features of upper secondary qualifications (program setting)				
	Technological Baccalaureate	3	Completion of lower secondary education	Four types of programs (sciences and tertiary technologies, sciences and industrial technologies, sciences and laboratory technologies, medico-social sciences). Three specific programs for the hotel trade, applied arts, music and dance. Core and elective subjects	National written and/ or oral examinations in core and elective subjects	Passing grades in examinations	University	18.9
	Professional (Vocational) Baccalaureate	2	Completion of lower secondary education	Compulsory general subjects and professional studies relevant to different occupations and industries	Written, practical and oral examinations in core and elective subjects, as well as work and training assessments during the course	Successfully completed examination and program work	Work, further education, university	12.5

Country		Certificate	Years	Entry requirement	Compulsory general subjects and professional studies	Tests or exercises	Completion	Leads to	%
		Certificat d'aptitude professionnelle (CAP) or Brevet d'etudes professionnelles (BEP)	2	Completion of lower secondary education	Compulsory general subjects and professional studies relevant to different occupations and industries	Tests or exercises based on compulsory subjects and professional studies	Successfully completed examination and program work	Work, further education	17.0
Germany	Separate	Zeugnis der Allgemeinen Hochschulreife	3	Dependent on type of school attended and academic achievement	Small number of majors selected from three areas (languages, literature and the arts; social sciences; mathematics, natural sciences and technology) with each area needing to be included	Abitur examination (written and oral exams)	Passing grades in at least four subjects	University	27.3
		Vocational leaving and apprenticeship certificates (Dual System)	2–4	Open	Workplace training and school-based formal curricula established by the lander. Training covers 350 professions	Final examination before an examination board relevant to the training industry. Practical and written component	Successful completion of the exam	Trades and occupations	48.5

(continued)

Table 2.2 (continued)

				Features of upper secondary qualifications (program setting)				Cohort grad. rate
Structure	Qualification	Duration (Years)	Entry requirements	Content	Form of assessment	Minimum completion requirements	Provides access to:	%
	Technical and professional certificates (such as the *Fachgebundene Hochschulreife* and the *Fach-hochschulreife*	2-3	Dependent on type of school attended and academic achievement	Specialise in subject areas such as engineering, economics, farming, the welfare system, and design. Students are also usually required to study core subjects (such as German, social sciences, mathematics, natural sciences, one foreign language and sport) from the three general subject areas	Final written and oral exams	Successful completion of the exam	Trades, occupations, higher education	12.2

Iceland	Separate	Matriculation examination certificate (*studentsprof*)	4	Varied admission based on results at end of compulsory education	Three main academic programs: foreign languages, natural sciences and social sciences. Students required to take core subjects (regardless of program), specialised subjects according to particular program of study, and electives	Examination and continuous assessment	Successfully completed examinations. Can also be awarded from the accumulation of internally set unit-credits.	University	39.4
		Journeyman's examination certificate (*sveinsprof*)	4	Open	Study comprises general academic subjects, theoretical vocational subjects and practical vocational subjects. Students must take a certain number of credits in general academic subjects	Journeyman's examination and continuous assessment of practical and theory work	Passing grades in exam and course work	Trades and occupations	40.6

(continued)

Table 2.2 (continued)

Structure	Qualification	Duration (Years)	Entry requirements	Content	Form of assessment	Minimum completion requirements	Provides access to:	Cohort grad. rate %
			Features of upper secondary qualifications (program setting)					
Italy								
Separate	Upper secondary leaving certificate (*diploma di Stato*) (*Classical/ Linguistica/ Scientifica/Tecnica/ Professionale/ Magistrale/Artistica*)	5	Lower secondary diploma (*primo ciclo di istruzione*)	Core and elective subjects, with electives varying by specialisation	Three written examinations and one oral examination	Successful completion of exams with a minimum grade point average	University	63.5
	Professional skills qualification (*Diploma di Qualifica Professionale*)	3–5	Lower secondary diploma (*primo ciclo di istruzione*)	Core and elective subjects, with electives varying by vocational specialisation. Specialisation involves basic training in either agriculture, industry and crafts, or the service sector	Examination	Successful completion of exam and course work	Work, further vocational education	5.8

Japan	Separate	Upper secondary school leaving certificate (academic)	3	Entrance exam	Credit-based system of core subjects (Japanese language; geography and history; civics; mathematics; science; health and physical education; art; home economics) and small number of possible electives	School-based assessment	Achieving threshold of credits (80) by successfully completing the required number of core and elective subjects	University entrance exam	66.1
		Upper secondary school leaving certificate (vocational/ technical)	3	Entrance exam	Credit-based system of core subjects and specialised vocational or technical electives	School-based assessment	Achieving threshold of credits (80) by successfully completing the required number of core and elective subjects	University and work	24.7
		High school graduation qualification test		Individuals who have not graduated upper secondary school	Exams cover core subjects in the general upper secondary curriculum	Examination	Passing grades in exams	University entrance exam	

(continued)

Table 2.2 (continued)

	Structure	Qualification	Duration (Years)	Entry requirements	Content	Form of assessment	Minimum completion requirements	Provides access to:	Cohort grad. rate %
					Features of upper secondary qualifications (program setting)				
Nether-lands	Separate	Upper Secondary Preparatory Diploma (VWO)	5	Achievement and school recom-mendation	Four programs (science and technology; science and health; economics and society; culture and society) with some common core subjects	National examination and school exam/ assessment	Passing final grades with minimum overall grade	University	22.9
		Upper Secondary General Education Diploma (HAVO)	6	Achievement and school recom-mendation	Four programs (science and technology; science and health; economics and society; culture and society) with some common core subjects	National examination and school exam/ assessment	Passing final grades with minimum overall grade	Professional higher education, VWO	21.2
		Upper Secondary Vocational Diploma (VMBO)	4	Achievement and school recom-mendation	Four programs associated with four industry or business sectors, each with its own combination of exam subjects	National and school-based examinations	Passing final grades with minimum overall grade	Work, further education	41.0

Country	System	Certificate	Years	Admission/Promotion	Programs/Streams	Assessment	Requirements	Destination	%
Norway	Separate	Upper Secondary Leaving Certificate (general)	3	Initially open, promotion can depend on achievement	Three general programs (general and business studies; music, dance and drama; sports and physical education)	Written and/or oral examinations and school-based assessment	Passes in all subjects and exams required for each program with minimum level of achievement in core subjects	University	44.0
		Vocational qualification/trade or journeyman's certificate	3	Open	Twelve vocational streams	Centrally set theoretical and practical examinations	Passes in all subjects and exams required for each program with minimum level of achievement in core subjects	Work, further education	29.9
Scotland	Integrated	National Qualification Certificates	1–3	Initially open, level of study depends on achievement	National Qualifications are available at five levels: Access, Intermediate 1, Intermediate 2, Higher, and Advanced Higher. Courses cover both general and vocational subjects. There are no compulsory subjects. National courses often involve three subject-related units	Internal and external assessment	National Course Qualifications are awarded to those who pass all of the internally assessed components and achieve a passing grade in the external exam for the course	University, work, further education	

(continued)

Table 2.2 (continued)

	Structure	Qualification	Duration (Years)	Entry requirements	Content	Form of assessment	Minimum completion requirements	Provides access to:	Cohort grad. rate %
					Features of upper secondary qualifications (program setting)				
Spain	Separate	Baccalaureate Certificate (*Bachillerato*)	2	Lower secondary certificate (*Graduado en Educación Secundaria*)	Four programs (arts; natural science and health; humanities and social studies; technology) with some common or core subjects	School-based assessment	Pass grade in all subjects	University entrance exam, advanced level specific vocational training	45.0
		Intermediate Specific Vocational Training Certificate (*Técnico*)	1–2	Lower secondary certificate (*Graduado en Educación Secundaria*)	Modules of theoretical and practical training based on 22 vocational fields, with some core subjects and field-specific options. Workplace module is compulsory	School-based and workplace assessment	Pass grade in all subjects and modules	Work, advanced level specific vocational training	21.0

Sweden	Integrated	Upper secondary leaving certificate (*Slutbetyg från gymnasieskolan*)	3	Lower secondary certificate (*grundskola*)	Two academic and 16 vocational strands. There are core subjects (Swedish, English, mathematics, civics, religion, science studies, physical education and health, and artistic activities) common to all strands plus specialist subjects	School-based with national tests in three core subjects (Swedish, English, mathematics)	Requisite number of credits with a pass grade in at least 90% for a completed course of studies, including a pass in a compulsory upper secondary certificate project	University, work, further education	88.0

Table 2.2 (continued)

	Structure	Qualification	Duration (Years)	Entry requirements	Content	Form of assessment	Minimum completion requirements	Provides access to:	Cohort grad. rate %
					Features of upper secondary qualifications (program setting)				
United States	Integrated	High School Diploma (Regular/ Standard, Vocational, Honor/ Regents, College Preparatory)	3	Open	Subjects can be clustered into vocational, general and academic tracks based on system of core subjects (often English, mathematics, social studies, science, health and physical education) and electives	School assessment on the basis of grades and work over the year	Satisfactory completion of a specified number of subjects (credits), designated for each diploma, varying by State. Minimum exit exam achievement scores in some states.	Higher education and work	75.0
		General Educational Development Certificate (GED)		Individuals who have not graduated from high school	Tests cover writing, social studies, science, reading and mathematics	Examination	Pass grade in all tests	Higher education and work	11.0

* = Not mutually exclusive

Sources: Qualifications and Curriculum Authority, International Review of Curriculum and Assessment Frameworks Archive; Eurydice: Eurybase – the information database on education systems in Europe; National Ministries of Education – Austria, Denmark, France, Finland, Germany, Iceland, Italy, Japan, Netherlands, Norway, Spain, Sweden; U.S. Department of Education, National Center for Educational Statistics; Department for Children, Schools and Families, England; National Statistics Bureaus: Australia, Austria, Denmark, France, Finland, Germany, Iceland, Italy, Japan, Netherlands, Norway, Spain, Sweden.

Table 2.3 Comparisons of pathways to completion: selected outcome indicators

	Mathematics achievement (PISA)			Access		Transition		
						% of 20- to 24-year-olds not in education and unemployed by attainment		
	% of between-school variance in mathematics achievement	% of between-school variance explained by SES of students and schools	% in programs in compulsory years leading to upper secondary vocational education	% of 25- to 34-year-old dropouts	% of 15- to 19-year-olds not in education or employment	Dropouts	Graduates	% deviation from OECD average in university entry
Australia	22.0	15.4	0.0	23.0		11.1	3.1	
Austria	55.5	35.2	42.9	13.0	10.2	12.0	4.2	−16
Denmark	13.1	9.3	0.0	14.0	3.0	6.0	4.7	+2
England	21.1[a]	15.3[a]	na	30.0[a]	9.4[a]	10.7[a]	3.7[a]	−1[a]
Finland	3.9	0.9	0.0	11.0	9.8	10.5	6.0	+20
France	na	na	9.5	20.0	14.0	23.7	9.8	
Germany	56.4	43.8	47.1[b]	15.0	4.7	12.6	8.8	−16
Iceland	3.6	0.3	0.0	32.0	4.3			+26
Italy	56.8	30.5	na	36.0	10.5	16.2	8.0	+2
Japan	62.1	42.0	25.4	6.0				−10
Netherlands	54.5	40.7	61.3	20.0	4.6	7.4	2.7	−20
Norway	6.5	2.9	0.0	4.0	2.7	10.9	4.0	+16
Scotland	21.1[a]	15.3[a]	na	30.0[a]	9.4[a]	10.7[a]	3.7[a]	−1[a]

(continued)

Table 2.3 (continued)

	Mathematics achievement (PISA)		Selected outcome indicators					
			Access			Transition		
	% of between-school variance in mathematics achievement	% of between-school variance explained by SES of students and schools	% in programs in compulsory years leading to upper secondary vocational education	% of 25- to 34-year-old dropouts	% of 15- to 19-year-olds not in education or employment	% of 20- to 24-year-olds not in education and unemployed by attainment		% deviation from OECD average in university entry
						Dropouts	Graduates	
Spain	17.2	9.8	0.0	39.0	7.3	7.3	2.8	–6
Sweden	10.9	5.8	0.0	9.0	4.2	11.9	8.2	+26
United States	27.1	18.7	0.0	13.0	7.0	11.3	5.1	+10

a = Figures are for United Kingdom

b = Figure from Secretariat of the Standing Conference of the Ministers of Education and Cultural Affairs of the Länder, Federal Republic of Germany (2009)

na = not available

Sources: OECD (2004, 2006).

and administered by GCE examining boards. High standards are required to pass a subject and gain accreditation, but the subjects can be of the student's own choosing. In terms of accreditation, this could be described as a system of standards, but standards without subject or knowledge prescription. For example, students could achieve high levels of learning in particular fields, such as history, while having poorly developed skills in other areas, such as mathematics. University preparation is sponsored in the areas of intensive study, and supported through a rigorous system of external examinations. However, accreditation is not based on a minimum number of subjects designed as a 'course' and covering a range of learning areas.

In other systems, the academic curriculum at upper secondary level is much more prescribed. In Austria, for example, students undertaking the matriculation certificate (*Reifeprufung*) must study three compulsory subjects – mathematics, German, and a foreign language – and additional subjects from a range of specialist and interdisciplinary electives. The electives provide for some specialisation in certain areas depending on the school. The focus can be on classical languages, mathematics and the sciences, economics and business, instrumental music or art. Similarly, in Finland, students are required to study four compulsory subjects (mathematics, general studies, mother tongue, foreign language) and at least one elective. In both systems, assessment involves academically competitive examinations and graduation based on minimum grades.

Another common model is one involving a range of core and elective subjects grouped into specialist programs, with the course requirements varying depending on the length or duration of study. Denmark, for example, offers two main types of academic programs, one focused on languages and the other on mathematics. There are core subjects common to both programs (Danish, history, biology, music, geography, visual arts, religious education, classical studies, physical education) as well as core subjects unique to each program and specialist electives within each program. Graduation requires successful completion of externally administered written and oral exams with a minimum grade point average. France, Italy, the Netherlands, Norway, Spain, Sweden and Iceland all operate versions of this model of provision – separate specialist academic programs with core subjects common across all strands and either prescribed subjects or electives within each specialist course. Graduation is largely based on examinations, sometimes competitive national exams as in France and the Netherlands, with minimum passing grades or scores for individual subjects and a minimum overall score. Some systems, such as Sweden and Spain, use school-based assessment, though even in these systems there is sensitivity and pressure related to the issue of 'academic standards'. In Sweden, this has seen the introduction of national tests in key core subjects (mathematics, English, Swedish) which have to be used by teachers in the awarding of grades in these subjects.

Graduation (sometimes referred to as matriculation, or *matura*) in most countries requires successful completion of a minimum number of subjects. In Sweden, this means gaining a requisite number of subject credits through successfully completing a course of study. In many systems the requirement is for achieving minimum grades in at least five subjects including a set number of compulsory subjects covering different key learning areas (such as mathematics and native language). An overall score, the equivalent of a grade point average derived from a minimum number of subjects, is sometimes used to set a threshold or standard for the successful completion of the award.

The function of academic programs in all systems, and the requirements around graduation and certification, are influenced by the process and needs of university selection. But there are some important differences in how this works. In some systems, successful completion of academic credentials at the end of schooling automatically qualifies students for entry to university without the need for further selection. In Germany, for example, candidates who are successful in the *Abitur* (the achievement examination taken on completion of upper secondary education) are awarded a general higher education entrance qualification (*Allgemeine Hochschulreife*). The *Abitur* grants access to all courses of study at universities and other higher education institutions. Similarly, in Austria, the *Reifeprüfung* or *Matura* entitles its holders to enrol in university studies of their choice, even though access to some specialist courses may require additional subject study and assessment. In the Netherlands, there may be different programs of academic study, but the VWO (matriculation) certificate qualifies pupils to enter university and higher professional education without further selection.

The onus of selection for university is removed from universities themselves in such countries because the whole organisational structure of schooling, programs and qualifications works to regulate the quality of students, delivering to universities a pool of academically selected and prepared students, homogeneous in skills, training and orientation. Numbers of students are also regulated because academic selection tends to occur early, more rigorously and more overtly than in other systems. The universities can distance themselves from involvement in the business of selection for entry because school organisation from an early stage is geared to the needs of academic recruitment and the promotion through matriculation of a minority of highly selected students. In all three systems (Germany, Austria and the Netherlands), the separation of students along academic lines occurs at the end of primary school or shortly thereafter. The majority of students in each system are channelled away from academic programs into vocational, professional and technical education paths at an early age. Table 2.3 shows that the three systems have the highest proportions of students in primary school and junior secondary years enrolled in programs leading to vocational education in high school (42.9% in Austria, 61.3% in the Netherlands and 47.1% in Germany). A minority of students – between 20% and 40% – are grouped into schools delivering intensive academic training leading to matriculation and university entry. The differentiation mainly occurs on the basis of students' ability and preference, and already orients students towards post-school study (university, higher education or other forms) or to the labour market on completion of school. Consequently, the rates of entry to university tend to be well below OECD averages in the three systems (see Table 2.3). These countries also tend to have high levels of variation in academic achievement across schools. Approximately 56% of the variance in mathematics achievement among 15-year-olds in Germany is due to between-school differences (compared to 27.1% in the United States, 10.9% in Sweden and 3.9% in Finland, see Table 2.3).[2] In Austria, the rate was 55.5% and in the Netherlands 54.5%. Social differences in intake account for much of the between-school differences in all three countries (43.8% in Germany, 40.7% in the Netherlands and 35.2% in Austria). This is an indication that the school systems are highly segregated along social as well as academic lines.

University selection also influences the graduation requirements in other countries. However, where systems are more comprehensive and secondary education less differentiated, both in terms of school organisation and program structure, universities tend to undertake their own selection process or be heavily involved in the establishment of selection criteria. They are less likely to rely on school qualifications as the sole requirement for admission. In Sweden, for example, which has some similar features in school organisation to the United States, all upper secondary programs give access to higher education, formally at least. Admission decisions on the selection of students are made by the individual universities. This occurs within a national framework of credit points based on teacher assessment, other specific tests such as the university standard aptitude test, and previous education and work experience. In Spain, successful completion of the *bachillerato* (baccalaureate) grants access to the university selection process. To enter university, students must currently, in addition to obtaining the *bachillerato*, pass a national admissions examination.

The academic courses and graduation criteria work in such systems to provide access to the opportunity to compete for university selection, rather than to a university place itself (as would happen in Austria or Germany). The most extreme version of this is in Japan where, despite highly competitive academic exams at different stages of schooling, at which success is necessary for access to the next stage, students who graduate with a high school 'leaving certificate' still have to sit for a competitive national university entrance exam in order to be considered for admission to university.

In such systems, the universities do not rely on the school qualification alone as the entry status marker. This is in part because the number of university places falls far short of the numbers of students graduating from the academic school programs. In some countries, such as Australia, the response is to use high school subject grades translated into a university entrance score. In other systems, such as in Sweden and Spain, it is to impose further selection requirements such as entry exams. It may be no coincidence that such practices occur in countries that have

---

[2] These figures were derived through an analysis of mathematics achievement using the PISA mathematics scale (see OECD, 2004, pp. 161–163 for an explanation of method). Variance was measured based on percentages of the average variance between OECD countries in student performance. For example, the total variance in student performance in the United States was 9,016 compared to the average OECD variance level of 8,593 giving a percentage of 104.9. For each country, variance is divided between that attributable to achievement levels of students in different schools (between-school differences) and that attributable to the range of student results within schools (within-school differences).

been successful in promoting higher proportions of students into academic programs in secondary school by delaying selection of branches of study to much later in schooling. A sizeable group of countries possess a largely comprehensive model in which students continue with a core curriculum until the end of the compulsory years (often at age 16). This is the model that exists in England and Scotland, many of the Nordic countries, as well as Spain, France and Italy. In these countries, students only choose a particular branch or type of schooling at the end of the compulsory phase, often following exams or assessments that lead to an accredited school certificate or qualification. Few countries have the system of secondary schooling that characterises the United States, Canada and most states of Australia in which there is no secondary school certificate or formal assessment to mark the end of the compulsory years.

Countries that postpone the point at which students have to choose a particular branch or type of schooling (those with no or low percentages of students in programs in the junior years tracking to high school vocational courses, see Table 2.3) do tend to encourage more students into academic programs leading to higher education. This can operate within the structure of a single certificate arrangement, as in the United States, where all students who graduate formally or technically qualify for higher education, or in a diversified high school program and accreditation structure as in Norway, Denmark, Spain, Japan and France where there are academic and alternative qualifications and only part of the student population enters a program oriented to university entry, even though the latter tends to be the majority of students.

Systems that defer the point of program choice tend to encourage more students into academic courses. But it would be wrong to conclude that institutional and program arrangements in such systems are not geared around the selective requirements of academic preparation for university entry. Even the most integrated and formally open secondary school systems tend to be organised around the needs of academic selection. Norway, for example, offers a wide range of general and vocational upper secondary programs which work to accommodate diversity in aptitudes and interests, while maintaining a more homogeneous group of the most academically skilled in the university-preparatory courses. Graduation from the academic preparatory courses is based on examination success and minimum grades in core subjects. In the United States, tracking serves the same purpose. Subject selection or more formal ability selection can work to group higher achieving students together in higher tracks, usually in mathematics and science classes, and low achieving students in lower track classes. The system of college preparatory classes for advanced students and general education and vocational classes for others sifts and sorts along academic lines, working to serve the needs of academic selection as the primary function.

The standards debate around graduation, and the push in the United States to install hurdle requirements through exit examinations and high-stakes testing, is usually focused on the standards of those who are not college-bound and the minimum skill levels they should possess or display in order to earn a diploma. A problem is that if higher standards are set (and high-quality learning and achievement for all is a worthy national goal for education), it is important to ensure that the conditions are in place to deliver that high-quality learning for all. Currently, the upper secondary structures in most countries effectively prepare selected numbers of students for academic pathways. The challenge is around how effectively they deal with the learning needs and achievement standards of the remaining groups of students.

Alternative Pathways

Not all students are able to or want to pursue academic pathways leading to university. While traditionally upper secondary courses were designed mainly for an academic elite, most countries have developed alternative courses and qualifications to enable an increasing number of young people, with a wider range of abilities, to complete school and graduate with a relevant qualification. The alternatives mainly involve technical or vocational education. In these developments, one challenge for systems has been to ensure that the programs are of high quality, fostering commitment to learning and personal development, and having valued employment or further education and training outcomes. Another challenge has been to ensure that the programs provide standards of learning that enable continued study in further education once students leave school, rather than being terminal options. The quality of programs is critical in addressing the problems of dropout because it is often the sorts of students at risk of dropping out – those who are not achieving well, those who have tended to become disaffected with school and formal academic work – who are likely to be attracted to available alternatives.

Countries have taken different approaches to these challenges. They differ, for example, in terms of whether vocational and general streams run in parallel or in integrated programs, in terms of the range and organisation of vocational qualifications, in terms of the timing and nature of the choices that young people have to make between distinct pathways and post-school destinations, and in terms of assessment and graduation requirements. Three broad approaches are evident, and these are discussed in detail below.

The first type of approach is to integrate or incorporate vocational options within the general structure and organisation of a more traditional school curriculum. This often involves offering a menu of vocational subject or unit options from which students choose, in combination with general and academic subjects, options that can be used as part of credit sequences which accumulate and are counted with other credits to meet completion requirements. This approach could be described as an 'education or school-based' model of vocational provision because it attempts to incorporate vocational education into the existing structure and logic of more traditional secondary school studies. Even though vocational units or subjects can be organised around areas of employment, industry or occupation, the modules of study tend to be school-based and school-delivered, designed in line with assessment and syllabus requirements of traditional school subjects. This approach is more frequently provided in systems that have comprehensive school settings in the upper secondary years attended by university-bound students as well as those pursuing other destinations.

One example is provided by the United States where students have vocational choices as part of a menu of subject options. The vocational subjects tend to be designed around specific occupations in particular industries such as agriculture, business or health care. The sort of pathway vocational-track students would follow to graduation is to take a minimum number of credits in compulsory areas (such as English, mathematics, social studies, science, health and physical education), along with a number of credits in elective subjects from a menu including vocational options. The vocational electives can represent as much as one third of the required high school study. Alternatively, students may choose not to take any vocational subjects, since most high school students are free to take as much – or as little – vocational coursework as they want. This means that there can be varying levels of intensity of study in vocational education. Figures from the 1990s reveal that while the majority of high school students in the United States took at least one vocational education course (defined very broadly to cover a range of subjects from occupationally specific labour market preparation subjects to consumer education and technology), about 21% took a concentrated sequence of units that could be described as a vocational program or track (Laird et al., 2006). The rest enrolled in either a college-preparatory track (38%) or a general track (neither college-preparatory nor vocational, 41%). Of those taking largely a vocational program, about a quarter also completed a college-preparatory curriculum.

Based on outcomes data, vocational programs would appear to deliver some benefits as an alternative pathway for potential dropouts. Bishop and Mane (2004) reported that compared to other course takers, students taking larger numbers of vocational education units or subjects were more often lower achievers (based on Grade 8 grade point average) and from lower socioeconomic status (SES) backgrounds. Even so, in an analysis of short- and long-term returns to high school study, Bishop and Mane found that compared to other school leavers, those who opted for more vocational education tended, all else equal, to spend more time employed both in the initial post-school years and 8 years later. Other studies report equivalent employment outcomes, through lower levels of participation and completion in post-secondary education and lower earnings for those with stronger vocational preparation in school (Laird et al., 2006; Levesque et al., 2000). Bishop and Mane (2004) noted that stronger emphasis on vocational preparation courses in upper secondary education tended to increase school attendance of 15- to 19-year-olds. Other work also suggests that, all else equal, the more vocational education classes the students take, the less likely they are to drop out (Mertens et al., 1982, for example), and that part of the reason for this is the positive effects of vocational education courses on student engagement resulting from participation in applied, work-based learning (Hughes et al., 2001; Steinberg, 1998).

A similar model of vocational education to that found in the United States operates in Australian schools. The majority of young people enter a general education pathway at the end of compulsory education (Year 10 in most states). Usually completed over 2 years, students can take vocational education subjects as part of their sen_or school certificate. To qualify for a certificate, students must generally complete a sequence of elective units or subjects with most final year students needing to successfully complete a minimum number of subjects, including English. One difference from the United States is that as well as obtaining a secondary school certificate, students enrolled in vocational education courses can also obtain a separate certificate for their vocational study, effectively providing a dual qualification. Vocational education programs can consist of stand-alone, nationally recognised, industry-specific courses based on industry training packages, which are also accredited for the secondary school certificate, though integration into school certificates varies across states. Some of the vocational education programs contain structured workplace learning with expected competency-based learning outcomes included in assessment.

In 2001, about 21% of Year 12 (final school year) students in Australian schools enrolled in at least one vocational education subject or course (Lamb & Vickers, 2006).[3] The rate was 29% for students from low SES backgrounds, and 11% for those from high SES backgrounds. The chances of unemployment in the first post-school year were lower among graduates who had undertaken some vocational preparation than among dropouts, and about the same as graduates who did not take any vocational education, though this varied depending on the type of program studied. There is also some evidence that students who studied vocational education courses in school were more likely to complete school because their study (including experiences in the workplace) helped them to form more positive views about learning and school. Students in Year 9 who reported plans to drop out more often completed school if they entered vocational courses rather than academic or general programs (Lamb & Vickers, 2006).

A second broad approach to the provision of alternative upper secondary pathways is to provide stand-alone vocational education qualifications where there is little or no attempt at integration with the academic or general high school curriculum. Instead, the alternative pathways have much stronger connections to employment and enterprises. The content of programs (including identified occupation skills and competencies) and assessment are often designed by agencies associated with employer and craft guilds, usually accredited or administered by labour and commerce ministries rather than education departments, and often legally governed by vocational training or commerce acts rather than education statutes. In such systems, vocational programs and qualifications have close links with the labour market and weak links with higher education, even though further education is often possible in the same vocational area. The programs are therefore sharply differentiated from academic programs where the main focus is preparing students for university. The programs and qualifications are mainly provided in separate schools. It is also a feature of such systems that separation based on selection or preferences tends to occur earlier in

---

[3]The rate is closer to 14% using the approach applied in the United States by Laird et al. (2006) in defining a vocational program or course as a concentrated sequence of vocational units or subjects.

school, and students sometimes enter schools and courses in lower secondary education that already orient them towards vocational programs in upper secondary education. There are several examples.

In Austria, young people choose between a general education and several vocational pathways at a relatively young age. Most opt for vocational/technical pathways, with about 20% of all students completing their ninth year of compulsory schooling at a 1-year pre-vocational school (*Polytechnische Schule*), which qualifies them for transition to apprenticeship training within the dual system. There are a number of different types of schools offering technical and vocational education programs in the upper secondary years. In general, there are two pathways, the first involving apprenticeships as part of the dual system, and the second involving study either at a secondary technical or vocational school (*Berufsbildende mittlere Schule*), which provides intermediate vocational training, or at an advanced-level secondary vocational school (*Berufsbildende höhere Schule*). After reaching the end of the compulsory years, over 50% of students enter a school-based vocational route or an apprenticeship.

Similar structures are found in Germany, Switzerland, the Netherlands and Denmark. In Germany, after the universal 4-year primary-school period, educational pathways diverge within the secondary school system, which consists of vocationally focused schools (*Hauptschule*), general secondary schools (*Realschule*), academic schools (*Gymnasium*) and schools that combine these elements (*Gesamtschule*). The different pathways often converge within the dual system, which accepts graduates of all schools. At upper secondary level, the majority of German students (two thirds of each age cohort) undertake vocational training. In the Netherlands, secondary education, compulsory until the age of 16, is offered at several levels. Lower secondary vocational education (VMBO) programs combine general and vocational education, after which pupils can continue in upper secondary vocational education and training (MBO). Upper secondary vocational education (MBO) is offered in the areas of economics, technology, health, personal care, social welfare and agriculture. MBO programs vary in length from 1 to 4 years, as well as varying in level (from 1 to 4). About half of all upper secondary students take vocational programs.

There are variations to this broad approach, with some systems delaying the separation of students along academic and vocational pathways until the post-compulsory years. Examples are provided by Italy, Spain, Japan and France. In France, for example, many children enter vocational school after finishing lower secondary school. In vocational school, they do either a *certificate d'aptitude professionnelle (CAP)* or a *brevet d'études professionnelles (BEP)*. Neither of these qualifications gives access to tertiary-level courses, but most young people who do enter vocational school leave for work. Both courses are taken over 2 years, and both offer training in a wide range of occupations in industrial, commercial and service sectors. It is possible for pupils who pass the BEP to do a further 2 years study to get the *baccalauréat professionnel* (or *bac pro*), giving access to university. About 40% of secondary school students enrol in vocational programs, and about 17% leave school having completed the CAP or BEP. In Japan, of the 30% of high school students who take a vocationally based program, approximately two thirds enter vocational high schools (either special training colleges or miscellaneous schools) for a 3-year course. The remaining third enter colleges of technology for a 5-year course. Vocational programs combine learning modes, with theoretical and practical education at a vocational school or college alternating with practical training in an approved company or organisation. Courses are based on promoting applied technical skills linked to key occupations.

A third broad approach to the provision of alternative pathways is one in which separate vocational education programs are offered in upper secondary education, but these programs retain links with academic and general education and keep open avenues to higher education. Examples are provided in several Nordic countries, in particular Sweden, Norway and Finland. In Sweden and Norway, upper secondary education is largely provided in comprehensive schools as in the United States and Australia. In Sweden, after completing compulsory schooling, students proceed to a 3-year upper secondary school. Starting upper secondary education means choosing between a wide set of different educational tracks or programs. There are 17 national programs and numerous regional special programs. Over 50% of students embark on one of 14 national vocational programs when they enter the post-compulsory years, with the remaining students taking up one of two general or academic courses. All programs include a common set of core subjects (Swedish/Swedish as a second language, English, mathematics, religion, civics, science studies, physical education and health, and artistic activities) with the core subjects accounting for about one third of the tuition. The remaining time, pupils study program-specific subjects and choices. The national programs are frameworks within which the pupils can choose various specialisations, based on a sequence of credit-based units, with graduation requiring successful completion of a requisite number of core and other credits. The vocational programs are based on specific occupations and industries. All national programs qualify students for further study including higher education.

Completion of basic education in Finland leads to a choice in upper secondary school between general education or a vocational program. Both alternatives last 3 years and completion of the studies provides eligibility to apply for higher education. About 50% of high school students undertake vocational education. There are 52 vocational qualifications which provide generic basic vocational skills for work (in any field) and more specialised skills in one employment sector. For every program, 25% is core or elective and 75% is vocational studies, including about 15% in on-the-job learning. As in Norway, a vocational qualification can be obtained either through school-based education, or in the form of apprenticeship training. Apprenticeship training is based on an employment agreement (apprenticeship contract) between the student and the employer, confirmed by the education provider. The completion of a vocational qualification takes 3 years and provides, formally at least, access to higher education.

In Norway, upper secondary education is split into 15 education programs: 3 prepare for higher education and 12 are vocational. About half of the commencing cohort enters vocational pathways, though it is possible for students to transfer to the general education pathway in order to qualify for tertiary education. As in

Sweden, students undertake a set of common core and specialist subjects. Each educational program comprises a more basic first year, and 2 years of specialisation. Most vocational programs convert the last year of specialisation into 2 years of apprenticeship training in enterprises. The vocational preparation is based on specific occupations and industries.

Impact of Alternative Pathways

There are few robust comparative evaluations of the effectiveness of the various alternative pathways looking at the issues of differentiation, inclusiveness and outcomes. It is possible to look in a descriptive way at the relationship between vocational pathways and graduation rates across countries by mapping rates of school completion against proportions of vocational graduates. This information is displayed in Fig. 2.1. The completion rates presented in Fig. 2.1 are cohort-based rates rather than the OECD measure using the percentage of upper secondary graduates to the population at the typical age of graduation. The rates were derived from reports provided by individual Ministries of Education and National Bureaus of Statistics.[4]

Figure 2.1 suggests that the different approaches to providing vocational pathways are related, on the surface at least, to differences in overall rates of completion. It shows that there is a tendency for countries that have higher completion rates to also have higher proportions of vocational education graduates.

The group of nations that operate vocational education programs as separate qualifications or tracks, including Germany, Austria, Denmark and the Netherlands, tend to have the highest rates of school completion. Sweden, which offers vocational programs that can qualify students for higher education, also has a relatively high graduation rate. Other factors need to be considered before drawing any causal conclusions, but the patterns suggest that systems enrolling more students in vocational education tend to have high rates of school completion.

Do high school completion rates promoted through program diversification come at the cost of stronger levels of social stratification? Diversification does contribute to social and achievement differentiation within nations: participation in different pathways is strongly linked to family background, and the different pathways promote social stratification. One measure of this is provided by OECD research using PISA data on the achievement of 15-year-olds collected from more than 35 OECD and other nations in 2000 (OECD, 2005). The data were used to measure the degree of institutional differentiation in each education system, and revealed that the countries that have more program and institutional diversification, such as Germany, Austria and the Netherlands, also have substantially higher levels of between-school variance in SES (OECD, 2005, p. 54). Differences in SES

---

[4]For a comparison using OECD estimates of graduation, see Bishop and Mane (2004, pp. 384–385).

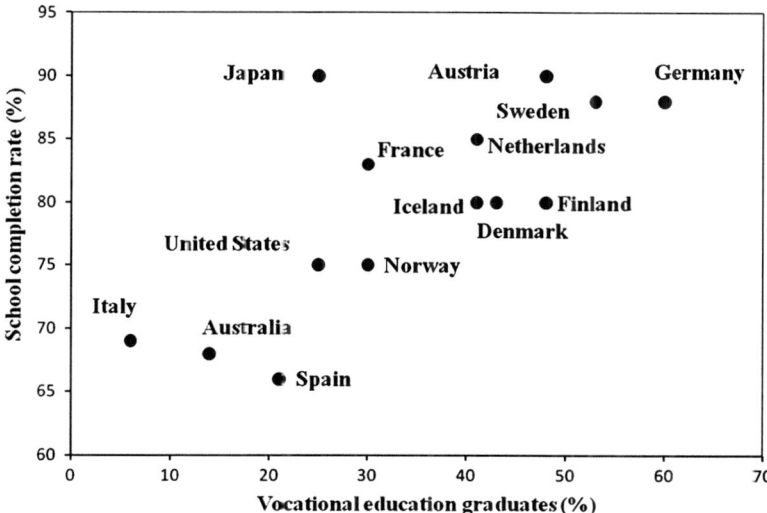

Fig. 2.1 Upper secondary vocational education graduates, by school completion rates: selected OECD nations (Sources: see list at bottom of Table 2.2)

composition are more marked in those systems that promote selection of students into different schools and tracks at younger ages, even if these systems ultimately achieve high rates of school completion. Levels of social stratification across schools and programs are lower in systems that operate more comprehensive models of schooling. In highly diversified or segmented systems, social background is strongly linked to the school one attends and the curriculum track one takes.

Program and institutional diversification also promote stronger inequality in achievement. The second column in Table 2.3 shows cross-national differences in the levels of between-school variance in student mathematics achievement reported by the OECD using PISA data from the 2003 survey. The proportion of between-school variance in student performance was obtained through multilevel analysis and expressed as a percentage of total variance in student performance within a country (OECD, 2006). Total variance for each country is an aggregate of estimated levels of differences between schools and differences between students within schools. The figures show that the more diversified systems had the highest levels of between-school differences in achievement. Austria (55.5%), Germany (56.4%) and the Netherlands (54.5%) recorded between-school variance in mathematics achievement for 15-year-olds at rates more than double the rates for the United States (27.1%), England (21.1%), Spain (17.2%) and Sweden (10.9%). In the more diversified systems, students' achievement levels are strongly affected by the schools that they attend and the courses that they take. Recent *Education at a Glance* figures (OECD, 2007, p. 279) show that in many countries, even after controlling for social and other background differences, achievement levels of vocational education students are significantly lower than for students in academic and general programs. This suggests that the vocational education pathways attract lower achieving students and can also be associated with lower standards of learning and achievement in areas such as mathematics (OECD, 2007).

A measure of the impact of social segregation on achievement in highly segmented systems is provided in the amount of between-school variance in student achievement that is accounted for by differences in student and school SES. Column 3 in Table 2.3 reports the percentage of variance in mathematics achievement explained by student SES and school social intake. In the highly segmented systems, student and school SES account for high proportions of between-school achievement differences. In Austria (35.2%), Germany (43.8%) and the Netherlands (40.7%), the percentage of between-school variance explained by the SES of students and schools is nearly double or more than the level of the United States (18.7%), and larger again when compared against England (15.3%), Spain (9.8%), Sweden (5.8%) and Australia (15.4%). Highly segmented systems are also more socially segregated.

While heightened social stratification may well be a risk of program and institutional diversification implemented as a means to achieving high upper secondary completion rates, this may be offset to some extent if the vocational and other alternative qualifications provide tangible benefits. This is a point made by Shavit and Muller (2000) in their cross-national study of vocational secondary education. They argue that alternative pathways provided by vocational education can work as a safety net, enhancing students' chances of finding gainful employment as skilled workers, while at the same time operating as a mechanism of social reproduction by diverting working-class students from upper secondary programs that lead to higher education and the professions. From this perspective, students who remain at school and complete a vocational or other non-academic upper secondary qualification are in a better position than those who drop out without completing any qualification, even if gaining the qualification has been achieved by being diverted away from more highly valued academic programs.

Do the alternative pathways offered in different systems provide good outcomes for students? Do they enhance students' chances of finding gainful employment as skilled workers? Estimates of economic prospects in the transition to the labour market suggest that there are returns to upper secondary qualifications in aggregate. OECD-derived estimates of unemployment among 20- to 24-year-olds show that unemployment rates are much lower for those with an upper secondary qualification than for those without, and as much as three times lower in some countries (see columns 7 and 8 in Table 2.3 for comparative rates across countries). However, these estimates do not separate out the effects of different types of upper secondary qualifications and pathways. While there are few robust international comparative evaluations of the effectiveness of the various alternative pathways, assessments of impact are available for individual systems and they tend to highlight the importance and value of vocational education qualifications, at least in comparison with dropping out and not gaining an upper secondary qualification.

Figure 2.2, for example, shows employment and unemployment experiences of a sample of 1998 school leavers over seven post-school years in France, by school attainment (Moncel, 2007). Long-term unemployment refers to those with either long

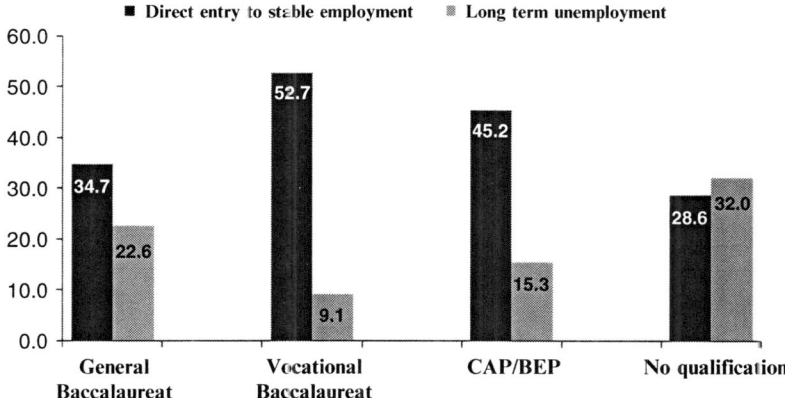

Fig. 2.2 Stable employment and long-term unemployment as main labour market experiences over seven post-school years, by attainment: France (%) (Source: Moncel, 2007)

periods looking for work over the first seven post-school years, or recurrent spells of unemployment over that time. The patterns suggest that school leavers with vocational qualifications, either vocational baccalaureate or the shorter CAP and BEP certificates, are far less likely to experience long-term unemployment (9.1% and 15.3%, respectively) compared to either those who graduate with a general baccalaureate (22.6%) or those who do not gain any upper secondary qualification (32%). Those with vocational qualifications are also more successful at gaining early direct entry from school to stable long-term employment. The results suggest positive returns to alternative pathways in France.

The results in France are consistent with patterns in other countries. Figure 2.3 presents unemployment rates by qualification in four countries: the Netherlands, Ireland, Scotland and Sweden. The figures were derived by Ianelli and Raffe (2007) from national school leavers' surveys undertaken in the mid-1990s and are based on activities of leavers up to 4 years after leaving school. The results show that in each country, there is a lower rate of unemployment amongst those who have upper secondary qualifications than amongst dropouts (those with less than an upper secondary qualification). The gap can be quite large. In Sweden, for example, the rate of unemployment for those with vocational qualifications is almost three times lower than the rate for dropouts. In Scotland and Ireland, there are also positive effects for vocational qualifications. In the Netherlands, young people with vocational non-apprenticeship qualifications are half as likely to be unemployed as those without an upper secondary qualification. In all countries, those with an academic qualification were least likely to be unemployed.

The results for France and these other four nations are consistent with studies in other countries showing positive effects for upper secondary vocational qualifications compared to lower secondary education only or no qualifications (Payne, 1995; Dearden et al., 2001; Ryan, 2001, 2003; Van de Werfhorst, 2002; Gangl, 2003; Silverberg et al., 2004).

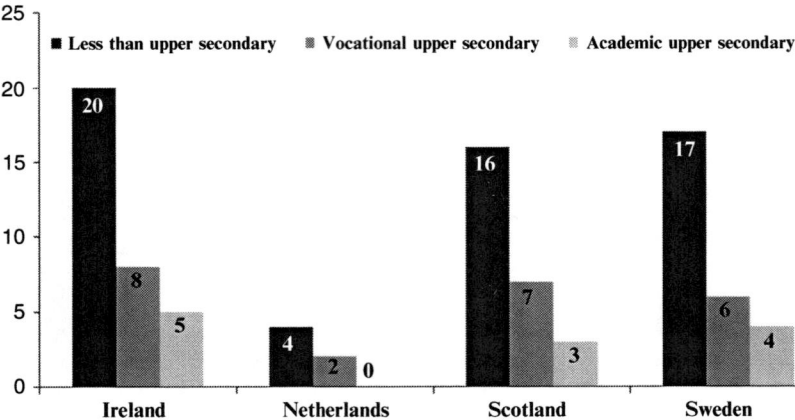

Fig. 2.3 Unemployment rates, by school attainment and qualification type: Ireland, Netherlands, Scotland and Sweden (%) (Source: Ianelli & Raffe, 2007)

The results for France shown in Fig. 2.2 reveal an unexpected feature, which is the suggestion that there are positive returns for vocational qualifications when compared with academic qualifications, at least as measured by long-term unemployment. The results on other labour market outcome measures, however, reverse this pattern. According to Moncel's (2007) analysis, fewer graduates from vocational compared to academic programs enter higher education, and for those in the labour market, the vocational education effect is not evident when it comes to earnings or occupational prestige, at least for those with a CAP or BEP certificate compared to those with a general baccalaureate.

Making valid cross-national comparisons of the impact of different models of program provision and pathways on student outcomes is not a simple matter, partly because there are so few comparisons and little available comparative data that can support robust analytical modelling. In terms of inclusiveness, at a broad system level, the simple comparisons shown in Tables 2.2 and 2.3 and Fig. 2.1 suggest that despite the social segregation, the highly diversified models of provision in countries such as Germany, the Netherlands, Denmark and Austria can promote high levels of completion. The percentage of 15- to 19-year-olds not in education or training is relatively low in countries that have such arrangements (4.7% in Germany, 4.6 in the Netherlands and 3.0% in Denmark). This is partly due to older compulsory leaving age (at least in Germany) and long duration of all of the pathways, but also due to the diversity of programs that these systems offer to meet the needs and interests of a wide range of young people. The attainment levels of 20- to 24-year-olds suggest that these systems do well in getting high proportions of school leavers to graduate with an upper secondary qualification, even if for the majority it is from a vocational education pathway.

The highest attainment levels are in the systems that provide separate vocational programs in upper secondary education, but which permit movement between such programs and academic or general education and provide avenues from alternative pathways to higher education. In Finland and Sweden, fewer than 10% of 20- to 24-year-olds are without an upper secondary qualification or not in education and training. Furthermore, these countries have comparatively high rates of graduation from general and academic pathways and strong entry rates into higher education (20% or more above the OECD average).

In terms of labour market outcomes, the simple comparisons at a system level shown in Table 2.3 may reflect at least in part the nature and structure of pathways taken. In every country, the percentage of 20- to 24-year-olds not in education and unemployed in 2004 is larger for those who left school without an upper secondary qualification than for those who left with a qualification. In some countries, the rates of unemployment are quite large. For example, the rates of unemployment in France are comparatively high for both groups (23.7% for dropouts and 9.8% for graduates). Yet, the large gap between the two groups suggests, particularly when viewed in conjunction with the cohort graduation rates presented in Fig. 2.2, some capacity for the vocational pathways in France to connect a proportion of young people to the labour market in the initial school-to-work transition period. In some countries, the provision of alternative pathways can also be associated with high rates of transition to higher education, suggesting that the range of upper secondary pathways is providing part of the youth cohort with high-quality vocational education qualifications combined with university entry certification. Sweden and Finland both have above average rates of entry to higher education, high rates of school completion, low rates of social segregation across schools and strong returns to upper secondary qualifications when compared against those outcomes for dropouts.

It is difficult to conclude much from the comparisons of outcomes in Table 2.3, however, because the results do not separate out the effects of the different alternative pathways in each country. Nor do they take account of differences between the populations of students who did and did not graduate, which is needed to assess the independent effects of the alternative qualifications. It is not possible to accurately measure effects without more rigorous modelling of the returns to qualifications. Such studies comparing returns to upper secondary qualifications, particularly cross-national studies, are rare. One exception is the study by Shavit and Muller (1998, 2000). They examined the impact of vocational education qualifications on occupational attainment in the early post-school years using similarly structured country data sets (from the 1980s and 1990s). Some of their results are presented in Table 2.4.

The results in columns 2 and 3 of the table are the log odds ratios of getting a first job as a skilled rather than unskilled worker. The numbers (presented as log odds ratios) are a way of representing the probability of gaining skilled work rather than unskilled work. The larger the number above 1, the more positive the effect of vocational education in helping graduates gain a job as a skilled worker. The results suggest that in most countries, upper secondary vocational qualifications have positive effects compared against dropout (not gaining any school qualifications), though not in Sweden or the United States. There are mixed patterns when effects of vocational qualifications are compared against academic education. In the

Table 2.4 Country differences in the effects of vocational education qualifications on occupational outcomes for males

	Log chances of entering labour market as skilled rather than unskilled worker		Occupational prestige (standard deviation units)
	Compared to dropout	Compared to academic qualification	Compared to academic qualification
Australia	2.53	2.57	0.04
United Kingdom	1.72	0.62	–0.15
France	1.54	0.45	–0.28
Germany	3.05	na	–0.30
Italy	1.11	0.22	–0.16
Netherlands	1.14	1.10	–0.36
Sweden	0.59	0.52	–0.51
United States	0.71	0.20	–0.11

Source: Shavit & Muller (2000).

Netherlands and Australia, the results are positive (numbers greater than 1) for vocational qualifications, suggesting that there are gains to vocational training in school. In all of the other countries, the results favour academic education. The same is true in looking at the results for occupational prestige (the social standing or status of occupations). The authors claim that cross-national differences in effects of vocational education are in part related to differences in institutional characteristics and program design, with effects bigger in countries where programs have a strong occupational specificity and where there are strong linkages with labour market organisations (Shavit & Muller, 2000). It is important to note that the results relate only to the first job on entry to the labour market and may not reflect longer-term career effects. Vocational education effects in career beginnings may be short-lived as students who gained academic training take advantage of better career advancement. No account is taken of rates of entry to higher education and further study. Furthermore, in some countries such as Australia, the data relate to periods when vocational education in schools was undeveloped and involved only very small numbers.

A more recent study of four countries by Iannelli and Raffe (2007) examined employment outcomes for young people making the transition from school to work in four countries: the Netherlands, Ireland, Scotland and Sweden. They compared outcomes according to different types of school qualifications and across countries. The study included calculations of the probabilities of employment outcomes controlling for country, qualification level and grades. The findings revealed that at a broad level vocational qualifications were more likely than lower secondary education to lead to participation in post-secondary education (at least for males). Vocational education options were less likely than academic qualifications to lead to study in post-secondary education. There was a positive vocational education effect for entry to employment rather than being unemployed when compared with dropouts, but no effect in comparison with academic graduates. Differences were also reported across countries, with the vocational education effects appearing stronger in the country that emphasised employment-linked or employment-based vocational programs.

Pathways to Completion for School Dropouts

Despite the range of alternative programs offered to encourage more young people to remain in school and complete, most countries have numbers of students who drop out before gaining a qualification and the numbers can be large. In Australia, the dropout rate is about 30% (Lamb et al., 2004). In the United Kingdom, one estimate places it at about 25%, though much higher if it includes those who did not obtain five or more A* to C grade General Certificate of Secondary Education (end of compulsory education) results – this would place the dropout rate at closer to 40% according to estimates for 2005/2006 published by the Office for National Statistics (2006). For the Netherlands, the level is around 15%, with a rate of 10% for those entering vocational pathways and 4% for those in general or academic programs (ven de Steeg & Webbink, 2006; Ministry of Education, Culture and Science, 2007). In Denmark and Finland, it is about 10% (Ministry of Education, 2005; Statistics Finland, 2007), in Spain over 30% (Ministry of Education and Science, 2006), and in France around 17% (Moncel, 2007).

Systems have responded to the problem of dropout in different ways. Some have resorted to legal and rather blunt measures by increasing the compulsory school leaving age, a measure which may keep students at school, but does not guarantee successful graduation, in part because it does not address the reasons why young people want to quit school in the first place. But many have responded by strengthening or putting in place opportunities for dropouts to gain upper secondary or equivalent qualifications outside of school. These external or post-school alternative pathways provide opportunities for study and graduation mainly through a range of educational or employment-based schemes. Some of these measures are occasionally criticised for their potential to encourage or induce young people to drop out of school – young people who may otherwise have remained in school and obtained a qualification. One pattern that may reflect this is the gender difference in dropout rates. The tendency for males to drop out of school at a greater rate than females in some countries may be linked to the availability of a wider range of alternatives for males, such as apprenticeships, as well as changes in labour demand (for example, in Australia, see Lamb et al., 2004). Some alternatives may work this way; however, systems face a critical dilemma – students may choose to drop out even if alternatives are not available. With large existing numbers of dropouts in an era where skills and education are more important than ever, can systems afford to restrict opportunities for young people to re-engage in study? Some econometric modelling of alternatives in the United States suggests that while alternative schemes may encourage some to drop out, their removal would not necessarily produce major reductions in dropout rates (Agodini & Dynarski, 2000; Tyler, 2003).

This section will look briefly at some of the main alternative pathways for dropouts to gain upper secondary or equivalent qualifications. There are three main categories examined: (1) those that are equivalent upper secondary credentialing programs, (2) those that provide employment-based education and training pathways such as apprenticeships, and (3) those that involve education-based qualifications through tertiary education institutions.

Upper Secondary Credential Equivalents

Some systems have developed equivalency credentialing programs for young people who do not gain a school-based diploma or certificate. The programs represent equivalents to the general or main high school graduation qualifications. There are two main examples. The first is the General Educational Development (GED) tests in the United States and Canada – a series of tests (in writing, social studies, science, reading and mathematics) that can be taken by those who have not gained a high school diploma. If successful in these tests, a qualification is awarded attesting to the achievement of high-school level academic skills.

The second scheme is the high school graduation proficiency qualification test in Japan. It is similar to the GED in that it is open to those who have not gained their high school diploma (usually those who have been truant from school or home schooled) and it aims to assess the level of skills across key subject areas to secondary school graduation level. The examination gives young people the opportunity to be certified that they have an academic ability equivalent to mainstream secondary school graduates. Success in the tests gives candidates the opportunity to then take the competitive university entry examinations.

In the United States, according to recent figures, about 9% of school leavers successfully complete a GED within 8 years of leaving school (National Center for Education Statistics, 2004). Studies on returns suggest that those who obtain a GED are less likely to go to college than those who obtain a traditional high school diploma, and they have lower earnings in later life (Cameron & Heckman, 1993; Murnane et al., 2000; Rumberger & Lamb, 2003). Murnane et al. (2000) estimate that about 30% of GED recipients had entered college by age 27 compared to 69% of those with a regular diploma. Recent work suggests that in terms of returns the benefits of completing the GED work differently depending on skill levels, providing benefits mainly to those dropouts with the lowest cognitive skills. For dropouts with stronger skills, completion of the GED is not associated with higher earnings (Boesel et al., 1998; Murnane et al., 2000; Tyler et al., 2000). While the returns for those who gain a GED may not be as positive as for those who achieve a high school diploma, GED certification does play a role in the educational attainment of high school dropouts (a point made by Maralani, 2003). Many dropouts resume their schooling at some point and go on to earn a GED. According to a study by the National Center for Education Statistics (1998), those who gain a GED are three times more likely to enter a post-secondary institution than dropouts who do not earn a high school credential.

Apprenticeship Qualifications

In some nations, apprenticeship training is an important pathway for school drop-outs. While in countries such as Germany and Austria, through the dual system, apprenticeships are linked to the school system, in other countries such as Canada, Australia and the United Kingdom, they are generally provided as post-secondary education and training. Apprenticeship-type programs generally involve an indenture or contractual agreement with an employer where a young person is expected to undertake a period of formal training in a classroom setting, sometimes referred to as *block release*, as well as on-the-job experience. The programs are designed to equip young people with the skills associated with a particular craft or trade and to provide certification through widely recognised qualifications. In most systems, apprenticeships are a structured program of vocational preparation sponsored by an employer, involving both part-time education and on-the-job training and work experience, leading to a recognised vocational qualification, and taking up to 4 years to complete. Such schemes are often appealing to young people who drop out of school because they provide a wage while learning (often a training wage, and usually below average earnings for young people not in training). They also involve the acquisition of skills through applied learning in workplaces, again often appealing to dropouts who have become disengaged from formal classroom learning in school settings, providing an alternative for young people not attracted by full-time school. Formally, most systems provide the possibility for moving to higher levels of training after completion of apprenticeship qualifications, though actual progression rates are often low (Centre Européen pour le Développement de la Formation Professionnelle [CEDEFOP], 2001).

Apprenticeships and apprenticeship arrangements vary widely across nations. In some countries, such as the United States, apprenticeships are less well developed as a system of training for young people, organised around a smaller number of occupations, and mainly operate for young adults; therefore, they play less of a role for dropouts. In other systems, such as Australia, they are the major form of education and training available to dropouts. Across nations, apprenticeship programs vary on such matters as length of training (from 6 months to 4 years), how they are entered (through employment contract or formal college enrolment), the requirements around formal learning (initial period of formal training, or on-going mixture of workplace and classroom training, for example), time in the workplace and areas of training. The traditional model of apprenticeship in many systems has been a 4-year indenture in a traditional craft area such as an electrical trade, plumbing, carpentry or automotive trade. However, there have been major reforms in several countries, expanding the areas of occupational training and the length of training. In Ireland and Australia, for example, traineeships have been introduced which provide training in white-collar occupations, such as clerical work (Barry, 2007; Dockery et al., 2005). The traineeships are usually for 12 months rather than 4 years. Modern apprenticeships in the United Kingdom can be short in duration – less than 12 months – and resemble more a program of youth training than a formal apprenticeship indenture program (Ryan & Unwin, 2001; Ryan, 2001).

The evidence available to compare the effects and value of apprenticeships as a pathway for dropouts across nations is meagre. There is information available on individual systems comparing the relative merits of apprenticeships with other qualifications, though. In Australia, for example, the national school dropout rate (numbers of young people entering secondary school and leaving without having gained a senior school qualification) is about 30%, 36% for males and 24% for females (Lamb et al., 2004). In the 1990s, up to 36% of male dropouts took up an apprenticeship and 28% gained a qualification by age 24 (Lamb et al., 1998). For females, the rate of take-up was about 8% and the qualification rate was about 6%. Recent figures suggest similar levels (Lamb & Mason, 2008). Traineeships extend structured training programs to a wider range of occupations than those represented by apprenticeships. Like apprenticeships, traineeships provide wages, but these are usually lower than those of apprenticeships, and traineeships generally provide one year of training rather than four. About 12% of male dropouts gain a traineeship qualification and about 9% of female dropouts do.

Returns to apprenticeships in Australia appear favourable for male dropouts. Regression estimates of the length of time unemployed at age 24 suggest that males gaining apprenticeship qualifications spend significantly less time unemployed than dropouts without qualifications and those with other types of vocational qualifications (Lamb et al., 1998). The rate is similar to that for school graduates. The patterns are similar for females with apprenticeship qualifications though the gaps are not significant. In terms of earnings, average weekly earnings regression equations for 24-year-old full-time workers suggest that males who complete apprenticeships earn 10–11% more than male 24-year-old graduates who do not undertake any post-school education or training. The wage benefits for females are lower, with female apprenticeship graduates earning 2% more than 24-year-olds who had graduated from high school without undertaking any further study.

The effects may hold over careers. Borland et al. (2000) estimated returns using the results of a wage regression equation for male weekly earnings from 1997 data. The equation was estimated for employed males (full- and part-time) aged 18–59. The estimates suggest that those with trade or apprenticeship qualifications earn marginally less than school graduates (3% less), but they earn significantly more than dropouts without any qualifications (14% more).

Evidence from other countries suggests some differences in effects. In France, compared to other labour market entrants, apprentices are likely to have more stable early labour market experiences, spending more of their early working lives in employment compared to other labour market entrants, though their pay is lower at the end of 5 years (Bonnal et al., 1999). In the United Kingdom, apprenticeship graduates tend to have higher employment rates, though only for moderate and low achievers. They also tend to have higher earnings, but only for males (Payne, 1995). In several countries, apprenticeship training appears to do less for women than for men, in terms of entry rates, occupational access and subsequent labour market outcomes. This may be because there is considerable gender segregation in the areas of apprenticeship training, consistent with patterns of gender segmentation in occupations and labour markets.

In sum, apprenticeships provide an important alternative pathway for school drop-outs. Compared to those who attempt to enter the labour market without post-school education and training, apprenticeship graduates enjoy benefits in terms of stable employment, less risk of unemployment and higher earnings. Apprenticeship shows up particularly well in such comparisons, being associated with gains in pay as well as employment. The returns may not hold up as well compared against mainstream high school qualifications, but for male dropouts the evidence suggests that they are an important avenue of successful transition from school to full-time work.

Vocational Education Qualifications

Another avenue for school dropouts to obtain qualifications is the range of vocational education qualifications usually offered through tertiary institutions such as further education colleges, polytechnics, and adult and community colleges, depending on the country. In many countries, more and more young people have come to rely on opportunities in community and adult education and training as they make the transition from school to work. As a result, the numbers of school leavers who enter employment without participating in some recognised form of further education or training have declined (for example, see OECD, 2006, p. 329, for trends in participation in education and training of 20- to 24-year-olds). It is through the tertiary education and training system that dropouts who struggle to find work can acquire the skills and attain the upper secondary or equivalent qualifications that can help make them more competitive in the labour market. The parts of the tertiary education sector that offer opportunities for dropouts to gain vocational qualifications comprise a vast number of public and private providers catering to the needs of a wide range of clients. The principal role they play for dropouts is to help provide alternative pathways through which dropouts can enter study, gain qualifications and pursue work, as well as proceed to higher levels of vocational education and general study within the vocational or the higher education sector.

The evidence available for comparisons of the way tertiary education opportunities work for dropouts in different countries is meagre. Data on individual systems looking at comparative returns to qualifications are more readily available. One such study in the United Kingdom was undertaken by McIntosh (2004) who studied the outcomes of the vocational qualifications pathways for 25% of school leavers at 23–25 years of age who had dropped out of school without any qualifications. The study took data on the cohort of individuals who left school in 1993, 1994 and 1995, and examined their further education decisions and early labour market outcomes. The results revealed that 56% of male and 54% of female dropouts gained at least one vocational qualification by their mid-20s. Vocational qualifications are provided at different levels associated with length of study and depth of skills training, with Level 3 qualifications equivalent to A levels (academic high school qualifications). Table 2.5 shows the proportions of dropouts gaining qualifications at each level from Level 1 (low) to Level 3 and above (high).

Table 2.5 Qualification pathways of 23- to 25-year-old dropouts: United Kingdom

No school qualifications	Males (%)	Females (%)
+ no vocational qualification	44.1	46.1
+ vocational level 1 (GCSE D-G standard)	30.7	29.9
+ vocational level 2 (GCSE A-C standard)	11.1	10.8
+ vocational level 3 (A levels)	5.4	4.1
+ above level 3	8.7	9.1

Source: McIntosh (2004).

Table 2.6 Employment and earnings of 23- to 25-year-old school leavers with no qualifications: United Kingdom

	Females		Males	
	Employed (%)	HRLY wage	Employed (%)	HRLY wage
No school qualifications				
+ no vocational qualification	30.6	5.53	68.2	6.05
+ vocational level 1	58.3	7.35	75.3	7.25
+ vocational level 2	70.3	5.44	88.7	7.14
+ vocational level 3	77.4	5.79	94.3	6.22
+ above level 3	93.5	8.23	77.9	9.45
High school qualifications				
+ no vocational qualification	83.9	6.87	94.4	8.14
+ vocational level 1	90.6	7.81	91.5	7.38
+ vocational level 2	78.0	6.69	94.8	7.98
+ vocational level 3	90.5	8.19	95.8	8.18
+ above level 3	92.0	8.85	91.6	10.03

Source: McIntosh (2004).

The analysis then went on to show that vocational qualifications can significantly impact labour market success, with the group of unqualified school leavers being much less likely to be employed than both dropouts who later gained vocational qualifications, and school leavers who had obtained upper secondary qualifications at school (see Table 2.6). The analysis reveals that those dropouts who do obtain vocational Level 2 or 3 qualifications are much more likely to be in employment than those who do not, their employment likelihood closing significantly on that of those individuals who reach these levels via the academic route at school. To a lesser extent, the wage gap also closes with vocational qualification acquisition, at least for initially unqualified males.

Results obtained in similar studies undertaken for dropouts in Australia are more equivocal. As in the United Kingdom, vocational qualifications in Australia are provided at different levels associated with length of study and depth of skills training. Basic and middle level vocational qualifications, which are the main qualifications undertaken by dropouts in their initial post-school years, are associated with weak, sometimes negative, employment and earnings returns when compared against school graduation, and provide little advantage over dropouts who do not undertake any further study (Lamb et al., 1998). This is not the case with higher level vocational qualifications, which show positive returns, but the participation and graduation rates for dropouts at these levels are low. In the 1990s, approximately 18% of male dropouts gained basic or middle-level vocational qualifications by age 24, with 3% of male and 7% of female dropouts gaining high-level vocational qualifications.

Figures are available on rates of entry to post-secondary education and training for dropouts in other countries (see for example, Berktold et al., 1998, for results on the subsequent educational attainment of dropouts in the United States, and Human Resources Development Canada, 2000, for Canadian estimates). However, data are not readily available to assess the outcomes of gaining alternative qualifications.

Conclusion

In building mass systems of secondary schooling, all nations face the challenge of finding ways to deal with pupil diversity – of finding a place for all – while maintaining high standards of learning. Some nations have been more successful in doing this than others. Historically, the development of the comprehensive high school and the high school diploma in the United States led the way in providing an architecture for secondary education that was inclusive and could promote mass rates of completion. This did not mean that the largely elective-based model did not continue to act as a powerful mechanism of social stratification, but it did help provide a system of mass delivery well in advance of other systems. Today, however, it is a different picture. Rates of graduation in the United States have tended to become stable, entrenched, whereas in other countries the rates have continued to grow, with some systems now achieving high levels of upper secondary completion.

Improvements in other countries have been partly achieved through developments based on the United States model. The Nordic countries of Sweden, Norway and Finland have all reformed their secondary school systems, implementing a comprehensive school model. In addition, during the 1980s and 1990s, these three nations implemented a number of educational reforms to upper secondary program provision focusing largely on vocational education as a means of encouraging students to stay in school. The approach in Sweden, for example, involves a group of vocational and general programs incorporated into a single school certificate. There are 14 vocational programs, structured around different occupational fields. All programs have a number of common subjects (providing a broad-based, general education) as well as generic and specialist options within vocational fields. The structure bridges the divide between vocational and general education by providing a stronger initial foundation in the early stages of all programs to prepare students for further learning. Foundation learning is followed by specialised training. Assessment is continuous with successful completion involving national tests for core subjects. Sweden has a fairly high proportion of vocational graduates, and a comparatively high overall graduation rate.

Another approach to dealing with the issues of pupil diversity and dropout is through offering an array of programs leading to separate qualifications, rather than a single certificate. National models that deal with the problem of pupil diversity through institutional, program and certificate diversification – providing alternative pathways through separate qualifications or certificates (academic, vocational, technical, specialist) – can also successfully promote high rates of graduation. Austria and Germany are good examples; they achieve high overall graduation rates. Vocational education graduates make up the majority of school graduates. Both systems have frameworks that find a place for everyone, though the places are not necessarily of equal value in terms of access to knowledge, learning and outcomes. They are also based on early selection, with students grouped along different school and program paths well before the senior years. The system is based on a selective rather than comprehensive school model. Social divisions across the different levels of qualifications in such systems can be quite marked. In such systems, inclusion can come at the cost of relegation for students from working class backgrounds. This leads to weaker opportunities for social mobility and a greater tendency for the reproduction of social differences in education across generations, even if the vocational alternatives provide positive labour market returns and work as a safety net.

As systems implement further reforms to raise completion rates and eliminate dropout, they will need to build programs and institutional arrangements that can cater for students from diverse backgrounds and with varying talents. The challenge for systems in doing this will be to ensure quality and consistency in the standards of learning for all students across all programs. To date, some nations have been more successful in doing this than others. Providing rigorous and meaningful alternative pathways, built on common foundations of learning that keep open further study options for all, will be the key.

References

Agodini, R., & Dynarski, M. (2000). *Understanding the trend toward alternative certification for high school graduates*. Princeton, NJ: Mathematica Policy Research.

Barry, M. (2007). *Vocational education and training in Ireland: Thematic overview*. Dublin: Training and Employment Authority. Retrieved from http://www.fas.ie/NR/rdonlyres/9ABC5EE1-CF20-4AA5-ACA4-C5B81DD9FE5E/437/PDFonline_vet_in_ireland_2009994.pdf

Berktold, J., Geis, S., & Kaufman, P. (1998). *Subsequent educational attainment of high school dropouts*. Washington, DC: National Center for Education Statistics.

Bishop, J., & Mane, F. (2004). The impacts of career-technical education on high school labour market success. *Economics of Education Review, 23*, 381–402.

Boesel, D., Alsalam, N., & Smith, T. (1998). *Educational and labour market outcomes of GED certification*. Washington, DC: National Library of Education, Office of Educational Research and Improvement, U.S. Department of Education.

Bonnal, L., Fleury, L., & Rochard, M. (1999). L'Insertion Professionnelle des Apprentis et des Lycéens Professionnels: des Emplois Proches des Formations Suivis. *Économie et Statistique, 323*, 3–30.

Borland, J., Dawkins, P., Johnson, D., & Williams, R. (2000). *Returns to investment in higher education* (The Melbourne Economics of Higher Education Research Program Report No. 1). Melbourne: University of Melbourne.

Cameron, S., & Heckman, J. (1993). The nonequivalence of high school equivalents. *Journal of Labour Economics, 11,* 1–47.

Centre Européen pour le Développement de la Formation Professionnelle (CEDEFOP). (2001). *The transition from education to working life: Key data on vocational training in the European Union* (CEDEFOP Reference Series No. 3). Luxembourg: Office for Official Publications of the European Communities. (ERIC Document Reproduction Service No. ED456225)

Dearden, L., McIntosh, S., Myck, M., & Vignoles, A. (2001). *The returns to academic, vocational and basic skills in Britain* (Skills Task Force Research Paper). London: CEP, London School of Economics.

Dockery, M., Koshy, P., & Stromback, T. (2005). *From school to work: The role of traineeships.* Adelaide: NCVER.

Federal Ministry of Education and Research (Germany). (2005). *Basic and structural data, 2005.* Berlin: Federal Ministry of Education and Research.

Gangl, M. (2003). The structure of labour market entry in Europe: A typological analysis. In W. Müller & M. Gangl (Eds.), *Transitions from education to work in Europe* (pp. 95–116). Oxford: Oxford University Press

Hughes, K., Bailey, T., & Mechur, M. (2001). *School-to-work: Making a difference in education. A research report to America.* New York: Institute on Education and the Economy, Teachers College, Columbia University. Retrieved from http://www.tc.columbia.edu/iee/PAPERS/Stw.pdf

Human Resource Development Canada. (2000). *Dropping out of high school: Definitions and costs.* Human Resources and Social Development Canada. Retrieved from http://www.hrsdc.gc.ca/ en/cs/sp/hrsd/prc/publications/research/2000-000063/page00.shtml

Iannelli, C., & Raffe, D. (2007). Vocational upper-secondary education and the transition from school. *European Sociological Review, 23*(1), 49–63.

Laird, J., Chen, X., & Levesque, K. (2006). *The postsecondary educational experiences of high school career and technical education concentrators: Selected results from the NELS·88/2000 postsecondary education transcript study (PETS) 2000* (NCES 2006–309rev). Washington, DC: National Center for Education Statistics, U.S. Department of Education.

Lamb, S., Long, M., & Baldwin, G. (2004). *Performance of the Australian education and training system.* Report for the Victorian Department of Premier and Cabinet, Melbourne. Retrieved from http://www.dpc.vic.gov.au/CA256D800027B102/Lookup/CommonwealthStateRelations report/$file/perf%20of%20aust%20education.pdf

Lamb, S., Long, M., & Malley, J. (1998). *Access and equity in vocational education and training: Results from longitudinal surveys of Australian youth.* ACER Research Monograph No. 55. Melbourne: ACER.

Lamb, S., & Mason, K. (2008). *How young people are faring, 2008.* Report for the Foundation for Young Australians. Melbourne: Foundation for Young Australians.

Lamb, S., & Vickers, M. (2006). *Variations in VET provision across Australian schools and their effects on student outcomes.* LSAY Research Report No. 48. Melbourne: ACER.

Levesque, K., Lauen, D., Teitelbaum, P., Alt, M., & Librera, S. (2000). *Vocational education in the United States: Toward the year 2000* (NCES 2000–029). Washington, DC: National Center for Education Statistics, U.S. Department of Education.

Maralani, V. (2003). *From GED to college: The role of age and timing in educational stratification.* Los Angeles: UCLA, California Center for Population Research. Retrieved from http://escholarship.org/uc/item/9gv1f20x

McIntosh, S. (2004, April). *What difference does it make? Vocational education for low-achieving school-leavers.* Paper presented at the Royal Economic Society Annual Conference, Swansea, Wales. Retrieved from http://repec.org/res2004/McIntosh.pdf

Mertens, D., Seitz, P., & Cox, S. (1982). *Vocational education and the high school dropout.* Columbus, OH: The National Center for Research in Vocational Education, The Ohio State University.

Ministry of Education (Denmark). (2005). *Facts and figures 2005: Education indicators, Denmark, 2005.* Copenhagen: Danish Ministry of Education.

Ministry of Education, Culture and Science (Netherlands). (2007). *Key figures 2002–2006: Education, culture and science in the Netherlands.* Amsterdam: The Ministry of Education, Culture and Science. Retrieved from http://www.minocw.nl/documenten/KEYFIGURES2002_2006.pdf

Ministry of Education and Science (Spain). (2006). *Las Cifras de la Educación en España. Estadísticas e Indicadores* (Edición 2006). Madrid: Ministerio de Educación y Ciencia. Oficina de Estadística.

Moncel, N. (2007). Recent trends in education and labour market policy for school-to-work transition of secondary education school leavers in France. In The Japan Institute for Labour Policy and Training (JILPT Report No. 5), *Transition Support Policy for Young People with Low Educational Background* (pp. 39–59). Tokyo: The Japan Institute for Labour Policy and Training.

Murnane, R., Willett, J., & Tyler, J. (2000). Who benefits from obtaining a GED? Evidence from high school and beyond. *Review of Economics and Statistics, 82*, 23–37.

National Center for Education Statistics. (1998). *Subsequent educational attainment of high school dropouts* (NCES 98–085). Washington, DC: National Center for Education Statistics, U.S. Department of Education.

National Center for Education Statistics. (2004). *Issue brief: Educational attainment of high school dropouts 8 years later*. Washington, DC: National Center for Education Statistics, US Department of Education. Retrieved from http://nces.ed.gov/pubs2005/2005026.pdf

Office for National Statistics. (2006). *Education and training highlights*. Retrieved October 5, 2009, from http://www.statistics.gov.uk/CCI/nugget.asp?ID=1963&Pos=3&ColRank=2&Rank=352

Organisation for Economic Co-operation and Development (OECD). (2004). *Learning for tomorrow's world – First results from PISA 2003*. Paris: OECD.

Organisation for Economic Co-operation and Development (OECD). (2005). *School factors related to quality and equity: Results from PISA 2000*. Paris: OECD.

Organisation for Economic Co-operation and Development (OECD). (2006). *Education at a glance: OECD indicators 2006*. Paris: OECD.

Organisation for Economic Co-operation and Development (OECD). (2007). *Education at a glance 2007: Education indicators*. Paris: OECD.

Payne, J. (1995). *Options at 16 and outcomes at 24: A comparison of academic and vocational education and training routes* (Youth Cohort Report No. 35). Sheffield: Department for Education and Employment.

Rumberger, R. W., & Lamb, S. (2003). The early employment and further education experiences of high school dropouts: A comparative study of the United States and Australia. *Economics of Education Review, 22*(4), 353–366.

Ryan, P. (2001). The school-to-work transition: A cross-national perspective. *Journal of Economic Literature, 39*(1), 34–92.

Ryan, P. (2003). Evaluating vocationalism. *European Journal of Education, 38*, 147–162.

Ryan, P., & Unwin, L. (2001). Apprenticeship in the British 'training market'. *National Institute Economic Review, 178*, 99–114.

Shavit, Y., & Muller, W. (1998). *From school to work: A comparative study of educational qualifications and occupational destinations*. Oxford: Clarendon Press.

Shavit, Y., & Muller, W. (2000). Vocational secondary education, tracking and social stratification. In M. Hallinan (Ed.), *Handbook of the sociology of education* (pp. 437–452). New York: Springer.

Silverberg, M., Warner, E., Fong, M., & Goodwin, D. (2004). *National assessment of vocational education: Final report to congress*. Washington: U.S. Department of Education. Retrieved from www.ed.gov/rschstat/eval/sectech/nave/reports.html4

Statistics Finland. (2007). *Finland in figures: 2007*. Helsinki: Statistics Finland.

Steinberg, A. (1998). *Real learning, real work: School-to-work as high school reform*. New York: Routledge.

Tyler, J. (2003). The economic benefits of the GED: Lessons from recent research. *Review of Educational Research, 73*(3), 369–403.

Tyler, J., Murnane, R., & Willett, J. (2000). Estimating the labour market signaling value of the GED. *Quarterly Journal of Economics, 115*, 431–468.

Van de Werfhorst, H. (2002). A detailed examination of the role of education in intergenerational social-class mobility. *Social Science Information, 41*, 407–438.

Ven de Steeg, M. W., & Webbink, H. D. (2006). Voortijdig schoolverlater in Nederland: omvang, beleid en resultaten, CPB Document 107.

Willms, D. (2006). *Learning divides: Ten policy questions about the performance and equity of schools and schooling systems* (UNESCO Institute for Statistics Working Paper No. 5). Montreal: UIS.

Part II
Case Studies

Introduction to the European Education Systems

Stephen Lamb

Historically, in European nations school dropout was not an issue that received much research attention. Secondary school systems were largely designed to be selective and dropout was a natural consequence. The traditional academic second-ary school, such as the *lycée*, *gymnasium* or *grammar school*, provided a classical education preparing a selected few from the wealthy classes for higher status posi-tions and lifestyles. By their nature these schools were selective, serving the filter-ing and preparation needs of universities and the professions.[1]

The modern need for expansion of secondary education saw the development of alternative forms of school and the diversification of programs, though academic selection remained a dominating feature. Programs at upper secondary level have diversified to include shorter and longer cycles of study, often without common standards of learning and achievement – meaning that while some streams of study prepare students for higher education, others are short-term and terminal, preparing students for the labour market rather than further study.

Therefore, nowadays not all streams of study or training in upper secondary education in European countries give access to tertiary education. In many coun-tries, schools are divided into different types. Some types are more vocational, others are academic. The most obvious example is Germany. Here, many children (although in declining numbers) enter the *Hauptschule*. This ends with the *Hauptschulabschluss* – a certificate which does not give access to tertiary studies. Many children also enter the *Realschule*. This is concluded by the *Realschulabschluss*. If students do well enough, they can then transfer to a *Fachoberschule* (a vocational college). If they graduate with the *Fachhochschulreife*, they can then enter a *Fachhochschule* or a *Gymnasium*, from which they can access university or other

---

[1] See Benavot's paper (The diversification of secondary education: School curricula in compara-tive perspective, *Revista de currículum y formación del profesorado*, 10(1), 1–26, 2006) and the study by Mueller, Ringer and Simon (*The Rise of the Modern Education System*, Cambridge, UK: Cambridge University Press, 1987) for more extensive discussion of these issues.

S. Lamb (✉)
Centre for Post-Compulsory Education and Lifelong Learning,
University of Melbourne, Australia

S. Lamb et al. (Eds.), *School Dropout and Completion: International Comparative Studies in Theory and Policy*, DOI 10.1007/978-90-481-9763-7_3,
© Springer Science+Business Media B.V. 2011

types of tertiary education. Thus children who enter either a *Hauptschule* or a *Realschule* and successfully complete their studies are not able to go directly into tertiary-level courses. They must do further studies and be successful at these higher levels.

Some other countries such as Switzerland and Poland have similar systems, so the German model can be considered important and of fairly wide relevance.

Another example is France. Many children there enter vocational school after finishing lower secondary education. In vocational school, they study towards either a *certificate d'aptitude professionnelle (CAP)* or a *brevet d'études professionnelles (BEP)*. Neither of these qualifications gives access to tertiary-level courses, and most young people who do enter vocational school leave for work. This pathway involves a large number of young people. The problems that it poses by not providing access to tertiary level courses have been officially recognised. As a result, these days an increasing number of young people who do the BEP are taking further vocational training by enrolling in the *baccalauréat professionnel* (or *bac pro*). This can lead to tertiary study, but the great majority (around two thirds) of *bac pro* students leave for work. If they do continue, only about three in ten actually finish the tertiary course because they do not have the academic preparation.

Spain also has important differences between curriculum streams. High school students who undertake intermediate-level vocational studies (*Ciclos Formativos de Grado Medio*) go to work or further training (*Grado Superior*). If they wish to go to university, they must either enrol in the *Bachillerato* and gain their *Título de Bachiller*, or graduate with the *Técnico Superior* which then gives access to university.

Briefly, also, England and Scotland offer various alternative streams of study to young people at the end of compulsory education. Traditional '*A levels*' (England) or *Advanced Highers* (Scotland) can be taken by students wanting to enter university, while other students may take a range of alternatives including vocational qualifications leading to work or further training.

Germany, France, England, Scotland, Switzerland, Poland, and Spain do things differently. But importantly, all of these countries have internally different streams and types of schools that (1) take in young people with different characteristics, and (2) lead in different directions. Thus differences between young people come to be associated with different directions. The implications of these differences for rates of dropout and completion vary between the countries, as the following case studies reveal.

Chapter 3
The Question of School Dropout: A French Perspective

Marianne Blanchard and Rémi Sinthon*

Introduction

At the start of the 1980s, with unemployment rates continuing to rise, the French government targeted the particular difficulties faced by young people who were entering the workforce without qualifications.[1] The Minister for Education called for higher qualification levels from the French population, and this objective was later made official in the law relating to education and careers guidance of 1989. This projected a development over the next decade in which the whole of the age-group would attain a recognised qualification of at least the level of basic vocational awards – the Certificate of Vocational Aptitude (CAP) or the Certificate of Vocational Studies (BEP).[2] This law would contribute to the issue of school dropout coming fully onto the political agenda at the beginning of the 1990s.

The government-led effort to increase qualification rates was reinforced in the course of the next decade by European Union directives. At the time of the Lisbon Summit in 2000, the member states of the Union emphasised the need to train a skilled workforce. Given that it was the least well-qualified individuals who were also the most affected by unemployment, the priority became one of reducing early school leaving. Today, the objective is to ensure that by 2010 at least 80% of young people aged 20–24 years have an upper secondary qualification.

In France, the growing government concern about early school leavers, along with the development of research in the area, has resulted in a fuller understanding of a phenomenon whose contours can be described as fluid. To understand the specific features of the French context, the discussion begins with a sketch of the organisation of the education system. Following that, there is an overview of how

---

*(translated by Richard Teese)

[1]In 1985, the unemployment rate in France for young people aged 15–24 years was 23.7%. It was 19.7% in 2007.

[2]CAP and BEP are awards granted at the end of 2 years of vocational study in school.

M. Blanchard (✉) and R. Sinthon (✉)
Centre Maurice Halbwachs, École Normale Supérieure, France

S. Lamb et al. (Eds.), *School Dropout and Completion: International Comparative Studies in Theory and Policy*, DOI 10.1007/978-90-481-9763-7_4,
© Springer Science+Business Media B.V. 2011

much is known about the issue of dropout. Finally the discussion turns to public policies aimed at tackling the issue.

The French Context of Schooling: A Centralised System, Strongly Hierarchical and Recently Transformed to a Mass System

The French school system is entirely centralised. The powers delegated to regional and local authorities – *région*, *département*, and local councils – mainly relate to the management of buildings and equipment. The French state takes charge of the broader directions of educational policy, including curriculum, timetable and school year, examinations, and recruitment and management of staff. Centralised, the French schooling system is also equally very hierarchical. It is true that the creation of a common junior high school (*collège unique*) in 1975 displayed a will to offer comprehensive schooling to the whole of an age cohort. However, from the end of junior high school, the system becomes complex and breaks into numerous streams which are markedly hierarchical. Thus, only the 'better' student reaches academic senior high school (*lycée général*).

Lower Secondary Education: Junior High School (Collège)

In 1975, the reforms led by the Minister of National Education, René Haby, ended the streamed programs of lower secondary education and created the common junior high school (*collège unique*). The guiding concern was to avoid early selection of pupils (separation into different streams), and through this approach to raise general levels of achievement.

Junior high school is organised into four year-levels, starting with the class of 'the sixth' and ending with the class of 'the third'. All pupils are expected to follow the same educational program over these 4 years across a range of subject areas: French, mathematics, history, geography and physical sciences. In contrast to primary schools, where class teachers usually teach all subjects, in junior high school teachers usually teach one or two subjects to different classes.

Today, almost all children continue their studies until the end of the fourth year of junior high school: the continuation rate in 2001 was 97%. However, junior high school is not as 'common' as it might appear. Of pupils entering the fourth and final year in 2001, 85% came from the mainstream general program, while 15% had been guided into special streams. Since 1996, junior high schools have been able to make specific arrangements for students in difficulty, covering both programs and timetables (Ministry of Education Nationale, 2008). These arrangements differ according to year-level. In the penultimate year, 'support classes' are run to help students reintegrate into the mainstream program. Teaching is organised around 'projects' within defined subject areas, but linked with the world of work through short placements.

In the final year of junior high school, 'transition classes' are more directly geared to vocational training, with work placements taking up half of the student's total time.

Pupils who have experienced the greatest difficulties in primary school are oriented from the start of junior high school to pre-vocational classes (*classes préparatoires à l'apprentissage* [CPA], and *classes d'initiation préprofessionnelle par alternance* [CLIPA]) or to adaptation classes (*section d'enseignement général et professionnel adapté* [SEGPA]). Pre-vocational classes are located in apprenticeship centres and concern only a small minority of students (9,700 in 2007–08). The SEGPA stream enables children judged to be 'poorly adjusted' to school to continue their schooling until age 16. There were more than 100,000 pupils in SEGPA classes in 2006, 70% of whose parents were in blue-collar jobs, were unemployed or were not in the labour force, and 61% of whom were boys. Each class comprises about 16 pupils, and this enables individualised study programs to be developed. Pupils follow a general program of the type that mainstream pupils in the first and second year of junior high school follow, with the difference being in how SEGPA pupils are managed, that is, smaller classes, an individualised learning program, and a combination of general and vocational studies. From the third year of the program, the emphasis falls more on vocational training.

At the end of junior high school, and regardless of stream, all pupils sit their *brevet* (or school certificate) examination. Results are based on written tests and also continuous assessment in French, mathematics and history-geography. The national success rate in 2008 was 81.7%. Almost all of each new cohort now gains this award: in 2007, only 3.2% of 15- to 19-year-olds did not hold it, while amongst people over 65 years of age, the rate is 64.6%.

But behind these aggregate figures important differences are found. In fact, junior high school is far from being 'comprehensive', even within the 'general' stream. For a start, there are quite sharp differences between schools themselves, linked to their location. Numerous studies, spanning urban sociology and the sociology of education, have demonstrated the magnitude of inequalities between schools in different locations in terms of social composition, teaching conditions, and rates of success. For example, in the city of Paris, the rate of success in attaining the school leaving certificate (*brevet*) varies from ∠4% to 100%, depending on the school.

General and Technological Education

While earlier stages of schooling are marked by a policy of wide pupil mix and common core of curricular subjects, senior high school divides into distinct programs through choice of educational routes. Thus, at the end of the last year of junior high school, pupils are guided through a counselling process into either a general or technological senior high school or a vocational senior high school. Among students enrolled in the final year of junior high school in 2006, 57% entered the general and technological stream in senior high school in 2007, and 27% took the vocational route. A further 6% were repeating the year, while 10% did not continue in education (at least in schools or training under the control of the

Ministry of Education). This figure includes both dropouts and young people entering education or training programs under the control of other Ministries, including work-study or work-training programs.

The program in general and technological high schools lasts for 3 years ('second form', 'first form', and 'final year'). During the first year, pupils follow a common program of study. At the same time, they are expected to choose two components which are 'determinative' in their later allocation to specialised streams, based on options. At the end of the first year of senior high school, pupils are separated between the 'general' stream and the 'technological' stream. Orientation towards stream is often based on results in the first year of the high school course, with more successful pupils entering the general stream. This route, which recruits about 60% of students completing the first year of senior high, is designed to prepare for extended study. It comprises three series: economics and social science (ES), humanities/arts (L), and science (S). Depending on the series, the course of study will differ.

The 'technological' stream includes both 'general' subjects (French, mathematics, history-geography, science, English) and 'technological' studies which comprise vocational studies, like accounting. There are many areas of specialisation in the technological stream, the most important of which are laboratory technology, industrial technology, management, health and social welfare. When students complete the third and final year of senior high school, they sit for the national *baccalaureat* examination which opens the way to higher education.

Vocational Training: Institutional Duality

Vocational Senior High School and Apprenticeship Centres

Vocational training currently enrols about 40% of young people who complete junior high school. Courses lead to the award of various qualifications – BEP, CAP, vocational baccalaureat. These programs prepare young people for employment or, in some cases, tertiary education. They mostly enrol students from low socioeconomic status (SES) backgrounds: in 2007–08, those from a low SES background accounted for 63% of students studying for a CAP, 54.2% of those studying for a BEP and 51.4% studying for a vocational baccalaureat. While the general and technological streams of the baccalaureat are frequently offered in the same school, vocational courses are delivered in two different institutions: either vocational high schools or apprenticeship centres.

In vocational senior high schools, pupils have the status of a tertiary education student (*statut d'étudiant*) and, in addition to campus-based studies, undertake a work placement. But in CFA (apprenticeship centres), they work under contract with a business and are paid wages. They do both theoretical and practical studies in the apprenticeship centres for about one week in every four. For the most part, apprentices are young people judged to have failed at school. One in three has been excluded from mainstream programs from the end of the second year of junior high school.

Qualifications

Young people in vocational training can work towards the award of a BEP, CAP, or a vocational baccalaureat. The CAP and the BEP give the same level of qualification, while the vocational baccalaureat gives selective access to higher education.

The CAP (*certificat d'aptitude professionnelle*) takes 2 years, and is offered in more than 200 specialities. The program includes general studies (French, history, mathematics) as well as vocational training. CAP courses also include work placements, which vary according to specialisation. Numbers in CAP programs have been declining over the long term – 264,000 enrolments in 1980–81 compared to only 110,000 in 2007–08. Fifty-two per cent of CAP students are females. Today, a majority of CAP students undertake their training in an apprenticeship centre – 74,000 compared to 46,000 in vocational senior high school.

The BEP (*brevet d'études professionnelles*) aims to be more general than the CAP. There are some 50 specialities, with courses generally running for 2 years. Where with a CAP, the choice of training is fairly specific – 'butcher', 'fishmonger', 'small meats butcher', etc. – BEP courses relate to a family of occupations or an industry area, such as the 'food industry'. In 2007–08, 403,459 students were preparing a BEP, of whom 44.3% were female.

CAP graduates usually enter the workforce, while a majority of BEP graduates undertake either a technological or a vocational baccalaureat. In 2007–08, of the total number of pupils enrolled in the second year of CAP, 5.6% had repeated a grade, 11.7% were streamed into BEP, 10.7 % had chosen to enrol in a vocational baccalaureat, and 65% had left the education system (information not available on the remaining 7%).

Regarding BEP pupils, 8.3% repeated a grade, 42.5% were streamed into a vocational baccalaureat, 10.9% took a technological baccalaureat over 2 years (the first of which is an 'adaptation' year), and 35% had left the education system.

The vocational baccalaureat was created in 1985 in a context when BEP and CAP courses appeared inadequate, especially in industry areas such as information technology (IT) or communications. The idea was to allow students with a CAP or a BEP to prepare for this exam in 2 years. Incorporating a minimum of 16 weeks work placement, the vocational baccalaureat was conceived of as a qualification giving direct access to the labour market; however, nearly a third of graduates enter tertiary education courses.

Since 2007, it has been possible to study for the vocational baccalaureat over 3 years. From 2010, this approach will be generalised and will bring to an end the total training period of 4 years (CAP/BEP plus vocational baccalaureat). According to the Minister of National Education, Xavier Darcos:

> The baccalaureat in 3 years should change outlooks on vocational courses by ensuring that there is 'parity of esteem' between general baccalaureats and vocational. The objective is also to help more young people reach baccalaureat level. For while 6 months after completing a vocational baccalaureat 60% of young people have a job, less than 50% of BEP graduates do.

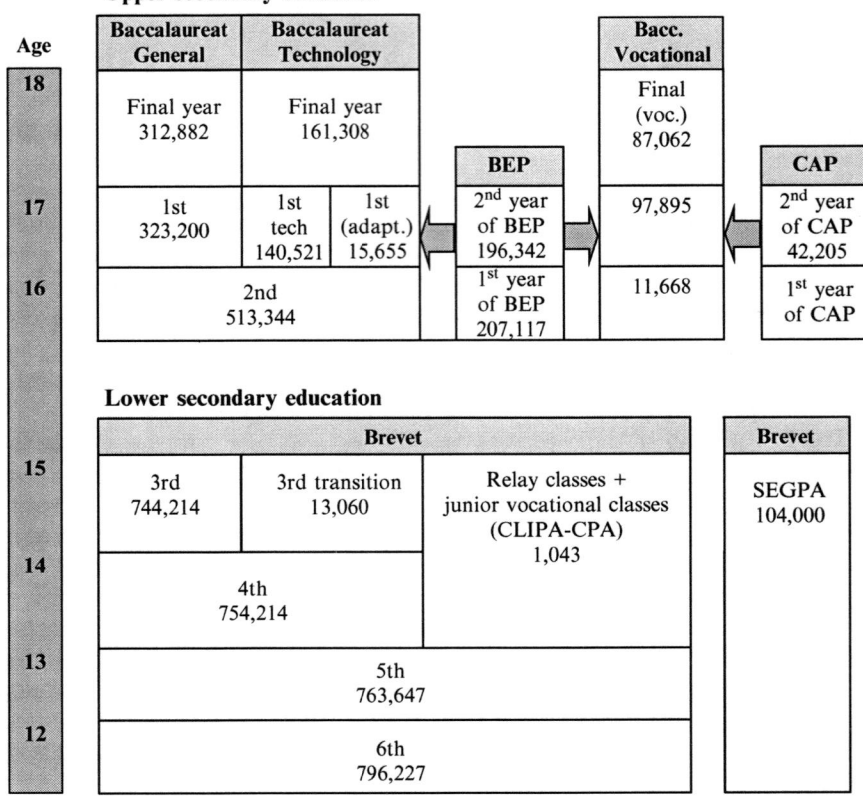

Fig. 3.1 Numbers of students in secondary education in France in 2007–08, by major stream or section

The structure of secondary education in France, with student numbers to show the relative importance of each of the different types of upper secondary qualifications, is provided in Fig. 3.1.

Graduation Rates: Trends Over Time

Democratisation: Qualitative or Quantitative?

Appearing on the agenda during the 19th century, the theme of 'democratisation' of education has remained very much to the fore in France. It has been linked with republican meritocratic ideology, according to which individuals should no longer inherit, but should earn their social position. Since the Ferry laws which established free, compulsory and secular schooling in the early 1880s, the objective of reformers has been not only to raise rates of participation in school as well as length of schooling, but also to ensure that educational success is more equally experienced. The historian Antoine Prost (1997) describes this kind of democratisation as 'qualititative' to the extent that it involves a weakening of the link between social origin and eventual social position. He contrasts this with quantitative democratisation – or 'massification' – which describes an increase in numbers of pupils, but without social inequalities disappearing. The latter are simply displaced into other forms.

What kind of democratisation has occurred in France? From a purely quantitative perspective, the chances of access to secondary education have undoubtedly increased. Following government policy to raise general levels of education, the decade of 1985–95 saw an unprecedented rise in senior high school numbers and in graduations from senior high school (see Fig. 3.2). The proportion of a generation holding a general, technological or vocational baccalaureat rose from 5% in 1950 to 29.4% in 1985, and to 62.7% in 1995. It stood at 64.2% in 2007. It should be stressed that this increase is due in large measure to the creation and expansion of the technological baccalaureat (1965) and vocational baccalaureat (1985).

Nevertheless, if qualification rates in the population have continued to grow, social inequalities in access to different levels of schooling and different streams have continued. Expansion in high school graduations has not been uniformly experienced across all social ranks. Amongst graduates in the general (or academic) streams of the baccalaureat, more than a third are from a senior management or liberal professions background, a category representing only about 8.4% of the

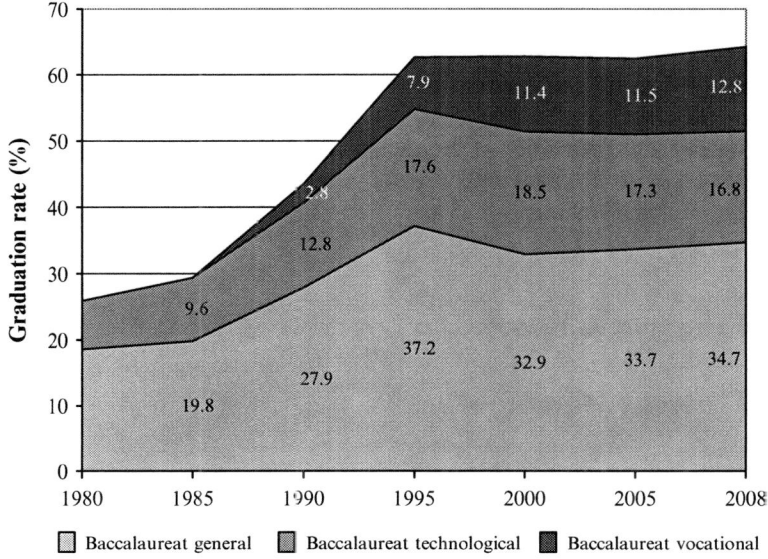

Fig. 3.2 Evolution of graduation rates, by type of baccalaureat: 1980–2008

French workforce. On the other hand, every fourth graduate in the vocational stream is from a manual worker's home, and only eight in 100 are from a high SES family.

Similarly, geographical inequalities persist both across France and within particular localities and regions. For example, within the academic region of the city of Lille, the proportion of young people holding the baccalaureat is 60% compared to 80% in Paris. And within the greater region of Paris, success at the baccalaureat exams varies widely according to school. In 2005, 100% of candidates in the prestigious and selective establishments of the inner city and rich suburbs succeeded, as opposed to fewer than 50% in some senior high schools located in areas with the most disadvantaged populations.

An Increasingly Qualified Population

In 1985, nearly one in ten 16-year-olds discontinued studies, with the majority of these leaving school without any qualification. In 1989, the Orientation and Guidance law laid down an objective of 80% of a generation reaching baccalaureat level, announcing, in effect, that the whole of an age cohort should attain a level of schooling at least equivalent to a CAP or BEP. It was an ambitious goal to take all young people beyond compulsory schooling and to ensure that the whole of the population should hold a qualification of recognised value in the labour market.

In France, the proportion of young people who quit school or other education without a qualification has remained at about 18% for some time. These are young people who have not graduated from upper secondary education, and they have no baccalaureat, CAP or BEP. Between 1982 and 2007, amongst young people from working class backgrounds, the rate has fallen from 53% to 32%, but remains very much higher than for the children of professionals and senior managers (5% in 2007) or office-workers (18.7%).

An ongoing high proportion of dropout has contributed to an ever-growing interest on the part of government and of social scientists. What then, is the state of our knowledge of this phenomenon?

School Dropout in France: An Overview of What We Know

School Dropout Meaning What?

'School dropout' (*décrochage scolaire*), 'disconnection from school' (*déscolarisation*), 'early leaving' (*abandon scolaire*), 'leaving school without a qualification' (*arrêt d'études sans qualification*) – there exists no single term in French corresponding to the term, school dropout. A range of terms is used by researchers and observers in the education system, testifying to the relatively recent nature of policy and scholarly interest in this question in France. Indeed, attention was for a long time centred on the question of 'scholastic failure' and on democratisation and equality of opportunity. But vagueness in language can equally be read as vagueness in the nature of the phenomenon itself. Strictly speaking, early termination of studies could be defined as leaving the school system before the statutory age of 16. However, this concerns only a very small group, kept small by the high rate of grade-repeating and a set of institutional processes discussed later in this chapter.

The level of education and training in France has traditionally been assessed using measures established in 1969. These define early leavers as young people who have quit education without reaching the final year of the CAP or BEP, or the first year of the general or technological baccalaureat (Léger, 2008). In France, the size of this group has fallen from 25% of a generation (or 170,000 young people) in 1975, to only 6%, or 42,000 young people, in 2005.

However, the statistical concept of early leaving as 'not reaching a defined stage of schooling' has progressively been abandoned in favour of the concept of 'not completing qualifications'. The Lisbon protocol, to which France is a signatory, views the issue as one of completing upper secondary education, obtaining a diploma and accessing employment. What matters from this perspective is failure to complete a program – cessation of studies before obtaining an award (CAP, BEP, baccalauréat). Since 2000, completion of an upper secondary program has been considered as the minimum necessary level of qualification. Applied to France in 2005 to 2007, the numbers failing this test would represent about 134,000 young people, or 18% of the relevant school population.

Thus, there are in France two different statistical concepts in circulation: an older approach in which the highest stage of schooling attempted is the issue, and a newer approach in which a minimum level of qualification is the criterion.

Fluidity in the Measure, and Measurement of Flows

As well as definitional problems, it should be stressed that estimating the number of pupils who fail to reach a certain stage of schooling or who fail to complete a qualification is far from an exact science. There does not exist in France any definition which is common to different administrative departments, and definitions can also vary from one academic region to another. It is thus difficult to do a precise stocktake at a local level, given that numbers can vary simply as a function of the particular organisation processing them. A report by the general inspectorate of national education stresses, indeed, that figures given for the same region can vary from 8% to 25% (Dubreuil et al., 2005).

Despite the vagueness which surrounds the concept of dropout and the difficulties of measurement, it is possible to establish a number of tendencies at a national level.

Who Are the Dropouts? A Statistical Profile

Most statistical series highlight the fact that dropout is a big issue. Far from being a marginal tendency, they show that growing official concern with school dropout is fully justified by its magnitude. Secondly, dropout involves pupils from as young as 14- to 15-years-old, and the level rises with age. Finally, all studies of the phenomenon have demonstrated the over-representation of pupils from working-class backgrounds.

All the data show a general tendency for 'exits without qualifications' to decline. But at the same time, they reveal a maintenance of social inequalities. Moreover, they testify to the importance of a pupil's 'school career' – for grade repeating prior to entry to secondary school plays a big role.

Logistic regression enables us to demonstrate the relative weight of different factors, and notably the importance of curriculum stream, in explaining school dropout. The analysis is based on the 'cohort of 1995' panel study conducted by the *Direction de l'évaluation, de la prospective et de la performance, Ministère de l'Éducation Nationale.*

The two senior high school streams of the general and the technological baccalaureat are clearly distinguished from the others by the low probability of dropout. The difference could perhaps be explained by the general, as compared to the vocational, nature of a baccalaureat stream, but hinges more on the social prestige hierarchy of the different streams which is implicit, but widely understood. The more that a stream is considered as prestigious, the weaker the likelihood of abandoning it. The importance of stream points to the fundamental role played by school guidance.

As Table 3.1 suggests, school career plays an important role in what happens to a young person since, all other factors remaining equal, repeating a grade in primary school makes dropping out likely (66.6% of those repeating a grade drop out). This confirms the results of numerous qualitative studies (as cited above) which show that early learning difficulties lead eventually to dropping out.

There is a slight tendency for boys to quit school more often than girls. But family background factors play a much bigger role than gender. The chances of dropout weaken as parental level of education rises. This is consistent with analyses inspired by Bourdieu's notion of cultural capital, or more specifically with studies based on interviews or small-scale surveys which show that poorly-educated parents experience more difficulties helping their children with the demands of school or assisting them to construct an academic or vocational plan (Terrail & Bedi, 2002).

At a given level of parental education, children whose fathers are in intermediate professional jobs have a lower chance of dropping out than those from a skilled manual worker's background; while the children of semi-skilled manual workers and even more those where the fathers have never worked or where job is not reported have a higher chance of dropping out. There are several possible explanations which are relevant here. When parents have a stable job which permits them to live comfortably, the family environment is in itself more stable for the child and

Table 3.1 Determinants of school dropout

Categories	Per cent (%)	Estimate
(Intercept)	35.3	0.12*
Gender		
Boy	40.4	Reference
Girl	29.9	−0.14***
Stream		
Senior high (general)	4.8	−3.02***
Senior high (tech)	10.9	−2.69***
BEP	58.0	Reference
CAP	69.2	0.40***
Never enrolled in above	74.4	0.65***
Father's occupation		
Manager, professional	16.2	−0.08
Associate professional	23.2	−0.18***
Small business, indep.	36.0	0.09
Office worker	35.1	−0.05
Skilled manual	43.0	Reference
Semi-skilled manual	53.1	0.16**
Unknown/never worked	55.1	0.27***
Parents' highest level of qualification		
Higher education	13.0	−0.25***
Baccalaureat or equivalent	22.6	−0.14*
BEP	31.5	−0.13*
CAP	40.7	Reference
Leaving certificate (brevet)	44.1	0.07
No qualification	55.2	0.29***
No response	52.2	0.36***
Type of municipality of junior high school attended		
Paris region	35.3	0.22***
Over 100,000 inhabitants	34.1	0.11*
20,000 up to 100,000	34.3	Reference
5,000 up to 20,000	37.0	0.00
Less than 5,000 inhabitants	36.7	0.03
Repeated a grade in primary school		
No	30.7	Reference
Yes	66.6	0.57***

Notes: *, **, *** = 10%, 5% and 1% thresholds.

the parents offer a role model of success, giving meaning to achievement at school. Moreover, parents try to prevent any social demotion of their children and are thus so much more conscious of the problems of incomplete schooling (*déscolarisation*) which risks the future social position of their children.

Finally, it is important to note the higher probability of dropping out associated with attending a junior high school in the Paris region by comparison with going to an establishment located in a municipality of between 20,000 and 100,000 inhabitants. This highlights the importance of the geographical context of schooling.

Analyses of the Dropout Phenomenon in French Sociology

Studies of school dropout have multiplied in France in the course of the 1990s, notably under the influence of several Ministries which launched a very large research project on the question in 1999. Most research has been conducted from a qualitative view.

Moreover, in the last few years most French researchers have studied dropping out of school as a 'combinatory process' (Millet & Thin, 2003), with research based on a reconstruction of schooling histories. Starting from the premise that 'the comprehension of the processes of dropping out cannot be reduced to the search for determinant factors', the task has been to show how family life, school life and peer culture interact.

A distinctively sociological approach to the process of dropping out takes differences of situation as a key element. The sociologist adopts a critical view of the concept of dropout itself, instead of merely inheriting it from institutional authority. As Stephane Bonnéry (2004) shows, 'the emergence of the category of dropout used by schools to depict the problems it faces runs the risk of homogenising under a single de-sociological term the different processes which lead pupils to cease attending school or at least to show no interest in schooling'.

Bonnéry rejects, moreover, a fatalistic vision which presupposes a link between 'pupil origin' and academic future. To him, if school dropout is more frequent amongst working classes, this is a question in the first place of achievement problems. Thus, the task is to understand why it is that pupils struggle to learn.

Conceptualising Dropping Out as a Process

Research by Glasman (2000) questions the assumed 'specificity' of school dropouts.

In terms of objective and quantifiable attributes, there does not appear to be any radical difference between senior high school students who drop out and those who, poorly motivated by school work as they may be, remain on the inside of school. Given this, the task should be to study how the objectives of dropouts differ from students who continue – the particular processes which distinguish trajectories – rather than looking at how pupils themselves might differ.

Taking dropout as the outcome of a cumulative process of difficulties, Broccolichi's originality lies in having looked at the antecedents of dropping out (2000). Focusing on the relationship between the dropout and school knowledge, Broccolichi has demonstrated the central role of 'cognitive disengagement' (*décrochage cognitif*). This concerns an often 'silent' phenomenon, not marked by displays of indiscipline, violence, or absenteeism. Pupils do not reach the point of entry to their 'craft' as 'students', the demands of which are not clear to them, and they lose perspective on the meaning of school work, thus breaking with the expectations of the system even while remaining 'on the inside' of school.

The Role of the Institution

Not focused simply on pathways of young people, most French researchers insist on the fact that dropping out calls into question how well schooling works as an institution, and particularly its capacity to give positive meaning to the experience of school and to help guide young people within it.

Reaching junior high school often marks a turning point in the trajectory of dropouts. Learning difficulties and a feeling of demoralisation tend to increase once children enter this new institution where demands on students increase and the experience of deepening failure is no longer offset by a personal link with the teacher (Broccolichi & Ben Ayed, 1999). On the basis of the personal accounts they reviewed, Broccolichi and Ben Ayed observe that 'this type of situation leads logically to indiscipline in classes where the possibilities exist for connivance in it on the part of other pupils, similarly motivated'.

Besides changes linked to conditions under which learning occurs, junior high school as an institution also plays a role in how pupils perceive and respond to schooling, in that school can oppose the pathways that pupils might wish to take, notably at the end of the second last year. Indeed, a decision on stream that is imposed and not wanted by either parent or pupil contributes to a loss of meaning and can encourage a progressive disengagement from school.

Public Policies and Programs Put in Place to Reduce Dropout

For many years in France, dropout was considered to be a marginal problem, limited to particular populations, such as gypsies or recent arrivals. In fact, it is only from around the second half of the 1990s that it is possible to really speak of an institutional concern for young people with 'incomplete schooling' (*élèves désco-larisés*), a concern that was matched by the implementation of specific educational interventions. That school dropout could occur before that time without becoming an issue recognised by educational institutions or by researchers is linked to a convergence of factors (Glasman, 2000): 'Giving up school had less visibility as long as the labour market could absorb unskilled labour' and school was thus not seen as necessary for workforce transition. Moreover the institutional priority was on 'democratisation' of school, particularly access to senior high school: the issue was above all how to raise the general level of school qualifications in order to meet the needs of the economy.

In fact, most of the education policies implemented since the 1960s (at both system and school level) have been aimed at lifting the general level of qualification of the population, checking failure of school, and promoting equal opportunity. The emergence of dropout as a 'policy problem' seems to have favoured the development of intervention measures at an individual level.

System Level

At the system level, major structural changes mark the history of French schooling and its much greater democratisation since the 1960s. From the outset, these changes involved transforming the mixed types of lower secondary education into a new type of school: the *collège* (junior high school). Between 1966 and 1975, some 2,354 junior high schools were built to accommodate pupils from the formerly diverse range of school types that once represented lower secondary education. From the 1980s, the concern shifted to promoting the greatest access to senior high school and the baccalaureat. Between 1982 and 1992, the rate of access to the final year of the baccalaureat rose from 35.7% to 66%. In 1993, the different streams of senior high school were reorganised with a view to 'parity of esteem' for all specialisations and to put an end to the supremacy of mathematics. This involved allowing greater individual support and supervision for the weakest learners, and the establishment of supplementary classes for small groups. As it has turned out, this reform has had few positive effects, and since 1995 there has been stagnation in the number of senior high school graduates as well as a maintenance of the hierarchy of difficult streams.

School Level

At the start of the 1980s, French education policy took an important turn. While, since the 1960s, the idea had been to create a uniform system to offer the same programs to all students, the 1980s saw a switch to give 'more to those who have less', with the implementation in 1981 of Education Priority Zones or EPZ.

Born of the 'observation that educational inequalities are due to the great diversity of social and cultural settings', Educational Priority Zones involve designating selected schools (both senior high and junior high) to receive supplementary funding.

The effectiveness of the EPZ is, however, increasingly disputed. According to a study by the national statistics institute (INSEE) relating to the period 1982–93, 'the implementation of Education Priority Zones has had no significant effect on the success of pupils'. Indeed according to this study, all additional funds benefit teachers – who, since 1991, have received a premium of €1,097 per year – rather than pupils directly. Moreover the EPZ label is seen by parents as a signal that a school is 'bad', and thus plays the role of stigmatising. As a result, the numbers of pupils attending EPZ schools has been in continuous decline, with many parents seeking to avoid them.

In 2006, the Educational Priority Zone policy was revamped and Ambition to Succeed networks were established, initially involving 249 junior high schools. These establishments are former EPZ schools, but selected from amongst the most disadvantaged. Under the reform, these schools were intended to receive a reinforcement of four 'guiding teachers' (*professeurs referents*) – innovative teachers intended to help the teams already in place. Teaching assistants – university students under supervision – have also been promised. In practice, it appears that these measures have not always been applied to the letter and have been criticised by some teacher unions.

Individual Level

The measures implemented at a system and a school level show that the emphasis of public policy has not been on school dropout as such. It is helpful to recall the convergence of factors that resulted in 'dropout' being placed on the policy agenda (Glasman, 2003) in the 1990s. Firstly, there was a concern for public order. Pupils who are not where they should be are considered a threat. Secondly, young people with no qualifications represent the 'hard core' of teenage unemployment, and while successive governments have made tackling unemployment a priority, the workforce transition of young unqualified people has never been more problematic. Finally, in an epoch when half the age cohort stays on at school until age 20, those who leave before age 18 and without qualifications appear out of step.

As Bonnéry (2004) recalls, before early leaving became an issue in national education policy, it was 'scholastic failure' which mobilised agencies within the Ministry of Education, and led to policies at the individual level. According to Bonnéry, dropout is often seen as an advanced form of scholastic failure. As a consequence, the arrangements set in place to tackle failure – an 'old' phenomenon – have been redefined as targeting early leaving, more recently identified.

More precisely, measures combined to control early leaving have a double genealogy. They are not only heirs of strategies to tackle failure at school: the arrangements put in place by public authorities to tackle unemployment amongst young people now serve to support actions to reduce dropping out. Given these dual origins, it is difficult to isolate those measures that specifically address the problem of early leaving in the jungle of individual intervention. In fact, the missions of reducing failure at school, preventing dropout, and facilitating workforce transition are closely linked.

A Brief History of Intervention

Starting in the middle of the 1980s, the question of workforce transition became increasingly important in educational policy, and the 'alternance' model of training and transition schemes expanded (Geay, 2003). In 1986, the program Transition Provision for Young People in the Education System (DIJEN, *dispositive d'insertion des jeunes de l'éducation nationale*) was established. This brought together the totality of diverse and localised measures for young people quitting junior high school or senior high school without a qualification. The General Transition Mission (MGI, *Mission générale d'insertion*) replaced the DIJEN in 1992. As well as coordinating local arrangements, the MGI is meant to map students exiting from school who do not enrol in another school. Its role is also to intervene directly with families and young people and to encourage schools to adopt policies to prevent early leaving.

In 1999, the measures that were piloted under the MGI were formalised and expanded through the adoption of the New Chances program (*Nouvelle Chance*). Three major principles have guided this new program. Firstly is the idea that 'there is no uniformly valid solution for each young person, but rather a personal response'. The policy thus favoured individualised pathways. Secondly, the aim was to encourage innovation in teaching and experimental approaches. Finally, links with the world of work were necessary.

Given the large numbers of measures implemented under the MGI and their strongly local nature, it is possible to offer only a general overview here. Discussion will be limited to some preventative measures and training programs under the MGI and leave to one side other actions which relate directly to transition. Finally, it should be stressed that counter dropout measures do not all fall under the MGI banner. Many interventions occur at the local level, managed by schools or other agencies, and are too various and numerous to be reviewed here.

Prevention Measures Under Mission Générale d'Insertion, MGI

These solutions aim at identifying pupils who are struggling with school work from junior high school on. The aim is to provide them with personalised support through 'on-site interviews' in which each young person can discuss issues with a psychology and guidance counsellor. Transition Support Groups (GAIN, *Groupes d'Aides à l'insertion*), also called 'oversight cells' (*cellules de veille*), are responsible for the tasks of monitoring and support. The groups are organised locally by school principals.

In 2006–07, nearly three in four of the 54,364 students benefitting from these one-to-one interviews subsequently undertook a training program; 3% entered the labour market.

Training Programs Under Mission Générale d'Insertion, MGI

MGI networks also organise training programs. These can be part-time or full-time, and aim either to give short-term assistance to a young person or help them complete a recognised program of study or training.

1. Preparatory programs undertaken part-time

There are numerous schemes under this broad heading. In some cases, the larger group comprises young people who at the beginning of the school year are not enrolled in a school and who come under the wing of local guidance agencies. In other cases, the target group involves students in mainstream schooling, who in view of the difficulties they are experiencing, undertake supplementary classes or 're-engagement modules' (*modules de remotivation*) for a period ranging from several weeks to a full school year.

Amongst these measures, it is possible to distinguish 'relay classes' (*classes relais*), implemented from 1998 to 1999, and 'relay workshops' (*ateliers relais*) since 2002. The objective is to help 'tackle under-achievement and prevent social marginalisation' (Circular, 12 June 1998). 'Relay' programs enrol students from junior high school (and ultimately also senior high school) who are considered to have 'entered into a process of rejection of school' (*un processus de reject de l'institution scolaire*) as evident in 'failure to observe internal rules, persistent absenteeism from class, and even absence from school'. Relay classes are based on a partnership led by different government departments (education, justice, local government) and involve regional authorities and the voluntary sector.

Since their creation in 1998, the number of these programs has continued to grow. In 1999–2000, there were 180 with an intake of 2,600 students; this had grown to 360 by 2005–06, including 254 relay classes and 106 relay workshops. About 6,511 students were enrolled in the relay programs that year (Alluin, 2007; Poncet & Alluin, 2003)

Participation in these programs is overwhelmingly male: 78% in 2004–05, generally from 13 to 15 years old Students usually come from the first to the fourth (and final) year of junior high school, mainly the general or mainstream programs (88% of all participants in 2004–05).

On average, students spend about 3 months in these programs. In 2004–05, 74% of students subsequently returned to junior high school and 4% entered vocational senior high school. No solution was found for 1–2% of participants.

After-exit statistics on participating students are weak: for all existing cohorts in 2003–04, non-response to a (follow-up) survey 6 months after exit was 35%.

2. Full-time programs

Full-time programs enrol students defined as having 'broken with school' and whose likelihood of completing a qualification within the usual time appears weak, given that they have already left school or are in the course of doing so. These programs run for varying periods, with year-round enrolment of students. They are characterised by individual support and supervision, workplace experience, and a focus on the 'basics' (literacy, numeracy).

Finally, some programs are designed mainly for young people exiting from the final year of vocational, technological or general senior high school streams who have failed the exams at least twice, or who have experienced severe problems in their school work. The aim is to help them prepare for the exams or to re-sit an examination.

Of the students who took part in a special learning program (N = 32,458), some 64% returned to a mainstream education program or undertook a new program, while 8% entered the labour market. Figures produced by the administering authority (MGI) tend to show that these initiatives, as well as preventative ones, are relatively effective. However, there is no available information on long-term outcomes, and the proportion of students who have neither returned to study nor found work is not small.

Alternative Pathways

Outside of the measures which aim to prevent dropout or to intervene at the first signs of early leaving, there are few possibilities for dropouts to resume study once they have left. A 'second chance' school – the first to be created – was opened in 1998 in Marseille in response to the European Commission. Today, 36 such schools (called E2C or *école de la seconde chance*) enable about 4,000 young people aged 16–25 years and who left school at least 2 years ago to reacquire the fundamentals – reading, writing, numeracy – for a period of between 6 and 24 months, all the while learning for a job through a work placement. The training course is free. The schools are operated by associations which bring together numerous agencies within the local economy and various public authorities (Ministry of National Education, the council of the region, National Employment Association, municipalities, chambers of commerce, etc.) For the moment, no data are available on the outcomes from these second-chance schools.

Regarding continuing education, this has been progressively developed since 1971 under the umbrella of the Ministry of National Education. But by comparison with other European countries, this sector is fairly small. According to Eurostat, only 7.4% of adults aged 25–64 years took a 'formal' course in 2007 – that is, one leading to a qualification – or a 'non-formal' course designed by teaching staff, whereas the average for the European Union reaches 9.7%.

Critical Views

While a solid statistical picture of outcomes is lacking in the medium to long term, certain aspects of the 'relay' programs (programs designed for those who have or are becoming disengaged from school) have been criticised. Geay (2005), in particular, has attacked the multiplication of relay measures in the absence of a debate about the stakes involved, whether social or academic.

With the 'massification' of school, which has occurred in a context of underemployment, segmentations internal to the population of school have developed. The diversification of tools to manage populations judged to be 'academically deviant' answers to this new state of play in which schooling becomes organised to cope with diversity through the establishment of alternative programs that become treated as legitimate pathways rather than through tools to combat the antecedents of dropout.

The multiplication of localised programs would, on this interpretation, be symptomatic of a 'massified' school system which, unable to offer adaptive conditions of learning – to avoid difficulties from the outset – does not succeed in treating its dysfunctions other than through specific and localised initiatives, thus throwing into question the notion of genuine comprehensive schooling (*l'école unique*).

What 'Lines of Action' Are Needed for Reconnection with School?

Concluding a study of dropping out, Glasman has sought to identify 'lines of action', keeping in mind that reflection on what is possible and pertinent should not assume that there is one set of solutions corresponding to a set of typical situations: 'there's nothing to say that what reconnects one student will reconnect another' (Glasman & Oeuvrard, 2004). Glasman also invites us to consider the problem under its wider social aspect, and thus not to ask schooling to do what it cannot do. For research shows that the practices of disconnecting from school are fuelled largely by the socioeconomic conditions of families, influenced directly by poverty, unemployment and precariousness.

Stressing these limits, what are the lines of action for a 'reconnection with school'? Disengagement from school owes its origins in many cases to a failure to connect and progress in school, and this can occur from the youngest age – the point of entry to school. Given this, it would be necessary to address growing gaps in student learning in primary school, with support in the first and second years of junior high school often coming too late (even if early learning problems are not always detectable).

References

Alluin, F. (2007). Le suivi et le devenir des élèves accueillis en classes-relais 2004-2005. Les notes d'évaluation- D.E.P.P., 07.11, mars. Retrieved from media.education.gouv.fr/file/62/8/4628.pdf

Bonnery, S. (2004). Un 'problème social' émergent ? Les réponses institutionnel-les au décrochage scolaire en France. *Revue internationale d'éducation*, Sè-vres, no. 35, avril, 81–88.

Broccolichi, S. (2000). Désagrégation des liens pédagogiques et situations de rup-tures. *VEI Enjeux, le décrochage scolaire: Une fatalité?*, no. 122, septembre, 36–47.

Broccolichi, S., & Ben Ayed, C. (1999). L'institution scolaire et la réussite de tous aujourd'hui : (Pourrait mieux faire). *Revue française de pédagogie*, no. 129, 39–51.

Dubreuil, P., Morin, E., Fort, M., & Ravat, J.-C. (2005). Les sorties sans qualification : Analyse des causes, des évolutions, des solutions pour y remédier. Rapport à Monsieur le Ministre de l'éducation nationale, de l'enseignement supérieur et de la recherche, à Monsieur le Ministre délégué à l'enseignement supérieur et à la recherche, no. 2005-074, from www.ladocumentationfrancaise.fr/rapports-publics/054000542/index.shtml

Geay, B. (2003). Du 'cancre' au 'sauvageon'. *Actes de la Recherche en Sciences*, no.149, 21–31.

Geay, B. (2005). Les déscolarisés: Les enjeux d'une categorisation. *Cahiers de recherche*, no. 20, 2nd quarter.

Glasman, D. (2000). Le décrochage scolaire: Une question sociale et institution-nelle. *VEI Enjeux, le décrochage scolaire: Une fatalité?*, no. 122, septembre, 10–25.

Glasman, D. (2003). Quelques acquis d'un programme de recherche sur la désco-larisation. *VEI-Enjeux, Prévenir les ruptures scolaires*, no. 132, mars, 8–18.

Glasman, D., & Oeuvrard, F. (Eds.). (2004). *La déscolarisation*. Paris: La Dispute.

Léger, F. (2008). Sorties sans qualification, la baisse se poursuit. Les notes d'in-formation-D.E.P.P., 08.05. Retrieved from http://www.education.gouv.fr/cid20801/les-sorties-sans-qualification-la-baisse-se-poursuit.html

Millet, M., & Thin, D. (2003). La 'déscolarisation' comme processus combinatoire. *VEI-Enjeux, Prévenir les ruptures scolaires*, no. 132, mars, 46–58.

Ministry of Education Nationale. (2008). The state of education. Issue no. 18, 2008. Paris: Le ministère de l'Education nationale et le ministère de l'Enseignement supérieur et de la Recherche.

Poncet, P., & Alluin, F. (2003). Les dispositifs relais 1999–2003. Les notes d'évaluations. D.E.P.P, 04–11, novembre. Retrieved from ftp://trf.education.gouv.fr/pub/edutel/dpd/noteeval/eva0411.pdf

Prost, A. (1997). *Éducation, société et politiques. Une histoire de l'enseignement en France, de 1945 à nos jours*. Paris: Éditions du Seuil.

Terrail, J.-P., & Bedi, A. (2002). Histoire scolaire et histoire familiale des décrocheurs. In E. Bautier, S. Bonnéry, J.-P. Terrail, A. Bebi, S. Branca-Rosoff, & B. Lesort (Eds.), *Décrochage scolaire: Genèse et logique des parcours*. Rapport de recherche pour la DPD/MEN (pp. 20–37).

Chapter 4
School Dropout and Completion in Spain

Rafael Merino and Maribel Garcia

What Are the Main Features of Spain's Upper Secondary Education and Training Provision?

Secondary education in Spain is structured into two parts. Lower secondary education (*Educación Secundaria Obligatoria*) is compulsory and lasts over four school years divided into two cycles each of 2 years. It begins after the conclusion of primary school at the age of 12; therefore, when a student finishes compulsory education, he or she is 16 years old. After this period, upper secondary education begins, which includes three main tracks: the academic (baccalaureate), the professional and the occupational.

Until the 1990 Educational Reform, only primary schooling was comprehensive; secondary schools were divided into baccalaureate secondary schools (*institutos de bachillerato*) and vocational training schools (*institutos de formación profesional*). However, the 1990 Reform extended the comprehensive curriculum to compulsory secondary education, and integrated the two types of training into secondary education schools (*institutos de enseñanza secundaria*), although keeping separate academic and professional tracks.

The application of comprehensiveness to compulsory secondary education has caused much controversy within the educational community and in political debates. It may be said that, at present, and since the educational reform of 2006, the comprehensiveness of compulsory secondary education is limited. This is because the Programs of Curricular Diversification (*Programas de Diversificación Curricular*), in which the curriculum is adapted to low-performing students by means of less abstract learning and more practical activities, are implemented in the second cycle. Although it is not accurate to say that upper secondary education is comprehensive, more and more links are being fostered between academic and professional tracks,

R. Merino (✉)
Education and Work Research Group (GRET), Autonomous University of Barcelona, Spain

M. Garcia (✉)
Department of Sociology, Autonomous University of Barcelona, Spain

S. Lamb et al. (Eds.), *School Dropout and Completion: International Comparative Studies in Theory and Policy*, DOI 10.1007/978-90-481-9763-7_5,
© Springer Science+Business Media B.V. 2011

thus moving from a tracked system to a linked one (Raffe & Spours, 1997). It should also be added that although there is only one curriculum within compulsory educa-tion, there are important differences between schools, as will be shown later on – for instance, between state-supported and private schools.

The students who succeed in acquiring the basic competences contained in the compulsory secondary education curriculum obtain the Secondary Education Certificate (*Graduado en Secundaria*). The evaluation to award this certificate is done by the secondary school's team of teachers; they may also give the certificate to students who have not passed two or, exceptionally, three subjects. There is no external evaluation on a national level: each secondary school and each team of teachers within it carries out the evaluation based on the aims and the criteria estab-lished by the educational administration. Students who have not achieved the goals of the cycle receive something similar to an O-level Certificate (*Certificado de Escolaridad*) that has no academic value.

To access the baccalaureate or the Intermediate Level of Vocational Training (*Formación Profesional de Grado Medio*), it is necessary to hold the Secondary Education Certificate (*Graduado en Secundaria*).

Baccalaureate studies are taken over two school years, though owing to a high rate of students repeating a year, and also a high rate of dropout, the possibility of studying it over three school years is being discussed by policy-makers. There are five branches of study: nature and health sciences, sciences and engineering, social sciences, human-ities and arts (although the latter is taught in only a few secondary schools). Approximately half the subjects (language, philosophy, history, physical education) are common across all branches, 40% are in the specialism, and 10% are optional, although there may be regional differences according to each Autonomous Community.[1] To obtain the Baccalaureate Certificate (*Título de Bachiller*), students must pass all the subjects, with an evaluation being carried out by the school team of teachers.

There is no external test for validating the Baccalaureate Certificate – an attempt to impose such a test in 2002 aroused large-scale opposition. Instead, there is an admission examination to access university (*selectividad*), the aim of which is to order the students' preferences according to the grade they obtained (using the aver-age grade between the baccalaureate and the admission examination).

Vocational training in upper secondary education includes two levels: Intermediate Vocational Training (*Ciclos Formativos de Grado Medio*, CFGM) and Advanced Vocational Training (*Ciclos Formativos de Grado Superior*, CFGS). To access CFGM, students must hold the Secondary Education Certificate (*Graduado de Secundaria*) or pass an admission examination; to access CFGS, students must hold the Baccalaureate Certificate (*Título de Bachiller*) or pass an admission examination. It should be noted

---

[1] Although Spain is not a federal state, educational powers have been transferred to the regional or territorial governments, the so-called Autonomous Communities (*Comunidades Autónomas*). Even though the general regulation of the system is still carried out by the state government, the development of the curriculum, the management of the schools and some important educational policies such as, for instance, the prevention of school failure depend on the autonomous govern-ments, in collaboration with the local authorities.

that there is no direct access for students completing a CFGM and willing to study a CFGS; for those students, the normal track would be to study the baccalaureate. This has provoked many complaints that have led to the establishment, still in an experimental stage, of some promotion courses for those students holding a CFGM Certificate who are preparing themselves for the admission examinations to CFGS.

Both CFGM and CFGS are taught in secondary schools; they require about 1,300 and 2,000 hours, usually distributed over two school years. The curriculum is vocationally driven, with no optional subjects, and includes 25% work-based learning, with the remaining time being spent in the school. However, there are experiments in some Autonomous Communities, with more hours being spent in companies. Courses are provided in 26 special fields or professional families and correspond to Level 2 (CFGM) and Level 3 (CFGS) of the National Catalogue of Professional Qualifications (*Catálogo Nacional de Cualificaciones Profesionales*).

Students who pass a CFGM obtain the Technician Diploma (*Título de Técnico*), and those who pass a CFGS, the Higher Technician Diploma (*Título de Técnico Superior*). Assessments are carried out by the teachers in the secondary school. Students holding a Higher Technician Diploma may access university, especially the first cycles of technical degrees. One of the problems of these qualifications is that they do not yet have a clear correspondence with the occupational categories defined in collective agreements. Except for some very unusual cases for which the qualification is a requirement in order to be able to work in a specific profession (as in the case of healthcare, for instance), the fact of having obtained such a vocational qualification does not provide students with clear guarantees of obtaining a job related to their training. Furthermore, there is a paradox: some of the requirements to carry out a specific job are obtained in the training for the unemployed, which is provided outside of the educational system.

The students who do not obtain the Secondary Education Certificate (*Graduado en Secundaria*) have the possibility of joining some programs of First-Level Vocational Training (*Programas de Formación Profesional de Nivel 1*), presently called Programs of Initial Professional Qualification (*Programas de Cualificación Profesional Inicial*), which last for a school year (between 800 and 1,200 hours). These programs are provided in secondary schools or in authorised schools (non-profit making foundations, city councils or guilds), and have a small component of work-based training. They give students access to professional certificates (*certificados de profesionalidad*) issued by the work authority, or a second chance at the Secondary Education Certificate (*Graduado de Secundaria*) if they study a specific and voluntary module of basic skills. These programs will be analysed more thoroughly later in this chapter.

What Are the Main Rates of School Graduation or Dropout? Have These Changed from Previous Decades?

In Spain, the debate on school failure has been very important and has involved much controversy. For many years, it was considered that school failure was the result of the student's lack of adaptation, in accordance with deficit or handicap theories.

According to these theories, the students who failed in school had their own characteristics, psychological and social, which distanced them from their classmates. The introduction of the sociological theories of Bourdieu and Bernstein, among others, shifted the focus to the role of school as the cause of school failure. In the last few years, the discourse on inclusive school has introduced the concept of 'school failure', which holds that the *institution* is responsible for student failure, because of its inability to adjust to the different needs and motivations of its students.

Although there are many dimensions of school failure, there is some consensus on the basic indicator of failure, which is the rate of non-graduation at the end of compulsory education; that is, the percentage of an age cohort that does not succeed in obtaining the Secondary Education Certificate when completing compulsory secondary education.

Another indicator is that of the 'schooling net participation rate', defined as the number of students enrolled according to age, divided by the total number of the population belonging to the age group. The dropout concept is also used, but related to school absenteeism; that is to say, the number of boys and girls who do not succeed in completing compulsory secondary education, although this phenomenon is much more complex to analyse and measure (Garcia, 2008). But it is the rate of non-graduation that appears in the official statistics.

The concept of dropout in post-compulsory education, which is the number of students who have enrolled in the baccalaureate or in vocational training but who do not complete it, is also commonly used. Finally, and according to the Lisbon Goals, a standard and comparable indicator of school success presently being used is the percentage of young people between 20- and 24-years-old holding a certificate of post-compulsory education.

First is an analysis of the schooling net participation rate, allowing examination of changes over the last 3 decades. According to the official statistics of the Ministry of Education, these rates at ages 15 and 17 are shown in Table 4.1.

Full schooling by the age of 15 was not achieved until the end of the 1990s for two reasons. Until the 1990s, compulsory primary education lasted up to age 14, and although, theoretically, the students who did not pass this cycle were compelled to follow a program of initial vocational training, in practice, many students did not attend it or quit it during the first course (Merino & Llosada, 2007). Educational and social policies were not able (or it was not considered a priority objective enough) to do something more for this group. In 1990, the Law on the General Planning of the Educational System (*Ley de Ordenación General del Sistema Educativo*, LOGSE) was passed that established compulsory secondary education (*Educación Secundaria Obligatoria*) from 12 to 16 years. Despite its many problems, it has achieved almost full schooling of students at age 15. However, some aspects of the quality of this schooling have been very much criticised, such as high rates of school failure. The percentage in schooling at age 17 (that is, in the post-compulsory stage) has steadily increased: from the beginning of the 1980s to the middle of the 1990s, it rose from 50% to 75% of the cohort. But since the end of the 1990s, this figure has not changed, especially due to the persistence of a high 30% rate of school failure in compulsory education. Spanish educational authorities and the public are well aware of these data, which show that the country is far from

Table 4.1 Schooling net participation rates at significant ages, 1983–84 to 2006–07

Schooling net rate	At age 15	At age 17
1983–84	71.3	48.3
1984–85	73.8	50.9
1985–86	76.7	51.9
1986–87	79.4	53.6
1987–88	82.6	56.6
1988–89	83.7	59.6
1989–90	86.2	62.1
1990–91	89.5	64.3
1991–92	91.5	66.6
1992–93	93.8	69.1
1993–94	n.d	71.7
1994–95	n.d	73.3
1995–96	n.d	74.4
1996–97	n.d	75.1
1997–98	n.d	76.1
1998–99	n.d	75.9
1999–2000	100	74.9
2000–01	100	74.8
2001–02	100	75.7
2002–03	100	75.3
2003–04	100	74.9
2004–05	100	74.8
2005–06	100	75.5
2006–07	100	75.7(p)

n.d = no data available; p = provisional
Source: Estadística de la Enseñanza en España
(Statistics of Education in Spain). Several years.
Ministry of Science and Education.

achieving the goal of 85% of young people between 18- and 24-years-old holding a certificate of post-compulsory education, as established by the Lisbon Strategy.

To calculate the rates of students who obtain the Secondary Education Certificate and the rates of dropout at the different levels and educational stages, two approaches may be used. The first approach is based on official statistics. Figure 4.1 shows the flows of students in the transition from compulsory education to the different post-compulsory pathways over the period 2000–05 (Merino & Garcia, 2008).

Percentages have been calculated for each level and program; those in brackets are for the total age cohort. The first point to note is the student failure to complete compulsory secondary education, which happens in about a third (33%) of the cohort. For this group, the 1990 Law designed the Social Guarantee Program (*Programa de Garantía Social*), which offered a first-level vocational training. However, it was scarcely appealing, for it did not allow students to continue on in the educational system. If added to that is the lack of resources allotted to these programs, it may very well be understood why only a little over one quarter (27%)

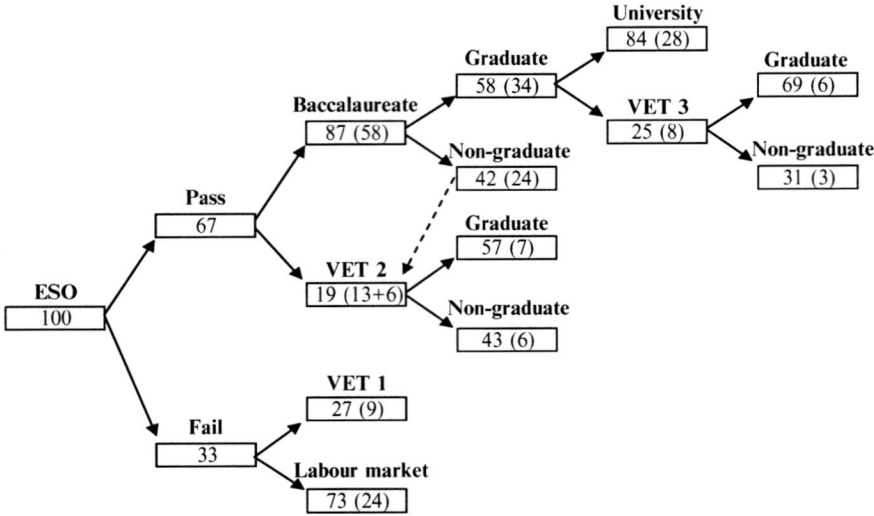

Fig. 4.1 Educational flows in Spain, 2000–05 (%)

of those who had failed have enrolled in these programs. The others, about one quarter of the age cohort (this figure is similar to the schooling net participation rate at the age of 17), are facing a transition to the labour market without any kind of certificate or professional training.

The academic track, the baccalaureate, shows a non-graduation rate of just over 40%, including both those students who drop out and those who do not pass. To reduce this percentage, in the last few years some measures of flexibility have been undertaken, such as the possibility of studying a third year, but only the subjects that the students have not passed. Another set of students who have dropped out of the academic track reorient into vocational training, thus contributing to the image of vocational training as the place where students who have failed the baccalaureate end up going (Merino, 2007).

Intermediate Vocational Training (CFGM), taken by almost 20% of the young people who have passed compulsory secondary education, shows a dropout rate of 43%. This very high rate may be accounted for by many who take up employment opportunities that have been offered, thus raising the opportunity costs of pursuing studies (Merino, 2006). It may well be that what happens during the economic crisis that began in 2008, which is predicted to be a long one, will lower these opportunity costs, and, therefore, will (potentially) reduce the very high dropout rate. Some indices regarding occupational training point to this trend.

After the 1990 reform, a professional track – the Advanced Vocational Training (*Ciclos Formativos de Grado Superior*, CFGS) – was established for those students who completed the baccalaureate, partly as an alternative to the academic track in university. This newly created higher professional track has ended up attracting 25% of the students holding a baccalaureate certificate. However, it is not exactly an alternative track to the university, for a significant percentage of these students use Advanced Vocational Training (CFGS) as a different pathway to attain the former, as sample data will show. Although to a lesser extent than in Intermediate Vocational Training (CFGM), due to students joining the labour market, the drop-out rate in these courses is about 30%.

Figure 4.1 was built on official enrolment data gathered and published by the Ministry of Education. But these are stock data, and the flow reconstruction has important limitations. For instance, it does not show the real tracks that young people follow when they go from first-level programs to Intermediate Vocational Training through admission examinations or special preparation courses. To analyse these tracks, it is necessary to use data from a survey carried out in 2005 showing the educational options in a sample of young people including both those holding and others who did not hold the Compulsory Education Certificate (*Graduado en ESO*) from school year 2000–01 to school year 2004–05. The relevant data appear in Fig. 4.2.

These data, which come from a different statistical source, are similar but not identical, and confirm some previously described trends, such as the preference of young Spanish people for the academic pathway and for considering vocational training a second option when the previous one fails. This is also confirmed by the fact that a third of Intermediate Vocational Training (CFGM) students have failed in the baccalaureate, and that the students who have taken more years to complete the baccalaureate are those who tend to choose Advanced Vocational Training rather than university study. They also account for phenomena that do not appear in official statistics, such as the dropout from the educational system of those students who obtained the Secondary Education Certificate. Although the latter do not represent a large percentage (3.5% of the whole age cohort, 5% of those who have

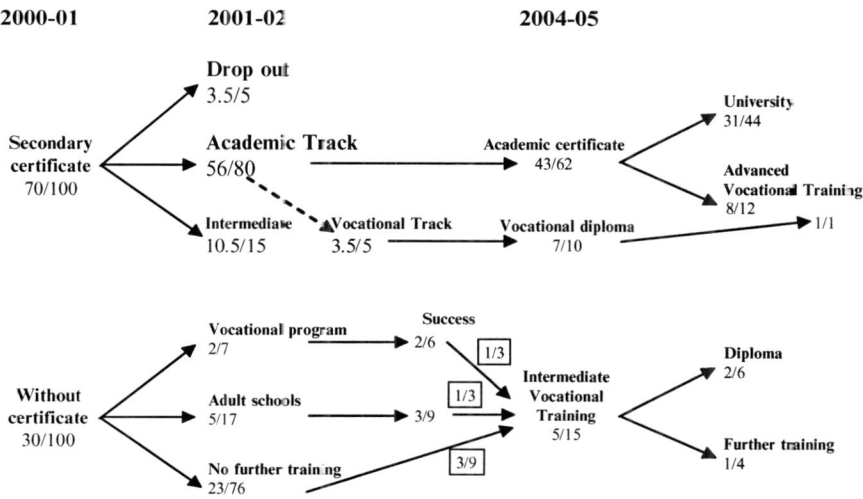

Fig. 4.2 Educational flows based on Spanish young people's pathways, 2000–05 (Source: ETEFIL)

obtained the Certificate, as shown in Fig. 4.2), they deserve to be thoroughly studied. This dropout makes failure in the baccalaureate appear to be less than the one detected in official statistics; however, one out of every four students enrolled do not complete it. Of those, some move into vocational training, where dropout also occurs: almost 50% do not obtain the Technician Diploma. Another phenomenon that official statistics do not show is the transition from Intermediate Vocational Training to Advanced Vocational Training: although it is not a major pathway, the fact that it exists is nevertheless significant in itself. Legislation is being introduced so that this transition may take place more easily.

There is much more information, apart from the official statistics, about the students who do not obtain the Certificate. Approximately one quarter (24%) of these students start a program of recovery, be it a vocational or an academic one, to obtain the Secondary Education Certificate. The vocational programs (the so-called Social Guarantee Programs) have less weight, for they enjoy very little prestige and almost all the students who enrol (2% of the cohort, or 8% of those not obtaining their Secondary Education Certificate) complete them. The academic programs (taken by 5% of the cohort, or 17% of those without a Certificate) are available in adult schools and are not necessarily courses aimed at young people who have not obtained the Certificate; rather these programs have been designed for the general adult population. They are less successful but allow students to obtain an official certificate. At any rate, the most interesting success or recovery measure is the access to Intermediate Vocational Training, which involves one out of every six students (16%) who have not obtained the Secondary General Certificate. These students have been able to continue post-compulsory studies, although a third of them have not been able to complete them.

In summary, the Spanish educational system faces a very important challenge when compared with the other countries of the Organisation for Economic Co-operation and Development (OECD): almost one quarter of each age cohort does not continue post-compulsory studies. Of the students who do undertake these academic studies or vocational training, almost one third do not complete them. And of those who do not enrol for them, only a small percentage make use of the recovery programs, which are far from being a true recovery for a significant percentage of the potential population.

Who Graduates and Who Drops Out?

In the empirical studies on school failure, the classic variables of social inequalities have been used: those that are related to social class, gender and ethnic groups. Regarding social class, basically two variables have been used: the type of work or occupation and the parents' level of education. The parents' career appears in several surveys, mainly in the EPA (*Encuesta de población activa*; Survey of the Working Population), and is classified according to the National Classification of Occupations (*Clasificación Nacional de Ocupaciones*) matrix. Based on this classification, different socioeconomic classifications may be carried out that are an approximation to the reference social class.

According to the data analysed by Martínez (2007a), a child from an upper class family had a 5.8% (1 in 17) chance of not obtaining the certificate of compulsory education by the age of 20. whereas for a child of a working class family it was a 24.4% (1 in 4) chance, and for a child of a farmer's family, a 31.4% (1 in 3) chance. These differences have remained more or less equal since compulsory schooling was introduced. In 1995, a book was published in Catalonia on school success and failure that prompted some debate, for it showed the social differences of students obtaining the certificate at the end of compulsory education, but also that middle class children did not avoid the risk of non-completion: 13% had not obtained the certificate (Cirem, 1995). Despite economic means, and despite the educational strategies of families, school failure was not only a problem affecting the working class.

Regarding the level of education, the relationship between the parents' education and their children's school performance has been demonstrated, especially mother's level of education (Calero, 2006). Using data from the European Household Panel and multinomial logistic regression, this author analysed the different probabilities of pursuing the academic path in post-compulsory education; the most discriminating variable was mother's level of education. Although the latter is not a specific indicator of school success or failure, it is nevertheless related to it, for students who study the baccalaureate have the best results in compulsory education.

The studies based on statistical correlations are somewhat limited when interpreting data. First, they do not explain non-expected situations; for instance, why some working class boys and girls obtain good results and pursue their studies and even go to university. Second, and related to this first aspect, they do not account for the specific mechanisms that cause parents' social inequality to bring about their children's educational inequality. To do this requires studies of a qualitative kind that analyse how, based on similar objective conditions (of occupation and education), families belonging to the same social class are different regarding expectations and educational strategies. This is what a team of Spanish sociologists have attempted to do (Martín Criado et al., 2000), that is to say to study the different attitudes of working class families regarding education. Thus, subjective aspects such as the relationships established with school, the priority given to studying by the family environment or passing responsibilities on to the children must be incorporated into the explanation of the different school outcomes and of the probabilities of school success or failure.

Gender and educational inequalities have also prompted much debate in the scientific community and, no doubt, in the educational one. The new datum is that over the last decades, school failure has been more frequent among male students; also, more female students are in post-compulsory secondary education (mostly in baccalaureate) and even the university. This phenomenon has taken place in many countries from the 1980s onwards (Baudelot & Establet, 1992). Several explanations have been provided (Merino et al., 2006a) ranging from biological to cultural factors. At any rate, female students have adapted much better overall than male students to school environment, which has paradoxically caused the phenomenon of girls' school failure to become 'invisible'. This has consequences for the programs of transition to work, as will be seen in the following section; these programs are often designed for occupational areas to which young women with low skills have very few opportunities to access.

Regarding ethnic groups, in Spain, studies have been carried out on the schooling of the Rom population, an ethnic group with an established presence that has traditionally been marginalised in several domains – work, housing and obviously in education too. In fact, the incorporation of Rom girls and boys into compulsory education has involved difficulties, and, still today, for this group absenteeism rates in secondary education are high. Many boys quit school when they are 14 years of age due to a lack of interest or because they must help to financially support the household; girls quit even earlier to help the family with housework or due to the reluctance of the family to allow them to continue their studies. Furthermore, the presence of ethnic boys and girls in post-compulsory and higher education is difficult to quantify. Neither statistics on education nor national population surveys record the Rom people as a different group; thus, most studies that have been carried out are on a local level or are qualitative approximations. It should be pointed out that a study by a team of anthropologists analysed school success factors in Rom boys and girls (Abajo & Carrasco, 2004), in which, by means of qualitative methods, they found factors of school success, among which non-segregated schooling stood out; however, the risk of non-segregated schooling is that it may lead to a process of acculturation.

The relationship between the ethnic groups and educational inequalities has undergone a very important development in the last few years due to the very important arrival of immigrants. In a 10-year span, Spain has gone from being a country of emigrants to becoming a country of immigrants (from 2.3% of foreigners in 2000 to 10% in 2008; the percentage of students in compulsory education has also followed this pace) and, therefore, a multicultural country. This situation has remarkably changed the social scenery in urban and rural areas, and has provoked conflicts and tensions, the most important setting of which has been school. Prompted by social and political concern regarding this issue, in the last few years a considerable number of research studies have been carried out on the access and incorporation of children who, together with their families, go through their migratory or second-generation processes. Although sometimes the media exaggerate the negative impact of immigrant students entering the educational system, it clearly appears to be harder for immigrant students to obtain the compulsory education certificate and to continue in post-compulsory education. Whereas for Spain as a whole, in the 2007–08 school year, 10% of the students in compulsory secondary education were foreigners, they only amounted to 4% of baccalaureate students and to 6% of vocational training students (Carabaña, 2008). The explanations for such differences are more or less the same ones that were used to explain school failure among working class young people, perhaps just emphasising more the cultural dimensions, but it is very difficult to establish correlations with a situation as heterogeneous as immigration.

From a statistical point of view, only citizenship (Spanish or foreign) is recorded. This in itself causes problems as increasingly more and more people from immigrant origins obtain Spanish citizenship. However, from the point of view of the internal composition of immigration, there is large diversity. Although majority groups come from Latin America (especially Ecuador and Colombia), or from Morocco, families also come from Argentina, Romania, Senegal, Pakistan or China, to name a few, to settle in Spain. This is a recent phenomenon, and there is still need to study in depth the education and training trajectories of these young men and women.

In addition to factors related to the biographic profile of the students and their families, another factor partially explaining differences in rates of school failure is the regional context, more specifically, the economic structure and local labour markets. In the early 1990s, it was already clear that school failure was very different in areas of Spain such as Catalonia, Galicia and Andalusia (Planas & Comas, 1994). Whereas in Catalonia, the non-graduation rate when finishing compulsory education was 30%, in Andalusia and Galicia it was only 20%. The explanation is twofold. The industrial structure of Catalonia provided more job opportunities, thus vocational training was more attractive. Instead, the tendency to pursue studies is higher in areas where the economy is weaker and where the educational system functions as a temporary buffer. But this tendency happened with the educational system defined by the Law of 1970, which made it compulsory for students who did not pass primary education to enrol in lower-level vocational training (*Formación Profesional de Primer Grado*). With the application of the educational reform of 1990, this mandatory connection disappeared, and so this factor could no longer explain the higher level of school failure in Catalonia.

Furthermore, in the beginning of the 1990s, the Spanish economy was in recession. Then, from 1996 onwards, there was a cycle of great economic growth, when millions of jobs were created, partially explaining the increase in the immigrant workforce (although this was generally in those sectors requiring low skills, such as construction and tourism). This economic boom accounts for the fact that in the last few years, the differences in school failure have increased throughout the country. In the 'Mediterranean Arc', where there are high levels of employment, dropout and school failure rates are higher than in other areas of the country. It is relevant to highlight the case of the Balearic Islands, with a school failure rate of almost 40% (Calero, 2006), which is a case of a labour market that basically offers low-quality jobs related to mass tourism. This often encourages students to give up their studies and enter the labour market. This is referring to what economists call 'opportunity cost': the lack of difficulty finding a job and a salary means a lack of incentive to make an effort to study and to pursue secondary education. This phenomenon is well known in vocational training, where between 30% and 50% of enrolled students do not complete the course, generally because they find a job (Merino, in press). The period of economic growth ceased in the first part of 2008, with increasing numbers of unemployed people. It is still necessary to verify empirically if this economic downturn will lower opportunity costs and therefore encourage young people to continue studying, or whether school failure rates will continue to be as high as they are now.

To sum up, explanatory factors for school failure can be found in the 'supply-side' characteristics of individuals and their families and in the 'demand-side' characteristics of local labour markets. To these two sets of factors can be added a third, which here is called the 'institutional' factors – what schools can do and actually do to increase or reduce school failure. This issue is analysed in the following section.

Programs, Policies and Practices to Reduce Dropout

There is a general consensus today in Spain that the dropout and school failure rate is too high. Over previous decades, political priority was given to schooling participation rates, to ensure that schooling during compulsory primary education (and in the last few years, in the non-compulsory pre-school period) was provided to all children. In this way, historical discrimination experienced by many generations excluded from school was rectified. But once participation rates of almost 100% in compulsory education and 70% in post-compulsory education had been achieved, emphasis has been put on the efficiency of the system. The public agenda has moved from quantity to quality. When the data on non-graduation from compulsory education for students who are aged 16 are compared, the Spanish rate is far from the average of the other countries in the European Union or the OECD.

Every time a survey or a report (such as PISA) discussing graduation and dropout rates is made public, the focus of Spain's media, in its political debates, and within the educational community is that something has to be done to reduce the school failure rate of approximately 30%. The problem is to achieve consensus in what must be done, which inevitably involves hardships. In addition to logical (and legitimate) ideological differences regarding the definition and treatment that school failure deserves, there are important intrinsic difficulties, such as the appearance of unwanted effects.

If the diagnosis is focused on *individual* variables, then emphasis is put on the *compensatory* dimension of the programs to be implemented; they focus on offering more hours to the students so that they may be able to follow the normal pace of the group. Compensatory education may be private; for instance, a middle class family that provides private lessons to their child, because he or she learns more slowly than other classmates. It may be state-supported, like the support programs of afternoon centres for students with such family problems that they cannot normally follow their studies. It may also be mixed, with the collaboration of the Administration and of cooperative and associative networks to carry out so-called 'school reinforcement' (*refuerzo escolar*).

If the diagnosis focuses on the *external* variable, eventual solutions are very difficult. This is another of the weak points of statistical correlations when trying to give them shape in political proposals. The fact that working class young people or those who have illiterate mothers have a higher probability of failing in school tells us little about what could be done, for neither their class nor their mothers can be changed. Grant policies may be established (and they actually are) to compensate for the direct and indirect school costs, but they have greater impact on access to the different educational levels than on school performance (Martínez, 2007b). In addition, it is also very difficult to impinge on the structure of the labour market; although the knowledge economy might be fostered, reality is reality and the demand for a low-skilled workforce will continue to be a lack of incentive for educational endeavour. Calls for active employment programs focus on training and operate under the assumption that unemployed individuals are those who do not adjust to the requirements of the labour market, so that they appear as responsible for their situation (Walther & Stauber, 2002).

Finally, what can schools do? Educational policy has been the scene of strong ideological, political and academic debates about the steps to be taken to reduce school failure. As discussed in the first section, one of the aims of every educational reform from the last 40 years in Spain has been to reduce the rate of early dropout and non-graduation in compulsory education. To achieve this aim, basically two kinds of proposals have been made: organisational and didactic, each of them focusing on discussion of the positive and negative aspects of comprehensive education. In the 1980s, consensus was reached regarding 14 as the age for students to complete compulsory education, and to decide between the academic path and the professional one. The 1990 reform extended the common curriculum by 2 years and fostered the methodology of significant learning based on constructivist theories to address the obvious difficulty of managing classes with a greater diversity of students. The first years of the application of this reform were extremely conflicted; the second cycle of compulsory secondary school, from ages 14 to 16, was the most difficult one. Many teenagers behaved badly and they started to be called 'school objectors' (*objetores escolares*); also, many teachers complained about the increasing impossibility of controlling their classrooms and secondary schools, about the lack of resources and the unavoidable fall in the levels of school performance of all students. Many families also complained about the fact that interested and motivated students were combined in classrooms with students who wanted to quit school (Merino, 2005).

At the bottom line of this whole debate, beyond biased exaggerations, the internalisation or externalisation of school failure was being debated (Planas et al., 1998), as well as the role and aims of compulsory education. Either school engages itself to make every student acquire the so-called 'basic competences', or it has only a fundamentally classificatory function to sort students according to their attainment. The responses to school failure very much depend on this dilemma.

From the first point of view, the response is basically a didactic one: methodology should be changed and teachers' training should be improved. From the second point of view, the response to school failure is clear: the reason why students fail at school is because it cannot offer them anything that may interest them. Therefore, what school should do is to diversify its curriculum, for example, by offering programs based on manual skills with a vocational orientation, even if this is at the risk of creating a hierarchy of status among the different paths of the curriculum; or these programs could be provided by institutions outside the secondary school system.

The 1990 educational reform chose the former way, whereas the 2002 reform chose the latter. In a law passed in 2006, the importance of didactic orientation was partly reinforced, but doors were also opened to curricular diversification, which *de facto* already existed in many secondary schools.

This first important debate focuses on how to reduce school failure at the end of compulsory education; however, there is a second important debate on what to do with the students who have not obtained the Secondary Education Certificate. As already mentioned, the 1990 reform prevented these students from entering school-based vocational training and instead established specific programs called Social Guarantee Programs (*Programas de Garantía Social*, PGS). These had a vocational orientation, but greater possibilities of becoming stigmatised programs. In fact, the PGS have only interested a third of the students who have not obtained their Secondary Education Certificate, and most classes have been provided in institutions outside the secondary school system despite serious problems maintaining stability (Merino et al., 2006b). The idea was to establish programs that lasted one school year and that were based on professional-skill modules. However, they did not enable students to either obtain the Secondary Education Certificate or pursue vocational training studies.

The *Ley Orgánica de Educación* (Organic Law on Education) of 2006 rectified these fundamental problems by establishing the Programs of Initial Professional Qualification (*Programas de Cualificación Profesional Inicial*, PCPI), which are programs that last 2 years, incorporate a module of basic skills that allows students to obtain the compulsory Secondary Education Certificate and makes access to intermediate-level vocational training (*Formación Profesional de Grado Medio*, CFGM) easier. Although the external character of educational institutions has been maintained, it seems that educational administrators have taken the structuring and follow-up of these programs more seriously. Because they were to be implemented for the first time in the 2008–09 school year, it is still too early to carry out an assessment of the programs as to whether they become a true second opportunity for students who have failed in school.

The evaluation of educational reforms, in general, and of the policies against school failure, in particular, is not easy to resolve. To the technical difficulty related to this kind of assessment should be added the ongoing ideological and political disputes regarding the best way of approaching the problem of school failure. An example of this is the substitution of the new Programs of Initial Professional Qualification (*Programas de Cualificación Profesional Inicial*, PCPI) for Social Guarantee Programs (*Programas de Garantía Social*, PGS). The PGSs have been criticised, but no assessment of their strong and weak points has been carried out. In November 2006, when the Ministry of Education was beginning to enforce the LOE (*Ley Orgánica de Educación*, Organic Law of Education), a monograph on how the new PCPIs should be implemented was published, in which the present authors participated (Merino et al., 2006a). However, this was done without an assessment of the results over the previous 15 years that PGSs have been in operation.

One possibility for obtaining the Secondary Education Certificate, for those who did not obtain it while they were at secondary school, is to attend courses in adult schools. These schools, which in the beginning were a response to the high rate of illiteracy of the adult population, are increasingly 'being rejuvenated' as a result of this possibility (Planas & Monturiol, 2006). According to some data of the Ministry of Education, in the 2006–07 school year, 40% of students who enrolled in adult schools to obtain the Secondary Education Certificate were aged under 20. At these schools, students can also prepare themselves for the examinations to enter vocational training; however, not many young people actually do so.

An aspect that must be taken into account is that Spain is a strongly decentralised country with regard to education. Although the State Administration still holds power over the general regulation of the educational system, territorial or regional governments (the Autonomous Communities) have some regulatory power and, more than anything else, a management role. In the curriculum of compulsory secondary education, for instance, some Communities have transformed the optional subjects to obligatory ones in either the academic or vocational paths. Also, some specific devices have been set up for groups of students with special difficulties, such as language immersion classrooms (*aulas de enlace*) for teenagers of immigrant origin who join the educational system but who are not literate in Spanish. Some Communities have designed their own Social Guarantee Programs, such as the Programs of Transition to Work (*Programas de Transición al Trabajo*) in Catalonia, in very close collaboration with the local administrations.

Despite having virtually no powers in educational matters, these local administrations have taken on great responsibility in the establishment of programs to encourage school success; many of the problems derived from early dropout and school failure are concentrated in some specific areas, and are usually linked to social problems that appear in the local community. It is worth highlighting the programs against school absenteeism (Garcia, 2008), launched by many city councils with the participation of the social services, the local police and other agencies in order to identify those children and teenagers not attending school. The network of municipal institutions of occupational training is also very important; these institutions provide a broad offering of training courses, counselling workshops and other resources for young people who lack academic training. Although part of this counselling and training is regulated by the Ministry of Employment and the Autonomous Governments (with the financing of the European Funds), city councils are in charge of giving momentum to and managing many programs. All of the programs managed or fostered by local administrations have two main problems, which make them less efficient: not enough financing, since financing is unstable and subject to political or administrative changes in the higher levels; and lack of networking among various areas and departments.

Finally, many secondary schools have developed innovative projects to reduce their dropout and/or school failure rates. While there may not be official records of these projects, some research has been carried out on them (Ferrer, 2007). The vast majority of these projects are based on diversification or on curricular adaptation, with some degree of external training, which provides students with different educational agents and environments. The aim of these projects is to offer something more interesting and appealing than mathematics, language or history to the percentage of teenagers (who, depending on the school, may number between 40% and 50%) who are not motivated regarding their studies. Project classrooms (*aulas de proyecto*) or open classrooms (*aulas abiertas*) replace the ordinary curriculum, with practical activities within or outside the school premises, often with the collaboration of local associations and companies that take these students for some hours in order to get them away from the routine of secondary school and to increase their motivation in a 'real' environment.

Basically, these projects have two limitations: they are mostly fostered and carried out on the initiative of teachers who are very motivated and feel empathy for these students, with no clear institutional support, and they may have a boomerang effect, increasing the temptation of ordinary teachers to direct more students towards these programs so that the complex management of mainstream classrooms diminishes.

The problem of school failure is on the public agenda, especially in the context of the common aim of the European Union countries that was part of the Lisbon Declaration. Spain is still far from the 10% dropout rate that European countries established as a goal for 2010, and, even worse, there is not any downward trend in the rate of dropout. The structural programs may make it difficult to find solutions in the mid and long run, which is the reason why the challenge for the educational community and for policy-makers is much greater and more urgent.

The importance of this issue is such that on November 11, 2008, an agreement between the Ministry of Education and the Autonomous Governments was announced. This was to develop a plan to combat premature school dropout, aiming at reducing by half the dropout rate in 2012 and thus getting closer to the OECD average. This plan has been provided with funds (the idea is to obtain €240 million) and will focus on strengthening the aforementioned strategies (including PCPI, admission examinations to vocational training, schools for adults, improved counselling and teacher training), as well as completely new ones, such as schools for parents, and the recognition of non-formal learning. The hope is that it will be more than just another plan, and that it will be implemented over the next few years.

References

Abajo, J.E., & Carrasco, S. (Eds.). (2004). *Experiencias y trayectorias de éxito escolar de gitanas y gitanos en España*. Madrid, Spain: Instituto de la Mujer-CIDE.
Baudelot, C., & Establet, R. (1992). *Allez les filles!* Paris: Le Seuil.
Calero, J. (2006). *Desigualdades tras la educación obligatoria: Nuevas evidencias*. Madrid, Spain: Fundación Alternativas.
Carabaña, J. (2008). *El impacto de la inmigración en el sistema educativo español* (ARI 63/2008 – 17/06/). Real Instituto Elcano. Retrieved from www.realinstitutoelcano.org/wps/portal
Cirem. (1995). *Èxit i fracàs escolar a Catalunya*. Barcelona, Spain: Fundació Bofill.
Ferrer, M.T. (2007). Les aules obertes. Experiències escolars compartides: Una línia de futur per al rendiment escolar. *Perspectiva Escolar, 311*, 66–71.
Garcia, M. (2008). Role of secondary schools in the face of student absenteeism: A study of schools in socially underprivileged areas. *International Journal of Inclusive Education, 12*(3), 263–280.

Martín Criado, E., Gómez Bueno, C., Fernández Palomares, F., & Rodríguez Monge, A. (2000). *Familias de Clase Obrera y Escuela*. Bilbao, Spain: Iralka.

Martínez, J.S. (2007a). Fracaso escolar, clase social y política educative. *Viejo Topo, 238,* 44–49.

Martínez, J.S. (2007b). Clase social, género y desigualdad de oportunidades educativas. *Revista de Educación, 342,* 287–306.

Merino, R. (2005). De la LOGSE a la LOCE. Discursos y estrategias de alumnos y profesores ante la reforma educativa. *Revista de Educación, 336,* 475–502.

Merino, R. (2006). Two or three pathways for vocational training? Assessment of educational reforms in Spain. *European Journal of Vocational Training, 37,* 52–67.

Merino, R. (in press). *La formación profesional reglada en España: Tendencias y debates.*

Merino, R., & Garcia, M. (2008). Spain, educational system. *Formazione & Insegnamento, 1/2,* 99–137.

Merino, R., García, M., & Casal, J. (2006a). De los Programas de Garantía Social a los Programas de Cualificación Inicial. Sobre perfiles y dispositivos locales. *Revista de Educación, 341,* 81–98.

Merino, R., & Llosada, J. (2007). ¿Puede una reforma hacer que más jóvenes escojan formación profesional? Flujos e itinerarios de formación profesional de los jóvenes españoles. *Témpora. Revista de sociología de la educación, 10,* 215–244.

Merino, R., Sala, G., & Troiano, H. (2006b). Desigualdades de clase, género y etnia en educación. In F. Fernández Palomares (Ed.), *Sociología de la Educación*. Madrid, Spain: Pearson Educación S.A.

Planas, J., & Comas, M. (1994). *Prévention de l'échec scolaire et de la marginalisation des jeunes dans la période de transition de l'école à la vie adulte et professionnelle en Espagne*. Barcelona, Spain: ICE-UAB.

Planas, J., Garcia, M., & Casal, J. (1998). Las reformas en los dispositivos de formación para combatir el fracaso escolar en Europa: Paradojas de un éxito. *Revista de Educación, 317,* 301–317.

Planas, J., & Monturiol, M. (2006). *Improving teaching and learning for adults with basic skill needs*. Spanish background report. Paris: OECD.

Raffe, D., & Spours, K. (1997). *The unification of post-compulsory education: Towards a conceptual framework* (Working Paper No. 2). London: Institute of Education, University of London.

Walther, A., & Stauber, B. (Eds.). (2002). *Misleading trajectories. Integration policies for young adults in Europe?* Opladen, Germany: Leske &Budrich.

Chapter 5
Towards Compulsory Participation in England

Alice Sullivan and Lorna Unwin

Introduction

Children in England who started secondary school in September 2008 have a special claim to fame: they form the first cohort obliged by law to participate in some form of officially recognised education or training until they reach their 17th birthday (Department of Children, Schools and Families [DCSF], 2007). This is because they will be 16 in 2013, the date that marks the first stage in the government's plan to raise what it refers to as the 'participation age'. In 2015, the second stage of the plan will require all young people to participate until they are 18. There have been calls for the school-leaving age to be extended to 18 since the end of the First World War (see Simon, 1986). The current age at which young people can leave school has stood at 16 since 1972, having risen from 14 to 15 in 1947 following the 1944 Education Act. The Act also announced that although young people could leave school at 15 and enter the labour market, they would be required to attend county colleges for the purposes of part-time 'continuation education'. In her discussion of these proposals, Tinkler (2001, p. 79) explains that policy-makers of the time felt that anyone who left school at 15 had 'received an education inadequate to their needs as individuals, citizens and workers', and that 'no wage earning occupation could in itself be a "proper" education for those who had left school at 15'. Furthermore, it was argued that young people would be happier and have richer lives if they remained in contact with an educational institution for some years after entering employment, particularly as the jobs they were likely to get might promote 'physical, mental and moral degeneration'.

The county colleges were never built and the call for 'continuation education' was dropped, but the ambition to make education or training compulsory in some form or other has been a matter of debate ever since. The focus in the 1944 Education Act on the protection of young people from the potential dangers of the labour market and the desire to continue their intellectual development for as long as possible has given way to a new set of imperatives for keeping young people in some form of officially

A. Sullivan (✉) and L. Unwin (✉)
Institute of Education, University of London, UK

S. Lamb et al. (Eds.), *School Dropout and Completion: International Comparative Studies in Theory and Policy*, DOI 10.1007/978-90-481-9763-7_6,
© Springer Science+Business Media B.V. 2011

recognised education or training. The main focus of today's policy-makers is on the economic and social consequences of early leaving (for the individual, the economy and society), plus a desire to arrest England's poor showing in the league tables from the Organisation for Economic Co-operation and Development (OECD) for national participation and 'dropout' rates. The current participation rate in post-compulsory education and training has not changed since 1994 when it plateaued at around 75%. These concerns are set within what the government refers to as a context of change (economic and social), and thus the background paper for the new legislation argued that:

> Young people growing up now can expect a life of change – and we must equip them not just with the cognitive capacity but also with the personal capabilities, resilience, interpersonal skills and the attitudes that will enable them to benefit from the opportunities this will bring. (Department for Education and Skills [DfES], 2007, p. 10)

It is important to draw attention at this stage to the fact that the new legislation is significantly different from previous changes to the school-leaving age. In 2013, the compulsory phase of schooling will still end at 16, and young people will be able to leave school. The new requirement to continue participating means young people will have to find a place in one of the following parts of the English system:

Full-time education – including school, college and home education
Work-based learning – such as an apprenticeship or other form of government-supported training (GST) program
Part-time education or training – if they are employed, self-employed or volunteering more than 20 hours a week

Although this variety of contexts means that the concept of 'school dropout', as used in other countries, still won't apply in England, the new legislation will build stronger walls around the publicly funded education and training system to the age of 18. The prison metaphor is not inappropriate: those young people who refuse to 'participate' will be subject to a series of penalties, the highest level of which would result in them appearing before a youth court and their parents or guardians being subjected to a 'parenting order' (DCSF, 2007). A parenting order, which can last for up to 12 months, is issued by a magistrate's court and usually requires the parent or guardian to attend counselling or guidance sessions for a period of up to 3 months. In some cases, they may have to attend meetings with teachers at their child's school, ensure their child does not visit a particular place unsupervised or make sure their child is at home at particular times. Failure to meet these requirements can result in prosecution.

This chapter examines the current inequalities in terms of the outcomes of the English system for young people aged 16–18. It is argued that whilst the ambition to raise the levels of participation in education and training beyond 16 is justified, much will need to be done to ensure that the education and training programs available to young people are of equal quality.

The chapter is divided into four further sections: the first discusses the nature of compulsory education in England to the age of 16; the second discusses the different pathways that comprise post-compulsory education and training; the third examines the impact of gender in relation to education and training; and the fourth provides some concluding remarks.

Compulsory Education in England

Children in England enter the 'primary stage' of education in the year in which they have their fifth birthday. Prior to this, children from the age of 3 who attend some form of pre-school provision are in what the 2002 Education Act termed the Foundation Stage of education. At the age of 11, children then transfer to new schools to start the 'secondary stage' of education. Depending on the part of the country, some secondary schools take pupils to the age of 18, and some to the age of 16. A minority of 'middle schools', which take pupils from the age of 8 or 9 to the age of 12 or 13, still exist. The vast majority of schools are funded and maintained by the state, but there are privately funded primary and secondary schools (which usually refer to themselves as 'independent' schools), and they have a significant impact on the rest of the system. The status of private schools in Britain is quite different from that of the private schools in either the United States or continental Europe. Whereas in most developed countries, private schools are primarily religious and often highly subsidised (by church or state), British private schools are in the main socially and (often) academically exclusive institutions, which, being unsubsidised, are far too expensive for the bulk of the population. Because Britain incorporated most denominational schools within the state sector, its private sector is relatively small. As Hillman (1994, p. 403) puts it: 'In most countries private schools provide for religious, ethnic and cultural diversity. In Britain they provide an often high-powered preparation for a significant proportion of the future members of high-status occupations.' The domination of elite occupations by alumni of the top private schools (often, for historical reasons, termed 'public schools') has long been apparent (Boyd, 1973). The majority of secondary schools do not select by ability, but there are still 164 state-funded grammar schools covering pupils in around one third of England, entry to which is determined by an entrance examination taken at the age of 11. Grammar schools also exist in Northern Ireland, but not in Wales or Scotland. In 2007, only 7% of pupils at the end of Key Stage 4 (Year 11) were attending private schools. Sixty per cent of private school pupils gained five or more A*-C grade passes in their General Certificate of Secondary Education (GCSE) exams, including English and mathematics, compared with 46% of state-maintained school pupils. Evidence suggests that a substantial proportion of the apparent academic advantage at the private schools is due to the academically and socially selective nature of their intake (Sullivan & Heath, 2003). Pupils at state schools defined as 'selective' outperformed private school pupils at GCSE, with 98% gaining (five or more) 5 − A*−C GCSE exam passes.[1] Despite efforts towards 'widening participation', students from private schools still gain a disproportionate level of places at elite universities. For example, nearly half of the home undergraduates at Oxford University come from private schools (Oxford University Gazette, 2008).

---

[1] Source: Table 3 http://www.dcsf.gov.uk/rsgateway/DB/SFR/s000768/revisedGCSE2008sfrables.xls

Under both Conservative and Labour governments, education policy over the past 20 years or so has promoted 'diversity' (of types of school) and 'parental choice' within the state system in England. In contrast, and as Raffe (2010) notes, the advocacy of diversity is something that Scotland has resisted. Where once, Labour governments regarded the shift to a totally non-selective comprehensive system of secondary schooling as crucial to creating a more equal society (see Lodge & Blackstone, 1982), Tony Blair's New Labour government elected in 1997 signalled a significant change to the so-called old Labour principles. This saw the introduction of various initiatives to encourage greater involvement from employers and other interested parties from the wider community in the running of schools. Part of the argument is that schools (and other educational institutions) need to learn how to innovate and be more enterprising, and this is connected to a belief that it is only through such an approach that so-called failing schools, mainly found in deprived areas, will be turned around. Sammons (2008) argues that the origins of the intense pressure on schools to improve their performance since the election of the New Labour government, and since 2007, under Blair's successor, Gordon Brown, can be traced to a lecture in 1995 given by Michael Barber (now Lord Barber) who was a key New Labour education adviser and former Professor of Education at the Institute of Education, University of London. Barber advocated the need to challenge what he saw as deep-rooted low expectations and poor quality of education in schools in disadvantaged communities.

In 2000, the Labour government announced that it intended to create a number of 'academies', a new type of secondary school partly inspired by the previous Conservative government's establishment of city technology colleges (CTCs) and which, in turn, had been influenced by the charter schools initiative in the United States. Academies are state-funded schools, which are established and managed by sponsors, including existing schools and colleges of further education, universities, philanthropists, businesses, the voluntary sector and the faith communities. Government claims that sponsors will challenge traditional thinking on how schools are run and, hence, help to reverse cultures of low aspiration in areas of the country where school results are deemed to be unacceptable. The sponsor's role is to set up an endowment fund to be used by a board of trustees to run the school, with particular emphasis on initiatives to stem the impact of deprivation on education in their local communities. Woods et al. (2007, p. 240) describe academies as 'hybrid organisations' in that they combine 'private characteristics', such as being 'independently managed', backing by independent sponsors and freedom to innovate, with '...public characteristics, such as dependence on government funding and expectations to contribute to social goals by tackling educational inequalities and contributing to the regeneration of communities'.

Between 2002 and 2005, over 50 academies had been opened or approved and current plans are to increase their number to 400. Academies are set up with the backing of the local education authority (LEA) in the area, and the LEA has a seat on each academy's governing body. When academies are co-sponsored by their local authority, the LEA will have two seats on the governing body. Academies are not maintained by an LEA, but they collaborate closely with it, and with other schools in the area. Research suggests that academies do not actually achieve better examination results than schools with comparable intakes of students (Gerard, 2005). The government has also pledged to support the expansion of faith school provision within the state sector. This now includes Muslim, Hindu and Sikh schools, as well as Christian and Jewish schools. Both academies and faith schools have been accused of covert social and academic selection of pupils.

From 1988 until 1994, all pupils in English secondary schools followed a 10-subject national curriculum divided into four 'key stages', ending with external assessment at ages 7, 11, 14 and 16. From 2009, the testing of young people at 14 was to be dropped, following consistent and intense pressure on government to ease the assessment burden. From 1994 onwards, various interventions were made by government to provide more flexibility for schools to adapt what was seen as an overly prescriptive and unwieldy curriculum framework. In 2002, the Increased Flexibility Programme (IFP) went a considerable step further, and allowed schools to release some 14- to 16-year-olds from parts of the national curriculum so that they could attend vocational courses for up to 3 days a week at their local further education college. From their evaluation of the IFP, Higham and Yeomans (2007) concluded that government had been 'pushing at an open door' as far as schools were concerned because the majority of teachers believed that the 10-subject national curriculum had compelled large numbers of young people to take subjects that did not motivate or interest them. There are also Youth Apprenticeships for 14- to 16-year-olds, which involve work experience with local employers.

The ability to 'choose' which subjects to study is part of the government's desire to develop a 'personalised' approach to education:

> The central characteristic of such a new system will be personalisation – so that the system fits to the individual rather than the individual having to fit to the system. This is not a vague liberal notion about letting people have what they want. It is about having a system which will genuinely give high standards for all…and the corollary of this is that the system must be both freer and more diverse – with more flexibility to help meet individual needs; and more choices between courses and types of provider, so that there really are different and personalised opportunities available. (DfES, 2004, foreword)

Whilst what has been termed the 'choice' agenda is being implemented throughout the country's public services, Avis (2004, p. 209) has warned, however, that the creation of multiple and differentiated pathways in education may serve to 'reproduce the patterns of inequality and structural differentiation present in wider society'.

With regard to the themes explored in this book, the key assessment stage in England takes place at 16 when pupils sit external examinations in a range of subjects (sciences, humanities, modern languages and vocational subjects) to be awarded the GCSE. This assessment comes at the end of 2 years of study; hence young people have to choose their GCSE subjects at the end of their third year in secondary school. These choices are important because they ultimately affect the extent to which young people can then gain access to subjects at a more advanced level, including at university. GCSEs are graded from A* to G, but the benchmark for success is to attain at least five GCSEs at grades A* to C, including English and mathematics. The attainment of five GCSEs at the higher levels, formally classified as a Level 2 achievement, is regarded as the entry requirement for the more prestigious apprenticeships, for jobs with training, and as the platform for progression to the next level of academic qualifications, known as 'A Levels', which are required to gain entry to higher education. Thus, the English system is characterised by this seismic break at the age of 16. Those young people who do not achieve the magic five GCSEs at grades A* to C are regarded as failures, for the system has no way of recognising the attainment of lower-level GCSEs even though a young person may, for example, have passed several at grades D to G. Those who do climb over the GCSE threshold are then able, if they wish, to remain in full-time education, either at school or at a further education college catering for the 16–18 age group, to study for A Levels.

Hodgson and Spours (2008) have identified the following five characteristics of the English general education system:

- Qualifications-led and dominated by GCSEs and A Levels
- Selective at 16+
- 'Elective' with considerable learner choice in terms of individual qualifications post-16 and increasingly post-14
- Individual subject focused rather than programatic
- Little curriculum breadth – particularly post-16

These characteristics have resulted in the system being criticised for forcing young people to take increasingly narrow groups of subjects and for favouring those who can most easily succeed. In order to counter such criticisms, since 2000, a major thrust of education policy in England has been to construct a 14–19 phase of education that will encourage young people to remain in full-time education or government-funded training and overcome the terminal status of the GCSE stage at the age of 16 (for detailed reviews, see Hodgson & Spours, 2003, 2008). The most recent initiative to emerge is the introduction of 14–19 Diplomas covering a range of vocational areas of study (e.g., information technology, engineering and creative and media) from September 2008. They will be delivered through partnerships between schools and colleges, and young people will be able to combine them with GCSE and A-level study. Decisions about the content of the diplomas have been led by Sector Skills Councils (SSCs), which represent employers in 25 areas of the economy, and universities have been involved to some extent in relation to stipulating how much general education would be required for a diploma to be recognised for entry to a degree course.

The design of and inspiration for the new diplomas came from the Tomlinson Working Group on 14–19 Reform (led by Sir Mike Tomlinson) set up by government in 2003. The group recommended that GCSEs and A Levels be replaced by a new overarching diploma covering all 14–19 learning. Despite considerable enthusiasm for this model from significant numbers of teachers, teacher unions, parts of the academic community, some employer organisations and other interested parties, the idea was rejected by Tony Blair and his government in 2005. Government decided, however, that the concept of a diploma could be introduced as a way to create a more substantive vocational offering within schools and colleges for full-time students. Despite the fact that colleges of further education had been running full-time vocational courses for young people aged 16 and over for many years, the new 14–19 Diplomas are being promoted as 'the' vocational program. The first students enrolled in September 2008, so it is too early to pronounce on the effectiveness of this new pathway, but there are considerable concerns that these new qualifications are being introduced too quickly without adequate pilots, that there is too much inconsistency across the subject lines, and that they are already overly academic in terms of their content and forms of assessment (see Stanton, 2008).

There has been considerable change to the governance and funding arrangements related to schools in England over the past 10 years or so. The 'Every Child Matters' agenda and the Children Act 2004 placed the responsibility on the city- and county-based local authorities that administer school-based education to establish new departments to bring together all services covering children and young people. This so-called inter-agency approach (involving schools, health services, the police and the voluntary sector) was enshrined in the government's decision in July 2007, when Gordon Brown took over from Tony Blair as Prime Minister, to split the existing DfES into two new departments: the Department for Children, Schools and Families (DCSF) and the Department for Innovation, Universities and Skills (DIUS). DCSF is responsible for children and young people (and hence their education and training) up to the age of 18, whilst DIUS looks after education and training beyond 18. This was seen as a particularly problematic split for further education colleges, which cater for students from the age of 14 (as part of a program that allows school pupils to spend part of the week attending courses in college) to adults at and beyond retirement age (see Huddleston & Unwin, 2007, for an overview of the colleges' remit).

Pring (2008, p. 678) argues that the 'Every Child Matters' agenda has had the result that:

> Education is now officially seen as one aspect of 'well-being' (howsoever this is defined) and, reciprocally, 'well-being' is seen as a condition, generally speaking, for educational achievement.

This conflation of education with broader concerns for young people's personal and social development is reflected in the legislation to increase the participation age to 18:

> Young people who participate between the ages of 16 and 18 are less likely to experience teenage pregnancy, behave anti-socially, be involved in crime or go to prison. They are more likely to be healthy and to develop good social skills, which makes it easier for them to find work and succeed in life. (DCSF, 2007, p. 4)

Post-Compulsory Education and Training in England

At the age of 16, young people can:

- Remain in full-time education in school or college
- Study part-time at college
- Enter employment, full-time or part-time

- Enter government supported work-based learning – apprenticeship (available at Levels 2 and 3) or a pre-employment program
- Become classified as NEET (Not in Education, Employment or Training)

To encourage full-time participation, young people whose parents/guardians earn less than £30,000 a year can apply for the means-tested Education Maintenance Allowance (EMA) worth up to £30 per week.

The latest figures for England, as provided in Table 5.1, show that 71% of 17-year-olds are in full-time further education or government supported training (GST). The prevalence of GST is the highest in the North East of England (13%), and lowest in London (4%).[2]

As these national statistics show, there are regional variations, but further break-downs at the level of wards within cities would show even starker contrasts from one area to another. For example, there are substantial differences in the levels of educational attainment in different London boroughs (Lupton & Sullivan, 2007). These gaps between rich and poor areas are apparent in all cities, to varying degrees. Nottingham is another city of stark contrasts between areas. In 2007, 64% of pupils in Nottingham North gained five or more A*-C grades at GCSE, compared to 49% in Nottingham South.[3] Between 1991 and 2006, the proportion of school-leavers who continued in education rose from 61% to 78%. At the end of compulsory schooling in 2006, girls were more likely to continue in education (82%) than boys (74%), while boys were more likely than girls to be in employment or GST. Rates of unemployment or NEET were similar between the sexes (7% for females and 8% for males).[4] The proportion of 16- to 18-year-olds who were classed as NEET was at a high during the mid-1980s, which was a time of high unemployment. However, levels have been fairly flat since the early 1990s. In addition to the classification as 'NEET', young people can be classed as 'NET' (Not in any Education or Training). In practice, this category provides an overestimate of the number of young people who are receiving no education or training at all, as government classifies anyone in a job that does not involve some form of government-supported or recognised form of training as NET. Recent qualitative case study research suggests that some young people in this category are receiving both on- and off-the-job training as part of their job (see Maguire et al., 2008). In addition, research shows that it is very misleading to treat both the NEET and NET categories as homogeneous, as they include young people who have a range of reasons and motives for not participating in officially recognised pathways.

---

[2]The 29% of 17-year-olds not participating in education and training may well be considered, in line with definitions in other parts of this book, as 'dropouts' in other countries, recognising though the difficulties that this concept presents in the English context, difficulties discussed in this chapter. The rates may be even higher than those suggested here because no account is taken of actual completion of education and training (Editors' note).

[3]Source: DCSF http://www.dcsf.gov.uk/inyourarea/statics/pcons_lea_892_4.shtml

[4]Source: DCSF Education and Training Statistics for the United Kingdom, 2007, Table 3.10.

Table 5.1 Post-compulsory education and training rates of 17-year-olds 2005–06

	In further education			Government supported training (GST)	All in full-time education and GST
	At school	Full-time	Part-time		
North East	22	34	7	13	70
North West	21	40	5	11	71
Yorkshire and the Humber	24	32	6	10	66
East Midlands	30	29	6	9	68
West Midlands	26	35	6	9	69
Eastern	33	31	5	7	70
London	36	35	5	4	75
South East	32	34	5	7	72
South West	31	32	6	8	71
England	29	34	5	8	71

Source: DCSF Education and Training Statistics for the United Kingdom (2007), Table 2.2.

Within the 16–18 category, the risk of NEET increases with age. In 2006, 6.7% of 16-year-olds, 9.8% of 17-year-olds, and 14.7% of 18-year-olds were classified as NEET (source as above). Nevertheless, NEET status is often short term, and data from the Youth Cohort Study (YCS) suggest that the majority of 16-year-olds who were NEET in 2004 were no longer NEET by 2006. By age 18, 37% of those who had been NEET at 16 remained in this category. Only a minority of young people classified as NEET at any point in time are 'long-term NEET', and many will be NEET only for a brief period, or will 'churn' in and out of this status (Hayward et al., 2008).

Parents' social class is strongly associated with the likelihood of being NEET at the age of 18. However, prior academic attainment is an even more powerful predictor of NEET status. Eighteen-year-olds who had attained fewer than five D-G grade GCSEs in Year 11 (age 15/16) were 10 times more likely to be NEET than those with eight or more A*–C grades.

Similarly, the most powerful predictor of academic attainment by 18 is earlier attainment in the final year of compulsory schooling. Of those with eight or more GCSE A*–C grades at 16, 84% gained Level 3 qualifications by 18 years of age, compared to just 3–4% of those with no A*–C passes. Qualifications in the UK are organised according to levels. Level 2 is regarded as the benchmark for employability and, hence, the level that should be achieved by the end of compulsory schooling. Level 3 qualifications include A Levels and intermediate vocational qualifications. Parents' social class background is also linked to qualifications at the age of 18 years in a predictable way, with the offspring of parents from the professional classes and of graduates being the most likely to gain Level 3 qualifications, but intermediate and lower supervisory class individuals being more likely to gain vocational qualifications at both Level 2 and Level 3. Women were substantially more likely than men to achieve at Level 3.

Data from the Youth Cohort Study show that young people from Indian backgrounds had the highest rates of academic attainment at the age of 18 years, followed by whites, with black, Pakistani and Bangladeshi attainment being lower. To put this in context, Indians in England are relatively well-educated and disproportionately found among the professional classes compared to the white majority, while all other minority ethnic groups are relatively economically disadvantaged. Bangladeshi and Pakistani parents are more likely to be recent immigrants who are not fluent in English, and these communities have high rates of poverty. Nevertheless, it is striking that all of the major minority ethnic groups have higher rates of participation in further and higher education than the white majority. According to the Youth Cohort Study data cited above, 44% of white 18-year-olds were in full-time education in 2006, compared to 77% of blacks, 62% of Pakistani and Bangladeshis, and 84% of Indians.[5]

The fact that whites, and white males in particular, are relatively unlikely to persist in further and higher education has led to claims that white working-class males are 'the new underclass' (Paton, 2008). This adds a new dimension to the anti-feminist backlash of anxiety regarding girls' persistent trouncing of the boys in the battle of the GCSE grades. Now, to add insult to injury, not just females, but blacks too, are out-doing the white males (at least in terms of participation). Policy and media pronouncements on this new 'disadvantaged group' would never lead one to suspect that being a white male is still a major advantage in the English labour market and the wider society. Indeed, the heavy investment that ethnic minority youth make in education and training is driven at least partly by their relatively disadvantaged labour market positions, and the anticipation of labour market discrimination (Connor et al., 1996; Heath & McMahon, 1997; Heath & Smith, 2003). A lack of immediate job opportunities may also remove the incentive for ethnic minority youth to quit education (Leslie & Drinkwater, 1999; Rivkin, 1995). According to the Youth Cohort Study data cited above, 25% of white 18-year-olds in 2006 were in full-time jobs, compared to 9% of blacks and 9% of the Pakistani/ Bangladeshi category. The figures for unemployment (i.e., NEET) were: whites 8%, blacks 9%, Pakistani/Bangladeshi 11%. Low-qualified women are also particularly disadvantaged in the labour market, and therefore have stronger incentives to invest in education and training than their male peers. The interaction between gender and ethnicity in determining educational participation is important; however, and, in contrast to other ethnic groups, there are more Pakistani and Bangladeshi men than women in higher education in Britain (Bhattacharyya et al., 2003; Dwyer et al., 2006).

The same source shows that 3% of 18-year-olds had gained vocational A-levels (AVCEs), and 7% had gained National Vocational Qualifications (NVQs) or equivalent. A quarter of the cohort had vocational qualifications at Level 2 or higher, compared to 57% with academic qualifications at this level.

---

[5]Source: The activities and experiences of 18-year-olds: England & Wales, 2006. Table B. http://www.dcsf.gov.uk/rsgateway/DB/SFR/s000695/SFR47–2006.pdf

Those young people who leave compulsory schooling and enter one of England's vocational education and training (VET) pathways find themselves within an expanding, unbounded territory encompassing schools, colleges, workplaces and voluntary organisations. Some of the territory's activity is publicly funded and some through private sources (such as employers paying for workforce development or students paying full costs for courses), both bolstered through a level of cross-subsidy, which is poorly understood. The territory is populated by a range of stakeholders, with varying degrees of power and influence, and its activities take place in a multitude of buildings including village halls and decaying warehouses, school and college classrooms, state-of-the-art laboratories and the production plants of multinational companies.

The majority of young people who enter the VET territory are in the 50% of the cohort that has failed to achieve the GCSE benchmark. As a result, they will be required to continue to try and improve their basic or 'functional' skills in 'communication', 'application of number' and information technology. These young people will also be restricted to the Level 2 apprenticeship programs and, hence, are less likely to have access to off-the-job learning. Furthermore, young people who fail to reach the GCSE benchmark, but want to remain in full-time education, will have to leave school and enter further education colleges. This means that colleges have a higher proportion of students from disadvantaged backgrounds than any other type of educational establishment (Stanton, 2008; Fletcher & Perry. 2008). Colleges, however, receive less funding per student than schools, and hence disadvantage would appear to beget disadvantage.

The complexity of the VET pathways brings young people into contact with a wide range of organisations in the public and private sector, the boundary between which is often blurred. For example, a young person might seek an apprenticeship in childcare. She might start by being referred by the careers advice service to a training provider who will register her and try to find an employer willing to recruit her on an apprenticeship basis. She might then return to the provider for off-the-job training or the provider might visit her in the workplace to carry out assessment towards a vocational qualification. This provider may be a private company, or a quasi-company which is part of the 'enterprise' section of a local further education college. Thus, negotiating a path between these different organisations quickly becomes part of the young person's post-school journey. The young person who remains in full-time education, however, has far less to negotiate and those who study for academic qualifications may never leave the comfort of the school or college. Complexity, it seems, is judged to be more suitable for those young people who are likely to have achieved less educationally (and hence, more likely to be from less advantaged backgrounds) up to the age of 16.

Evans (2002) uses the concept of 'Bounded Agency' to explain how young people try to exert control over their circumstances and decision-making, but find themselves restricted or impeded by structural barriers that are deep-rooted and very difficult to overcome. She stresses the need for agencies working with young people to 'emphasise brokerage and advocacy as a primary aim and function, to the extent that young adults perceive and experience this to be as real as the emphasis that is currently placed on their "deficits"' (ibid., p. 265).

Gender Segregation in Education, Training and Work

A particular concern regarding the 'choice' agenda is that it may exacerbate the influence of gender stereotypes on the types of qualifications that young people are able to achieve. Concerns about 'boys' underachievement', driven by the gender gap in GCSE passes, have dominated the policy agenda to such a degree that it has become difficult to raise wider gender issues, such as women's continued disadvantage in the labour market, and the fact that young women who leave school with low levels of qualifications are more disadvantaged in the labour market than comparable young men (Bynner et al., 1997; Howieson & Ianelli, 2008; Rake, 2000). Young women who are NEET also face an increased risk of early child-bearing and mental health problems (Bynner et al., 1997).

As the level of qualifications gained by the general population has expanded, it matters more than ever, not simply what level of qualifications an individual has, but what area this qualification is in. There is a clear link between gender segregation in qualifications and gender segregation in the labour market, yet schools and colleges have not addressed the way in which girls continue to be over-represented in those domains with the weakest labour market value. The tendency to see these gendered patterns as an unproblematic consequence of individual choices ignores the social pressures on young people to abide by gendered norms of behaviour. In addition, it is unrealistic to assume that young people possess (and are able to process) information regarding the long-term consequences of their teenage decisions for their adult labour-market positions (Manski, 1993).

While females have overtaken males in terms of overall academic attainment, traditional patterns of participation in particular fields of study have persisted. At A level, the most popular subjects for females (excluding general studies) are English, psychology, biology, art and design and mathematics. For males, they are mathematics, English, history, biology and physics. Figure 5.1 shows the number of A-level entries for these subjects according to sex. English, psychology and art and design are heavily female-dominated, while mathematics and physics are heavily male-dominated, despite the fact that girls and boys have similar attainments in mathematics at age 16.

Vocational qualifications are even more segregated by gender than academic qualifications. Females are concentrated in 'health and social care', and a full 40% of female qualifications in this category are accounted for by this one subject. The most popular subjects for males are Information Communications and Technology (ICT) and business.[6]

The biggest pull factor leading young people away from full-time education continues to be the labour market. It is known from research that the majority of 16- to 19-year-olds work part-time, and many have some work experience from the age of 14, so that 'earning and learning' has become the common experience for young

---

[6]Source: DCSF Education and Training Statistics for the United Kingdom, 2007, Table 3.5

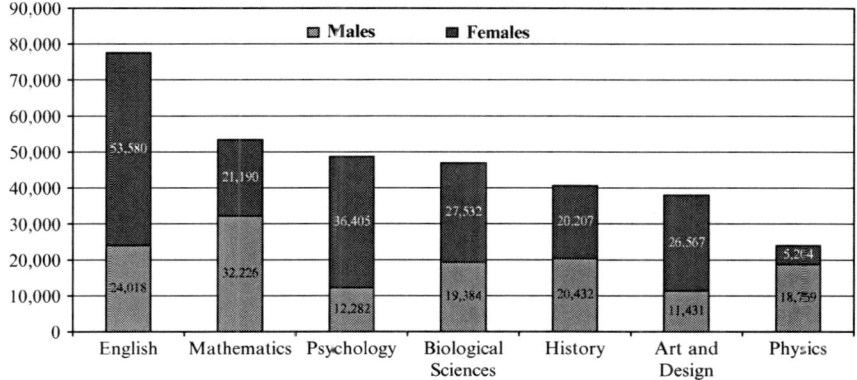

Fig. 5.1   A level subject entries by sex for 16- to 18-year-olds in England 2006–07[7]

people (Hodgson & Spours, 2001, p. 386). The massive growth of service industries has benefited from a willing army of young, part-time workers whose identity shifts, often on a daily basis, between student, employee and consumer. Employers can offer flexible hours, the possibility of working long shifts to earn extra money, and employment close to home. These employers will often demand little in the way of prior experience or qualifications, but require applicants to meet the emerging requirements of the 'aesthetic labour market' (see Nickson et al., 2003). For a teenager concerned to earn just enough money to cover their social life and mobile phone bills, such jobs are very attractive. That attraction may, in turn, lead to a decision to stay with a job that offers few long-term prospects but in which the young person feels safe. This may have particularly damaging consequences for young women as figures from the 'Apprenticeships' program indicate (see Fuller et al., 2005).

The government-funded 'Apprenticeships' program in England covers three work-based pathways (see Fuller & Unwin, 2008). 'Young Apprenticeship' is for 14- to 16-year-olds and involves work experience alongside full-time study in school and college. The two main pathways for 16- to 25-year-olds are 'Apprenticeship', which leads to Level 2 qualifications, and 'Advanced Apprenticeship', which leads to Level 3 qualifications. Apprenticeships are available in around 100 occupational areas, but, as is shown below, the majority of apprentices are found in 12 sectors. Apprentices usually spend 4 days a week in the workplace and 1 day in an off-the-job setting in a college, in a company-based workshop, or with another form of training provider. The majority have 'employed' status. The length of apprenticeships varies from around 1 to 3 years according to the requirements of the sector, and the content of the training program is determined by Sector Skills Councils (SSCs). Government funding covers the cost of training to meet the mandatory qualification requirements, and employers pay the apprentices' wages.

---

[7]Source: DCSF: GCE/VCE A/AS and Equivalent Examination Results in England, 2006/07, Tables 2, 2m, 2f. http://www.dcsf.gov.uk/rsgateway/DB/SFR/s000755/

Table 5.2 Sixteen to 18-year-olds, 'average in learning' 2006–07
(12 months) by gender and apprenticeship level

	Female	Male	Total
Advanced Apprenticeship L3	10,217	42,800	**53,017**
Apprenticeship L2	40,541	56,690	**97,231**
Total	**50,758**	**99,490**	**150,248**

Source: Learning and Skills Council, http:www.apprenticeships.
org.uk/partners/frameworks/apprenticeshipsdata/reports20062007

Table 5.3 Aged 19+, 'average in learning' 2006–07 (12 months)
by gender and apprenticeship level

	Female	Male	Total
Advanced Apprenticeship L3	20,585	25,558	**46,143**
Apprenticeship L2	22,138	25,315	**47,453**
Total	**42,723**	**50,873**	**93,596**

Source: Learning and Skills Council, http:www.apprenticeships.
org.uk/partners/frameworks/apprenticeshipsdata/reports20062007

Given that employment structures in the UK are highly segregated by gender, it is perhaps no surprise that the Apprenticeships program mirrors such divisions, as Tables 5.2 and 5.3 show. The segregation of vocational training by sector has strong implications for the *level* of qualifications that can be attained.

Two important points about apprenticeship participation emerge from these statistics. First, the majority of participants in the program are male, with the male–female imbalance being the starkest in the Advanced Apprenticeship. Second, the majority of participants are in the younger, 16–18 age group, and most of them are in the Level 2 program.

Despite apprenticeships currently being available in over 100 sectors, over three quarters of apprentices are found in just 12 sectors. Nonetheless, the diversity of occupations and jobs covered in these sectors is indicative of the very different types of workplace settings in which young people on apprenticeships find themselves. One key difference is in the proportion of participants following L2 and L3 programs. In electrotechnical, the vast majority are following the Advanced Apprenticeship; whereas in retail, hairdressing and construction, over 8 out of 10 are following the L2 program. The 12 most populated apprenticeship sectors are as follows, in descending order:

• Construction
• Hairdressing
• Business administration
• Customer care

- Hospitality
- Childcare and early years
- Engineering
- Vehicle maintenance
- Retail
- Health and social care
- Electrotechnical
- Plumbing

The extent of the segregation is, however, of considerable concern, particularly because the structure of the program into Level 2 and Level 3 pathways exacerbates the impoverished position of young women. In their analysis of gender segregation in England and Wales, Fuller et al. (2005) showed that, although there are roughly the same number of female apprentices as male, the females are more likely to be found in Level 2 apprenticeships. This is because females dominate apprenticeships in the service industries (e.g., health and social care, retailing, hairdressing), which, in turn, offer far more Level 2 than Level 3 apprenticeships. The economic returns to Level 2 vocational qualifications are poor compared to Level 3 (Dearden et al., 2000; Jenkins et al., 2007) and female apprentices have fewer opportunities for progression than their male counterparts.

This troubled part of the VET territory is particularly affected by the refusal of successive governments to regulate employer behaviour. In addition, the very notion of an apprenticeship model of training will come under increasing pressure as the current global economic crisis continues to have an impact over the coming years. Despite the fact that many young people benefit from involvement in government-funded youth training programs (see Unwin & Wellington, 2001), this provision has been heavily criticised since the late 1970s, and the current 'Apprenticeships' program bears all the problematic hallmarks of its predecessors (see Fuller & Unwin, 2008).

Conclusion

This chapter has described the complex landscape of both compulsory and post-compulsory education and training in England. Whilst examinations at age 16 still mark a watershed in terms of the extent to which young people's futures will be determined by their relative success or failure, the concept of 'dropout' from the system cannot be strictly applied.[8] Rather, the majority of young people continue to participate in the system by joining one of the many pathways that open up after

---

[8]The notion of 'not in education, employment or training (NEET)', though, can be used to identify those within a cohort who are no longer in school and do not hold upper secondary or equivalent qualifications and can be considered 'dropouts' as defined in other countries. This could be applied at an age, such as 17-year-olds, as in Table 5.1 of this chapter (Editors' note).

the compulsory phase of education has ended. Some young people switch between pathways, trying one and then another, and some who become classified as NEET or NET may reappear in an official pathway at a later stage.

The concept of 'graduation' to mark the end of compulsory schooling in England was first discussed by government in 1999 as a contribution to combating the dangers of social exclusion created by an education system that labeled 50% of 16-year-olds as failures. A report from the then Social Exclusion Unit (SEU) argued that:

> Graduation would be a challenging but achievable goal requiring as a minimum the Level 2 standard of achievement in formal qualifications (academic, vocational or occupational), and also involving the key skills of communication, use of numeracy and a range of options for arts, sport and community activity. (SEU, 1999, p. 11)

When the concept was piloted in three areas of the country, young people, parents, employers and teachers were found to support the idea, but the disadvantages were felt to be too great. As Lindsay and Maguire (2002, p. 8) explain, the very fact that graduation would require young people to meet certain thresholds would still mean some, and probably the most disadvantaged, would remain excluded.

It is clear from the data and discussion presented here that the age-old fault lines of social class, gender and ethnicity still have a serious impact on the fortunes of individuals, and that failure to achieve early on in life can prove to be a profound impediment to later progression. Despite the considerable expansion of the numbers of young people entering higher education over the past 10 years, and the 'widening participation' agenda, the impact of social class on the chances of participation in higher education remains strong. In addition, only 78% of young people who start (towards a) full-time degree are now expected to gain a degree, and completion rates vary widely according to the prestige of the institution (Higher Education Statistics Agency, 2008). Employment and wage rates on graduation also vary widely across institutions (Chevalier & Conlon, 2003).

In 2013, England will see whether the first 16-year-olds obliged to remain in some form of education or training until they are 18 have conformed with the government's wishes. In a highly critical review of the new legislation, Wolf (2008, p. 7) argues that it runs counter to our understanding about the relationship between motivation and learning. Furthermore, she states that it will have a negative impact on the youth labour market as many businesses that currently employ 16- and 17-year-olds will stop doing so because of the requirement to provide them with formal recognised training. This will, according to Wolf, have the self-defeating effect of harming the most disadvantaged and marginalised young people (ibid.). The counter arguments are that for too long, England has allowed employers to recruit young people without any requirement to provide them with the necessary vocational education and training to enable them to progress both within and beyond their current employment. This neglect is regarded as being harmful for the well-being of both the country's economy and for the individual.

Regardless of the effects of the new legislation, however, it is clear from this chapter that it is unlikely on its own to solve the deep-rooted inequalities in the

English system. Whilst much progress has been made over the past 20 or so years in terms of the numbers of young people acquiring qualifications at the end of their compulsory phase of schooling and in terms of the numbers who progress to further and higher education, it is still the case that social class and, to some extent, geography, remain tough barriers to overcome.

References

Avis, J. (2004). Work-based learning and social justice: 'Learning to labour' and the new vocationalism in England. *Journal of Education and Work, 17*(2), 197–217.

Bhattacharyya, G., Ison, L., & Blair, M. (2003). *Minority ethnic attainment and participation in education and training: The evidence* (Department for Education and Skills, Research Topic Paper RTP01–03). London: DfES.

Boyd, D. (1973). *Elites and their education.* Slough, UK: NFER.

Bynner, J., Morphy, L., & Parsons, S. (1997). Women, employment and skills. In H. Metcalf (Ed.), *Half our future.* London: Policy Studies Institute.

Chevalier, A., & Conlon, G. (2003). *Does it pay to attend a prestigious university?* (Working Paper No. CEEDP0040). London: Centre for the Economics of Education, London School of Economics.

Connor, H., Lavalle, I., Yackey, N.D., & Perryman, S. (1996). Ethnic minority graduates: Differences by degree. *Labour Market Trends, 104*, 395–396.

Dearden, L., McIntosh, S., Myck, M., & Vignoles, A. (2000). *The returns to academic and vocational qualifications in Britain.* London: Centre for Economic Performance, London School of Economics.

Department of Children, Schools and Families (DCSF). (2007). *Raising expectations: Staying in education and training post-16 – From policy to legislation.* Nottingham, UK: Department of Children, Schools and Families.

Department for Education and Skills (DfES). (2004). *Five year strategy for children and learners* (Cm 6272). London: HMSO.

Department for Education and Skills (DfES). (2007). *Raising expectations: Staying in education or training post-16* (Cm 7065). London: HMSO.

Dwyer, C., Modood, T., Sanghera, G., Shah, B., & Thapar-Bjorket, S. (2006). Ethnicity as social capital? Explaining the differential educational achievements of young British Pakistani men and women. Paper presented at the 'Ethnicity, Mobility and Society' Leverhulme Programme Conference, University of Bristol, Bristol, UK.

Evans, K. (2002). Taking control of their lives? Agency in young adult transitions in England and the New Germany. *Journal of Youth Studies, 5*(3), 245–269.

Fletcher, M., & Perry, A. (2008). *By accident or design. Is our system of post-16 provision fit for purpose?* London: CfBT.

Fuller, A., Beck, V., & Unwin, L. (2005). The gendered nature of apprenticeship: Employers' and young people's perspectives. *Education and Training, 47*(4/5), 298–311.

Fuller, A., & Unwin, L. (2008). *Towards expansive apprenticeships, a commentary for the ESRC's teaching and learning research programme.* London: Institute of Education.

Gorard, S. (2005). Academies as the 'future of schooling': Is this an evidence-based policy? *Journal of Education Policy, 3,* 369–377.

Hayward, G., Wilde, S., & Williams, R. (2008). *Rathbone/Nuffield review engaging youth enquiry.* Consultation report. Retrieved from. www.nuffield14–19review.org.uk

Heath, A., & McMahon, D. (1997). Education and occupational attainments: The impact of ethnic origins. In A. H. Halsey, H. Lauder, P. Brown, & A. Stuart Wells (Eds.), *Education: Culture, economy and society.* Oxford, UK: OUP.

Heath, A., & Smith, S. (2003). Mobility and ethnic minorities. *New Economy, 10*(4), 199–204.

Higham, J.J.S., & Yeomans, D.J. (2007). Curriculum choice, flexibility and differentiation 14–19: The way forward or flawed prospectus? *London Review of Education, 5*(3), 281–297.

Higher Education Statistics Agency. (2008). *Performance indicators in higher education in the UK 2006/07.* Retrieved from http://www.hesa.ac.uk/index.php/content/view/1166/141/

Hillman, J. (1994). Independent schools. In Paul Hamlyn Foundation Commission into Education (Ed.), *Insights into education and training* (pp. 403–444). London: Heinemann.

Hodgson, A., & Spours, K. (2001). Part-time work and full-time education in the UK: The emergence of a curriculum and a policy issue. *Journal of Education and Work, 14*(3), 373–388.

Hodgson, A., & Spours, K. (2003). *Beyond A levels: Curriculum 2000 and the reform of 14–19.* London: Kogan Page.

Hodgson, A., & Spours, K. (2008). *Education and training 14–19: Qualifications, curriculum and organisation.* London: Routledge.

Howieson, C., & Ianelli, C. (2008). The effects of low attainment on young people's outcomes at age 22–23 in Scotland. *British Educational Research Journal, 34*(2), 269–290.

Huddleston, P., & Unwin, L. (2007). *Teaching and learning in further education* (3rd ed.). London: Routledge.

Jenkins, A., Greenwood, C., & Vignoles, A. (2007). *The returns to qualifications in England: Updating the evidence base on level 2 and level 3 vocational qualifications.* Discussion Paper. London: Centre for the Economics of Education, London School of Economics.

Leslie, D., & Drinkwater, S. (1999). Staying on in full-time education: Reasons for high participation among ethnic minority males and females. *Economica, 66,* 63–77.

Lindsay, G., & Maguire, M. (2002). *Modelling the implications of graduation for 16 year olds in three geographical areas* (DfEE Research Report 340). London: HMSO.

Lodge, P., & Blackstone, T. (1982). *Educational policy and educational inequality.* Oxford, UK: Martin Robertson.

Lupton, R., & Sullivan, A. (2007). London: Opportunity and challenge. In T. Brighouse, & L. Fullick (Eds.), *Education in a global city: Essays from London.* London: Bedford Way Publishing.

Maguire, S., Huddleston, P., Thompson, J., & Hirst, C. (2008). *Young people in jobs without training.* Warwick, UK: Centre for Education and Industry, University of Warwick.

Manski, C. F. (1993). Adolescent econometricians. In C. T. Clotfelter, & M. Rothschild (Eds.), *Studies of supply and demand in higher education.* Chicago: University of Chicago Press.

Nickson, D., Warhurst, C., Cullen, A. M., & Watt, A. (2003). Bringing in the excluded? Aesthetic labour, skills and training in the 'new' economy'. *Journal of Education and Work, 16*(2), 185–203.

Oxford University Gazette. (2008). *Statistical information on the University of Oxford.* Oxford, UK: University of Oxford.

Paton, G. (2008, June 19) White working-class boys becoming an underclass. *Daily Telegraph.*

Pring, R. (2008). 14–19. *Oxford Review of Education, 34*(6), 677–688.

Raffe, D. (2010). Participation in post-compulsory learning in Scotland. In S. Lamb, E. Markussen, R. Teese, N. Sandberg, & J. Polesel (Eds.), *School dropout and completion: International comparative studies in theory and policy.* Dordrecht, The Netherlands: Springer.

Rake, K. (2000). *Women's incomes over the lifetime.* London: The Cabinet Office.

Rivkin, S.G. (1995). Black-white differences in schooling and employment. *Journal of Human Resources, 30*(4), 826–852.

Sammons, P. (2008). Zero tolerance of failure and New Labour approaches to school improvement in England. *Oxford Review of Education, 34*(6), 651–664.

Simon, B. (1986). The 1944 Education Act: A conservative measure? *History of Education, 15*(1), 31–43.

Social Exclusion Unit (SEU). (1999). *Bridging the gap: New opportunities for 16–18 year olds not in education, employment or training* (Cm 4405). London: Social Exclusion Unit.

Stanton, G. (2008). *Making the 14–19 reforms work for learners.* London: CfBT.

Sullivan, A., & Heath, A. (2003). Intakes and examination results at State and private schools. In G. Walford (Ed.), *British private schools: Research on policy and practice*. London: Woburn Press.

Tinkler, P. (2001). Youth's opportunity? The Education Act of 1944 and proposals for part-time continuation education. *History of Education, 30*(1), 77–94.

Unwin, L., & Wellington, J. (2001). *Young people's perspectives on education, training and employment*. London: Kogan Page.

Wolf, A. (2008). *Diminished returns. How raising the leaving age will harm young people and the labour market*. London: Policy Exchange.

Woods, P. A., Woods, G. J., & Gunter, H. (2007). Academy schools and entrepreneurialism in education. *Journal of Education Policy, 22*(2), 237–259.

Chapter 6
Participation in Post-Compulsory Learning in Scotland

David Raffe

Introduction

The Scottish education system has no generally recognised concept of school completion or graduation. After the age of 16, when education ceases to be compulsory, the level, duration, mode and content of learning vary widely, and there is no standard or benchmark by which to judge whether an individual has completed secondary education. The system's key characteristic is flexibility; post-compulsory education and training comprise a 'climbing frame' with multiple entry and exit points rather than pre-determined lines or programs leading to fixed standards to be achieved by all learners. This chapter therefore focuses on levels of participation in post-compulsory learning. It also refers more briefly to the attainment of those who participate, although unlike many other countries, 'participation' and 'attainment' are the subjects of separate discourses in Scotland.

The Scottish education system is generally perceived to perform well. Recent strategic audits have identified education as a source of Scottish comparative advantage (McConnell, 2006). However, this strong performance is blemished by low participation in post-compulsory learning, compounded by low attainment among many of those who participate, by a large number of teenagers not in education, employment or training (NEET), and by inequalities in participation and attainment. The United Kingdom as a whole has lower participation in post-16 education and training than most of its comparator countries, and participation is lower in Scotland than in the rest of the UK. According to one recent report, 62% of 15- to 19-year-olds in Scotland were in education and training in 2003, the lowest percentage of any country in the Organisation for Economic Co-operation and Development (OECD) (Scottish Funding Council [SFC], 2008a).[1] Scotland has

---

[1] An earlier report cited a figure of 'just under 70%' for the same year (Scottish Executive, 2006a). A more recent estimate, supplied by the Scottish Government, shows 72.4% of Scottish 15- to 19-year-olds in education in 2006 (this includes apprenticeships but excludes Skillseeker training programs). The comparable figure for the UK was 75.7% and the OECD average was 83.0%.

D. Raffe (✉)
Centre for Educational Sociology, University of Edinburgh, UK

S. Lamb et al. (Eds.), *School Dropout and Completion: International Comparative Studies in Theory and Policy*, DOI 10.1007/978-90-481-9763-7_7,
© Springer Science+Business Media B.V. 2011

one of the OECD's highest proportions of 15- to 19-year-olds who are NEET; it also has one of the highest proportions of 15- to 19-year-olds in employment without education, suggesting that the NEET problem is one of low participation in education rather than a shortage of employment (Scottish Executive, 2006a). Early in 2007, Scotland's First Minister Jack McConnell commissioned a report on extending compulsory education beyond the current minimum leaving age of 16; his government lost office after the 2007 election and the report was never published. Later in the same year, an OECD team reviewed the *Quality and Equity of Schooling in Scotland* (OECD, 2007). It concluded that Scottish schools had important strengths but faced two main challenges: an achievement gap between children from different socioeconomic backgrounds, and low and socially unequal participation and attainment in learning beyond compulsory schooling. The first challenge is shared with many other countries, which have similar levels of social inequality; the second challenge – of low post-compulsory participation and attainment – is faced by Scotland to a greater extent than most other European or OECD countries.

Low participation makes it harder to achieve national policy objectives such as raising skill levels and ensuring their wide distribution. It also matters for the young people themselves: early leavers face disadvantage in education and the labour market, especially females and the lowest qualified, whose risk of unemployment or unstable employment is greatest (Howieson, 2003; Hannan et al., 1998). Many become NEET, and some of these find it difficult to escape from their NEET status.

The social science literature offers at least three explanatory frameworks for low participation.

Cultural explanations focus on the cultures or sub-cultures of young people and of the education system. Such explanations attribute low participation in Scottish post-16 education to a 'British' youth sub-culture, which celebrates early transitions to adulthood (Jones & Wallace, 1992), and to the disengagement produced by the cultural distance between the school system and many young people. The OECD review of Scottish education blamed the academic ethos of schools for failing to engage and motivate weaker learners. Cultural explanations draw on the theories of sociologists such as Bernstein (1971) and Bourdieu (1997) who analyse the cultural foundations of curricula, pedagogies and school organisation in relation to those of young people and their class backgrounds. Cultural explanations figure prominently in policy debates, reflected in exhortations to raise aspirations, in calls for programs to be made more 'relevant' and in the belief that 'parity of esteem' is the answer to low participation in vocational learning.

Rational explanations argue that young people respond in a rational (or at least, 'situationally' or 'pragmatically' rational: Goldthorpe, 2000; Hodkinson et al., 1996) way to the opportunities, incentives, costs and constraints associated with participation in education. They attribute low participation in Scotland to educational pathways which offer poor prospects of success for low-attaining young people, to the weak links between education and employment, to the weak incentives of a polarised labour market with many low-skilled jobs which require few qualifications, and to the lack of transparency of pathways and the destinations to which they lead. Rational explanations draw on the rational-action theories of writers such as Boudon (1974) and Goldthorpe (2000), and are used especially to predict 'secondary effects' of social class on choices at key decision points such as the end of compulsory schooling, as distinct from 'primary effects' on attainment. Rational explanations also feature in policy analyses and prescriptions, such as the 'pathways engineering' approach proposed by the OECD (1998).

Developmental explanations focus on aspects of young people's psychological or social development, which affect their capacity or disposition to participate in education. Young people may drop out of learning because they lack self-esteem, self-efficacy or resilience, because they lack cognitive or social skills, or because of dependency on drugs or alcohol. Such 'deficits' are the product, in part, of the family and social environment; low educational participation in Scotland may reflect relatively high levels of poverty and deprivation, as well as parenting behaviours and social environments which result in developmental trajectories associated with dropout from education. Developmental explanations draw primarily on psychology and on theories of individual and social development, although they have recently received attention from economists and life-course researchers (Heckman & Masterov, 2004; Feinstein et al., 2008). Unlike cultural and rational explanations, they imply a 'deficit' model of dropout. They have been influential in recent policy debates, reflected in support for early interventions and in increased government concern with parenting skills and family influences on individual development.

These three explanations are not mutually exclusive, nor are they exhaustive (other explanatory frameworks, such as social capital, may also help to explain participation). They were developed primarily to explain social inequalities in educational participation and attainment, but they can equally be used to explain the overall level of participation and trends over time. Cultural and rational explanatory frameworks have been widely employed in macro-sociological research, so they may be more suitable for comparative analysis than 'micro' perspectives such as the developmental explanation described earlier. The three explanations are used in this chapter as a loose framework on which to base a review of post-compulsory participation in Scotland. The chapter is divided into seven sections. After a brief description of Scottish education in the following (second) section, the third section reviews the level, trend and distribution of post-compulsory participation. The fourth, fifth and sixth sections use the three explanatory frameworks to compare possible policy strategies and describe recent and current policy initiatives. The final section draws conclusions.

The Scottish Education System

Schooling in Scotland is compulsory from age 5 to 16. Pupils spend 7 years at primary school and a minimum of 4 years at secondary school. Except for private schools, which serve about 5% of the age group, schools are comprehensive and co-educational, run by local authorities and linked with geographical catchment areas, although parents can choose schools in other catchments if places are available. The school system is uniform: Scotland has avoided the 'school diversity' agenda of England and some other countries. All schools are funded and administered on a similar basis, school standards are consistent, school social segregation is among the lowest in Europe and differential school effects are small.

School students progress with the same year group through the 11 years of compulsory schooling; grade repetition is virtually unknown. At the end of S4 (fourth year of secondary school), at age 15 or 16, pupils take Standard Grade (or equivalent) examinations. Standard Grades are single-subject, graded qualifications, typically attempted in eight subjects. They will be replaced in 2013–14 by re-designed single-subject qualifications following a public consultation in 2008 (Scottish Government, 2008a, b).

At present, Standard Grades mark the end of compulsory education, and they strongly influence subsequent destinations. It is not necessary to achieve a given level of performance in order to continue into post-compulsory education, but the grade achieved in a particular subject typically determines the level at which that subject can be studied in upper-secondary schooling, and young people with lower grades are relatively likely to enter college or training rather than stay on at school, or to leave learning altogether.

About a third of young people leave school at the end of compulsory education, at age 16. At least half of these 16-year-old leavers continue full-time learning either in colleges or in work-based national training programs. Colleges are all-purpose institutions offering a variety of vocational and general programs to students of all ages, including school leavers aged 16, 17 and 18. College programs are available at a range of levels up to and including Higher National (short-cycle higher education) qualifications. Most programs are designed for full-time study over 1 or 2 years. The main national training programs are Modern Apprenticeships, available to entrants of all ages, although 16- to 24-year-olds have priority, and Skillseekers, a program for 16- to 18-year-olds, mostly at a level below Modern Apprenticeships. A few early leavers enter part-time education or training outside of national training programs, usually provided or funded by their employer. All 16- and 17-year-olds not in education or training are entitled to work-based training under a Youth Guarantee introduced in 1988, when benefit entitlements were withdrawn from unemployed under-18-year-olds.

Formally, the different institutional pathways beyond 16 have equal legitimacy, and their diversity is celebrated as a strength of the system. In practice, they form a status hierarchy headed by schools. School staying-on rates continue to be used as key indicators of participation and, before 2007, separate government departments covered school and post-school education. Destination statistics are published for school-leaver groups, rather than for school-year groups who complete compulsory education at the same time. This makes it difficult to compare school and post-school options as equivalent destinations.

As noted earlier, there is no recognised concept of upper-secondary completion or graduation in Scottish education, and the level, duration, mode and content of learning vary widely. One reason for this is the diversity of pathways; another reason is the diversity of programs within each pathway, and their open-ended character. The upper-secondary school curriculum is elective: students choose a mixture of single-subject courses at a variety of possible levels over 1 or 2 years. Each course is separately certificated. High-attaining students aiming for university typically take five 'Higher' courses in the first post-compulsory year, followed by a mixture of additional Highers, re-sits and/or 'Advanced Highers' in the second. For lower-attaining students, the volume and level of study is more variable; many take 'Intermediate' courses possibly combined with one or two Highers. About a third of students who stay on in post-compulsory schooling leave after 1 year, often to enter college or an apprenticeship. Most full-time college provision consists of set 1-year programs at a choice of levels with opportunities to progress between programs. Work-based provision is also organised around set programs, but these vary in duration and demand.

All post-compulsory courses and programs are unit-based and describable in terms of credit values and levels of the Scottish Credit and Qualifications Framework (SCQF). It would be possible, therefore, to define benchmarks for graduation based on defined volumes and levels of study, and required subjects or competences. In practice, however, this is not the way the Scottish system works – or has worked hitherto. New Scottish Baccalaureates in languages and science are being introduced to encourage study of those subjects. They will be awarded for combinations of existing qualifications (two Advanced Highers and one Higher) in the relevant subject area together with an interdisciplinary project, and they will cover only part of a full-time program. They are neither graduation certificates nor baccalaureates as these terms are understood in other countries. Scotland's open or flexible system contrasts with the more structured pathways characteristic of most other European systems. Scottish schools may expect students to take particular subjects (usually English, sometimes mathematics), but otherwise students choose the courses that match their interests, ambitions and abilities, strongly influenced by the perceived requirements of 'end-users' such as universities and employers. However, this flexibility affects some students more than others: for students following the royal road to elite universities, the choices are relatively simple; for other students, and especially the least qualified who may need most support to navigate their pathways, the options are less clearly defined.

Nearly half of young people (47% in 2006) enter full-time higher education before the age of 21; about a third of these take sub-degree courses at college. The higher education (HE) system is stratified, not only between universities and colleges, but also according to universities' ability to select their students, with the lower-status 'recruiter' institutions typically showing greater flexibility in recruitment and in the requirements for entry. Admission to higher education is decentralised, and school qualifications do not confer an entitlement. A majority of young people who enter HE do so on the basis of Highers and other school qualifications, but a minority follow a college route into HE, often progressing from non-advanced vocational programs to sub-degree programs, and sometimes progressing from these to university degree courses using articulation or credit transfer arrangements based on the SCQF.

The Scottish labour market is closely integrated with the rest of the UK. It is weakly regulated and has weak occupational labour markets. Selection procedures are flexible; qualifications are important signals in the labour market but only in a small range of occupations do they provide a licence to practise.

The Level, Trend and Distribution of Post-Compulsory Participation

In the absence of a concept of secondary completion or graduation, Scottish research on participation or dropout in post-compulsory education has typically focused on participation in the spring after S4, the last compulsory school year. Much of this research has been based on the Scottish School Leavers Survey (SSLS), a series of surveys conducted from the early 1970s until 2005. From 1984 to 2005, the SSLS followed representative samples of year groups for 3 years (occasionally more) beyond compulsory schooling. Table 6.1 shows the 'main activities' of

Table 6.1 Main activity of four Scottish year groups at age 16–17 and at age 18–19 (%)

Completed S4 in:	1984	1990	1998	2002
Main activity at age 16–17	**1985**	**1991**	**1999**	**2003**
School	42	59	65	68
College	4	4	8	9
Training program	23	18	8	8
Job	18	13	11	8
Unemployed	11	6	7	4
Other	2	1	2	4
Total	101	101	101	101
Weighted n	(6,422)	(4,416)	(7,534)	(4,712)
Main activity at age 18/19	**1987**	**1993**	**2001**	**2005**
Full-time education	21	34	45	45
Training program	5	8	11	9
Job	53	40	33	35
Unemployed	15	11	8	7
Other	6	7	3	4
Total	100	100	100	100
Weighted n	(3,858)	(2,724)	(4,933)	(3,200)

Note: S4 is the last compulsory school year. Most members of each year group celebrated their 16th birthday between March 1 of the S4 year and the end of the following February.
Source: Scottish School Leavers Survey. Tables 6.1 and 6.2 are based on a data set constructed by Linda Croxford for the ESRC-funded Education and Youth Transitions project, and subsequently extended for Scotland for the Scottish Government-funded Scottish Trends project (see Croxford et al., 2007; Croxford, 2009).

four SSLS year groups at age 16–17 (in the spring after S4) and at age 18–19, 2 years later. Between the 1980s and the early 2000s, participation at age 16–17 in full-time education rose substantially; it rose even more, in proportionate terms, at age 18–19. Of those in the year group which completed S4 in 2002, more than three quarters were still in full-time education at age 16–17, and nearly half were in full-time education at age 18–19 (about three quarters of these were in higher education). The proportion in training programs at age 16–17 fell sharply over the period, while the proportion in these programs at age 18–19 increased slightly; this partly reflects a shift in their function from absorbing the consequences of mass school-leaver unemployment to developing skills for the economy.

Table 6.1 suggests that the growth in participation in school, college or other full-time education had slowed down by the early 2000s. The 2002 S4 cohort was the last to be surveyed by the SSLS. More recent trends are indicated by official statistics, which suggest that participation has stopped increasing during the current decade. Between 1999–2000 and 2006–07, the proportion staying on at school beyond the compulsory leaving age fell by a percentage point, from 68.4% to 67.4% (Scottish Government, 2008c). The participation rate of under-21-year-olds in higher education fell from a peak of 51.5% in 2000 and 2001 to 47.1% in 2006 (Scottish Government, 2007a). The number of 16- to 24-year-olds in national training programs has shown no clear trend since 1999; it stood at around 38,000 in 2007 (Scottish Government, 2007b). The one type of participation that has continued to rise is in full-time college programs (excluding higher education), which attracted 23% of school leavers (of all ages) in 2006, compared with 19% in 1999 (ibid.), but this has not been enough to increase total participation levels significantly.

Table 6.2 shows how participation in different forms of learning at age 16–17 among members of the 2002 S4 cohort varied according to gender and educational and family background. More young women than young men continued in full-time education, but more males entered work-based training. The strongest single predictor of participation was attainment at Standard Grade. A majority of the two highest attainment categories continued at school; those with lower qualifications were more likely to enter college or training, but they still had much lower participation rates overall. Social class and family structure were also associated with participation. And more than half of young people who truanted for days or weeks at a time during their last compulsory year did not continue formal learning thereafter. Table 6.2 shows simple bivariate associations, but more detailed studies confirm that gender, educational attainment and parental class are independently associated with participation (e g., Paterson & Raffe, 1995; Howieson, 2003). They also show that these determinants have changed little over time, even when total participation rates were rising, although there has been some weakening of the correlation between S4 attainment and full-time participation, associated especially with a trend for less-qualified young people to enter college.

A substantial proportion of young people who continue in education or training beyond 16, and especially those from disadvantaged backgrounds, either crop out of their post-16 courses or achieve relatively poor attainments. Less-qualified young people who continue at school beyond 16 have an uncertain chance of

Table 6.2 Main activity in spring 2003 (at age 16–17) of young people who completed
S4 in 2002, by gender, educational and social background (%)

	School	College	Training	Other	Total (n)
Gender					
Male	65	8	11	16	100 (2,380)
Female	71	10	5	15	101 (2,332)
Standard Grade attainment					
5+ Credit awards	94	1	1	4	100 (1,845)
5+ General awards	60	13	10	16	99 (2,116)
5+ Foundation awards	26	20	19	35	100 (533)
Others	23	13	14	50	100 (171)
Parents' social class					
Prof and managerial	83	6	4	8	101 (1,830)
Intermediate	65	9	11	16	101 (1,378)
Working	55	15	10	21	101 (1,086)
Unclassified	50	13	10	27	100 (416)
Family structure					
Mother and father	73	8	8	12	101 (3,328)
Step parent(s)	59	9	10	21	99 (360)
Lone parent	56	14	7	23	100 (896)
Other	53	13	8	26	100 (103)
Truancy in S4					
Days/weeks at a time	20	15	13	53	101 (287)
Less frequent or never	71	9	7	13	100 (4,412)

substantially improving on their low attainment (Howieson & Iannelli, 2008).
Recent reforms enhanced low-attainers' access to post-compulsory school courses,
but had a less favourable impact on their subsequent progression (Raffe et al.,
2007). Completion rates for college programs have risen in recent years and are
currently about 70%; some students drop out and do not complete because they are
offered a job (SFC, 2008b). Completion rates from training programs have also
risen in recent years, but they are still relatively low. In 2005, only half of 16- to
24-year-olds leaving Modern Apprenticeships had completed their programs; reasons for non-completion included: company closure, finding another job, disciplin-
ary reasons, loss of interest, or finding that the training was not what they were
looking for (Cambridge Policy Consultants [CPC], 2006). Success or failure in
post-compulsory learning is not random: social inequalities in participation and
attainment increase between the ages of 16 and 18 (Raffe et al., 2006).

An estimated 53% of young people in the last SSLS cohort gained Higher
pass(es) at school, which could represent a very crude indicator of school completion. The proportions completing college and training programs could be estimated
by multiplying the percentages in these programs at age 16–17 (9% and 8%: see
Table 6.1) by the respective completion rates reported above (70% and 50%). This
yields a total completion rate of about 63% of the cohort (53% + [9% × 70%]
+ [8% × 50%]). This is the percentage of the cohort who 'complete' some form of

education and training. It is an underestimate, partly because the figures in Table 6.1 already exclude a substantial proportion of those who dropped out of college and training programs, and partly because it takes no account of part-time education and training, or of programs entered after the first post-compulsory year. Moreover, it fails to respect the logic of the system, which treats all post-compulsory learning as valid regardless of its level or duration.

The SSLS evidence on patterns of participation does not provide a clear basis for choosing among the three explanatory frameworks discussed earlier. This is hardly surprising, because each of these frameworks was developed to explain such patterns, and especially to explain social inequalities. Thus, the cultural theories framework argues that the cultural distance between the school system and young people varies with social background: the school system legitimates and validates the cultural capital of the dominant classes. It also argues that youth sub-cultures are socially variable, and cultural pressures for early leaving are strongest in the case of white, working-class males. Rationalist theories attribute inequalities in participation to the different goals, resources and opportunities of young people from different backgrounds. And developmental theories note that poverty and social deprivation, and related experiences such as dependence on social care, frequently give rise to developmental trajectories characterised by educational failure and dropout.

The growth in participation can similarly be attributed to either cultural or rational factors, although it is less likely to have a developmental explanation. Thus, it could reflect the growth of cultural capital among young people,[2] changes in youth sub-cultures and past educational reforms which reduced the cultural distance between schooling and young people. Rising levels of parental education explain some (but not all) of the rise in attainment and participation, and increasing proportions of SSLS sample members who stay on at school say that they do so partly because of an intrinsic interest in their subjects (Paterson & Raffe, 1995). However, SSLS sample members also give strongly instrumental explanations for their decisions. The growth in participation could also reflect the changing balance of opportunities and incentives created by rising compulsory-school attainments, the collapse of the teenage labour market, more flexible educational pathways, increased opportunities in higher education and a growth in occupations requiring higher-level qualifications. Such factors create the 'context' of education which, over several decades of SSLS research, has been shown to be a major determinant of the success or failure of educational reform (Raffe, 1984).

If empirical data fail to differentiate among the explanatory frameworks, this may be because, at least in part, they describe different aspects of the same processes. Sub-cultures may mediate the influence of opportunity structures and their situational logic on young people's choices, culturally conditioned behaviours may give rise to developmental problems, and rational action may be one element in

---

[2] However, more determinist interpretations of cultural theories suggest that the total stock of cultural capital is fixed. Goldthorpe (2000) makes this point to argue that cultural-capital theories cannot account for educational expansion.

a culturally shaped repertoire (Hatcher, 1998). The OECD review's analysis combines all three explanations. It attributes working-class disengagement and failure to the academic Scottish curriculum, to weak intrinsic and extrinsic incentives, and to low self-confidence and self-esteem, and it argues that these three processes reinforce each other.

Nevertheless, the three theoretical frameworks point towards different policy responses to the problem of low participation. The following sections describe current Scottish policies, grouped according to whether the underlying strategy most directly addresses cultural, rational or developmental determinants of low participation. These are described respectively as culturalist, rationalist and developmentalist strategies, although these terms are not used in official documents, and many current policies combine elements of different strategies.

Culturalist Strategies

Culturalist strategies aim to reduce the cultural distance between potential early leavers and the education system by changing the culture of the former or (more realistically) by changing the curriculum, pedagogy and culture of the latter. Young people may become disengaged well before the end of compulsory education: culturalist strategies therefore seek cultural change in compulsory schooling as well as in post-compulsory education and training. Most of these interventions have much broader objectives than raising participation.

An example is *A Curriculum for Excellence*, one of the flagship programs of the current government, which aims to transform the curriculum for 3- to 18-year-olds so that all young people become 'successful learners, confident individuals, responsible citizens and effective contributors to society and at work' (Curriculum Review Group, 2004, p. 12). These 'four capacities' are to be developed through changes in pedagogy and school organisation, as well as in curricular content; the reform is premised on a concept of curriculum, which embraces interdisciplinary learning, the ethos and life of school as a community and opportunities for personal achievement, as well as curriculum areas and subjects (Scottish Government, 2008b). The reform is more advanced in primary than in secondary schools, and details of how it will work in the 'senior phase', which covers learning between the ages of 15 and 18 whether at school, college or elsewhere, are still being worked out. In 2008, the government announced a new entitlement: all young people are entitled to a senior phase of education in which they continue to develop the four capacities and which, among other things, 'prepares them well for achieving qualifications to the highest level of which they are capable' (ibid., p. 15). The model for planning this entitlement, under the title *16 + Learning Choices*, 'envisages all young people, well in advance of their school leaving date, being made an offer of an appropriate, attractive place in learning post-16' (ibid., p. 4).

The OECD (2007) review of Scottish schooling commended the vision of *A Curriculum for Excellence* and its potential to effect the cultural change, which it judged necessary. However, it criticised its separation from other relevant curriculum initiatives, and especially from *Skills for Work* courses which, although formally subsumed within *A Curriculum for Excellence*, had in practice developed as a parallel but separate initiative. *Skills for Work* courses were introduced as pilots in 2005 and 'rolled out' nationally in 2007. They offer applied and experiential learning in particular occupational areas, mainly for 14- to 16-year-old school pupils, usually provided in partnership with a college (occasionally with an employer). Each course is similar in volume to a single Standard Grade subject. The courses appear to recruit middle- and lower-attaining students, although there are no reliable data on this. Evaluations show generally favourable reactions from learners and teachers, with positive effects on self-confidence, self-esteem, motivation and vocational skills and knowledge (Her Majesty's Inspectorate of Education, 2007; Spielhofer & Walker, 2008).

So far, there is no evidence of the impact of *Skills for Work* courses on post-compulsory participation. Of course, they were not designed primarily to increase post-16 participation – their formal objective is to develop general 'employability skills' – but they are part of a general move to broaden and diversify the curriculum, with the expectation that this will stimulate engagement and learning among a wider range of young people. *Skills for Work* courses also reflect a tendency in recent Scottish debates to see vocational learning as the solution to problems of engagement and participation. Policy-makers in Scotland, as in many other countries, see an expansion of vocational learning and an improvement in its status as a means to expand participation in post-compulsory learning as well as to achieve the desired curriculum diversity and cultural change. This approach receives *prima facie* support from the trend for countries where more upper-secondary students take vocational programs to have higher total participation or graduation rates (Leney, 2004; Lamb, 2008).

Apprenticeships are often seen as a way of attracting young people and raising participation. They offer applied and 'relevant' learning, in a cultural setting very different from school, through which young people acquire an occupational identity and adult status. Scottish Modern Apprenticeships are seen to be successful and improving (CPC, 2006; Scottish Executive, 2006b). However, their quality is uneven and they are subject to important supply constraints. The history of work-based training in Scotland since the 1980s reveals a tension between quality and quantity, and a related tension between the goals of social inclusion and of economic development (the same tensions are identified elsewhere in the UK Fuller & Unwin, 2003). Apprenticeships tend to be successful under specific sectoral and labour-market conditions, and they cannot be expanded indefinitely to sectors or labour-market contexts where these conditions are not satisfied. The cognitive and behavioural demands of many apprenticeships make them less suitable for the lowest qualified school leavers, and their recruitment tends to be skewed in favour of white males. They are an important component of a diverse learning system but they cannot be used as the principal means of attracting and motivating young people who would otherwise drop out of learning.

Another way to boost vocational provision is through expanding full-time programs at college. However, as we have seen, Scottish colleges already provide a range of vocational programs. Simply providing such programs is not sufficient to guarantee high participation. Moreover, evidence from other countries suggests that vocational programs may not be the most appropriate ways to engage the most disaffected young people (Steedman & Stoney, 2004). This is supported by the experience of *Skills for Work*: participation in these courses requires (for instance) a certain level of maturity, and colleges have resisted their use as 'dumping grounds' for problem students.

16+ Learning Choices proposes 'a new focus … on those young people for whom school is not the right option post-16' (Scottish Government, 2008d, p. 2). It aims to include not only 'vocational' college and training programs, but also non-formal learning opportunities in community settings, including programs run by voluntary organisations, youth work and volunteering schemes. It argues that such opportunities, backed up by intensive advice and guidance, may be more appropriate for the most vulnerable young people at the greatest risk of dropping out. It proposes to place these options on an equal footing with formal learning opportunities, with the same level and consistency of financial and other support.

Rationalist Strategies

Rationalist strategies aim to change the balance of opportunities, incentives and costs in order to make participation a 'rational' choice for more young people.

One rationalist strategy focuses on the opportunities, incentives and costs which arise from the organisation of the education system itself. An example is 'pathways engineering', which tries to structure educational pathways to encourage participation (OECD, 1998). This typically involves making the system more flexible, designing post-compulsory programs on which low-attaining students have a higher probability of success, and increasing the range of destinations to which each pathway may lead. Measures of pathways engineering in Scotland have focused in particular on the qualifications system and the ways in which it structures access and progression. A series of reforms since the 1980s have created a more flexible, unified and seamless qualifications system, which embraces vocational and academic learning and facilitates access, transfer and progression. The SCQF is an outcome of these reforms (Raffe, 2007). They have created a more open system, but their impact on participation and progression, especially among young people, has been relatively modest. Young people with low prior attainments have continued to experience high failure rates on the new progression pathways, and the 'intrinsic logic' of a unified qualifications system has proved weaker than the 'institutional logic' in which it is embedded (Raffe et al., 2007). And improving pathways to educational qualifications may be an ineffective rationalist strategy if the labour market offers little incentive for young people to achieve these qualifications.

A second rationalist strategy focuses on opportunities, incentives and costs that arise from outside the education system, and especially from the labour market.

Like pathways engineering, this strategy often targets vocational programs. The evidence base for rates of return to Scottish programs is weak, but it is possible that the recent increases in college participation reflect positive labour-market returns (Gasteen et al., 2003). One way to increase labour-market returns to vocational programs is to enhance their quality and ensure that they meet current employment needs. Successive governments have sought to do this through a variety of measures, although 'employer engagement' remains one of the unsolved problems of Scottish (and British) education and training policy (Scottish Government, 2007c). *More Choices More Chances*, the report which outlined the Scottish government's NEET strategy, requires local authorities to lead partnerships of providers, employers and other agencies to coordinate opportunities and support for at-risk school leavers in their areas (Scottish Executive, 2006a). A more radical way to increase the labour-market returns to learning is to increase the utilisation of, and demand for, the skills that are acquired. This is the current policy of the Scottish Government (2007c) but it has relatively few policy levers to give it effect.

Participation decisions may also be influenced by more immediate financial considerations. Educational Maintenance Allowances (EMAs) of up to £30 per week are available to 16- to 19-year-olds from low-income families in full-time education. An evaluation of the first pilot EMAs estimated that they increased participation rates by 7 percentage points overall, and by 9 percentage points among young people from low-income families (Croxford et al., 2002). A subsequent evaluation suggested that increased participation was also reflected in increased attainment (Croxford et al., 2004). However, arrangements for financial support vary across different learning options, potentially influencing educational choices in favour of the options that pay best rather than those that best meet young people's learning needs. Moreover, support tends to be less available and less predictable for participation in the non-formal learning opportunities which may be most appropriate for disengaged young people. The government recently consulted on ways to reduce these inconsistencies (Scottish Government, 2008d).

Information, advice and guidance services frequently form part of rationalist strategies on the basis that rational decision-making requires good information. The current all-age guidance service, Careers Scotland, was established in 2002, and in 2008 it was brought into a new organisation with wider skills-related responsibilities. Enhanced information, advice and guidance will form an element of *16+ Learning Choices*, possibly following a model of 'activity agreements' already piloted in England.

The SCQF provides a potential basis for introducing what Scotland has lacked since 1950 – a Graduation Certificate to mark the completion of upper secondary education. The OECD review recommended that a flexible Graduation Certificate be introduced at different levels to recognise learning at school, college and the workplace. Such a certificate would not automatically result in increased participation: its design would need to be sufficiently flexible to attract low-attaining young people and offer reasonable prospects of success, but not so flexible as to undermine the currency of the award and its value, compared with the existing qualifications. The government has formally rejected the OECD recommendation

(Scottish Government, 2008a), but some commentators, including the present writer, have suggested that the idea deserves further consideration.

Developmentalist Strategies

Developmentalist strategies focus on the most vulnerable young people and on those who drop out, or are at risk of dropping out, because of specific developmental and social problems. Young people who drop out, and especially those who become NEET, are disproportionately likely to have low self-esteem and self-efficacy, low social, personal and cognitive skills, family problems, and/or a history of offending, alcohol and drug use or teenage pregnancy (York Consulting, 2005). Not all these problems are strictly described as 'developmental', but they all invite responses which focus primarily on the individual and his or her problems, rather than on the education system and its cultures and opportunity structures.

Interventions in pursuit of this strategy are diverse, reflecting the diversity of individual young people and their needs. Many are local programs organised by voluntary organisations; relevant national programs are also diverse and flexible in their targeting, content and organisation. They tend to involve a variety of agencies, reflecting the variety of problems faced by the young people concerned (family, education, housing, employment, physical and mental health, addiction, and so on). Effective partnership working is an important (if, in practice, variable) component of developmentalist approaches. Another important component is a Key Worker who provides a single personal contact point for the young person concerned, and can help to coordinate the work of different agencies on their behalf. Many interventions focus on employability and employment as their main objectives rather than continued participation in education and training.

In 1999, a government-appointed committee reviewed the needs and provision of services for 16- to 24-year-olds with additional support needs (Scottish Executive, 1999). It identified gaps in the existing provision and inadequate coordination among the variety of agencies involved and made a number of recommendations, including the proposal for Key Workers. Careers Scotland played a leading role in taking these recommendations forward; a series of local Inclusiveness Projects were introduced, and subsequently absorbed into mainstream provision. Careers Scotland is also responsible for programs such as *Activate*, which aims to boost core skills and employability skills for at-risk young people in their final year of compulsory education. Other programs designed for young people in this group are local and organised by, or in partnership with, voluntary organisations. However, as a recent study to inform the curricular response to the NEET problem concluded, 'curricular solutions cannot fully address social problems' (Finlay et al., 2008, p. 9).

Get Ready for Work is a work-based program (previously part of Skillseekers), which offers varying forms and amounts of support for young people who require additional support to enter employment. It is intended that many of these young people should progress to mainstream work-based training programs, but evaluations have criticised the small proportions of leavers who actually make this transition (Smart Consultancy and Eddy Adams Consultants, 2006).

Evaluations and reviews of 'developmentalist' initiatives confirm the value of the Key Worker approach and, related to this, the need to support clients through advocacy and the need for different support agencies to be coordinated. Other themes include the importance of a progression focus, the need to expect setbacks and to have a strategy for dealing with them, and the need to involve young people in the design of interventions (Eddy Adams Consultants and Smart Consultancy, 2005; SQW, 2005; Scottish Executive, 2005). The current *16 + Learning Choices* consultation proposes to make such opportunities available as part of a more coherent package focused on the delivery of an individual entitlement. It aims to put all options on an equal footing, with the same level and consistency of financial and other support. '[L]earning which might previously have been described as an "alternative" curriculum offer must be considered just as mainstream as Highers are for those young people who remain at school' (Scottish Government, 2008d, p. 2). It also asks whether some particularly vulnerable young people might benefit from a 'broker' to negotiate on their behalf for opportunities which are not currently available (Scottish Government, 2008d).

Discussion

Many of the policy measures reviewed in this chapter operate at the system level: they aim to change the curriculum, provide new programs and qualifications or new mechanisms for coordinating the supply of learning opportunities. Some focus on the institutional level, at least in the sense of promoting particular types of institutional provision (through colleges, apprenticeships or the voluntary sector) Others focus on the individual, for example, by providing financial support, increased information, advice and guidance or key workers. The difference between these three levels does not correspond very closely to the distinction between culturalist, rationalist or developmentalist policy strategies. It is not possible, from this brief review, to conclude which of these strategies has been most effective. All three may be necessary components of a concerted effort to reduce dropout and raise participation in post-compulsory learning.

Different strategies may be more effective in different contexts and for different groups. It is probable that as participation has risen over time, a larger proportion of those who continue to drop out do so for reasons labelled in this chapter as 'developmental', suggesting that developmental strategies become more important. Nevertheless, studies of early leavers and NEET young people consistently draw attention to their heterogeneity (Finlay et al., 2008). *More Choices, More Chances* distinguished between the 'hardest to help' NEET young people and an intermediate group who were 'quietly disaffected', for whom less intensive interventions could make a 'massive difference' (Scottish Executive, 2006a). It is possible that this latter group would be more likely to respond to culturalist or rationalist strategies.

Moreover, an emphasis on all three strategies helps to challenge the individualistic focus of many policy documents, including *More Choices, More Chances*. Disengagement and dropout are not just individual problems; they also reflect broader social trends as well as problems in the school system and its relationship to the labour market and other social institutions, which are addressed by the culturalist and rationalist strategies.

Our framework also helps us to question another tendency in Scottish policy debates: the tendency to see vocational learning as a simple remedy for the problems associated with low participation. In the first place, this review has raised the question of supply and demand: Scotland already offers a diverse range of post-compulsory vocational opportunities, but this supply does not create its own demand. Conversely, the supply of some vocational opportunities, especially those based in the workplace, may be severely constrained. Second, vocational learning should not be used as shorthand for curricular diversity. The features that make many 'vocational' interventions effective have little to do with their vocational content. Third, genuinely vocational programs are unsuitable ways to engage young people who have important developmental issues. And fourth, if vocational programs expand faster than the labour market's demand for their qualifications, the incentive to participate will diminish. Vocational learning has an important role both as a component of general education and as a principle for organising some learning pathways, but its potential contributions to the problems discussed above are both specific and limited.

I have suggested that developmental explanations for low participation may have become more important over time, as total dropout rates have fallen. Subject to this, 3 decades of SSLS-based research on the range of participation decisions – including decisions on the choice of program as well as whether to participate or not – point to the importance of rational factors in explaining broader patterns and trends in participation. If this analysis is still valid, an important reason for high dropout in Scottish education may be the polarised demand for skills from an 'hourglass' economy. Unlike successive UK governments, the Scottish government has accepted the argument that the solution to the skills problem lies as much with the demand for skills as with their supply, and has set the policy goal of increasing the utilisation of, and demand for, skills. It has few policy instruments for doing this, but even if it is only partly successful, this could be an important means by which participation in post-compulsory learning is raised.

References

Bernstein, B. (1971). *Class, codes and control* (Vol. 1). London: Routledge and Kegan Paul.
Boudon, R. (1974). *Education, opportunity and social inequality*. New York: Wiley.
Bourdieu, P. (1997). The forms of capital. In A. H. Halsey, H. Lauder, P. Brown, & A. Stuart Wells (Eds.), *Education: Culture, economy, society* (pp. 46–58). Oxford, UK: Oxford University Press.
Cambridge Policy Consultants (CPC). (2006). *Evaluation of modern apprenticeships and skill-seekers*. Final Report. Cambridge, UK: CPC.

Croxford, L. (2009). *Change over time in the contexts, outcomes and inequalities of secondary schooling in Scotland, 1985–2005.* Edinburgh, UK: The Scottish Government.

Croxford, L., Howieson, C., Iannelli, C., & Ozga, J. (2002). *Education Maintenance Allowances: Evaluation of the East Ayrshire pilot.* Edinburgh, UK: Scottish Executive.

Croxford, L., Iannelli, C., & Shapira, M. (2007). *Documentation of youth cohort time series* (EYT Working Paper 20). Edinburgh, UK: CES, University of Edinburgh.

Croxford, L., Ozga, J., & Provan, F. (2004). *Education Maintenance Allowances: Attainment of national qualifications in the Scottish pilots.* Edinburgh, UK: Scottish Executive.

Curriculum Review Group. (2004). *A curriculum for excellence.* Edinburgh, UK: Scottish Executive.

Eddy Adams Consultants and Smart Consultancy. (2005). *Mapping employability and support services for disengaged young people.* Edinburgh, UK: Scottish Executive.

Feinstein, L., Duckworth, K., & Sabates, R. (2008). *Education and the family: Passing success across the generations.* London: Routledge.

Finlay, I., Sheridan, M., McKay, J., & Nudzor, H. (2008, September). Young people on the margins: In need of more choices and more chances. Paper to BERA Annual Conference, Edinburgh, UK.

Fuller, A., & Unwin, L. (2003). Creating a 'Modern Apprenticeship': A critique of the UK's multi-sector, social inclusion approach. *Journal of Education and Work, 16*(1), 5–25.

Gasteen, A., Houston, J., & Davidson, C. (2003). *Scottish educational qualifications: The returns to educational routes.* Research Report for the Scottish Economic Policy Network (Scotecon), Stirling, from scotecon.net.

Goldthorpe, J. (2000). *On sociology.* Oxford, UK: Oxford University Press.

Hannan, D., Smyth, E., Raffe, D., Martin, C., Brannen, K., Rutjes, H., Becker, K., & Werquin, P. (1998). *Education, vocational training and labour market transitions among lower level school leavers in four European countries.* Final Report. Dublin, Ireland: ESRI.

Hatcher, R. (1998). Class differentiation in education: Rational choices? *British Journal of Sociology of Education, 19*(1), 5–24.

Heckman, J., & Masterov, D. (2004). *The productivity argument for investing in young children* (Working Paper 5). Invest in Kids Working Group, Committee for Economic Development. Retrieved December 19, 2008, from. http://jenni.uchicago.edu/Invest

Her Majesty's Inspectorate of Education (HMIE). (2007). *Preparing for work: A report on the Skills for Work pilot programme.* Livingston, Scotland: HMIE.

Hodkinson, P., Sparkes, A., & Hodkinson, H. (1996). *Triumphs and tears: Young people, markets and the transition from school to work.* London: David Fulton.

Howieson, C. (2003). *Destinations of early leavers* (Special CES Briefing No. 28). Edinburgh, UK: CES, University of Edinburgh.

Howieson, C., & Iannelli, C. (2008). The effects of low attainment on young people's outcomes at age 22–23 in Scotland. *British Journal of Educational Research, 34*(2), 269–290.

Jones, G., & Wallace, C. (1992). *Youth, family and citizenship.* Buckingham, UK: Open University Press.

Lamb, S. (2008). *Alternative pathways to high school graduation: An international comparison* (Report No. 7, California Dropout Research Project). Santa Barbara, CA: UCSB.

Leney, T. (2004). *Achieving the Lisbon goal: The contribution of VET.* Final Report to the European Commission. London: QCA.

McConnell, J. (2006). *Scotland's future: Thinking for the long term.* Edinburgh, UK: Scottish Executive.

Organisation for Economic Co-operation and Development (OECD). (1998). *Pathways and participation in vocational and technical education and training.* Paris: OECD.

Organisation for Economic Co-operation and Development (OECD). (2007). *Quality and equity of schooling in Scotland.* Paris: OECD.

Paterson, L., & Raffe, D. (1995). Staying-on in Scotland: 1985–1991. *Oxford Review of Education, 21*(1), 3–23.

Raffe, D. (1984). *Fourteen to eighteen: The changing pattern of schooling in Scotland.* Aberdeen, UK: Aberdeen University Press.

Raffe, D. (2007). Making haste slowly: The evolution of a unified qualifications framework in Scotland. *European Journal of Education, 42*(4), 485–502.

Raffe, D., Croxford, L., Iannelli, C., Shapira, M., & Howieson, C. (2006). *Social-class inequalities in education in England and Scotland* (Special CES Briefing No. 40). Edinburgh, UK: CES, University of Edinburgh.

Raffe, D., Howieson, C., & Tinklin, T. (2007). The impact of a unified curriculum and qualifications system: The Higher Still reform of post-16 education in Scotland. *British Educational Research Journal, 33*(4), 479–508.

Scottish Executive. (1999). *Implementing inclusiveness, realising potential.* Edinburgh, UK: Scottish Executive.

Scottish Executive. (2005). *Employability framework for Scotland: Report of the NEET workstream.* Edinburgh, UK: Scottish Executive.

Scottish Executive. (2006a). *More Choices, More Chances: A strategy to reduce the proportion of young people not in education, employment or training in Scotland.* Edinburgh, UK: Scottish Executive.

Scottish Executive. (2006b). *Building on our success: Improving modern apprenticeships* (Consultation Paper). Edinburgh, UK: Scottish Executive.

Scottish Funding Council (SFC). (2008a). *Learning for all: Second update report on measures of success.* Edinburgh, UK: SFC.

Scottish Funding Council (SFC). (2008b). *Student and staff performance indicators for further education colleges in Scotland 2006–07.* Edinburgh, UK: SFC.

Scottish Government. (2007a). *The age participation index for Scotland 2005–06* (Statistics Publication Notice). Edinburgh, UK: Scottish Government.

Scottish Government. (2007b). *Destinations of leavers from Scottish schools: 2006/07* (Statistics Publication Notice). Edinburgh, UK: Scottish Government.

Scottish Government. (2007c). *Skills for Scotland: A lifelong skills strategy* (Statistics Publication Notice). Edinburgh, UK: Scottish Government.

Scottish Government. (2008a). *A consultation on the next generation of national qualifications in Scotland.* Edinburgh, UK: Scottish Government.

Scottish Government. (2008b). *Curriculum for excellence: Building the curriculum 3: A framework for teaching and learning.* Edinburgh, UK: Scottish Government.

Scottish Government. (2008c). *Pupils in Scotland, 2007* (Statistical Bulletin Edn/B1/2008/1). Edinburgh, UK: Scottish Government.

Scottish Government. (2008d). *16+ Learning Choices: First step activity and consultation report* (Consultation Document). Edinburgh, UK: Scottish Government.

Smart Consultancy and Eddy Adams Consultants. (2006). *Scottish Enterprise National Get Ready for Work programme: Evaluation 2002–2006.* Glasgow, UK: Scottish Enterprise.

Spielhofer, T., & Walker, M. (2008). *Evaluation of Skills for Work pilot courses.* Edinburgh, UK: Scottish Government.

SQW. (2005). *The national evaluation of the Careers Scotland Inclusiveness Projects.* Edinburgh, UK: Scottish Executive.

Steedman, H., & Stoney, S. (2004). *Disengagement 14-16: Context and evidence* (Discussion Paper 654). London: Centre for Economic Performance, London School of Economics.

York Consulting. (2005). *Literature review of the NEET group.* Edinburgh, UK: Scottish Executive.

Chapter 7
Germany's Education System and the Problem of Dropouts: Institutional Segregation and Program Diversification

Andrea Reupold and Rudolf Tippelt

Introduction

In light of the large number of individuals deemed 'underprivileged' in the education system, it is especially important within the context of the ongoing qualifications debate to focus on the young people in Germany who do not possess a formal academic qualification. As a result of the differentiated system in the secondary phase of schooling in Germany, dropouts come from many pathways including the Secondary General School, the Intermediate Secondary School and the Grammar School, as well as from vocational training schools, Dual System apprenticeships and special-needs schools.

The Secondary General School (*Hauptschule*) represents the school type that is at the lowest academic level. It is compulsory until Grade 9 and in some federal states until Grade 10, by which time students are aged 15 or 16. This type of school provides a general education that is mainly seen as a basis for practical vocational training. The Intermediate Secondary School (*Realschule*) provides extended general education until Grade 10. With the Intermediate Certificate, students have access to all types of medium-level occupations, to the dual apprenticeship system and also have the option to transfer to a Grammar School or to specific subject-related grammar schools that provide access to universities of applied sciences (*Fachhochschulen*). The Grammar School (*Gymnasium*) offers schooling from Grade 5 to Grade 12 or 13, and with the final exams (A-levels, or *Abitur*) students qualify for studies at all institutions of higher education. Normally, about two thirds of these school leavers transfer to universities, while others enter the Dual System.

This divided school system is seen as one of the main causes of social selection and inequality as it provides the grounds for the tracking or streaming of students (e.g., see the PISA[1]-studies: PISA-Konsortium Deutschland, 2004). On the other

---

[1] Programme for International Student Assessment.

A. Reupold and R. Tippelt (✉)
Institute of Pedagogy and Educational Research, Ludwig-Maximilians-University, Munich, Germany

S. Lamb et al. (Eds.), *School Dropout and Completion: International Comparative Studies in Theory and Policy*, DOI 10.1007/978-90-481-9763-7_8,
© Springer Science+Business Media B.V. 2011

hand, this system, which attempts to qualify young people at the educational level that best suits their capabilities and interests, can result in comparatively high completion rates.

Youth without an educational or vocational qualification have greatly reduced options within the educational system and also in the job market (e.g., see Hillmert & Mayer, 2004; Friebel, 1999; Max-Planck-Institut für Bildungsforschung, 1995). To design policies that reduce dropout rates, it is essential to identify the influences and also those institutions and agencies that are accountable. In Germany, responsibility for these problems is scattered throughout the federal political and educational system, with the 16 states having responsibility for educational legislation and administration. In order to ensure agreements on educational matters of supra-regional importance, there is a national committee that fosters cooperation and coordination: the Standing Conference of the Ministers of Educational and Cultural Affairs (*Kultusministerkonferenz*). Some of the common regulations concern compulsory full-time school attendance, which is 9 years in 12 federal states, and 10 years in four federal states (for a more thorough description of the system, see Reich et al., 2008).

Main Features of Secondary Education and Training Provision

In general, Germany's education and training system is relatively complex, even at the school level. After Pre-School (ages 5–6) and Primary education (ages 6–10), the early diversification of secondary school pathways starts when the pupils are aged 10, and is completed after an orientation stage of 2 years. During this orientation stage of Secondary Level I, students are selected for the different school types according to their performance as shown in their grades, their general capacity to perform as assessed by their teachers, and the students and their parents' inclinations.

As previously indicated, there are basically three different types of schools that offer secondary education in Germany: the Grammar School (*Gymnasium*), which prepares for a more academic track; the Intermediate Secondary School (*Realschule*), which mainly prepares for specialist technical training; and the Secondary General School (*Hauptschule*), which has a more vocational focus. Thus, as early as in the lower secondary level, students aged between 10 and 15 and their parents need to make decisions concerning different pathways within the educational system, based on the student's interests and aptitudes. When compared with other countries, this selection process is sometimes criticised as occurring too early.

The Secondary Level II stage starts when students are aged 15, and offers a wide range of options to qualify them for academia or the job market. The following sections present an overview of the broad variety of options that are available.

Secondary Level 1

Attending Secondary General Schools mainly provides access to the dual apprenticeship system. The form of assessment is school-based and in some federal states there are state-wide exams. The certificates that can be obtained after graduation are the Basic School Certificate (*Hauptschulabschluss*) and the Qualified Main School Certificate (*Qualifizierender Hauptschulabschluss*).[2]

Intermediate Secondary Schools prepare for all vocational tracks – not just the Dual System but also for Technical Secondary Schools (*Fachoberschulen*) that provide access to a more academic track at universities of applied sciences. By graduating from Intermediate Secondary School, students obtain a Middle School Certificate. The form of assessment is the same as in Secondary General Schools: school-based and in some federal states, state-wide exams.

In Grammar Schools, students are prepared for the academic tracks but can also access all vocational tracks by graduating with their A-levels (*Abitur*). The form of assessment is again the same as in Secondary General Schools and Intermediate Secondary Schools.

Aside from these three secondary school types, there are two other sorts of school in which only very small numbers of students are enrolled: Comprehensive Schools that combine the above described three school types in one institution, and schools for children with special needs. Half of all young people who leave school without a Secondary General School leaving certificate come from Special Schools. Some 77% of all Special School students leave school without a basic certificate or a higher qualifying certificate. This group of school leavers represents about 4% of the 15- to 17-year-old population (Autorengruppe Bildungsberichterstattung, 2008, p. 89).

Decisions about where to study made at this Secondary Level I stage do not limit students to a certain track at Secondary Level II, but changing track takes more effort than following one pathway through the two stages. Often, therefore, the choices at Level I predispose decisions on a pathway in Level II.

Data from the working group on educational reporting (Autorengruppe Bildungsberichterstattung, 2008) show changes in the decade from 1996 to 2006 in the number of graduates from each type of school and the proportion of the relevant age-group that they represent. In absolute terms, graduates from the Secondary Intermediate School (*Realschule*) make up the largest group, and also the group that has shown most growth over the period 1996–2006 – from 46.4% of 16- to 18-year-olds to 49.6%. By contrast, the number of graduates from the Secondary General School (*Hauptschule*) fell during the decade, and they also represent a declining proportion of the age-group 15–17 years (30.6% down to 28.5%). The biggest change in proportional terms occurred in the Technical Secondary Schools – the smallest sector – whose graduates represented 8.5% of 18- to 21-year-olds in 1996 rising to 13.6% in 2006. Graduates with A-levels (*Hochschulreife*) represented 28.2% of 18- to 21-year-olds in 1996, falling to 25.6% in 2001, before rising to 29.9% in 2006 (Autorengruppe Bildungsberichterstattung, 2008, pp. 87–88, p. 269).

---

[2] The difference between the two certificates is that the Qualified Main School Certificate involves a special exam that can also be taken by students from any of the other school types and that qualifies for the 2-year full-time vocational schools, commercial schools and more complex vocational training. The certificate improves the opportunities of the graduate to get a training contract or – with a good grading – to continue in their schooling and access an Intermediate Secondary School.

Secondary Level II

Secondary Level II education in Germany is basically separated into two main tracks: vocational education and general education. General education concludes with an A-level certificate at Grammar Schools for university access, whereas vocational education includes the Dual System, full-time intermediate technical schools (*Berufsfachschulen*) and higher technical schools (*Fachoberschulen*).

In terms of numbers of students, the Dual System is the most significant pathway in Germany: 60% of young people take part in vocational training within this system, which had over 1.6 million trainees in 2007, and more than 600,000 new training contracts[3] per year. There are more than 300 nationally recognised training occupations available through the system. Even with over 150,000 vocational experts in the examination boards of the Chambers of Commerce and Industries working on an honorary basis, the average cost per trainee within the Dual System stands at €18,000 per year. The overall cost to the German economy for this vocational training is €30 billion per year.

The Dual System is open to all Secondary Level I graduates, and students participate in on-the-job training as well as vocational training over a period of 2 to 3.5 years (Konsortium Bildungsberichterstattung, 2006; Autorengruppe Bildungsberichterstattung, 2008). Training regulations focus on the duration of training, as well as the content in terms of knowledge and skills required for designated occupations, and are developed by the federal government, trade unions and the federal states.

Intermediate vocational schools (*Berufsfachschulen*) provide general and vocational training and differ in their definitions of entrance levels as well as in the duration of their programs (from 1 to 3 years). Some call for students to have an Intermediate Certificate, but others are also open to Secondary General School graduates.

Technical Secondary Schools (*Fachoberschulen*) offer specialised education for various areas and provide students with a certificate that allows access to higher education (*Fachhochschulen*).

There have been changes in the backgrounds of trainees entering the Dual System, based on their prior school certificates. In a longitudinal comparison, data from the Federal Statistical Office show that in 1970, 80% of trainees had completed lower secondary schooling (Secondary General School, *Hauptschule*), 19% had graduated from Intermediate Secondary Schools (*Realschulen*), and only 1% had A-levels (*Abitur*). By 2004, these percentages had shifted markedly: a much smaller 37% of the trainees had graduated from lower secondary schools, while

---

[3] A training contract is arranged between a (private) training organisation and the trainee. The contract runs for the official training period and guarantees a place for training, adequate payment during the training and the educational standards defined by the state. In the context of the Dual System the student attends a vocational school 1 or 2 days a week on average. Most training takes place in the enterprise under the supervision of vocational trainers.

46% were from Intermediate Secondary Schools and 17% from Grammar Schools with A-levels (*Abitur*). In other words, students holding university entrance qualifications have increasingly taken up options that were traditionally intended for those who graduated from lower secondary schools (Konsortium Bildungsberichterstattung, 2006; Tippelt & van Cleve, 1996). Thus, as well as a general shortage of trainee positions in the Dual System due to the economic situation, there is increasing competition among graduates from the different school types who are all trying to get one of the limited number of training positions. Demand and supply of training positions should, in theory, be balanced, but in reality, because of the decreasing number of training positions and the attractiveness of the Dual System in Germany, the demand for places is greater than the supply.

Having described the German educational system and its Secondary Level II pathways, the next section provides an overview of the possible stages at which dropout can occur: this can be from each of the different school types and training programs. Dropout numbers and rates will be given where they are available.

Rates of School Graduation and Dropout

Dropout from Secondary Level II in Germany occurs within both the general school system and in vocational education. Moreover, Germany's school organisation has a very specific feature that contributes to delayed school careers: *grade-repeating* (or *retake*). It is possible for students to repeat a year at either the same type of school they attended, or to change school type 'downwards', for example from Grammar School to Intermediate Secondary School, and repeat the year there. The assumption in the latter case would be that Grammar School was not the appropriate school for that student, and the student would be more successful at an Intermediate Secondary School. These early problems in a student's educational career are sometimes first indicators for the identification of young adults at risk of dropping out. In this section, the main focus is on dropout rates, but in order to provide a more comprehensive picture, some numbers on grade-repeating are also presented.

Grade Repeating and School Dropouts

In Germany, three in every hundred pupils have their school careers delayed through grade-repeating. In absolute numbers, for the year 2006–07, 234,000 students (or about 2.7% of the total school population) retook a grade between Primary and Secondary Level II (Autorengruppe Bildungsberichterstattung, 2008, p. 258). By looking at the changes in the numbers of grade repeaters and comparing the numbers from 1995–96 with those of 2006–07, a differentiated picture can be drawn.

With regard to type of school, the educational report of 2008 (Autorengruppe Bildungsberichterstattung, 2008) points out that Intermediate Secondary Schools have the highest rates of grade repeating (around 5%, compared with 4% for Secondary General Schools and 2% for Grammar Schools). But compared with 1995–96, the rates for Intermediate Secondary Schools have tended to decrease. Grammar Schools have relatively low rates (2.9% in 1995–96, 3.2% in 2006–07). This might be due to the fact that Grammar Schools lose students to other school types, but have to take in students from these other schools only to a very limited degree. This would be consistent with the observation of rising rates in Secondary General Schools (from 3.4% in 1995–96 to 4.1% in 2006–07).

Regarding the gender-specific data, it is a general trend across all school types and all years that young male students tend to repeat grades more often than female students. Moreover, young students from migrant backgrounds are more likely to repeat than German students. In the national educational report that was published in 2006, it was shown that this trend starts in primary education and only starts to weaken in the Secondary I Level.

Repeating classes as well as dropping out of Secondary II general schooling happens in all three different school types. Depending on the school type, dropping out of school – in contrast to repeating classes – means leaving school without any official qualification or certificate. The only exceptions are students dropping out from Grammar School after Grade 10. In this case – when they have finished Grade 10 successfully – they automatically receive the Secondary Intermediate School certificate. In every other dropout scenario, students have no school certificate unless they take extra courses and/or exams.

The numbers shown in Fig. 7.1 refer to school leavers from general education aged 15–17 years without a basic school certificate. Here, the overall national rate was at

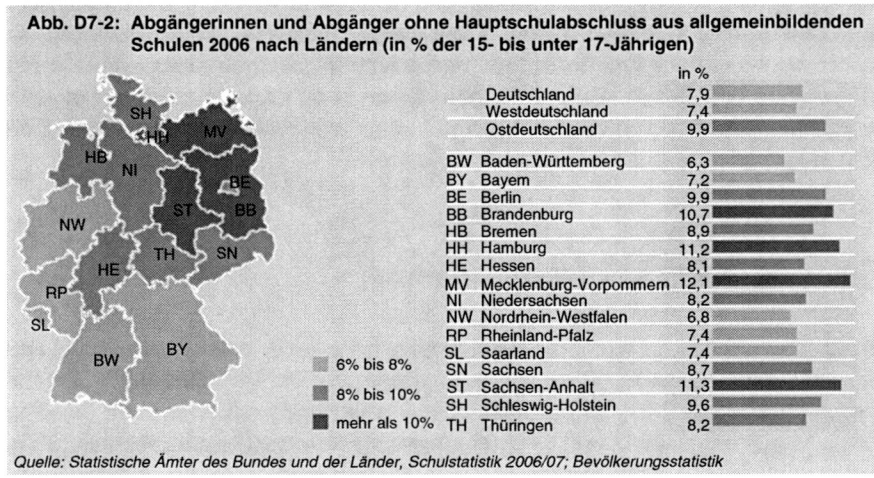

Abb. D7-2: Abgängerinnen und Abgänger ohne Hauptschulabschluss aus allgemeinbildenden Schulen 2006 nach Ländern (in % der 15- bis unter 17-Jährigen)

		in %
	Deutschland	7,9
	Westdeutschland	7,4
	Ostdeutschland	9,9
BW	Baden-Württemberg	6,3
BY	Bayern	7,2
BE	Berlin	9,9
BB	Brandenburg	10,7
HB	Bremen	8,9
HH	Hamburg	11,2
HE	Hessen	8,1
MV	Mecklenburg-Vorpommern	12,1
NI	Niedersachsen	8,2
NW	Nordrhein-Westfalen	6,8
RP	Rheinland-Pfalz	7,4
SL	Saarland	7,4
SN	Sachsen	8,7
ST	Sachsen-Anhalt	11,3
SH	Schleswig-Holstein	9,6
TH	Thüringen	8,2

6% bis 8%
8% bis 10%
mehr als 10%

Quelle: Statistische Ämter des Bundes und der Länder, Schulstatistik 2006/07; Bevölkerungsstatistik

Fig. 7.1 School-leavers without basic school certificate from general schools (% of all 15- to 17-year-olds) (Source: Autorengruppe Bildungsberichterstattung, 2008, p. 87)

7.9% (n = 76,000) in 2006, while the rates for federal states differ considerably. What this chart reveals is that in the northern and eastern parts of Germany, dropout rates are generally higher than in the western and southern parts. On average, West Germany's dropout rate lies at 7.4% and East Germany's at 9.9%. The highest rate (12.1%) was measured in the state of Mecklenburg-Vorpommern (MV) and the lowest in Baden-Württemberg (6.3%). Overall, 2.4% of all young adults in Germany aged 18–24 years have not graduated from the Secondary I Level (Autorengruppe Bildungsberichterstattung, 2008).

Up to a point, dropping out is compensated for by access to the Dual System for some young people without a school leaving certificate. Longitudinal studies show that 38% of this group find a position within the Dual System within 30 months, while others enrol in full-time vocational school or in one of the diverse set of programs known collectively as the 'transition system' (Übergangssystem).[4]

While there are no cohort-equivalent graduation or dropout rates for Germany that would allow a follow-up of the school careers of cohorts of young people, numbers for 2000 and 2004 clearly show a tendency for students who have no school gradua- tion certificate to take up offers in the 'transition system' that prepares them to enter the Dual System. In 2004, of all commencing students in vocational training who did not hold a Secondary General School leaving certificate, 84.0% attended courses in the transition system (83.9% in 2000). In 2000, merely 15.8% (and 15.5% in 2004) of this 'unqualified' group of students successfully entered the Dual System directly, and only a very small number (0.3% in 2000 and 0.5% in 2004) entered the full-time vocational schooling system (Konsortium Bildungsberichterstattung, 2006, pp. 82–83).

In contrast, among those students who in 2004 entered vocational training hold- ing a Secondary General School certificate, 40.2% started directly in the Dual System (47.3% in 2000); and of those with a Secondary Intermediate Secondary certificate, 48.5% did so (54.1% in 2000).

In terms of transition to vocational training, the most successful students are those with the highest school certificate: A-levels (Abitur). The numbers here are intriguing. In 2000, 69.7% of Abitur students who entered vocational training did so in the Dual System, with a further 24.8% in full-time Technical High Schools. Only 5.4% started vocational training in the transition system. In 2004, the pattern was very similar: 68.2% entered the Dual System, 28.9% full-time vocational schooling, and only 2.9% began in the transition system.

A longitudinal study conducted by the Federal Institute for Vocational Education and Training (BIBB) on the pathways of young adults whose highest schooling is that of a Secondary General certificate focused on three test intervals: 6, 18 and 30 months after leaving the general school system. The results show that after 6 months,

---

[4]The transition system is a third form of vocational education besides the Dual System and voca- tional schools that was developed during the 1990s. It consists of a variety of short-term educa- tional measures that are intended to support the transition from the general educational school to award-bearing vocational education. The transition system is at the moment in terms of numbers of students nearly as big as the Dual System. Especially in Eastern Germany, the transition system plays an important role in the process of vocational integration.

27.5% were in enterprise-based vocational training, 15.7% in non-enterprise-based[5] vocational training, 38.2% in the transition system, and only 18.7% were not in any kind of training.

After 30 months, three main groups could be identified. The first group consisted of those young adults who started training in either enterprise-based or non-enterprise-based training (around 43%) during the first 6 months after leaving school. The trajectory of this group was very stable as only very few dropped out. By 18 months, another 14% had joined this group (i.e., they had commenced enterprise-based or non-enterprise based training), and by 30 months, a further 3% had joined it. These later entries mainly came from the transition system and increased the total number in enterprise-based or non-enterprise-based training to 60% (Autorengruppe Bildungsberichterstattung, 2008).

The second group of young adults entered the transition system (38.2%) and can be characterised as those who only rarely succeeded in finding a training position after 18 months (only 33% of this group had a training position). Even after 18 months, more than half of this group were still in the transition system. At the 30th month, a certain percentage had succeeded in entering a fully qualifying training position, so that about half of this group made the transition into the vocational training system. In general, the transition paths of this group of young adults were more of an odyssey than a systematic model of successful educational continuity (Autorengruppe Bildungsberichterstattung, 2008).

The third group (19%) consisted of those who did not attend school in any way and who did not find a job or a training position. Only a minority of this group (33%) were able to find a fully qualifying position, leading to the level of a skilled worker, within the 30 months.

These numbers show that the initial rate of students who are identified as dropouts (those who have left school and do not have any kind of school-leaving certificate) might even be higher if those who have graduated, but are not successfully integrated into vocational education or the job market, are taken into account.

Training Dropouts

When students enter the Dual System they are, on the one hand, still students during their vocational schooling phases, but on the other hand they are educated and socialised as *employees* in their on-the-job-training phases, and here they sign a contract with their employer. Students in the Dual System are meant to attend vocational school and for the whole period of training remain at the company that offered the contract to them. If students break-off the training and the contract, or if they do not attend vocational school, or if they do not successfully pass the exams at the end of their training phase, they are not granted a certificate and are regarded as dropouts in the Dual System.

---

[5]Enterprise-based training is delivered (partly) within a firm, while non-enterprise-based training is delivered in a school setting.

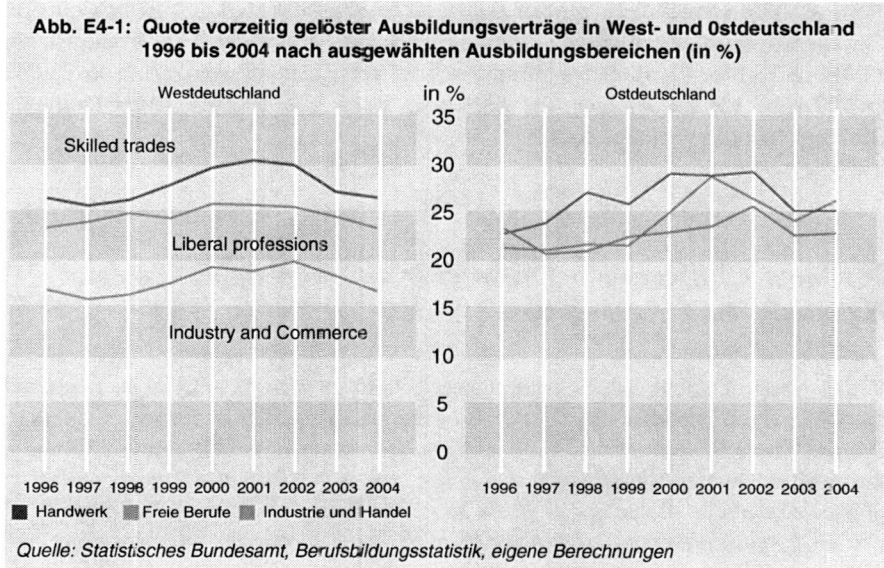

Abb. E4-1: Quote vorzeitig gelöster Ausbildungsverträge in West- und Ostdeutschland 1996 bis 2004 nach ausgewählten Ausbildungsbereichen (in %)

Quelle: Statistisches Bundesamt, Berufsbildungsstatistik, eigene Berechnungen

Fig. 7.2 Changes in training dropout rates, 1996–2004, West and East Germany (%) (Source Konsortium Bildungsberichterstattung, 2006, p. 93)

Dropouts from the Dual System pose a big challenge for vocational education in companies and are a high financial risk for them. Interestingly, dropout numbers have been rising dramatically in the last 40 years: rates were at 5% for longer-lasting contracts and at about 15% for recently signed contracts before the 1980s. At the end of the 1980s, these numbers almost doubled: in 2000 the rates were at 25.1% for the recently signed contracts.

Figure 7.2 illustrates the rates in more recent years (1996–2004) for three different occupational areas for both West and East Germany.

The overall national rate for these prematurely dissolved contracts is at about 26% for Germany, and is thus regarded as very high. In order to reduce this figure, there are a number of programs and projects that, for example, focus on better matching processes or early counselling models. Later in this chapter, there will be further discussion of the reasons for dropout and the measures to reduce it.

In general, the last two educational reports on Germany (Autorengruppe Bildungsberichterstattung, 2006, 2008) have highlighted a trend in which school qualifications have become partly disconnected from the types of school that normally award them. In the German context, this is referred to as 'permeability' in that a qualification increasingly penetrates different types of schools rather than being uniquely available from one of them. Increased permeability is evident, for example, in the fact that a Secondary General School certificate (*Hauptschulabschluss*) can be acquired at a Secondary Intermediate school (*Realschule*) and that the certificate normally awarded by this school can also be gained elsewhere through additional courses and/or examinations. A higher level of school graduation can also be obtained belatedly through job-related education. The 10-year period from

1996 to 2006 shows the extent of the trend to obtain school certificates outside the normal institutional route: (1) rates for basic school certificates grew from 12.1% to 13.5%; (2) rates for middle school certificates increased from 13.5% to 17% and (3) for A-levels the rates rose from 11% to 15% (Autorengruppe Bildungsberichterstattung, 2008).

Dropouts – Differentiated According to School Type, Gender, Nationality and Socioeconomic Status

If the group of young adults without any school certificate in 2004 is examined more closely, it becomes clear that half of the group consists of former students of Special Needs Schools and 35% come from Secondary General Schools. Although the numbers do vary, these are the two major groups that form the largest proportion of the dropouts in all compared years. In general, dropouts have fewer chances of getting a training position within the Dual System: 13 months after dropping out, only half of this group succeeded in signing a contract with a training company. After 2.5 years, only 69% of them had achieved that goal.

More young men than young women are likely to drop out of school. In 2004, 9.5% of German males aged 15 to 17 did not have a school certificate, compared with 5.6% of females. Young people from migrant backgrounds were also much less likely than Germans to have completed a school certificate, with the same difference by gender: 19.7% of males and 12.9% of females were in this category (Konsortium Bildungsberichterstattung, 2006, p. 254).

In a more detailed analysis of these numbers, and controlling for the socioeconomic status of young adults, the relative likelihood of obtaining A-levels is almost the same for students from Germany and for students with a migrant background from other European Union countries, the United States, East Asia, the former Soviet Union, Italy, Turkey, Morocco, and East and Middle Europe. For students who originally come from Greece, Spain, Portugal, Vietnam and other South Asian countries, there is even a positive effect of nationality on the chance of attaining A-levels. Without controlling for socioeconomic status, these chances differ a great deal: for example, students from Italian or Turkish backgrounds have one half to one third the likelihood of obtaining A-levels, compared with Germans (Autorengruppe Bildungsberichterstattung, 2008).

After further differentiating socioeconomic status, the educational levels of the parents are found to be the most important influences on the level of achievement in school. If the first family attachment figure (normally the father) has a university-level degree rather than being a dropout with no educational certificates, the likelihood for the young adult to also achieve A-levels is three times as high. If the second parent (normally the mother) has A-levels as well, chances are four times as high, compared to having a second parent without any schooling certificates. Additionally, young adults obtain A-levels less often when their parents have a lower family income, even if the parents may have equally high educational attainments and vocational positions compared to the latter group.

Explanations for Dropouts in Germany

The reasons for dropping out can be seen as individual (the motivational and cognitive attributes of the young person) as well as related to external factors concerning the school and vocational training system. More intensive research in this field is necessary, but it can be said that the reasons for dropout are multifaceted and originate basically in four areas: family background (e.g., socioeconomic status), the schooling system (e.g., lack of permeability), organisational issues (e.g., the quality of the curriculum), and issues concerning school effectiveness (Ditton, 2007. for an overview on school effectiveness criteria, see Seidel, 2008). Krekel and Ulrich (2009) point to four individual determining aspects associated with not being able to find a trainee position in the Dual System: (1) achievement, (2) family background, (3) migration background and (4) gender.

In qualitative studies on dropout in the training and vocational system (Weiss, 2002), the main reasons that have been found include:

- A lack of interest in the occupation
- A lack of achievement, mainly concerning attainment at vocational schooling
- Trainee deviance, mainly absence without permission
- Conflicts in the training company

Additional reasons relate to health or family issues, as well as lack of training quality. However, these reasons given in case studies cannot explain the continuing rise of dropouts in the Dual System. Since there is no evidence basis for a decline in the quality of instruction, several reasons can be found when looking at the surrounding conditions.

One of these concerns the ratio of training offers from companies to school leavers seeking an apprenticeship. Assuming that a discontented trainee would only dissolve his contract with one company when he or she can be sure of already having a new contract with another company, the risk of high dropout rates is greater in years of trainee position over-supply. This hypothesis sounds convincing, and there is a certain correlation; however, it does not hold for the continuing rise in dropout rates ever since the 1970s (Weiss, 2002).

A second important factor is the preparatory education of the trainees. The number of students without any basic certificate in the Dual System has hardly changed at all, but the number of students with basic certificates fell considerably (from 47.3% in 2000 to 40.2% in 2004). The relative numbers of students with A-levels more than doubled since 1979 (Weiss, 2002). As Weiss noted in 1982, it is mainly graduates from Grammar Schools who tend to dissolve their trainee contracts. So the numbers of dropouts in the Dual System might have risen because the students entering it have a higher formal school education. But again, this can only be a partial reason because this group represents a relatively small number (15% in 1999) in relation to all trainees in the Dual System.

A further option to explain the rising dropout rate is a change in student value systems and attitudes to work. Since training for a certain occupation does not guarantee a lifelong position in a company anymore, and staying with one company is no longer necessarily regarded as a positive sign, students do not accept a vocation and its regulations as a given order that needs to be rigidly followed. Rather, they see a vocation as a discretionary goal that is chosen by them, and leaving one track in favour of another is just part of a personal search process for the right job (Fischer, 2002, p. 17).

Prevention and Reduction of Dropout Numbers in Germany

The educational report in 2008 (Autorengruppe Bildungsberichterstattung, 2008) states that in the years to come, a meaningful reduction in the number of students who drop out of school without any certificate is a core challenge for the quality of the German educational system. Measures that help to reduce this number are seen as an urgent matter also by the ministries of the federal states, but such acknowledgement has not yet been followed by research initiatives. As Stamm (2006) points out, there are no national programs for dropouts, and theoretical discussion is only in its early phase. However, some first conceptual frameworks for action are being developed and implemented at different provider levels (school/training) and at different policy levels (individual/organisational/systemic).

Reduction of School Dropouts

Many programs and projects have been initiated in Germany in order to prevent school dropout. They mainly focus on individual support, increased school quality, improved teacher skills and counselling services at schools, and the development and implementation of educational standards. The choice and implementation of programs varies according to the specific needs and priorities of the federal states.

The integration of the educationally disadvantaged through educational counselling, learning centres and new learning cultures has set a major goal involving the expansion of continuing education through such programs as 'Learning Regions', creating networks and synergies between different institutions and agencies, with finance from the European Union and German Ministry for Education and Research (Tippelt et al., 2008).

Reduction of Training Dropouts

To reduce the rate of training dropout in Germany requires addressing issues in each of the three systems involved: (1) the Dual System, (2) the vocational schooling system, and (3) the vocational transition system.

Since the reasons for dropout are multifaceted, preventative policies focus on a variety of aspects, for example, strengthening the Dual System; promoting better cooperation between the educational system and the labour market; providing module-based curricula; enhancing the quality of instructors; intensifying access tests, educational counselling and matching services; as well as concentrating on problem-based, project-oriented teaching and learning methods.

Employers and training companies focus on preventive measures that create a positive learning and working culture that supports the trainees' motivation and their openness to new learning experiences. A culture of trust that encourages but also challenges young adults can help to reduce the risk of dropout. Moreover, additional qualifications and coaching or mentoring offered to the trainees, further education for the companies' vocational trainers, and a close collaboration with the vocational school system are useful in reducing dropout (Dobischat & Düsseldorff, 2009, p. 383f).

Alternative Pathways

School graduation and a leaving certificate are the minimum requirements for a successful transition into the training system and employment market. But as shown in Fig. 7.1, the proportion of young adults who leave school without a minimum certificate is, on average, about 8%. Though the assumption that successful school graduation is an important requirement in Germany for integrating young adults into the labour market is widely shared, the effects of not successfully graduating are rarely researched. Gaupp et al. (2008) summarise the results of the most relevant studies done in Germany in this field (Braun et al., 2009; Solga, 2004, 2005; Prein, 2006; Lex, 1997; Dietz et al., 1997) as follows:

1. Young adults without Secondary General graduation have lower options to immediately make the transition into the vocational system.
2. They rarely take the option of going back to school, though this would enhance their chances of finding a position in the vocational system.
3. They are often dependent on support programs and measures.
4. They have a high risk of being 'decoupled' from the regular vocational training system by attending a series of supportive measures and phases of unemployment.

The results also show that a segment of these young adults still find training positions and other vocational education opportunities. How this kind of resilience is gained or how it works is not yet sufficiently researched, but should be a subject of future research.

Aside from entering the labour market or taking up vocational education opportunities, there are also alternative pathways for students in Germany to gain a school certificate. The programs that are highest in numbers are firstly the option to attend special courses at Adult Education Centres (*Volkshochschulen*) in order to complete the Secondary General certificate. Secondly, there are programs called *Praxisklassen* for young students at Secondary General Schools who have exceptional learning and achievement problems. This dropout prevention model focuses on special support in order to contribute to the student's positive learning and working attitudes. In close cooperation with companies, youth welfare services and vocational counselling institutes, internships are organised so that a smooth transition into working life is achieved. As part of these reform initiatives, those involved in vocational training, social work and school psychology are working together intensively to build a network of organisations to address the dropout situation (Tippelt et al., 2008).

Policies on Three Different Levels Aiming at Prevention of Dropout

Germany's education policies can be summarised as being implemented on three different levels: micro (individual), meso (organisational) and macro (system). All countries have their own distinctive approaches to the issue of preventing dropout. In Germany, policies to address the problem can be seen within this framework (see also Krekel & Ulrich, 2009):

Individual strategies focus on individual factors, such as providing potential dropouts with developmental support strategies. There are a multitude of different smaller and larger programs that are directed at the most vulnerable young adults, and these vary according to the particular conditions in each federal state. An overall view as to what these programs aim at, or should focus on in the future, is given below:

- To enable students to better understand their own achievement and learning situation, they should be given continuous feedback on school and learning performance (not only grades). This also helps them to take responsibility for their own learning biography and options in life.
- To facilitate successful implementation of the above, teacher education must be intensified so that teachers are skilled at dealing with the challenges at hand.
- Further professional development for teachers, as well as training for other educators, is needed here.

Organisational strategies take into account the responsibilities of schools, training organisations and relevant personnel. Some key principles are given below:

- In school and training environments, over-straining and under-challenging of students has to be avoided, and the didactics as well as the learning culture in schools need to be modified.

- Pedagogical approaches in schools are often generalised and groups of students are targeted rather than individuals. To individualise the pedagogical approach is thus a core strategy to better identify students at risk of dropping out, and to help to prevent it.
- In line with this argument is the challenge of developing educational options and support programs for weak learners who will most likely have low school achievement, and who are thus a group at risk of dropout.
- In order to provide this support, individualisation, etc., vocational counselling, school psychology and social work in schools need to be integrated systematically.
- Since social cohesion at school encourages students to remain at school, participation in extra-curricula activities (sport, cultural activities, youth welfare service, youth social work) should be fostered.

Systemic strategies concentrate on institutional factors, such as change in school learning and teaching culture, and take into account historical as well as regional and political conditions. Here, reduction of the discrepancy between the number of available and required trainee positions, as well as the qualitative differences between them, is at the centre of attention (Krekel & Urlich, 2009). Key approaches in this area are given below:

- Curricular educational standards need to be revised and a multi-stakeholder approach needs to be applied, so that the stakeholders' interests are included and transitional phases are easier for the individual students.
- The system needs to be more permeable or seamless, to allow for different educational alternatives even if one pathway has been chosen at a certain time during the educational biography of a person. This way, more options to 'correct' or adjust school, vocational and academic careers can be created, as well as second chances for dropouts.

While giving a perspective on future developments, Krekel & Ulrich (2009) report on reverse tendencies: the critical economic situation that will negatively influence the number of offered trainee positions and demographic developments that will reduce the number of trainees in the medium term.

In Germany, there is a pressing need for a positive image of a new learning culture, which is supportive and sensitive to the needs of youngsters who require extra help and support to succeed.

References

Autorengruppe Bildungsberichterstattung im Auftrag der Ständigen Konferenz der Kultusminister der Länder in der Bundesrepublik Deutschland und des Bundesministeriums für Bildung und Forschung (Eds.). (2008). Bildung in Deutschland 2008. *Ein indikatorengestützter Bericht mit einer Analyse zu Übergängen im Anschluss an den Sekundarbereich I.* Bielefeld: Bertelsmann.

Braun, F., Reißig, B., & Skrobanek, J. (2009). Jugendarbeitslosigkeit und Benachteiligtenförderung. In R. Tippelt & B. Schmidt (Eds.), *Handbuch Bildungsforschung. 2* (pp. 953–966). Aufl., Wiesbaden: VS Verlag.

Ditton, H. (2007). Schulquaität – Modelle zwischen Konstruktion, empirischen Befunden und Implementierung. In J. Buer & C. von Wagner (Eds.), *Qualität von Schule* (pp. 83–92). Frankfurt am Main: Lang.

Dietz, G., Matt, E., Schumann, K., & Seus, L. (1997). *"Lehre tut viel…"– Berufsbildung, Lebensplanung und Delinquenz bei Arbeiterjugendlichen.* Münster: Votum.

Dobischat, R., & Düsseldorff, K. (2009). Berufsbildung und Berufsbildungsforschung. In R. Tippelt & B. Schmidt (Eds.), *Handbuch Bildungsforschung. 2* (pp. 383–404). Aufl., Wiesbaden: VS Verlag.

Fischer, A. (2002). Erfahrungen der vom Ausbildungsabbruch betroffenen Personengruppen. In S. Bohlinger & K. Jenewein (Eds.), *Ausbildungsabbrecher – Verlierer der Wissensgesellschaft? Konzepte, Risiken und Chancen aktueller Handlungsansätze aus der Berufsbildungsforschung und –praxis* (pp. 17–26). Bielefeld: Bertelsmann.

Friebel, H. (1999). *Bildungsbeteiligung: Chancen und Risiken. Eine Längsschnitt-Studie über Bildungs- und Weiterbildungskarrieren in der Moderne.* Opladen: Leske & Budrich.

Gaupp, N., Lex, T., & Reißig, B. (2008). Ohne Schulabschluss in die Berufsausbildung: Ergebnisse einer Längsschnittuntersuchung. *Zeitschrift für Erziehungswissenschaften, 11*(3), 388–405.

Hillmert, S., & Mayer, K. (Eds.). (2004). *Geboren 1964 und 1971. Neuere Untersuchungen zu den Ausbildungs- und Berufschancen in Westdeutschland.* Wiesbaden: VS Verlag.

Konsortium Bildungsberichterstattung im Auftrag der Ständigen Konferenz der Kultusminister der Länder in der Bundesrepublik Deutschland und des Bundesministeriums für Bildung und Forschung (Eds.). (2006). *Bildung in Deutschland. Ein indikatorengestützter Bericht mit einer Analyse zu Bildung und Migration.* Bielefeld: Bertelsmann.

Krekel, E., & Ulrich, J. (2009). *Jugendliche ohne Berufsabschluss. Handlungsempfehlungen für die berufliche Bildung.* Berlin.

Lex, T. (1997). *Berufswege Jugendlicher zwischen Integration und Ausgrenzung.* München: Verlag.

Prein, G. (2006). Schulerfahrungen und Berufsverläufe benachteiligter Jugendlichen. In H. Fördster, R. Kuhnke & J. Skrobanek (Eds.), *Am Individuum ansetzen. Strategien und Effekte der beruflichen Förderung von benachteiligten Jugendlichen* (pp. 27–61). München: DJI Verlag.

Max-Planck-Institut für Bildungsforschung (Ed.). (1995). *Bildungsverläufe und psychosoziale Entwicklung im Jugendalter (BIJU). Zwischenbericht für die Schulen.* Berlin: MPIB.

PISA-Konsortium Deutschland (Ed.). (2004). *PISA 2003. Der Bildungsstand der Jugendlichen in Deutschland – Ergebnisse des zweiten internationalen Vergleichs.* Münster: Waxmann.

Reich, J., Edelmann, D., & Tippelt, R. (2008). Education and training of 15–20 years-olds in Germany. *Formazione & Insegnamento, 1/2*, 69–97.

Seidel, T. (2008). Stichwort: Schuleffektivitätskriterien in der internationalen empirischen Forschung. *Zeitschrift für Erziehungswissenschaften, 11*(3), 348–367.

Solga, H. (2004). Ausgrenzungsgefahren trotz Integration – die Übergangsbiographien von Jugendlichen ohne Schulabschluss. In S. Hillmert & K. Mayaer (Eds.), *Geboren 1964 und 1971. Neuere Untersuchungen zu den Ausbildungs- und Berufschancen in Westdeutschland* (pp. 39–64). Wiesbaden: VS Verlag.

Solga, H. (2005). *Ohne Abschluss in die Bildungsgesellschaft.* Opladen: Verlag Barbara Budrich.

Stamm, M. (2006). Schulabbrecher oder: Wer bricht denn hier was ab? *Unsere Jugend,* 7+8, 323–332.

Tippelt, R., & van Cleve, B. (1995). *Verfehlte Bildung? Bildungsexpansion und Qualifikationsbedarf.* Darmstadt: Wissenschaftliche Buchgesellschaft.

Tippelt, R., Reupold, A., Strobel, A., & Kuwan, H. (2008). *Lernende Regionen – Netzwerke gestalten*. Bielefeld: Bertelsmann.

Weiss, R. (2002). Ausbildungsabbruch – Eine Herausforderung für die betriebliche Berufsausbildung. In S. Bohlinger & K. Jenewein (Eds.), *Ausbildungsabbrecher – Verlierer der Wissensgesellschaft? Konzepte, Risiken und Chancen aktueller Handlungsansätze aus der Berufsbildungsforschung und –praxis* (pp. 5–16). Bielefeld: Bertelsmann.

Chapter 8
School Dropout in Secondary Education: The Case of Poland

Piotr Mikiewicz

Introduction

It is generally assumed that school dropout is not much of a problem in Poland. According to Eurostat (2008), the rate of early school leaving is only 5.5%, which means that only a small proportion of young people aged 18–24 have not obtained an upper secondary qualification. Rapid and wide expansion of education at the secondary and tertiary levels suggests that the quality of Polish education is high and so too is its effectiveness. This chapter presents a contrary point of view. The author will try to show the impact of educational change in contemporary Polish education, particularly in terms of social inequalities. The processes of change have led to an illusion of democratic and effective schooling but, as will be argued, the mechanical involvement of larger and larger numbers of students in education is not sufficient to overcome social inequalities or to open up opportunities to all. As will be shown, dropout (or potential dropout) is not as low as might be expected and differs according to the type of secondary education.

The first part of this chapter presents a general overview of changes in the contemporary education system in Poland and its general structure. The second part presents estimates of dropout rates in secondary schooling. Finally, some institutional strategies to assist students at risk of dropping out are discussed.

Changes in Poland's Contemporary Educational System

In Poland, one can observe the same processes of educational expansion as in all industrialised countries, however, these processes started much later than in the West. As was the case with industrialisation, educational expansion started in Poland after World War II. After a period spent dealing with the challenge of

P. Mikiewicz (✉)
International Institute for the Study of Culture and Education,
University of Lower Silesia, Poland

S. Lamb et al. (Eds.), *School Dropout and Completion: International Comparative Studies in Theory and Policy*, DOI 10.1007/978-90-481-9763-7_9,
© Springer Science+Business Media B.V. 2011

illiteracy, the number of years of schooling rose and the proportion of young people in secondary and tertiary education expanded. In the school year 1960–61, 65% of young people aged 15–18 studied in secondary schools, in the school year 1970–71 the figure had risen to 74%, in 1979–80 it reached 81% and by 1986–87 it was 84%. Participation in tertiary education lagged behind: in the school year 1980–81 the gross participation rate at the tertiary level (age 19–24, not compulsory) was 11.5% and 10 years later it was not much higher – 12.9% (Statistical Yearbook of Poland, 1970, 1980, 1991).

Until the collapse of the socialist regime in 1989, the Polish education system was mainly concerned with training a low qualifications workforce. Hence, until 1989, basic vocational education was the major element of secondary education. In that year, there were 1,177 general upper secondary schools (*lyceums*) in Poland, which recruited 21% of the graduates from primary schools, and 3,404 basic vocational schools (BVS) attended by 50% of all 15-year-olds (Statistical Yearbook of Poland, 1991). The education system was of course associated with an economic model based on heavy industry and the political circumstances of the former socialist regime, which emphasised the labour force as 'the leading class of the nation'.

In the social history of Poland, 1989 was without a doubt a ground-breaking year. The term 'social transformation' is used as a description of the processes that took place in Poland after 1989, to explain the dynamics of change observed in the country. Next to the spheres of politics and the economy, the field of education is the one in which changes are most visible. As with all other spheres of social life, education was involved in change from the time of the social transformation. The educational system, freed from political restrictions and allowed to operate under a free market economy has, over the past 20 years, been transformed.

It is hard to identify any individual factor responsible for changes in the education system. Nevertheless, one of the most prominent is the economy (Niezgoda, 1993). The change from 'central planning' to a 'free market system' forced the (r)evolution of the structure of the economy. From the beginning of the 1990s, one can observe a slow but evident shift from mass production in industry to a more service-oriented market (typical of the more highly developed countries of Western Europe). This change of logic in the economy and the implementation of new technologies caused the emergence of a previously unknown phenomenon – mass unemployment. This unemployment was structural in character, mainly affecting individuals with insufficient skills for the new market. The first wave of unemployment affected low-skilled workers, who had obtained only basic vocational education. Highly qualified people, with high educational achievement, tended to find jobs in the new occupational structure. It was a clear signal to society that education matters. Young Poles who entered the school system in the 1990s heard the message clearly. Through their 'push on education', they produced a change in the structure and functions of the school system. As Kwieciński (2002, p. 10) pointed out, 'people in new governmental and economical circumstances through their decisions produced the structural changes in secondary education'.

As an effect of that 'push' dynamic, it is possible to observe changes in the structure of secondary education (without formal change to the system, however).

In the school year 1994–95, only 36% of primary school graduates entered basic vocational schools. By contrast, 31% entered general education schools (GES), providing students with general education and leading directly to higher education – this was 10% more than 5 years earlier. In the school year 1999–2000, there were 2,156 general education schools (*lyceums*), and the number of basic vocational schools decreased to 2,408. In the same year, 38% of 15-year-olds started their education in lyceums, while 26% started in basic vocational schools (Education in the school year 2001/2002; Statistical Yearbook of Poland, 2000).

In 1999, the educational reform act emphasised general academic education, and vocational training was marginalised even more. Two years later, in the school year 2001–02, the number of students attending basic vocational school decreased to 2,372 and covered only 22% of primary education graduates. After several years of implementation of the reform, basic vocational schools now serve only 16% of graduates.

The dynamics of change at the tertiary education level have been equally deep. In the time of the socialist regime in Poland, expansion of this sector was restricted. In 1960, 50 higher education institutions had been established. By the school year 1989–90, this had increased to 98. After 1990, the possibility of private education emerged, which caused an avalanche of growth of new higher education institutions. In 1991, there were 112 higher education institutions in Poland, in the school year 1995–96 there were 179 and by 2000 this had risen to 283. After 2000, growth was even stronger, with an increase of almost 30 such institutions each year. In the school year 2000–01, there were 310, in the next year 344 and now there are 455 institutions (public and private) serving the rapidly growing number of students. In the 1990s, the number of students at tertiary level grew by a factor of almost four. In 1989, there were 374,200 tertiary students, and in 1999, this had risen to 1,425,800. Now in Poland, higher education institutions offer their services to 1,937,400 students (Wincławski, 2003; Wasielewski, 2003; Concise Statistical Yearbook of Poland, 2008).

The Contemporary Educational System in Poland

In 1999, the reform of the education system was implemented. This has resulted in deep structural and curricular change, aimed at linking education more closely with changes in the market and in general social life. New schools should teach how to flexibly adapt to a changing world. The best tool to achieve this is (it is argued) general and academic education. But vocational education has been marginalised. Let us have a closer look at the new educational structure.

Children can enter the educational system at the age of 3 by attendance at nursery schools, which serve children aged 3–5 or 3–6. At 6 years of age, children attend compulsory pre-school preparatory classes: so-called 'Class 0'. Education in nursery schools is usually fee-paying. Currently only 50% of children aged 3–5 are enrolled in this level of education.

Regular education starts at the age of 7, when children are enrolled in primary schools. Primary schooling lasts for 6 years and is divided into two phases. First, Grades 1–3 (ages 7–9) comprise the so-called early-school education. After this preparatory time, equipped with basic competences, children start education in the regular class-lesson system, Grades 4–6 (ages 10–12). Education in primary school ends with an external examination of the pupils' skills. This examination has no selective function and is designed to measure the level of skills, which constitute the starting point of work for teachers at the next stage of education in the *gymnasium*.

After primary education, children are enrolled in lower secondary school, which is still compulsory: the *gymnasium*. Education here lasts for 3 years, Grades 7–9 (ages 12–15). The aim of the *gymnasium* is to prepare students for education at the upper secondary level. *Gymnasium* concludes with another external exam assessing levels of achievement. The external exam after *gymnasium* is important because the score obtained is the basis for enrolment in one of the tracks and different types of schools in upper secondary education. Secondary schools establish cut-off scores, and based on these scores, selection of pupils to a given type of secondary school takes place. Following the reform of 1999, education at the upper secondary level is offered in the following educational pathways (provided in separate schools):

General upper secondary schools (GES): 3-year schools providing general education for those preparing to take up university studies. Education at these schools concludes with an externally assessed examination – the *Matura* ('A level' examination).

Specialised upper secondary schools (SSS): 3-year schools providing specialist professional education, preparing students to take up university studies, but also allowing students to obtain professional qualifications. Students in specialised upper secondary schools can choose from 15 specialisations: chemical tests of the environment, business and administration, electronics, electrotechnology, fashion design, shaping the environment, forestry and wood technology, mechanical techniques of production, mechatronics, agricultural and food processing, art and usable metal craft, social, transport and dispatching, services and economics, and information management. Over half the students in specialised secondary schools choose two specialisations: business and administration and information management. Education in specialised secondary schools concludes with an externally assessed examination – the *Matura* ('A level' examination).

Technical schools (TS): 4-year secondary schools providing the possibility of sitting the *Matura* and going to university, but also allowing students to obtain a vocational technician diploma in a narrow range of technical professions. Students in technical secondary schools and complementary technical secondary schools can choose, among others, from professions that belong to the following groups: technicians, mid-level personnel in the fields of biological sciences and health safety, salaried personnel in the remaining specialisations, money management, customer service and others (including personal services and security). Education in technical schools concludes with externally assessed examinations – the *Matura* ('A level' examination) and an examination of vocational competencies.

Basic vocational schools (BVS): 2- or 3-year vocational schools, narrow-range, aimed at delivering concrete vocational competencies, they provide the possibility of further education in *complementary general* or *technical upper secondary schools*, which then enable students to continue learning at universities. Basic vocational schools provide education for occupations that belong to the following groups: farmers, miners and builders; metal processing workers and mechanics (the most popular among men and women); makers of haberdashery, printing workers and related; other industrial workers and craftsmen; operators and fitters of mining and processing machines; drivers and vehicle operators; and a few other occupations such as personal services and security workers, models, shop assistants and demonstrators.

In general, as shown above, vocational secondary education contains three tracks: (1) specialised secondary schools, (2) technical schools and (3) basic vocational schools, although only the latter two provide students with a vocational certificate. Education in specialised secondary schools concludes with the same credentials as in general upper secondary schools: the school leaving certificate and the *Matura* diploma. Students in technical schools can additionally gain a vocational diploma. Graduates from these three tracks (specialised secondary schools, general education schools and technical schools) have open access to education at tertiary level. By contrast, graduates from basic vocational schools gain a school leaving certificate and a vocational diploma, which do not give access to tertiary education.

At present only basic vocational schools provide a direct vocational track. Vocational certificates (and competencies) earned in technical schools have little relevance in the labour market. These schools are more an academic track (leading to tertiary education) for lower achievers in the *gymnasium*.

Vocational training in basic vocational schools can be provided in two ways. The first way is school-based vocational training, at workshops located in school. The second mode is similar to the German dual model, as students can have the status of a young worker and have vocational training in the workplace. This means that the students spend part of the week (2 days) at school, while the rest is devoted to work. This kind of vocational training is based on a bilateral agreement between student and employer. Students receive a salary no less than 4% of the average salary in the country in the first year of schooling, 5% in the second and 6% in the third year. According to official data, in the school year 2007–08 almost half (47.6%) of basic vocational school students took part in the second mode of vocational training.

The biggest segment of post-lower secondary schooling in Poland is, at present, general upper secondary school, with 44% of lower secondary graduates; followed by technical upper secondary school (33.4%), basic vocational school (14.8%) and specialised secondary school (6.8%).[1] Specialised secondary schools are not very popular, despite the fact that their aim is to provide a middle way between technical

---

[1] Source: Concise Statistical Yearbook of Poland, 2008

secondary school and traditional secondary school. It is clear that young people prefer an educational pathway leading to a *Matura* examination and opening the door to universities.

Girls more often than boys choose general upper secondary schools, but more rarely technical upper secondary schools and basic vocational schools. However, there has been an increase in the number of boys in upper secondary schools (from 19.1% in 1995–96 to 39% in 2005–06). Therefore, while in the school year 1995–96 there were 213 females for every 100 males in general upper secondary school, in the school year 2005–06 there were 151 females for every 100 males. According to official statistics for the school year 2007–08, the gender division in upper secondary education was as follows:

- Basic vocational school: 29% female and 71% male
- General upper secondary school: 61% female and 39% male
- Specialised secondary school: 59.9% female and 40.1% male
- Technical upper secondary school: 38.9% female and 61.1% male[2]

Selection Processes in Secondary Schooling

The changes described above have led to the situation in which 85% of graduates of compulsory education enter educational pathways leading to *Matura* and are (at least potentially) able to start education at the tertiary level. Academically oriented secondary education is dominant and it is possible to see a change in the role of education within society. In older cohorts, vocational education is the most common background, but the younger cohorts are more and more academically educated. What is relevant is that changes in the distribution of educational enrolments in secondary education were pushed by the aspirations of young people, and free-market education has responded to this need. Secondary education seems to be universal and the obvious minimum level of education, replacing primary education, which was the threshold in the past.

In general, in Poland today, there is much more emphasis on academically oriented education than vocational schooling. This is a change in perception, since at the beginning of the 1990s while general education and university entrance were perceived as something better and an asset, vocational education was not treated as something worse or worthless. It was simply enough to obtain a basic vocational education to get a good job. It was possible to observe positive selection into the best educational pathways, that is, the track *primary school*, *lyceum*, and *university*, which used to be called the 'royal path of education' leading to the best occupational and social positions (Kozakiewicz, 1973). Until the beginning of the 1990s, the main mechanism of selection was inclusion of the best skilled pupils into general education secondary schools. Much research showed that this

[2] Source: Concise Statistical Yearbook of Poland, 2008

educational pathway involved mainly children from families of higher socioeconomic status (Kwieciński, 1995). This mechanism changed in the mid-1990s, when the inclusion of the best turned into *exclusion* of the *worst* (educationally) into basic vocational schools. Currently, students of basic vocational schools are excluded from the academic or main education pathway in what could be described as the beginning of a process of social exclusion – because children identified as not being fit for general education school are disproportionately from low socioeconomic status backgrounds (Kwieciński, 1995). This is a very homogenous group, both with respect to their school competence and social background (Kwieciński, 2002; Domalewski & Mikiewicz, 2004).

Selection and enrolment into different educational strands in upper secondary schooling in Poland are based on two forms of pupil evaluation: external examination after lower secondary school (*gymnasium*), and grades obtained during the *gymnasium* years. Each school at the secondary level estimates an entry score. This leads to educational differentiation within secondary education based on a dual process. First, particular tracks (perceived differently in terms of prestige, with general education considered by the public as superior to vocational) have different degrees of openness to students based on their educational achievements at the lower secondary level. Specialised secondary schools and technical schools are attended by young people of average and below average educational competence according to their performance in the external examination after *gymnasium*. Basic vocational schools attract students with the lowest school achievement. General education schools are more differentiated, but as can be clearly seen, they attract the strongest lower secondary school graduates (Domalewski & Mikiewicz, 2004).

The second level of differentiation within secondary schooling is that between particular schools, especially within the general education school track. As it is the largest segment of upper secondary education, it is not surprising that general education schools vary greatly from each other. Some of them are attended by young people with outstanding educational achievements (in terms of grades and scores achieved in the external examination), others by pupils with above average achievements; and there are also schools that group together pupils with average and below average competence, so in fact these schools do not differ in this respect from technical and specialised secondary schools. It has turned out that a rise in the number of general education school pupils has resulted in lowering the threshold for access to this type of education. Practically everybody who has achieved average school results has the opportunity to enter general education school. But this does not mean that the competence of pupils attending different schools is equivalent. According to data gathered in research from 2003 (Domalewski & Mikiewicz, 2004), it was possible to discern five categories of secondary schools, based on the achievement profile of students:

Schools of category A grouping together young people with outstanding achievements (lyceums)

Schools of category B grouping together young people with above average achievements (lyceums)

Schools of category C grouping together young people with average achievements (basic vocational, specialised secondary schools and also lyceums)

Schools of category D grouping together young people with below average achievements (basic vocational, specialised secondary schools and also lyceums)

Schools of category E grouping together young people with the lowest achievements (basic vocational schools)

As recently as the mid-1990s, pupils with average and below average school achievement, who now attend general secondary schools, would not have had a chance of entering an academic track owing to their lower level academic skills. The educational potential of these young people is much lower compared to the potential of their peers attending those general secondary schools which group together pupils with above average and outstanding school achievements. This means that it is impossible to implement curricula at a similar level in all general education schools, despite the fact that the schools are formally obliged to follow the same program of education. The equalisation of opportunities provided by placing a pupil in a school that formally provides the same education as a traditional general education school, but where all youngsters attending the school are below average in their assessed academic skills, can be seen as a fiction and a sort of deception.

Secondary schools differ not only in regard to the school competence of their pupils, but also in regard to their social background (socioeconomic status), as shown in Table 8.1. This, of course, is rooted in the correlation between school attainment and the status of the family of origin (Domalewski & Mikiewicz, 2004). Therefore, different school environments which are formed as a result of different levels of their pupils' competence, also constitute separate social environments.

Table 8.1 Social composition of particular types and categories of school (%)

Social status	School profile					
	GES	SSS	TS	BVS	Total	
Low	8.7	16.3	22.0	38.2	15.8	
Lower middle	15.0	21.3	28.2	30.9	20.5	
Middle	47.0	51.5	43.2	28.3	44.3	
Higher middle	14.0	8.4	4.7	2.1	9.9	
High	15.3	2.5	1.9	0.5	9.4	
Total	100.0	100.0	100.0	100.0	100.0	
Social status	School category					
	Cat. A	Cat. B	Cat. C	Cat. D	Cat. E	Total
Low	1.4	6.5	14.7	22.4	38.2	15.8
Lower middle	7.2	13.3	22.1	26.5	30.9	20.5
Middle	33.7	49.0	51.2	44.0	28.3	44.3
Higher middle	23.1	16.4	7.2	5.1	2.2	9.9
High	34.6	14.7	4.7	1.9	0.5	9.4
Total	100.0	100.0	100.0	100.0	100.0	100.0

Source: Domalewski & Mikiewicz (2004).

Consequently, school selection continues to be social in character – it channels young people with different backgrounds into separate educational paths. Despite the fact that young people from families with lower social status now have easier access to schools qualifying for university entry, most of them attend technical schools, specialised secondary schools and those general education schools that group together pupils representing average and below average school competence (school categories C and D).

In brief, the Polish secondary education structure is divided into three social worlds: (1) the world of basic vocational schools, dominated by young people from families of low social positions; (2) the world of schools qualifying graduates for university entry (lyceums, specialised secondary schools, technical schools), which are more varied socially and are dominated by pupils from families of medium social status, with a considerably strong presence of young people from low-status families; and (3) the world of schools forming socially elitist environments, dominated by pupils from high-status families.

Students' Educational Aspirations

Coming back to the issue of school dropout in secondary education, a focus on the educational aspirations of young people would be helpful in better understanding the issue. Research done in 2003 provides an interesting overview. In that research, 16-year-olds in different schools were asked about their educational aspirations (see Domalewski & Mikiewicz, 2004; also Table 8.2). Although it is still quite early in terms of their schooling, educational aspirations of 16-year-olds can be treated as a predictor of their future decisions. More importantly, in the context of school dropout, educational aspirations can explain different levels of commitment to school. Students planning long educational pathways will probably be more committed.

Table 8.2 shows that there are differences in the educational aspirations between students from different types of secondary schools – for example, general education school students have aspirations that are different from the aspirations of students from other school types, especially those from basic vocational school. Also, importantly, most of the students in the first year of basic vocational school planned for a higher level of education than they were actually obtaining, with most of them wanting to continue education in complementary general education schools or technical schools. Still, they had much lower aspirations than their peers from the general education schools, most of whom wanted to obtain at least a masters degree. It can be clearly observed that different types of schools gather pupils with different levels of aspirations. General education schools are places for ambitious pupils, basic vocational schools are for those with lower level aspirations, whilst technical schools and specialised secondary schools are places in the structure where young people aspire to middle-level educational positions. These groupings are an effect of selection processes at the entrance to secondary school: as stated previously, institutions select candidates according to their achievements at the *gymnasium* level.

Table 8.2 Educational aspirations according to school type and category

Educational aspirations	Type and category of school									
	GES Cat. A	GES Cat. B	GES Cat. C	SSS Cat. C	TS Cat. C	GES Cat. D	SSS Cat. D	TS Cat. D	BVS	Total
Basic vocational	–	–	–	–	–	–	–	–	7.2	0.8
Upper secondary	0.5	1.8	10.4	31.4	23.7	20.7	39.7	53.3	75.8	24.5
Bachelors degree	2.7	7.8	14.3	14.0	22.8	14.9	19.2	19.6	8.0	12.8
Masters degree	56.2	62.0	59.4	30.6	41.8	50.8	24.7	19.4	4.1	43.2
Masters degree plus (doctoral degree and others)	40.6	28.4	15.9	24.0	11.7	13.6	16.4	7.7	4.8	18.7
Total	100.0	100.0	100.0	100.0	100.0	100.0	100.0	100.0	100.0	100.0

Source: Domalewski & Mikiewicz (2004).

Educational aspirations are clearly linked to the level of students' skills. In addition, schools enrolling better students (in terms of educational achievements) deal with much more committed individuals.

But the situation is even more complicated. As described above, it is possible to observe a division not only by the different types of schools, but also by different categories of schools within the same type. In lyceums of category D (gathering pupils with relatively low level school competencies), over 20% of students planned to obtain only a secondary education, whilst 50% planned to get a masters degree in the future. At the same time, students in schools of category A were much more ambitious – 56% planned to get a masters degree, and almost the same proportion were ready to strive for something more (such as a doctoral degree). This is the case for students aged 16! If education is treated as a road to adulthood and a social position in the future, it is evident that from quite early on, young people are aware of the pathways to which they are predestined.

(Potential) School Dropout in Upper Secondary Education

The issue of school dropout is associated with the processes of selection within education. The structure of the educational system (organisationally and socially) as presented above is the background to these processes. Selection in the Polish educational system is both internal and external in character. Generally speaking, there are two major forms of selection:

1. *End-of-school selection*, which involves the mechanisms of qualification and enrolment into separate tracks and certain schools, made on the basis of two elements: the outcomes of the external examination after *gymnasium*, and grades achieved at the end of lower secondary school
2. *Within-school selection* (the 'educational sieve'), whereby the school evaluates the pupil and decides his/her fate – promotion or not at the end of each year of study with selection occurring in three ways: promotion to the next stage, grade repeating or early school leaving (dropout).

As there is no official body in Poland that gathers information about leaving school before the expected time, acquiring accurate estimates of the dropout rate poses major difficulty. It is necessary to use approximate indicators dealing with information of different sorts. School participation can be measured as the proportion of school students in an age cohort compared with the population of that age cohort (*school participation rate*). In the Polish context, this would be the proportion of school students aged 16–18 compared with the population of 16- to 18-year-olds, which was 90.3% in the school year 2006–07, and 89.3% in the year 2007–08 (Education in the school year 2006/2007, 2007/2008). School dropout is the proportion of the age group that is not in school. This means that about 10% of those aged 16–18 are out of school, equating to about 167,000 people.

That indicator refers to how many young people are not in the education system, but another definition of dropouts estimates the number who started their education in a school and leave before the end of the planned or regular period of schooling (Kwieciński, 1972; Fatyga et al., 2001). In the Polish literature, the following types of school dropouts have been identified:

- **Natural school dropouts:** those who fall victim to natural causes such as death, accidents, suicide, etc.
- **Apparent school dropouts:** students who move to another city, country or type of school
- **Actual school dropouts:** students who enter the system and do not finish school
- **Potential school dropouts:** pupils who are in the system, but are more or less likely to exit school before the planned time (e.g., due to repetition and other forms of selection within the system) (Fatyga et al., 2001; Putkiewicz & Zahorska, 2001)

Calculation of the dropout rate is very complicated, if possible at all. Even if there was access to data about students who leave particular schools, it is still not known if they are in the group of apparent school dropouts who move to another school or city. The best (i.e., least problematic) ways of measuring the dropout rate could be through the *'non-graduation in time' rate* – the proportion of non-graduated students in the 'normal period', and the *repetition rate* – the proportion of non-promoted students (i.e., the number of students who do not graduate to the next year of schooling).

Both of the above are indicators of potential dropout, as students who do not succeed in education are probably more likely to drop out of the system, although this is not necessarily the case. How do these two indicators look in the Polish secondary education system?

Table 8.3 shows that the overall 'non-graduation in time' rate is about 16.5%, but it differs among tracks. The lowest rate is for general education schools, giving the impression that it is quite 'easy' to finish this sort of education within the expected

Table 8.3 Proportion of potential school dropouts[a]

School type	Class I School year 2003–04	Graduates 2005–06 (and 2006–07 for TS)	Number of students who did not finish education in time	Proportion of non-graduates in time (%)
BVS[3]	102,157	75,675	26,482	**25.9**
GES	252,849	235,987	16,862	**6.7**
SSS	87,275	68,955	18,320	**21.0**
TS	140,631	106,395	34,236	**24.3**
Total	**582,912**	**487,012**	**95,900**	**16.5**

[a] Those students who didn't complete school in the 'normal' period of time
Source: Concise Statistical Yearbook of Poland (2004, 2008).

[3] Without division into 2- and 3-year schools (most BVS are 3-year schools)

time (surprisingly, given that it is officially the most demanding pathway leading directly to further education at the tertiary level, and is the largest part of the struc-ture). Partly, the low rate can be explained by the fact that such schools are attended by relatively 'good' students in terms of their educational performance (although not only the best students, as shown in previous sections). Other tracks are not so 'easy' – one fifth of the specialised secondary schools 'starters' do not finish in time, and for technical schools and basic vocational schools the figure is one quarter. A similar picture is seen when looking at repetition rates for each track (see Table 8.4).

The rates given in each column of Table 8.4 show the proportion of students not promoted at each stage of upper secondary schooling. The non-promotion rate decreases at the higher year-levels in each type of school. General selection (the *sieve effect*) takes place heavily at the beginning and at the end of the first year of schooling. It seems that a high proportion of students fail promotion in the first year of each school type, possibly because they are not as committed to school requirements and expectations – they do not know how to 'play' the school game, adequately recognise the field (in the Bourdieu sense) and follow the rules and regulations. It is also clear that in 3-year basic vocational schools, a high level of non-promotion also takes place at the end of the second year. Again it is possible to observe much lower rates of non-promotion in general education schools than in other tracks.

Table 8.4 Rates of non-promotion, by type of school: Lower Silesia, Poland, 2006–07

Type of upper secondary school	School year				
(a) General education schools	**Year 1**	**Year 2**	**Year 3**		**Total**
Number of students	17,203	16,867	17,050		51,120
Number of students not promoted	678	575	233		1,486
Percentage not promoted (%)	**3.94**	**3.41**	**1.37**		**2.91**
(b) Basic vocational schools – 2 years	**Year 1**	**Year 2**			**Total**
Number of students	2,142	1,801			3,943
Number of students not promoted	296	101			397
Percentage not promoted (%)	**13.82**	**5.61**			**10.07**
(c) Basic vocational schools – 3 years	**Year 1**	**Year 2**	**Year 3**		**Total**
Number of students	3,694	3,086	3,242		10,022
Number of students not promoted	557	346	189		1,092
Percentage not promoted (%)	**15.08**	**11.21**	**5.83**		**10.90**
(d) Specialised secondary schools	**Year 1**	**Year 2**	**Year 3**		**Total**
Number of students	5,699	6,800	6,824		19,323
Number of students not promoted	833	623	207		1,663
Percentage not promoted (%)	**14.62**	**9.16**	**3.03**		**8.61**
(e) Technical schools	**Year 1**	**Year 2**	**Year 3**	**Year 4**	**Total**
Number of students	8,116	6,479	5,775	5,208	25,578
Number of students not promoted	929	520	271	79	1,799
Percentage not promoted (%)	**11.45**	**8.03**	**4.69**	**1.52**	**7.03**

Source: Education in Lower Silesia in the school year 2006/2007.

This picture is not complete, as it is not possible to estimate the graduation rates and non-promotion rates for different school categories according to the educational potential of students gathered there after initial school selection (school categories A–E). As these are separate pathways indicated in field research but not in official structures, there is no chance of obtaining official statistics in that respect. However, if it is remembered that in terms of their students' educational skills and social backgrounds, lyceums of categories C and D are similar to technical schools and specialised secondary schools, it can expected that such schools will also be similar in terms of 'non-graduation in time' and non-promotion rates.

The above analyses allow us to draw a sketch of diversified secondary schooling. It is a world divided in two. The first is the world of general education school (*lyceums*), which enrol students selected for their academic talent based on test scores and academic achievement, students recognised and rewarded for possessing the highest educational aspirations. These student characteristics probably account for the very low 'non-graduation in time' rates and non-promotion or repetition rates recorded by general education schools. The second is the world consisting of technical schools, specialised schools and basic vocational schools: this tends to be the world of students more or less excluded from mainstream secondary education (*lyceums*). Schools in this world are relegated, enrolling students with much lower educational competence and aspirations, a relegation that pools students identified through their weak exam results and poor academic progress as not worthy of a *lyceum* education. Pupils located in this 'school world' can be viewed as students at risk of dropout.

Mechanisms of Assistance for Students at Risk

Although school dropout is not perceived by policy-makers as a major issue for educational policy, there are some institutional mechanisms to assist students at risk. The main ones are special job-training schools, which are school-based preparatory units for the least skilled students. In the school year of 2007–08, this form of education enrolled 7,200 students. Students who are not able to meet secondary school expectations are trained in simple-skilled occupations and are able to enter the labour market.

Youth Work Services (YWS) has a similar role. YWS is a state organisational unit of the public finances sector and is supervised by the Ministry of Labour. It cooperates with units of territorial self-government in educating, training and employing youth. These tasks are performed by 16 regional offices, 10 inter-regional centres of education and approximately 400 organisational units all over the country. YWS concentrates in particular on education and rehabilitation, as well as on providing help to youth at risk of unemployment, socially maladjusted youth, and youth requiring special care and influence.

Mention should also be made of the state education centres that provide psychological and pedagogical counselling services. Their main task is to support the psycho-physical development and effectiveness of the learning of children and youth and to provide psychological, pedagogical and speech-therapy assistance to all needy people. Assistance is available to children and youth at different ages, including youth under 19 who are not studying or working. The institutions support schools in the following areas: overall development of children and youth; learning effectiveness; acquiring and developing social communication skills including negotiating skills for solving conflicts and problems; preventing addictions and other problems affecting children and youth; providing psychological and peda-gogical help to children and youth from at-risk groups; providing therapy for devel-opment disorders and dysfunctions; helping children choose the direction of their education, their profession and how to plan a career; helping parents and teachers in diagnosing and developing the potential and strengths of students; and support-ing the educational functions of schools.

The aim of the counselling services is to support children and youth develop-ment and the effectiveness of learning, as well as providing parents or guardians, teachers and pedagogues with psychological, pedagogical and speech-therapy help. Psychological and pedagogical counselling services are generally accessible. In the school year 2004–05, there were 557 state psychological and pedagogical counsel-ling services operating.

The third institutional device worth noting is Institutions of Professional Training (IPT), a non-government educational organisation that has 24 branches all over Poland, some of which have over a 100-year history. Together they create one of the most widespread, versatile and ubiquitous networks of non-state educational centres in the country. They consist of education centres for youth and adults at the upper secondary level, offering courses, seminars and workshops to improve pro-fessional skills as well as workshops for practical acquisition of specific vocational skills. These IPT centres offer education within the scope of job training, teaching job skills and offering qualifications, training and improvement of already-held qualifications (for more, see Kurantowicz et al., 2008).

This short list indicates that, in Poland, policies to address the issue of dropouts are based on strategies targeting individuals – these strategies include various means to help students at risk. It seems that dropout is not considered to be a very important issue for social policy. This is partly explained by officially low dropout rates, even from secondary education. In this context, early school leaving is viewed as an individual problem and should be solved at the individual or familial level. The state and social policy systems provide some tools to assist in this indi-vidual struggle.

Polish educational policy can be summarised by the motto *keep them at school as long as possible*. However, from another perspective, it can be argued that this small 'educational miracle' (the rapid expansion of secondary and higher education) is just an illusion, the result of lowering the expectation bar on the higher levels of education – for instance by establishing a minimum score of only 30% to pass the *Matura* exam. This conceals problems that could arise if the demands of the system were set higher. Dropout is one such concealed issue.

Conclusions

Despite the rise of educational aspirations in society as a whole, there are 'traditional' social divisions in educational outcomes within each cohort of young people in Poland's current educational system. These divisions start at home, in the family, when young people are equipped with basic competences (*habitus*), and later are enacted in the school world, leading to differential educational achievement. Rapid and deep changes in the post-Soviet country that is contemporary Poland might suggest that the vicious circle of social reproduction through education has been broken. A closer examination shows that this is an illusion.

There are separate tracks of schooling within the structure of secondary education, with the different paths the product of four factors: the type of education, the educational competence of pupils, the social composition of the school and educational aspirations of pupils gathered in a given school. Secondary education is a platform for the 'splitting of the social worlds': particular attitudes towards school are fostered and the differences between schools evident at the start of secondary education become much more pronounced. In the elitist general education schools (schools of category A), a culture of conformity is created and a mode of cooperation between teachers and pupils can be established. At the opposite end of the secondary school structure, in basic vocational schools (and in vocational education as a whole), a culture of resistance makes cooperation harder (sometimes impossible) and the struggle with school work leads to further educational and social marginalisation of pupils channelled into that track (see Mikiewicz, 2005). Dropout is much more likely in the latter educational and social reality.

In the case of Poland, dropout seems relatively unimportant, or less obvious. The rise of educational aspirations and a kind of scholastic culture creates the space for long-term education and the illusion of democratic schooling. Compared to other Western countries, the Polish education system looks more successful and seems to meet European benchmarks and expectations. Much more relevant issues now are the internal differentiation of secondary and tertiary education and the overall consequences of such differentiation. The school selection which occurs at the first selection threshold, marks the beginning of the channelling of pupils' biographies. The result of this channelling appears as early as the moment of selecting the type of university or college education. As mass secondary education is becoming increasingly varied internally, tertiary education is also becoming subject to differentiation.

Considering the nature of young people's educational aspirations, one can expect deep changes in the structure of the nation's education. The young are well aware of the requirements of the contemporary labour market and want to gain qualifications which their parents do not have. This generation will definitely achieve a higher level of formal education than their parents did. Education in the changed school system, adjusted to new economic conditions, has a different character: one of its basic features is the duration of schooling – for young Poles, education certainly will last longer than it did for their parents. Thus, a shift to a higher level of education – to at least secondary level – is clearly evident.

A separate issue is the question of distances between social classes. Looking at the differences in educational aspirations of young people depending on the status of their family of origin, it is apparent that despite relatively high hopes for the future in all social groups, these ambitions have different ceilings for different social groups. The young people from families in which parents have university-level education are relatively more ambitious than those from low-status families. The popularisation of education at the secondary and tertiary levels does not mean that class differences are reduced. Instead, university degrees are devalued and the whole population moves one step upwards in the education hierarchy. Consequently, there is now a situation where a university degree is not a guarantee of employment nor of prestige, yet individuals without such a degree are excluded from the mainstream of social life (Beck, 2003). It can be said that to have a good education is not a 'big deal', but *not* to have one is a disaster. That is why the issue of dropout, or potential dropout, within secondary education has become so important.

References

Beck, U. (2003). *Społeczeństwo ryzyka* [Risk society]. Warsaw: Scholar.
Concise Statistical Yearbook of Poland (2004, 2008). Warsaw: GUS.
Domalewski, J., & Mikiewicz, P. (2004). *Młodzież w zreformowanym systemie szkolnym* [Young people in the reformed educational system]. Toruń – Warsaw: IRWiR PAN.
Education in the school year 2001/2002, Oświata i wychowanie w roku szkolnym 2001/2002. Warsaw: GUS.
Education in the school year 2006/2007, Oświata i wychowanie w roku szkolnym 2006/2007. Warsaw: GUS.
Education in the school year 2007/2008, Oświata i wychowanie w roku szkolnym 2007/2008. Warsaw: GUS.
Eurostat. (2008). *Europe in Figures - Eurostat Yearbook 2008*. Luxembourg: Office for Official Publications of the European Communities. Retrieved from http://epp.eurostat.ec.europa.eu
Fatyga, B., Tyszkiewicz, A., & Zieliński, P. (2001). *Skala i powody wypadania uczniów z systemu edukacji w Polsce* [The scale and reasons for loss of students from the education system in Poland]. Warsaw: ISP.
Kozakiewicz, M. (1973). *Bariery awansu poprzez wykształcenie* [Barriers to advancement through education]. Warsaw: PWN.
Kurantowicz, E., Mikiewicz P., & Nizińska, A. (2008). Education and training in Poland, *Formazione Insegnamento, 1*, 43–68.
Kwieciński, Z. (1972). *Odpad szkolny na wsi*. Warsaw: IRWiR PAN.
Kwieciński, Z. (1995). *Dynamika funkcjonowania szkoły* [The dynamics of the functioning of the school]. Toruń: UMK.
Kwieciński, Z. (2002). *Wykluczanie* [Exclusion]. Toruń: UMK.
Mikiewicz, P. (2005). *Społeczny świat szkół średnich – od trajektorii marginesu do trajektorii elit* [The social world of secondary schools - From the marginal trajectory to the elite trajectory]. Wrocław: DSWE.
Niezgoda, M. (1993). *Oświata i procesy rozwoju społecznego: Przypadek Polski* [Education and processes of social development: The Polish case]. Kraków: UJ.
Putkiewicz E., & Zahorska, M. (2001). *Społeczne nierówności edukacyjne – studium sześciu gmin* [Social inequalities in education – A study of six districts]. Warsaw: ISP.
Statistical Yearbook of Poland (1970, 1980, 1991, 2000). Warsaw: GUS.

Wasielewski, K. (2003). Studia socjologiczne na tel sporów o współczesny model wyższej uczelni. In K. Szafraniec & W. Wincławski (Eds.), *Socjologia w szkołach wyższych w Polsce. Kształcenie Socjologów i nauczanie socjologii po roku 1989* (pp. 181–220). Toruń: UMK.

Wincławski, W. (2003). Studia socjologiczne w polskim szkolnictwie wyższym dawniej i dziś. In K. Szafraniec & W. Wincławski (Eds.), *Socjologia w szkołach wyższych w Polsce. Kształcenie Socjologów i nauczanie socjologii po roku 1989* (pp. 11–36). Toruń: UMK.

Chapter 9
School Dropout and Completion in Switzerland

Elisabetta Pagnossin

Introduction

Today, the Swiss education and training system is in the process of fundamental changes aimed at harmonising and rationalising some essential structural elements at the different educational levels. The complexity of the Swiss education system comes from the historical and cultural characteristics of the country. By way of introduction, a short description of its key features will permit a better understanding of the main tendencies of the current reforms and of the aims pursued at the political level.

At the end of compulsory education, at age 15, the majority (more than 70%) of Swiss young people opt for vocational training. However, progressively, and for many reasons, young people are now less keen to pursue this kind of education immediately after compulsory schooling. There is a tendency for an increasing proportion of young people to spend 1 or 2 years attending a 'transitional program' before going on to post-compulsory schools. Most of those who have attended one of these programs re-enter the official educational system and obtain a diploma of post-compulsory education some years later; only very few do not and therefore leave the school system without a qualification. The integration into the labour market of those without a qualification is highly compromised; therefore, their risk of unemployment and need for social assistance are quite high.

All these elements will be discussed in detail in the different sections of this chapter.

E. Pagnossin (✉)
Institut de Recherche et de Documentation pédagogique, Switzerland

S. Lamb et al. (Eds.), *School Dropout and Completion: International Comparative Studies in Theory and Policy*, DOI 10.1007/978-90-481-9763-7_10,
© Springer Science+Business Media B.V. 2011

The Contextual Framework: The Swiss Education System

The Swiss education system[1] (shown diagrammatically in Fig. 9.1) is characterised by federalism and decentralisation based on the principle of subsidiarity.[2]

The sharing of responsibilities in education between the federal and canton levels is quite complex, and varies depending on the educational level and on the political institution(s) concerned. In fact, in the context of what is called 'cooperative

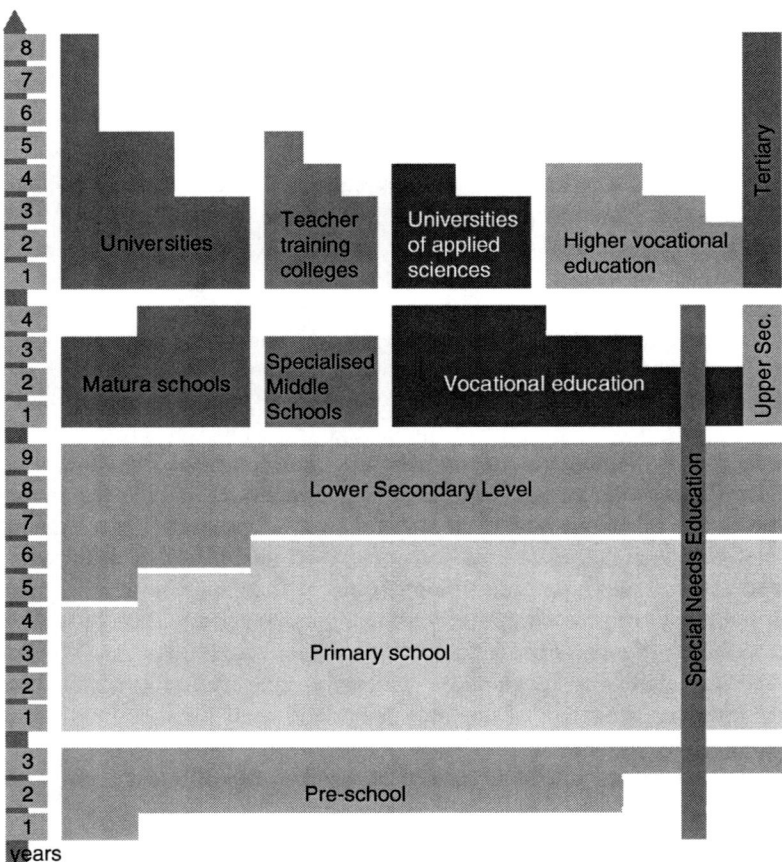

Fig. 9.1 Simplified diagram of the Swiss education system

---

[1] All data cited in this chapter come from the data bank of the Swiss Federal Statistical Office (http://www.bfs.admin.ch.bfs/portal/fr/index/themen/15.html) if not otherwise stated.

[2] According to this principle, superior levels (Confederation or cantons) can pass regulations or undertake tasks where and when the subordinate levels are not in a position to do so. The application of this principle results in a highly decentralised system where municipalities hold strong political responsibilities.

federalism', each of the 26 cantons[3] that form the country has its own education system, organised with substantial autonomy.

The coexistence of so many cantonal education systems implies the existence of different structures for compulsory schooling, with advanced or basic requirement tracks, which prepare respectively for academic/general versus vocational curricula. Compulsory education is divided into two cycles: the primary school and the lower secondary level, but their structures are not uniform between cantons. Nevertheless, for the majority of children, selection[4] starts at the lower secondary level, when they are 11–12 years old, on the basis of the requirements of the track[5] in which they are allowed to enrol. Under some conditions, changes from one type of track into another are possible even before the end of compulsory schooling. In reality, it is quite difficult. In 2006, 29.9% of the children at the lower secondary level were enrolled in a basic requirement track; 61.3% in an advanced one and 8.8% in a school without a specific track (see Fig. 9.2).

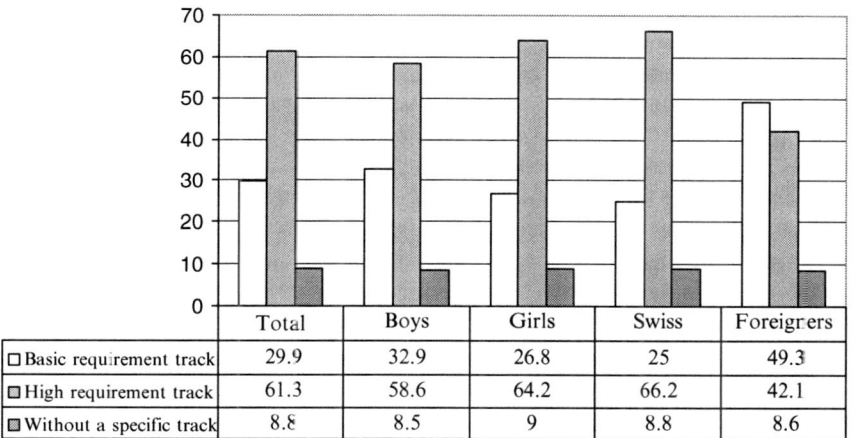

	Total	Boys	Girls	Swiss	Foreigners
☐ Basic requirement track	29.9	32.9	26.8	25	49.3
☐ High requirement track	61.3	58.6	64.2	66.2	42.1
☐ Without a specific track	8.8	8.5	9	8.8	8.6

Fig. 9.2 Participation in different tracks within lower secondary education in Switzerland in 2006 (%)

---

[3] The Swiss Conference of Cantonal Ministers of Education (CDIP – EDK) is the council which brings together the 26 Ministers of Education. It is divided into four regional conferences that partly reflect the multilingualism of the country. Intercantonal agreements ('concordats') are the most binding instruments that permit cooperation between the signatory cantons. The Intercantonal Agreement on Education Coordination (dating from 1970) forms the concrete legal basis for intercantonal collaboration concerning compulsory education.

[4] It is not really true to say that children choose the type of education they are going to follow, as they are about 10 years old. The selection is made on teachers' decisions that are taken mainly on the basis of the school marks obtained and the performances students have reached. In some places cantonal tests are important. Therefore, teachers propose the type of school they consider suitable for the children; their parents have, under some conditions, the right to oppose those decisions. In theory, switches from one type of school to another are possible, but they are quite difficult to make.

[5] Depending on the canton, there are between one and four tracks.

It is important to note the higher proportion of boys (32.9%) and foreign children (49.3%)[6] in the basic requirement classes. Conversely, two thirds of girls (64.2%) and Swiss students (66.2%) follow advanced requirement curricula.

At the end of compulsory schooling (the ninth year), children's options are already dependent on the previous kind of education received, and the choices are successively more restricted. The upper secondary level is split up into two main pathways: general/academic education and lower vocational education and training.

The first pathway, which lasts 3 or 4 years, is through the Matura schools[7] and provides the possibility of direct entrance to the cantonal universities and the federal institutes of technology. There are also specialised middle schools which prepare pupils for higher vocational education (universities of applied sciences), for instance, in the fields of healthcare, communications and information technology, and the social sciences.

In the second pathway, the most common form of lower vocational training is the 'dual system' (apprenticeship) that combines practical and theoretical learning. Students can choose from more than 200 careers involving both training in firms and courses in vocational schools (Dubs, 2006; Hanhart & Schulz, 1998). This training lasts at least 2 years, depending on the subject and the qualification attained (basic or advanced federal certificate). Full-time vocational training in school also exists, but it is quite rare. The federal professional baccalaureate can be obtained after having completed studies in addition to the vocational education and training, either at the same time or after the apprenticeship. This also gives students access to universities of applied sciences.[8]

Most pupils enter an upper secondary school immediately after finishing compulsory education. However, a growing minority of students do not continue directly into this stage. In fact, over the last decade, transitional short length courses, which do not end with a qualification, have been increasing.

A very small proportion of pupils enter the workforce after compulsory school and abandon further formal education without obtaining an upper secondary level diploma.

The Current Reforms in the Swiss Education System

Many changes are taking place within the Swiss education system. The national political authorities are willing to adopt the requirements that are shared worldwide due to the internationalisation of education systems, and to address issues such as mobility, harmonisation, quality, equity, accountability, efficiency and many others.

---

[6] Depending on the type of data available, it is not always possible to characterise foreigners by their socioeconomic status. First generation young immigrants are often, but not always, of lower socioeconomic status.

[7] It is possible to sit for the final examination and to get the certification at any age and without attending a school. Private courses exist for supporting students in their preparation.

[8] In 2006, 80% of students were enrolled in a tertiary level institution (67% in a university, 33% in a university of applied sciences) and 20% followed an upper vocational institution.

All the levels of the education system have already been or are being reformed. For instance, the general education tracks underwent profound reform a decade ago, and this reform is currently being evaluated. A new law on vocational education came into force in 2004 and the landscape of tertiary education is being reorganised.

A new intercantonal Agreement on Education Coordination of Compulsory Schooling ('*Harmos Concordat*') has been announced and came into force on August 1, 2009 for the signatory cantons.[9] It is the first step of a formal process towards the harmonisation of some basic educational structures at the national level.[10] At the same time, but independently, popular demand for harmonisation and coordination of education at the intercantonal level has been given clear political expression, thanks to the role of 'direct democracy'.[11] In fact, on May 21, 2006, Swiss citizens accepted some changes in the articles of the Federal Constitution concerning education and training in the country.

These two national projects aim at better coordination and collaboration between cantons on compulsory schooling and on the conditions that define and precede the transition to post-compulsory education.

The Target: 95% of Teenagers with a Diploma of Post-Compulsory Education by 2015

In 2005, the proportion of young Swiss who obtained a qualification at the end of post-compulsory education was 89%. This percentage is quite high compared with the mean of 82% among the Organisation for Economic Co-operation and Development (OECD) countries, and 83% among the European Union's member States (OECD, 2005). In light of that data, the Swiss Conference of Cantonal Ministers of Education declared its eagerness to reach the target of 95% of teenagers with a post-compulsory certificate by 2015.[12] The rationale for increasing the proportion of boys and girls who complete their upper secondary education comes from the consideration that it has become an essential qualification to enter the workforce and to start a professional life.

It is possible to analyse the distribution of the two types of diplomas in Switzerland. Over time, the percentage of teenagers choosing vocational training

---

[9] At the same time, another Convention has been signed between the French-speaking cantons ('*Convention scolaire romande*') aiming at a stronger coordination and harmonisation than the national one ('*Harmos Concordat*'). See www.ciip.ch and www.edk.ch

[10] For instance, changes concerning the structure and the duration of compulsory education (which will start earlier), as well as the curricula that will be harmonised at the regional linguistic level.

[11] Direct democracy is a system of democracy giving citizens more direct participation in the legislation process through such tools as referendums.

[12] The Swiss Conference of Cantonal Minister of Education (CDIP), *Lignes directrices du projet Transition, communiqué de presse du 27.10.2006*. The European Union declared that their target is 85% of young people with a certificate of post-compulsory schooling by 2010.

has diminished.[13] The reasons put forward to explain this trend are numerous and will be discussed later. Nonetheless, the choice of the type of education remains quite differentiated with regard to cultural and linguistic areas inside the country, to gender and, to a lesser extent, nationality. In fact, boys, foreigners and German-speaking pupils more often choose vocational education.[14]

An analysis of the evolution of the diploma in terms of numbers completing confirms the increase in teenagers who complete upper secondary education (see Fig. 9.3). The rate of increase since 1990 is greater for girls than for boys, though girls have not yet reached the same level as boys in attaining this standard of education.

The decrease in the proportion of diplomas delivered in vocational education is mostly due to girls' diminishing interest for this type of training. At the same time, the increase in the percentage of females who obtain a qualification of general education is significant.

In order to increase the number of young people who obtain a post-compulsory education qualification, it is also important that they can do it as quickly as possible, to minimise the possibility of abandoning their study in the meantime. One of the strategies to increase completion is to reduce the amount of time and money it takes for the individual and the community. Some of the factors that add to that cost include changes in the educational pathway (e.g., with the breaking of an apprenticeship contract); a lack of apprenticeships available in the desired fields; and the necessity to wait 1 year in a transitional course before starting the training or education curriculum.

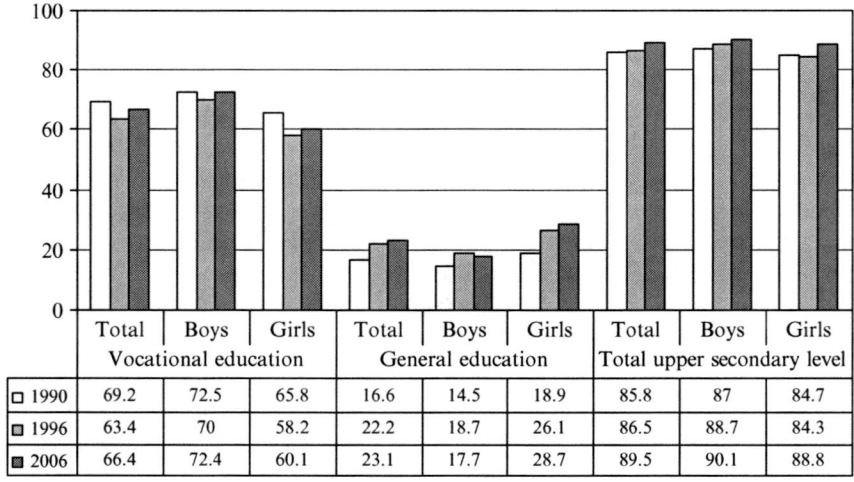

	Total	Boys	Girls	Total	Boys	Girls	Total	Boys	Girls
	Vocational education			General education			Total upper secondary level		
□ 1990	69.2	72.5	65.8	16.6	14.5	18.9	85.8	87	84.7
▨ 1996	63.4	70	58.2	22.2	18.7	26.1	86.5	88.7	84.3
▩ 2006	66.4	72.4	60.1	23.1	17.7	28.7	89.5	90.1	88.8

Fig. 9.3 Trend in students obtaining an upper secondary education diploma in Switzerland (%)

---

[13] It was 76.3% in 1990 and 72.7% in 2006.

[14] In 2006, at the upper secondary level, 79.4% of boys and 65.7% of girls were enrolled in vocational education, as were 72.4% of Swiss students and 74.6% of foreigners.

Analysis of the percentage of young people who enter post-compulsory education immediately after finishing the compulsory phase shows an important increase in the role of transitional courses.[15]

The choice of general education has risen slightly. On the other hand, direct entry into vocational training has diminished considerably over time. The decrease of the proportion of boys entering vocational training is not compensated by an increase in entry to a general/academic education stream, as it is for girls. However, the increase in the proportion of registrations for a transitional solution is roughly the same for both sexes.

Two major trends, obviously interwoven, can be identified: on the one hand, the decreasing number of young people in lower vocational training, and, on the other, the increasing number of enrolments in transitional programs. These two trends will be discussed in the following sections.

Trends in Lower Vocational Training

A major problem has developed concerning opportunities for apprenticeship training that has its roots in changes in industry that have affected the apprenticeship contracts' market. At the end of compulsory education, there is now a shortage of contracts in the fields of vocational training preferred by young people. There are several reasons that can explain this situation.

Number and Types of Firms Providing Apprenticeships Is Changing

The number of firms that provide apprenticeships – the essential partners of the dual vocational training system – is progressively decreasing, especially in some fields. For instance, in 2007, only 32% of Swiss firms supplied apprenticeship contracts (Burri & Brunner, 2007a, p. 4). They provided 79,000 apprenticeship places,[16] but 3,000 of these remained vacant (about 3% every year). Among the firms providing apprenticeships, nearly 70% are large (with more than 100 employees), even though 60% of Swiss firms are small (fewer than 10 employees) (Mühlemann et al., 2004).

---

[15] TREE (Transitions from School to Work) is a longitudinal research study on school-to-work transitions carried out in Switzerland at the national level. This study largely confirms the data presented by the Swiss Federal Statistical Office (Amos et al., 2003; Meyer, 2005).

[16] This number represents a slight increase (+3%) compared to that of the previous year. Since 2000, the small positive and negative fluctuations tend to result in an overall stable situation (Burri & Brunner, 2007a, p. 10).

Costs and Benefits of Apprentice Training

The proportion of firms providing training is relatively small, even if it seems that apprentice training is economically attractive. Many research studies conclude that, in Switzerland, firms make profits from the work of nearly two thirds of the apprentices trained. For the other one third of apprenticeship contracts that cannot be considered as lucrative, engaging the trained apprentice[17] at the end of his or her contract can reduce the costs for the firm because it removes the recruitment costs and those arising from the training of a new employee. During the last year of their apprenticeship, the young trainees reach a level of competence that equals two thirds of the productivity of a qualified employee in that particular field (Mühlemann, 2008; Mühlemann & Wolter, 2007). For the firm, the training costs are compensated by the benefit arising from the apprentice's productive labour. The cost-benefit ratio depends on the firm's size and on its appreciation of the expected cost-benefit balance when the enrolment of an apprentice is decided.

Employers apply many selection criteria when they choose their future apprentice. A survey has been conducted in order to evaluate employer priorities: the way in which the profession has been chosen;[18] the motivation[19] and the skills[20] for it are considered as the most important elements (respectively 65%, 62% and 58%) in the candidate selection. The other criteria are: subjective impressions (47%), the candidate's school career (37%), his or her more personal characteristics[21] (10%) and personal interests[22] (5%) (Burri & Brunner, 2007a, p. 18, b, pp. 37–38).

The qualifications and qualities of the young candidate are also quite important, as firms want to engage people who correspond to the firm's aspirations and expectations (Mühlemann & Wolter, 2007, p. 46). As mentioned before, qualifications and education skills are not the most important selection criteria for a firm. However, the educational gaps of their apprentices oblige them to invest more time in their training, which also raises their costs. Of course, the educational gaps of a candidate can deter a company from engaging him or her. Nonetheless, other factors are considered in calculating the cost-benefit ratio, whose balance is always fundamental in determining the offer of apprenticeship contracts. Most reasons

---

[17] The proportion of apprentices who remain in the same firm is a good indicator for understanding the willingness of a firm to plan its staff renewal. The proportion depends on the company's size. In large firms (more than 250 employees) more than half (58%) of the apprentices trained remain at least 1 year after the end of their training; in the small ones (0–4 employees) the proportion is 18%. In between, the progression is linear. Differences appear according to sectors of activity: in the secondary sector, about half of the apprentices trained remain. In the tertiary sector, the volatility is much more important, with only one third of the trainees being re-engaged.

[18] This can include aptitude tests and the job interview.

[19] This means the interest shown for the profession and for the company.

[20] They include technical, methodological, social and personal competencies, as well as the general state of health.

[21] Characteristics such as age, sex, nationality and place of residence.

[22] For example, hobbies, sport and membership of different types of associations.

invoked by firms for training apprentices (or not) are bound to this rational calculation (that is, too low a benefit expected in relation to the time needed, or not sufficient work available for the apprentice). The short- or long-term perspectives are also always taken into account.

Number and Types of Apprenticeship Contracts

The evolution of the apprenticeship contracts' market is bound to that of the job market: the economic situation determines both. Two other trends that influence the economic situation (Flückiger, 2007) must be taken into account: economic globalisation and technological development that reduces the need for particular skills. The consequences are relocation, demand for mobility, expansion of the tertiary sector and reduction of small-scale and industrial production. They concern precisely the types of jobs in which the apprenticeship contracts were previously the most numerous and appropriate, and they have not been compensated by apprenticeships created in the service sector.

There is an imbalance,[23] which has become constant, between the supply of and the demand for apprenticeship contracts, not only from a quantitative point of view, but also from a qualitative one, and which depends on the fields considered. From a quantitative point of view, this vocational system is healthy if there are sufficient apprenticeship positions available – that is, there are at least 12% more contracts available than contract requests by young people looking for vocational training (Puippe, 2003). From the qualitative point of view, it is important to note the lack of apprenticeship positions in the professional branches that will be in particularly high demand in the future (that is, in the sectors of information and communication technologies, health and the retail trade). Conversely, the supply of positions is too high in some fields that will not guarantee a job in the future (Puippe, 2003, p. 20).

However, the imbalance is relative, as every year there are some apprenticeship positions that remain vacant in certain economic sectors (for instance, the building industry and hotel services).

It is possible that some contracts are not signed due to the uncertain future of certain professions, leading subsequently to problems of retraining, and the transfer of acquired skills into another profession or qualification.

Since apprenticeship salaries are not high (Schwaab, 2008) and the costs of the training vary considerably among young people and among firms, another reason some contracts are not signed can be due to the location of the position, obliging the candidate apprentice to incur possibly prohibitively high mobility costs.

---

[23] Since 2006, many initiatives have been created in order to change this situation: they are directed towards the candidates for vocational training (for example, an Internet platform with all the apprenticeships contracts supplied) and also to firms, in order to make them more aware of the advantages of this training activity.

It is now important to analyse the apprenticeship places that remain vacant. For instance, in August 2007, 96% of the contracts supplied that year were signed.[24] A few training possibilities were still open, in particular in the building, painting, and carpentry professions (8%) and in metal or machine production (6%). On the other hand, apprenticeship positions in trade/office and technical drawing professions were almost all assigned. The attribution of contracts for the health professions rapidly reached 99% (Burri & Brunner, 2007a, p. 15).

Finally, although demographic trends can partly influence the availability of apprenticeship contracts, researchers consider these as a minor factor.

Apprentices' Satisfaction with Their Field of Training

A survey concluded that 71% of young people engaged in apprenticeship training in 2007 declared that it was in the field that they wanted to be in; 6% of them said that they were trained for a profession that they didn't desire, and 16% for a profession that they considered a second choice[25] (Burri & Brunner, 2007b, p. 54).

The lack of satisfaction with the profession in which they are trained can have consequences for the young apprentices in the more or less short term, with the breaking of the training contract or with substantial difficulties in entering the professional world (Herzog et al., 2004b; Kaiser et al., 2007). Consequently, it is very important to avoid the situation of limited choices in which teenagers must start training for a profession that doesn't reflect their desires and expectations (Rastoldo, 2006). The lack of interest and motivation can re-emerge later (Finzi et al., 2008; Meyer Schweizer, 2009; Schmid & Stalder, 2007b). The proportion of rescinded apprenticeship contracts reaches nearly 20% every year.[26] This proportion is quite high, and it is harmful both for the teenager and the firm. For the teenager, such a situation causes a delay for his or her training (with much time and energy lost) and the uneasy feeling of failure, which can cause health problems (Michaud, 2001; Neuenschwander, 2008; Neuenschwander & Süss, 2004; Stalder & Schmid, 2006b). Firms are also losers, as the cancellation of a contract during the schooling year causes additional costs and organisational problems, and naturally a feeling of failure too, that can induce discouragement for training apprentices.

A research study conducted in the canton of Bern (Moser et al., 2008; Schmid & Stalder, 2007a; Stalder & Schmid, 2006a) shows that in the group of teenagers

---

[24] More than half (61%) of the new candidates who start an apprenticeship are boys. The gender division of labour in the different groups of professions is still very marked. Boys are trained for professions in metallurgy (95%), the building industry (85%) and in technical fields (70%). The majority of girls are in the health sector (85%), retail (75%), clerical sector (65%) and hotel services (60%) (Burri & Brunner, 2007b, p. 33).

[25] The remaining 7% of young people interviewed didn't reply.

[26] Bessey & Backes-Gellner, 2008; Masdonati & Lamamra, 2007; Masdonati et al., 2007; Stalder & Schmid, 2006b.

who rescinded an apprenticeship contract, half of them very quickly signed another one, mostly in the same field but with another firm. For the others, only one in three hadn't found a solution after 18 months; most of them were immigrants and had already rescinded an apprenticeship contract. Their dropout was very often definitive. Another qualitative research study conducted in Geneva canton generally confirmed these conclusions (Rastoldo et al., 2009).

Recruiting apprentices has become very selective (Haeberlin et al., 2004), as the number of apprentice contracts has become more scarce. A study has concluded that a young candidate must write on average 18 applications in order to obtain a contract. Big differences appear among the various groups of professions. A candidate must apply more often for a place in retail services (on average 29 times), for desk or office jobs and health services (for both of these, 25 applications), and for places in hotel and household services (24). It seems to be somewhat easier to get a contract in the fields of the building, painting and wooden industries (10), metallurgy and machine industries (12) and in the drawing and technical professions (17) (Burri & Brunner, 2007a, p. 19).

Some significant differences concern the nationality of the candidates seeking a contract. In 2007, young foreigners wrote on average 39 applications before finding an apprenticeship place, while young Swiss made only 14 applications. More than 20% of young foreigners had to write more than 50 applications, and 10% wrote even more than 100 (Burri & Brunner, 2007b, p. 72; Fibbi et al., 2003). And while boys had to write on average 15 applications, girls had to send about 20 letters. It is clear that some individual characteristics influence, in a positive or negative way, the chances of a candidate obtaining an apprenticeship contract.

The motivation and the opportunity to mobilise social resources must be added to these socioeconomic and demographic factors, which include social origin, nationality, gender and age.[27]

Overall, if employers want to enrol a new apprentice, they have an abundance of choice. Normally, they prefer the best candidates, those who have finished the higher requirement tracks and have been good students, with good marks. With the shortage of contracts available and the consequent candidate selection process, the result is a tendency towards young people who are over-qualified for the position obtained. Furthermore, as the number of low qualification jobs progressively decreases, every young person must obtain a diploma if he or she wants to be able to integrate into the labour market.

On the one hand young people can consider their personal interests, values, aptitudes and aspirations and the expectations of other people (including parents) in determining their career choices, but on the other hand a degree of rationality induces some young people to make choices depending on the actual opportunities available, and on the realities of the labour.[28]

---

[27] It seems that employers prefer to engage candidates who are not too young.

[28] Research has analysed the various stages of the process leading to the choice of the professional field from the teenagers' perspective, describing the different constraints and successive decisions (Herzog et al., 2004a; Schulz, 2007).

Apart from all of the factors already mentioned (economic, political, demographic and personal), the education system must recognise its responsibilities. First of all, it does not enable all students to acquire the fundamental skills required to start an apprenticeship. Secondly, the skills transmitted do not match those needed in the job market. Finally, its mode of organisation favours discrimination against young people when they are hired. If the education system doesn't prepare students with curricula that are adapted to the needs of the economy, then the expectations that the job market has of the education system have not been made clear enough. The economic world and the education system are both responsible for the gap teenagers must face. Therefore, the gap between the skills taught at school and those demanded from the job market must be filled by the development of better collaboration and cooperation between the two parties. Nonetheless, if the preparation of students for a professional life is one of the missions of the educational system, it is not the only one (Perriard, 2005, pp. 16, 20).

The lack of apprenticeship places, especially those that need only basic qualifications, combined with increasing numbers of young people who complete compulsory education and are ready to start vocational training, means that more young people do not have any alternative, and are obliged to enter transitional courses. Generally, attendance in one of these short educational or vocational programs, before starting training that leads to some certification, is chosen by default by the teenager. One exception should be mentioned: those who must wait until they turn 18 before starting special vocational training (for example, health or child care training). The 1 or 2 years spent in such transitional programs lengthens the overall time before entering the workforce, causing costs for the young person and the community. The discussion on the advantages and disadvantages of these programs is still open. These options are positive experiences if they permit most of the teenagers who follow them to subsequently obtain a diploma instead of remaining without a qualification.

The Transitional Programs

The programs defined as 'transitional' or 'intermediate' generally follow post-compulsory education and precede upper secondary training. They do not provide a professional qualification. They are extremely varied, depending on the objectives pursued, but also according to the field and type of training. They are not coordinated at the national level, and they vary between cantons. The majority are organised at the public level, but private initiatives also exist. Each program can concern a different target group, as the age or the required skills can differ. Their content and organisation can also be extremely different. Participants must pay for most of them or receive a small remuneration, as in the case of courses organised by the unemployment insurance.

For instance, in 2005, young people involved in these kinds of training were distributed in the different programs in the following proportions:

- Programs with training in schools exclusively: 38%
- Programs combining theory and practice training: 27%

- Programs organised by the unemployment insurance: 29%
- Other types of learning (various information and training periods, language courses, etc.): 2%
- No information: 4% (Egger et al., 2007, p. 24).

According to Böni (2003, p. 98), the transitional programs do not fundamentally differ in content from an underpaid professional activity; they are similar to vocational training but they do not lead to a training certificate. Therefore, they have a lesser value on the job market.

Most of the transitional programs last 1 year. For 2006, figures are as follows:

- 1–6 months: 32%
- 7–12 months: 38%
- More than 12 months: 5%
- Don't know/no reply: 25% (Burri & Brunner, 2007b, p. 59).

The proportion of young people who spend a few months in a transitional program has progressively risen over the years;[29] it was 13.6% in 1990, 16.6% in 1995, 17.4% in 2000 and 19.7% in 2005.[30] In 2005, girls in the program (22.4%) outnumbered boys (16.9%); young foreigners (35.9%) outnumbered Swiss nationals (15.8%); and young people from the French-speaking part of the country (23.9%) outnumbered those from the German-speaking (18.8%) and the Italian-speaking regions (7.3%).[31]

A survey was conducted in 2007 on the upcoming activities planned by the 1,370 young people enrolled that year in a transitional option in Switzerland. The following figures were obtained in relation to where the young people interviewed anticipated they would be in a few months time:

- Searching (again) for an apprenticeship contract: 34%
  - In the preferred profession: 79%
  - In another profession: 21%
- Enrolled in another school: 23%
- Searching for a job: 13%
- Starting a supplementary training/language course: 7%
- Starting the apprenticeship contract already signed: 3%
- Other: 6%
- Don't know/no reply: 14% (Burri & Brunner, 2007b, p. 60).

Between two thirds and three quarters of young people, after having attended one of these transitional programs, subsequently started some certifying educational or vocational training (Egger et al., 2007, p. 50).

---

[29] This is calculated as the percentage of the total number of pupils who were enrolled the previous year in the ninth (and last) year of compulsory schooling.

[30] For instance, the absolute numbers were 9,693 teenagers in 1990 and 16,870 in 2005.

[31] Regional differences can be easily explained by the diversity in the cantonal education systems.

The choice and the availability of these intermediate or transitional programs is mostly dependent on external factors, such as the economic situation in the country: when the economy weakens, firms offer fewer apprenticeship contracts and these are allocated to the most qualified candidates (Fuhrer & Wolter, 2007). But personal factors can also play a role in the decision to undertake a transitional program, when it may be the only alternative for the young candidate. For instance, delaying for a year the decision to choose a profession to follow can be helpful for many young people.

Another important function of these programs is that they provide an opportunity to improve low educational skills. They are also useful when an apprenticeship contract has not yet been found, or prior to entry to vocational training that requires a minimum age.

Young People Without a Post-Compulsory Diploma

A typology of young people without a post-compulsory qualification has been established (Eckmann-Saillant et al., 1994). It is divided into six categories. The first one is composed of young people in 'a precarious situation' who are exposed to various social risks, for instance, physical or psychological problems, marginality, immigrant status and low social and economic status. The second category is that of the young 'new immigrants', who are characterised not only by cultural traits (as that of a foreign language) but also by an underprivileged legal status. The uncertainty concerning the length of their stay in Switzerland can prevent them from seriously starting any long-term training. The 'passive conformists' are middle-class young people who haven't yet acquired the economic independence to live according to their aspirations. The 'rebellious' are in conflict with parents, school and society, a situation that can delay their entry into professional life. The 'second generation immigrants' are torn between two cultures and are not able to decide on the profession they will enter, since different professions are viewed and valued differently by the two cultures. The last category, the 'young workers' want to be economically independent as soon as possible.

The proportion of teenagers who leave the education and training system without a post-compulsory school qualification can be seen as an indicator of the education system's failure in its effectiveness in retaining and training the young generation (every youth whatever his or her situation) until the threshold that permits minimal personal and professional development and provides the basis for lifelong learning.[32]

One indicator is the proportion of young people aged 18–24 who leave school without finishing a post-compulsory education and who do not enter another type of training. An international comparison shows that the Swiss dropout rate[33] is among the lowest; its level already nears the benchmark of 10% aimed at by the

---

[32] The responsibility of the educational system for giving all young citizens the fundamental right to education and training is a Constitutional principle (Federal Constitution, art. 41), and one of the objectives of the Harmos project (art. 3) is to give everyone the possibility of integrating into the labour market and develop according to his or her capacity.

[33] It is important to note that the national definition of the rate of dropout is slightly different from that used for the international comparison on the basis of Eurostat data. The differences concern the length of time spent without training (4 weeks or 1 year) and the higher level of education obtained.

European Union for 2010, as declared within the framework of the Lisbon Strategy This international comparison of dropout rates reveals major differences betweer countries, with percentages that range from 5% to 50%.

Between 1996 and 2006, the proportion of Swiss young people who left school prematurely[34] rose from 5.5% to 10.4%, with a decrease to 8.5% in the following year (see Fig. 9.4).

The factors that can lead to dropping out are numerous and quite complex giver the multiplicity of life experiences and situations of each individual. The circumstances that can influence the decision to stop upper secondary education can be caused by socioeconomic, cultural and geographical elements or be linked to the family situation and the environment. Other factors such as conditions in the labour market, the organisation or functioning of the education system or the demographic context can also be determinants. In Switzerland, the transition from compulsory to post-compulsory education can be tricky, as mentioned earlier, for instance arising from the problems engendered by the lack of apprenticeship contracts. A recently published report (Häfeli & Schellenberg, 2009) presents findings about the different factors that can encourage the vocational training of at-risk youth.

In the past dozen years, there has been no consistent gender differentiation in dropout rates; the trend alternates with small fluctuations around an overall stability. On the other hand, gender has some influence on the direct or indirect entrance to post-compulsory training that results in a qualification,[35] and also the type of training attended (Vouillot, 2007).

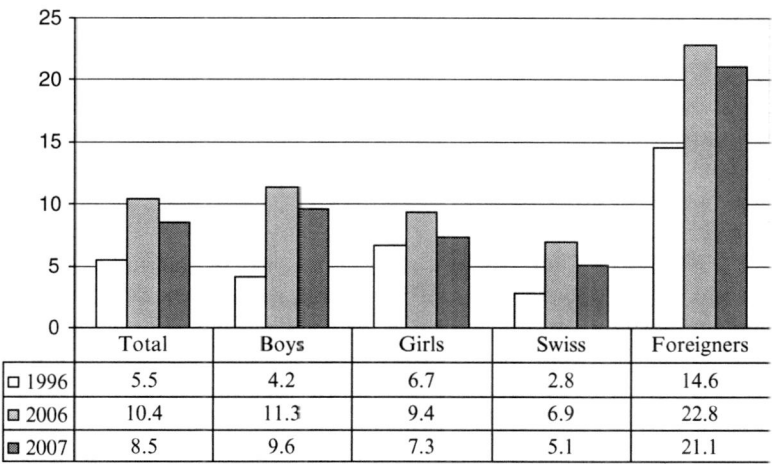

	Total	Boys	Girls	Swiss	Foreigners
□ 1996	5.5	4.2	6.7	2.8	14.6
▨ 2006	10.4	11.3	9.4	6.9	22.8
▣ 2007	8.5	9.6	7.3	5.1	21.1

Fig. 9.4 Rates of dropout in Switzerland (% of 18- to 24-year-olds without post-compulsory education)

---

[34] Increasingly, it is extremely difficult to have a profession without a post-compulsory qualification; those in this situation are at risk of being excluded from active life with the important economic and social consequences that this implies.

[35] For instance, young people, especially girls, who want to acquire a profession in the health sector must wait until 18 years of age. In the meantime, they start a transitional program of 1 or 2 years.

Since 1996, there has been a clear difference between the proportion of young Swiss and foreigners who give up school. The dropout rate is about 5% for Swiss teenagers and between 15% and 25% for foreign students.[36] But foreigners do not constitute a unique homogeneous category and their situations can differ considerably, especially according to socioeconomic background.[37]

Every year, a cohort of approximately 2,000–2,500 young people (that is, 2.5–3% of every cohort) gives up education but is not able, in the mid-term, to enter either a new education or training program at upper secondary level or the labour market. These young people are at a serious risk of being dependent on social security benefits, perhaps over a lengthy period of time.

Today, as a result of the 'knowledge society' and changes in the economy, an upper secondary qualification has become the minimal criterion for gaining a place in the job market and avoiding job insecurity, unemployment or dependence on social security.

The unemployment rate for 20- to 24-year-olds is relatively high: it reached 6.1% in 2005 and 3.4% for those aged 15–19, compared to the national average of 3.8% (Office fédéral de la formation professionnelle et de la technologie [OFFT], 2004; Weber, 2004, 2005, 2007).

For the same year, the average proportion of the adult population obtaining social security benefits in Switzerland was 3.3%; this percentage was the highest among the younger age groups (for those aged up to 17 years, and 18–25 years, it was 4.9% and 4.5%, respectively).

Very often, people in this situation have multiple problems; they combine lack of skills with personal problems, social and family difficulties, and have different degrees of motivation for further training.[38] Most of the time, the young who are motivated can more easily find a solution (even if a transitional one) than those who are not (or are less) motivated. Once excluded, they are in a situation in which the cantonal social services do not re-contact them, and so do not try to help those who probably need much more support than those who are helped. Providing support is then difficult as they rapidly disappear from the lists of regular students. There is no census or coordinated long-term monitoring for this category, and it is inevitable that their records are lost.

Since 2006, the political authorities have become increasingly aware of the problem and have adopted some measures that should prevent these situations. At the individual level, a national project, 'case management – vocational training', was launched for the 13- to 18-year-olds identified as having difficulties in following vocational training or entering the workforce (OFFT, 2007; Pagnossin, 2009).[39]

---

[36] In 2006, the proportion was 6.9% for Swiss nationals and 22.8% for foreigners.

[37] The TREE longitudinal study shows that young people who dropped out come mostly from a lower socioeconomic status (Meyer, 2005).

[38] The level of motivation of these young people is often discussed and questioned. For example, Böni (2003) concludes that most of the teenagers who, 2 years after having finished compulsory education are still without a professional solution, remain motivated and pursue their efforts in searching for an apprenticeship contract or a training alternative.

[39] The following year a second project, 'case management +', was launched and concerns 18- to 24-year-olds.

The implementation is actually taking place at the cantonal level; it will be fully operational in 2011. On the one hand, the need for cross-institutional coordination has been recognised. It should include educational and social authorities, as well as those involved in the vocational training and economic sectors. All of these stakeholders should closely collaborate in order to identify those students who are still in compulsory schooling but are potentially in a precarious situation. In order to help them enter upper secondary education and, subsequently, the job market, objectives and measures must be jointly decided and coordinated by those who will be responsible for their planning and implementation. The accompanying measures must also be individualised and would be defined as successful when the young person finds his or her professional direction. On the other hand, 'case management' or coaching should be applied to those students identified as at-risk before finishing their compulsory education and they should be individually accompanied until they have acquired a qualification and are integrated into the workforce.

At the same time, a special program developed by national and cantonal authorities with the economic sector will involve private firms. It aims at helping them in some aspects that can be a source of difficulty in their role of training. Special attention will be given to administrative and social aspects in order to help them in their (present and future) training partnerships.

All these measures are quite expensive and will need much energy and organisation for them to be adopted. But young people without a qualification or a job are also expensive in the long term. Hopefully this coordinated plan will be successful, but it is too early yet to evaluate it.

Conclusion

The choice of a profession is a long process, carried out over various stages and during which time many people can inform and/or influence the teenagers' decisions. Contextual factors, such as the responsibilities of the educational system and the economic situation of the country must also be taken into account, as they can produce various important effects. Most research is on transition, either as a global process or focused on analysing its determinants and influences at the individual level (Masdonati, 2007; Neuenschwander, 2007; Neuenschwander et al., 2006).

Vocational training is the most popular pathway within upper secondary education – hence the economic partnership in the dual system attracts much attention. In fact, some problems, the origins of which are external to the educational system, have important vocational training consequences. It has been seen that economic aspects (such as costs and profits, selection criteria) and the sociological ones (including influences of immigration, lower socioeconomic status, exclusion and discrimination) all have an impact on vocational training.

The Swiss VET system promotes inequity[40] as it develops a specific mode of selection that is different from selection procedures of exclusively based programs

---

[40] As concluded by a German study (Maaz et al., 2008).

(Hupka et al., 2006). It should be added that this selection intervenes after the program-based selection at the lower secondary level; these institutional aspects must not be forgotten. A good level of achievement at school is also, but not always, important (Imdorf, 2007a, b).

Completing post-compulsory education has become essential for successful integration into the workforce. Young people who enter into the job market directly after compulsory schooling are very rare, but many teenagers spend a year or two in transitional courses before starting upper secondary education. The debate on the usefulness of these short-term training courses, increasingly praised by young people for different reasons, even if they do not lead to certification, is still open. They are, however, flourishing, partly because of the problems encountered due to the lack of apprenticeship places, and because vocational training is extremely popular in Switzerland. Three quarters of teenagers initially choose vocational training as their upper secondary education pathway, even if this proportion is declining slightly. Most of the remaining students (nearly one quarter) enter a general/academic education. Nonetheless, a very small minority of about 2–3% of every cohort do not acquire a qualification, risking unemployment or dependency on social security benefits during their future life.

Research on dropping out is mostly reported in studies on vocational training or transitional solutions. Short interruptions or 'deviations' from the standard pathways do not always imply that teenagers have definitely abandoned the educational and training system, but only delayed; they can re-enter it later.

It appears that having not obtained an apprenticeship contract in the desired field, or having already gone through a transitional program, are the best predictors of rescinding an apprenticeship contract (Kaiser et al., 2007). Other research adds that being immigrants, of low socioeconomic status, living in an urban region, and/or having low school achievement, are the most usual characteristics of teenagers who stop, at least once, their vocational training (Bertschy et al., 2007, 2008a, b). Qualitative research on young people rescinding their apprenticeship contract has concluded that stopping a vocational training program is a phenomenon that cannot be easily generalised, as it is extremely complex, but that it is not always synonymous with definitively dropping out (Lamamra & Masdonati, 2009; Rastoldo et al., 2009).

Currently 89% of young Swiss people have attained an upper secondary school qualification, a high percentage by international standards. The target is to reach 95% of young people living in Switzerland with this level of qualification. Many measures have been considered to attain this objective. Most of them are based on better coordination and cooperation at the national level, and concern those pupils who are thought to be at risk before finishing compulsory schooling. It is too early to evaluate these measures since they have not yet been completely implemented; many of them are just political declarations of intention and the success of their realisation cannot be assessed for many years.

References

Amos, J., Böni, E., Donati, M., Hupka, S., Meyer, T., & Stalder, B. E. (Eds.). (2003). *Parcours vers les formations postobligatoires. Les deux premières années après l'école obligatoire. Résultats intermédiaires de l'étude longitudinale TREE* [Pathways to post-compulsory training. The first two years after leaving school. Interim results of the longitudinal study TREE]. Neuchâtel: Office fédéral de la statistique (OFS).

Bertschy, K., Böni, E., & Meyer, T. (2007). *Les jeunes en transition de la formation au monde du travail. Survol de résultats de la recherche longitudinale TREE, mise à jour 2007* [Young people in transition from training to work. Overview of results of TREE longitudinal research, updated 2007]. Berne: TREE.

Bertschy, K., Cattaneo, M.A., & Wolter, S.C. (2008a). L'entrée sur le marché du travail - un chemin parsemé d'obstacles [Entry into the labour market – a path strewn with obstacles]. *Panorama*, 18–19.

Bertschy, K., Cattaneo, M.A., & Wolter, S.C. (2008b). *What happened to the PISA 2000 participants five years later?* (Working paper). Zürich: Institut für Strategie und Unternehmensökonomik (ISU).

Bessey, D., & Backes-Gellner, U. (2008). Pourquoi certains jeunes abandonnent leur formation [Why some young people leave their training]. *Panorama*, 20–21.

Böni, E. (2003). Parcours discontinus et jeunes sans formation. In J. Amos, E. Böni, M. Donati, S. Hupka, T. Meyer & B. E. Stalder (Eds.), *Parcours vers les formations postobligatoires. Les deux premières années après l'école obligatoire. Résultats intermédiaires de l'étude longitudinale TREE* (pp. 81–99). Neuchâtel: Office fédéral de la statistique (OFS).

Burri, B., & Brunner, T. (2007a). *Baromètre des places d'apprentissage. Août 2007 (Rapport condensé)*. Berne: Office fédéral de la formation professionnelle et de la technologie (OFFT).

Burri, B., & Brunner, T. (2007b). *Baromètre des places d'apprentissage. Août 2007 (Rapport détaillé)*. Berne: Office fédéral de la formation professionnelle et de la technologie (OFFT).

Dubs, R. (2006). *An appraisal of the Swiss vocational education and training system.* Berne: h.e.p.

Eckmann-Saillant, M., Bolzman, C., & de Rham, G. (1994). *Jeunes sans qualification: trajectoires, situations et stratégies* [Unskilled youth: Pathways, situations and strategies]. Geneva: Institut d'études sociales (IES).

Egger, M., Dreher, T., & Partner. (2007). *Etude approfondie sur les offres de formation transitoires entre scolarité obligatoire et formation professionnelle. Rapport.* Berne: Office fédéral de la formation professionnelle et de la technologie (OFFT).

Fibbi, R., Kaya, B., & Piguet, E. (2003). *Nomen est omen: Quand s'appeler Pierre, Afrim ou Mehmet fait la différence.* Berne/Arau: Direction du program PRN 43 en collaboration avec le Forum Formation et emploi et le Centre suisse de coordination pour la recherche en éducation (CSRE).

Finzi, I., Müller, B., Mulatero, F., & Schweri, J. (2008). Changement de métier après l'apprentissage [Change of job after apprenticeship]. *Panorama*, 11.

Flückiger, Y. (2007). Le système suisse de formation face aux mutations du marché de travail. Formation Emploi. *Revue française de sciences sociales, 100*, 5–14.

Fuhrer, M., & Wolter, S.C. (2007). Ne donne-t-on qu'à ceux qui sont déjà pourvus? *Panorama, 4*, 15–16.

Haeberlin, U., Imdorf, C., & Kronig, W. (2004). *Chancenungleichheit bei der Lehrstellensuche* [Inequality of opportunity in apprenticeships]. Berne/Arau: Direction du program PRN 43 en collaboration avec le Forum Formation et emploi et le Centre suisse de coordination pour la recherche en éducation.

Häfeli, K., & Schellenberg, C. (2009). *Facteurs de réussite dans la formation professionnelle des jeunes à risque* [Success factors in training for at-risk youth] (Final Report – unedited version). Zurich: Haute école intercantonale de pédagogie spécialisée.

Hanhart, S., & Schulz, H.-R. (1998). *La formation des apprentis en Suisse.* Lausanne/Paris: Delachaux et Niestlé.

Herzog, W., Neuenschwander, M., & Wannack, E. (2004a). *Im engen Bahnen: Berufswahlprozess bei Jugendlichen.* Berne/Arau: Direction du program PRN 43 en collaboration avec le Forum Formation et emploi et le Centre suisse de coordination pour la recherche en éducation (CSRE).

Herzog, W., Neuenschwander, M., & Wannack, E. (2004b). Wie verlaufen Berufswahlprozesse? *Panorama, 2,* 36–37.

Hupka, S., Sacchi, S., & Stalder, B. E. (2006, September 7–9). *Does the Swiss VET system encourage inequity?* Paper presented at the European Research Network on Transitions in Youth TIY, Marseilles.

Imdorf, C. (2007a). On ne demande pas les meilleurs, mais les discrets. *ZeSo, 2,* 28–29.

Imdorf, C. (2007b). Weshalb ausländische Jugendliche besonders grosse Probleme haben, eine Lehrstelle zu finden. In H.-U. Grunder & L. von Mandach (Eds.), *Choisir et être choisi. Intégration et exclusion des jeunes et jeunes adultes dans la scolarité et l'emploi* (pp. 100–111). Zürich: Seismo.

Kaiser, C., Davaud, C., Evrard, A., & Rastoldo, F. (2007). *Les jeunes en formation professionnelle. Rapport II: Comment les jeunes interprètent leur parcours de formation* [Young people in vocational training. Report II: How youth interpret their training program]. Geneva: Service de la recherche en éducation (SRED).

Lamamra, N., & Masdonati, J. (2009). *Arrêter une formation professionnelle. Mots et maux d'apprentis* [Stop job training. Words and woes of apprentices]. Lausanne: Antipodes.

Maaz, K., Trautwein, U., Lüdtke, O., & Baumert, J. (2008). Educational transitions and differential learning environments: How explicit between-school tracking contributes to social inequality in educational outcomes. *Child Development Perspectives, 2*(2), 99–106.

Masdonati, J. (2007). *La transition entre école et monde du travail. Préparer les jeunes à l'entrée en formation professionnelle* [The transition between school and the workplace. Preparing young people for entry into vocational training]. Berne: Peter Lang.

Masdonati, J., & Lamamra, N. (2007, October 24–26). *La formation professionnelle entre continuités et ruptures: Témoignages de jeunes en situation de décrochage.* Paper presented at the '3èmes Rencontres Jeunes & Sociétés en Europe et autour de la Méditerranée', Marseille.

Masdonati, J., Lamamra, N., Gay-des-Combes, B., & De Puy, J. (2007). Les enjeux identitaires de la formation professionnelle duale en Suisse: un tableau en demi-teinte. Formation Emploi. *Revue française de sciences sociales, 100,* 15–29.

Meyer Schweizer, R. (2009). Un jeune sur trois choisirait une autre profession [One youth in three would choose another profession]. *Panorama, 2,* 20–21.

Meyer, T. (2005). *School-to-work transition in Switzerland. Results as of 2004 from the TREE panel survey.* Berne: TREE.

Michaud, P.-A. (2001). Prévenir les ruptures, limiter leurs conséquences [Prevent disruptions, limit their consequences]. *Panorama, 6,* 8–10.

Moser, C., Stalder, B.E., & Schmid, E. (2008). Lehrvertragsauflösung: Die Situation von ausländischen und Schweizer Jugendlichen. Ergebnisse aus dem Projekt LEVA. Berne: Bildungsplanung und Evaluation der Erziehungsdirektion.

Mühlemann, S. (2008). Apprentis allemands moins productifs que ceux en Suisse [German apprentices less productive than those in Switzerland]. *Panorama,* 14–15.

Mühlemann, S., Schweri, J., & Wolter, S.C. (2004). Pourquoi les entreprises ne forment pas d'apprentis et que faire pour y remédier [Why companies do not train apprentices and what to do about it]. *La Vie économique. Revue de politique économique, 9,* 43–48.

Mühlemann, S., & Wolter, S.C. (2007). La formation d'apprentis est une activité rentable. [Apprenticeship training is a profitable activity]. *La Vie économique. Revue de politique économique, 10,* 44–47.

Neuenschwander, M. (2007). Comment l'école et la famille influencent le choix professionnel [How school and family influence career choice]. *Panorama, 4,* 26–28.

Neuenschwander, M. (2008). L'intégration professionnelle au coeur des débats. *Actualités de la formation professionnelle*, *210*, 1–3.

Neuenschwander, M., Balmer, T., Gasser, A., Goltz, S., Hirt, U., Ryser, H., et al. (2006). *Schule und Familie – was sie zum Schulerfolg beitragen* [School and family – What they contribute to academic attainment]. Berne: Haupt.

Neuenschwander, M., & Süss, D. (2004). Risks and problems of apprentice drop-outs - Results of empirical studies. In OFSP (Ed.), *Suchtforschung des BAG - Recherches de l'OFSP en matière de dépendances 1999–2001: Vol 2/3. Prévention* (pp. 93–99). Berne: EDMZ.

Organisation for Economic Co-operation and Development (OECD). (2005). *Education at a glance*. Paris: OECD.

Office fédéral de la formation professionnelle et de la technologie (OFFT). (2004). *Places d'apprentissage. Chômage des jeunes* [Apprenticeships. Youth unemployment]. Berne: OFFT.

Office fédéral de la formation professionnelle et de la technologie (OFFT). (2007). *Le case management 'formation professionnelle'. Principes et mise en oeuvre dans les cantons*. Berne OFFT.

Pagnossin, E. (2009, June 25–27). *Le case management 'formation professionnelle' en Suisse romande*. Paper presented at the Colloque international de l'Association francophone d'éducation comparée (AFEC). IREDU Dijon.

Perriard, V. (2005). *Transition de l'école obligatoire vers la formation professionnelle: les facteurs explicatifs des difficultés actuelles. Analyse de la littérature* [Transition from compulsory education to vocational training: Factors explaining the current difficulties. Analysis of the literature]. Lausanne: Unité de recherche pour le pilotage des systèmes pédagogiques.

Puippe, P.-Y. (2003). Formation professionnelle: 'le chemin de la promotion' [Vocational training: 'the way of promotion']. *Panorama*, *6*, 20–22.

Rastoldo, F. (2006). Les élèves de 9e s'expriment sur leur choix d'orientation. *Panorama*, *1*, 19–20.

Rastoldo, F., Amos, J., & Davaud, C. (2009). *Rapport III: Le devenir des jeunes abandonnant leur apprentissage*. Geneva: Service de la recherche en éducation (SRED).

Schmid, E., & Stalder, B.E. (2007a). Lehrvertragsauflösung: direkter Wechsel und vorläufiger Ausstieg. Ergebnisse aus dem Projekt LEVA. Berne: Bildungsplanung und Evaluation der Erziehungsdirektion.

Schmid, E., & Stalder, B.E. (2007b). Pourquoi les jeunes changent de métier durant l'apprentissage. *Panorama*, *5*, 10–11.

Schulz, H.-R. (2007). *Coûts et bénéfices de la formation professionnelle. Plaidoyer pour une optique plus large d'appréciation* [Costs and benefits of vocational training. Advocating a broader appreciation]. Bâle: Fédération des écoles techniques (FET).

Schwaab, J.C. (2008). L'USS demande un renforcement des bourses pour les apprenti(e)s! [USS requires a strengthening of scholarships for trainee(s)!] *USS-Infos*, 7, 1–2.

Stalder, B.E., & Schmid, E. (2006a). Lehrvertragsauflösung, ihre Ursachen un Konsequenzen. Ergebnisse aus dem Projekt LEVA. Berne: Bildungsplanung und Evaluation der Erziehungsdirektion.

Stalder, B.E., & Schmid, E. (2006b) Raisons et conséquences des abandons d'apprentissage [Reasons and consequences of dropping out of learning]. *Panorama*, 2, 13–14.

Vouillot, F. (2007). Formation et orientation: l'empreinte du genre [Training and orientation: The imprint of gender]. *Travail, genre et société*, 2(18), 23–26.

Weber, B. (2004). Le chômage des jeunes en Suisse [Youth unemployment in Switzerland]. *La Vie économique. Revue de politique économique*, 10, 43–46.

Weber, B. (2005). Le chômage des jeunes en relation avec la conjoncture. *Panorama*, 6, 4–5.

Weber, B. (2007). La situation des jeunes sur le marché suisse du travail [The situation of young people in the Swiss labour market]. *La Vie économique. Revue de politique économique*, 3, 52–54.

Introduction to the Nordic Education Systems

Eifred Markussen

The following chapters have a closer look at dropout and completion in three of the five Nordic countries: Iceland, Finland and Norway.

In all of the Nordic countries upper secondary education builds on a compulsory education lasting 9–10 years. A common feature of the compulsory education systems in all the Nordic countries is that they are unitary: the children are kept in common schools and there is no tracking within compulsory education. After completing compulsory education most continue into post-compulsory, with transition levels varying from 93% in Iceland and Finland to 98% in Norway.

Upper secondary education is structured differently in the three countries. The academic programs are organised in more or less similar ways, but vocational education is very different – both in the content of the education and how it is organised. In Norway, there is a '2 + 2' model, where half of the vocational education (2 years) is carried out as a student in school and the other half (2 years) as an apprentice in a workplace. Iceland has a model that resembles that of Norway, but with far fewer apprentices. Finland has mainly a school-based system for both vocational education and academic courses.

Dropout is considered a large social problem in all of the Nordic countries. There is a shared view across the countries that failure to complete upper secondary education is a loss not only for the individual, but also for society more broadly. Persons who fail to gain an upper secondary qualification find it harder to get jobs and end up in weaker labour market positions compared to those who achieve a qualification, and for the community this represents a loss of potential skills and human capital.

Measurement of dropout and completion varies across the countries. In Iceland, 62% of those born in 1982 had completed upper secondary education at the age of 24, 30% had dropped out, and 7% were still in upper secondary education. In Norway, 68% of those that started in upper secondary education in 2003 had completed 5 years later, at the age of 20–21, while 19% had dropped out, 8% had gone

E. Markussen (✉)
NIFU Nordic Institute for Studies in Innovation,
Research and Education, Norway

S. Lamb et al. (Eds.), *School Dropout and Completion: International Comparative Studies in Theory and Policy*, DOI 10.1007/978-90-481-9763-7_11,
© Springer Science+Business Media B.V. 2011

through all the years but without meeting all requirements, and 6% were still in upper secondary education. In Finland, the focus is on those not in education, employment or training (NEET), and in 2004, 11.8% of all persons between 15 and 24 years of age were in this category.

Even though Nordic education systems may be viewed as part of an egalitarian, redistributive model, where education has been considered a means of reducing social inequalities and the focus has been on developing common schools and inclusive programs, dropout stands out as a serious problem and challenge. In this context, it is also worth noting that social background is identified as an important variable predicting dropout in each system, that research concludes social inequalities are reproduced through the education system, and that one of the outcomes of this reproduction is dropout from upper secondary education.

The following country chapters on Iceland, Finland and Norway, in addition to outlining trends and patterns in dropout and completion, examine and discuss different measures implemented to reduce dropout and increase completion. Many of these measures, recently implemented, have not been evaluated or are being evaluated at the moment, but there is a preliminary view that many of them seem to have had little or short lasting impact only. This has not always been the case. The Nordic countries have been the source of major educational policy reforms over the last 2 decades – reforms that have re-shaped upper secondary school provision and produced major changes in participation. One such measure that has had a significant impact on reducing dropout and increasing completion is the Norwegian Reform of 1994 (Reform 94), which opened up upper secondary education for whole cohorts and helped democratise participation. Similar reform efforts have occurred across the Nordic countries, as the following chapters reveal.

Chapter 10
Dropout and Completion in Upper Secondary Education in Finland

Risto Rinne and Tero Järvinen

The Structure of the Finnish Educational System

The basic structure of the Finnish education system is rather simple (see Fig. 10.1). Compulsory education starts from the year in which children turn 7 and ends when they are 16 years old. In addition, all 6-year-olds are entitled to pre-school education for 1 year before starting comprehensive school.

The Finnish comprehensive school includes primary and lower secondary schools and is uniform in nature; different tracks leading to different educational outcomes are not part of the system. However, inside the comprehensive school there is an extensive special education system for at-risk students, which has expanded systematically and rapidly since the comprehensive school reform in the early 1970s (Kivirauma, 1989; Simola et al., 1999; Jahnukainen, 2003; Myllyniemi, 2008) (Fig. 10.2). Special education can be either full-time or part-time in nature, the latter alternative being more common. The number of special education students in Finland is high by international standards. Approximately 8% of those in comprehensive school can be classified as full-time special education students (officially transferred to special education – mainly full-time) and some 22% as part-time special education students (Kivirauma et al., 2004; Statistics Finland 2005, 2008).

This new division within the common comprehensive school has seen not only a growing numbers of pupils going to the special education track, but also a growing *proportion* of pupils going there. The proportion of pupils transferred to special education in Finnish primary schools, for instance, has consistently increased over the past 10 years.

The post-compulsory upper secondary level comprises general and vocational education, which are delivered in different schools. Education in upper secondary general schools is based on courses, without traditional year classes, and ends in a nationally comparable matriculation examination. This usually takes 3 years.

R. Rinne (✉) and T. Järvinen
Centre for Research on Lifelong Learning and Education, University of Turku, Finland

S. Lamb et al. (Eds.), *School Dropout and Completion: International Comparative Studies in Theory and Policy*, DOI 10.1007/978-90-481-9763-7_12,
© Springer Science+Business Media B.V. 2011

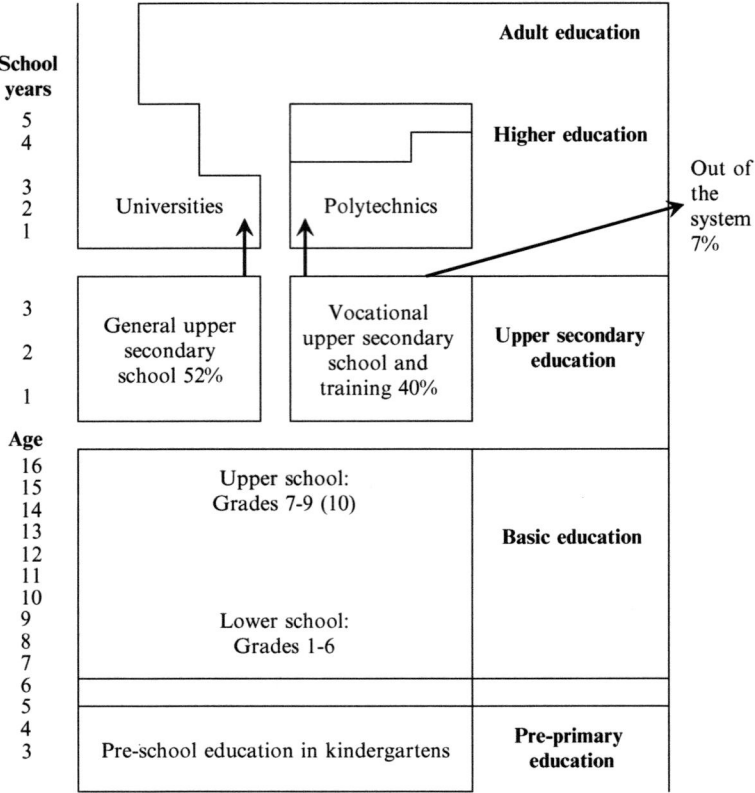

Fig. 10.1 The Finnish educational system in 2007
Note: The flow sizes of pupils into the secondary branches of education and out of the educational system after completing comprehensive school are based on estimates derived for 2006. See Vanttaja & Rinne (2008)

In vocational education and training, study is primarily organised in year classes, meaning full-time studies for 3 years. The admission requirement for upper secondary education is a comprehensive school certificate. Students apply to both forms of education through a joint application system, and the selection is based on students' school reports.

Basic vocational education and training consists of eight study fields, the most popular fields being technology and transport, business and administration, and health and social services. The study fields are further divided into 119 study programs, leading to 53 basic vocational qualifications. For example, the field of technology and transport consists of 60 study programs leading to 26 basic vocational educational qualifications. Dividing study fields into specific programs is based on the aim of providing students both basic occupational skills as well as more specialised skills in some areas.

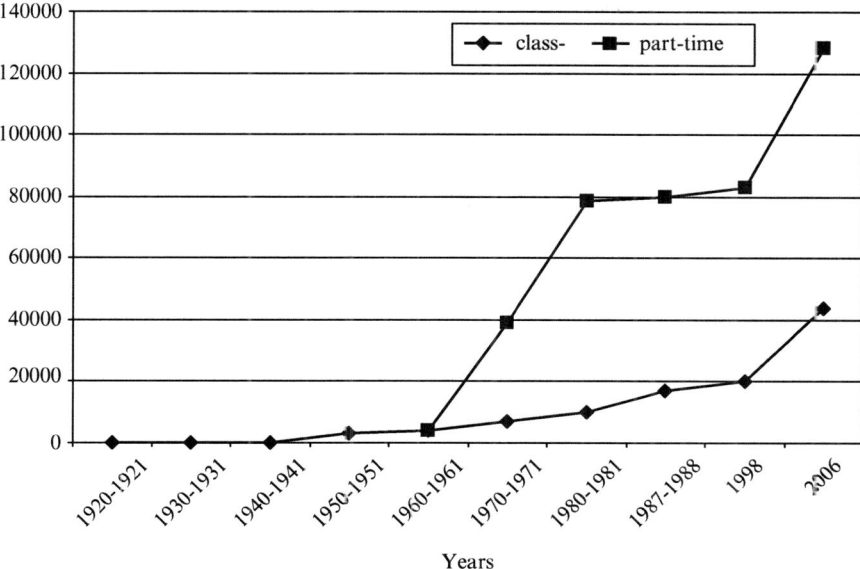

Fig. 10.2 The numbers of pupils participating in special education in Finland in the years 1920–2006 (Sources: Rinne & Kivirauma, 2005; Statistics Finland, 2008)

Upper secondary general school and a school-based vocational education are not, however, the only educational alternatives after completing compulsory education in Finland. A small minority (about 2–5%) of the comprehensive school leavers continues their studies in some other educational institutions, for example in voluntary additional basic education (Grade 10) or in adult education centres.

Finland also has an apprenticeship training system, although compared to some other European countries, such as Germany or Norway, it has traditionally been quite a marginal educational route. The popularity of apprenticeship training has, however, gradually increased. In 2006, 18% of all vocational upper secondary qualifications were based on apprenticeship training (Statistics Finland, 2008). As the apprenticeship training is based on a work contract, the practical training periods take place at the workplace in connection with ordinary work assignments. This is complemented by theoretical studies arranged at educational institutions, typically at institutions providing vocational education and training. Furthermore, upper secondary vocational qualifications may also be obtained through competence tests, independent of how the vocational skills have been acquired. In 2006, 17% of all basic vocational qualifications were obtained through competence tests (Statistics Finland, 2008).

At the tertiary level, Finland established, in 1996, a dual model of higher education, which includes universities and polytechnics. Every student who has completed upper secondary school is allowed to apply for tertiary level education. Upper secondary general school certificates and vocational school certificates are not, however, comparable, since there is no national exam included in vocational education and training, but in general education there is. In Finland, the selection of university students is based both on entrance examination and applicants' upper secondary school certificates, and universities and faculties usually have their own minor subject quota for those students who have completed vocational school. In practice, quite a few vocational school graduates continue their studies in universities, polytechnics being the more common alternative, in addition to going to the labour market.

Both upper secondary and higher education are free of charge in Finland, which means that there are no tuition fees; students only need to pay for the study materials they use. There is also a multiform and extensive adult education system in Finland. Participation in adult education is among the highest in the world (Tuijnman & Hellström, 2001; Antikainen, 2005; Rubensson, 2005; Raivola et al., 2006).

Finland at the Top of the World Rankings

As a result of globalisation, and the increased influence of supranational organisations in particular, nation states such as Finland have come under increasing pressure to follow neo-liberal orthodoxy in educational policy and planning. By examining the policy documents and practices of the World Bank, the Organisation for Economic Co-operation and Development (OECD) and the European Union, for instance, it is possible to see the heavy influence of free-market neo-liberalism in the thinking about educational reform and policy-making, and almost no nation state can avoid its profound influence.[1]

It is, however, important to remember that even if the same policy discourse does enter the policy systems of different countries, policy implementation is a highly complicated and fortuitous affair. National policy-making is always inevitably a process of bricolage: a matter of borrowing and copying bits and pieces of ideas, amending locally tried approaches, theories, research, trends and fashions and flailing around for anything that might work. Many policies are ramshackle, compromise, hit and miss affairs, which are reworked and tinkered with and inflected through complex processes of influence and ultimately re-creation in the national or local context of practice (cf. Ball 1994, 2001).

The OECD differs from the other supranational organisations, in that its influence over the education policy of the member states is based on information management. The OECD has not made any legally binding decisions or issued any obligatory education policy recommendations. On the other hand, the OECD has become established as a kind of *éminence grise* in the setting of educational policy in all industrialised countries (Rinne et al., 2004; Kallo, 2009.)

The OECD has been quite diligent in making and publishing country reviews, as well as thematic reviews, concerning educational issues. In addition to organising

---

[1] Many studies related to supranational/global influences on national educational policies have recently been carried out within Centre for Research on Lifelong Leaning and Education (CELE), in the University of Turku (e.g., Kallo & Rinne, 2006; Niukko, 2006; Seppänen, 2006; Kallo, 2009), but in the framework of this article it is not possible to concentrate on these in detail.

Table 10.1   The ranking of Finnish comprehensive school students in PISA studies in the years 2000–06

Year	Reading	Mathematics	Natural science	Problem-solving
2000	1	4	3	na
2003	1	2	1[a]	2[a]
2006	2	2	1	na

na   Research results are missing
[a]   Tied position
Source: OECD (2006).

numerous meetings and consultations on educational politics, its impressive book series *Education at a Glance*, in which countries are ranked on the basis of various educational indicators, has had a great influence in steering the direction of education politics in many countries.

Countries have also been ranked three times with the help of a new vehicle of evaluation, the OECD Programme for International Student Assessment (PISA), and every time, in 2000, 2003 and 2006, Finland has been at the very top of the ranking. The ranked lists presented in Table 10.1, based on PISA studies, show the excellent ranking of Finnish comprehensive school students (15-year-olds, 57 countries involved in the latest study). In addition, although differences in the performance of the students representing different sexes, regional areas and social backgrounds were also clear in Finland, these differences were among the smallest in the populations studied.

Recently, there has been a lot of discussion, both nationally and internationally, related to Finland's huge success in PISA competitions. For example, high-quality teacher education and especially the Finnish comprehensive school system related to junior years of schooling have been seen as explaining the success of Finnish students. In Finland, study results, especially those presented in the PISA 2000 study, have been enormously important in damping down heavy criticism directed towards the comprehensive school, the critics of which appeared in Finland in the early 1990s in the wake of global neo-liberal educational politics. Without PISA, the turn of the tide in educational policy would undoubtedly have been stronger, and the post-war tradition of equality in educational opportunities might have weakened more drastically than it has. The neo-liberal voices criticising the comprehensive school, as well as educational equality as one of the most important aims of the Finnish educational system, have been dampened, but have not altogether vanished.

The Main Patterns of Post-Compulsory Graduation and Dropping Out

One reason the dropout rate in Finnish comprehensive school has been minimal since the 1960s is the extensive special education system within the comprehensive school (Simola et al., 1999). For instance, in the 2006–07 school year, only

0.23% of the comprehensive school leavers, 152 pupils, did not succeed in obtaining the basic education school leaving certificate (Myllyniemi, 2008).

Annually, more than 90% of Finnish compulsory school leavers continue their studies either in upper secondary general schools or in vocational institutions. During the past 10–15 years, a little more than half of the comprehensive school graduates have continued their post-compulsory studies in general upper secondary schools, whereas the share of those continuing in vocational education and training has varied between 33% and 40%. Nowadays, it is also possible to study and get certificates simultaneously in both institutions, but this opportunity has not been popular among young people so far.

General upper secondary school has been a popular choice, especially among girls and young people from more advantaged social backgrounds, while boys and working-class youth have been over-represented in vocational schools. In addition, many fields of education are either male- or female-dominated in vocational education, with technology and transport being the most male-dominated (84% male students in 2006), and social and health services the most female-dominated field (90% female students) (Rinne, 2007; Statistics Finland, 2008). In 2006, half of the students who completed compulsory school continued their post-compulsory studies in general upper secondary education (females: 60%, males: 43%) and 40% continued their studies in vocational schools (females: 31%, males: 49%) (Myllyniemi, 2008).

In Finland, different upper secondary school forms have traditionally had different societal functions. The aim of the general schools has been to prepare students for higher education studies with higher status, whereas the objective of vocational schools has been to produce skilled (mostly manual) workers for different sectors of the labour market. It is more typical for the general school students to continue their studies after graduation, whereas the risk of being unemployed is higher among the vocational education students. While 45% of those who graduated from the general schools in 1998 were still studying in 2005, the corresponding figure among those who had graduated from vocational education and training was only 16%. The unemployment rate 7 years after graduation was 8% among the former vocational education students, whereas it was only 4% among those who had graduated from general schools (Statistics Finland, 2008).

In a situation where over 90% of those finishing comprehensive school continue their studies, upper secondary education can, in practice, be considered a part of compulsory education in Finland. Annually, only 5–8% of 16-year-olds drop out of the education system immediately after comprehensive school (Myllyniemi, 2008). On the basis of official statistics and other nationally representative data available, it is not possible to give exact numbers about how many of these dropouts will recommence their studies later on. What is known is the fact that 12% of Finnish young people aged 15–24 were outside both education and working life in 2005. Although this statistical group of 'outsiders' consists mainly of the young unemployed, it also includes those in military service, young housewives/-husbands and those whose situation is unknown (Länsi-Suomen lääninhallitus, 2007).

The risk of dropping out of upper secondary education has slightly increased during the past few years. Previously, students who had succeeded best in comprehensive school almost exclusively chose the general educational route. Now, some of them are choosing the vocational route, which means that the least successful students have more difficulty getting into vocational schools than before. In 2006, 7% of those Finnish young people who completed their compulsory education did not continue their studies in post-compulsory education, while the proportion of early school leavers in the previous year was 5% (Myllyniemi, 2008).

Despite the increased popularity of vocational schools, and the fact that dropout in vocational education has evenly diminished during the first years of the new millennium, vocational schools still have the greatest dropout in the context of upper secondary education in Finland. In addition, among vocational school dropouts, interruption of studies almost exclusively (90% in the school year 2004–05) means dropping out of the whole educational system – at least temporarily; whereas for half of the general school dropouts, the interruption of studies means continuing in some other form of education (Statistics Finland, 2008).

Interruption of upper secondary education was more common among males than females in Finland until the school year 2004–05, when the situation changed in vocational education and training. However, dropping out of the educational system altogether is more typical for boys than girls, for whom dropping out more often means continuing in some other form of vocational education (Statistics Finland, 2008).

Main Predictors of Dropping Out

It has become a widely held assumption that those young people between the ages of 16 and 18 who are outside all education, training or employment are condemned to an economically and socially marginalised future. Difficulties in the early stages in one's labour market career are seen as leading to an increased risk of subsequent unemployment or insecure employment. Prolonged unemployment, in turn, has been found to be connected with health and social problems, and as a result, with economic, social and political exclusion (e.g., Bynner & Parsons, 2002; Korpi et al., 2003).

In international discourse, it has been stated that after being 2 years outside education, employment opportunities are seriously diminished and returning to education becomes less probable (Vanttaja & Järvinen, 2006; Myllyniemi, 2008). As a result, those young people who are outside both education and working life at the age of 16–18 have been called 'youth at risk'. It is worthwhile to notice that in the Finnish context, the dropout phenomenon has been examined as an issue wider than just school interruption, and it has usually been connected with those young people who are outside both education and working life. As a result, the category 'NEET' (Not in Education, Employment or Training) is much closer than that of 'early school leavers' when speaking of dropout youth in the Finnish context.

During the past few decades, Finnish girls and boys have had almost an equally great likelihood of being outside education and working life at the age of 16–18. In turn, young people from disadvantaged social backgrounds, immigrant youth, disabled young people as well as former full-time special education pupils have had the greatest risk of being excluded from education and working life immediately after comprehensive school. These groups are not mutually exclusive, but partially overlapping. For instance, both the disabled and immigrants can be found among the typical group of special education pupils (Järvinen & Vanttaja, 2001; Järvinen & Jahnukainen, 2008).

In Finland, on average, the children of parents in weak labour market positions, with low incomes and basic education, have a greater probability of being excluded from education and working life at the age of 16–18 than the rest of the population (Järvinen & Vanttaja, 2001; Vanttaja, 2005). The connection between social background and one's educational career has long been known, and it has been documented in many studies in Finland and elsewhere (e.g., Kivinen & Rinne, 1995; Järvinen, 2003; Kivinen et al., 2007). On the other hand, the educational situation of immigrant youth, including Finnish-born youth with immigrant parents, is relatively new in Finland, since the number of immigrants has increased in Finland only during the past few decades.

Unfortunately, there is no information available in official Finnish statistics related to the social, regional and ethnic background of young people outside both education and working life. However, based on the census register data gathered for research related to the living conditions of Finnish young people (Autio et al., 2008), it is possible to examine the different background factors related to being outside education and working life among Finnish young people aged 15–24. This information is presented in Table 10.2.[2]

Gender and region are not very closely connected with young people's exclusion from education and working life in contemporary Finland, whereas the educational level of parents, and especially immigrant status, are strong determinants of young people dropping out of those fields. The less educated the mother or father is, the greater the likelihood that their offspring is outside education and working life. In the whole population aged 15–24, the proportion of these young outsiders was 11.8% in 2004, whereas among those whose mother had not continued schooling after compulsory school, the proportion of dropout youth was 18.3%. Among immigrant youth, the proportion of those outside education and working life was 30%, and among those born outside the European Union as many as 38.6% were outside education and simultaneously without a job in 2004.

According to research, finding employment is difficult for immigrants in Finland (e.g., Jaakkola, 2000; Forsander, 2002). The employment status of immigrants weakened especially in the 1990s due to the recession, and this affected both those who had been in Finland for a longer time and new arrivals. In a few years the unemployment rates increased several-fold, and at worst, that of immigrants was over 50%. In addition to high unemployment rates, the problems that immigrants face include unstable work careers and, in the case of more highly educated immigrants, finding work that corresponds to their level of education and professional training, as they are usually employed in jobs for which they are over-educated. Immigrants also often work in jobs that are of low status

---

[2] Those in military service or retired are not included in the numbers presented in the Table 10.2; the group under examination hence consists mainly of unemployed youth and those at home with their children.

Table 10.2 The proportion of young people outside education and working life in the Finnish population aged 15–24 by gender, region, country of birth and parents' educational level in 2004 (%)

Background characteristic	Rate
Gender	
Males	11.3
Females	12.0
Both sexes	11.8
Region	
Countryside	12.1
Small town	11.4
City	11.3
Country of birth	
Finland	11.0
Other European Union country	22.9
Countries outside the European Union	38.6
Mother's educational level	
Basic education	18.3
Upper secondary education	11.9
Higher Ed./Bachelor's degree	7.8
Higher Ed./Master's degree	5.7
Father's educational level	
Basic education	16.3
Upper secondary education	11.7
Higher Ed./Bachelor's degree	7.4
Higher Ed./Master's degree	5.8

Source: Statistics Finland (2008).

where it is difficult to motivate Finnish employees to accept them (Forsander & Alitolppa-Niitamo, 2000; Kyhä, 2006).

The problems of the post-compulsory education of immigrant youth have been examined in several studies, many of which are local in nature (e.g., Romakkaniemi & Ruutu, 2001). One problem relates to participation in post-compulsory, secondary level education. The difference in participation between immigrant youth and the other Finnish youth is significant. First of all, immigrant youth complete secondary education (general or vocational) at an older age than among the general population. Of those young people born in Finland, 65% have completed some sort of secondary education by the age of 19, while among immigrant youth over half do so only at the age of 21. Secondly, only 14% of the general population have completed only compulsory education at the age of 24, but among immigrants of the same age the corresponding figure is as high as 43%. Thirdly, although one half of all 20- to 24-year-old Finnish-born youth are general upper secondary school graduates, only 3 out of 10 immigrants of the same age are, and among those of African background, the proportion is as low as 1 out of 10 (Järvinen & Jahnukainen, 2008).

The consequences of exclusion from education and work on the later lives of Finnish young people have also been studied using longitudinal data and methods

(Järvinen & Vanttaja, 2006; Vanttaja & Järvinen, 2006; Järvinen et al., 2007).[3] Based on the results of this follow-up study, it seems that on average, the assumption that unemployment at the beginning of one's work career combined with limited education has negative consequences on one's later life course holds true. Those Finnish young people who are outside both education and working life at the age of 16–18 often end up in weaker labour market positions and with lower income levels as adults than others belonging to the same age cohort. As young adults, half of the target group had been either unemployed, or for some other reason outside the labour market (e.g., on a disability pension). Over half of the women and two thirds of the men had not completed any kind of education after compulsory education, and hence still had only a basic education at the age of 31–33 (Vanttaja & Järvinen, 2006). In addition, less than one third of the early school leavers had managed to carve out a stable labour market career (Järvinen & Vanttaja, 2006).

Although integration into society had been more difficult for those belonging to the group of unemployed early school leavers than in the population as a whole, life courses representing both exclusion and inclusion were found in the study. Despite the weak 'societal prediction', there were many in the group of early school leavers who had continued their education at a later age and succeeded in finding their place in the world of work. About 10% had continued higher education and ended up in the high-income group. The correlation between one's total education and career was strong. Those who had participated in adult education, especially those who had completed a higher education qualification, most often ended up in a successful labour market career; whereas those with only basic education had most often ended up outside the active labour force and/or in the low-income group (Vanttaja & Järvinen, 2006). Also, the social background of early school leavers was closely connected with the kind of labour market careers they came to have, and the link between parents' educational level and the later success of their offspring was especially strong (Järvinen & Vanttaja, 2006).

Programs, Policies and Practices in Reducing Dropout in Finland

Since the 1990s, and especially after Finland's entry into the European Union in 1995, different types of educational and labour market projects and practices intended to reduce the social exclusion of young people have become more common. In the course of time, the emphasis in these practices has shifted from offering employment to offering education, with combinations of education and work-based training being more and more common. Despite the fact that the youth unemployment rates have been higher in Finland than in European Union and OECD countries on average

---

[3] In this particular research project, the target group consisted of a 50% sample of all Finnish youth aged 16–18 (except those in military service) who were unemployed and had not continued their schooling after compulsory school in 1985 (n = 6,983). The life courses of these young people were followed at 5-year intervals up to and including the year 2000.

during the past 10–15 years, the length of unemployment periods are usually quite short for most young people (Järvinen, 2006). This is not, however, the situation in the case of the least educated young people, who have serious difficulties in both getting and keeping a job, and who quite often have problems in their personal lives as well. To support these young people, alternative forms of education, new kinds of pedagogical practices and vocational guidance as well as various methods supporting young people's life management have increasingly been developed during the past 10–15 years (Järvinen & Jahnukainen, 2001; Silvennoinen, 2002; Opetusministeriö, 2005).

Transition from basic to secondary education has been seen as a critical stage from the points of view of the educational and social exclusion of young people. In 2005, the Finnish Ministry of Education appointed a committee whose task was to make proposals for action which will guarantee that the whole age group has opportunities for further education and training. The committee's final report set a goal that in the year 2009, 97.5% of compulsory education school leavers would start in upper secondary education or training, or in additional basic education (Opetusministeriö, 2005).

Related to transition from basic to secondary education, two main problems in Finland are young people's dropping out of the educational system immediately after compulsory school, and failure to complete vocational education. During the past few decades, an attempt has been made to reduce young people dropping out of education as well as interruption of (vocational) schooling, for example by increasing vocational guidance and individual counselling (both in basic and secondary education), by adding more work-based learning into the curriculum of vocational education; and by paying special attention to the teaching and learning of certain 'risk-groups' of young people, such as immigrant youth, disabled youth and young people with learning difficulties or social problems.

In Finland, instead of emphasising the societal nature of the dropout phenomenon and concentrating, for example, on the social inequalities related to it, the problem of dropout has typically been viewed as an individual-level phenomenon. Partly as a result of this kind of understanding, system-wide reforms in reducing dropout have been unusual in Finland.

However, besides the extensive special education system described earlier, the establishment of additional basic education (Grade 10) can also be mentioned as an example of these kinds of system-wide reforms. This educational program – targeted at those young people who have difficulties in continuing their schooling after compulsory school or who have difficulties in making their educational choices – started as a project as early as 1977, and it was systemised several years later, in 1985. Under the circumstances of rapidly increased youth unemployment rates in the late 1970s, the aim was to offer an extra year in basic education for those young people who had dropped out of education immediately after compulsory school, or who wanted to improve their grades in order to get into the educational track of their choice (Silvennoinen, 2002).

Those young people who have completed basic education in the same or the previous year are eligible to apply for this program. Instruction is often carried out in cooperation with compulsory schools and vocational schools, and representatives of working life are also often included in the cooperation, mainly by offering places for students' practical training, which is an important element in this form of education. Another key element in this training program is individualised vocational guidance.

An individual study plan is formulated for every student, often in cooperation with the representatives of the local employment authority (Opetusministeriö, 2005).

Since the beginning of the 1990s, measures of support targeted at young people considered 'youth at risk' have expanded, and partly as a result of this, the number of pupils in additional basic education has decreased (Opetusministeriö, 2005). At the beginning of the 1990s, about 5% of those completing their basic education continued their studies in additional basic education annually. During the first years of the new millennium the proportions varied from 2% to 3%, the proportion being 2% in 2006 (Statistics Finland, 1993, 1994, 1996, 1998; Myllyniemi, 2008).

Despite the decline in the number of students in additional basic education, it is still seen as an important measure of support in combating the educational exclusion of young people. In its report, a committee appointed by the Ministry of Education proposed that voluntary additional basic education must be made the young person's statutory subjective right, and participation in this form of education should be made possible not only for school leavers of the same and previous year, but also for those who have finished their schooling 2 years earlier (Opetusministeriö, 2005).

In addition, the gender division of students in voluntary basic education has changed over the course of time. At the beginning, most of the students were boys, whereas the majority are now girls. It seems that boys who have problems in transition from basic to secondary education prefer work to education, and try to get a foothold on the labour market as soon as possible. Their participation in education varies depending on the youth labour market situation, whereas girls take a more positive stand on education as a means to improve one's possibilities of getting a job. Although the proportion of boys in additional basic education declined in the course of the 1980s, it increased again immediately at the beginning of the 1990s, when youth unemployment rates rose rapidly in Finland (Silvennoinen, 2002).

Another supporting measure worth mentioning is a program called youth workshop activities, which in the range of public sector services is located partly in the field of social work and partly in the fields of education and labour markets, and as such is a multidisciplinary activity. This also means that the measures of support offered by youth workshops are based on multi-professional cooperation between the representatives of the educational system, employment authorities, and welfare, health care and youth work (Opetusministeriö, 2005; Ministry of Education, 2008).

Youth workshops have developed from projects to permanent services. Currently, approximately half of the Finnish municipalities organise youth workshop activities, and about 7,000 young people participate in these activities (Ministry of Education, 2008). The aim of the youth workshops is to promote young people's integration into labour markets, as well as to support their future planning and life management. The workshops offer young people a chance to work under the supervision of a youth workshop trainer, as well as an individually tailored path to education or working life. In the youth workshops, the participants work and receive on-the-job training while simultaneously improving their life-management skills. Individual counselling and life-management support is offered by a multidisciplinary team consisting of special education teachers, psychologists, guidance counsellors, social and youth workers and representatives of the health service (Opetusministeriö, 2005; Ministry of Education, 2008).

Young people involved in activities offered by youth workshops can be either unemployed or still in education, in which case the aim is ensuring that they get a basic or vocational school certificate. The typical client involved in youth workshop activities is a young person who is under 25 years of age, unemployed and who has not completed any post-compulsory schooling. Since immigrants are quite well represented among young people involved in youth workshop activities, the need for experts in immigrant work has increased during the past few years. In 2006, a total of 52 different mother tongues were spoken in the workshops. The duration of youth workshops is individually determined; they usually last 1 year, but shorter periods are also possible (Opetusministeriö, 2005; Ministry of Education, 2008)

In vocational education and training, the correspondence of education to the world of work has been a key development focus area. For example, the proportion of studying at the workplace through learning at work has been increased and competence tests as a form of quality assurance have been included in the study program. Since 1998, and with the financial support of the European Union, various types of workshop activities have also been introduced in regular vocational education and training in Finland. The central idea of vocational schools' own workshops is learning by doing, which has been seen as an efficient method of increasing commitment in those young people who have difficulties in handling the theoretical contents of instruction in vocational education. Students can be involved in workshop activities a few hours a day on a regular basis, or they can get individual guidance a few times a week or month, or even more rarely, depending on their personal needs (Opetusministeriö, 2005; Ministry of Education, 2008).

One of the recently introduced measures of support targeted at young people at risk of educational exclusion is preparatory training for vocational education, from which students can flexibly move on to attain education leading to qualification. This program involves vocational counselling as well as teaching and learning the basic study skills that are needed for completing vocational education. The aim of the preparatory training is also to strengthen the general life-management skills of the students. The length of the study period in preparatory education varies individually; the aim is that students can move from preparatory to vocational training, leading to a qualification as soon as it is seen as appropriate from the point of view of each individual student. In preparatory training, special attention has been paid to the learning and schooling of certain groups of young people, such as disabled youth and immigrant youth (Opetusministeriö, 2005; Ministry of Education, 2008).

Individual support for young people at risk of educational and social exclusion is also offered by local employment authorities in Finland. Young people outside educational institutes have the opportunity to utilise the educational and occupational career counselling services of employment offices. Despite scarce resources, the social guarantee that has been implemented since the beginning of 2005 obliges local employment authorities to offer an activation plan for every unemployed job seeker below 25 years of age after they have been unemployed for 3 months. Activation plans can include offering education, work-based training, preparatory training of different kinds or employment, with offering education being the prime measure of support for those young people who lack upper secondary education qualifications.

Some Conclusions and Widening the Perspective: Finland – Not at the Top After All?

Finland is riding along on its fame in the OECD international educational rankings. In the latest country review (OECD, 2006), Finland received first place in natural sciences as well as second place in reading and mathematics. In 2000 and 2003 Finland was also ranked among the best, awarded first place in reading in both reviews, and thus the national success story seems steady enough. In addition, in the Finnish comprehensive school, the interdependent differences in achievement are comparatively small in international comparison.

Further, Finnish young people are more highly educated compared to youth in many other OECD countries, and young people's exclusion from both education and working life is also less of a problem in Finland than in many other countries belonging to the European Union (European Commission, 2005; OECD, 2008).

On the other hand, success at school, choice of educational careers and climbing up the educational ladder are still closely connected with one's parents' social status and level of education, even in the Finland of the 21st century (Järvinen, 2003; Kivinen et al., 2007). Even though the significance of the home as the definer of school success has weakened during recent decades, the clear discrepancies have not disappeared anywhere. Due to the recession in the beginning of the 1990s, and the simultaneous new course taken in educational policy, clear internal differentiation in the school establishment as well as the genesis of educational routes for the 'haves' and the 'have-nots' can be seen. For instance, in relation to choices concerning secondary education, choosing general school is more common among children with highly educated parents than among children of less educated parents (Rinne, 2007), and it is even eightfold more probable for the offspring from a highly educated family to end up in a university than for a child from a family with lower education (Kivinen et al., 2007).

It is also of utmost importance to note that Finnish children do not reach the PISA kind of top rankings in all the other comparative research. For example, in an international comparative study by the World Health Organization (2004, pp. 43–44), it came to light that only a small minority (5%) of Finnish children and young people truly enjoy being at school. When comparing 15-year-olds regarding this issue, Finnish young people brought up the rear.

In a comparative study published by UNICEF regarding the overall well-being of children and young people, Finland was ranked as third out of 15 countries in 2005. Only the Netherlands and Sweden were ahead of Finland in this study. However, even in this comparison, Finland received low scores when comparing the 'family and friend relations' of children (12th), and the 'experience of subjective well-being' of children (9th). Regarding those issues, Finland's ranking was clearly below average (Kangas, 2008).

In Finland, there has recently been a lot of discussion related to the polarisation of young people into those who are coping well in many areas of life and those who are at serious risk of social exclusion. Fear has been expressed that these groups of young people are becoming increasingly separated from each other (Autio & Eräranta, 2008). Based on available official statistics as well as recent survey studies, one can argue that on a general level, this polarisation hypothesis holds true. It seems that the proportion of young people who are at risk of social exclusion has increased during the past 15 years in Finland. Firstly, exclusion from the family sphere has become more common among children and young people: the proportion of children and young people placed outside their home or in custody has constantly increased during the years 1991–2006. Also, the proportion of young people with both low incomes and mental health problems has increased during the same period. Although the employment situation of young people has become better during the past few years, youth unemployment rates are still higher in Finland than in other countries belonging to the European Union on average (e.g., Järvinen & Vanttaja, 2005; Myllyriemi, 2008).

There are several differences related to the well-being of boys and girls in Finland. Loneliness, for instance, is more common among young males than among young females, as is a negative attitude towards schooling. Mental health problems, in turn, are more common among girls than boys. One must note, however, that although risk of becoming socially excluded has somewhat increased during the past 10–15 years, the great majority of Finnish young people are satisfied with their life as a whole, and with their health and social relations in particular. In a nationally representative study, when asked what school grade (using the Finnish scale of 4–10) young people aged 15–29 would give to their overall life satisfaction, 92% of them responded at least 8/10. In all, it seems that the life situation of the majority of Finnish young people is good or even extremely good, whereas the minority of young people have serious life-management problems and severe difficulties in many areas of life. In this respect, the above-mentioned polarisation hypothesis holds true (Myllyniemi, 2008).

This small, although growing minority of Finnish children and youth seems to be at risk of wider social exclusion, and this social truth has strong influences on both everyday life at school and the whole educational system. The idea of raising the educational level of the entire population and establishing educational equality has been at the centre of Finnish education policy since World War II. For over a century, the country has struggled to guarantee the offspring of all families an optimal level of education in every possible way, despite their economic, social, regional or educational background or status, and regardless of gender or ethnic origin. In Finland, there has been a strong faith in national solidarity, which means that the weakest have also been taken care of.

Over the past 2 decades, however, there have been clear signs of change in the thinking around the aims, delivery and organisation of education. The provision of education has more radically than before been based on ever hardening competition. There has been a tendency to regard education more and more as being the servant of the production economy and in terms of economic investment and efficiency. These steps towards ever deeper neo-liberalistic educational policy may threaten to marginalise and cause difficulties to an ever-growing number of children and young people.

The signs of change are clear enough to warrant stopping to contemplate further, and more widely, the goals of education: to ask seriously what the future of Finnish children and young people will be like, not only as regards their academic success, but also concerning their well-being at school and the quality of their future.

References

Antikainen, A. (2005). Aikuiskoulutukseen osallistumisen erojen syyt. In U. Rönnberg (Ed.), *Aikuiskoulutuksen vuosikirja. Tilastotietoja aikuisten opiskelusta 2003* (pp. 23–32). Helsinki: Opetusministeriö.

Autio, M., & Eräranta, K. (2008). Johdanto: polarisaatio käsitteenä ja empiirisesti koeteltuna tutkimusteesinä. In M. Autio, K. Eräranta, & S. Myllyniemi (Eds.), *Polarisoituva nuoruus. Nuorten elinolot vuosikirja 2008* (pp. 8–15). Helsinki: Nuorisotutkimusverkosto & Nuorisoasiain neuvottelukunta & Stakes.

Autio, M., Eräranta, K., & Myllyniemi, S. (Eds.). (2008). *Polarisoituva nuoruus. Nuorten elinolot vuosikirja 2008*. Helsinki: Nuorisotutkimusverkosto & Nuorisoasiain neuvottelukunta & Stakes.

Ball, S. J. (1994). *Education reform: A critical and post-structural approach*. Buckingham: Open University Press.

Ball, S. J. (2001). Globaalit toimintaperiaatteet ja kansalliset politiikat eurooppalaisessa koulutuksessa. In A. Jauhiainen, R. Rinne, & J. Tähtinen (Eds.), *Koulutuspolitiikka Suomessa ja ylikansalliset mallit* (pp. 21–44). Turku: Suomen kasvatustieteellinen seura.

Bynner, J., & Parsons, S. (2002). Social exclusion and the transition from school to work: The case of young people not in education, employment or training (NEET). *Journal of Vocational Behavior, 60*(2), 289–309.

European Commission. (2005). *Modernising education and training: a vital contribution to prosperity and social cohesion in Europe*. 2006 Joint Interim Report of the Council and of the Commission on progress under the 'Education & Training 2010' work program. Brussels: The European Commission.

Forsander, A. (2002). *Luottamuksen ehdot. Maahanmuuttajat 1990-luvulla suomalaisilla työmarkkinoilla*. Helsinki: Väestöliitto.

Forsander, A., & Alitolppa-Niitamo, A. (2000). *Maahanmuuttajien työllistyminen ja työhallinto. Keitä, miten ja minne*. Helsinki: Työministeriö.

Jaakkola, T. (2000). *Maahanmuuttajat ja etniset vähemmistöt työhönotossa ja työelämässä*. Helsinki: Työministeriö.

Jahnukainen, M. (2003). Laman lapset? Peruskoulussa erityisopetusta saaneiden oppilaiden osuuksien tarkastelua vuodesta 1987–2001. *Yhteiskuntapolitiikka, 68*(5), 501–507.

Järvinen, T. (2003). *Urheilijoita, taiteilijoita ja IB-nuoria. Lukioiden erikoistuminen ja koulukasvatuksen murros*. Helsinki: Nuorisotutkimusverkosto.

Järvinen, T. (2006). Nuoret ja työmarkkinoiden muutos uuden vuosituhannen alussa. In J. Autio (Ed.), *Kymmenvuotiskatsaus 2005. Teemana yritystoiminta*. Helsinki: Tilastokeskus.

Järvinen, T., & Jahnukainen, M. (2001). Kuka meistä onkaan syrjäytynyt? Marginalisaation ja syrjäytymisen käsitteellistä tarkastelua. In M. Suutari (Ed.), *Vallattomat marginaalit. Yhteisöllisyyksiä nuoruudessa ja yhteiskunnan reunoilla* (pp. 125–151). Helsinki: Nuorisotutkimusverkosto.

Järvinen, T., & Jahnukainen, M. (2008). Koulutus, polarisaatio ja tasa-arvo: hyvä- ja huono-osaistuminen perus- ja keskiasteen koulutuksessa. In M. Autio, K. Eräranta, & S. Myllyniemi (Eds.), *Polarisoituva nuoruus. Nuorten elinolot – vuosikirja 2008* (pp. 140–149). Helsinki: Nuorisotutkimusverkosto & Nuorisoasiain neuvottelukunta & Stakes.

Järvinen, T., & Vanttaja, M. (2001). Young people, education and work: Trends and changes in Finland in the 1990s. *Journal of Youth Studies*, *4*(2), 195–207.

Järvinen, T., & Vanttaja, M. (2005). *Nuoret koulutus ja työmarkkinoilla*. Helsinki: Nuorisoasian neuvottelukunta. Retrieved June 1, 2009, from http://www.minedu.fi/nuora

Järvinen, T., & Vanttaja, M. (2006). Koulupudokkaiden työurat. *Yhteiskuntapolitiikka*, *71*(1), 14–22.

Järvinen, T., Vanttaja, M., & Aro, M. (2007). Koulupudokkaista menestyjiksi. In M. Kuorelahti, & K. Lappalainen (Eds.), *Ruohon juurella – tutkimusta ja näkemystä* (pp. 116–134). Joensuu: Joensuun yliopisto.

Kallo, J. (2009). *Comparative and historical study on the OECD education policies, with a particular focus on the thematic reviews on tertiary education. Manuscript of dissertation.* CELE, University of Turku.

Kallo, J., & Rinne, R. (Eds.). (2006). *Supranational regimes and national education policies – Encountering challenge. Research in educational sciences 24.* Turku: Finnish Educational Research Association.

Kangas, O. (2008). Pohjoismaat – maailman paras kolkka? *Yhteiskuntapolitiikka*, *73*(4), 357–367.

Kivinen, O., & Rinne, R. (1995). *The social inheritance of education. Equality of educational opportunity among young people in Finland.* Helsinki: Statistics Finland and Research Unit for the Sociology of Education, University of Turku.

Kivinen, O., Hedman, J., & Kaipainen, P. (2007). From elite university to mass education. Educational expansion, equality of opportunities and returns to university education. *Acta Sociologica*, *50*(3), 231–247.

Kivirauma, J. (1989). *Erityisopetus ja suomalainen oppivelvollisuuskoulu vuosina 1921–1985.* Turku: Turun yliopisto.

Kivirauma, J., Rinne, R., & Klemelä, K. (Eds.). (2004). *Erityisopetus laajenevana koulutienä.* Turku: Turun yliopiston kasvatustieteiden tiedekunta.

Korpi, T., De Graaf, P., Hendrickx, J., & Layte, R. (2003). Vocational training and employment precariousness in Great Britain. *Acta Sociologica*, *46*(1), 17–30.

Kyhä, H. (2006). Miksi lääkäri ei kelpaa lääkäriksi? Korkeakoulutetut maahanmuuttajat Suomen työmarkkinoilla. *Aikuiskasvatus*, *26*(2), 123–129.

Länsi-Suomen lääninhallitus. (2007). *Polarisaatiomuistio.* (Ed. by E. Häggman). Retrieved September 16, 2008 from http://www.laaninhallitus.fi/

Ministry of Education. (2008). *The Finnish government's child and youth policy programme 2007–2111.* Publications of the Ministry of Education, Finland 2008: 21. Helsinki: The Ministry of Education.

Myllyniemi, S. (2008). Tilasto-osio. In M. Autio, K. Eräranta, & S. Myllyniemi (Eds), *Polarisoituva nuoruus? Nuorten elinolot vuosikirja 2008* (pp. 18–81). Helsinki: Nuorisotutkimusverkosto & Nuorisoasiain neuvottelukunta & Stakes.

Niukko, S. (2006). *Yhteistyötä ilman riskejä? OECD:n rooli Suomen koulutuspolitiikassa.* Turku: Turun yliopisto.

Opetusministeriö. (2005). *Perusopetuksen ja toisen asteen koulutuksen nivelvaiheen kehittämistyöryhmän muistio.* Opetusministeriön työryhmämuistioita ja selvityksiä 2005: 33. Helsinki: Opetusministeriö.

Organisation for Economic Co-operation and Development (OECD). (2006). (PISA 2006) *The Programme for International Student Assessment. Results.* Paris: OECD.

Organisation for Economic Co-operation and Development (OECD). (2008). *Education at a glance.* Paris: OECD.

Raivola, R., Heikkinen, A., Kauppi, A., Nuotio, P., Oulasvirta, L., Rinne, R., Kamppi, P., & Silvennoinen, H. (2006). *Aikuisten opiskelumahdollisuudet ja järjestäjäverkko toisen asteen ammatillisessa koulutuksessa.* Jyväskylä: Koulutuksen arviointineuvosto.

Rinne, R. (2007). Lukionkäynti vanhempien näkemänä. In K. Klemelä, E. Olkinuora, R. Rinne & A. Virta (Eds.), *Lukio nuorten opiskelutienä. Turkulainen lukio opiskelijoiden, vanhempien ja opettajien silmin 2000-luvun alussa* (pp. 207–260). Turku: Turun yliopiston kasvatustieteiden tiedekunta.

Rinne, S. (2007). Kodin merkitys lukiolaisten opiskelumenestykseen ja valintoihin. In K. Klemelä, E. Olkinuora, R. Rinne & A. Virta (Eds.), *Lukio nuorten opiskelutienä. Turkulainen lukio opiskelijoiden, vanhempien ja opettajien silmin 2000-luvun alussa* (pp. 261–294). Turku: Turun yliopiston kasvatustieteiden tiedekunta.

Rinne, R., Kallo, J., & Hokka, S. (2004). Too eager to comply? OECD education policies and the Finnish response. *European Educational Research Journal, 3*(2), 454–485.

Rinne, R., & Kivirauma, J. (2005). The historical formation of modern education and the junction of the 'educational lower class'. *Paedagogica Historica. International Journal of History of Education, 41*(1&2), 61–78.

Romakkaniemi, H., & Ruutu, S. (2001). *Unelma ammatista. Kokemuksia maahanmuuttajien valmistavasta koulutuksesta Helsingin ammatillisissa oppilaitoksissa.* Helsinki: Helsingin kaupungin opetusvirasto.

Rubensson, K. (2005). *The state of equality in adult education in Nordic and OECD countries.* Paper presented at 'Adult Education – Liberty, Fraternity, Equality?' Conference, CELE, University of Turku, Finland, May 13–14, 2005.

Seppänen, P. (2006). *Kouluvalintapolitiikka perusopetuksessa. Suomalaiskaupunkien koulumarkkinat kansainvälisessä valossa.* Turku: Suomen Kasvatustieteellinen Seura.

Silvennoinen, H. (2002). *Koulutus marginalisaation hallintana.* Helsinki: Gaudeamus.

Simola, H., Rinne, R., & Kivirauma, J. (1999). Finland. National changes in education and education governance. In S. Lindblad & T. Popkewitz (Eds.), *Education governance and social integration and exclusion: National cases of educational systems and recent reforms* (pp. 42–64). Uppsala: Uppsala University.

Statistics Finland. (1993). Koulutus 1993:7. *Koulutuksen kysyntä 1991.* Helsinki: Tilastokeskus.

Statistics Finland. (1994). Koulutus 1994:3. *Education in Finland 1994. Statistics and indicators.* Helsinki: Tilastokeskus.

Statistics Finland. (1996). Koulutus 1996:13. *Koulutuksen kysyntä 1995.* Helsinki: Tilastokeskus.

Statistics Finland. (1998). Koulutus 1998:5. *Oppilaitostilastot 1998.* Helsinki: Tilastokeskus.

Statistics Finland. (2005). Koulutus 2005:3. *Oppilaitostilastot 2005.* Helsinki: Tilastokeskus.

Statistics Finland. (2008). *Oppilaitostilastot 2007.* Helsinki: Statistics Finland.

Tuijnman, A., & Hellström, Z. (Eds.). (2001). *Curious minds: Nordic adult education compared.* Copenhagen: Nordic Council of Ministers.

Vanttaja, M. (2005). Koulutuksesta ja työstä karsiutuneiden nuorten kotitaustan ja myöhempien elämänvaiheiden tarkastelua. *Yhteiskuntapolitiikka, 70*(4), 411–416.

Vanttaja, M., & Järvinen, T. (2006). The young outsiders: The later life courses of 'drop-out youth'. *International Journal of Lifelong Education, 25*(2), 173–184.

Vanttaja, M., & Rinne, R. (2008). Suomalainen koulutusjärjestelmä ja koulutuspolitiikka 1990- ja 2000-luvuilla. In R. Rinne, L. Jögi, R. Leppänen, M. Korppas & K. Kemelä (Eds.), *Suomalainen ja virolainen koulutus ja Euroopan unionin uusi koulutuspolitiikka.* Turku: Turun yliopiston kasvatustieteiden tiedekunta.

World Health Organization (WHO). (2004). Young people's health in context. Health Behaviour in School-aged Children (HBSC) study: International report from 2001/2002. Denmark: WHO.

Chapter 11
Dropout in a Small Society: Is the Icelandic Case Somehow Different?

Kristjana Stella Blondal, JónTorfi Jónasson and Anne-Christin Tannhäuser

Icelandic Education

Early in the 20th century, the Icelandic education system was poorly developed, with no compulsory education and no legal framework for primary education. During the next 100 years, however, the system became mature, flexible and fairly advanced – largely on par with systems in the other Nordic countries (Guttormsson, 2008). While the total Icelandic population did not reach 300,000 until the 21st century, numerous studies have shown that Icelandic education developed in ways similar to much larger systems, both in qualitative and quantitative terms, and apparently dealt with many of the same problems (e.g., Jóhannsdóttir, 2006; Jónasson, 1999, 2003; Jónasson & Tuijnman, 2001). Such studies draw attention to important similarities between different systems and warn against over-emphasising their differences, though they of course exist. The conclusion is that much can be learned about various aspects of many major problems in Iceland simply by analysing studies from its neighbours. Moreover, these neighbours may also benefit from Iceland's experience, as information about a number of issues is relatively easy to come by in the quite well-documented Icelandic setting.

By comparison, the Icelandic system still faces one outstanding problem: an extremely high dropout rate in upper secondary education. This phenomenon is considered so crucial that recent legal reform has focused particularly on it. This chapter will describe the Icelandic education system with an emphasis on upper secondary education, present Icelandic findings on the problem of school dropout, and describe the programs and policies that have been developed to address this issue.

Icelandic society generally emphasises education, with an eye to ensuring that every child and young person has an equal right to education, free of charge, in both compulsory and upper secondary school. The following statement reflects a fundamental principle of the Icelandic education system:

K.S. Blondal (✉), J.T. Jónasson and A.-C. Tannhäuser
University of Iceland, Iceland

S. Lamb et al. (Eds.), *School Dropout and Completion: International Comparative Studies in Theory and Policy*, DOI 10.1007/978-90-481-9763-7_13,
© Springer Science+Business Media B.V. 2011

... everyone should have equal opportunities to acquire an education, irrespective of sex, economic status, residential location, religion, possible handicap, and cultural or social background. (Ministry of Education, Science and Culture, 2002, p. 7)

Icelandic children normally start school at the age of 6 and progress automatically from one year to the next throughout 10 years of compulsory education as shown in Fig. 11.1. Implicit in the main principle of an equal right to education is the compulsory schools' responsibility to attend to the educational needs of each student. Pupils with special needs have the right to study support, based on evaluation of their needs. Special educational support can take place in the special education classroom, in the general classroom, or in both, which is most often the case. Less than 0.5% of each cohort attends special schools; on the other hand, around 20% receive special educational support while attending mainstream classes (Statistics Iceland, 2007).

After completing compulsory education at the age of 16, most students proceed directly to upper secondary school, despite it being non-compulsory (see Fig. 11.1). Since 2000, over 90% of 16-year-olds have enrolled in upper secondary level each year (Statistics Iceland, 2006a, 2008a). Upper secondary studies are typically 4-year programs (with some notable exceptions, however), and are supposed to comprise students in the age group of 16 to 20.

The compulsory system, comprising primary and lower secondary schools, is financed and operated by the municipalities. The upper secondary system, in contrast, is operated and financed by the central government, except that the municipalities provide up to 40% of construction costs. According to the Upper Secondary School Act of 1996, upper secondary school administration is based on legislation regulations and the curriculum guide issued by the central government. The structure of the

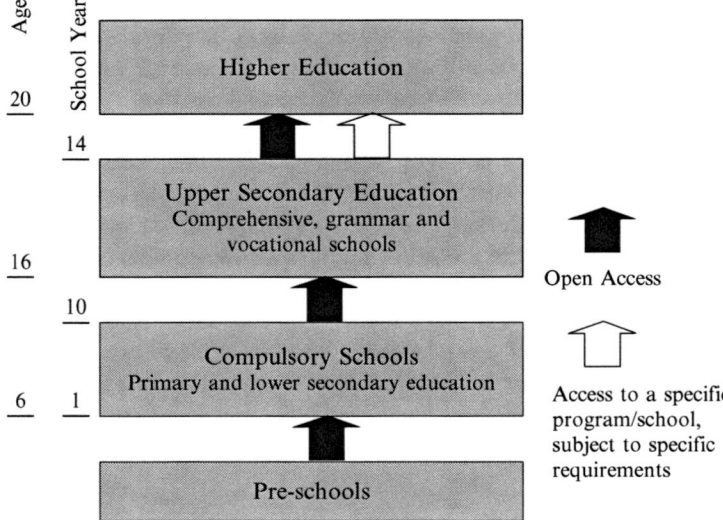

Fig. 11.1 The structure of the Icelandic educational system (Source: Ministry of Education, Science and Culture, 2005)

system and the curriculum framework is dictated by the central government, albeit the schools have a rather limited but increasing scope for independent action. Thus, the administrative structure is essentially two-layered, where one layer represents the central government and the other the individual schools. A new Upper Secondary School Act was passed in 2008; it is meant to take effect gradually and enter into full force no later than 2011. We will describe the system in terms of the previous (1996) Act, as this has moulded the system and remains in effect to a great extent, but we will also point out changes implicit in the new Act.

Upper Secondary School in Iceland

The Icelandic school year is 9 months long. Some upper secondary schools offer evening adult education classes and distance education. While distance education is organised independent of age, evening classes are organised specifically for adults. Distance education has been on the rise since 2003, while special adult education classes have diminished (Statistics Iceland, 2008b). Generally there is no tuition charge for upper secondary schooling, though vocational students pay part of their materials costs. In addition, students in adult and distance education pay partial tuition (Ministry of Education, Science and Culture, 2002, 2005).

In the last grade of compulsory school, students have until now taken nationally coordinated examinations in up to six subjects (Icelandic, mathematics, Danish, English, social science and natural science); these have in fact been optional, but entrance into different upper secondary programs has been to a varying degree conditional on passing at least some of them, as determined by the ministry. The decision regarding entrance requirements has now been moved from the ministry to individual schools under the new Upper Secondary School Act (2008), and at the same time the national examinations have been abolished in their current form. The changes are, though, not dramatic; everyone had the legal right of entrance into the upper secondary school level, irrespective of academic results, at the end of compulsory education under the Upper Secondary School Act of 1996. However, admittance into many specific programs was contingent on student outcome in the national examinations. Therefore, those not taking any such examination or performing poorly had somewhat limited options at the upper secondary level.

Upper secondary studies are typically 4-year programs (with some notable exceptions, mainly involving expressly shorter-duration programs) and are supposed to cover the age group of 16 to 19 (with graduation at the age of 20). There are about 30 upper secondary schools in the country, and they fall into three main categories. Firstly, there are traditional grammar schools offering only matriculation examination programs. For a long time, such schools formed the homogeneous backbone of the secondary system. Secondly, various vocational schools developed from the late 19th century onwards. Such schools were specialised, with those offering programs for the industrial arts emerging as the most prominent. Thirdly, since the late 1970s, comprehensive schools have been established in accordance with the government's policy of opening schools that offer both vocational programs and academic programs for the university entrance examination (UEE). Comprehensive schools combine the two former types of schools, following not only the rationale of economy in rural areas, but also fundamentally the goal of eradicating as much as possible any question of status difference between the different types of programs, and facilitating transfers between programs and schools whenever students so desire. The explicit rationale for building up the comprehensive system was that students could easily change tracks. But implicit was that they could move from the academic or *gymnasium* track to the vocational tracks if they could not cope with the former (Jónasson, 1997). In fact, this did not happen frequently; rather, what transpired fairly soon was that academically able vocational students, especially in the comprehensive schools, switched to academic programs (Jónasson, 1994). In the years 2007 and 2008, more than half of all 16- to 19-year-old students attended comprehensive schools, roughly one third attended grammar schools, and about 7% vocational schools.

Recently, the vocational schools have been permitted to offer matriculation programs, typically in combination with their vocational programs. This merging of academic and vocational programs has been a leading development since the 1970s (Jónasson, 1997, 2008). It is also a major principle behind the most recent law on upper secondary education, where the explicit rhetoric is to claim that the status of vocational and academic education should be equivalent within a holistic system, such that the university entrance examination might be completed from both the vocational and academic tracks (Ministry of Education, Science and Culture, n.d.).

Around 100 branches of study are offered at the upper secondary school level, of which over 80 are vocational. Every branch offers pathways to further education. The main pathways are as follows: (1) academic programs; (2) an arts program; (3) a multitude of vocational programs such as the industrial arts, which have been the mainstay of vocational schooling; (4) a general program; and (5) a variety of (normally short-term) work-related programs. These programs are defined in terms of credits. Usually the students are expected to complete 17 to 18 credits per semester (Ministry of Education, Science and Culture, 2008), but in most schools they are allowed to take more or fewer credits per semester. The matriculation examination usually requires 140 credits.

Academic programs typically take eight semesters (4 years) and conclude with the matriculation examination. Four different study programs are offered: social sciences, natural sciences, languages, and business and economics.

The *arts program* takes 3 years and is designed to prepare students for further education in the field.

The category of *vocational programs* exhibits by far the greatest variety of courses, generally taking six to eight semesters, but with very few exceptions of shorter- or longer-term programs. Vocational programs may be divided into two categories: study in certified trades which confer professional licences in the respective professions, and study that prepares students for certain jobs but gives no legally protected qualifications. Study in certified trades is conducted either through a master training program or through school-based vocational training. The vocational training for students in master training programs is primarily in the workplace in companies or with a master craftsman, but students complete the academic portion of their studies in a school according to a set curriculum. Students in school-based vocational education and training (VET) programs receive their general and special training in a school, followed by training in the workplace. In both programs, students are responsible for obtaining a work contract or workplace training position themselves. Students in other forms of vocational education study largely in a school environment, although training in the workplace is frequently part of the program (Ministry of Education, Science and Culture, 2007a).

Students can complete matriculation examinations both from vocational programs and the arts programs by taking additional courses (Ministry of Education, Science and Culture, 2007a, 2008). The proportion of students completing matriculation examinations using this option has been growing over the last years. From 1996 to 2002, around 3% of matriculations were of this type, with a steady increase since. In 2002, 6% of those completing matriculation did so by taking additional courses, as compared to 15% in 2007 (Statistics Iceland, 2009a).

The *general program* takes 1–2 years and is mostly intended for those who do not fulfil admission requirements for other courses of study and thus need to improve their academic skills in core subjects before entering other lines of study. This program is also for students who have not yet decided which path to pursue (Ministry of Education, Science and Culture, 2008). In a sense, this option can be regarded as a simple prolongation of the compulsory lower secondary school.

Work-related programs are designed for students who have had extensive special education in compulsory school and are unable on academic grounds to participate in other courses of study (Ministry of Education, Science and Culture, 2008). The work-related programs are part of the mainstream system and some of the comprehensive schools make a special effort to offer such programs.

As in other Organisation for Economic Co-operation and Development (OECD) countries, most students complete programs giving access to higher education. Academic programs attract by far the most students. Statistics from 2008 show that roughly half of the 16- to 19-year-old cohort attended academic programs, 16% were in VET (including apprenticeships), 8% were in apprenticeships, around 10% in general studies, and 1% in work-related studies. One fifth were not registered in upper secondary school. Roughly 70% of the 16- to 19-year-old students in academic courses were either in natural or social sciences. Almost one third of the apprentices were in building and construction branches (30%); 22% in electrical industry branches; 14% in vehicles and transport branches; 13% in hairdressing and beauty therapy; and 12% in metal, machinery technique, and production branches (Statistics Iceland, n.d.). Moreover, males are more likely to opt for the vocational programs than females (Jónasson & Blondal, 2002a).

The upper secondary school level emphasises flexibility. In the introduction to the booklet on upper secondary education in Iceland that every student receives during the last grade of compulsory school, the Minister of Education, Science and

Culture emphasises that students in academic programs can easily switch to vocational courses, and students in vocational programs can pursue further studies to complete the matriculation examination. Also, students can transfer credits between different schools and fields, augmenting the ease of changing programs, both for students who want to switch tracks from vocational to academic studies and vice versa, as well as within fields (Ministry of Education, Science and Culture, 2008). The credit unit system introduced with the new Upper Secondary School Act should make transferring between schools or study programs easier yet, since the system will thereupon be further harmonised (see below).

The educational reform of the entire school system that the Icelandic central government is currently undertaking is of particular relevance here because the dropout issue was given absolute priority in the most recent legislation (the Preschool Act, No. 90/2008; the Compulsory School Act, No. 91/2008; the Upper Secondary School Act, No. 92/2008). The intention explicit in the reform is that education shall be organised so as to meet the requirements and expectations of students, substantially increase curriculum flexibility, add to the number of educational pathways offered, facilitate the completion of upper secondary programs in 3 rather than the normative 4 years, and create conditions for more students to complete defined study programs, with a view to decreasing school dropout (Ministry of Education, Science and Culture, n.d.). The possibility of completing traditional 4-year studies in a shorter period of time has existed since the early 1970s, when the unit credit system was implemented parallel to the sequential class (first by the relatively new grammar school, *Menntaskólinn við Hamrahlíð*, in 1972). Most students, however, complete their studies in 4 years or more, rather than in fewer than 4 years (Jónasson & Blondal, 2002a). The special emphasis on facilitating completion of upper secondary school in a shorter time than 4 years might change this, but the laws are not clear in the sense that they do not state how many credit units students need to complete for their graduation. This will probably be stated in the new national curriculum that is under development, and if not, each school will have to define it in its curriculum and submit it for ministerial approval.

The following discussion involves the provisions directly related to dropout. The 2008 legislation provides for a new qualification called the *upper secondary school leaving certificate*, requiring 1½ or 2 years of study, but not entailing any specific courses. Other qualifications provided for are vocational certificates which confer professional licences in the respective professions, the matriculation examination (i.e., UEE), and other final examinations which are defined by upper secondary schools and prepare students for certain jobs but give no legally protected qualifications. Finally, upper secondary schools may now begin to offer post-secondary education (the Upper Secondary School Act, No. 92/2008).

The new upper secondary school leaving certificate is aimed at students who do not plan to complete further qualifications, and one of its main purposes is to decrease school dropout at the secondary level. Whether the certificate will make much difference to students is not clear, since it conveys no rights except to further study at the same school level, which the students have anyway (Ministry of Education, Science and Culture, n.d.). However, the certificate may induce students to complete at least 1½ years of upper secondary education, instead of the 1 year which many have typically completed before dropping out. This remains to be seen.

Finally, it is important to emphasise two important principles inherent in the reform. One is making vocational education equivalent to academic education. For example, the academic and vocational matriculation examinations are rendered equivalent. This is the official statement but it is not made explicit in the legislation as to how this is to be effected, so the exact ramifications remain unclear. The second principle, and in fact one of the major aims of the new legislation, is decentralising the upper secondary school system, even though the schools have to obey guidelines set by the ministry (Ministry of Education, Science and Culture, n.d.). Again, it is unclear how the ministry will balance its control with that of the schools, but there is no doubt that the government continues its effort to bolster vocational education, apparently against the odds of it actually being effective (Jónasson, 1998, 2003, 2008). Schools themselves, by being given extra freedom, may find ways to diminish the dropout rate.

Tertiary Education

The Icelandic tertiary system is essentially a unitary one, kindred to the United Kingdom and perhaps the Swedish systems, and thus it fits the 5A level of UNESCO's International Standard Classification of Education (ISCED) (Jónasson, 2004). In terms of the European Bologna framework for higher education, the university level is largely a $3 + 2 + 3$-cycle system, with essentially no post-secondary, non-university track. This refers to a first cycle of 3 years (bachelor's level), 2 years at master's level, and 3 years at doctoral level.

Because Icelandic students do not normally complete their studies at upper secondary school until the age of 20, they might be expected to graduate from university at somewhat older ages than their peers in neighbouring countries, especially as it is not uncommon for Icelandic students to take a year off after matriculation. Comparison of the proportions of students in Iceland, Sweden and Denmark who completed a matriculation examination and bachelor's degree in 2000 and 2001 as a percentage of the reference cohorts indicates that the picture is not so clear-cut. While Icelandic students graduate from upper secondary school somewhat older than in Denmark or particularly in Sweden, the Icelanders are not as distinct in age from the Danish students as the formal systems might lead us to expect. Moreover, the differences largely disappear when moving to the level of higher education: in all three countries, the highest proportion of students graduated at the same age, at around 24–26 years (Jónasson, 2002). Note that these points are only meant to bring out qualitative aspects, that is, to show that the basic profiles of the three countries are quite similar. In any case, the formal system descriptions fail to tell the full story. Such descriptions would imply that Icelandic students should lag behind the Danish and Swedish students by a whole year, but they do not.

Patterns of School Dropout

At the age of 16, most students proceed directly to upper secondary school. Nonetheless, early school leaving is more common in Iceland than in many other OECD countries. An Icelandic study of a cohort born in 1975 showed that around 40% had not yet finished upper secondary school at the age of 24 (keeping in mind that the normal completion age for most study programs is 20). This result resembles that from a comparable Icelandic study of a cohort born in 1969. On the other hand, of those who had not completed the upper secondary level, around 16% were studying at that level at the age of 24 (Jónasson & Blondal, 2002a; Jónasson & Jónsdóttir, 1992). A recent study on early school leavers (European Commission Directorate General for Education and Culture, 2005) showed the Icelandic situation to be somewhat special, in that the Icelandic population gradually does complete school, showing changes even in cohorts aged over 30. As shown in Fig. 11.2, the dropout rate is quite high for both males and females of every age group, but it gradually decreases with age to reach a low of around 20% for females in their 30s, and for males in their 40s. Thereafter it increases with age.

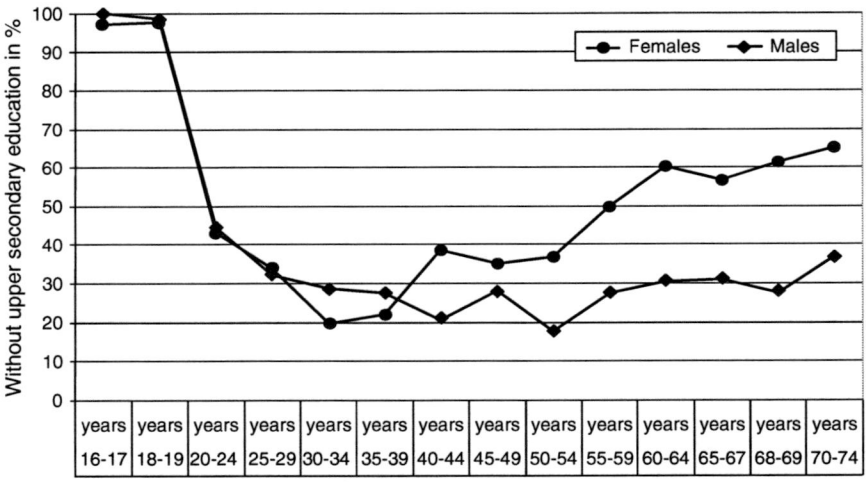

Fig. 11.2 Proportion of a cohort which has not obtained any formal certificate after compulsory education in Iceland, 2003 (Source: Jónasson & Dofradóttir, 2008)

It should be noted that even though Iceland's dropout rate is high and of great concern, the system is actually flexible in a modest but compensating way. This is demonstrated by the fact that the upper secondary programs stay open to older cohorts than the system is mainly tailored for. While the system accepts students of any age, it is based on an age range of 16–19. Still, statistics show that over the last 10 years, only about 60% of students in upper secondary schools have been in this age range. A little less than 30% have been 21- to 29-year-olds, and roughly 10% have been older (Statistics Iceland, 2006a). Understandably, many older students opt to attend evening classes or register for distance education, in both cases more so with increasing age.

The dropout rate is greater among males than females. Furthermore, the rate is greater outside the capital region and among students from families with low socio-economic status (Blondal & Jónasson, 2003; Blondal & Adalbjarnardottir, in press). In addition, dropout is greater from vocational programs than from academic programs (Statistics Iceland, 2004).

Through the years, students in the capital region have, on average, achieved higher grades than students outside it in the nationally coordinated examinations at the end of compulsory school (Jónasson & Blondal, 2002a, 2002b; Námsmatsstofnun, 2006). The surveys of student cohorts born in 1969 and 1975 showed that the dropout rate was higher outside of the capital region. When controlled for academic achievement in the national examinations at the end of compulsory school, however, the difference in dropout rate between the capital region and other regions disappeared (Jónasson & Blondal, 2002a). This suggests that the problem of varying regional educational attainment at upper secondary level can be traced to academic achievement in elementary school. Similar analyses showed much lesser effects of gender and students' socioeconomic background when academic achievement was taken into account.

The Icelandic study of the cohort born in 1975 showed that at age 24, almost a quarter of the cohort had either never enrolled in upper secondary school (7.3%) or had not completed any courses there (15.3%). Moreover, of the students who dropped out, over half (55%) left before completing the equivalent of one school year. This means that they completed less than one quarter of the majority of programs offered at this school level, whether towards matriculation examinations or the many vocational programs. As for completing the equivalent of two school years, about 80% of the group that quit left before that stage (Jónasson & Blondal, 2002a). Similar findings were obtained in the comparable study of the cohort born in 1969 (Jónasson & Jónsdóttir, 1992).

Why Do Students Drop Out? Theorisation and Explanations

In an earlier study on the education, attitudes to school and psychological characteristics of the Icelandic cohort born in 1975 (4,180 individuals), dropout was examined from three different perspective (Jónasson & Blondal, 2005a). It was looked at from the *system perspective*, where there was speculation on the extent to which dropping out can be attributed to the Icelandic work and education infrastructure and to the curricular choices open to students; the *school perspective*, where consideration was given to how various schools operate; and finally the *individual perspective*, where dropout causes are understood in terms of the attributes of the individual, or in terms of the individual's immediate social environment.

The System Perspective

Consider first the *system*[1] *perspective*. The explanations hitherto given for Iceland's high dropout rates, based on the educational system, are primarily four:

1. There is the general assumption in the system that upper secondary education may take too many years, in any case longer than in other Nordic countries (Jónasson, 2002). (As discussed previously, upper secondary education has typically been characterised by 4-year programs.) This assumption is probably based on the notion that those students who succeed in completing the first half of the studies would be less likely to drop out if they had 1 year left instead of 2.
2. The school system may be overly flexible, allowing students to come and go as they please, so that they lack compulsion to complete their studies. Whereas flexibility is normally seen as an advantage, here it is considered a disadvantage.
3. The implicit societal emphasis on general rather than vocational education seems to influence many students to make apparently non-intuitive choices; thus, despite having deeper interest in vocational subjects, they choose academic tracks. The Icelandic system leaves the choice of upper secondary tracks completely up to the students except in those relatively few instances where they do not fulfil the prerequisites of a specific program. There is considerable evidence that students feel pressure to choose academic tracks even though their basic interests fit vocational tracks.
4. The labour market attracts students out of school. This explanation points out how expansion of the Icelandic labour market in recent years has resulted in unusually enticing job opportunities for young people with little formal educational qualifications, compared to other European countries (European Commission Directorate General for Education and Culture, 2005). In the Icelandic cohort study, job opportunities were one of the three main reasons students gave for quitting school (Jónasson & Blondal, 2002a).

Working along with school has been very common in Iceland. In 2003–05, around 60% of 16- to 24-year-old students either in upper secondary or tertiary-level education worked along with studying, and on average worked for 28 hours per week! Additionally, 8–9% of students not working during their studies were in fact looking for work (Statistics Iceland, 2006b).

---

[1] Alternative terms to *system* might be *external environment* or *macro context*.

The School Perspective

It is possible to divide the perspectives that schools have into two types, based on their image or role in society. On the one hand, some exceptionally prestigious schools mainly have the aim of preparing their students for higher education, and even for a few special fields of higher education, such as medicine or engineering. On the other hand, the remaining schools have the broader aim of educating a very diverse student group that will not necessarily continue studying after upper secondary schooling. The prestigious schools are not seen to effectively encourage students who do not meet their educational standards to continue; these schools do not necessarily see it as a problem when students leave before completion. The schools with broader aims try to retain their students (admittedly to a varying extent), and unequivocally attempt to decrease their dropout rates.

Added to all this are school finances, which are quite complex. A significant portion of school funding is on a per capita basis, related to the number of students completing their courses, irrespective of their level of achievement. This is supposed to support the government policy of encouraging schools to retain students. However, how sensitive a school is to this pressure depends on the type of students it generally accepts, on how retention is measured, and how the individual school balances the pros and cons of retaining educationally weak students with respect to the funding system.[2]

Although school effectiveness has not been a major focus of Iceland's school dropout discussion, a study of this matter is now underway under the leadership of the present authors. Also, an Icelandic study has previously indicated that the relationship between different upper secondary schools and student progress at university level, controlled for previous academic achievement, is far from simple (Jónasson & Blondal, 2005b). It was not the case that students coming from the so-called best schools progressed faster through university than those coming from schools which definitely had a lower overall status.

The Individual's Perspective

In the Icelandic cohort study, those defined as school dropouts (i.e., those not currently studying and not having completed an upper secondary education by the age of 24) were asked about their main reasons for leaving school (Jónasson & Blondal, 2002a). The most common reasons given by both males and females were categorised under the headings 'I was bored with my studies' and 'I had

---

[2]Recently, a number of schoolmasters were reprimanded formally by the Ministry of Education for incorrect bookkeeping on this issue, an action they find unfair. The controversy centres on the precise moment at which a student is to be counted as a dropout. School appropriations are related to the number of students who have not dropped out.

financial difficulties'. A common category for males was 'I got a good job,' and for females, 'I had a child'. The findings also showed that around half of the dropout group, looking back (at age 24), felt that leaving school had been the right decision, considering their situation at that time. It should also be pointed out, however, that half of the group thought their situation in the labour market would be better if they had completed upper secondary education. Practically everyone wanted to add to their education, although 60% believed it would be difficult to start studying again within the formal education system. Although these findings give insight into why students leave school, it should be noted that the phenomenon of dropout is complicated; many different factors come into play, often during different periods in the student's life. The individual factors that have most often been identified are students' academic performance and school engagement (see Rumberger, 2004).

Performance in academic programs at the lower secondary (compulsory) level has been clearly demonstrated to be one of the strongest predictors for upper secondary dropout, in Iceland as well as elsewhere (see Battin-Pearson et al., 2000). Figure 11.3 shows the percentage of a cohort of Icelandic students who had completed upper secondary education – either matriculation or vocational programs – by the age of 24, as a function of grades in a standardised test in Icelandic at the end of compulsory school (age 16). It also shows the percentage of the cohort that got certain grades (the line), for example 5% of the cohort got grades lower than 3, and 31% got grades higher than 7 (the grade system is from 1 to 10).

The figure demonstrates three points. First, grades clearly predict the graduates from academic programs: the higher the grades, the more likely the students are to

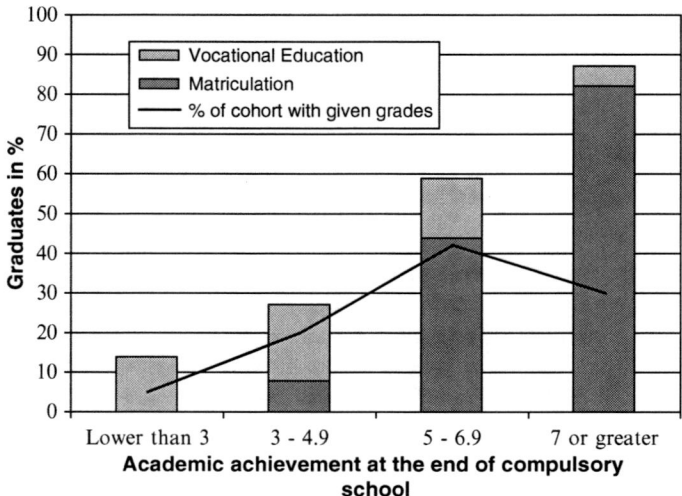

Fig. 11.3 Proportion of a cohort who completed upper secondary education by program in light of academic achievement at the end of compulsory school (Source: Derived from Jónasson & Blondal, 2002a)

have completed the matriculation examination by the age of 24. Second, grades do not predict completion of vocational programs; and third, the figure also shows that only 60% of the group with average grades (5–6.9) completed upper secondary education. This means that while the relationship between academic achievement and educational outcome is robust and clear, very little is known about the most numerous groups, despite realizing that their probability of graduation is 60% and therefore their chance of dropping out is 40%.

The Icelandic cohort study also showed that students who had low grades at the end of their compulsory education, and later dropped out of school, had generally lower self-esteem when aged 24. Moreover, to some extent they had different attitudes towards school and education than their peers who completed the matriculation examination. Interestingly, the attitudes of those who left school were similar to the attitudes of those who actually completed a vocational education. The findings indicated that, compared to those who completed a matriculation examination, those who left school and those who completed a vocational education were not as pleased with either the institution they attended or their studies, and had been more interested in vocational than academic subjects during lower secondary school (Jónasson & Blondal, 2002a).

Programs, Policies and Practices for Reducing Dropout

In Icelandic politics, dropout is generally viewed in the context of the competitive national economy, of school efficiency, and of flexibility in providing educational opportunities. Dropout is seldom associated with how employable individuals might be. For years, the reason has been 'unusually good job opportunities for workers with few formal educational qualifications' (European Commission Directorate General for Education and Culture, 2005, p. 95). In 2008, this changed with the global financial crisis that seriously affected the Icelandic economy. It is possible to discuss the changes at three levels: the governmental or systematic level, the school level, and the informal institutional level.

The *governmental level* has two threads. The first has been discussed in relation to the new legislation which was partially aimed at reducing dropout. The second is gradually increased emphasis on counselling within the educational system. At the *school level*, the strategies can be characterised as the preventive initiatives. The third level, *the informal institutional level*, has two strands: the adult education provisions at the upper secondary level, and a variety of remedial initiatives that have government support but little direct government involvement.

Prevention Measures

Two of the recent measures taken by the Icelandic government in order to lessen school dropout are in line with recent recommendations of the OECD (Field et al., 2007). More flexibility and diversity shall be guaranteed in the course supply at upper secondary level, along with increasing freedom of student choice within the tracks they choose. The plan is to achieve this by further decentralizing curriculum design at the upper secondary level. Schools are encouraged to develop further and more flexible lines of study to fit the needs of their students (Ministry of Education, Science and Culture, n.d.). This, of course, begs the question of what grounds students have to compose their own tracks.

A second measure in line with the OECD recommendations is changing the framework of the system by encouraging, but not requiring, a shortening of the general length of upper secondary school courses from 4 to 3 years. This has been discussed in Iceland for several years now (Ministry of Education, Science and Culture, n.d.; the Upper Secondary School Act, No. 80/1996). A remoulding of the credit system allows schools to organise study programs which will lead to the matriculation examination within 3 years, although it is not yet clear to what extent schools will take the government's torch and carry out this idea.

The legal framework is furthermore aimed at facilitating the combination of academic and vocational tracks, by making the formal character of the system more comprehensive than before. Access to higher education is to be eased from both directions. This valorisation of vocational training is expected to help combat dropout in the Icelandic context, since many students seem to opt for academic programs for reasons of prestige or the desire to keep their options open, even when their skills or interests lie elsewhere. Directing these students to the 'right' program for them is now, as in the past, hoped to reduce dropout. However, it remains quite uncertain how the next level higher – universities – will react to this modification.

Schools have gradually put considerable emphasis on counselling, inter alia, to increase school retention. This development has been supported with government regulation. Both compulsory and upper secondary schools have been obliged to provide access to counselling (the Compulsory School Act, No. 66/1995; the Upper Secondary School Act, No. 80/1996). Some primary schools have developed career education programs that are a part of the school's formal curriculum and should ease the transition to upper secondary school. Supportive programs, career counselling and guidance have been further expanded by the Upper Secondary School Act of 2008. Each school shall describe arrangements for counselling and guidance in its school syllabus. The new legislation makes it mandatory for schools to provide support to students with special needs, including social or emotional problems as well as specific (and even perhaps cognitive) problems such as dyslexia. Although none of the legislation demands the professionalising of guidance posts, it is worth noting that the University of Iceland offers masters' and doctoral programs in career counselling and guidance.

In a wider perspective, various social and welfare programs are connected to dropout prevention at the compulsory level. Many communities have been experimenting with or implementing policies in this regard. The Olweus Bullying Prevention Program receives financial support from the continuing education fund for compulsory schools. Some schools have adopted School Management Training (SMT), which aims at providing a positive learning environment for students, including positive experiences in both academic and social life.

Remedial Initiatives

There are a host of remedial initiatives operating in Iceland, run largely by different organisations, often closely connected to the municipalities, sometimes supported by the government but not under its purview (Jónasson & Tannhäuser, 2009). It is important to note that, in general, current policies target most of all those who dropped out from upper secondary school and those who completed only compulsory school without ever enrolling in the next level higher. It is possible to identify three separate providers of 'second-chance' schooling: (1) upper secondary schools (2) lifelong learning centres, and (3) traditional providers of continuing education and various labour market bodies. All three types of providers share two general objectives: to educate unskilled workers in the labour market, and to lead individuals with a disrupted school or employment history back into the educational system or labour market.

By tradition, the Icelandic upper secondary system is one system for all age groups, which means one can enter the system at any age. This is very visibly demonstrated in the industrial arts. However, from the early 1970s, adult education classes were established at many of the upper secondary schools, which essentially ran the day program (normally at some greater pace) in the evenings (Jónasson, 2006). In some sense it was a separate arrangement, even though the system was the same (the same teachers, curriculum and credentials). These evening programs were strong for a roughly 30-year period but now seem to be waning somewhat, perhaps because of substantial options offered by distance education. An objective of public policy, expressly aimed at reaching out to adults, is to increase distance and distributed learning at upper secondary level as an alternative to evening classes. In 2008, 77% of upper secondary students attended day school, 16% registered in distance education programs, but only 7% were in evening school. This is in contrast to 12% in evening school in 2001 (Statistics Iceland, 2009b).

The Upper Secondary School Act of 1996 provided for the structure of 'senior departments', allowing them to be organised in collaboration with the municipalities and specified craft associations or employers. In line with the provisions of the Act, schools have participated in the development of lifelong learning centres and government financial allocations have been provided. These are now seen as a very important addition to post-school opportunities, especially for those with the least educational background.

Additionally, both the central and municipal governments have cooperated with an agency (the Education and Training Service Centre, run by the Confederation of Icelandic Employers) and trade unions to develop schemes that assess real competency, as an alternative to enrolling in upper secondary courses and completing them. This again seems a notable feature of the educational spectrum for two reasons. The first is the extent to which the labour market players have united in this endeavour, and the second is the way the agency attempts to reach the least skilled, inter alia, providing a strong emphasis on recognising the real competence these people have and equating it with school credits. This facilitates re-enrolment in appropriate courses even after having dropped out, with individual competence being evaluated through guidelines developed by the Education and Training Service Centre (Education and Training Service Centre, n.d.).

Nine municipalities outside of the capital region run lifelong learning centres that endeavour to serve the entire community in regard to second-chance education. These centres are partly based on the Upper Secondary School Act of 1996 and provide educational opportunities related to local needs and available educators. They are non-profit, independent corporations, run in collaboration with the local authorities, local school authorities, and local trade unions (Ministry of Education, Science and Culture, 2007b). One of their missions is to provide second-chance schools for adults, along with career counselling. They received a considerable stimulus through the agenda set forth by the former Icelandic government in 2003, since it emphasised the development of a powerful lifelong learning network, in collaboration with social partners. Furthermore, the government provides funds for counselling, enabling the centres to reach out to regional companies with career guidance.

Conclusions and Future Perspectives

Are students who drop out in Iceland somehow special in comparison to peers in other countries? Since so many Icelanders leave school early, could their composition as a group be 'different' from the parallel groups in countries with high graduation rates? There is no question that Icelandic dropouts are very diverse; they certainly do not form a homogeneous group from any perspective, but lacking are comparative data for asserting that this is any different from other countries. In particular there is a need to investigate in comparative terms how the employment situation affects the composition of the group, but perhaps a dramatically changing employment situation in Iceland may hand us a valuable longitudinal design.

The very strong and simple relationship between dropout and standardised marks at the end of compulsory education presents a double paradox (see Fig. 11.3). One part is that there is a strong linear relationship between these marks and the likelihood of graduating or dropping out, where a non-linear relationship would have been more understandable. While the relationship is very robust and clear, we know very little about the most numerous group, despite realising that their probability of dropping out is 40%.

The second part is precisely how many drop out with good school performance. The largest dropout group had average grades from primary school, and thus did not seem to have particular difficulties with studying. To explore this it may be necessary to move out of the statistical arena and divide the overall group of dropouts into three distinct groups on the basis of their academic performance at the end of compulsory education, since much of the information available is of a qualitative nature. Then it would be possible to speak more concretely about each separate dropout group. On that basis, it may be possible to pinpoint quite different causes for dropout in each group and be able to suggest differing, specific remedies, for instance for the academically weak group or the medium or strong one. If this proves a useful approach, one or more of the groups might be comparable to dropouts in countries with a low dropout rate, whereas the other one or more groups might not be.

It will be very interesting to observe what developments for dropout rates the recent reform in the Icelandic educational system will lead to; however, this will be somewhat complicated to assess. The patterns were changing, though admittedly very slowly, and perhaps very little indeed for males, during the period in which the employment market was stable. Concurrent with the employment market changes, the curricular composition will evolve as the system becomes even more comprehensive. Then the question may be: Will giving students more leeway in choosing their courses, and thus the composition of qualifications, influence those who are most likely to drop out to stay?

But there are, of course, a variety of complicating factors. There are a number of nearby environmental distractions (peers, siblings, parents who may oppose student desires, etc.) which a school should perhaps sense and may thus be able to counteract.

The short term will, unfortunately, see substantial increases in unemployment in Iceland. It will be instructive to investigate how this will influence school choice and both the dropout rate and dropout patterns.

References

Battin-Pearson, S., Newcomb, M. D., Abbott, R. D., Hill, K. G., Catalano, R. F., & Hawkins, D. (2000). Predictors of early high school dropout: A test of five theories. *Journal of Educational Psychology, 92*(3), 568–582.

Blondal, K. S., & Adalbjarnardottir, S. (in press). Parenting practices and school dropout: A longitudinal study. *Adolescence.*

Blondal, K. S., & Jónasson, J. T. (2003). Brottfall úr framhaldsskóla. Afstaða til skóla, stuðningur foreldra og bakgrunnur nemenda [School dropout. Attitudes to school, parental support and students' background]. In Friðrik H. Jónsson (Ed.), *Rannsóknir í félagsvísindum IV* (pp. 669–678). Reykjavík: University Press.

Education and Training Service Centre. (n.d.). Website. Retrieved August 26, 2008, from http://www.frae.is/english/education-and-training-service-centre/

European Commission Directorate General for Education and Culture (DG EAC). (2005). *Study on access to education and training, basic skills and early school leavers* (Ref. DG EAC 38/04). Lot 3: Early School Leavers. Final Report. Retrieved June 27, 2007, from http://ec.europa.eu/ education/doc/reports/doc/earlyleave.pdf

Field, S., Kuczera, M., & Pont, B. (2007). *No more failures: Ten steps to equity in education.* Paris: OECD.

Guttormsson, L. (Ed.). (2008). *Almenningsfræðsla á íslandi 1880–2007* [History of general education in Iceland, 1880–2007]. Reykjavík: University Press.

Jóhannsdóttir, G. (2006, September). *Convergence in the development of Nordic higher education systems prior to the Bologna reform process.* Paper presented at the CHER conference in Kassel, Germany. Retrieved September 10, 2008, from. http://www.uni-kassel.de/wz_/CHER/Welcome.html

Jónasson, J. T. (1994). Skipt um skoðun. Um flutning nemenda á milli þriggja flokka námsbrauta í framhaldsskóla [Change of mind. Transition of students between three different tracks at upper secondary school]. *Uppeldi og menntun, 3*(1), 63–82.

Jónasson, J. T. (1997). Students passing the Icelandic university entrance examination (UEE) 1911–94. *European Journal of Education, 32*(2), 209–220.

Jónasson, J. T. (1998). The foes of Icelandic vocational education at the upper secondary level. In A. Tjeldvoll (Ed.), *Education and the Scandinavian Welfare State in the Year 2000* (pp. 267–304). New York: Garland Publishing.

Jónasson, J. T. (1999). The predictability of educational expansion: Examples from secondary and higher education. In I. Fägerlind, I. Holmesland & G. Strömqvist (Eds.), *Higher education at the crossroads. Tradition or transformation?* (pp. 113–131). Stockholm: Institute of International Education. Stockholm University.

Jónasson, J. T. (2002). *Samanburður á skólakerfum Danmerkur, Íslands og Svíþjóðar* [Comparison of educational systems and student flow in Denmark, Iceland and Sweden. A part of a report commissioned by the Icelandic Ministry of Education as a part of the decision process to shorten the normal time spent in compulsory and secondary education]. Reykjavík: Social Science Research Institute, University of Iceland and School of Education.

Jónasson, J. T. (2003). Does the state expand schooling? A study based on five Nordic countries. *Comparative Education Review, 47*(2), 160–183.

Jónasson, J. T. (2004). Higher education reforms in Iceland at the transition into the twenty-first century. In I. Fägerlind & G. Strömqvist (Eds.), *Reforming higher education in the Nordic countries. Studies of change in Denmark, Finland, Iceland, Norway and Sweden* (pp. 137–188). Paris: International Institute for Educational Planning.

Jónasson, J. T. (2006). Símenntun: Símennt og fullorðinsfræðsla [Continuing education and adult education]. Unpublished manuscript.

Jónasson, J. T. (2008). Samræmdur framhaldsskóli í mótun [A comprehensive upper secondary school being moulded]. In Loftur Guttormsson (Ed.), *Almenningsfræðsla á Íslandi 1880–2007* (pp. 157–173). Reykjavik: University Press.

Jónasson, J. T., & Blondal, K. S. (2002a). *Ungt fólk og framhaldsskólinn. Rannsókn á námsgengi og afstöðu '75 árgangsins til náms* [Young people and upper secondary school: A study on student progress through the education system and attitudes of the '75 cohort to education]. Reykjavík: Social Science Research Institute, University of Iceland and University Press.

Jónasson, J. T., & Blondal, K. S. (2002b). *Námsferill, námslok og búseta. Rannsókn á námsferli '75 árgangsins* [Student progress, graduation and residence. Study of the 1975 cohort]. Reykjavík: Social Science Research Institute, University of Iceland.

Jónasson, J. T., & Blondal, K. S. (2005a). *Back on Track.* Articles, summaries and highlights from the Leonardo Valorisation Conference held in Reykjavík, Iceland 8–9 October 2004. Reykjavík: The Icelandic Leonardo National Agency.

Jónasson, J. T., & Blondal, K. S. (2005b). *Námsframvinda í háskóla í ljósi fyrri menntunar* [Student progress through higher education in light of previous education]. Reykjavík: Rannsóknarstofa um þróun menntamála. Social Science Research Institute, University of Iceland.

Jónasson, J. T., & Dofradóttir, A. G. (2008). *þátttaka í fræðslu á Íslandi. Niðurstöður úr Vinnumarkaðskönnun Hagstofu Íslands 2003* [Participation in lifelong learning in Iceland. Results from the labour market survey of Statistics Iceland]. Reykjavík: Rannsóknarstofa um menntakerfi. Social Science Research Institute, University of Iceland.

Jónasson, J. T., & Jónsdóttir, G. A. (1992). *Námsferill í framhaldsskóla* [Student progress through upper secondary school]. Reykjavík: Social Science Research Institute, University of Iceland.

Jónasson, J. T., & Tannhäuser, A.-C. (2009). Early school leaving in Iceland. Policies, monitoring and good practice to combat ESL. Unpublished manuscript.

Jónasson, J. T., & Tuijnman, A. (2001). Nordic adult education compared: Findings and interpretation. *Golden Riches. Nordic Adult Learning, 2001*(2), 6–11.

Ministry of Education, Science and Culture. (2002). *The educational system in Iceland.* Reykjavík: Ministry of Education, Science and Culture. Retrieved August 26, 2008, from http://bella.mrn. stjr.is/utgafur/skolenska.pdf

Ministry of Education, Science and Culture. (2005). *Ministry of Education, Science and Culture in Iceland*. Reykjavík: The Ministry of Education, Science and Culture. Retrieved August 28, 2008, from http://bella.mrn.stjr.is/utgafur/ummrnens.pdf

Ministry of Education, Science and Culture. (2007a). *The Icelandic National Curriculum Guide. General section 2004*. Reykjavík: The Ministry of Education, Science and Culture. Retrieved August 26, 2008, from http://bella.mrn.stjr.is/utgafur/almhluti_frhsk_enska.pdf

Ministry of Education, Science and Culture. (2007b). *2007 national report Iceland*. Reykjavík: The Ministry of Education, Science and Culture. Retrieved August 20, 2009, from http://ec.europa.eu/education/policies/2010/natreport07/ice_en.pdf

Ministry of Education, Science and Culture. (2008). *The upper secondary education in Iceland 2008*. Retrieved August 26, 2008, from http://bella.mrn.stjr.is/utgafur/namlok_2008_enska.pdf

Ministry of Education, Science and Culture. (n.d.). *Ný menntastefna. Metnaðarfullt, þroskandi og skapandi skólastarf. Framhaldsskólar. Greinargerð* [New educational policy. Upper secondary education. The rationale behind the act on upper secondary education adopted in May 2008]. Retrieved September 29, 2008, from http://www.nymenntastefna.is/log-um-framha.dsskcla/greinargerd

Námsmatsstofnun. (2006). *Meðaleinkunn eftir landshlutum* [Average grade by geographical areas]. Retrieved August 21, 2008, from http://www.namsmat.is/vefur/samr_prof/landshl_munur/4.isl_sta/ 4.isl_sta_landh.html

Rumberger, R. W. (2004). Why students drop out of school. In G. Orfield (Ed.), *Dropout in America* (pp. 131–155). Cambridge, MA: Harvard Educational Press.

Statistics Iceland. (2004). Brottfall nemenda úr framhaldsskólum 2002–2003 [Dropouts from upper secondary schools 2002–2003]. *Hagtíðindi, skólamál, 89*(45).

Statistics Iceland. (2006a). *News No. 50/2006: Enrolment in upper secondary and tertiary education in autumn 2005*. Retrieved October 19, 2008, from http://www.statice.is/?PageID=444&NewsID=1536

Statistics Iceland. (2006b). *Námsmenn – Atvinnuþátttaka, atvinnuleysi og fjöldi starfandi eftir ársfjórðungum 2003–2006* [Students – Employment participation rate, unemployment rate and working rate by quarters 2003–2006]. Retrieved September 17, 2008, from http://www.hagstofa.is/?PageID=637

Statistics Iceland. (2007). Nemendur í grunnskólum haustið 2006 [Pupils in compulsory schools in autumn 2006]. *Hagtíðindi, skólamál 92*(17). Retrieved September 7, 2009, from https://www.hagstofa.is/lisalib/getfile.aspx?ItemID=5991

Statistics Iceland. (2008a). *News No. 82/2008: Enrolment in upper secondary and tertiary education in autumn 2007*. Retrieved September 19, 2008, from http://www.statice.is/?PageID=444&NewsID=2994

Statistics Iceland. (2008b). *News No. 10/2008: Registered students in schools at the upper secondary and tertiary level in autumn 2007*. Retrieved September 17, 2008, from http://www.statice.is/Pages/444?NewsID=2989

Statistics Iceland. (2009a). *Graduations with matriculation examination at upper secondary level by line of study, type of examination and sex 1995–2007*. Retrieved July 20, 2009, from http://www.statice.is/Statistics/Education/Upper-secondary-schools

Statistics Iceland. (2009b). *Registered students by mode of teaching and type of school in autumn 1997–2008*. Retrieved July 20, 2009, from http://www.statice.is/Statistics/Education/Upper-secondary-schools

Statistics Iceland. (n.d.). Special analysis.

The Compulsory School Act No. 91/2008. Retrieved September 10, 2008, from http://www.nymenntastefna.is/media/frettir//Compulsory_school_Act.pdf

The Preschool Act No. 90/2008. Retrieved September 10, 2008, from http://www.nymenntastefna.is/media/frettir//Preschool_Act.pdf

The Upper Secondary School Act No. 80/1996. Retrieved September 10, 2008, from http://eng.menntamalaraduneyti.is/Acts/nr/2435

The Upper Secondary School Act No. 92/2008. Retrieved September 10, 2008, from http://www.nymenntastefna.is/media/frettir//Upper_secondary_school_Act.pdf

Chapter 12
Early Leaving, Non-Completion and Completion in Upper Secondary Education in Norway

Eifred Markussen, Mari Wigum Frøseth, Nina Sandberg, Berit Lødding and Jorunn Spord Borgen

Introduction

The Structure of Upper Secondary Education and Training

In one way, the Norwegian system of education can be understood as part of the Nordic model – an egalitarian, redistributive system. Upper secondary education is by and large public, as are other types of education. From an international perspective, the Norwegian Parliament was from very early on, as early as 1920, ready to adopt the principle of a common school for all (Dokka, 1988). The right to freely available public education was extended from 7 years at the end of the Second World War to 13 years from 1997; 10 of these years are compulsory.

Over the last 4 to 5 decades, Norway has also moved from a school system practising segregation to a school system focused on the principle of inclusion; for instance, in the case of special education, extended use of special classes and special schools has been substituted, at least in theory, by mainstreaming (Markussen, 2009). In this period, the concept of *equality* has also undergone change, from one of formal equality, via the principle of equality-of-resources and, later, equality-of-results, to the principle of equality-of-opportunities, which remains the focus today (Hernes, 1974; Aasen, 2006).

The project of modernising upper secondary education in Norway by developing an organised, public and universal system – including both general and vocational education – started in the 1960s. Integrating both vocational schools, with different traditions, and the apprenticeship system into the overall upper secondary education system has been a long and complicated process, characterised by tensions, conflicts and compromises (Olsen, 1996; Michelsen & Grove, 2005).

During these years, there has been considerable reform activity within Norwegian upper secondary education. As well as an ongoing process introducing small changes,

E. Markussen (✉), M. Wigum Frøseth, N. Sandberg, B. Lødding and J. Spord Borgen
NIFU Nordic Institute for Studies in Innovation,
Research and Education, Norway

S. Lamb et al. (Eds.), *School Dropout and Completion: International Comparative Studies in Theory and Policy*, DOI 10.1007/978-90-481-9763-7_14, © Springer Science+Business Media B.V. 2011

there have been three key or major reforms over the last 40 years. The first was in 1976, when the general, academic upper secondary schools (*gymnas*), which prepare students for higher education, and the vocational schools, which prepare students for the labour market, were merged into a common unified system of upper secondary education.

The second major reform – Reform 94 – more or less created the Norwegian upper secondary education as it is today, when it comes to structure and the qualification system. The main features of this reform were (1) to give every 15- to 16-year-old a statutory right to 3 years of upper secondary education, thereby making it possible for all students within vocational education and training (VET) to complete; (2) to give every student a right to a place in one out of three chosen study programs; (3) the reduction in the first year of upper secondary from 109 courses to 13 study programs; and (4) the introduction of a '2 + 2' model within VET (the model will be explained below). The main driving force behind this reform was the mismatch created by falling job opportunities in the youth labour market and an upper secondary system without the capacity to accommodate all the young people who were flocking to upper secondary.

The third comprehensive reform was in 2006, and it led to changes in primary as well as in lower and upper secondary education. In upper secondary it adjusted some of the structures; for example, reducing the number of vocational study programs from 12 to 9, and creating new subject structures within the different programs. Compared to Reform 94, which had really transformed upper secondary education, the reform of 2006, according to Markussen (2007), produced only small adjustments to structure and qualification systems.

It is possible to postpone commencement in upper secondary until 5 years after completion of compulsory education. Nevertheless, the large majority of students start immediately after lower secondary. There are no general entry requirements, apart from having completed compulsory education. While admission in general is fairly unrestricted, there are entry requirements to certain educational programs. If there are more applicants than the number of places, admission to a program depends on the grade point average (GPA) from 10th grade. Among those applying for upper secondary in 2005, 2006 and 2007, 83% were admitted to their program of first choice (Frøseth et al., 2008). This selection was based on GPA from the last year of compulsory education. Hence, GPA regulates admission to the most popular study programs. It also regulates entrance to the second and third years of upper secondary. Still, this is a restrained form of meritocracy, in so far as the counties are obliged to provide school places securing everyone admission to one out of three individual choices.

During transition from compulsory education, and through the different levels of upper secondary education in school or apprenticeship, the students have a 'right to necessary guidance on education, careers and social matters' (Opplæringslova [Education Act] § 9-2).

The Main Pathways

Upper secondary education consists of both general and vocational tracks (see Fig. 12.1). Within the general tracks there are three study programs: (1) general academic studies; (2) music, dance and drama; and (3) sports and physical

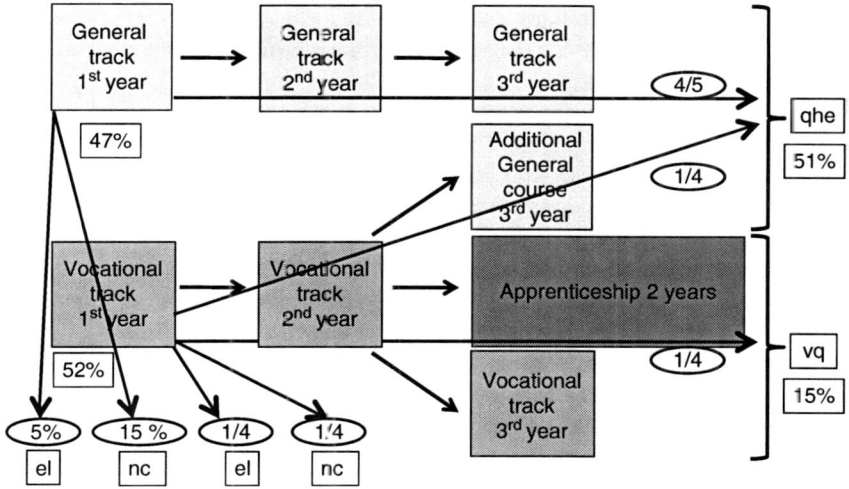

Note: qhe = qualification for higher education, vq = vocational qualification,
      el = early leaver, nc = non-completer

Fig. 12.1 Structure and throughput in upper secondary education in Norway (Source: Markussen et al., 2008)

education. The students in these programs follow a direct 3-year line through upper secondary. After finishing and passing all exams, they are qualified for entering higher education.

There are nine vocational study programs: (1) building and construction; (2) design, arts and crafts; (3) electricity and electronics; (4) health and social care; (5) media and communication; (6) agriculture, fishing and forestry; (7) restaurant and food processing; (8) service and transport; and (9) technical and industrial production. Starting in a vocational program, there are three paths through upper secondary (see Fig. 12.1).

The main road through VET is the so-called 2 + 2 model, which means that the students first complete 2 years of schooling and then 2 years of apprenticeship in a firm. It is important to stress that this is the normal model for vocational education and that VET, including the apprenticeship system, is a part of upper secondary education. The 2 + 2 model is a corporatist arrangement in which the public sector provides school places and the business sector provides apprenticeships. It is possible to qualify for around 180 different occupations through the 2 + 2 model, and when a person has gone through this education, passing all exams, he or she is able to start as a qualified worker within his or her given occupation. Approximately one sixth of all who start their third year of training/education in upper secondary are apprentices (Frøseth et al., 2008). However, only around 50% of the new apprentices are 18 years old, the rest are older. As in some other countries, there has traditionally been an age-related heterogeneity among apprentices in Norway. Should not enough apprenticeships be available for the 18-year-olds, the county authorities are obliged to offer them training at school in the form of a third-year course. Both these vocational tracks provide the students with a certificate after a craftsman's or journeyman's examination.

The second road within vocational education is a 3-year, school-based education structured towards an occupation. This is possible for 10 different occupations.

The third option for those who have started in a vocational study program is to switch to an additional general course. This is possible after 2 years in a vocational program, and those who complete after 3 years are qualified for higher education. It has turned out to be an option with a fast-growing popularity among vocational students, and has established itself as an important alternative to apprenticeship (Høst and Evensen, 2009). However it is not an easy pathway to higher education, as the students have to complete all the general subjects in 1 year. Statistics show that these students are more likely to fail by the end of third year than other students, and this happens for 30–40% of them (Markussen et al., 2008).

The system allows students to switch pathways. If students wish to change programs, the right to education is extended by 1 year. The structure of the system makes it easier to switch from a vocational to a general track than the other way around. The county can approve apprenticeship contracts which prescribe that the entire education, or larger parts than prescribed by the curricula, may be completed as on-the-job training. However, until now this has been available to only a limited number of students.

After qualifying from upper secondary education, students have achieved either (1) *qualification for higher education*, (2) *vocational qualification*, or (3) *competence at a lower level* (Opplæringslova [Education Act] §3-3).

Qualification for higher education is achieved mainly by completing within one of the three general programs. Vocational qualification is gained mainly by going through and passing all exams, including the journeyman's exam at the end of an apprenticeship, within one of the nine vocational programs. Competence at a lower level is obtained by all those not achieving qualification for higher education or vocational qualification. Students may obtain competence at a lower level in a planned manner, as the end of a consciously chosen track of education and training, or they may receive it by default. The latter is by far more common, and will be the case if the students, for instance, leave school, fail, or do not fulfil the requirements in one way or another (see below).

Governance of Upper Secondary Education

Upper secondary education is administered at two levels of government, the state and the county level. There are 19 counties in Norway. In cross-national comparisons, the Norwegian education system has traditionally been characterised as centralised (Telhaug & Mediås, 2002). However, developments in the governance of post-compulsory education since the 1990s have seen increasing decentralisation, as the state has passed on authority to counties and schools (NOU, 2003, p. 16).

The system for upper secondary education is managed within the framework of a mixed system of government, balancing centralised and decentralised authority, as well as corporate influence. The state defines the goals and provides the budgetary framework for post-compulsory education. The regional authorities are responsible for operating and developing the schools, and for developing strategies to attain national goals. The counties are to provide upper secondary education throughout the country, making equivalent educational courses available to everyone. Even though VET and apprenticeships are regarded as an integral part of the system, the responsibility to establish apprenticeship places rests with employers, and the numbers of apprenticeship places are dependent on market fluctuations.

Local authorities may delegate certain tasks to the local administration, to councils, and to the schools. Within nationally binding frameworks, determined by law and curricula, the counties, school principals and teachers may exert influence on subject matter, teaching aids and methods. Even if the reform of 2006 assumes an even larger degree of local freedom of action, new techniques of state administration such as audits and inspections/supervisions are gaining ground. Thus, the balance between modern technocracy and institutional trust, centralisation and decentralisation, is an unsettled empirical question.

After the adoption of the Norwegian Apprenticeship Act in 1950, the social partners – the main organisations representing the employers and the employees – were entrusted with a high level of autonomy for the administration and control of the apprenticeship system through professional self-government (Michelsen & Høst, 2004). From 1992, the secretariat for the National VET Council was formally integrated into the Ministry of Education, Research and Church Affairs. The National VET Council has, since 2004, had its mandate redefined. It no longer has any decision-making authority, for instance in approving new curricula and trades or dismantling existing ones, but is instead an advisory policy board for the national educational authorities. A corresponding shift in tasks has occurred in the VET boards at the county level (Høst, 2008).

Viewed from a neo-corporate perspective (Streeck & Schmitter, 1985), all of these changes can be understood as a movement away from self-government, in which the social partners were given considerable space for self-regulation in policy-making and policy administration, to a regime of participation, in which the social partners are consulted for advice, but are clearly subordinate to the state.

Main Patterns of Early Leaving, Non-Completion and Completion

Several studies of dropout and completion have documented that even though nearly the whole cohort enters upper secondary education, far from everybody completes (Markussen et al., 2008; Statistics Norway, 2009; Støren et al., 2007). This section will give a brief presentation of the main patterns of dropout and completion in upper secondary education in Norway.

Although upper secondary is voluntary, every year 98–99% of those completing compulsory education apply for a place. Figure 12.1 shows numbers based on a sample study within the cohort starting upper secondary in 2002 (Markussen et al., 2008). Around half the cohort applied for vocational programs and the other half for general programs. Thus, education is the main activity for young people, and around 91% of 16- to 18-year-olds are in upper secondary (Raabe, 2007). As the labour market in Norway has a lot of opportunities, including for youth, the unemployment rate for those under 20 years of age is usually low. It is also very common for young people to combine upper secondary education with work, and all together more than 40% of 15- to 19-year-olds take part in some form of paid work (Statistics Norway/AKU, 2008). This situation may contribute to a certain 'pull effect' on students to opt out of school.

In this book, 'dropout' is a term used to describe those who do not complete an upper secondary qualification. This chapter makes a distinction between two groups of young people that in other countries would be treated as one group, 'dropouts'. The term *early leaver* is used here to describe those young people leaving upper secondary education without finishing all the years required to complete; either 3 years as students or 4 years as apprentices. Those who stay the entire time but eventually end up not passing all of the required exams are labelled *non-completers*.[1] The two distinct terms are used when referring to results from the study *Early Leaving, Non-Completion or Completion?* (Markussen et al., 2008). Most studies on dropout do not distinguish between early leaving and non-completion, meaning that when referring to research in other countries, the term *dropout* will cover both early leaving and non-completion.

In this chapter the concern is with early leaving and non-completion only from upper secondary education. Early leaving in compulsory education does exist, but only in very small numbers. Non-completion in compulsory education does not even exist officially, although 7–8% complete without achieving grades in all subjects, or they achieve the lowest grade in one or more subjects (Frøseth et al., 2008). These students are eligible for studies in upper secondary education, but it is likely they will have difficulty successfully negotiating all upper secondary demands.

For the study by Markussen et al. (2008), a total of 9,749 young people in the south-eastern part of Norway were followed for 5½ years: from applying for a place in upper secondary in spring 2002, until autumn 2007 (the numbers in Fig. 12.1 are based on this study). The results show that 5 years after finishing compulsory school, two thirds (66%) had completed upper secondary. Among these, 51% achieved qualification for higher education, and 15% achieved vocational qualification. The remaining one third (34%) had not completed upper secondary within 5 years, thereby obtaining *competence at a lower level*. Of these, 15% had left early,

---

[1]Until 2007, Statistics Norway used the term 'dropout' to refer to both groups. The Norwegian translation 'frafall' literally translated means 'falling out'. From 2007, Statistics Norway have presented their yearly statistics on dropout and completion in a new way, distinguishing between 'completers', 'non-completers', 'dropouts' and 'continuers'.

and 19% ended up as non-completers after finishing all their years in upper secondary but without passing all of the required exams (Markussen et al., 2008).

Statistics Norway does a full-scale mapping of attainment of qualification for every cohort. According to Statistics Norway (2009), the throughput of students in upper secondary has been remarkably stable across cohorts after Reform 94. The share that completed within 5 years in the cohorts entering upper secondary in 1994, 1998, 2000, 2001, 2002 and 2003 varied between 68% and 72%. The above-mentioned studies report status of completion after 5 years, but it is worth mentioning that the vast majority complete in the prescribed 3 years for pupils or 4 years for apprentices (Markussen et al., 2008; Statistics Norway, 2009).

The throughput of students in upper secondary improved considerably after the implementation of Reform 94, especially among the students within VET As a result of this reform, completion among VET students doubled from 30% for the cohort entering upper secondary in 1991, to 60% for the cohort entering in 1994 (Støren et al., 1998). The main reason for this was that Reform 94 made it possible for all students to go through VET. Prior to the reform, many were stopped after the first or second year because there were too few places at the next level.

Despite this improvement, the completion rate remains significantly lower among students in vocational programs, as compared to students in general programs (Markussen et al., 2008; Statistics Norway, 2009; Støren et al., 2007). The average early leaving rate for all students based on the cohort study was 15%. Figure 12.1 shows that among those who started in a general track, around four out of five achieved qualification for higher education, while 5% dropped out, and 15% did not complete. Within the vocational programs, the situation was much worse: one quarter ended up with vocational qualification, one quarter with qualification for higher education, one quarter dropped out, and one quarter were non-completers. The differences in competence achievement between different education programs may be due to variations in the composition of students with regard to individual attributes such as GPA from lower secondary, records of absence, etc., and context variables such as different opportunities of obtaining an apprenticeship between different trades, and different pedagogical practices and learning cultures within the different programs (Markussen et al., 2008).

A proportion of those leaving early do this between the second and third year. Half of these early leavers appeared to be applicants for an apprenticeship who did not obtain a place, and as a consequence, opted out (Markussen & Sandberg, 2005). Thus, the process of obtaining an apprenticeship seems to affect early leaving among VET students.

To sum up, recent studies of completion, non-completion and early leaving in upper secondary education in Norway have shown that about two thirds complete upper secondary education within 5 years; while one third do not. Not completing upper secondary may be due both to early leaving or non-completion (not passing all exams required).

The reform of 2006 brought some changes in upper secondary, and one intention is to improve the throughput of students. It remains to be seen if and to what extent there will be any changes in the patterns of completion, non-completion and early leaving in upper secondary education as a consequence of this reform.

Main Predictors of Early Leaving, Non-Completion and Completion

Research results have revealed a significant variation in early leaving, non-completion and completion rates in upper secondary related to a large number of factors. Girls have better completion rates than boys, and students whose parents have higher education complete upper secondary to a greater extent than those who have parents with a lower educational level. Students from a minority background more often leave early or do not complete compared to other students, and there are large differences in the completion, non-completion and early leaving rates among students within different education programs. Several of these factors also correlate with each other. For instance, girls achieve better grades than boys, and there are large differences in the composition of students within different education programs with regard to the students' grades, and records of absence (Markussen et al., 2008).

This section will concentrate on results from multivariate analyses, and start by giving a short account of what have been identified as the main predictors of early leaving, non-completion and completion in upper secondary education in Norway. Finally, it will look more closely at apprentices and try to identify the factors that can explain variation in their achievement of competence.

Markussen et al. (2008) looked into the factors which influence early leaving, non-completion and completion in upper secondary education. They conducted a multinomial logistic regression analysis of the conditions that influence the likelihood of having either left early or not completed, as compared to having completed upper secondary education after 5 years. Several variables were included in the analysis, such as gender, family background, achievement from last year of compulsory school, educational content and working methods in compulsory school, adjustment to school, ambition and future plans, spare time activities, and education program and county.

GPA from the last year of compulsory school was found to be the most decisive factor influencing early leaving, non-completion or completion after 5 years in upper secondary. The better the grades, the lower the likelihood of both leaving early or not completing, as compared to completing (Markussen et al., 2008). Other studies have also provided evidence of the importance of school achievement during compulsory education for early leaving, non-completion or completion in upper secondary (Støren et al., 1998, 2007).

The influence of background variables on the likelihood of early leaving or not completing, as compared to completing upper secondary education within 5 years, was quite weak after controlling for grades from compulsory school. Analyses have revealed that background variables to a great extent affect the outcome of upper secondary education through the effect these variables have on school achievement (Markussen et al., 2008; Støren et al., 2007). However, even if the influence is fairly weak, a number of background variables have proven to have a statistically significant impact on the likelihood of early leaving, non-completion and completion in upper secondary education. These variables include gender, parents' educational level and their position in the labour market, with whom the young people lived as 15-year-olds (both parents or not), and majority/minority background (Markussen et al., 2008). Although the effect of each individual background variable was relatively weak, the collective effect of coming from a home where the parents lived together, had higher education, worked, etc. was highly significant both for grades in compulsory school and the attainment of qualification in upper secondary education. Thus, it makes sense to give a brief account of how these background variables have proven to affect the likelihood of early leaving or not completing, as compared to completing within 5 years. Below, all effects are referred to on the condition 'other things equal', and as compared to the likelihood of completing upper secondary education.

Boys have a higher likelihood of not completing within 5 years than girls, but there is no difference between boys and girls when it comes to the likelihood of early leaving. The parents' educational level had only a weak effect on competence achievement, but those who had parents with compulsory school as their highest educational level had a somewhat greater likelihood of leaving early than students who had parents with higher education. Students living with both parents as 15-year-olds had a lower probability of leaving early or not completing than students who did not live with both parents. Students with a minority background had a higher probability of leaving early or not completing within 5 years than students with a majority background (Markussen et al., 2008). Another study of the same data demonstrates that early leaving is far more common in vocational tracks among students with a minority background than among majority students. In the general track, non-completion stands out as a significantly greater problem among minority students than among majority students (Lødding, 2009).

All things equal, there has also proven to be great variation in the likelihood of early leaving or not completing, as compared to completing, among students in different educational programs. This indicates that there are conditions linked to the education programs which are related to competence achievement in upper secondary education – that is, even taking into account variations in the composition of students between education programs, with regard to, for example, school achievement and parents' educational level (Markussen et al., 2008).

Completion, Non-Completion and Early Leaving Among Apprentices

There have also been analyses conducted into which factors affect the likelihood of completing upper secondary education among apprentices, as compared to dropout (both early leaving and non-completion) (Markussen et al., 2008; Støren et al., 2007). GPA from compulsory school has a highly positive impact on the likelihood of apprentices completing upper secondary education within 5 years. The effect of background variables disappeared when controlling for GPA. This indicates that the influence of background variables on competence achievement among apprentices is transmitted via grades from compulsory school. Number of absences had a negative effect on the likelihood of completing upper secondary, while considering oneself as practically inclined and process-oriented, and focusing on homework, had a positive impact on the probability of completing upper secondary as an apprentice (Markussen et al., 2008).

These analyses showed that far fewer factors had an effect on completion, non-completion and early leaving among apprentices, when compared to the analysis of the entire group of young people. This may be explained by the fact that apprentices after all are a selected group.

The share of applicants obtaining an apprenticeship varied from 65% to 80% over the 5 years prior to 2008, dependent on variations in economic cycles (Høst, 2008). Analyses have shown that the probability of obtaining an apprenticeship increases with low records of absence and higher GPA from compulsory education, majority background, being a boy, having a father with vocational education and having a statutory right to upper secondary education (Markussen et al., 2008; Markussen & Sandberg, 2005; Støren et al., 1998, 2007; Støren & Skjersli, 1999; Vibe et al., 1997).

Analyses have also shown differences in the chances of obtaining an apprenticeship between trades (Markussen et al., 2008). According to the statutory right to upper secondary education/training, the county municipality is obliged to offer an alternative education in school to students who do not obtain an apprenticeship. In this context it is worth mentioning that research has indicated that the education/training offered in the alternative arrangement to an apprenticeship – the school-based track – does not seem to be of the same quality as the education offered within the apprentice scheme. Students who do not obtain an apprenticeship, and therefore are offered the school-based track leading to a trade or journeyman's certificate, have higher early leaving rates (Støren & Skjersli, 1999) and a larger share of these students fail in the qualifying examination (Støren et al., 2007). This is to some extent due to differences in earlier school achievement among those who obtain an apprenticeship and those who do not, but the differences do not disappear in multivariate analyses where variations in school achievements are taken into account. This suggests a difference in the quality of the education and training offered to apprentices and to those who do not obtain an apprenticeship (Støren et al., 2007).

Understanding Completion, Non-Completion and Early Leaving

Since 1994 about two thirds of every cohort has completed upper secondary education with a qualification for higher education or a vocational qualification. The remaining one third either leaves before finishing or stays through all years but without completing all requirements, and by doing so achieves competence at a lower level. The main predictive variable, when it comes to early leaving and also non-completion, is the student's schooling abilities, as measured by GPA from the last year of compulsory education.

The analyses within the project *Early Leaving, Non-Completion or Completion?* also identified some other school-related variables predicting early leaving and non-completion. Most important is the finding that low identification and engagement with the school, as measured by absence, misbehaviour, feeling socially excluded, having low ambitions and putting little effort into school work, have a negative effect on the probability of completing upper secondary education.

In addition, the analyses showed some demographic and background variables predicting early leaving and non-completion: gender, minority/majority background, parent's education, mother's labour-market status and family structure.

These findings are consistent with research in other countries (e.g., Alexander et al., 2001; Battin-Pearson et al., 2000; Ekstrom et al., 1986; Entwisle et al., 2005; Finn, 1989; Janosz et al., 1997; Lamb et al., 2004; Rumberger, 1987, 2004; Traag & van der Velden, 2008).

Prior to the *Early Leaving, Non-Completion or Completion?* project, there had not been any large-scale studies of early leaving conducted in Norway. One reason for this may be that early leaving has not been considered a real problem until recently. Until Reform 94, being outside upper secondary was not regarded as a problem; rather, it was common that many young people aged between 16 and 19 were working, or switching between education and work. Reform 94, with its strong structural, financial and normative means to make upper secondary normal for all 16- to 19-year-olds, was, however, implemented shortly after a deep recession, which resulted in unemployment for many young people. Thus, the construction of the early-leaver category in Norway may be seen as a consequence of both the state of the labour market and the reform giving every young person a statutory right to upper secondary education.

The launching of the research project *Early Leaving, Non-Completion or Completion?* was one response, as early leaving began to emerge as a problem. Because of the lack of earlier Norwegian research, it was necessary to turn to the international literature when trying to explain early leaving and non-completion and the results of the study. One might say that the study – and other Norwegian research on this topic – has been influenced by approaches employed by researchers internationally.

A three-step explanation will be used to try to explain early leaving and non-completion of upper secondary education in Norway:

1. Compulsory education produces students with a large variation in skills, and not everyone is equally prepared to successfully master upper secondary education.
2. In the transition from lower to upper secondary education, when advising students what kind of upper secondary education to choose, the system does not recognise this variation in knowledge, skills and attitudes.
3. When working with these students in upper secondary education, the system does not recognise this variation, either.

As shown above, GPA from the last year of compulsory education is the variable with the strongest predictive power for the outcome of upper secondary education. An important question is how GPA from compulsory education, as an expression of the students' knowledge, skills and attitudes, is produced. To attempt to answer this question, two contributions from the international research literature on the subject, by Finn (1989) and Rumberger (2004), will be called on.

Finn (1989) draws up two models for understanding dropout as a process starting in the early years of schooling. Following the 'Frustration–Self-Esteem Model', early school failure leads to an impaired self-view, making the individual oppose the school. This opposition may take the form of misbehaviour, truancy, and in the end total withdrawal. In the 'Participation–Identification Model', Finn focuses on participation as a starting point. If the students are not participating, this might lead to poor achievement, followed by low identification with school, and finally withdrawal.

Rumberger (2004) argues that to study dropout one has to include both an individual and an institutional perspective. His framework, based on the individual perspective, is built on three central elements: engagement, educational performance and background. Educational performance and engagement are related and affect each other. Background influences both performance and engagement. In this way, background, engagement and performance are mutually interrelated. In his institutional perspective he argues that people's actions are shaped by the settings in which they live, and that students' behaviour and achievements have to be studied within different contexts: families, peer groups, schools, local communities, and the larger environment (Rumberger, 2004).

Drawing on Finn (1989) and Rumberger (2004) it is possible to construct a conceptual framework to understand early leaving, non-completion and completion in Norwegian upper secondary education, as displayed in Fig. 12.2.

When children enter primary education, they differ in their relationship to school. Through their early years of living they have acquired different understandings of what the school is and how important schooling is. They also come into primary education with a varying level of knowledge and skills. As shown in Fig. 12.2, much of this variation is due to different backgrounds: gender, minority/majority background, family structure, parents' education, parents' labour market status and cultural capital.

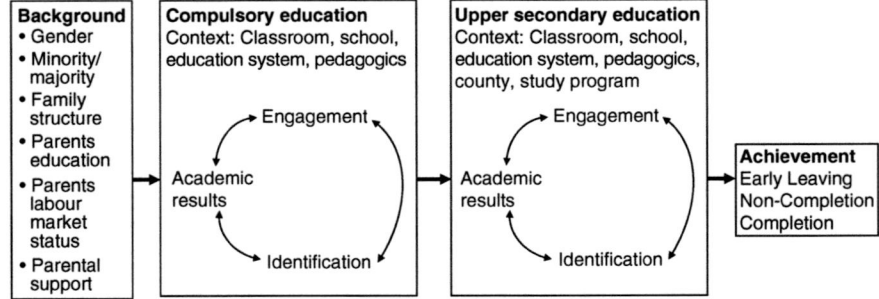

Fig. 12.2 Conceptual framework for understanding student achievement in Norwegian upper secondary education (Source: Markussen, Sandberg & Frøseth, forthcoming)

Some children then, meet school on their home ground, the school recognises them, they identify with school, and the school identifies with them. These children enter a positive circle (Fig. 12.2): they perform well academically, their identification with the school is strengthened, and they show a high level of engagement. Others enter a negative circle: they meet school on away ground, the school does not recognise them, they identify with school to a lesser extent, and vice versa.

These children do not perform as well academically, they do not obtain the same identification with the school, and they show a lower level of engagement (Finn, 1989; Ekstrom et al., 1986; Newmann et al., 1992; Rumberger, 2004; Wehlage et al., 1989). This happens because the school does not adjust its teaching to the variation in the students' knowledge, abilities and skills.

This process first takes place in compulsory education, resulting in varying achievements (see above). These varying achievements imply considerable variation in students' abilities to meet the requirements of upper secondary education. Based on studies of upper secondary education in Norway, it is argued that, as a result of the different lives they have lived with their families and in kindergarten and compulsory school, a large proportion of every cohort at the age of 15–16 has not acquired the necessary requirements (knowledge, skills, attitudes and engagement) to complete upper secondary education, at least not at this stage in life.

Even though this is the case, as many as 98–99% of the cohorts apply and start in upper secondary every year (Markussen, 2003; Frøseth et al., 2008). And nearly everyone applies for, and starts on, a track aiming at qualification for higher education or vocational qualification. Being aware of the great variation in abilities, and being aware of the demands to be fulfilled in order to complete, it could be argued that the education system is doing some students a disservice when leading those not capable of completing, into tracks aiming for full completion. Knowing that it has been possible since 1994, it is worth questioning why very few students (less than 1%) are offered alternative courses – for instance more practical courses aiming for full competence or courses aiming for competence at a lower level.

When these students start in upper secondary, many of them enter into a new negative circle of 'academic results–identification–engagement' (see Fig. 12.2). Teaching in upper secondary does not, as with the transition process to upper secondary, recognise the extent of variation among the students, and treats nearly everyone as if they are capable of completing. Many of the students aiming for completion are not capable of this, and when they experience low levels of identification and engagement, and low academic results, these students have – since upper secondary is not compulsory – the option to leave; and as shown above, many of them do.

The education system is acting upon a tacit assumption, that basically every single individual at the age of 16 has the ability to complete upper secondary education by achieving qualification for higher education or vocational qualification. Yet, it could be argued that many do not have the ability. Because of this, many students start out with goals they are not able to reach.

It may be better if this tacit assumption was replaced by a new basic understanding, explicitly stating that 15- to 16-year-olds at the point of leaving compulsory education have, through the lives they have lived in family, school and society, achieved very different knowledge, skills and attitudes. Not all of them have obtained the necessary abilities at this stage of life to achieve qualification for higher education or vocational qualification.

Building on this understanding, it would be better for upper secondary education to provide targeted programs, in accordance with students' abilities. For those with appropriate skills, this may be to help them achieve qualification for higher education or vocational qualification. Or it may be to help students aim for and achieve what is called *competence at a lower level*, a theme returned to below. Aiming at competence at a lower level is also targeted education that may break the negative version of the circle illustrated in Fig. 12.2.

Policies to Reduce Early Leaving and Non-Completion

Concern over high early leaving and non-completion rates in Norway has intensified the search for effective tools to (1) prevent young people from quitting, (2) channel early leavers back to school or into qualifying work, and (3) prevent those staying on from ending up as non-completers. Attention will now turn to describing some measures implemented on national and system-wide levels in order to reduce early leaving and non-completion and increase completion in Norway's upper secondary education.

In 1994, as described above, a comprehensive reform of upper secondary education in Norway was implemented. One of the main reasons for this reform was that upper secondary education was not able to cater for all those young persons aged 15–16 who had just finished compulsory education and who wanted to start upper secondary. Because of lack of capacity a large number of young people (those with the lowest GPA from compulsory education) at the age of 15–16 were being forced out of education, becoming early leavers without entering upper secondary education. Amongst other reasons, Reform 94 was introduced in order to put an end to this early leaving between the compulsory and post-compulsory stages of education that was forced upon young people by the system. And this was a success. As noted earlier, a result of this reform was that nearly everybody started in upper secondary education. Furthermore, the reform succeeded in improving throughput and completion: completion among VET students doubled from 30% in the cohort entering upper secondary in 1991, to 60% in the cohort entering in 1994 (Støren et al., 1998).

As mentioned above, in the decades prior to Reform 94, it was common for many young people aged 16–19 to be working or switching between education and work, so that being outside upper secondary education was not considered to be a problem. But when the opportunities in the labour market vanished and upper secondary education was opened up to everybody, the norm was created that every young person should attend upper secondary education. As this took place, not following the norm became a problem, and it could be argued that it was only after the implementation of Reform 94 that early leaving and dropout from upper secondary education emerged as a real problem. It is interesting that the reform that reduced the numbers of early leavers before post-compulsory education and increased the numbers of completers from upper secondary, also created early leaving and drop-out from upper secondary education as a problem and a challenge.

It was not only Reform 94 itself that was meant to reduce early leaving and improve completion. As part of the reform, some measures aimed at helping potential dropouts to stay in school were also introduced. Two of these measures, the *Follow-Up Service* and *competence at a lower level* are worth describing.

The main task of the Follow-Up Service is to help students who have a statutory right to upper secondary education but who are out of school or work, back into education or to work. The service still exists, but it has not been evaluated for nearly 10 years, so it is not possible, based on data, to say how it is working at present. From earlier evaluations it is known that the service has been struggling to fulfil its task, as almost the only options they had were to return early leavers to school (Grøgaard et al., 1999).

As a part of Reform 94, a new form of competence was introduced. The legislation in relation to upper secondary education stated that after finishing upper secondary education, the students should acquire one out of three possible forms of qualification: qualification for higher education, vocational qualification, or *documented partial competence*. From 2001 the name of this third form of qualification was changed to *competence at a lower level*. At the same time it became possible for students to undertake study towards this competence at a lower level qualification within their upper secondary education, and to work for this as a *learning candidate*, rather like an apprentice in a workplace. At the end of this education, the learning candidate does an exam called the *Competence Test*, and after passing this exam he or she receives a *Certificate of Competence*, documenting the qualifications he or she has acquired through upper secondary education. Competence at a lower level was introduced in order to give those not capable of achieving qualification for higher education or vocational qualification another option within the system, and can be seen as a measure to keep students in upper secondary education.

From 2007 a new way to achieve planned competence at a lower level, the *Certificate of Practice*, was introduced, allowing students to complete their upper secondary education over a 2-year period. The main part of the education is based on practical work in the work place, like an apprentice. When fulfilling these 2 years, and achieving a Certificate of Practice, students will have two options: either to end their education and apply for work on the basis of their Certificate of Practice, or to continue their education as an apprentice aiming for a full vocational education by obtaining a trade or a journeyman's certificate.

In 2003, a national *Plan of Action against Early Leaving in Upper Secondary Education* was launched. In an evaluation, Buland and Havn (2007) point out that a considerable diversity of strategies were developed throughout the country, including career and employment counselling; new systems for early warning; supplementary qualification for teachers in handling the challenges related to early leaving; special attention to the first few months of upper secondary school for students at risk; additional alternative possibilities for young people for working outside of ordinary school; and improved cooperation between schools in order to facilitate transition from one level of education to the next. These are seen by the practitioners involved as effective means for preventing early leaving and non-completion.

According to the analysis by Buland and Havn (2007), in order for work to reduce early leaving to be successful, it needs to be 'firmly rooted in the educational system on all levels, not as a project, but as an ongoing, ordinary part of the activities of every school'. Thus, they conclude, the task involves systematic, enduring, goal-oriented hard work in different arenas simultaneously. Two evaluations of projects on partnership for career guidance in compulsory education, and in a lifelong perspective, support the significance of these success criteria (Borgen et al., 2008; Røste & Borgen, 2008).

In 2006, a new comprehensive reform of all education for persons between 6 and 19 years of age was implemented. The Government and the Parliament gave many reasons for this reform, but in upper secondary education one of its main aims was said to be the reduction of early leaving and non-completion and the improvement of completion (St.meld. nr. 30, 2003–04).

As a part of the reform, several elements aiming at reduced dropout and increased completion were introduced. Three of these measures are worth mentioning: *career guidance*, the *Elective Program*, and the *In-Depth Study Project*.

Career guidance for young people was highlighted in the reform of 2006 as a measure for preventing early leaving and non-completion. The aim is to bring about a significant improvement of the guidance service through several means, including partnerships for career guidance, which involve a range of different actors at different levels and across sectors. Supplementary qualification for school counsellors is seen as crucial to the endeavours.

In order to strengthen students' basis for choosing educational programs and subjects in upper secondary, two new subjects have been established: the *Elective Program* is taught to all students in lower secondary throughout all 3 years; and the *In-Depth Study Project* is taught in the vocational tracks in upper secondary during the first and the second year.

The three main areas of the Elective Program are knowledge about the structure in upper secondary and working life; trialling of possible programs in upper secondary education; and training, mapping out, and discussing the implications of the student's own interests and circumstances concerning their individual educational and work life choices. The trialling of programs can take place in an upper secondary school or in a local workplace.

The objective of the In-Depth Study Project is that students should be able to try out one or more trades and gain experience with the content, tasks and working methods used in different vocational subjects before they select their own pathway.

Norway has implemented two comprehensive reforms, in 1994 and 2006, and in both cases an important reason for these reforms, amongst many others, was to reduce early leaving and non-completion and increase completion. It has been shown that Reform 94 succeeded in both reducing the numbers of early leavers between the compulsory and post-compulsory stages of education, and increasing the completion rates within upper secondary education. But early leaving and non-completion rates are still worryingly high and the 2006 Reform is aiming to improve this situation. Special measures seeking to reduce dropout and increase completion – better career guidance and the two new subjects (the Elective Program and the In-Depth Study Project) – have been designed, piloted and recently implemented, and are under evaluation at present. Thus, while it is impossible at the time of writing to say whether they will work as intended, the ongoing evaluations will hopefully tell us more.

References

Aasen, P. (2006). Utdanning og sosial utjevning [Education and the diminishing of social differences]. *Bedre Skole 3, 2006.* Oslo: Utdanningsforbundet.

Alexander, K. L., Entwisle, D. R., & Kabbani, N. S. (2001). The dropout process in life course perspective: Early risk factors at home and school. *Teachers College Record, 103*(5), 760–822.

Battin-Pearson, S., Newcomb, M. D., Abbott, R. D., Hill, K. G., Catalano, R. F., & Hawkins, J. D. (2000). Predictors of early high school dropout: A test of five theories. *Journal of Educational Psychology, 92*(3), 568–582.

Borgen, J. S., Vibe, N., & Røste, R. (2008). *Karriere Akershus: evaluering av Partnerskap for karriereveiledning i Akershus* [Career Akershus: Evaluation of partnership for career guidance in Akershus]. Report 11, 2008. Oslo: NIFU STEP.

Buland, T. & Havn, V. (2007). *Intet menneske er en øy. Rapport fra evalueringen av tiltak i Satsing mot frafall* [Evaluation of measures against dropout]. Trondheim: SINTEF Teknologi og samfunn. Gruppe for skole- og utdanningsforskning.

Dokka, H. J. (1988). *En skole gjennom 250 år: Den norske allmueskole, folkeskole, grunnskole 1739–1989* [The history of the Norwegian basic education through 250 years, 1739–1989]. Oslo: NKS-forlaget.

Ekstrom, R. B., Goertz, M. E., Pollack, J. M., & Rock, D. A. (1986). Who drops out of high school and why? Findings of a national study. *Teachers College Record, 87,* 3576–3730.

Entwisle, D. R., Alexander, K. L. & Olson, L. S. (2005). First grade and educational attainment by age 22: A new story. *The American Journal of Sociology, 110*(5), 1458–1502.

Finn, J. D. (1989). Withdrawing from school. *Review of Educational Research, 59*(2), 117–142.

Frøseth, M. W., Hovdhaugen, E., Høst, H., & Vibe, N. (2008). *Tilbudsstruktur og gjennomføring i videregående opplæring.* [Tracks and throughput in upper secondary education]. Report 40, 2008. Oslo: NIFU STEP.

Grove, K., & Michelsen, S. (2005). *Lærarforbundet - mangfald og fellesskap. Historia om Lærarforbundet og organisasjonane som danna forbundet* [The history of the Teachers Union]. Bergen: Forlaget Vigmostad/Bjørke.

Grøgaard, J. B., Midtsundstad, T., & Egge., M. (1999). *Følge opp – eller forfølge. Evaluering av Oppfølgingstjenesten i Reform 94* [Follow up or pursue. Evaluation of the Follow-Up Service in upper secondary education]. Fafo report 263. Oslo: Fafo.

Hernes, G. (1974). Om ulikhetens reproduksjon [On the reproduction of inequality]. In M. S. Mortensen (Ed.), *I forskningens lys.* Oslo: Universitetsforlaget.

Høst, H. (2004). *Kontinuitet og endring i pleie- og omsorgsutdanningene* [Continuity and change in care and nursing education]. Bergen. Rokkan-rapport 4–2004.

Høst, H. (Ed.). (2008). *Continuity and change in Norwegian vocational education and training (VET).* Report 29, 2008. Oslo: NIFU STEP.

Høst, H., & Evensen, M. (2009). *Ny struktur - tradisjonelle mønstre? Om Kunnskapsløftets strukturendringer i det videregående opplæringssystemet, og utforming av tilbud og dimensjonering i fylkeskommunene* [New structure – traditional patterns. About structural changes in upper secondary education in Reform 2006, and the construction of the educational options in the counties]. Report 28, 2009. Oslo: NIFU STEP.

Janosz, M., Le Blanc, M., Boulerice, B., & Tremblay, R. E. (1997). Disentangling the weight of school dropout predictors: A test on two longitudinal samples. *Journal of Youth and Adolescence, 26,* 733–762.

Kunnskapsdepartementet. (2006). *Tiltak for bedre gjennomføring i videregående opplæring.* [The Ministry of Education: Measures for better achievements in upper secondary education. The GIVO-report]. Oslo: Kunnskapsdepartementet.

Lamb, S., Walstab, A., Teese, R., Vickers, M., & Rumberger, R. (2004). *Staying on at school: Improving student retention in Australia.* Brisbane: Ministerial Council on Employment, Education and Training and Queensland Department of Education.

Lødding, B. (2009). English abstract of the NIFU STEP Report: *Quitters, strugglers and completers.* Retrieved from http://www.nifustep.no/norsk/publikasjoner/sluttere_slitere_og_sertifiserte

Markussen, E. (2009). Spesialundervisning i videregående virker ikke etter intensjonen – uendret etter Kunnskapsløftet [Special education in upper secondary does not work according to intentions]. In E. Markussen (Ed.), *Videregående opplæring for nesten alle [Upper secondary for (almost) everyone].* Oslo: Cappelen Damm.

Markussen, E. (2007). Reform 94 lever videre – men svikter hver femte ungdom? [Reform 94 lives on – But is letting every fifth youth down?]. In H. Hølleland (Ed.), *På vei mot Kunnskapsløftet.* Oslo: Cappelen Akademiske.

Markussen, E. (2003). *Valg og bortvalg. Om valg av studieretning i og bortvalg av videregående opplæring blant 16-åringer i 2002. Første delrapport i prosjektet Bortvalg og kompetanse* [About choice of study branch and dropout from upper secondary among 16-year-olds in 2002]. Skriftserie nr. 5, 2003. Oslo: NIFU.

Markussen, E., Frøseth, M. W., Lødding, B., & Sandberg, N. (2008). *Bortvalg og kompetanse. Gjennomføring, bortvalg og kompetanseoppnåelse i videregående opplæring blant 9749 ungdommer som gikk ut av grunnskolen på Østlandet våren 2002: hovedfunn, konklusjoner og implikasjoner fem år etter* [Early leaving, non-completion or completion? On early leaving, non-completion or completion in upper secondary education among 9749 young people that left lower secondary in the spring of 2002]. Report 13, 2008. Oslo: NIFU STEP.

Markussen, E., Sandberg, N., & Frøseth, M. W. (Forthcoming). Reaching for the unreachable: Identifying factors predicting early school leaving and non-completion in Norwegian upper secondary education.

Markussen, E., & Sandberg, N. (2005). *Stayere, sluttere og returnerte. Om 9756 ungdommer på Østlandet og deres karriere i videregående opplæring frem til midten av det tredje skoleåret* [Stayers, quitters and returners. About 9756 young people in the south-east of Norway and their career in upper secondary until the end of the third year of schooling]. Report 3, 2005. Oslo: NIFU STEP.

Markussen, E., Lødding B., Sandberg N., & Vibe, N. (2006). *Forskjell på folk – hva gjør skolen? Valg, bortvalg og kompetanseoppnåelse i videregående opplæring blant 9749 ungdommer som gikk ut av grunnskolen på Østlandet våren 2002* [People are different – what does the school do? Choice, dropout and achievement of qualification in upper secondary education among 9749 young people that left lower secondary in the spring of 2000]. Report 3, 2006. Oslo: NIFU STEP.

Michelsen, S., & Høst, H. (2004). Building the new governance in Norwegian apprenticeship organisation. In R. Husemann & A. Heikkinen (Eds.), *Governance and Marketisation in Vocational and Continuing Education.* Frankfurt am Main: Peter Lang.

NAV. (2008). http://www.nav.no/page?id=249

Newman, F. M., Wehlage, G.G., & Lamborn, S. D. (1992). The significance and sources of student engagement. In F. Newman (Ed.), *Student engagement and achievement in American secondary schools.* New York-London: Teachers College Press.

NOU. (2003:16). Utdannings- og forskningsdepartementet (2003). *I første rekke. Forsterket kvalitet i en grunnopplæring for alle* [Ministry of Education: A better education for all].

Olsen, O. J. (1996). Fagopplæring : omforming [VET in Change]. In O. J. Olsen (Ed.), *Yrkesutdanning og fagopplæring under en moderniseringsoffensiv. Opplegg for evaluering av Reform 94*. Bergen: AHS - Gruppe for flerfaglig arbeidslivsforskning, Universitetet i Bergen

Opplæringslova. LOV 1998-07-17 nr 61. Lov om grunnskolen og den vidaregåande opplæringa. Sist endret 27. juni 2008 [Education Act. Act relating to primary and secondary education. Last amended 27 June 2008].

Raabe, M. (2007). *Hovedtall for utdanning.* [Main figures on education. Statistics Norway]. Oslo, Kongsvinger: SSB.

Rumberger, R. W. (1987). High school dropouts: A review of issues and evidence. *Review of Educational Research,* 57(2), 101–121.

Rumberger, R. W. (2004). Why students drop out of school. In G. Orfield (Ed.), *Dropouts in America: Confronting the graduation rate crisis.* Cambridge, MA: Harvard Education Press.

Røste, R., & Borgen, J. S. (2008). *Erfaringsanalyse av Partnerskap for karriereveiledning i Telemark* [Experience analysis from partnership for career guidance in Telemark]. Report 7, 2008. Oslo: NIFU STEP.

Statistics Norway. (2009). *Starter på yrkesfag, ender med studiekompetanse* [Starting on a vocational program, ends up with qualification for higher education]. Statistics Norway. Retrieved from http://www.ssb.no/emner/04/02/30/vgogjen/

Statistics Norway/AKU. (2008). http://www.ssb.no/emner/06/01/aku/tab-2008–08–01–05.html

St.meld. nr. 30 (2003–2004). *Kultur for læring* [Culture for learning]. Oslo: Utdannings- og forskningsdepartementet.

Streeck, W., & Schmitter P. C. (1985). Community, market, state – and associations? The prospective contribution of interest governance to social order. In W. Streeck & P. C. Schmitter (Eds.), *Private Interest Government. Beyond Market and State.* SAGE-series in Neo-corporatism. London: Sage Publications.

Støren, L. A., Helland, H., & Grøgaard, J. B. (2007). *Og hvem stod igjen-? Sluttrapport fra prosjektet Gjennomstrømning i videregående opplæring blant elever som startet i videregående opplæring i årene 1999–2001* [Who was left behind? About achievement of qualification among students starting in upper secondary education in Norway in the years 1999–2001] Report 14, 2007. Oslo: NIFU STEP.

Støren, L. A., & Skjersli, S. (1999). Gjennomføring av videregående opplæring - sett i lys av retten til opplæring [Completion of secondary education – In light of the right to education] In R. Kvalsund, T. Deichman-Sørensen & P. O. Aamodt (Eds.), *Videregående opplæring - ved en skilleveg? Forskning fra den nasjonale evalueringen av Reform 94.* Oslo: Tano Aschehoug.

Støren, L.A., Skjersli, S., & Aamodt, P. O. (1998). *I mål? Evaluering av Reform 94: sluttrapport fra NIFUs hovedprosjekt.* [Crossing the finish line? Evaluation of Reform 94]. Report 18 1998. Oslo: NIFU.

Telhaug, A. O., & Mediås, O. A. (2000). *Fra sentral til desentralisert styring. Statlig, regional styring av utdanningen i Skandinavia fram mot år 2000* [From centralised to decentralised government. State and region in the governance of education in Scandinavia towards the Year 2000]. Steinkjer: Utdanning som nasjonsbygging.

Traag, T., & van der Velden, R. K. W. (2008). *Early school leaving in the Netherlands. The role of student-, family- and school factors for early school-leaving in lower secondary education.* Maastricht: Maastricht University.

Vibe, N., Edvardsen, R., & Sandberg, N. (1997). *Etter halvgått løp. Rekruttering og gjennomstrømning i videregående opplæring etter Reform 94* [Half way through. Recruitment and achievement of qualifications after Reform 94]. Report 1, 1997. Oslo: NIFU.

Wehlage, G. G., Rutter, R. A., Smith, G. A., Lesko, N., & Fernandez, R. R. (1989). *Reducing the risk. Schools as communities of support.* London - New York - Philadelphia: The Falmer Press.

Introduction to the New World Education Systems

Stephen Lamb

Dropout has attracted a lot of attention in countries sometimes referred to as the *new world* nations: the United States, Canada and Australia. Headlines such as 'high school dropout crisis continues in US',[1] 'high school dropout crisis threatens US economic growth',[2] 'battle to boost Year 12 completion rates' (Australia),[3] 'high-school dropouts – a black mark on Canada's secondary school system'[4] reflect deep-seated concerns in each country about the problem of dropout and its effects. Yet these nations, sharing similar colonial histories, have been at the vanguard of building modern, democratic secondary school systems. They have been very successful in transforming their secondary schools into mass systems. The continuing concerns over the problem of dropout are based on a sense of failure – a sense that the systems have failed to deliver on their promise of providing universal secondary education that is non-selective, meritocratic and provides equal chances of success to all regardless of social background, race and gender.

The United States led the way. According to Trow (1977, p 114),[5] mass secondary education in the United States was built through a system of comprehensive high schools, devoted initially to the education of the great mass of students for work and life and the preparation of a small minority for higher education which, over time, became the major function. Mass rates of high school completion were achieved as early as the middle of last century. The comprehensive high school was

---

[1]CNN, May 5, 2009, http://www.cnn.com/2009/US/05/05/dropout.rate.study/

[2]Committee on Education and Labor. May 12, 2009, http://edlabor.house.gov/newsroom/2009/05/high-school-dropout-crisis-thr.shtml

[3]*The Age* Newspaper, January 24, 2009.

[4]Communiqué of the CD Howe Institute, October 22, 2009, http://www.cdhowe.org/pdf/commentary_298pr.pdf

[5]Trow, M. (1977). The second transformation of the American school system. In J. Karabel, & A. H. Halsey (Eds.), *Power and ideology in education* (pp. 105–118). New York Oxford University Press.

S. Lamb (✉)
Centre for Post-Compulsory Education and Lifelong Learning,
University of Melbourne, Australia

S. Lamb et al. (Eds.), *School Dropout and Completion: International Comparative Studies in Theory and Policy*, DOI 10.1007/978-90-481-9763-7_15,
© Springer Science+Business Media B.V. 2011

important to these achievements. It removed the practice of channelling students into separate academic and vocational schools (or streams) at a relatively young age which was and remains common to many European systems. It catered to students from diverse backgrounds with diverse talents and abilities and it did so by establishing a single certificate, the high school diploma, which offered a broad range of common and elective options.[6] While comprehensive high schools and development of the graduate diploma contributed to the unprecedented growth of secondary education, they still act as a source of differentiation in pathways. They do this largely through the role of tracking, in which students take different programs (vocational, general, academic) based on their subject selections, despite being in the same school.

In Canada, there is considerable diversity across provinces, but the secondary school systems have developed many features similar to the United States. Comprehensive high schools are a common model with vocational and academic programs offered within the same school. Secondary school diplomas are awarded to students who complete the requisite number of compulsory and optional courses. In the main, students follow tracks or streams of study (vocational, academic, general) based on their elective choices.

In Australia, the comprehensive school is also the main model of schooling, though private and selective-entry schools are significant, depending on the state or territory. Widespread program reforms in the 1980s and 1990s, designed to democratise participation and improve rates of graduation, led to the development of school qualifications not dissimilar to the high school diploma in the United States.

Despite these efforts to develop truly universal models of secondary education, dropout remains an issue in each of the systems as the following case studies show.

---

[6]See Green's study *Education and State Formation: The Rise of Education Systems in England, France and USA*. New York: St. Martin's Press, 1999.

Chapter 13
High School Dropouts in the United States

Russell W. Rumberger

Introduction

One of the major educational challenges in virtually all industrialised nations is raising the education level of the workforce. This includes getting more students to complete upper secondary school or what is referred to as 'high school' in the United States. Completing high school is increasingly viewed as a minimal requirement for entry into the labour market and for further, post-secondary education. In fact, with the economy generating an increasing number of jobs that require at least some post-secondary schooling, students who earn no more than a high school diploma will most likely have diminishing economic prospects in the future economy.

Despite the growing importance of graduating from high school, a large segment of the student population in United States fails to complete it. Moreover, while an increasing percentage of adolescents have enrolled in high school over the last 4 decades, the percentage of students completing high school has actually declined. This chapter provides a brief overview of the United States educational system and then reviews research on the patterns of high school dropout and graduation, the causes of dropping out, and what programs and policies have been developed to reduce dropout and improve high school graduation rates.

The United States Educational System

The United States educational system is composed of both public and private schools, with about 89% of school-age children (ages 5–17) attending public schools (Snyder et al., 2009, Table 2). Public schools are governed and funded by the government, while private schools are governed by religious and non-religious authorities and generally funded privately, but do receive limited government funding for particular programs.

R.W. Rumberger (✉)
Gevirtz Graduate School of Education, University of California, Santa Barbara, United States

S. Lamb et al. (Eds.), *School Dropout and Completion: International Comparative Studies in Theory and Policy*, DOI 10.1007/978-90-481-9763-7_16,
© Springer Science+Business Media B.V. 2011

Because the constitutional authority for public education resides in states, the United States has 50 state educational systems and another one for the nation's capital, the District of Columbia. In addition, all states except Hawaii delegate substantial authority to the more than 15,000 local education agencies known as 'school districts', which are governed by locally elected school boards and range from very small, rural districts to very large, urban districts. As a result, there are widespread differences in schools throughout the United States in terms of funding, governance, school structure, the role of teacher unions, school practices and school 'quality', whether quality is defined in terms of resources, practices, or student outcomes (Card & Krueger, 1998). Public schools in the United States are also highly segregated, reflecting widespread differences in the demographic character- istics of students in terms of social class, race and ethnicity, immigration status and language background (Orfield & Lee, 2005).

Despite these differences, there is actually a fair amount of commonality among schools and state school systems, including the provision of secondary schooling. The most common school structure in the United States consists of three grade- level configurations: 'elementary schools', with grade spans typically ranging from kindergarten to Grade 5 enrolling students aged 5–10 years; 'middle schools', with grade spans typically ranging from Grade 6 to 8 enrolling students aged 11–13 years; and 'high schools', with grade spans typically ranging from Grades 9 to 12 enrolling students aged 14–17 years (see Fig. 13.1). But there are substantial varia- tions that often include only one or two grade-level configurations. For example, in some local school systems, elementary schools range from kindergarten to Grade 8; in other school systems, high schools range from Grades 7 to 12; and in some, typi- cally rural, school systems students attend a single school ranging from kindergar- ten to Grade 12. Of all public secondary schools in 2006–07 that included Grade 12, 58% were 4-year high schools (Grades 9–12), 13% were 6-year high schools (Grades 7–12), and 21% were combined elementary/secondary schools (Snyder et al., 2009, Tables 98, 100). Yet because combined schools are typically smaller, a higher proportion of students actually attend 4-year high schools.

Not only does the structure of secondary schools vary among states and locali- ties, so do requirements for attending and graduating. Each state specifies the compulsory schooling age, dictating the age that students must attend school. The minimum age that students can leave school ranges from 16 to 18 (Snyder et al., 2009, Table 165). Since it typically takes 4 years to complete the requirements for a high school diploma, students who leave before the age of 18 are not assured of earning a diploma.

Most states also specify the requirements for earning a high school diploma, although school districts can add additional requirements. These requirements vary among states and have changed over time. In 2006, among states that specified course requirements, the number of course credits[1] varied from a low of 13 in such states as California, Wisconsin and Wyoming, to a high of 24 in such states as

---

[1] A course credit is known as a Carnegie unit and represents the credit received for completing a 1-year course.

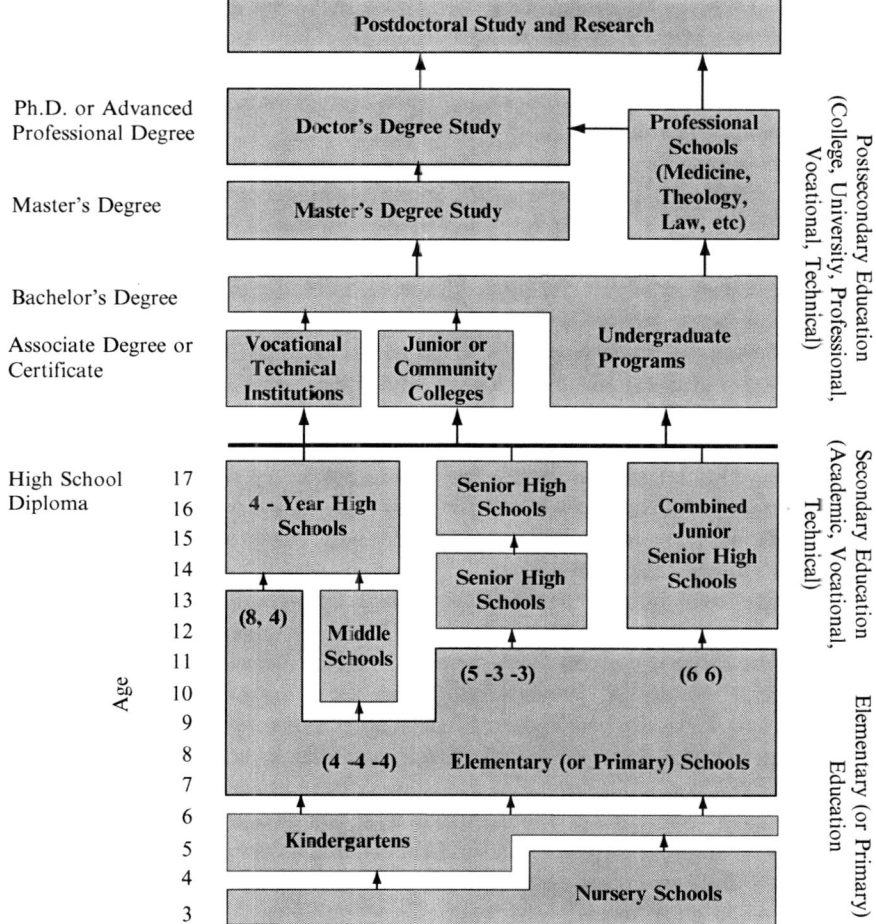

Fig. 13.1 Structure of education in the United States (Source: Snyder, 2009, Fig. 1)
Note: Adult education programs, while not separately delineated above, may provide instruction at the elementary, secondary or post-secondary education level. Chart reflects typical patterns of progression rather than all possible variations

Alabama, Florida and South Carolina (Snyder et al., 2009, Table 167). Alabama appears to have the most rigorous requirements: 4-year courses in English, social studies, science and mathematics, together with eight additional courses. This translates into four academic and two additional courses for each of the 4 years of high school. Such requirements leave little room for error – students who fail to earn six credits per year would not progress in school and would run the risk of not graduating in the expected 4 years.

Most of the requirements for earning a diploma focus on academic courses: English, social studies, science and mathematics. A few states require courses in the fine arts and foreign languages. Only two states, Arkansas and Delaware, require students to take any career and technical education courses (American Diploma Project, 2007), although all states offer them and many students take them: in 2004 high school graduates nationwide completed an average of 3.5 credits of career and technical education courses (Planty et al., 2007, Fig. 3).

Students in many states must also pass a high school exit exam in core subject areas, primarily English and mathematics, in addition to meeting course requirements. With the growth of the accountability movement and standards-based reform in the 1990s, assessments are used to ensure that students have mastered more rigorous, grade-level content standards. By 2006, 22 states required that students pass some sort of exit before being awarded a diploma, whereas previously or in other states, they only had to meet the course requirements (Snyder et al., 2009, Table 167).

Some states also use exams to award higher level diplomas that may benefit students' prospects for entering college. New York, for example, awards three levels of high school diplomas based on the types of course credits earned (all requiring 22 year-long credits), and on the number and scores on the Regents Exam: from a minimum score of 55 in five subjects for a Local Diploma, to a minimum score of 65 in eight subjects for a Regents Diploma with advanced designation (City University of New York, 2009).

In addition to determining the requirements for a regular high school diploma, states can award alternative or equivalency diplomas. These are typically awarded based on passing either a state or national examination. The most common national examination is the General Educational Development (GED) test administered by the American Council of Education, a private higher education organisation representing all sectors of United States degree-granting institutions (General Education Development Testing Service, 2008). The GED is a series of five subject exams in which, beginning in 1997, test-takers had to exceed the performance of at least 33% of traditional graduating high school seniors in order to pass the test. However, states establish their own criteria for using the GED results to issue high school certificates. Some states award regular diplomas, while other states award 'equivalency' diplomas or certificates based on either the GED or state-designed examinations. Some states also award other high school certificates in lieu of a regular diploma, such as certificates of attendance for students who fail to meet regular or alternative graduation requirements. Other states issue regular diplomas to all students who complete high school regardless of the requirements they meet, which makes it difficult to make comparisons across states.

Of all the high school completion certificates awarded in the United States in 2004–05, almost 94% were regular diplomas, 5% were equivalency diplomas, and less than 2% were other types of certificates.[2] But those percentages varied widely among states, with some states, such as California, awarding primarily regular diplomas (98%), while other states, such as Georgia, awarding much higher percentages of equivalency and other certificates (17%, compared with 83% regular diplomas).

---

[2]Based on Common Core Data. Retrieved February 7, 2009, from http://nces.ed.gov/ccd/bat/output.asp

The distinction between completing high school by earning a regular diploma and completing high school by earning an equivalency diploma is important for at least two reasons. First, research suggests that the economic benefits are not equivalent (Cameron & Heckman, 1993; Tyler, 2003). Second, the two types of diplomas help define both high school dropouts and high school graduates, as we now see.

Trends in Dropout and Graduation Rates

Identifying the number of students who drop out of school and graduate each year in the United States is complicated by the difficulty of tracking students over time, and the sources of data currently available to track them. There are also a number of measures of dropout and graduation rates that are used. Because these measures generate different rates, there has been considerable debate among scholars and government officials over the accuracy and use of these alternative measures (Heckman & LaFontaine, 2008; Mishel & Roy, 2006; Warren, 2005).

The federal government, in collecting dropout and graduation statistics from the states, defines a dropout as a previously enrolled student who has 'not graduated from high school or completed a state- or district-approved education program'.[3] The United States Census Bureau, which collects national population data, also defines a dropout as someone who has not completed high school by earning a high school diploma or alternative credential.[4] In other words, completing high school by any type of credential precludes someone from being considered a dropout by the federal government and by virtually all state governments. In fact, it is not even necessary to earn any type of high school credential to avoid being labelled a dropout – in California, for example, a student is not considered a dropout if 'the student has transferred to and is attending a college offering a baccalaureate or associate's program'.[5]

Yet not dropping out of school is not the same as graduating. The federal government also defines a high school graduate as someone who earns 'a regular high school diploma'.[6] Similarly, all of the nation's governors signed an agreement in 2005 to voluntarily implement a common formula for calculating their state's high school graduation rate, where graduation is defined as earning a diploma (National Governors Association Task Force on State High School Graduation Data, 2005, p. 15). Hence, keeping students from dropping out is not the same thing as getting

---

[3] See Defining and Calculating Event Dropout Rates Using the CCD. Retrieved July 20, 2009, from http://nces.ed.gov/pubs2007/dropout05/DefiningAndCalculating.asp

[4] See Defining and Calculating Dropout and Completion Rates Using the CPS. Retrieved July 20, 2009, from http://nces.ed.gov/pubs2007/dropout05/DefiningDropoutAndCompletion.asp

[5] See Dropout Guidelines for October 2008 CBEDS. Retrieved July 20, 2009, from http://www.cde.ca.gov/ds/sd/cb/dropoutguide.asp

[6] See final regulations for the federal Title I of the No Child Left Behind Act issued in October 2008. Retrieved July 20, 2009, from http://www.ed.gov/policy/elsec/reg/proposal/uniform-grad-rate.html

more students to graduate, and it is the latter that is most important to states and the federal government, and may be more lucrative for students.

The federal government calculates a number of different dropout and graduation rates (Laird et al., 2008):

- **Event dropout rate**. The percentage of persons in a population who drop out of school over a specified period of time, which is often a period of 1 year.
- **Status dropout rate**. The percentage of persons in a specified population who are not currently enrolled and have not completed school by earning a regular or an alternative (e.g., GED) high school credential.
- **Status completion rate**. The percentage of persons in a specified population who have completed high school by earning a regular or an alternative (e.g., GED) high school credential.
- **Cohort graduation rate**. The percentage of persons in a population who graduate – earn a regular high school diploma – over longer periods of time, such as the 4 year period from the beginning of Grade 9 to the end of Grade 12, and over multiple periods of time for the same population of students, such as the graduation rate over a 4-year period, a 5-year period, and a 6-year period.

State governments, too, calculate a number of different dropout, completion and graduation rates. In some cases, they are generated to satisfy federal reporting requirements; in other cases, they are used to satisfy state accountability and reporting requirements.

What do these rates reveal about the extent of the dropout problem in the United States? Based on the event dropout rate, 407,000 students dropped out of Grades 10–12 in the 2005–06 academic year, or about 3.8% of the students enrolled in United States schools (see Table 13.1). This is no doubt an undercount because it excludes students who dropped out before Grade 10. Annual dropout rates have been falling steadily over the last 25 years, from a high of 6.7% in 1979 to the current rate of 3.8% in 2006 (Laird et al., 2008, Table 4).

But annual dropout rates understate the likelihood that a student will drop out some time during his or her educational career. A better gauge is the proportion of dropouts in the population, referred to as the status dropout rate. Again, according to United States Census survey data, in October 2006 there were almost 3.5 million dropouts aged 16–24, representing 9.3% of the population (Table 13.1). These rates too have declined over the last 25 years, from a high of 14.6% in 1972 to the 2006 rate of 9.3% (Laird et al., 2008, Table 7).

Census data further reveal that 87.8% of the population aged 18–24 years had completed high school by October 2006 (see Table 13.1).

Dropout and graduation rates vary widely among demographic groups. First, dropout and completion rates vary by gender. Males are more likely to drop out and less likely to complete high school than females. Second, Blacks and Hispanic, who represent more than 30% of public school students (Snyder et al., 2009, Table 41), are more likely to drop out and less likely to complete high school than Whites and Asians. Third, students from low-income families are more likely to drop out of school than students from high-income families. Fourth, among Hispanics, foreign-born students have the highest dropout rates and the lowest completion rates,

Table 13.1 United States dropout and completion rates by demographic characteristics, October 2006

	Event dropout rates of 15- to 24-year-olds	Status dropout rates of 16- to 24-year-olds	Status completion rates of 18- to 24-year-olds
Total	3.8	9.3	87.8
Sex			
Male	4.1	10.3	86.5
Female	3.4	8.3	89.1
Race/ethnicity			
White, non-Hispanic	2.9	5.8	92.6
Black, non-Hispanic	3.8	10.7	84.8
Hispanic	7.0	22.1	70.9
Asian	4.1[a]	3.6	95.8
More than one race	3.1[a]	7.0	89.7
Family income			
Low income	9.0[a]		
Middle income	3.5		
High income	2.0		
Immigration status			
Foreign born			
Hispanic	10.0	36.2	57.7
Non-Hispanic	2.5[a]	4.2	95.0
First generation			
Hispanic	6.9	12.3	81.9
Non-Hispanic	4.7	4.2	95.0
Second generation or more			
Hispanic	4.8[a]	12.1	83.5
Non-Hispanic	3.0	6.9	91.2

[a]Interpret data with caution due to small sample size
Source: Laird et al. (2008, Tables 1, 6, 9)

while second generation and higher students have the lowest dropout rates and the highest completion rates. Among non-Hispanics, the picture is more complicated; first generation students appear to have both the highest event dropout rates, but the lowest status dropout rates, as well as the highest completion rates.

Yet dropout and completion rates alone may not be sufficient to reveal the extent of the problem. Census data have been criticised because they rely on respondents' self-reported educational status, which respondents may overstate, and because completion rates include persons who earn a GED, even though there is extensive evidence that alternative credentials do not provide the same economic benefits as a traditional high school diploma. Thus, both federal and state governments are attempting to measure the proportion of entering Grade 9 students who earn a regular diploma within 4 years, which is known as the *ninth-grade cohort gradua-tion rate*. Such a rate is particularly difficult to measure because it requires tracking students over several years. This is problematic, in part, because students often transfer from one educational setting to another during their high school careers.

In addition, some students are retained, especially in the ninth grade, when they fail to earn enough credits to be promoted to the next grade level.

A number of specific measures are currently used to estimate the ninth-grade graduation rate, and all have limitations (Miao & Haney, 2004; Mishel & Roy, 2006; Warren, 2005). Recently, the federal government has adopted one measure known as the *averaged freshman graduation rate*, and has produced estimates for the nations' public schools and for the public schools in each state. These estimates show a graduation rate of 75% nationally for all public schools in 2004–05, with state rates varying from a low of 60% in South Carolina to a high of 88% in Nebraska (Laird et al., 2008) Table 12. Graduation rates also vary widely among school districts in the United States, with some districts – such as New York City and Los Angles, the nation's two largest districts – having graduation rates of around 50% (Garofano & Sable, 2008, Table A-13).

Long-term trends show that the graduation rate was at its highest level in 1970 at 79% and then trended downward, reaching its lowest level of 71% in 1996 (see Fig. 13.2). The rate has trended upward since that time. Enrolment rates show different trends, reaching a low of 90% in 1980 and peaking at 95% in 2006. What accounts for those divergent trends is not clear.

Stagnating growth in high school graduation rates is not only problematic in itself, it is also problematic because it reflects the relative status of the United States in the global labour market. The Organisation for Economic Co-operation and Development (OECD) computes the percentage of upper secondary graduates to the population at the typical age of graduation. In 2006 the United States ranked 20th among OECD countries in the percentage of students who graduated from high school, with a graduation rate of 77% (OECD, 2008, Table A2.1). The average among all OECD countries in 2006 was 83%, and the average among the 19 OECD countries in the European Economic Union – those countries that represent out closest economic competitors – was 86% (OECD, 2008, Table A2.1). More disturbing, over the period from 1995 to

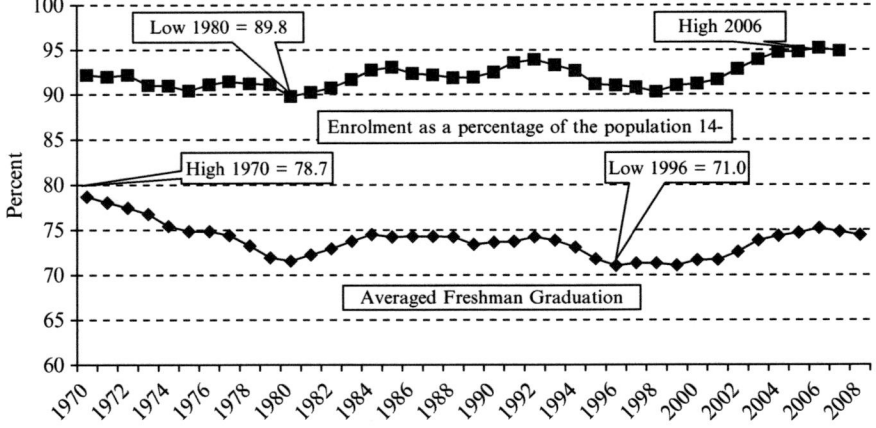

Fig. 13.2 Enrolment and graduation rates, 1970–04 (Source: Snyder et al., 2009, Tables 55, 104)

2005, the average graduation rate in the United States improved by a mere 3 percentage points, from 74% to 77% while the average graduation rate in OECD countries improved by 6 percentage points, from 77% to 83%. In other words, the United States is falling behind other countries in getting students to graduate from high school, hampering the ability to improve training and college participation beyond high school.

Why Do Students Drop Out?

Understanding why students drop out of school is the key to addressing this major educational problem; yet identifying the causes of dropping out is extremely difficult. Like other forms of educational achievement (e.g., test scores), the causes of dropping out are influenced by an array of proximal and distal factors related to both the individual student and to the family, school, and community settings in which the student lives.

Dropouts themselves report a variety of reasons for leaving school, including school-related reasons, family-related reasons and work-related reasons. The most specific reasons cited by a sample of 2002 10th-graders who dropped out were 'missed too many school days' (44%); 'thought it would be easier to get a GED' (41%); 'getting poor grades/failing school' (38%); 'did not like school' (37%); and 'could not keep up with schoolwork' (32%) (Rotermund, 2007a). But these reasons do not reveal the underlying causes of why students quit school, particularly those causes or factors in elementary or middle school that may have contributed to students' attitudes, behaviours and school performance immediately preceding their decision to leave school. Moreover, if many factors contribute to this phenomenon over a long period of time, it is virtually impossible to demonstrate a causal connection between any single factor and the decision to quit school.

Although existing research is unable, for the most part, to identify unique causes of dropping out, a vast empirical research literature has examined numerous predictors of high school dropout and graduation (Rumberger & Lim, 2008). The empirical research comes from a number of social science disciplines and has identified two types of factors: (1) individual factors associated with students themselves, such as their attitudes, behaviours, school performance and prior experiences; and (2) contextual factors found in students' families, schools and communities.

Individual Factors

A variety of individual factors are associated with dropping out, including several demographic factors. Generally, dropout rates are higher among males, Blacks and Hispanics, immigrants and students from non-English backgrounds. Attitudes also affect dropout rates. Dropout rates are higher among students who have low educational and occupational aspirations. Several activities and behaviours also predict dropout rates, including absenteeism, misbehaviour in school and pregnancy. Finally, poor academic achievement is a strong predictor of dropping out. Together, these factors support the idea that dropping out is influenced by both the social and academic experiences of students.

In addition to these proximal factors, a number of distal factors are associated with dropping out, such as student mobility. Both *residential* mobility (changing residences) and *school* mobility (changing schools) increase the risk of dropping out of high school (Haveman et al., 1991; Rumberger, 1995; Rumberger & Larson, 1998; Swanson & Schneider, 1999; Teachman et al., 1996). Student mobility may represent a less severe form of student disengagement or withdrawal from school. That is, students may voluntarily transfer or be forced to transfer by school officials in an attempt to find a more suitable or supportive school environment before quitting school altogether. For example, one study found that students typically attend two or more high schools before dropping out (Rumberger & Larson, 1998).

Another distal factor is grade retention. Although retention may have some positive impact on academic achievement in the short run, numerous studies have found that it greatly increases the likelihood that students will drop out of school (Rumberger & Lim, 2008). Finally, a number of long-term studies have found that lack of early academic achievement and engagement (e.g., attendance, misbehaviour) in elementary and middle school predicts withdrawal from high school.

Institutional Factors

While individual factors clearly contribute to students' decisions to drop out of school, individual attitudes and behaviours are shaped by the various settings or contexts in which students live. As noted by the Forum on Adolescence, created by the National Institute of Medicine and the National Research Council to bring authoritative, non-partisan research to bear on policy issues facing adolescents and their families: 'Another important insight of scientific inquiry is the profound influence of settings on adolescents' behaviour and development' (National Research Council and Institute of Medicine, 1999, pp. 11–12). This perspective is common in such social science disciplines as economics, sociology and anthropology, and more recently has been incorporated in an emerging paradigm in developmental psychology called *developmental behavioural science* (Jessor, 1993). This paradigm recognises that the various settings or contexts in which children live – families, schools and communities – all shape their attitudes, behaviours and experiences. For example, the National Research Council Panel on High-Risk Youth (1993) concluded that too much emphasis has been placed on 'high-risk' youth and not enough on the high-risk settings in which they live and go to school. Similarly, a 2004 review of the literature on childhood poverty identified a wide variety of family, school, and community environmental factors that impede the development of poor children (Evans, 2004). Both reviews reflect the growing emphasis on understanding how these contexts shape educational outcomes.

This new perspective has important implications for studying and understanding the problem of school dropout. Anthropologists, by studying the experiences of dropouts in particular settings, have long illustrated the importance of the family, school and community contexts in understanding dropouts (Trueba et al., 1989). Recent developments in statistics have also allowed quantitative researchers to study the influence of context, particularly the school setting, on academic performance across large numbers of schools (Lee, 2000; Rumberger & Palardy, 2004). This research has identified a number of factors within students' families, schools and communities (and peer relationships) that predict dropping out.

Families

Family background is widely recognised as the single most important contributor to success in school. Socioeconomic status, most commonly measured by *parental education* and *family income*, is a powerful predictor of school achievement and dropout behaviour. Parental education influences students' aspirations and educational support, while family income allows parents to provide more resources to support their children's education, including access to private schools, after-school and summer school programs and more support for learning within the home. In addition, students whose parents monitor and regulate their activities, provide emotional support, encourage independent decision-making (known as *authoritative parenting style*) and are generally more involved in their schooling are less likely to drop out of school (Rumberger et al., 1990; Rumberger, 1995). It has also been found that students in single-parent and step-families are more likely to drop out of school than students in two-parent families.

Schools

It is widely acknowledged that schools exert powerful influences on student achievement, including dropout rates. Four types of school characteristics influence student performance: social composition of the schools, structural characteristics, school resources, and school policies and practices (Rumberger & Lim, 2008).

The social composition of schools – the characteristics of students attending the schools, particularly the socioeconomic composition of the student body – predicts dropping out even after controlling for the individual factors that influence dropping out.

The second characteristic has to do with the *structural characteristics of schools*, such as size, location and school control (public versus private) (McNeal, 1997; Rumberger, 1995; Rumberger & Thomas, 2000). Dropout rates from Catholic and other private schools are lower than dropout rates from public schools, even after controlling for differences in the background characteristics of students. Yet students from private schools typically transfer to public schools instead of or before dropping out, so that student turnover rates in private schools are not statistically different to turnover rates in public schools. Smaller schools also have lower dropout rates. What is less clear is whether structural characteristics themselves account for these differences or whether they are related to differences in student characteristics and school resources often associated with the structural features of schools.

The third type of characteristic concerns *school resources*. Resources, in particular student/teacher ratios and teacher quality, appear to influence dropout rates even after controlling for a host of individual and contextual factors that might also influence dropout rates.

The final characteristic type has to do with *school policies and practices*. In particular, academic and social climate – as measured by school attendance rates, students taking advanced courses, and student perceptions of a fair discipline policy – predict school dropout rates, even after controlling for the background characteristics of students as well as the resource and structural characteristics of schools.

School factors contribute to student withdrawal in two ways. One way is indirectly, by creating conditions that influence student engagement and their *voluntary* withdrawal from school. Another way is directly, through explicit policies and conscious decisions by school personnel that cause students to *involuntarily* withdraw from school. These rules and actions may concern low grades, poor attendance, misbehaviour, or being over-age and may lead to students being forced to transfer to another regular or 'alternative' high school designed for students who do not fit into the regular school. This form of withdrawal is school-initiated and contrasts with the student-initiated form mentioned above. Some schools, for example, contribute to students' involuntary departure from school by systematically excluding and discharging 'troublemakers' and other problematic students (Fine, 1991; Riehl, 1999).

Communities

In addition to families and schools, communities can influence students' withdrawal from school. Differences in neighbourhood characteristics can help explain differences in dropout rates among communities, apart from the influence of families (Clark, 1992; Crane, 1991). Some evidence suggests that there is a threshold or tipping point on the quality of neighbourhoods that results in particularly high dropout rates in the most disadvantaged neighbourhoods. Poor communities may influence child and adolescent development through the lack of resources (playgrounds and parks, after-school programs) or negative peer influences (Hallinan & Williams, 1990; Wilson, 1987). Community residents may also influence parenting practices over and above parental education and income. Students living in poor communities may also be more likely to have dropouts as friends, which increases the likelihood of dropping out of school.

Another way that communities can influence dropout rates is by providing employment opportunities both during and after school. Relatively favourable employment opportunities for high school dropouts, as evidenced by low neighbourhood unemployment rates, appears to increase the likelihood that students will drop out, while more favourable economic returns to graduating, as evidenced by higher sala- ries of high school graduates compared to dropouts, tend to lower dropout rates (Clark, 1992; Bickel & Papagiannis, 1988). Working long hours outside of school can increase the likelihood of dropping out, although the impact of working in high school depends on the type of job held and on the student's gender.

Not only are settings important in influencing dropout behaviour, similar set- tings affect individuals differently. Why is it that some students persist in school while living in poor families or attending lower-quality schools? These different outcomes arise not only because of so-called 'objective' differences in individuals – intelligence, race or family situation – but also because of how individuals view or interpret their conditions. Thus, dropping out of school cannot be understood simply by studying the conditions of families and schools, or even the behaviours of students, but must also be understood by studying the views and interpretations of those conditions and behaviours by dropouts themselves. Anthropological stud- ies of dropouts are based on this premise.

Finally, to understand why students drop out requires looking at school experiences and performance over a long period of time. Dropping out is more of a process than an event. Students don't suddenly drop out of school. Many dropouts show patterns of early school failure – disruptive behaviour, failing grades, repeating – that eventually lead to students giving up or being forced to leave because of poor attendance or disruptive behaviour (Alexander et al., 2001; Barrington & Hendricks, 1989 Cairns et al., 1989; Ensminger & Slusacick, 1992; Garnier et al., 1997; Roderick, 1993).

These three features – the contexts or settings of families, schools and communi- ties; different interpretations of context; and school experiences over time – are all important for understanding why students (in the United States) drop out of school. In addition, dropping out must also be understood in relation to other activities or situations that youth face, such as school violence, gang involvement, teenage preg- nancy and problems at home.

Responding to the Dropout Crisis

Reducing the number of dropouts has become a national policy concern – sometimes labelled a 'crisis' – both inside and outside of the government. In February 2005, the nation's governors (elected heads of state government) held a 2-day summit on high schools where Microsoft chairman Bill Gates stated:

> America's high schools are obsolete. By obsolete, I don't just mean that our high schools are broken, flawed and under-funded – though a case could be made for every one of those points. By obsolete, I mean that our high schools – even when they're working exactly as designed – cannot teach our kids what they need to know today… This isn't an accident or a flaw in the system; it is the system (Gates, 2005).

On April 9, 2006, one of the nation's leading news magazines, *Time*, featured a cover labelled *Dropout Nation* along with a number of stories about the dropout crisis in America. And Former United States Secretary of State Colin Powell and his wife established a foundation in 1997, *America's Promise*, that is funding dropout summits in all 50 states and over 50 cities throughout the United States.

Both the government and private organisations are funding interventions to reduce dropout rates and improve high school performance. Because dropping out is influenced by both individual and institutional factors, intervention strategies focus on either or both sets of factors. *Programmatic strategies* provide would-be dropouts with additional resources and supports to help them stay in school without attempting to alter the characteristics of families, schools and communities that may place them at risk. *Institutional strategies* provide incentives, resources and supports to strengthen families, schools and communities. In addition, states have enacted a number of policies to improve high school outcomes. In general, few of these strategies to date have proven effective.

Programmatic Strategies

There are two programmatic approaches to dropout prevention. One approach is to provide supplemental services to students within an existing school program. The second approach is to provide a complete alternative school program, either within an existing comprehensive high school or in a separate facility (alternative school). Neither approach attempts to change existing institutions serving most students; instead they create alternative programs or institutions to target students who are somehow identified as being at risk of dropping out, or who have already dropped out.

Unfortunately, there is little scientific evidence on the effectiveness of these dropout interventions. One reason is that there have been relatively few rigorous evaluations of dropout intervention programs. Another reason is that the scientifically rigorous evaluations that do exist often fail to demonstrate program effectiveness. In 2002, the United States Department of Education established the What Works Clearinghouse (WWC) to review scientific evidence on the effectiveness of a variety of educational interventions, including dropout interventions (United States Department of Education, Institute of Education Sciences, 2009). To date, the WWC has identified only 16 interventions with scientifically rigorous evidence: seven were effective in reducing dropout rates, six were effective in improving students' progress toward graduation (such as earning credits toward graduation), but only four programs were effective in improving high school completion rates. Moreover, none of these four programs were effective in helping students earn a regular high school diploma; rather they helped students earn an equivalent diploma by passing the General Educational Development (GED) test.

Institutional Strategies

Institutional strategies have the potential to reduce dropping out for a much larger number of students by improving some of the environmental factors in families, schools and communities that contribute to dropout behaviour. Although the promise of systemic solutions to the dropout problem is great, the reality is not. The reason is simply that systemic changes are extremely difficult to achieve because they involve making fundamental changes in the way institutions work individually and within the system in which they are a part.

One institutional approach is to reform existing high schools under the assumption that as the school itself is not performing adequately for most students, then programmatic approaches would be insufficient to bring about the substantial improvement in student outcomes and high school performance. The most widespread approach for reforming existing high schools is known as comprehensive school reform (CSR). This approach involves multiple strategies to alter all facets of a school and 'is built on the premise that unified, coherent, and integrated strategies for improvement, knitted together into a comprehensive design, will work better than the same strategies implemented in isolation from each other' (United States Department of Education, 2002, p. 1).

Yet few CSR models have proven effective. A United States Department of Education centre, the Comprehensive School Reform Quality Center, found only 16 models that met their standards for rigorous evaluations: 10 were found to produce positive effects in student achievement, but only three were found to provide positive effects in dropout and graduation rates (Comprehensive School Reform Quality Center, 2006). An independent review of 10 comprehensive school reform models where at least half of the reform focused on secondary schools found only two evaluations conducted by outside evaluators that showed significant improvements in student outcomes (Borman et al., 2003). And the What Works Clearinghouse review of four CSR or new school models found that only one was effective at keeping students in school, two were effective in helping students progress in school, and none were effective in helping students to complete school (United States Department of Education, Institute of Education Sciences, What Works Clearinghouse, 2008).

One of the CSR models and one of the programmatic strategies found to be effective at keeping students in school utilised career and technical education as a component of the model. There is a growing interest among some educators and policy-makers to support and encourage different approaches – known as 'multiple pathways' – to help students meet rigorous academic standards, including career and technical programs and project-based learning (American Diploma Project, 2007; Oakes & Saunders, 2008). The idea is not to offer alternative credentials, but rather alternative ways to meet the requirements for a high school diploma.

Another institutional approach for improving high school performance is to close, rather than redesign, low-performing schools and replace them with new schools. The strategy is often coupled with creating a particular type of new school known as a 'charter school' – public schools that are established and managed outside the regular public education system, and that are freed from most of the regulations and requirements of regular public schools. Charter schools were established to provide choice within the public school system, to spur educational innovation, to create competition as a way to improve non-charter schools, and to improve student achievement. The extent to which charter schools have achieved those goals has been the subject of intense and often partisan debate (Carnoy et al., 2005; Finn et al., 2000; Henig, 2008; Zimmer et al., 2009). Nonetheless, their popularity continues to grow. In 2006–07, there were 4,132 charter schools in the United States, up from 2,179 in 2003–04, with 521 of those secondary charter schools (Snyder et al., 2009, Tables 98, 101). In California alone, the number of charter high schools increased from 97 in 2000–01 to 271 in 2005–06 (Rotermund, 2007b).

The research evidence on the effectiveness of charter schools is decidedly mixed, based on two recent studies. The first study examined 669 charter schools in five districts located within five different states, and state-wide in three other states, and found that middle and high school charters are producing achievement gains that are, on average, neither substantially better nor substantially worse than those of traditional public schools (Zimmer et al., 2009). The second study examined charter school performance in 15 states and the District of Columbia and found that 46% of the charter schools had mathematics gains that were indistinguishable from the average gains among matched students who attended traditional public schools (TPS), 17% had gains that exceeded the growth in TPS, and 37% had gains significantly below those in TPS (Center for Research on Education Outcomes [CREDO], 2009).

Efforts to reform other institutions that serve at-risk youth have also proved more difficult. One ambitious systemic reform effort was the New Futures Initiative, promoted and funded by the Annie E. Casey foundation beginning in 1988 (White & Wehlage, 1995). New Futures was an attempt to build new collaborative structures among existing public and private institutions in five cities (Dayton, Ohio; Lawrence, Massachusetts; Little Rock, Arkansas; Pittsburgh, Pennsylvania; Savannah, Georgia) to address the problems of at-risk youth, including school dropout. The key strategy was to establish an oversight collaborative in each city with representation from public and private sector agencies to 'identify youth problems, develop strategies, and set timelines for addressing these problems, coordinate joint agency activities, and restructure educational and social services' (White & Wehlage, 1995, p. 24). These collaborative organisations also included case managers who (1) brokered services among the disparate agencies serving at-risk youth and their families; (2) served as advocates for at-risk youth; and (3) served as the 'eyes and ears' of the collaboratives by providing information and feedback to the group about what reforms were needed. Evaluations of this ambitious, systemic reform effort found that it did little to reduce dropout rates and other problems of at-risk youth. As with other systemic reform efforts, the evaluations found little incentive or support from the intervention for changing the fundamental functioning of schools.

Systemic Reform Strategies

Three systemic reforms are designed to improve high school performance. One is to raise high school graduation requirements, either by increasing the number and rigor of courses needed to receive a diploma or by requiring students to pass a high school exit exam. Although earlier research studies found no or limited effects of exit exams, more recent studies have found that high school exit exams have lowered high school completion rates, especially among low-achieving students (Reardon et al., 2009).

Another systemic reform is to raise the compulsory schooling age to 18 (Bridgeland et al., 2008). A recent review of several studies that examined the relationship between the state compulsory schooling age and dropout or graduation rates found that states with higher compulsory schooling ages had lower dropout rates or higher graduation rates (Rumberger & Lim, 2008).

A third systemic reform strategy to improve high school performance is establishing dual enrolment programs, which allow high school students to take college classes while still completing their high school diploma. In 2003, 71% of United States high schools offered dual enrolment courses with more than one million students enrolled (Snyder et al., 2009, Table 152). A rigorous evaluation of one such program found that it did not improve dropout or graduation rates (Dynarski & Gleason, 1998).

Conclusion

Improving graduation rates has become a national concern in the United States. The federal and state governments, along with many private foundations, are pouring millions of dollars into dropout prevention programs and high school reform efforts. By and large, those efforts, at least to date, have not been successful.

Successfully addressing the dropout problem in the United States will require both capacity and will. Capacity requires technical expertise to develop and implement effective dropout prevention and recovery programs, as well as more ambitious systemic school reforms. While some schools have such capacity, most require additional resources, technical expertise, and incentives to restructure the existing schools. Such solutions have been tried, but have not succeeded. Research suggests why systemic reforms of schools and other agencies serving youth are problematic, but not how to address them.

The development of such capacity will require political will; but even with the will to reform schools, it is unlikely that the United States will ever eliminate disparities in dropout rates among racial and ethnic groups without eliminating disparities in the resources of families, schools and communities. To the extent that dropping out is a social and not just an educational problem, then effective solutions must address changes in families and communities as well as schools. But the more comprehensive the scope of change, the more difficult the change becomes. Ultimately, the ability to 'solve' the dropout problem in the United States may depend more on the country's ability to address widespread inequalities in the larger social and economic system (Rothstein, 2004).

References

Alexander, K. L., Entwisle, D. R., & Kabbini, N. S. (2001). The dropout process in life course perspective: Early risk factors at home and school. *Teachers College Record, 103,* 760–882.

American Diploma Project (2007). *Aligning high school graduation requirements with the real world: a road map for states.* Washington, DC: Achieve. Retrieved October 14, 2009, from http://www.achieve.org/AligningHighSchoolGradRequirements

Barrington, B. L., & Hendricks, B. (1989). Differentiating characteristics of high school graduates, dropouts, and nongraduates. *Journal of Educational Research, 82,* 309–319.

Bickel, R., & Papagiannis, G. (1988). Post-high school prospects and district-level dropout rates. *Youth & Society, 20,* 123–147.

Borman, G. D., Hewes, G. M., Overman, L. T., & Brown, S. (2003). Comprehensive school reform and achievement: A meta-analysis. *Review of Educational Research, 73,* 125–230.

Bridgeland, J. M., DiIulio Jr., J. J., & Streeter, R. (2008). *Raising the compulsory school attendance age: The case for reform.* Washington, DC: Civic Enterprises.

Cairns, R. B., Cairns, B. D., & Necherman, H. J. (1989). Early school dropout: Configurations and determinants. *Child Development, 60,* 1437–1452.

Cameron, S. V., & Heckman, J. J. (1993). The nonequivalence of high school equivalents. *Journal of Labor Economics, 11,* 1–47.

Card, D., & Krueger, A. B. (1998). School resources and student outcomes. *Annals of the American Academy of Political & Social Science, 559,* 39–53.

Carnoy, M., Jacobson, R., Mishel, L., & Rothstein, R. (2005). *The charter school dust-up: Examining the evidence on enrollment and achievement.* Washington, DC/New York: Economic Policy Institute and Teachers College Press.

Center for Research on Education Outcomes (CREDO). (2009). *Multiple choice: Charter school performance in 16 states. Executive Summary.* Stanford, CA: CREDO, Stanford University.

City University of New York. (2009). *College now, high school graduation: Credit and regents requirements.* New York City: Author. Retrieved from http://collegenow.cuny.edu/nextstop/finish_hs/creditreq/

Clark, R. L. (1992). *Neighborhood effects on dropping out of school among teenage boys.* Discussion paper. Washington, DC: The Urban Institute.

Comprehensive School Reform Quality Center. (2006). *CSRQ center report on middle and high school comprehensive school reform models.* Washington, DC: American Institutes for Research.

Crane, J. (1991). The epidemic theory of ghettos and neighborhood effects on dropping out and teenage childbearing. *American Journal of Sociology, 96,* 1226–1259.

Dynarski, M., Clarke, L., Cobb, B., Finn, J., Rumberger, R., & Smink, J. (2008). *Dropout prevention: A practice guide* (NCEE 2008–4025). Washington, DC: National Center for Education Evaluation and Regional Assistance, Institute of Education Sciences, United States Department of Education. Retrieved October 14, 2009, from http://ies.ed.gov/ncee/wwc

Dynarski, M., & Gleason, P. (1998). *How can we help? What we have learned from federal dropout-prevention programs.* Princeton, NJ: Mathematica Policy Research.

Ensminger, M. E., & Slusacick, A. L. (1992). Paths to high school graduation or dropout: A longitudinal study of a first-grade cohort. *Sociology of Education, 65,* 95–113.

Evans, G. W. (2004). The environment of childhood poverty. *American Psychologist, 59,* 77–92.

Fine, M. (1991). *Framing dropouts: Notes on the politics of an urban public high school.* Albany, NY: State University of New York Press.

Finn, Jr., C. E., Manno, B. V., & Vanourek, G. (2000). *Charter schools in action: Renewing public education.* Princeton, NJ: Princeton University Press.

Garnier, H. E., Stein, J. A., & Jacobs, J. K. (1997). The process of dropping out of high school: A 19-year perspective. *American Educational Research Journal, 34,* 395–419.

Garofano, A., & Sable, J. (2008). *Public elementary and secondary school districts in the United States: 2005–06* (NCES 2008–339). Washington, DC: United States Department of Education,

National Center for Education Statistics. Retrieved October 14, 2009, from http://nces.ed.gov/pubsearch/pubsinfo.asp?pubid=2008339

General Education Development Testing Service. (2008). *2007 GED testing program statistical report*. Washington, DC: Author.

Hallinan, M. T., & Williams, R. A. (1990). Students' characteristics and the peer-influence process. *Sociology of Education, 63*, 122–132.

Haveman, R., Wolfe, B., & Spaulding, J. (1991). Childhood events and circumstances influencing high school completion. *Demography, 28*, 133–157.

Heckman, J. J., & LaFontaine, P. A. (2008). *The American high school graduation rate: Trends and levels* (NBER Working Paper 13670). Cambridge, MA: National Bureau of Economic Research. Retrieved October 14, 2009, from http://www.nber.org/papers/w13670

Henig, J. R. (2008). *Spin cycle: How research is used in policy debate: The case of charter schools*. New York: Russell Sage Foundation.

Jessor, R. (1993). Successful adolescent development among youth in high-risk settings. *American Psychologist, 48*, 117–126.

Laird, J., Cataldi, E. F., KewalRamani, A., & Chapman, C. (2008). *Dropout and completion rates in the United States: 2006* (NCES 2008–043). Washington, DC: United States Department of Education, National Center for Education Statistics. Retrieved October 14, 2009, from http://nces.ed.gov/pubsearch/pubsinfo.asp?pubid=2008053

Lee, V. E. (2000). Using hierarchical linear modeling to study social contexts: The case of school effects. *Educational Psychologist, 35*, 125–141.

McNeal, R. B. (1997). High school dropouts: A closer examination of school effects. *Social Science Quarterly, 78*, 209–222.

Miao, J., & Haney, W. (2004). High school graduation rates: Alternative methods and implications. *Education Policy Analysis Archives, 12*. Retrieved October 14, 2009, from http://epaa.asu.edu/epaa/v12n55/

Mishel, L., & Roy, J. (2006). *Rethinking high school graduation rates and trends*. Washington, DC: Economic Policy Institute.

National Governors Association Task Force on State High School Graduation Data. (2005). *Graduation counts*. Washington, DC: Author. Retrieved October 14, 2009, from http://www.nga.org/Files/pdf/0507GRAD.PDF

National Research Council and Institute of Medicine (1999). Risks and opportunities: Synthesis of studies on adolescence. In M. D. Kipke (Ed.) *Forum on adolescence*. Washington, DC: National Academic Press.

Oakes, J., & Saunders, M. (Eds.) (2008). *Beyond tracking: Multiple pathways to college, career, and civic participation*. Cambridge, MA: Harvard Education Press.

Orfield, G., & Lee, C. (2005). *Why segregation matters: Poverty and educational inequality*. Cambridge, MA: The Civil Rights Project, Harvard University.

Organisation for Economic Co-operation and Development (OECD). (2008). *Education at a glance 2008*. Paris: OECD.

Planty, M., Provasnik, S., & Daniel, B. (2007). *High school coursetaking: Findings from the condition of education 2007* (NCES 2007–065). Washington, DC: National Center for Education Statistics.

Reardon, S. F., Atteberry, A., Arshan, N., & Kurlaender, M. (2009). *Effects of California High School Exit Exam on student persistence, achievement, and graduation*. Stanford, CA: Institute for Research on Education Policy & Practice, Stanford University. Retrieved October 14, 2009, from http://www.stanford.edu/group/irepp/cgi-bin/joomla/index.php

Riehl, C. (1999). Labeling and letting go: An organizational analysis of how high school students are discharged as dropouts. In A. M. Pallas (Ed.), *Research in sociology of education and socialization* (pp. 231–268). New York: JAI Press.

Roderick, M. (1993). *The path to dropping out*. Westport, CN: Auburn House.

Rotermund, S. (2007a). *Why students drop out of high school: Comparisons from three national surveys* (Statistical Brief 2). Santa Barbara, CA: California Dropout Research Project, University of California, Santa Barbara. Retrieved October 14, 2009, from http://cdrp.ucsb.edu/dropouts/ pubs_statbriefs.htm

Rotermund, S. (2007b). *Alternative education enrollment and dropouts in California high schools* (Statistical Brief 6). Santa Barbara, CA: California Dropout Research Project, University of California, Santa Barbara. Retrieved October 14, 2009, from http://cdrp.ucsb.edu/dropouts/pubs_statbriefs.htm

Rothstein, R. (2004). *Class and schools: Using social, economic, and educational reform to close the black-white achievement gap*. Washington, DC: Economic Policy Institute.

Rumberger, R. W. (1995). Dropping out of middle school: A multilevel analysis of students and schools. *American Educational Research Journal, 32*, 583–625.

Rumberger, R. W., Ghatak, R., Poulos, G., Ritter, P. L., & Dornbusch, S. M. (1990). Family influences on dropout behaviour in one California high school. *Sociology of Education, 63*, 283–299.

Rumberger, R. W., & Larson, K. A. (1998). Student mobility and the increased risk of high school drop out. *American Journal of Education, 107*, 1–35.

Rumberger, R. W., & Lim, S. A. (2008). *Why students drop out of school: A review of 25 years of research*. Santa Barbara, CA: California Dropout Research Project. Retrieved October 14, 2009, from http://cdrp.ucsb.edu/dropouts/pubs_reports.htm#15

Rumberger, R. W., & Palardy, G. J. (2004). Multilevel models for school effectiveness research. In D. Kaplan (Ed.), *Handbook of quantitative methodology for the social sciences* (pp. 235–258). Thousand Oaks, CA: Sage Publications.

Rumberger, R. W., & Thomas, S. L. (2000). The distribution of dropout and turnover rates among urban and suburban high schools. *Sociology of Education, 73*, 39–67.

Snyder, T. D. (2009). *Mini-digest of education statistics 2008* (NCES 2009–021). Washington, DC: United States Department of Education, National Center for Education Statistics. Retrieved October 14, 2009, from http://nces.ed.gov/pubsearch/pubsinfo.asp?pubid=2009021

Snyder, T. D., Dillow, S. A., & Hoffman, C. M. (2009). *Digest of education statistics, 2008* (NCES 2008–022). Washington, DC: United States Department of Education, National Center for Education Statistics. Retrieved October 14, 2009, from http://nces.ed.gov/pubsearch/pubsinfo.asp? pubid=2009020

Swanson, C. B., & Schneider, B. (1999). Students on the move: Residential and educational mobility in America's schools. *Sociology of Education, 72*, 54–67.

Teachman, J. D., Paasch, K., & Carver, K. (1996). School capital and dropping out of school. *Journal of Marriage and the Family, 58*, 773–783.

Trueba, H. T., Spindler, G., & Spindler, L. (Eds.). (1989). *What do anthropologists have to say about dropouts?* New York: Falmer Press.

Tyler, J. H. (2003). Economic benefits of the GED: Lessons from recent research. *Review of Educational Research, 73*, 369–398.

United States Department of Education. (2002). *Comprehensive School Reform (CSR) program guidance*. Washington, DC: Author. Retrieved October 14, 2009, from http://www.ed.gov/programs/compreform/legislation.html

United States Department of Education, Institute of Education Sciences. (2009). *What Works Clearinghouse*. Retrieved October 14, 2009, from http://ies.ed.gov/ncee/wwc/overview/

United States Department of Education, Institute of Education Sciences, What Works Clearinghouse. (2008). *WWC topic report: Dropout prevention*. Retrieved October 14, 2009, from http:z//ies.ed.gov/ncee/wwc/reports/topic.aspx?tid=06

Warren, J. R. (2005). State-level high school completion rates: Concepts, measures, and trends. *Education Policy Analysis Archives, 13*. Retrieved October 14, 2009, from http://epaa.asu.edu/epaa/v13n51/

White, J. A., & Wehlage, G. (1995). Community collaboration: If it is such a good idea, why is it so hard to do? *Educational Evaluation and Policy Analysis, 17*, 23–38.

Wilson, W. J. (1987). *The truly disadvantaged: The inner city, the underclass, and public policy*. Chicago: The University of Chicago Press.

Zimmer, R., Gill, B., Booker, K., Lavertu, S., Sass, T. R., & Witte, J. (2009). *Charter schools in eight states: Effects on achievement, attainment, integration, and competition*. Santa Monica, CA: Rand.

Chapter 14
Educational Systems and School Dropout in Canada

Michel Janosz, Sherri L. Bisset, Linda S. Pagani and Ben Levin

Introduction

Describing pathways of school graduation and dropout in Canada is no simple task. Canada is a confederation of ten provinces and three territories,[1] each responsible for their educational structure and curriculum, from pre-school to post-secondary education, including technical and vocational education. There is no federal ministry of education, nor are there national standards for graduation qualifications, making it difficult to describe the educational system in Canada. Each province and territory is characterised by a unique geopolitical, socio-demographic, cultural, historical, linguistic,[2] migration, labour and economic profile. Over time, these unique patterns have been incorporated into the structure, curriculum, assessment and accountability policies across educational jurisdictions (Council of Ministers of Education Canada [CMEC], 2008).

Discussions of schooling in the context of graduation/dropout tend to be focused on the ability of the education system to provide youth with the tools and opportunities they need to take part in the labour force. Indeed, although many jurisdictions are implementing reformed programs with broader human development

---

[1]Over half of the Canadian population is centred in Ontario or Quebec, and a very small proportion of Canadians live in the territories. Out of the approximate five million full-time equivalent enrolments across Canadian public elementary and secondary schools during the 2004/05 school year, about two million occurred in Ontario and one million in Quebec. More than 99% of the population (31 million inhabitants) live in one of the ten provinces. Canadian children and adolescents (5–19 years old) comprise 19% of the population.

[2]French and English are both official languages, and while all jurisdictions give access to public education in either language, few Francophones live outside Quebec. Just on 67.6% of the population speak English only, 13.3% speak French only, and 17.4% speak both French and English. More than 85% of French-mother-tongue Canadians live in the province of Quebec while only 4% of Anglophone Canadians live in Quebec (Census Canada, 2006).

M. Janosz, S.L. Bisset., L.S. Pagani
School Environment Research Group, University of Montreal, Canada

B. Levin
Ontario Institute for Studies in Education, University of Toronto, Canada

S. Lamb et al. (Eds.), *School Dropout and Completion: International Comparative Studies in Theory and Policy*, DOI 10.1007/978-90-481-9763-7_17,
© Springer Science+Business Media B.V. 2011

and socio-emotional aims, there is a clear preoccupation within the Canadian educational system to align students' educational experiences with the needs of the labour market. In response, there have been transformations in the programs and policies aiming to better prepare students for transition out of secondary school and into the labour market or on to further post-secondary education.

In order to situate the graduation/dropout experience in Canada within an international context, this chapter begins by highlighting the challenges inherent when constructing statistics that attempt to capture a single 'Canadian reality' by revealing the distinctiveness between jurisdictions. Once this variation is clarified, the discussion then identifies the commonalities among jurisdictions and in this respect, the aim is to draw a broad picture of the graduation/dropout situation in Canada, to identify principal determinants, and to describe some of the most important government initiatives to foster school success. The discussion begins by recalling the general structure of compulsory and post-compulsory education in Canada.

Compulsory and Post-Compulsory Education in Canada

Pre-School to Secondary Education

Subtle differences can be found in the organisation of the pre-school, elementary, secondary and post-secondary education systems across Canada (Fig. 14.1). Pre-school begins for most Canadian children 1 year prior to Grade 1, at between 4 and 5 years of age (in the form of junior and senior kindergarten, respectively). All Canadian children have access to pre-school; however, with the exception of two provinces (Nova Scotia and New Brunswick) schooling prior to Grade 1 is not mandatory. In some provinces, public school is offered 2 years prior to Grade 1 (Quebec, Ontario, Manitoba), and in some cases, 3 years prior to Grade 1 (Saskatchewan, Alberta). Beyond the regular pre-school programs, some jurisdictions offer pre-school programs to students who are disabled or at high risk of school failure.

The total duration of (compulsory) schooling is 12 years for all Canadian youth, with some exceptions: (1) in Quebec, combined elementary and secondary schooling lasts 11 years;[3] and (2) in Nova Scotia and New Brunswick, students are mandated to 13 years of education (due to pre-elementary education requirements).[4] Some jurisdictions mandate a middle school transition for students (i.e., Nova Scotia), whereas others leave middle school to the discretion of their districts. Thus, the amount of time students spend in high school ranges from 3 to 5 years. Students are generally mandated by law to stay in school until the age of 16 (or graduation) with two exceptions: in New Brunswick and Ontario the mandatory school leaving

---

[3]The typical age of graduation is thus 17 in Quebec, whereas it is 18 across all other jurisdictions.

[4]While pre-elementary schooling is not mandatory in the majority of jurisdictions, the overwhelming majority of children do attend pre-elementary schooling (i.e., 'senior and/or junior kindergarten' or *maternelle* in Quebec).

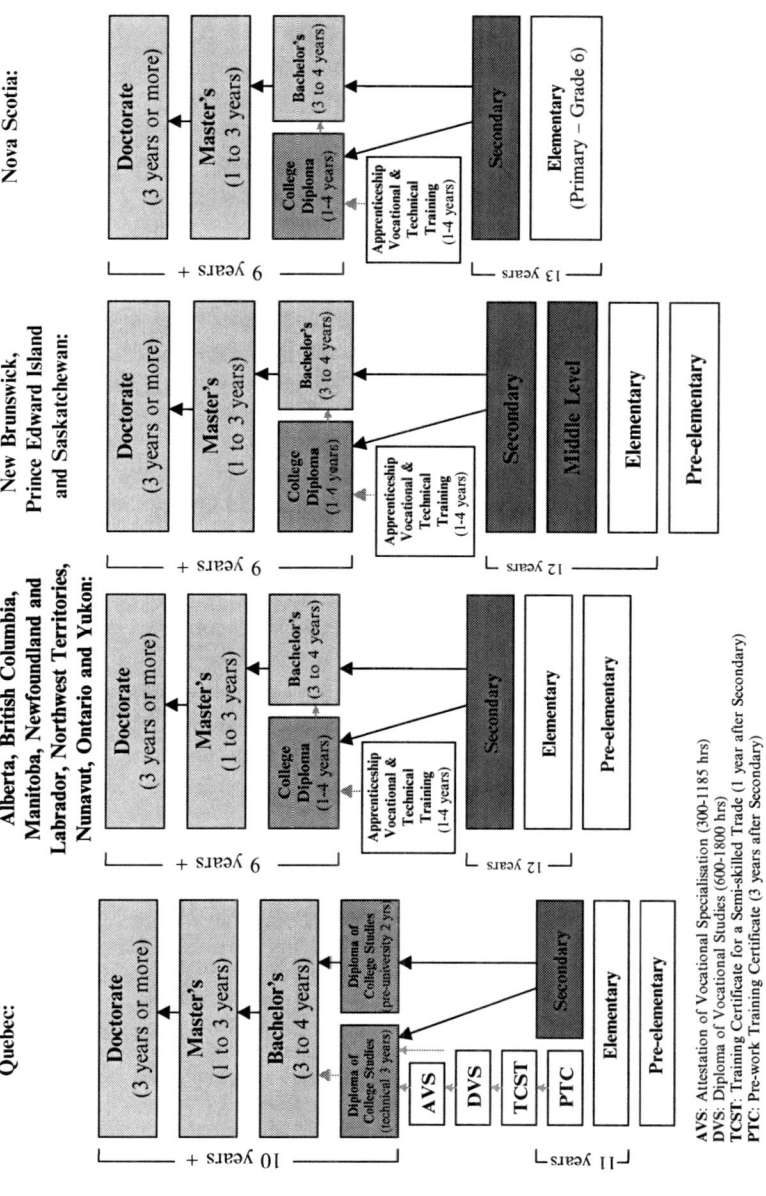

Fig. 14.1 Structure of Canada's education system (Source: Derived from 2008 Canadian Information Centre for International Credentials, Council of Education, Canada)

age is 18. These extensions to the mandatory school leaving age are recent: since 2000 for New Brunswick, and since 2006 for Ontario.[5]

International comparisons highlight institutional differentiation (i.e., students following discrete academic, professional or vocational streams attend different schools) and segregation (i.e., students attend separate schools according to academic performance, religion, ethnicity or socioeconomic status) (Lamb, 2008). Public Canadian schools are largely comprehensive; that is, students following a range of academic, professional or vocational programs are found within the same school and segregation according to performance, religion or socioeconomic status is minimal.[6] Segregation according to religion and language can be found in some jurisdictions such as Ontario and Quebec, respectively. Some segregation also exists with respect to entrance requirement for independent, private or special needs schools. Alternative schools cater to students with unique cognitive or behavioural challenges or offer a distinct curricular approach and give students more independence or provide additional instruction in language, arts or sports. However, the majority of programs that target special needs or high achievers (e.g., sports, dance, students with learning difficulties or emotional and behavioural disorders) are embedded within the mainstream secondary school curriculum.

It follows that the separation of students along academic lines occurs at the conclusion of secondary school, with the exception of Quebec. In Quebec, three different vocational programs are also offered as an alternative to an academic route. These programs last from 1 to 2 years and orient students either directly to the labour force or towards specialised technical and vocational education (TVE).[7] Aside from Quebec, Canada can be generally classified with countries which postpone the point at which students choose a particular branch or type of schooling. While students who obtain a secondary school diploma may choose to enter directly into the labour market or pursue post-secondary training, the secondary system in Canada tends to espouse values suggesting that 'good students' seek university-type tertiary education. Indeed, this has been identified as a key issue in Canada's 'dropout problem' (de Broucker, 2005).

---

[5]Extending the compulsory school attendance is identified as having the potential to have positive effects for all young people, especially young women. Several Canadian policy researchers, however, believe that this policy requires other supporting system changes to enhance interest among students to remain in school and to deter employers from hiring youth who are required to be in school (Oreaopolous, 2005; de Broucker, 2005).

[6]While we use the term 'segregation' to facilitate international comparisons, we acknowledge that with the exception of Quebec and for private and independent schools, families choose to enrol their children into religious or language-specific schools, many of them – depending on the province – being fully publicly funded. This being said, if not enrolled in a private or independent school, students are often obligated to attend the school in their neighbourhood where the composition of that school typically reflects the socioeconomic status of the neighbourhood. Choice is, however, restricted in Quebec where Quebec-born and immigrant families are obligated by law to enrol their children in the French-language educational system, unless one of the parents attended an English-language school in Canada (for Canadian citizens) or in Quebec (for immigrants).

[7]In Quebec, 17% of secondary school students are enrolled in a TVE. Information regarding the proportion of secondary students enrolled in TVE in other jurisdictions is not available.

Post-Secondary Education

Public (and private) colleges, specialised institutes, community colleges, institutes of technology, etc., offer a range of vocation-oriented programs in a wide variety of professional and technical fields, including business, health, applied arts, techno-logy and social services. In some jurisdictions, post-secondary programs can over-lap with secondary education programs, whereby students obtain 'dual-credits' or participate in joint work/study programs. Universities and university colleges focus on degree programs but may also offer some professional diplomas and certificates which permit entry into a specialised skill or professional order.

Secondary school graduates choosing college or university rarely pass through a preparatory college to get to university. The exception is in Quebec, where the majority of university students (83%) transition through an institution known as CEGEP (Hango & de Broucker, 2007). CEGEP is a French acronym for *Collège d'enseignement général et professionnel*, meaning 'College of General and Vocational Education'. The CEGEP was established in 1967 by the Quebec govern-ment with the purpose of improving access to post-secondary education. Training at the CEGEP level is either 2 or 3 years. Students wishing to pursue university attend a 2-year pre-university program, and those enrolled in specialised vocational training enrol in a 3-year program.

Alternative Pathways

Alternative pathways are provided to students who are either unable or uninter-ested in the typical high school education pathway leading to university or college (Lamb, 2008). As depicted in Fig. 14.1, Canadian secondary schools do indeed expect that the majority of students will transition directly from secondary school to a tertiary institution. Alternative pathways are typically followed by (1) students who want to focus upon TVE during their high school education, or (2) students who return to school to complete their formation, often in pursuit of a post-secondary program.

In Canada, the integration of alternative pathways into the regular secondary program is limited, with the exception of Quebec where TVE qualifications are part of the curriculum. Manitoba and Alberta also formally recognise a TVE specialisa-tion – however in contrast to Quebec, no distinct qualification is offered. Apprentice-ship and other TVE[8] programs are in fact part of all Canadian jurisdictions; still,

---

[8]TVE programs can vary in length from less than 1 year to 3 years, and entrance requirements do not necessarily require students to have a secondary school diploma. These students may however be awarded a certificate of achievement, and in this case would not be considered dropouts. Alternatively, if a certificate is not awarded from the high school, but sufficient credits were acquired to pursue a TVE program, the student would not be counted as a secondary school graduate.

important variation can be found within and between jurisdictions regarding their development and elaboration. For example, the program in Saskatchewan focuses on developing skills in a practical context and articulating with apprenticeship programs where applicable, while in Ontario and British Columbia, formalised programs which combine post-secondary courses and/or apprenticeships allow students to begin earning income and/or credits toward a vocation while in secondary school. Variation between jurisdictions in terms of the availability of TVE secondary school programs can have an impact on graduation rate, whereby students who are not offered this option may drop out of school in pursuit of vocational aspirations. Nonetheless, it is noteworthy that the integration of TVE into normative curricula is a rapidly evolving theme in Canada.

A second form of alternative pathway corresponds more to an 'external diversification strategy' (Lamb, 2008). In Canada, this strategy is referred to as a 'second chance' program, also known as Continuing or Adult Education.[9] The second chance program aims at the reintegration of students (typically in their adult years) who did not graduate. In principle, second chance programs emphasise flexible, student-focused learning and close relationships between students and teachers. School systems encourage the reintegration of older students by offering various alternative support programs as well as offering credits based on the accumulation of 'life' experiences, such as advancement in reading, travel and work. Quebec has legislated two sectors of education, a youth sector and an adult sector. After the age of 16, students may choose to go to a school in the adult sector. While this permits youth dropouts an interesting alternative, as discussed later, this also introduces challenges to the adult sector which may be less equipped to deal with the special needs of these students.

While, in theory, Continuing or Adult Education targets adults who return to school based on a specific objective, in practice this sector is responding to a growing proportion of young adults as a means to complete a high school diploma. In this regard, second chance programs risk encouraging students to leave their regular secondary school prior to completing a qualification (Lamb, 2008). When the second chance system is recognised among youth as being less authoritative and 'controlling' than the typical high school, students may leave high school with the intention of returning to school in the Adult Education sector. The 'freedom' and 'flexibility' provided in the Adult Education system may be well suited to some young adults, but nonetheless many students risk becoming 'lost' in the system, which tends to approach education from more of a 'laissez-faire' philosophy. As highlighted by Looker and Thiessen (2008), the Continuing or Adult Education system is not designed to motivate students who are struggling, but rather depends on students' self-motivation and independence. While there appears to be a need for a program for students who do not complete high school within the typical timeframe, in

---

[9]Depending upon the jurisdiction, the sector of Continuing or Adult Education may or may not be located within the Ministry of Education. This sector has two aims: to increase access for adults who wish to upgrade their qualifications and also to provide a second chance to young adult dropouts.

reality, '…in Canada it is often the students who pursue their "second chance" rather than the system specifically giving them a second chance' (Looker & Thiessen, 2008, p.7).

First-Nation Education Structure

Finally, attention must also be given to the small proportion of Canadian students who fall outside provincial jurisdiction, mainly Aboriginal students.[10] In particular, while First Nation students represent a very small proportion of Canadian students (1.3%) this is the fastest growing population in Canada. Moreover, regions of Canada where the majority of First Nations peoples live are also those with the highest prevalence of dropout. Thus, the distinctiveness of Aboriginal education represents a significant part of the landscape in Canada. The educational experience has changed dramatically over the past few decades. In the not-so-distant past, Aboriginal children had to move away from their community into religious schools for assimilation purposes. In contrast, Aboriginal communities today enforce their self-governing rights. The overwhelming majority of Aboriginal schools are under First Nation management (98%), and First Nations peoples are developing diploma credentials, teacher certification programs and decision-making structures, all of which are independent of federal and provincial jurisdiction. Aboriginal children complete elementary education close to their homes, on their territorial land reserves. Overall, approximately 40% of Aboriginal students complete their secondary education off reserve in provincial schools; however, this rate goes up to 70% in densely populated jurisdictions such as Ontario, where reserves are often close to urban centres. Aboriginal students going on to post-secondary studies are supported for tuition, books and living allowances.

The High School Diploma in Canada:
Forms and Requirements

The Minister of Education within each jurisdiction has the legal authority to define the form and requirements for secondary school graduation, and in so doing, maintains standards at a national level. The Minister delegates to local authorities (school boards/districts/divisions) power to administer (buildings, personnel, students' enrolment and graduation diplomas), structure and implement curriculum,

---

[10] First Nations, Inuit and Métis peoples constitute Canada's Aboriginal population. First Nations is a term that refers to the Canadian Indian bands which are recognised as collectivities of Indians 'for whose collective use and benefit lands have been set apart or money is held by the Canadian Crown, or declared to be a band for the purposes of the Indian Act' (http://www.ainc-inac.gc.ca/ap/fn/index-eng.asp).

and select from different programs or initiatives. Thus, jurisdictions differ among each other with respect to requirements and options provided to secondary school students toward completion of a high school diploma. Embedded into this variation, there is a range of solutions aiming to engage students in their educational experience and to validate this experience with legitimate credentials.

The only Canadian law that dictates jurisdictional functioning is the right of Canadian citizens to attend an institution of their maternal tongue (i.e., French or English). Northern territories are further mandated through national and territorial law to provide education in the Official Language.[11] Immersion programs provide students with instruction for the acquisition of two language proficiencies (typically in English and French, but can also include a Native language). Bilingualism is not a requirement in Canada.

Overall, the academic curriculum in Canada is prescribed; core subjects are required for all students to pass with a minimum grade. Core subjects are combined with optional (or elective) subjects (or credits) where the proportion of prescribed credits ranges from 50% to 80%, with the exception of New Brunswick (35%). Required credits tend to be based on building mathematics, language, social studies and science proficiencies. Several jurisdictions further prescribe physical activity (or health), art, career planning, life management and applied skills.

When students do not fulfil the requirements for a diploma they may graduate with a certificate of achievement. This qualification is clearly differentiated from the full diploma. In some jurisdictions, a certificate of achievement is uniquely given to students with special needs, whereas in others, its attribution is more flexible. In this latter circumstance, more decision-making latitude is attributed to districts and schools. This distinction can have an impact on the graduation rate, whereby jurisdictions with a more lenient approach to awarding certificates could be expected to have higher graduation rates.

Patterns of School Graduation and Dropout in Canada

The Canadian educational system's performance is ranked highly internationally, with respect to indicators of the overall educational attainment of the general population and the mathematics, reading and science capacities of youth (Organisation for Economic Co-operation and Development [OECD], 2007; Bussière et al., 2007). Judging the performance of Canada's educational system (both internationally and nationally) with graduation or dropout rate indicators has been, and remains, a challenge. Certainly, the diversities among educational systems across Canada have an influence on the way jurisdictions calculate a graduation rate. The challenges experienced by Canada in obtaining a collective measure, together with the

---

[11] There are 11 Official Languages in the North West Territories and the language of instruction is a decision which is taken at the level of the district and/or school. Here, when an Official Language other than English is the language of instruction, English as a language must be part of the education program.

development of a new survey methodology at the turn of the century, precluded the harmonisation of a Canadian statistic with that of the methodology used in the OECD *Education at a Glance* (EAG) Report. However more recent developments in this area have resulted in a Canadian statistic appearing in the 2008 EAG Report.

Calculating Canada's Graduation/Dropout Rate: What are the Challenges?

A key issue that has challenged the production of a national performance indicator for graduation rates is associated with change. Jurisdictions have been challenged to adjust performance indicators to capture a process which is continually adapting to local conditions, which themselves are unstable. An important adjustment in Ontario – namely the elimination of Grade 13 – resulted in data from Ontario (prior to 2008) also being inadmissible in calculating the overall Canadian graduation rate. Another change that has challenged the counting of graduates is the increasing number of students who pursue alternative pathways, such as Continuing or Adult Education or technical and vocational education (TVE). With the exception of Quebec, students who only take the courses required for TVE or alternative second-ary school certificates have been excluded from the graduate count. This is why, up until now, data from Quebec have been excluded from the Pan-Canadian Education Indicators Program (PCEIP) (Canadian Education Studies Council [CESC], 2008).[12] The statistic harmonised to the EAG Report includes graduates from trade/vocational secondary programs as well as upgrading programs at the secondary level across all jurisdictions, including Quebec.

Jurisdictions prefer to use methods of calculating graduation/dropout rates which reflect the internal mechanisms and underlying philosophies of their system. For example, some regions monitor the graduation/dropout rates based on the follow-up of cohorts of students (i.e., British Columbia, Alberta, Saskatchewan, Ontario); others aggregate transversal annual data (i.e., Manitoba, Nova Scotia); and still others (i.e., New Brunswick, Prince Edward Island, Northern Territories) uniquely report the OECD graduation rate definition.

Canada's Graduation and Dropout Rates

Graduation Rate

The current overall graduation rate in Canada is estimated at 72.1% (see Table 14.1). Inter-jurisdictional rates range from a low of 28.4% in the northern territories to a high of 86.0% in the eastern Atlantic Provinces (Blouin, 2008). These rates are not

---

[12] The 2009 PCEIP report will provide a Canadian measure with the inclusion of data from Quebec.

Table 14.1 Canadian secondary school graduation rates, dropout rates and PISA reading and mathematics performance measures

	Graduation rate[a] 2005/2006	Dropout rate[b] 2007	PISA reading[c] 2006 Average (SE)	PISA Math[d] 2006 Average (SE)
OECD Average	(82.0)[d]	(14.7)[e]	491 (0.6)	498 (0.5)
Canada	72.1	9.2	527 (2.4)	527 (2.0)
Newfoundland and Labrador	79.4	10.2	514 (3.2)	507 (2.5)
Prince Edward Island	86.0	10.0	497 (2.8)	501 (2.3)
Nova Scotia	82.3	11.1	505 (3.5)	506 (2.3)
New Brunswick	85.7	9.0	497 (2.3)	506 (2.1)
Quebec	76.4	11.4	522 (5.0)	540 (4.2)
Ontario	70.4	8.2	534 (4.6)	526 (3.7)
Manitoba	74.6	12.9	516 (3.5)	521 (3.3)
Saskatchewan	83.9	8.4	507 (4.2)	507 (3.3)
Alberta	67.9	9.8	535 (4.2)	530 (3.8)
British Columbia	73.9	6.7	528 (5.7)	523 (4.4)
Yukon	66.8	–	–	–
Northwest Territories	62.2	–	–	–
Nunuvut	28.4	–	–	–

[a] Graduation Rate = Total secondary graduates/(total population 17 and 18 years of age/2). Includes first time graduates only, excludes private school graduates, excludes graduates of upgrading programs at post-secondary levels (Blouin, 2008)
[b] Dropout rate = Proportion of 20- to 24-year-olds reporting not to have completed high school and not to be in school completing a high school or post-secondary formation (Elias & de Broucker, 2008)
[c] PISA performance measures http://www.cmec.ca/pisa/2006/indexe.stm
[d] OECD Average graduation rate includes private schools whereas Canadian rates do not (OECD Education at a Glance 2007). Please note that the Canada rate includes an estimate for private schools and is harmonised with the OECD rate for the Education at a Glance 2008 Report
[e] OECD Average dropout rate is based on reference year 2002 (Education at a Glance 2005)

directly comparable to the international OECD averages since the OECD figures include estimates for private and independent schools. When this key methodological adjustment is made (i.e., inclusion of graduates from private and independent schools) the overall Canadian average goes up to 80%[13] (OECD, 2008).

Owing to methodological adaptations over time, interpreting inter-jurisdictional changes in graduation rates based on PCEIP estimates must be done with caution. That said, reported changes over the past decade are low (no more than 7%) in all jurisdictions with the exception of the Yukon and Northwest Territories, where improvements are noteworthy (24% and 36% respectively) (Blouin, 2008).

[13] Public schools represent 93% of all Canadian students. Overall, 12% of schools are private in Canada. The number of private school ranges across jurisdictions: in Quebec, British Columbia, Ontario and Manitoba rates are higher (22%, 19%, 14% and 14%, respectively) than in the rest of Canada where the number of private schools ranges from 0% to 5% (CESC, 2008).

When making international comparisons, it is noteworthy that Canada's graduates almost all complete programs designed to prepare students for direct entry to tertiary study (77%), and very few graduate from vocational-type programs (8%) (OECD, 2008). This is consistent with the characterisation of the Canadian secondary school diploma as offering little differentiation in formal qualifications.

High School Completion Rates Based on Cohorts

Following a cohort of students from secondary school entry to graduation represents the ideal approach to deriving comparable statistics on graduation/dropout rates. Statistics of this nature include students who do not complete high school within the typical timeframe (4 or 5 years) by following them over time (from 4 to 6 years). Reporting an overall Canadian completion rate is not possible as: (1) not all provinces collect these data; and (2) those that do, do not use the same methodology (e.g., jurisdictions may follow cohorts beginning anywhere between Grades 8 and 10 for a time period ranging from 4 to 6 years). With these caveats in mind, it can be seen from Table 14.2 that approximately 75–80% of Canadian students complete high school within 5 years, with the exception of Quebec (69%).

Dropout Rate

Distinct from graduation rate, the dropout rate has served as an important performance indicator in Canada since the beginning of the 1990s. The dropout rate is defined as the percentage of 20- to 24-year-olds who have not successfully completed upper secondary school and who are not enrolled in education or in a work study program (OECD, 2005). Canadian policy researchers tend to prefer the dropout rate over the graduation rate, as the former captures the proportion of the population with limited job market prospects and compromised potential for long-term well-being (de Broucker, 2005). Moreover, the dropout rate takes into consideration that youth who do not graduate at the typical age of graduation may indeed return to school and graduate during young adulthood.

While some variation can be found in the definition of dropout[14] a fairly consistent approach permits rates of dropout to be compared over time among Canadian provinces (data are not collected in the three northern territories) and internationally. Data are derived from the Labour Force Survey (LFS), a household survey querying

---

[14]This definition of dropout excludes individuals who, despite not having completed a secondary school diploma, completed a PSE diploma. When the definition of dropout is adjusted to include individuals 20–24 years of age who have a PSE diploma in the numerator, the estimated dropout rate is higher by approximately 2–3 percentage points (Raymond, 2008).

Table 14.2 Canadian high school completion rates (cohort rates) where available across jurisdictions

Province		
Methodology	Year	Per cent
British Columbia		
Six year high school completion rate	1996/97	77
Calculated by following students for 6 years from the time they enrol in *Grade 8*	2000/01	79
Alberta		
Five year high school completion rate	1998/99	75.2
Calculated by following students for 5 years from the time they enrol in *Grade 10*	2002/03	79.5
Saskatchewan		
Five year high school completion rate	1999/2000	80.3
Percent of students in a cohort starting in *Grade 10* who complete Grade 12 within 5 years	2001/02	79.8
Manitoba		
Four year high school completion rate	June 2003	74.3
Percent of students completing Grade 12 as a percentage of *Grade 9* enrolments 4 years earlier	June 2006	77.1
Ontario		
Five year high school completion rate	1999/2000	68
Percentage of students who graduated within 5 years after starting *Grade 9*	2001/02	73
Quebec		
Five year high school completion rate	2001/02	68
Calculated by following students from the time they enrol in *Grade 7, and before they get to the age of 20*	2006/07	69
Nova Scotia		
Four year high school completion rate	2002/03	81.6
Percent of students completing Grade 12 as a percentage of *Grade 9* enrolments 4 years earlier	2006/07	84.8

families[15] on a range of employment and employability topics, including educational attainment and school attendance.

The overall dropout rate for Canada for 2007 is estimated at 9.2%[16] (see Table 14.1; updates provided by Elias & de Broucker, Statistics Canada, 2008). Interjurisdictional ranges (excluding northern territories) are from a low of 6.7% in British Columbia to a high of 12.9% in Manitoba. The average dropout rate has

---

[15]Sampling consists of approximately 54,000 households at any point in time. Households are interviewed monthly for a 6-month period after which a new household is sampled in and similarly followed for 6 months.

[16]Rates for 2007 are calculated slightly differently from rates calculated for OECD reports. This slightly modified definition of dropout includes those who reported to be in school in a program defined as 'other'. Formerly, these individuals were considered to be in school and thus not to be dropouts.

improved over the last decade in Canada. Early in the 1990s, the estimated 3-year average was 15.7% (1990–91 to 1992–93). This rate fell to 10.1% for the 3-year estimate early in the current decade (2002–03 to 2004–05) (Bowlby & McMullen, 2002). There has been a good deal of fluctuation over time regarding the ranking of provinces; however, Quebec and Manitoba have maintained the highest (between 11.4% and 13.9%), and British Columbia the lowest (between 6.7% and 7.7%) dropout rates over the past 5 years (Elias & de Broucker, 2008) Dropout rates have not significantly changed in the eastern Maritime Provinces Reductions in the dropout rate in Alberta are notable: the rate was among the highest in 2003 (13.9%) and declined to be just above the Canadian average (9.8%) in 2007.

Relations Between Graduation, Dropout Rates and Learning

Graduation and dropout rates must be analysed cautiously as indicators of the quality of Canadian educational systems. For example, using the data presented in Table 14.1, there is no correlation between the graduation rate (among the 17-year-old population) and the dropout rate (20- to 24-year-olds) ($r = 0.06$, $n = 10$). While this may be due in part to the bias that accompanies indicators derived from self-reported surveys (i.e., Labour Force Survey), it might also reflect important systematic difference across provinces in relation to the second-chance and alternative pathway programs. Moreover, when examining the relation between the provincial graduation and dropout rates, together with the average PISA scores of their students (see Table 14.1), there is an almost perfect *negative* association between PISA performance measures and the graduation rate ($r = -0.97$ (Reading) and $r = -0.81$ (Mathematics); $p < 0.001$, $n = 10$). While one might think that reflects a bias due to poor performers leaving the educational system early (i.e., prior to the age of 15 when the PISA is measured), this does not seem to be the case. There is no significant correlation between the dropout rates and PISA scores ($r = -0.21$ (Reading) and $r = 0.09$ (Mathematics); $p > 0.50$, $n = 10$) and this is consistent with the fact that dropout tends to occur closer to the senior years of high school (16–17 years old).

Rate of 'Continuers' Returning to School After Dropping Out

Canadian statistics also monitor the rate with which students who drop out then return to school (i.e., rate of 'continuers'). Statistics derived from the Labour Force Survey reveal that the proportion of dropouts returning to school has increased over time. In 1990–91, 10% and 12% of men and women, respectively, between the ages of 20 and 24 years had returned to school after having dropped out of high school. This proportion increased to 16% for men and 22% for women in 2004–05 (Raymond, 2008). Nonetheless, an increasingly large proportion of young adults who return to school do not complete their high school diploma, but instead choose to seek a post-secondary diploma or degree. This, as noted earlier, tends to overestimate the dropout rate as an indicator of education failure. During 2004–05, 36% of men and 31% of women returned to school to complete a high school diploma (these proportions were 57% and 44% in 1997–98) (Raymond, 2008). It must be further noted that a large proportion of students who return to school do not graduate. Overall, an estimated 40% of those who dropped out between the ages of 18 and 20 and who had returned to school, had left school again within 2 years without completing their certification (Raymond, 2008).

Quebec's educational system, distinct in Canada due to a separation of the adult and youth sector, is often referred to in terms of a 'strong' Canadian second-chance program, having the highest proportion of second-chance students (or continuers) in Canada. An estimated 14% of all Canadian 18- to 20-year-old dropouts return to complete their schooling within 2 years, while in Quebec this rate is 23% (Bushnick et al., 2004).[17] A Quebec longitudinal study based on a 1986 cohort of kindergarten students found that while one third of students had not obtained a high school by the age of 20, roughly two thirds of them were enrolled in night courses or adult professional training. Further follow-up revealed that one third of these students had indeed obtained a diploma by the age of 23 (Vitaro et al., 2005).

Finally, it is worthwhile noting that youths who have left school for at least a full year (they must be aged 16 or over in Quebec, and 18 or 19 years of age or over in the other provinces) can pass a Canadian version of the General Educational Development (GED) test. This internationally recognised credential administered by the American Council on Education can be used as an 'equivalent' high school diploma for employers and, in some cases, may be accepted for entry into post-secondary institutions. Nevertheless, the use of GED in Canada is relatively recent and still of marginal use by adult learners (around 3% of adults learners in larger provinces like British Columbia or Ontario are estimated to participate in GED testing) (Myers & de Broucker, 2006). According to available information, GED results are not taken into consideration in the calculation of dropout and graduation rates in Canada.

Determinants of School Graduation and Dropout in Canada

No single theory dominates the Canadian literature on school dropout, but several conceptual frameworks are recognisable. First, most Canadian research on school dropout considers secondary school dropout as a complex phenomenon whereby multiple factors (individual, social, familial, institutional, community, cultural,

---

[17] Another example: the graduation rate will rise from 69% to 85% when students 20 years of age and above are considered (Ministère de l'Éducation, du Loisir et du Sport [MELS], 2008).

socioeconomic) exert their influence over time. Second, dropping out is also considered as the ultimate end to a gradual process of disengagement. This process can begin as early as school entry, whereby the significance of school diminishes over time and students lose interest in what school is offering (Audas & Willms, 2001; Janosz et al., 2008; Ferguson et al., 2005; Thiessen, 2007a, b). These views are developmental as well as ecosystemic and transactional (Sameroff et al., 2004). Beliefs that school disengagement results from a misfit between school expectations and students' needs are also recognisable within a stage-environment fit theoretical framework (Eccles, 2004). The decision to return to school among young adults has also been studied through the rational decision framework based on the benefits and costs of continuing school (Chaplin et al., 2003; Eckstein & Wolpin, 1999; Parent, 2006; Raymond, 2008). This framework pays particular attention to 'intentionally temporary' and involuntary dropouts, whereby school leavers are forced to leave due to circumstances or constraints perceived as being temporary.

Governmental reports and academic studies continually reconfirm the negative impacts of leaving secondary school before graduation on individual well-being (Janssen et al., 2006; Sawatzky, 2005; Shields & Shooshtari, 2001; Wilson et al., 2001) as well as on the human and social capital of the Canadian society (Kozyrskyij et al., 2002; Lafleur, 1992; Veugelers et al., 2001; Wilson et al., 2001). Parallel to this, Canadian research has also concentrated on the characteristics and predictors of school dropout. Conclusions of these investigations are mostly similar and consistent with findings reported in the scientific literature for the past 50 years (Tessener & Tessener 1958; Janosz et al., 1997; Rumberger, 2004). Also, while it has been argued that previous work on school dropout was oriented toward individual factors, whereby students were presented as being responsible for their misfortune (Maxwell, 2005), much of the present work recognises the complexity and multidimensionality of the problem (Ferguson et al., 2005; Janosz et al., 2008; Thiessen, 2007a, b). The Canadian Policy Research Network (CPRN) adopts a perspective whereby the educational system is understood to have a clear responsibility to prevent permanent dropout among young adults (de Broucker, 2005; Raymond, 2008).

Our overview of determinants revisits this work by highlighting recurrent findings as well as those which bring a fresh regard to the process of dropping out, and at times, returning to school. This touches on the work of Canadian researchers situated in government agencies and universities. Many governmental researchers have studied school dropout determinants with a nationally representative longitudinal study of Canadian adolescents and young adults. The Youth in Transition Survey (YITS) began in 2000 following two cohorts: 15-year-olds ($n = 29,330$) and 18- to 20-year-olds ($n = 23,592$). Youth were interviewed at baseline, and again after 2 years (sample sizes then were 26,544 for the younger and 18,800 for the older cohort), and 4 years later (when sample sizes were 22,403 for younger and 14,817 for older cohorts) (Bowlby & McMullen, 2002; Bushnik et al., 2004; Knighton & Bussière, 2006; Looker & Thiessen, 2008; Raymond, 2008).

Economic Factors

Several structural or 'macro'-level determinants have been shown repeatedly to predict dropout. Parental income is clearly identified to predict dropout in Canada (Drolet, 2005; Pagani et al., 1999). Many government reports emphasise the importance of parental education and occupation over household income (Bowlby & McMullen, 2002), though some research has shown important reductions in the negative effects of low-household income once parental education was controlled (de Broucker, 2005; Janosz et al., 1997). Canadian students who work more than 20 hours per week or who do not work at all for pay are more likely to leave school early (Bowlby & McMullen, 2002; Hango & de Broucker, 2007; Looker & Thiessen, 2008; Parent, 2006). The association between the labour market and dropout is complex. While research and policy suggest that labour market opportunities provide a major incentive for students to leave school in pursuit of work (Hango & de Broucker, 2007; Looker & Thiessen, 2008; Parent, 2006), others discuss the possibility that students' decision to leave school is also driven by wage premiums (Raymond, 2008).

Socio-Demographic Factors

Women are consistently less likely than men to drop out of school, more likely to return if they do drop out, and more likely to transition directly from secondary school to post-secondary education (Hango & de Broucker, 2007). Others find that gender differences disappear once school risk factors are taken into account (Janosz et al., 1997). Effects of race/ethnicity are less certain. Unlike most other countries with a sizeable immigrant population,[18] Canada does not have a higher concentration of dropouts who are immigrants. In fact, immigrants have, in general, obtained higher levels of education than their Canadian-born counterparts. These different patterns are likely to be related to the role and characteristics of Canada's immigration policies (de Broucker, 2005). For example, Canadian immigrants are required to have a high school diploma from their country of origin. On the other hand, Aboriginal youth have a much higher risk of dropping out than other Canadians, particularly Aboriginal men (Gingras et al., 2001). Among this group, the main risk factors for dropping out have been characterised as the interplay between social class, adult role taking (i.e., taking care of siblings or parents, becoming a parent), attendance and distance to relocate or travel to school (Ferguson et al., 2005).

Youth from urban areas are more likely to have completed at least a secondary school diploma prior to entering the labour force, compared to their rural counterparts

---

[18]One in eight of 20- to 24-year-olds was born outside Canada.

(Hango & de Broucker, 2007). The determinants specific to rural communities have been characterised as offering safety but also boredom, and caring but also harsh, passive discipline. The personnel and culture of the school has been found to have a particularly important place in the process of dropping out among youth in rural areas (Ferguson et al., 2005).

School Environment

Beyond the rural/urban settings, the role of the school's organisation, principal's leadership, school climate, quality of teachers' educational and pedagogical practices, and the quality of teacher-student relationships are considered to be important determinants of dropping out among all Canadian communities (Audas & Willms, 2001). While there is limited empirical evidence, researchers assert that after the effects of individual and family are taken into consideration, school effects are believed to account for between one third (Thiessen, 2007b) and one half (Audas & Willms, 2001) of the variation in dropout rates in Canadian schools. An important proportion of academic differentials between various regions and jurisdictions can be explained by the ability of the educational system in general, and the school 'climate' in particular.

Family Structure and Functioning

Family structures, in terms of living in a two parents home (two parents, and non-step) and having fewer siblings, are known factors which influence educational attainment (Hango & de Broucker, 2007; Janosz et al., 1997). Also, students who have a child of their own or who live with a partner are more likely to drop out (Bushnik, 2003). As a predictor of dropout, parental education (Janosz et al., 1997) is described as influencing students more through the value they place on education and the way they communicate this to their children, and less about parental ability which could be inherited by children (Oreopoulos, 2005). Indeed, positive educational attitudes and practices have steadily been related to school completion (high expectations, high values toward education, supporting behaviour, supervision and communication, involvement in school activities, etc.) (Deslandes & Bertrand, 2005; Janosz et al., 1997; Bushnick et al., 2004; Ferguson et al., 2005).

Psycho-Social Adjustment

Several symptoms of psycho-social maladjustment have been found to predict school dropout in Canadian studies – these symptoms include aggressiveness, hyperactivity-inattentiveness, oppositional behaviours, social isolation, peer rejection, association to unconventional peers, drug use and internalising problem behaviours (Audas & Willms, 2001; Janosz et al., 1997; Pagani et al., 2008; Vitaro et al., 2005; Vitaro et al., 2001).

Individual School Experience

Academic difficulties, as measured by grade retention and achievement scores, have been identified as some of the stronger predictors of dropout (Janosz et al., 1997; Pagani et al., 2001). Factors associated with academic failure, such as (poor) reading skills, negative perception of academic competencies, perception that school is irrelevant, weak school motivation and engagement, absenteeism and learning difficulties, are among other school factors to have been found to predict school dropout among Canadian students (Archambault et al., in press; Bushnik, 2003; Guay et al., 2004; Knighton & Bussière, 2006; Janosz et al., 1997, 2008; Vallerand et al., 1997).

The Heterogeneous Dropout

All factors identified above highlight the multidimensionality and complexity of the dropout phenomenon. Some Canadian researchers have tried to tackle this complexity more directly, trying to unveil the multiple pathways leading to school dropout, as well as trying to understand what prevents potential dropouts from leaving school. For example, Janosz et al. (2000), studying school dropout in two longitudinal samples of French-Canadian adolescents, demonstrated that students who abandon school greatly differ among themselves in their overall level of school engagement or social integration. They found that around 40% of students who dropped out of school were highly engaged in school (*quiet* dropouts). The latter also showed similar, and sometimes even better, behavioural and psychological profiles than the average graduate. Another 40% of dropouts experienced severe levels of school and psychosocial difficulties (*maladjusted* dropouts). The researchers also found two other intermediate sub-groups. A small group (10%) was strongly unmotivated in school while still able to generate average marks and show no signs of behaviour or psychosocial distress (*disengaged* dropouts). Finally, an equally small group was typically unmotivated, with a school experience of failure, while not showing externalising problem behaviours (*low achiever* dropouts). These findings illustrate three important issues: first, students who drop out do not seem to follow the same paths of disengagement; second, many students do not manifest apparent risk for dropping out yet they interrupt their schooling anyway; last, dropouts experience a multitude of the established risk factors at varying levels of intensity. A recent study on the different patterns of school engagement in high school leads to the same conclusions (Janosz et al., 2008).

Canadian researchers have also looked specifically at students who follow anomalous education trajectories and how social support and resilience interacts with these pathways (Pagani et al., 2008; Thiessen, 2007a, b). Findings show that students who persevere despite academic challenges are those with a trusting and advising adult, a parent and a network of friends who value education, caring attentive teachers, and a school that provides opportunities to learn about work and education (Thiessen, 2007a, b). The importance of these relationships is found to be maintained even once academic achievement (e.g., grade point average) and academic programs (e.g., selecting pre-university levels of mathematics) are taken into consideration.

Overall, Canadian studies on the characteristics and life experiences of students who leave school without a diploma call for a mixed approach of universal and selective prevention (all students and at-risk students), targeting simultaneously the student, the school, the peer group, the family and the community, from early childhood to late adolescence.

Policy and Programming to Prevent Dropout

Whatever differences exist among Canadian jurisdictions, they all share the vision that learning opportunities should be of the highest quality, accessible to everyone and throughout the lifespan (CMEC, 2008).[19] In a recent joint declaration (Learn Canada 2020), all provincial and territorial ministers of education reaffirmed their commitment toward these goals and agreed on four pillars of lifelong learning:

1. *Early Childhood Learning and Development*: all children should have access to high quality early childhood education that ensures they arrive at school ready to learn.
2. *Elementary to High School System*: all children in the elementary to high school systems deserve teaching and learning opportunities that are inclusive and that provide them with world-class skills in literacy, numeracy and science.
3. *Post-secondary Education*: Canada must increase the number of students pursuing post-secondary education by increasing the quality and accessibility of post-secondary education.
4. *Adult Learning and Skills Development*: Canada must develop an accessible, diversified and integrated system of adult learning and skills development that delivers training when Canadians need it.

Secondary school dropout may not be identified here as a pan-Canadian priority but many provinces have recognised this issue as a priority by setting targets for

---

[19]The Council of Ministers of Education of Canada (CMEC) is an intergovernmental instance composed of the ministers of education from the provinces and territories. Through CMEC, ministers share information and undertake projects in areas of mutual interest and concern.

improved graduation rates. Ontario, for example, in its Student Success Strategy has set a priority to increase the graduation rate from 75% to 85% by 2011 (Ministry of Education of Ontario, 2005), whilst New Brunswick wants to reach a full graduation rate by 2013, according to the When Kids Come First plan (New Brunswick Department of Education, 2007).

Beyond setting targets, provincial governments have also implemented large-scale initiatives to prevent dropout. For example, Quebec recently invested more than $150 million dollars in 200 high schools to increase school success of students from disadvantaged communities (The New Approaches New Solutions Strategy – NANS) (MELS, 2002).[20] Similarly, in 2005, the Ontario government initiated a major effort to improve high school graduation rates – the Student Success Strategy. The latter strategy has multiple elements involving changes in curriculum, the creation of leadership teams for student success in every school and district, the creation of 'Student Success Teachers' in every secondary school, and a variety of other elements (Levin, 2008a; see also www.edu.gov.on.ca/studentsuccess). The strategy is supported by an extensive infrastructure at the provincial level and in each school district. Since 2004, Ontario's 5-year high school graduation rate has risen from 68% to 75%.

Three out of the four pillars described above (1, 2 and 4) can be considered as cornerstones of both a universal and selective approach to the prevention of school dropout. Indeed, many Canadian governmental initiatives, whether embedded in the official curriculum or presented as complementary measures, focus on school preparedness and early literacy, school improvement or alternative schooling and adult education. Furthermore, since school dropout is mainly conceived in Canada within a developmental, ecosystemic and transactional framework, most policies promote simultaneous actions at the individual, school and community levels. Despite the fact that education is a matter of provincial and territorial jurisdiction, several similarities can be found in the jurisdiction approaches toward the graduation/dropout issue, as highlighted later.[21]

Pre-Elementary and Pre-Kindergarten Education

As mentioned earlier, at least two Canadian provinces mandate pre-elementary education and others offer such educational opportunity to children considered at

---

[20] In fact, it is so important that Quebec has created a special research fund (FQRSC) to foster research on student retention and academic success. Results from a large-scale, longitudinal, multi-site evaluation of the implementation and impact of NANS were to be available by the end of 2009.

[21] Since we have previously noted the importance of alternative and second chance programs as universal, selected or targeted dropout prevention strategies, discussion of these measures will not be repeated in this section.

risk of school failure, mainly those from disadvantaged families and communities. The importance, efficiency and added-value of early learning (literacy in particular) is thus clearly recognised by Canadian jurisdictions (Heckman, 2006), and initiatives emerge in various forms and settings, including sectors and partnerships external to the Minister of Education.

Focus on (Early) Literacy

Since literacy has been demonstrated to be a major determinant of school success, many jurisdictions have placed emphasis on literacy competencies, from early childhood to late adolescence, and even adulthood, in their general educational strategy (e.g., ReadNowBC in British Columbia, SaskSmart in Saskatchewan, and the Parenting and Family Literacy Centers in Ontario).

School Improvement

Described and articulated at various levels, almost all jurisdictions have implemented measures to improve the educational potential of their schools. At least two major types of (educational reform) actions have recently emerged in Canadian provinces. A first orientation is to focus on professional development, building new competencies among principals and teachers, implementing research-based practices and sharing promising initiatives. A second focus is on accountability through (1) school and school board strategic planning (identification of clear and measurable objectives chosen after going through systematic self-evaluation of local strengths and weaknesses; choice of promising interventions coherent with those objectives), and (2) monitoring of the implementation of their plan, as well as evaluation of its impacts. Although the theoretical elaboration of this approach is rooted within Ontario's experience (Fullan, 2009; Levin, 2008b), many provinces are following this path.[22]

School Health and Safety (in) Schools

In Canada, schools are considered to be important not only for the academic development and preparation of the workforce, but also for socio-emotional development

---

[22]For example: Alberta initiative for School Improvement; Leadership and Professional Learning in Ontario; The New Approach, New Strategy in Quebec; When Kids Come First in New Brunswick; School Development: A Continuing Challenge for Excellence in Newfoundland; Learning for Life II: Brighter Futures Together in Nova Scotia; New Teacher Induction in the Northwest Territories.

and the learning of healthy lifestyles. As in many other countries, education is considered to be a cornerstone of the quality of life, health and well-being in Canada (Canadian Association for School Health [CASH], 2008). In that respect, school dropout can be considered a public health issue (Freudenberg, 2007) and school violence can be considered to jeopardise the educational potential of schools (Janosz et al., 2008). Thus, the vast majority of jurisdictions subscribe to the school health movement (CASH, 2008), aiming to increase health literacy and providing a healthy and secure environment.[23]

School-Family-Community Collaboration

Acknowledging the importance of family and community factors for school success, Canadian schools are actively trying to integrate parents into the daily life of school and provide them with support, as well as to coordinate their actions with other governmental and community services (i.e., health and social services). Although not an easy task, almost all Canadian jurisdictions have programs towards this end (e.g., StrongStartBC in British Columbia; KidsFirst in Saskatchewan; When Kids Come First in New Brunswick; The New Approach, New Strategy in Quebec).

Conclusion

This brief analysis of the graduation and dropout rates in Canada unveils the socio-geographical diversity of the phenomenon and the methodological challenges associated with its measurement. Like other confederated countries, Canada's educational system is a mosaic of autonomous systems, sharing fundamental values but each choosing to express these values somewhat distinctively. Unsurprisingly, graduation rates vary between jurisdictions. Not counting the Territories, these rates reach 85% in less populated provinces, but drop to the lower 70% in the largest jurisdictions such as Ontario and Quebec. Interestingly, variations are smaller when analysing dropout rates (between 7% and 13%). It is noteworthy that the capacity to compare Canadian jurisdictions on these issues is fairly recent. As the quality of comparable indicators grows, we will be better able to explain the observed variations within the Canadian provinces and territories in terms of graduation and dropout rates.

---

[23] For example: Healthy Schools in British Columbia, Ontario; Schools in Shape and Health in Quebec; Alberta's Bullying Prevention Strategy; Safe School in Manitoba and Ontario; Healthy and Safe schools in New Brunswick; Safe and Caring schools in Newfoundland; Healthy Children Initiative and Mental Health Task Force in Nunavut.

Another important conclusion relates to the fact that graduation and dropout rates express different aspects of the 'performance' of an educational system. As reported, no correlation was found between the two indicators. This is understandable since they measure students' trajectories at different stages of development (17 versus 24 years old) and because opportunities for obtaining some school certifications depend on the structural opportunities (e.g., second chance programs) provided by local and provincial educational authorities. Moreover, and perhaps the most fascinating finding of this paper: Canadian indicators of school graduation and dropout are not related to the quality of the learning experience. Higher graduation rates are not synonymous with better learning competencies. In fact, the contrary appears to be the case. Higher graduation rates are associated with lower average scores on PISA. One hypothesis could be that keeping at-risk students in school will necessarily affect the average performance of the school population. Alternatively, is this higher retention rate the result of schools doing a better job at supporting lower achievers to complete high school, or is it the consequences of a less challenging educational environment? Indeed, we also reported that the better scores on PISA by the provinces with the lower graduation rates could not be explained by attrition of low-achieving students. Thus, having more dropouts in an educational system does not suggest that the system is producing poorer learners. One explanation could be that educational systems with lower dropout rates are very stimulating and demanding, but may be too challenging for a proportion of students who cannot keep up with the demands, who will fail to 'pass the test', and who eventually disengage from school (albeit with the same level of competency that would have helped them graduate in a different system). Clearly, these issues call for a deeper investigation. It would also be important to verify to what extent these observations are unique to Canada.

In any case, the Canadian educational systems are collectively facing the same challenges: providing the best educational environment to every child, adolescent or adult. Defining and measuring the performance of the schooling system is still, however, a challenge for both policy makers and researchers (Rumberger & Palardy, 2005). A better understanding of how and why the multiple indicators across Canadian jurisdictions are related is needed, in order to increase capacity to measure and monitor the quality of the educational system.

References

Archambault, I., Janosz, M., Pagani, L., & Fallu, J. S. The multidimensionality of student engagement and its predictive relationship to high school dropout. *Journal of Adolescence* (in press).

Audas, R., & Willms, D. (2001). *Engagement and dropping out of school: A life-course perspective.* Hull, QC: Applied Research Branch, Strategic Policy, Human Resources Development Canada.

Blouin, P. (2008). *Summary* public *school indicators for the provinces and territories, 1999/2000 to 2005/2006.* Ottawa, ON: Statistic Canada.

Bowlby, J., & McMullen, K. (2002). *At a crossroads: First results for the 18 to 20-year old cohort of the Youth in Transition Survey.* Hull, QC: Human Resources and Social Development Canada & Statistics Canada.

Bushnik, T. (2003). *Learning, earning and leaving: The relationship between working while in high school and dropping out*. Ottawa, ON: Statistics Canada.

Bushnik, T., Barr-Telford, L., & Bussiere, P. (2004). *In and out of high school: First results from the second cycle of the Youth in Transition Survey*. Ottawa, ON: Statistics Canada.

Bussiere, P., Knighton, T., & Pennock, D. (2007). *Measuring up: Canadian results of the OECD PISA study. The performance of Canada's youth in mathematics, reading, and science (2006 first findings for Canadians aged 15)*. Ottawa, ON Human Resources and Social Development Canada & Statistics Canada.

Canadian Association for School Health (CASH). (2008). *Consensus statement*. Surrey, BC: Canadian Association for School Health.

Canadian Education Statistics Council (CESC). (2008). Education indicators in Canada. Report of the 2007 Pan-Canadian Education Indicators Program (PCEIP). Toronto, ON: Statistics Canada and the Council of Ministers of Education of Canada (CMEC).

Chaplin, D., Turner, M., & Pape, A. (2003). Minimum wages and school enrolment of teenagers: A look at the 1990's. *Economics of Education Review, 22*, 11–21.

Council of Ministers of Education Canada (CMEC). (2008). *Education in Canada*. Ottawa, ON: Council of Ministers of Education of Canada.

de Broucker, P. (2005). *Without a paddle: What to do about Canada's young dropouts*. Ottawa, ON: Canadian Policy Research Networks Inc.

Deslandes, R., & Bertrand, R. (2005). Parent involvement in schooling at the secondary level: Examination of the motivations. *The Journal of Educational Research, 98*, 164–175.

Drolet, M. (2005). *Participation in post-secondary education in Canada: Has the role of parental income and education changed over the 1990s?* Ottawa, ON: Statistics Canada.

Eccles, J. S. (2004). Schools, academic motivation, and stage-environment fit. In R. M. Lerner & L. Steinberg (Eds.), *Handbook of adolescent psychology* (2nd edn, pp. 125–153). Hoboken, NJ: Wiley.

Eckstein, Z., & Wolpin, K. (1999). Why youths dropout of high school: The impact of preferences, opportunities, and abilities. *Econometrica, 67*, 1295–1339.

Elias, A., & de Broucker, P. (2008). *Updates for Tables D1 and D3 of the report Without a paddle: What to do about Canada's young drop-outs. Provincial/regional statistical figures and tables – Supplement*, October 2005. Ottawa, ON: Canadian Policy Research Networks Inc.

Ferguson, B., Tilleczek, K., Boydell, K., & Rummens, J. (2005). *Early school leavers: Understanding the lived reality of student disengagement from secondary school*. Toronto, ON: Ontario Ministry of Education.

Freudenberg, N. (2007). Reframing school dropout as a public health issue. *Preventing Chronic Disease, 4*, 1–11.

Fullan, M. (2009). Have theory, will travel: a theory of action for system change. In M. Fullan & A. Hargreaves (Eds.), *Change wars* (pp. 275–293). Boston, MA: Solution Tree Publishers.

Gingras, Y., Bowlby, J., & Pilon, M. (2001). *The costs of dropping out of high school*. Toronto, ON: Statistics Canada and the Council of Ministers of Education of Canada (CMEC).

Guay, F., Larose, S., & Boivin, M. (2004). Academic self-concept and educational attainment level: A ten-year longitudinal study. *Self and Identity, 3*, 53–68.

Hango, D., & de Broucker, P. (2007). *Education-to-labour market pathways of Canadian youth: Findings from the Youth in Transition Survey*. Ottawa, ON: Canadian Policy Research Networks Inc.

Heckman, J. J. (2006). Skill formation and the economics of investing in disadvantaged children. *Science, 312*, 1900–1902.

Janosz, M., Archambault, I., Morizot, J., & Pagani, L. (2008). School engagement trajectories and their differential predictive relations to dropout. *Journal of Social Issues, 64*, 21–40.

Janosz, M., Archambault, I., Pagani, L. S., Morin, A. J. S., & Bowen, F. (2008). Are there detrimental effects of witnessing school violence in early adolescence? *Journal of Adolescent Health*, 600–608.

Janosz, M., LeBlanc, M., Boulerice, B., & Tremblay, R. (1997). Disentangling the weight of school dropout predictors: A test on two longitudinal samples. *Journal of Youth and Adolescence, 26*, 733–762.

Janosz, M., LeBlanc, M., Boulerice, B., & Tremblay, R. (2000). Predicting different types of school dropouts: A typological approach with two longitudinal samples. *Journal of Educational Psychology, 92*, 171–190.

Janssen, I., Boyce, W. F., Simpson, K., & Pickett, W. (2006). Influence of individual- and area-level measures of socioeconomic status on obesity, unhealthy eating, and physical inactivity in Canadian adolescents. *American Journal of Clinical Nutrition, 83*, 139–45.

Knighton, T., & Bussiere, P. (2006). *Educational outcomes at age 19 associated with reading ability at age 15*. Ottawa, ON: Statistics Canada.

Kozyrskyij, A. L., Fergusson, P., Bodnarchuk, J., Brownell, M., Burchill, C., & Mayer, T. (2002). Community resources and determinants of the future health of Manitobans. *Canadian Journal of Public Health, 93*(Suppl 2), 9–14.

Lafleur, B. (1992). *The costs of school dropout in Canada*. Ottawa, ON: Conference Board of Canada.

Lamb, S. (2008). *Alternative pathways to high school graduation: An international comparison* (California Dropout Research Project, Report No. 7). Santa Barbara, CA: University of California & Linguistic Minority Research Institute.

Levin, B. (2008a). Sustainable, large scale education renewal. *Journal of Educational Change, 8*, 323–336.

Levin, B. (2008b). Reform without (much) rancor. In M. Fullan & A. Hargreaves (Eds.), *Change wars* (pp. 259–274). Boston: Solution Tree Publishers.

Looker, D., & Thiessen, V. (2008). *The second chance system: Results from the three cycles of the Youth in Transition Survey*. Gatineau, QC: Human Resources and Social Development Canada.

Maxwell, J. (2005). *Forward to 'Without a paddle: What to do about Canada's young dropouts'*. Toronto, ON: Canadian Policy Research Network Inc.

Ministère de l'Éducation, du Loisir et du Sport (MELS). (2002). *New approaches, new solutions: Fostering success for secondary school students in disadvantaged areas*. Québec: Gouvernement du Québec.

Ministère de l'Éducation, du Loisir et du Sport (MELS). (2008). *Indicateurs de l'éducation 2007*. Québec: Gouvernement du Québec.

Ministry of Education of Ontario. (2005). The Student Success Strategy. Retrieved from http://www.edu.gov.on.ca/eng/teachers/studentsuccess/strategy.html

Myers, K., & de Broucker, P. (2006). *Too many left behind: Canada's adult education and training system*. Toronto: Canadian Policy Research Networks Inc.

New Brunswick Department of Education. (2007). When Kids Come First. Retrieved from http://www.gnb.ca/0000/publications/comm/4578_report_E.pdf

Oreopoulos, P. (2005). *Stay in school: New lessons on the benefits of raising the legal school leaving age*. Ottawa, ON: C.D. Howe Institute.

Organisation for Economic Co-operation and Development (OECD). (2005). *Education at a glance, 2005*. Paris, France: OECD.

Organisation for Economic Co-operation and Development (OECD). (2007). *Education at a glance, 2007*. Paris, France: OECD.

Organisation for Economic Co-operation and Development (OECD). (2008). *Education at a glance, 2008*. Paris, France: OECD.

Pagani, L., Boulerice, B., Vitaro, F., & Tremblay, R. E. (1999). Effects of poverty on academic failure and delinquency in boys: A change process model approach. *Journal of Child Psychology and Psychiatry, 40*, 1209–1219.

Pagani, L., Tremblay, R. E., Vitaro, F., Boulerice, B., & McDuff, P. (2001). Effects of grade retention on academic performance and behavioral development. *Development and Psychopathology, 13*, 297–315.

Pagani, L. S., Vitaro, F., Tremblay, R. E., McDuff, P., Japel, C., & Larose, S. (2008). When predictions fail: The case of unexpected pathways toward high school graduation. *Journal of Social Issues, 64*, 175–193.

Parent, D. (2006). Work while in high school in Canada: Its labour market and educational attainment effects. *Canadian Economics Association, 39*, 1125–1150.

Raymond, M. (2008). *High school dropouts returning to school*. Ottawa, ON: Culture, Tourism and the Centre for Education Statistics.

Rumberger, R. (2004). Why students dropout of school. In G. Orfield (Ed.), *Dropouts in America* (pp. 131–155). Cambridge, MA: Harvard Education Press.

Rumberger, R., & Palardy, G. J. (2005). Test scores, dropout rates, and transfer rates as alternative indicators of school performance. *American Education Research Journal, 41*, 3–42.

Sameroff, A. J., Peck, S. C., & Eccles, J. L. (2004). Changing ecological determinants of conduct problems from early adolescence to early adulthood. *Development and Psychopathology, 16*, 873–896.

Sawatzky, J.A. (2005). Cardiovascular health in Canadian women: The bigger picture revisited. *Canadian Journal of Cardiovascular Nursing, 15*, 53–62.

Shields, M., Shooshtari S. (2001). Determinants of self-perceived health. *Health Reports, 13*, 35–52.

Tessener, R., & Tessener, L. (1958). Review of the literature on school dropouts. *National Association of Secondary School Principals Bulletin, 42*, 141–153.

Thiessen, V. (2007a). *The impact of factors on trajectories that lead to a high school diploma and to participation in post-secondary education among those with low reading competencies at age 15*. Ottawa, ON: Human Resources and Social Development Canada.

Thiessen, V. (2007b). *The impact of factors on trajectories that lead to non-completion of high school diploma and to participation in post-secondary education among those with high reading competencies at age 15*. Ottawa, ON: Human Resources and Social Development Canada.

Vallerand, R. J., Fortier, M. S., & Guay, F. (1997). Self-determination and persistence in a real-life setting: Toward a motivational model of high school dropout. *Journal of Personality and Social Psychology, 72*, 1161–1176.

Veugelers P. J., Yip, A. M., & Kephart, G. (2001). Proximate and contextual socioeconomic determinants of mortality: Multilevel approaches in a setting with universal health care coverage. *American Journal of Epidemiology, 154*, 725–32.

Vitaro, F., Brenden, M., Larose, S., & Tremblay, R. E. (2005). Kindergarten disruptive behaviors, protective factors, and educational achievement by early adulthood. *Journal of Educational Psychology, 97*, 617–629.

Vitaro, F., Larocque, D., Janosz, M., & Tremblay, R. E. (2001). Negative social experiences and dropping out of school. *Educational Psychology, 21*, 401–415.

Wilson K., Jerrett M., & Eyles J. (2001). Testing relationships among determinants of health, health policy, and self-assessed health status in Quebec. *International Journal of Health Services, 31*, 67–68.

Chapter 15
School Dropout and Completion in Australia

Stephen Lamb

In 2008, the newly elected federal government in Australia announced a national target of a 90% Year 12 (final school year) completion rate to be achieved by the year 2020, later brought forward to 2015 (Council of Australian Governments [COAG], 2009).[1] This announcement follows the commitment of federal and state governments over recent years to a new National Reform Agenda, which includes the goal to significantly improve the proportion of young people making a smooth transition from school to further study and work (COAG, 2006). Increasing the rates of Year 12 completion is viewed as one of the main ways of improving the chances of young Australians making a smooth transition from school to work.

Achieving the goal of 90% Year 12 completion will not be an easy task. An estimate from the 2006 *Census of Population and Housing* suggests that the national rate is currently at about 68%, only a little higher than that recorded in the previous census 5 years earlier (Lamb & Mason, 2008). The rates vary markedly across states and territories, and by race, gender and social background. Among indigenous Australians, the rate is as low as 47%, while the rate for children from poor backgrounds (taken as those in the lowest quartile of socioeconomic status based on the student population) is at about 55% (Australian Bureau of Statistics [ABS], 2008a; Lamb & Mason, 2008). The rate for males is ten points below that for females.

There are many aspects of schooling and post-compulsory provision that will need to be considered in the development of policy if the new target is to be achieved. There is considerable diversity across states and territories in populations, economies and school and program provision. Australia is a federated system and there are different approaches, qualifications and completion requirements across jurisdictions. An important initial step will be to look at the current features of school organisation and program provision, how they vary across states and

---

[1] The target is for 90% completion of Year 12 or equivalent qualifications which includes vocational certificates treated as equivalent to Year 12 school certificates. References to Year 12 completion in the chapter are taken to include 'equivalent' qualifications.

S. Lamb (✉)
Centre for Post-Compulsory Education and Lifelong Learning,
University of Melbourne, Australia

S. Lamb et al. (Eds.), *School Dropout and Completion: International Comparative Studies in Theory and Policy*, DOI 10 1007/978-90-481-9763-7_18,
© Springer Science+Business Media B.V. 2011

territories, how patterns have changed over time, what contributes to differences in rates of graduation and dropout, and from previous evidence what sorts of programs, policies and practices are likely to help raise completion rates. This chapter will look at each of these matters in turn.

Main Features of Post-Compulsory Provision

Programs

In Australia, as in other federal systems, the states and territories have constitutional responsibility for school education, including primary and secondary schooling, student enrolment policies, curriculum, course accreditation and certification procedures, and methods of student assessment. The qualification arrangements related to school education are under state jurisdiction. There are mechanisms through which national coordination of school education across state and territory jurisdictions is achieved. These mechanisms centre around the agreements achieved through the Ministerial Council for Education, Early Childhood Development and Youth Affairs (MCEECDYA), which involves all relevant state, territory and federal government Ministers of Education.

Secondary education in all states and territories is based on a model of general education through to the end of the compulsory phase (usually Year 10), followed by a 2-year upper secondary program culminating in a senior school certificate. In the past, access to upper secondary education in most states was through an examination-based (intermediate) certificate at the end of compulsory schooling. These arrangements have almost entirely disappeared.[2] Every state and territory offers a senior school certificate, except for the state of Victoria, which offers two: the Victorian Certificate of Education (VCE) and the Victorian Certificate of Applied Learning (VCAL). The school certificates are developed, accredited and awarded by state or territory curriculum and assessment authorities. The majority of young people enter a certificate program at the end of compulsory education, though dropout rates at the end of Year 10 (before children enter post-compulsory or senior certificate programs) vary across jurisdictions and can be as high as 24% (the national rate is 11%). To qualify for a certificate (to graduate), generally students must successfully complete a sequence of elective units of study or subjects. English is the only prescribed study, in some states.

Teese & Helme (2007) note that in the design of senior certificates across Australia, certain key concepts recur:

- Curriculum authorities use the concept of a *study pattern* (New South Wales Higher School Certificate, Queensland Certificate of Education), *student program* (VCE), *package of studies* (Australian Capital Territory Year 12) or *learning program* (VCAL) to refer to the set of 'studies', 'subjects' or 'courses' taken by a student.
- Each 'subject', 'course' or 'study' has a syllabus or study design.

---

[2]Only the state of New South Wales maintains a certificate at the end of the compulsory phase of schooling.

- 'Subjects' or 'courses' or 'studies' are generally organised as semester Units, though their load in instructional hours may vary, depending on the certificate and the nature of the study.
- Successful student learning involves reaching certain standards or achieving pre-defined outcomes.
- Success generates credits, which accumulate.
- Satisfactory completion occurs when graduation requirements are met.

These key concepts are shared, even while the descriptive terminology varies.

But there are also differences in how certificates are designed. In one certificate – the Tasmanian Certificate of Education (TCE) – subjects have different levels of complexity or cognitive demand, and students therefore become 'banded' into skill levels. In another certificate – the Victorian Certificate of Applied Learning (VCAL) – the focus is on the learning needs of students who would otherwise not complete school. The emphasis is on personal growth, student interests, applied learning and multiple contexts of learning, making it clear that the studies leading to this certificate are practical in nature, and that the standard being sought through the way the certificate is designed is intended to have this character. It is designed as a pathway to work.

In most certificates (apart from VCAL), there are three broad types of study or programs provided. The first comprises traditional academic subjects such as English, literature, physics, chemistry, mathematics, languages, humanities and art.

The second includes studies that have become known as vocational education and training in school (VETiS). While VETiS options are provided in all certificates, there are real differences in how this is done and in how VETiS counts towards completion of the senior certificate. For example, there are differences in the number of VETiS subjects that can be counted for university admission and also in the use of graded assessments. VETiS is mainly provided as separate subject or study options, equivalent to any other subject or study, except for a small number of school-based apprenticeships which provide a much more structured program of study. One feature of VETiS is that, as well as contributing to a senior school certificate (and university entry), depending on the state they are in, students enrolled in many VETiS courses can also obtain a separate certificate for their VETiS study, effectively providing a dual qualification. School VETiS programs can consist of stand-alone, nationally recognised industry-specific courses based on industry training packages, which are also accredited for the senior school certificate, though integration varies across states. Some of the VETiS programs contain structured workplace learning with expected competency-based learning outcomes included in assessment. In 2001, at a national level, about 21% of Year 12 students enrolled in at least one VETiS subject or course (Lamb & Vickers, 2006).

The third type of study available in several certificates is a range of options which are neither academic nor vocational, but aim to provide students with a range of broad work-preparation and life skills, such as the options *Learning from the Community* and *Work Education*.

The different types of study or programs orient students towards different post-school outcomes. Students who enrol in and complete mainly academic study qualify more often for university entry, whereas those who undertake and complete mainly vocational education are more likely to enter other forms of tertiary education or go directly into the labour market at the end of secondary school. Students mainly taking the third type of program are more likely to pursue work or basic levels of further education.

Schools

The structure of primary and secondary schooling in Australia varies between states and territories. There are two basic patterns evident in formal schooling in Australia, as illustrated in Fig. 15.1.

In New South Wales, Victoria, Tasmania and the Australian Capital Territory, primary education comprises a Preparatory or Pre-Year 1 grade followed by Years 1–6. Secondary education comprises Years 7–12.

In Queensland, South Australia, Western Australia and the Northern Territory, primary education comprises a Preparatory or Pre-Year 1 grade followed by Years 1–7. Secondary education comprises Years 8–12.

Australia, in the main, has an integrated ('comprehensive') institutional structure for the delivery of school-based post-compulsory programs. Students tend not to be separated into different schools on the basis of the post-compulsory programs or qualifications in which they enrol. Most secondary schools offer courses leading to the senior school certificate provided in their state or territory. Separation of students often occurs within schools through subject, course and certificate choices, and many schools do not offer the full range of accredited subjects or courses, with availability of options often dependent on student demand and school size.

Grade	New South Wales, Victoria, Tasmania, Australian Capital Territory	Queensland, Western Australia, Northern Territory, South Australia
Year 12		
Year 11		
Year 10	Secondary	Secondary
Year 9		
Year 8		
Year 7		
Year 6		Primary
Year 5		
Year 4	Primary	
Year 3		
Year 2		
Year 1		
Prep (Pre-Year 1)		

Fig. 15.1 Schooling structures across Australia (Source: Australian Bureau of Statistics, 2008a)

Despite the appearance, when it comes to students (rather than programs), schooling in Australia is not based on a 'comprehensive' model. It is a highly divided, almost segregated system. Private schools accounted for 40.4% of all post-compulsory school enrolments in 2006 (students in Years 11 and 12), with 21.8% in Catholic schools and 18.6% in non-Catholic private schools (ABS, 2007). Enrolments in private schools have grown markedly over the past 3 decades thanks in part to large increases in unconditional recurrent funding from Australian governments. Some private schools have almost 90% of their funding met by government, without any conditions applied to the use of funds. Private schools contribute to social divisions in schooling. About 32% of students in Catholic schools and 51% in non-Catholic private schools are from high socioeconomic status backgrounds (taken as those in the highest quartile of socioeconomic status [SES] based on the student population) compared to only 17% of students in government schools (Lamb et al., 2006).

Government schools also divide students. Apart from the effects of residential segregation, most states also have 'selective-entry' schools which select students on the basis of academic aptitude, measured through achievement tests. In Victoria, Western Australia and Queensland, the numbers are small, accounting for less than 2% of all Year 12 students, though the number of such schools in Victoria is about to double (Lamb, 2008). In New South Wales, almost 1 in 11 of all secondary students is enrolled in a 'selective-entry' school. The schools contribute to academic and social divisions in schooling. In 2004, 55.2% of students in selective-entry schools in New South Wales were from high SES backgrounds (taken as those in the highest quartile of SES based on the student population) compared to 25% in remaining schools.[3] These selective-entry schools focus almost exclusively on the academic curriculum and university entry (see Lamb & Teese, 2005). Academic selection can also take place in mainstream government schools. Many secondary schools in Victoria, for example, have introduced Selective Entry Accelerated Learning (SEAL) programs and 'high achievers' programs, which identify high achieving students and group them together for all of their classes (streaming). Similarly, in Tasmanian secondary schools, until recently, students from Year 9 were grouped for subjects based on skill level, a form of streaming which contributed to social stratification (Lamb et al., 2001).

Other features of school organisation are also important to note. In two jurisdictions – Tasmania and the Australian Capital Territory – post-compulsory schooling is largely provided in senior colleges (Years 11 and 12). In most other states and territories, secondary schooling is delivered in schools that offer classes from Year 7 to Year 12 or from Year 8 to Year 12. There is considerable diversity, though. Increasingly, senior colleges and variations on a senior college model are being implemented to allow regions to concentrate student numbers in order for schools to offer a broader range of programs. In many rural areas of Australia, schools are often small, operate as Preparatory to Year 12 schools (combined primary and secondary grades in a single school), and struggle to deliver program breadth in the senior years.

---

[3]Figures derived by Stephen Lamb from data provided by the New South Wales Department of Education and Training.

Patterns of Year 12 Completion

Measures

Graduation rates are not provided or published in Australia. The traditional indicator of school completion has been the 'apparent retention rate'. The Year 12 apparent retention rate is measured as the number of full-time students in Year 12 in a given calendar year divided by the number of students who were in the first year of secondary school when that Year 12 cohort commenced secondary school (either Year 7 or 8, depending on the state). Retention rates have been used by school systems in Australia as a measure of system performance, treating the rates as a measure of completion. However, the rates are not a measure of graduation; they are based on school census enrolments taken in August of every year, and they take no account of whether students successfully meet the graduation requirements. Other factors also affect the retention rate as an accurate measure of completion, for instance, the measure takes no account of population changes, inclusion of mature-age students, grade repeating or the availability of part-time school study options, all of which can inflate or depress the rates from 'real' levels of completion or graduation.

It is possible to adjust retention rates to arrive at a more accurate measure of completion. This has been done in several studies (see Lamb et al., 2004). Adjustments for measurement issues associated with population and related factors generally reduce the retention rate by up to 4 percentage points, depending on the year. To take account of students who are in Year 12 in August, but do not graduate, would require further adjustments of up to 5 percentage points (Lamb et al., 2004). The gap between the 2006 published retention rate and the rate of Year 12 senior school certificate attainment derived from the 2006 national *Census of Population and Housing* suggests that the apparent retention rate is about 8 percentage points above what might be considered a graduation rate (see Lamb & Mason, 2008; ABS, 2007).

The patterns presented in the following discussion are largely based on 'retention' rates, which are described using the term 'completion', though the limitations just mentioned need to be kept in mind.

Trends in Completion

The long-term trends in Year 12 school completion are displayed in Fig. 15.2. Since 1967, the proportion of young people completing school in Australia has more than trebled. In 2008, it was at 74.5%, about three points down on its peak of 77.1% reached in 1992. The trend shows a series of phases: (1) the steady growth from the late 1960s to the mid-1970s, fuelled by a buoyant economy and rising social aspirations; (2) the 1970s downturn, associated with a faltering economy and rising youth unemployment; (3) the upsurge in completion during the 1980s, initially spurred by the 1982–83 recession and falling teenage employment, reaching a peak in 1992; and

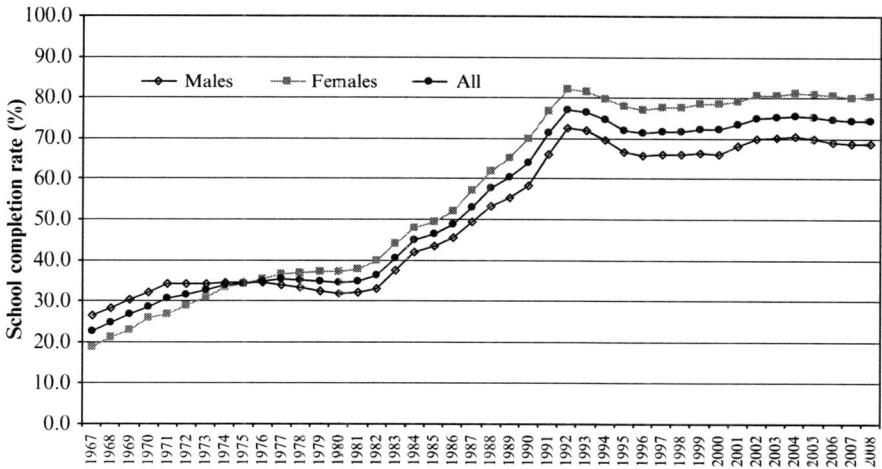

Fig. 15.2 School completion rates (Year 7/8–Year 12), Australia: 1967–2008 (Source: Australian Bureau of Statistics, *Schools Australia*, various years, Cat no. 4221.0 (ABS, 2008a))

(4) the stagnant years beginning in the 1990s when completion rates dipped and then plateaued (for elaboration on these phases, see Teese, 2002; Lamb, 1993; Lamb et al., 2004).

The most dramatic period of growth occurred in the 1980s. In the early 1980s, more than 60% of all secondary school students left school before Year 12. However, by the end of the decade, the vast majority were continuing through to Year 12. Rates of Year 12 completion, as low as 36% only 10 years earlier, reached a peak of 77.1% in 1992. At that time, optimistic predictions were made of almost universal completion by the end of the decade (Taskforce On Pathways In Education and Training, 1992; Centre for Skill Formation Research and Development, 1993). Many factors contributed to the growth over this period. Accelerated by falling teenage employment, sharp increases were recorded following the 1982–83 recession. Other factors were also influential, including increased government financial assistance (study allowances) for young people in families of low income, and the abolition of unemployment benefits for 16- to 17-year-olds. Important also were changes in school programs; in several states, major changes were made to the provision of the senior secondary school curriculum to accommodate a broader range of students. Together these changes supported a decade of great expansion in senior schooling, a decade in which Australian states moved rapidly and impressively towards developing mass systems of secondary education.

The downturn in the years after 1992 indicated that this phase of building stalled. Despite the remarkable period of expansion during the 1980s, the growth in school completion came to an end. Over a 5-year period from 1992, the rates of Year 12 completion fell by almost 6 percentage points. By 1997, according to apparent retention rates, non-completion of school again affected close to 30% of all students. Therefore, rather than having become a marginal consideration towards the close of the decade – affecting only a small residual group – non-completion of school involved a large number of young Australians and remained an important issue.

Since 1999, there has been some recovery, with completion rates pushing back up to the heights reached in the early 1990s. Even so, across Australia, one in every four secondary school entrants drops out of school before Year 12.

National completion rates tend to conceal differences across states and territories. Variations in economies, in labour market opportunities, in senior school program development, in institutional reforms, as well as in populations can affect school completion rates. During the period of growth in school completion rates in the 1980s, states displayed similar patterns of improvement, though the amount of growth varied. The states which began the 1980s with the weakest levels of completion – Tasmania and New South Wales – experienced weaker rates of growth compared to other states (see Lamb, 1998). This tended to widen the gaps over the decade: whereas in 1981, less than 15 percentage points separated the six states in the rates of completion, in 1992 over 30 points separated them. For the two largest systems (Victoria and New South Wales), there was only a 1 percentage point gap in the rate of completion in 1981; by 1991, this gap had increased to 12 percentage points. Differences between states grew until the early 1990s. Differential downturn in rates of completion from 1992 led to some convergence across the states and territories in rates of school completion, returning to the patterns of the early 1980s. In 2008, about 20 percentage points separated the states and territories, with the highest rate of 86% in the Australian Capital Territory and the lowest of 66% in the Northern Territory.

Demographic Patterns of School Completion

National and state completion rates mask large variations by gender, region, social group, school sector, ethnicity and indigenous background.

Girls complete school more frequently than boys do. In 2008, the national completion rate for girls was 80.5% as against 68.8% for boys (ABS, 2008a). Girls have not always completed school in greater numbers (see Fig. 15.2). The trend became established in the mid-1970s and reflected a number of major changes in the social and economic environment – the long-term loss of full-time jobs in the teenage labour market which disproportionately affected girls, the growth of employment in the services sector (a sector with high levels of female employment) requiring higher qualifications, the continuing relative lack of access to trade apprenticeships for girls, rising entry-levels to key professions (especially nursing), and improved career aspirations for girls as compared to 35 years ago (Sweet, 1995; Lamb et al., 2004).

Completion rates also vary by school type. Published rates in 2008 show that students attending non-Catholic private schools have the highest rates of completion (93.9%), followed by students attending Catholic schools (78.3%), and then students attending government schools (68.3%) (ABS, 2008a). Much of the gap between private and government schools is due to differences in the SES backgrounds of children attending the different types of schools. Private schools, particularly non-Catholic private schools, have much higher concentrations of children from high SES origins (Lamb et al., 2004).

There are wide variations in Year 12 completion based on social background. Children from high SES families – families in which parents are often university-educated and tend to have professional or managerial occupations and higher levels of cultural resources in the home such as books and computers – are far more likely to complete school compared to children from low SES backgrounds. One estimate suggests that by age 24, about 64% of Australians from low SES families have completed Year 12, while the rate for those from high SES families is 86% (Lamb & Mason, 2008).

Completing school is also related to where families live (see, for example, Teese, 2002). Reflecting a long-term pattern, children of families living in rural areas, where schools are often smaller and less able to offer a comprehensive range of curriculum options and families tend to have lower incomes, less often complete school by comparison with children living in urban areas. According to a recent study using 2006 Census data, the gaps between children living in rural areas and those living in urban areas can be as high as 20 percentage points (ABS, 2008b).

Studies also suggest that the language background of families is linked to levels of completion. Young people whose language background is not English (i.e., those from families in which the main language spoken at home is not English) are more likely to complete school compared to those whose main language at home is English. The difference is about 8 percentage points, according to a recent national study (Lamb et al., 2004). This finding is in line with research which has shown that even though the average educational attainment of parents in non-English speaking families is lower than their native English-speaking peers, they have higher educational aspirations for their children and place a premium on completing Year 12 as a way of enhancing their children's future prospects (Miller & Volker, 1989).

Indigenous students have low rates of school completion. The gap between indigenous and non-indigenous students in 2008 was almost 30 percentage points – 46.5% for indigenous students compared to 75.6% for non-indigenous students (ABS, 2008a). The last decade has seen improvement in the rates for the indigenous population, rising by over 10 percentage points, but still more than one in two indigenous children drops out of school before the final year (ABS, 2008a).

Factors Influencing Year 12 Completion

A considerable amount of research has been conducted into the reasons why young people complete school or drop out. Previous work suggests that there are several important groups of factors to consider. One group relates to *political and economic context* and includes such things as economy and labour market (employment and unemployment, apprenticeships, industry, recession and growth, teenage labour market opportunities) and government policies (school funding, resources, targets, initiatives). A second is linked to what might be called *school and system context* and covers such things as school organisation (sector, selective-entry schools, rural provision, school type), school-level policies and practices (pathways and careers education, intake, interventions), teachers and teaching (teacher quality, pedagogy, teaching styles, assessment) and curriculum and certification (breadth of offerings, VET in schools, senior school certificate requirements, alternative programs, university entry requirements). A third group is related to *student context* and includes such things as social and demographic factors (gender, region, ethnicity, socioeconomic status, race), personal factors (finances, physical and mental health, disability, psychology, pregnancy, drug use, transport, family obligations, family breakdown, homelessness) and prior student achievement (early school achievement and academic progress).

Political and Economic Context

Historically, in Australia, one strand of analysis on the factors influencing Year 12 completion has focused on the alternatives open to 15- to 19-year-olds. These include labour market factors as well as changes in the provision of education and training (such as post-school education and training programs). The state of the economy, particularly the youth labour market, has figured strongly in explanations of dropout and completion. For example, a report by the Commonwealth Tertiary Education Commission in the early 1980s argued that change in labour demand associated with recession was the underlying cause of fluctuating completion rates in the 1970s (CTEC, 1982).

Measured over the long term, there is a fairly weak relationship between school completion rates and the state of the youth labour market. As Fig. 15.3 illustrates, the recession in the early 1980s (1981–83) and the early 1990s (1990–92) produced

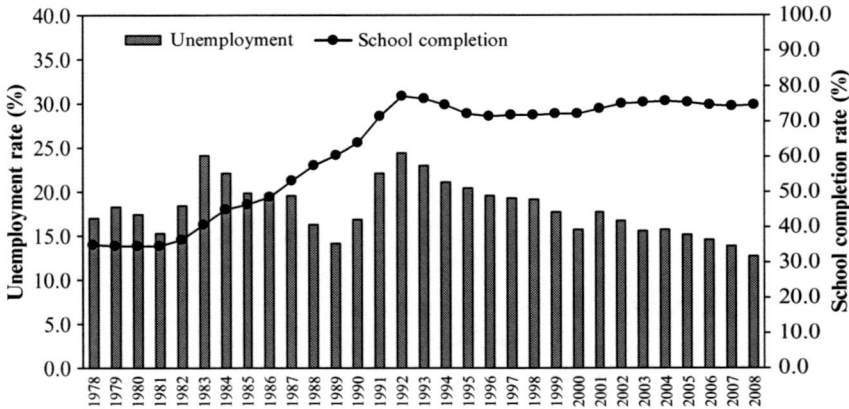

Fig. 15.3 Unemployment rates for 15- to 19-year-olds and school completion rates: Australia, 1978–2008 (Sources: Unemployment rates derived from Labour Force Australia (Cat. No. 6202.0) (ABS, 2009); School completion rates derived from Schools Australia (Cat. No. 4221.0) (ABS, 2008a))

rises in youth unemployment. The deterioration of the youth labour market, measured in terms of increases in youth unemployment, tended to be matched by growth in Year 12 completion rates. As jobs dried up, young people tended to remain longer at school. The relationship, though, is not consistent. Improvements in employment can occur without changes in completion trends (for example, as in the late 1980s and from 2001).

Despite the inconsistent relationship between school completion and unemployment, economic conditions may well affect the availability of employment and also the school leaving plans of students. Several major changes have taken place in the Australian labour market that have affected the opportunities for young people to find full-time work.

One of the changes has been a long-term fall in full-time teenage job opportunities. Structural changes to the Australian economy over the last 25 years have gradually, but dramatically, changed the number of jobs available to young people. The analyses of the youth labour market by Sweet (1992), Freeland (1996), Lewis and McLean (1998) and Wooden (1999) have drawn attention to the long-term fall in full-time job opportunities for teenagers. Between the early 1980s and 2006, for example, the proportion of 15- to 19-year-olds in full-time work fell from 39% to 15% and 'between May 1988 and May 1999, the number of full-time jobs held by teenagers aged 15–19 years fell by 49%' (Dusselldorp Skills Forum, 1999, p. 5). Accompanying the fall in full-time work has been a substantial growth in the numbers of part-time jobs. These have been focused largely in the retail and service areas, which overwhelmingly employ young people still in the education system (Wooden, 1999).

The relationship between economic trends and school completion suggest that the conditions of the teenage labour market – and the availability of jobs as an alternative to schooling – may influence students' decisions to stay on at school. Other labour market and government policy factors that have been identified as influences on school completion rates include policies on income support, and state and federal government policies on alternative forms of post-compulsory education and training, such as apprenticeships and adult education (Teese et al., 2000; Department of Family and Community Services, 2002). For example, alternative forms of education and training provided outside of school can work to reduce rates of school completion. Some states and territories have changed their legislation around school leaving ages to recognise alternative activities as equivalent to being in school. The policy, known as 'earning and learning', accepts full-time work or full-time study in school, or training or study outside of school, as fulfilling the legal requirement (see, for example, Rann, 2007). Work and alternative forms of study can function to draw students away from school and reduce Year 12 completion rates.

Student and School Contexts

Several studies have attempted to identify the most influential factors shaping school completion in Australia using a variety of statistical techniques such as multivariate logistic regression (see, for example, Long et al., 1999). Most highlight the influence of attributes associated with individuals and their family and school contexts.

A major study undertaken in 2004 using a large national sample of students participating in a longitudinal survey found that in terms of individual student characteristics, gender, indigenous status and having a disability or not have significant independent influences on completion (Lamb et al., 2004). All else equal, girls are much more likely to remain to Year 12 than boys. Also, indigenous Australians are far less likely to complete school than students from non-indigenous backgrounds. This is also true for students with disabilities or health problems who are less likely to remain to Year 12 than those without a disability.

Family background variables – SES, language background, family size and parental aspirations – all have strong independent effects on school completion. Students from higher rather than lower SES families, those from a non-English-speaking rather than English-speaking family, those from smaller rather than larger families, and those in families where the parents have tertiary education ambitions for their children, are significantly more likely to complete Year 12.

School setting is also important. The social and academic intakes of schools, measured through mean SES of schools and mean student achievement, are significantly related to the likelihood of students graduating from school. Other things equal, schools with a higher mean SES or achievement intake have significantly higher rates of completion.

School type has an important independent effect on completion. Other things equal, students attending Catholic schools are more likely to complete school than to drop out. This does not always apply to other independent schools, suggesting that the much higher completion rates for non-Catholic independent schools are linked to intake rather than any additional effect.

Other school factors reported as exerting an influence on completion include quality of teaching and learning: schools with more teachers who are perceived by students as having strong content knowledge of the subjects they teach, those who are perceived as having expertise in teaching, and those who display strong interest in students, are associated with higher levels of completion (Lamb et al., 2004).

Academic achievement and aspirations, as they form and are formed in school in conjunction with the influence of family, are major predictors of completion. Young people who achieve well in school tend to complete school far more often than those who are not achieving well. Similarly, academic motivation as measured by the number of hours of homework undertaken and the incidence of doing extra homework (beyond what is set) have independent effects on completion (Lamb et al., 2004).

Policies to Raise Completion Rates

System-Level Initiatives

Relatively little Australian research exists on the strategies school systems and schools use to improve student engagement and increase Year 12 completion. However, the past decade has seen the implementation of a number of completion initiatives in various parts of Australia. At a national level, changes to income support were introduced in 1998 to encourage students from poor backgrounds to remain in school or other forms of education and training. Youth Allowance (YA), the main income support program, is a means-tested payment made to students from poor backgrounds who are 16 years of age or older and in formal education and training, or looking for work. One important criterion for receiving YA is the requirement that young people under 18 years of age be in full-time education or training to receive payment. There is some evidence to suggest that this initiative has helped increase school completion (Department of Family and Community Services, 2002).

At a state or system level, a key initiative to help raise school completion rates has been to increase the compulsory leaving age. The government of South Australia, for example, increased its school leaving age from 15 years to 16 years in 2003, and has more recently extended it to 17 (in 2009). Similar changes have been made in Victoria and Western Australia. The school leaving age in Tasmania has been set at 16 for a considerable number of years, but there is a new requirement that after Year 10 young people need to continue in education or training for 2 years or until they turn 17. Governments have introduced these changes largely because of the view that it will lead to increases in school completion. As reported by one jurisdiction, 'the government decided to raise the school leaving age to 16 to require students to stay at school or participate in an approved course of instruction [because] research shows that where students complete 12 years of education their long-term prospects of employment increase' (Government of South Australia, 2009).

The main program initiative at a system level to raise rates of school completion has been the implementation and development of Vocational Education and Training in Schools (VETiS). As in other countries, VETiS has developed as an alternative to traditional academic programs to enable an increasing number of young people, with a wider range of abilities, to participate in upper secondary courses and obtain relevant qualifications. At the post-compulsory level, students can generally undertake as many VETiS subjects as part of their senior school certificate as they wish. However, while most do, not all schools offer VETiS. Students enrolled in VETiS courses can often obtain a separate certificate for their VETiS study, effectively providing a dual qualification.

There is some evidence to suggest that the availability of VETiS courses can improve the likelihood of school completion. A longitudinal study of students in Year 9 who reported plans to drop out of school before Year 12 more often graduated if they entered VETiS courses rather than academic or general programs (Lamb & Vickers, 2006). This is consistent with some overseas studies suggesting that, all else equal, the more VETiS classes students take, the less likely they are to drop out (Mertens et al., 1982, for example), and with findings based on studies of the effects of work-based learning programs, where similar evidence emerges concerning the positive effects on student engagement that result from participation in work-based learning (Hughes et al., 2001; Steinberg, 1998).

Another key initiative has been the introduction of pathways planning programs. In Victoria, for example, there has been the implementation in government secondary schools of the Managed Individual Pathways (MIPs) program and the recent development of the Student Mapping Tool to help schools identify students at risk of disengagement and dropout (see Lamb & Rice, 2008). MIPs is a scheme which offers all students aged 15 and over individual assistance to develop pathways plans. It is based on a case management model and provides a framework for schools to develop individualised pathways plans and provide targeted careers counselling. A review of the scheme found that MIPs had, across many schools, improved student engagement and staff–student relations, increased the responsiveness of school staff to the needs of all students and helped raise Year 12 completion (Asquith Group, 2005).

School-Level Policies

Schools can also employ at a local level targeted approaches to improve Year 12 completion rates. A recent study of schools effective in raising Year 12 completion rates for at-risk students identified a number of school-level practices or strategies. What emerged as central to improving school engagement and completion for at-risk students was a series of targeted interventions and programs underpinned by a supportive school culture or climate. The elements of school culture central to maximising student engagement and completion included a shared vision across the school community, high expectations of students, flexibility and responsiveness to individual student needs, a commitment to success for all students and a drive for continuous improvement (Lamb & Rice, 2008).

The targeted initiatives included student-focused strategies such as mentoring, early and more intensive pathways and careers planning, fine-grained coordination of welfare needs, family outreach, programs to improve students' social skills, tutoring and peer tutoring, targeted financial support, case management and targeted assistance for skill development among low achievers.

They also included school-wide strategies, for example familial-based forms of organisation such as mini-schools, team-based approaches to teaching, learning and pastoral care, early intervention to support literacy and numeracy skill growth, project-based and applied approaches to learning, strategic use of teachers and teaching resources, initiatives to improve connections with parents, priority professional development and high expectations on attendance and behaviour.

The schools with the greatest success in improving completion rates combined a range of these strategies, working to develop whole-of-staff commitment to engaging students, and constantly refining approaches as student and parent needs shift.

Pathways for Dropouts

There are opportunities in Australia for young people who do drop out of school to complete an upper secondary school certificate or equivalent. These alternative pathways come in various forms depending on the state or territory.

One pathway is to return to study to complete a senior school certificate. Some states, such as South Australia and Queensland, provide adult re-entry schools established as second chance schools to provide dropouts with the opportunity to complete school and graduate with a senior school certificate. Study for an upper secondary school certificate is also possible at Technical and Further Education (TAFE) institutions, or, in some states, through adult education providers such as the Centre for Adult Education (CAE) or a range of Adult and Community Education (ACE) providers. Accurate estimates of the numbers of students who return to complete a senior school certificate at a national level are not available. While a number of studies have examined the role and characteristics of re-entry schools (see, for example, Goldman & Bradley, 1996, 1997), they do not provide reliable estimates of the numbers who participate or complete. Data from one source suggest that at any one time up to 4% of dropouts aged 15–19 are enrolled in study for a senior school certificate at a TAFE or ACE provider in the state of Victoria, and about 3% in New South Wales.[4] National estimates, using longitudinal data, of enrolments of dropouts in a senior school certificate at a TAFE institution, ACE provider or by returning to school suggest that the rates are less than 5% (McMillan & Marks, 2003). Completion figures, though, are not available.

The main alternative pathway pursued by dropouts involves study or training for 'senior school certificate equivalent' qualifications, usually undertaken at a TAFE institution or private provider. The most popular of these are apprenticeships and traineeships. Apprenticeships generally involve an indenture or contractual agreement with an employer where a young person is expected to undertake a period of formal training in a classroom setting, sometimes referred to as *block release*, as well as on-the-job experience. The formal training component is generally provided by TAFE Colleges, private providers or group training schemes (though small numbers of school-based apprenticeships are available). Traditionally, apprenticeships involve a 4-year indenture in a traditional craft or trade area such as electrical trades, plumbing, carpentry and automotive trades. However, recent reforms have expanded the areas of training and the length of training. One variation has been the introduction of traineeships which provide training in a range of fields including white-collar occupations, such as clerical work. Traineeships are usually for 12 months rather than 4 years. Apprenticeships and traineeships often appeal to young people who drop out of school because they provide a wage while learning. They also involve the acquisition of skills through applied learning in workplaces, again often appealing to dropouts who have become disengaged from formal classroom learning in school settings, providing an alternative for young people not attracted by full-time school.

The importance of apprenticeships and traineeships to dropouts is highlighted in Table 15.1, which shows the patterns of take-up and completion over a 7-year period after leaving school. The estimates are from a national longitudinal study of over 13,000 students who were in Year 9 in 1995 and surveyed annually. The patterns show that almost 45% of dropouts had entered an apprenticeship or traineeship.

---

[4] Figures derived by Anne Walstab from the Australian Vocational Education and Training Management Information Statistical Standard for 2004.

Table 15.1 Pathways and completion of school-certificate equivalent qualifications for dropouts across seven post-school years

Pathways beyond school	Percentage
Education and training	**70.6**
Completed a senior secondary certificate equivalent qualification (39.9)	
High-level vocational qualification (AQF Level 4 or above)	5.5
Apprenticeship	23.9
Traineeship	10.5
Completed a lower-level certificate (10.8)	
Other forms of education and training (AQF Level 3 or below)	10.8
Enrolled in study but did not complete (19.9)	
High-level vocational qualification (AQF Level 4 or above)	6.3
Apprenticeship	5.9
Traineeship	4.4
Other forms of education and training (AQF Level 3 or below)	3.3
No further education and training	**29.4**
Total	**100.0**

Source: Figures derived from the Y95 cohort of the Longitudinal Surveys of Australian Youth (LSAY).

About one quarter did not complete their training. After seven post-school years, 23.9% of dropouts had successfully completed an apprenticeship. A further 10.5% had completed a traineeship.

In addition to apprenticeships and traineeships, a small number of dropouts study and complete high-level VET qualifications, also considered to be school certificate equivalent qualifications. This level of qualification can be used as an avenue to university. Table 15.1 reports a rate of completion for dropouts of 5.5% over the first seven post-school years.

Using estimates based on the results from the national longitudinal survey of young people reported in Table 15.1, it can be seen that high school equivalent qualifications are gained by roughly 40% of dropouts. When combined with data on the rates of school completion it suggests that currently about 81% of young Australians gain a school certificate or equivalent qualification – 68% successfully graduating from school and a further 13% gaining qualifications through alternative post-school pathways.

Conclusion

As the brief analysis presented in this chapter indicates, it will not be easy for the Australian government to achieve its ambitious goal to have 90% of young people attaining an upper secondary school qualification or equivalent by 2015. Rates of school completion reached a peak in the early 1990s and since that time have been stubbornly resistant to further growth. Unless there is a sustained labour market crisis, a recipe for completion growth in the past, it is difficult to see how further growth will occur. While completion, according to the last Census of Population and

Housing, was at 68%, nationally, and completion of school equivalent qualifications by dropouts adds a further 10–13 percentage points, the remaining growth that is needed will be difficult to achieve given the profile of dropouts. High levels of additional need (welfare and personal), low levels of achievement, higher absenteeism, negative views of school, low aspirations, disadvantage associated with low SES family backgrounds characterise many of those who fail to complete. Without targeted and effective interventions, without widespread reform to the curriculum to make it more meaningful and yet rigorous, and without attempts at improving the quality of teaching and learning, it is not easy to see how schools can deliver what is needed.

This leaves aside maybe a more important issue. Achieving high levels of completion by itself, without regard to the quality of completion, may have little real benefit to young people, the labour force or the community. If gains in completion are achieved simply by expanding the criteria of 'equivalent' qualifications and multiplying the number of alternatives without regard to the quality of learning and consistency in the standards of skills achieved by school leavers, there may be little gained even if the target for completion is achieved. It is of little use providing alternatives if they promote stratification, leading to inequality in outcomes, as effectively as if the alternatives did not exist. There is a need in moving forward to ensure that all programs at upper secondary level provide a similar foundation of learning and deliver access to the full range of further education and work opportunities for all. That will make achieving the national target truly meaningful.

References

Asquith Group (2005). Review of Managed Individual Pathways in government schools. Report for Victorian Department of Education and Early Childhood Development. Retrieved from http://www.eduweb.vic.gov.au/edulibrary/public/postcomp/mipsreview2006.doc

Australian Bureau of Statistics (ABS). (2007). *Schools Australia 2006. Catalogue No. 4221.0.* Canberra: ABS.

Australian Bureau of Statistics (ABS) (2008a). *Schools Australia 2007. Catalogue No. 4221.0.* Canberra: ABS.

Australian Bureau of Statistics (ABS). (2008b). *Australian social trends 2008. Catalogue No. 4102.0.* Canberra: ABS.

Australian Bureau of Statistics (ABS). (2009). *Labour force Australia. Catalogue No. 6202.0. Time Series Spreadsheets.* ABS: Canberra.

Centre for Skill Formation Research and Development (CSF). (1993). *After competence: The future of post-compulsory education and training* (Vol. 1). Brisbane: Griffith University.

Commonwealth Tertiary Education Commission (CTEC). (1982). *Learning and earning.* Canberra: Australian Government Publishing Service.

Council of Australian Governments (COAG). (2006). Council of Australian Governments meeting, 14 July 2006, Communiqué. Retrieved from http://www.coag.gov.au/coag_meeting_outcomes/2006-07-14/docs/ccag140706.pdf

Council of Australian Governments (COAG). (2009). Council of Australian Governments meeting, 30 April 2009, Communiqué. Retrieved from http://www.coag.gov.au/coag_meeting_outcomes/2009-04-30/docs/20090430_communique.rtf

Department of Family and Community Services. (2002). *Youth Allowance evaluation.* Canberra: Australian Government Publishing Service.

Dusselldorp Skills Forum. (1999, August). Key indicators 1999: How young people are faring.

Freeland, J. (1996). Citizenship postponed: Young people and an active citizenship. In J. Spierings, I. Voorendt, & J. Spoehr (Eds.), *Jobs for young Australians*. Adelaide: Social Justice Research Foundation.

Goldman, J. D., & Bradley, G. L. (1996). A profile of Australian high school dropouts who return to school. *Studies in the Education of Adults, 28*(2), 185–210.

Goldman, J. D., & Bradley, G. L. (1997). The educational experiences of Australian high school dropouts who return to school. *International Journal of Lifelong Education, 16*(1), 18–38.

Government of South Australia. (2009). Increase in school leaving age. Adelaide: Department of Education and Children Services. Retrieved July 29, 2009, from http://www.decs.sa.gov.au/community/pages/speced2/leavingage/.

Hughes, K. L., Bailey, T. R., & Mechur, M. J. (2001). School-to-Work: Making a difference in education. A research report to America. New York: Institute on Education and the Economy, Teachers College, Columbia University. Retrieved from http://www.tc.columbia.edu/~iee/PAPERS/ Stw.pdf

Lamb, S. (1998). Completing school in Australia: Trends in the 1990s. *Australian Journal of Education, 42*(1), 5–31.

Lamb, S. (2008). Selective-entry schools: Time for a re-think. *Professional Voice, 5*(3), 17–22.

Lamb, S., Hogan D., & Johnson, T. (2001). The stratification of learning opportunities and achievement in Tasmanian secondary schools. *Australian Journal of Education, 45*(2), 153–167.

Lamb, S., Long, M., & Baldwin, G. (2006). *Performance of the Australian education and training system.* Report for the Victorian Department of Premier and Cabinet. Retrieved from http://www.dpc.vic.gov.au/CA256D800027B102/Lookup/CommonwealthStateRelationsrep0rt/$file/perf%20of%20aust%20education.pdf

Lamb, S., & Mason, K. (2008). *How young people are faring, 2008.* Report for the Foundation for Young Australians. Melbourne: Foundation for Young Australians.

Lamb, S., & Rice, S. (2008). *Effective interventions to increase school completion.* Report for the Victorian Department of Education and Early Childhood Development.

Lamb, S., & Teese, R. (2005). *Equity programs for government schools in New South Wales: A review.* Report for the New South Wales Department of Education and Training. Retrieved from https://www.det.nsw.edu.au/media/downloads/research/completedprojects/nswequityrev.pdf

Lamb, S., & Vickers, M. (2006). *Variations in VET provision across Australian schools and their effects on student outcomes.* Longitudinal Surveys of Australian Youth Research Report No. 48. Melbourne: Australian Council for Educational Research.

Lamb, S., Walstab, A., Teese, R., Vickers, M., & Rumberger, R. (2004). *Staying on at school: Improving student retention in Australia.* Brisbane: Ministerial Council on Employment, Education and Training and the Queensland Department of Education: Brisbane. Retrieved from www.mceetya.edu.au/verve/_resources/studentretention_main_file.pdf

Lewis, P. E. T., & McLean, B. (1998, November). The youth labour in Australia. Paper presented to the Productivity Commission workshop on youth unemployment, Australian National University.

Long, M., Carpenter, P., & Hayden, M. (1999). *Participation in education and training 1980–1994.* Longitduinal Surveys of Australian Youth Research Report No. 13. Melbourne: Australian Council for Educational Research.

McMillan, J., & Marks, G. (2003). *School leavers in Australia: Profiles and pathways.* Longitduinal Surveys of Australian Youth Research Report No. 31. Melbourne: Australian Council for Educational Research.

Mertens, D. M., Seitz, P., & Cox, S. (1982). *Vocational education and the high school dropout.* Columbus, OH: National Center for Research on Vocational Education. (ERIC Document Reproduction Service No. ED228297)

Miller, P., & Volker, P. (1989). Socioeconomic influences on educational attainment: evidence and implications for the tertiary education finance debate. *Australian Journal of Statistics, 31A*, 47–70.

Rann, M. (2007). New school leaving age for South Australia. Statement by the Premier of South Australia. Retrieved from http://www.premier.sa.gov.au/news.php?id=1552&print=1

Steinberg, A. (1998). *Real learning, real work: School-to-work as high school reform.* New York: Routledge.

Sweet, R. (1992). Can Finn deliver vocational competence? *Unicorn, 18*(1), 31–43.

Sweet, R. (1995). *Linking schools and workplaces: Lessons from Australia and overseas.* Sydney: Australian Student Traineeship Foundation.

Taskforce on Pathways in Education and Training. (1992). *Information paper: Current and future trends in Victorian post-compulsory education and training.* Melbourne: Department of School Education.

Teese, R. (2002). *Early leaving in Victoria: Geographical patterns, origins, and strategic issues.* Melbourne: Educational Outcomes Research Unit, University of Melbourne.

Teese, R., & Helme, S. (2007). Examination of the principles, concepts and definitions underpinning Year 12 standards in Australian states and territories. Report for the Australasian Curriculum, Assessment and Certification Authorities. University of Melbourne (unpublished report).

Teese, R., Polesel, J., O'Brien, K., Jones, B., Davies, M., Walstab, A., & Maughan, A. (2000). *Early school leaving: A review of the literature.* Brisbane: Australian National Training Authority.

Wooden, M. (1999). *Impediments to the employment of young people.* Leabrook: National Centre for Vocational Education Research.

Part III
Programs, Equity and Policy

Chapter 16
Vocational Education and Training in France and Germany: Friend or Foe of the Educationally Disadvantaged?

Richard Teese

Introduction

The modern history of education systems in the developed world shows two striking trends which are related – the mass use of secondary education and widening vulnerability to failure at school. The more that young people have stayed on at school, the wider the net that school has thrown over the population and the greater the exposure of weaker groups to the demands of school. In the early decades after the Second World War, the majority of children from working-class backgrounds did not attempt extended secondary schooling. Many were considered to be underachievers. They repeated grades and were not admitted to academic secondary schools, or if they were admitted, they were placed in terminal courses. Thus failure came early and was definitive. Massification came later – though national chronologies vary – and, along with this, insecurity at a higher level of schooling. The children who had once completed only compulsory schooling (if that) and who had found refuge of sorts in the labour market progressively surrendered this protection which the stagnating economies of the late 1970s had greatly undermined. They were now trapped between the failure of economic institutions – to deliver more growth, especially in accessible areas of employment – and the failure that educational institutions could and would visit upon them.

Governments of the late 1970s and 1980s implemented both education and labour market policies to reduce continuing high levels of youth unemployment. Education policies are of particular importance because they were intended to tackle underlying structural problems, whereas labour market programs – typically more diverse and transitory – could at best soften the effects of cyclical downturn. The root problem was the widening gap between industry change in the economy and the educational levels of new generations entering the workforce. Large groups of young people were treated by school systems as if the jobs they would have

R. Teese (✉)
Centre for Post-Compulsory Education and Lifelong Learning, University of Melbourne, Australia

S. Lamb et al. (Eds.), *School Dropout and Completion: International Comparative Studies in Theory and Policy*, DOI 10.1007/978-90-481-9763-7_19,
© Springer Science+Business Media B.V. 2011

entered before the first oil shock still existed. Recovery in the mid-1980s exposed these young people to the contradictory demands of an economy looking forward and a school system looking backwards – on an economic and a social past.

Structural unemployment underlines the distinctive nature of the response of governments of the time – reforming the curriculum of secondary schools, particularly through vocational education. The objectives of this reform have been conceived in broader or narrower terms, depending on the country. In some, perhaps most cases, vocational education has been seen as adding provision of a different kind, without changing a predominantly academic or university-preparatory curriculum. In other cases, a more expansive and radical approach has been taken in which the whole of the upper secondary curriculum has been renovated to blur the boundaries between academic and vocational (for an international overview of approaches in the context of school dropout, see Lamb, 2008). But in all cases vocational education has supplied the key material to reconstruct the secondary school curriculum, partly or wholly, and to adjust the trajectories of young people to the directions of occupational and employment change.

It could be argued that reliance on diversification of the upper secondary curriculum through vocational education represents a conservative strategy which protects both the academic core and its beneficiaries, while supporting growth in areas that pose no threat to the established social pattern of outcomes (Shavit & Müller, 2000). The beneficiaries of this strategy are both social and professional – both parents and teachers. For by confining growth to low-prestige areas of the curriculum, educational policy creates a means of relegating difficult and unsuccessful students to a 'reserve space' and insulating more academic students and their teachers from this group. In effect, the use of vocational studies to expand educational participation without trespassing on high-prestige programs operates as a form of social engineering for the benefit of the most academically minded parents, their children and the teachers of their children.

While this argument is a familiar one, the implications are not always fully drawn out. The most important result of this conservative expansionary strategy is the failure to effectively tackle the roots of under-achievement in school. Indeed the very policy of operating a hierarchical structure of programs in upper secondary education helps ensure that low achievement has a rightful place, that is, a set of lower level opportunities are provided, access to which compensates for the inability of school to correct early and cumulative social disadvantage. Traditionally represented as a friend of the working class, vocational education could thus be considered its enemy. But everything depends on the specific ways in which vocational education has been used to reform curricula, the framework of opportunities that is created – both curriculum structure and school provision – and the extent to which under-achievement is tackled in the compulsory years of school. Vocational education is neither friend nor foe, except in the wider context of school system and education policy.

To demonstrate this and to draw out the implications, we examine two contrasting examples of how vocational education has been used to expand educational participation, but in each case has failed to protect young people from the effects of academic selection. The contrast we have chosen is between a predominantly *school-based* approach to using vocational education (France) and a predominantly *employment-based* approach to doing so (Germany). There is some overlap in these two approaches as, on the one hand, France also uses apprenticeship, while on the other hand Germany also runs full-time vocational schools. Neither of these two national models is an example of fundamental reform, and each retains a high degree of social selectivity through academic programs and differentiated provision. However, each provides insights into the more general way in which reform through vocational provision is checked and how failure accumulates in school systems in the course of educational expansion. Long-term improvement, including through the implementation of more inclusive approaches to upper secondary education, hinges on showing how more conservative approaches fail to deliver, not only on the equity front, but on the human capital front as well.

France

The use of vocational courses to increase participation in school is a longstanding feature of education policy in France. For example, in the early 1960s nearly half of all secondary school students were enrolled in vocational courses (Delion, 1973, pp. 89, 99). Many also began pre-vocational and pre-apprenticeship courses when they were 14–15 years old. School-based vocational courses were upgraded from the mid-1960s and continued to enrol a high proportion of secondary school students (41% in 1972–73) (Delion, 1973, p. 99). That vocational courses enrolled academically weaker children is evident from rates of grade-repeating and also, more problematically, from dropout rates – nearly one in five commencing students in short-cycle courses (CAP, *certificat d'aptitude professionnelle*, and BEP. *brevet d'études professionnelles*) (Delion, 1973, p. 93). The rejection of school by dropping out was not economically fatal in these years just before the first oil shock, but the individual and social costs of leaving school without a qualification became unsustainable with the onset of high youth unemployment. The introduction of a technological baccalaureat in the late 1960s – which today contributes half as many baccalaureat graduates as the academic or 'general' award (Ministère de l'Éducation nationale [MEN], 2007, p. 235) – and the development of short-cycle higher education programs, including in senior high school itself, reflect a determination to open schooling to an economy generating opportunities at a higher skill level and condemning unqualified school leavers to prolonged unemployment. But to lay the foundation for higher levels of training, access to vocational courses from early in secondary school was curtailed, the courses were revamped, and in theory they were restricted to students who completed at least 4 years of secondary school (Prost, 1992, pp. 73–88; Rault. 1994, pp. 9–24). As more and more young people stayed on at school – in the absence of full-time work or a broader system of apprenticeship – further reforms were made. In the mid-1980s, the vocational baccalaureat was introduced to enable students to earn a qualification of equivalent status to the general and technological baccalaureats once they had successfully completed a 2-year basic vocational course (the BEP) (Agulhon, 2000, pp. 46–47). In recent decades, the *bac pro* (vocational baccalaureat) has played a major role in expanding participation in upper secondary education, and over the most recent decade has been the only baccalaureat to register growth (MEN, 2007, p. 235).

If policy-makers in France have returned again and again to vocational training as a vehicle of educational reform, this does not mean that mainstream academic programs have been neglected. On the contrary, there is an equally long history of attempting to create a common lower secondary school curriculum, accessible to all, with no early tracking or streaming. The objective has been to raise achievement for children from all social backgrounds. Were this objective to succeed, it would have major implications for the nature of the 2-year basic vocational courses in upper secondary education (CAP, BEP). For these are filled through the processes of academic selection which continue to operate in the common junior high school (*collège*), an institution that is regarded as much as a factory of failure as success (see, for example, *Le Monde de l'Éducation*, no. 311, Février, 2003). The fact that students do have access to vocational courses in upper secondary school arguably relieves the pressure both on curriculum and on teachers to reduce under-achievement in lower secondary school (and earlier). In effect, this is to subordinate the objectives of common schooling to the 'needs' of hierarchical, differentiated schooling.

Policy-makers have endeavoured to reduce early selection and tracking, not only in lower secondary education, but also in mainstream academic programs in upper secondary school. Early specialisation in these 3-year programs has been curtailed in favour of a core with relatively few options in the first year, and more options in the second year. But running parallel to the general and technological baccalaureats, there continue to be the short-cycle vocational courses which represent a 'refuge' from under-achievement in the *collège* (Establet, 2005, p. 150).

This hasty sketch would be quite incomplete if we omitted to discuss a key factor in the production of failure itself: differences in the quality of the learning environments between junior high schools serving different communities (van Zanten, 2001). Put generally, failure comes about because the cognitive and cultural demands made by school grow more difficult the higher the level of schooling, while the home and school resources of poor families become more inadequate. But the widening gap between the demands of school and the cultural and pedagogical resources available to meet them is not experienced uniformly across a school system (for an overview, see Teese, 2007). In France, as in other OECD countries, there are major differences in school environments and these are associated with performance differences. The *collège unique* (common junior high school) is, in practice, not common, but highly differentiated by location, intake and achievement. The marked differences in achievement which are observed at the end of the 4-year program are linked to socioeconomic status (SES), gender and ethnicity. But pooling of multiple 'at-risk' groups of students intensifies the likelihood of failure. Even after controlling for individual characteristics, achievement is significantly lower in the most segregated schools than in others (Felouzis et al., 2005, pp. 56–57). The scope for segregation is becoming wider, thanks to measures to end zoning (*la carte scolaire*) and to free parents to choose (Terrail, 1997, p. 34; van Zanten & Obin,

2008; 'Carte scolaire', 2009). Thus, if the hierarchy of academic and vocational courses in upper secondary education dulls the pedagogical incentive to improve standards for lower SES children – and gives teachers the tools to select (e.g., the class guidance committee, *conseil de classe*) – the social conditions under which these children are educated frustrates and discourages teachers and lower their expectations (Dubet & Duru-Bellat, 2000, pp. 30–35). Access to vocational studies becomes a critical, compensating factor which relieves the stress of pedagogical failure. Parents themselves frequently accept decisions about stream placement (and grade repeating), as if these decisions help them, too, in managing the needs of their failing children. But the children themselves cannot escape the perception of failure and loss of respect which occurs through relegation to the vocational track.

From this perspective, vocational studies are called on to solve not only the problem of individual failure, but of group failure linked to school provision and inferior learning environments. Not only is the status of vocational studies affected by this task, but so too is the effectiveness with which courses work as judged by outcomes – who graduates, who gets a job, what kind of job, what the career prospects are, who continues in study or training, how successful they are. As an illustration, holders of basic vocational awards (CAP, BEP) were the only group of young people exiting the education system in 2004 whose unemployment rate after 3 years was greater than for the cohort of 2001 (around 17%). Those who undertook training for jobs in the services sector had an unemployment rate after 3 years of 22% (BREF, 2008, p. 248).

The French experience illustrates how vocational training has been used to expand educational participation in school without on the other hand protecting vulnerable populations from scholastic failure. A crucial aspect of this experience has been the clear separation between 'academic' and 'vocational'. These concepts have been used to distinguish between programs and to create streams in an ordered hierarchy which can also operate – and in practice do operate – as social streams. Instead of changing the quality of programs in teaching and learning terms, academic and vocational remain separate program structures, but pushed further up to the senior years, delaying choice rather than changing the range and nature of the choices or indeed merging them in more pedagogically inclusive programs. Massification has not brought about reforms based on how children learn, for example, shifting the emphasis from teacher-centred, formal instructional practice to more student-centred approaches. In short, the policy has been not only to put off student choice until later – which in fact does not delay their exposure to the most conservative teaching approaches and expectations – but to put off indefinitely curriculum reform of a more fundamental kind.

Germany

It might be thought that the weaknesses associated with school-based vocational training, as in France, are avoided in countries where apprenticeship plays a very large, even preponderant role. The Dual System in Germany is seen as having kept youth unemployment low over the long term and also, notably, during the recent world economic crisis. 'That Germany – like Austria and the Netherlands – records such a low rate of youth unemployment', writes the *Frankfurter Allgemeiner* (Arbeitslose Jugendliche, 2010), 'is linked to the dual training system'. The strength of this system in securing access to skilled, well-paid jobs for a majority of young people involves positive perceptions on the part of young people themselves, their parents and employers. Apprenticeship is not seen as compensation for failure at school, but as a source of security in a labour market that penalises the unqualified. Moreover, the big role that apprenticeship plays not only underpins a high overall level of participation by young people in education and training, but has protected them up to a point from structural change in the economy and resulting high levels of unemployment. By reducing young people's reliance on formal schooling, the German education system, it could be argued, also reduces their exposure to the scholastic failure evident in countries like France, whose school systems have become 'massified'. In this context, vocational training plays a crucial role, but it does so because it is employment-based and not annexed to schooling.

This argument draws support from comparative unemployment statistics and from adaptability over the long term to changes in industry and occupational patterns in the German economy, at least until fairly recently (Anweiler, 1996, p. 43). However, it ignores important features, both of the school system itself and of the Dual System as an evolving (and only partial) approach to vocational training.

Over time, the Dual System has shown increasing signs of stress and lack of adaptation to labour market changes. Long viewed as socially integrative – compensating for under-achievement at school or for lack of social promotion for low SES children through educational success – the Dual System today recruits from a higher level of schooling than in the past. Young trainees are, on average, graduates of intermediate secondary school (*Realschule*), when in earlier decades they came predominantly from basic secondary school (*Hauptschule*) (Baethge, 2008, p. 568). Increasing numbers of entrants to the Dual System have completed academic schooling and are qualified to enter higher education. The rising qualification level of trainees implies that success at school is playing an increasing role, and conversely that failure to reach higher levels of schooling is growing more important.

While the Dual System remains the most employment-effective sector of vocational training in Germany, it is declining in relative size when compared with other sectors as well as becoming more educationally selective. The other sectors in which young people undertake vocational training include vocational schools and the 'transition system' (*Übergangssystem*). Full-time vocational schooling is provided by intermediate vocational schools (*Berufsfachschulen*) and technical secondary schools (*Fachoberschulen*), from which students can progress to technical higher education. The full-time school sector of vocational training is fairly small in Germany – in contrast, for example, to France – and its share of commencing students in the vocational training system as a whole has remained stable over the last decade at about 17% (Baethge, 2008, p. 556). The 'transition system' covers a mix of different programs which act as bridges for school leavers, but do not themselves lead to a qualification. This diverse bridging sector accounts for almost as many new entrants to vocational training as the Dual System, and its share has been growing (from 32% in 1995 to 40% in 2004). Given the stability of shares in the full-time school sector of vocational training in Germany, this implies that the 'transition system' has grown at the expense of the Dual System (whose share of new entrants fell from 51% to 43% over the same period) (Baethge, 2008, p. 556).

The declining relative importance of the Dual System is symptomatic, not only of problems in adjusting to shifts in industry and employment patterns associated, for example, with the growth of the knowledge economy, but of a growing pattern of exclusion of poorly qualified school leavers. In other words, failure at school increasingly follows the under-achiever into the training market where he or she experiences what could be called 'secondary relegation' (i.e., relegation following a first phase represented by dropout or exclusion from school). The weakest learners, if they do undertake vocational training, more frequently enter the non-qualifying sector – the 'transition system' – in the hope of improving their competitiveness in the labour market, including obtaining an apprenticeship in the Dual System, direct access to which is progressively closing to them. This pattern suggests that the principle of academic selection which delivers low achievers to the labour market both earlier and at a lower level has extended into the operation of the training market. The employment-rich sector of the Dual System and the award-bearing courses offered by full-time vocational courses are becoming less accessible to low achievers, whose academic past haunts them. If the training system does continue to offer a 'safety net', this appears to have many holes, and these have been punctured by the school system. This is apparent, not only from trends in the Dual System – exclusive attention to which gives a distorted picture – but above all in the scale of activity in the 'transition system'. As Baethge observes, 'the critical outcome of structural shift in the vocational training system is the drastic increase in insecurity and the risk of failure at the start of (young people's) working lives which ties them to an expanding transition system' (2008, p. 558).

While, within the training system as a whole, the Dual System is shrinking and also becoming more educationally 'gentrified', it is losing ground to academic schooling and higher education in terms of transition across the whole education system. Between 1992 and 2004, new entrants to the Dual System fell by around 20 percentage points, while the number of commencing students in higher education grew by about 10 percentage points (Baethge, 2008, pp. 554, 555). This confirms the wider trend in OECD countries towards higher levels of participation in upper secondary education – in academic or general programs as distinct from vocational and employment-based training. But it also points to the second trend we noted at the start of this chapter – the widening exposure of the population to scholastic failure. The greater the social emphasis on higher education – as marked by enrolment trends – the more the population as a whole relies on gaining access to the paths of academic promotion in the school system and also on successful passage along these paths.

Social access to academic schooling is markedly unequal in Germany, thanks to early selection, the tripartite division of schools, and the processes of institutional social selection as well as cultural self-selection which this discriminating framework supports (Geißler, 2008, pp. 77–78; Müller & Pollak, 2008, p. 308). These are persistent, though changing features of German education. In the 1960s, only about 15% of 14-year-olds attended grammar school (*Gymnasium*). Social gaps were very large. Working-class children made up only 10% of Grade 10 students (though their fathers represented 45% of the workforce), while the children of civil servants (who made up only 9% of the workforce) took 25% of places (Arbeitsgruppe Bildungsbericht, 1994, p. 507). While these sharp disparities have been significantly reduced, they continue to be very marked. Children from high SES families are three times more likely than low SES children to enrol in a *Gymnasium* (Maaz et al., 2008, p. 205). Many children from less-educated families who do enrol leave at the end of Grade 10 (Rosner, 2006, p. 17), so that the low SES share of Grade 13 classes falls to 14% (compared to a workforce representation of 40%). Teacher judgement and parental perceptions and priorities contribute to early selection, even among children of similar measured ability. In one study it was found, for example, that low SES children had to achieve at about 50% higher than high SES children to gain a recommendation from primary school to go to a *Gymnasium* (cited in Rosner, 2006, p. 12).

Early selection into different types of secondary school varies by region (federal state) in Germany, but in general produces a set of secondary consequences which extend and deepen social disadvantage (Müller & Pollak, 2008, pp. 308–313). The lowest ranking type of school (the *Hauptschule*) has undergone a process of residualisation which has made it at once the socially most homogeneous type of school and the one in which multiple disadvantages of poverty, gender and ethnicity are concentrated (Solga & Wagner, 2008; Geißler, 2008, pp. 74–75). Social and academic filtering of intakes creates different learning environments which either promote achievement or weaken it, and which involve higher or lower expectations on the part of teachers. Differentiation of opportunity on the basis of early selection creates conditions in which both advantage and disadvantage are multiplied, and it is not surprising that large differences in competencies are recorded in PISA tests, both within and between different types of school (PISA-Konsortium, 2004, pp. 243–247).

Progress over time thus presents a mixed picture. If anything, the most vulnerable social groups – immigrant children from poorly educated backgrounds – are worse off today because the schools in which they are disproportionately concentrated have been residualised. On the other hand, access to intermediate secondary education through the *Realschule* has improved to the point where social chances now converge (Geißler, 2008, pp. 74–75; PISA-Konsortium, 2004, p. 244). This is significant because graduating from this type of school improves access to the Dual System, while also opening the door to technical higher education. But progress beyond intermediate secondary education – in the *Gymnasium* and in higher education as a whole, including university – has been much more limited or non-existent. As reflected in the distribution of 15-year-olds, the share of *Gymnasium* places held by young people from the lowest SES quartile is only about 6% (PISA-Konsortium, 2004, p. 244). Poorer relative achievement of low SES students and the comparative economic security represented by the Dual System are factors which keep this share low and prevent more equitable growth in university participation. More of the 'talented poor' steer away. Over the last 20 years, there has been practically no improvement in relative social access to university, with the children of manual workers representing about 17% of students (as against a workforce share of about 40%) (Mayer, 2008, p. 624).

The tripartite organisation of the German school system, while weakening in its rigidity through the declining role of the *Hauptschule* in a number of federal states, thus remains a structure of social exclusion, guarding and multiplying the advantages of the most well-educated families in Germany, and limiting more severely than in most other developed nations the chances of low SES children (Dravenau & Groh-Samberg, 2008, p. 103). This conservative role is compatible with educational expansion (Maaz et al., 2008, p. 214), but depends on flexibility in the sectors of education and training that are not 'high stakes', are able to absorb growth and can dissipate social tension through access to relative benefits. The Dual System does offer these benefits, but its pattern of social use is changing and its relative importance as measured by shares of new entrants to the training system as a whole is declining.

Young people in Germany are increasingly dependent on extended secondary schooling, and as a consequence their exposure to scholastic failure has widened. In the past, children from poorer families were protected from this by the Dual System. But this protection has weakened as the role of qualifications intensifies. To quote Baethge (2008, p. 568), 'A clear qualifications-based segmentation of the German vocational training system is evident in which the fully qualifying channels of training are occupied in the main by teenagers and young adults with intermediate or higher qualifications from school, while the transition system enrols mainly the poorly qualified'. Today failure at school in the form of holding no qualification or only a leaving certificate from a basic secondary school (*Hauptschulabschluss*) increasingly operates to *prevent* entrance to apprenticeship. The devaluation of the basic certificate and economic uncertainty resulting from this constrain young people to make greater use of school or to take refuge in the vocational 'transition system', which itself is a sector of uncertainty, issuing no qualifications and offering only limited and delayed access to apprenticeship. The vocational training system only 'solves' failure by creating a subordinate sector which is uncompetitive and disarmed and made all too accessible through lack of award-bearing courses. It is difficult to escape the impression that social advantage is being protected through the creation of multiple 'buffer zones', both within the school system itself and on its fringes in the vocational training system. The institutional site which shows the least social perturbation, the *Gymnasium*, is guarded on all sides – by lower-level schools, early selection and a hierarchy of vocational options. As the vocational compensations for scholastic failure decline, the dependence of the whole system on the early and largely irreversible production of failure becomes more overt.

Different Systems, Common Functions

Both the French and German systems display an increasing use of extended secondary schooling accompanied by a widening vulnerability of the population to scholastic failure. Vocational training provides only limited compensation for the continuing marked patterns of social selection and exclusion which operate through scholastic failure. Moreover if, as in France, training is provided mainly through schools, trainees are exposed to the logic of preparation for further study within a hierarchy of qualifications as compared to preparation for work. A most telling illustration of this concerns the evolution of the largest basic vocational certificate in France, the BEP (*brevet d'études professionnelles*). As Prost observes (1992, p. 202), by making the BEP a preparatory step to the vocational baccalaureat, policy-makers constrained teachers to prepare students for higher-level studies and to shift the emphasis away from preparation for work, with the resulting risk of reinstalling academic discrimination into a stream of study already fed by failure.

Although the French and German models of vocational training differ sharply, the same underlying functions of absorbing failure and channelling under-achievers into the lower reaches of the labour market are performed. Historically the German vocational training system can claim much lower rates of youth unemployment, and the Dual System in particular has proved adaptable, if to a declining degree. In contrast, vocational training in France has been engineered in the main through the school system. New and higher-level qualifications, based on a broader industry as opposed to a craft orientation, have been deployed. But youth unemployment has remained high, the period leading up to effective insertion into the employed work-force has lengthened, and the system appears to offer little protection against cyclical downturn. However, these differences from a labour market perspective in the performance of the vocational sectors of education systems mask underlying commonalities in institutional functions. These are of great interest from an equity perspective and also in the long run from a human capital angle.

Both the German and the French vocational training systems are constrained by how their school systems work. These display a remarkable historical contrast which is real enough in terms of chronologies, but deceptive as regards function. The tripartite system in Germany has clear parallels with the segmented system of post-primary schooling which existed in France on the eve of the great reforms of the late 1950s and 1960s. French policy-makers could pride themselves on having dismantled this system which, on the contrary, was retained in Germany, despite a major push for reform during the same period and the successful creation of a comprehensive model in the *Gesamptschule*. Germany retained early selection from around the age of 10 to support its segmented system, while France progressively abandoned it, having embraced a comprehensive model. But in fact selection went 'underground' in the *collège unique*. It continues to operate informally through options (like German and Latin), through guidance procedures, but above all through a still strongly teacher-centred academic curriculum working in sharply different and increasingly segregated social settings. Early selection in Germany has not spared socially disadvantaged populations from the demoralisation and relegation they experience in French schools. Indeed, as we have seen, tripartite organisation in Germany, even while evolving towards a more integrated system, has allowed adverse conditions to accumulate at the lowest point in the hierarchy (the *Hauptschule*) and this has worsened educational chances. Again if failure has delayed formal selection until the end of the 4-year junior high school program in

France, the complex hierarchical structure of the upper secondary curriculum and the operation of different types of school at this level (*lycée général et technologique, lycée professionnel*) create an environment of reference which shapes teacher behaviour and student perceptions in the officially unstreamed *collége* (Dubet & Duru-Bellat, 2000, pp. 30–35). There selection starts just as early, but is internalised in teaching and assessment rather than formalised in recommendations at the end of primary school.

Differences of form thus conceal commonalities of function. It is these that influence how well vocational training works and for whom. The function of academic selection operates through different structures, but discriminates through essentially the same cultural organs – school subjects. The consolidation of particular cognitive and generic cultural demands in academic subjects which have an enduring identity and a legal status requires specialisation of teaching effort, a filtering of classes and bureaucratic organisation to deliver competitive results. If Germany achieves this through the *Gymnasium*, France has its *lycées*, and each depends on a subject hierarchy which is more or less structured to marshal the discriminating demands that are made on students. Access to the 'hard' subjects which dominate the hierarchy of the curriculum ensures that social advantage can be converted into academic distinction. It is the preservation of this curriculum hierarchy, albeit in different national forms, which has ensured that progressive expansion of upper secondary education has been accompanied by widening social exposure to failure.

Going Forward

Seen in the perspective of how school systems work, vocational training can be regarded both as the friend that offers protection *and* the foe that delays reform. The broad implications for reform are clear. On the one hand, every effort must be made to close the achievement gap in the early years of school (and indeed poor cognitive growth before then) (Leschinsky, 2008, p. 387). This is borne out by international research on the long-term and cumulative impact of socio-cultural disadvantage (e.g., Feinstein et al., 2004). But, on the other hand, unless intervention in the early years is sustained into higher levels of schooling and backed by consequential structural reforms, the efforts made in the early years risk being wasted. On the premise that a substantial and sustainable raising of achievement amongst low SES and minority children is achieved, where would this leave the hierarchical school systems of Germany and France? What place would there be for a vertical hierarchy of curriculum served by a differentiated school system, if large achievement gaps between rich and poor were drastically reduced? But then it must be asked would it even be possible to compress these gaps if the institutions of academic differentiation in secondary school remained in place? For so long as *Hauptschule, Realschule* and *Gymnasium* exist, so long as *lycée professionnel* subserves *lycée général*, even small relative differences in achievement in primary school will continue to matter and the external signs that mark social origin will suggest that small test scores are even bigger than they are and of wider import.

In a context in which the use of extended secondary school is rising and with it the range of the population exposed to failure, reforming the curriculum of secondary schools cannot consist simply of adding vocational streams, as if what was required was a sanctuary or asylum free of academic scrutiny. The German example shows that hierarchies develop *within training systems*, that the most valuable locations are increasingly reserved for better qualified candidates. Furthermore, a larger and larger system is required to compensate for the relative lack of training places, while being prevented, on the other hand, from challenging the 'gold standard' of regulated apprenticeship by issuing its own awards. Generations of young people experience discrimination through this system which, at the same time, lowers their productivity as workers over the long term, increases the risk of anti-social behaviour, and drives up the social costs associated with unemployment, disability, welfare dependency and criminal justice.

The French example of relying on vocational options in school to support rising levels of educational attainment shows how vulnerability operates through the way in which preparation for higher study overrules preparation for work, thus refusing escape from academic discrimination, even for low achievers. Moreover, the French experience brings out even more forcefully the sense of injustice associated with relegation – as manifest in street violence and car burnings – and driven home by persistent, sometimes astronomic levels of youth unemployment. Over the last 20 years, the unemployment rate for 15- to 24-year-olds has never fallen below 18% (Goux & Nouveau, 2007, p. 84). But it also reveals injustice at the high end of a hierarchical system. For there, the pursuit of academic excellence leads to a virtual social monopoly at the most lucrative sites of the education system, and these consume resources on a scale incompatible with raising achievement in the schools of the poor. Expenditure per student in the preparatory classes of the *grandes écoles* is 1.75 times higher than expenditure on pupils in junior high school (MEN, 2007: 333), while within higher education there are even larger gaps between elite and mass sectors (Maurin, 2007, pp. 235–236; Renaut, 2002, p. 81).

If, in France, the dismantling of the structures of academic selection in junior high school has been checked by re-erecting them in senior high school (and beyond), this is because segregating more academic pupils – first by type of school and then by stream – also creates a culture of teaching and learning and a veneration of theoretical and abstract studies which marginalises innovation and reform in the sectors or in the schools deserted by the elite. The insights into student learning which have been gained through years of experience in comprehensive schooling and in vocational education and training can gain no foothold in academic schooling. There the aim is to distinguish between children through the most conservative means of teaching and assessment. Writing of the policy of building bridges between academic and vocational streams in France, Rault observes: 'Instead of being enriched by teaching and learning in vocational and technical training, secondary education has been content to open a few doors to a few deserters from an inferior stream…and to enhance the prestige of the 'noble' and much coveted stream by creating bridges. In this way, not only are vocational studies condemned, but academic schooling is impoverished' (1994, p. 15).

Applied, collaborative and problem-based learning – which might summarise the philosophy of vocational education and training – should extend into the territory of the most academically demanding subjects so that they become interesting and manageable thanks to the manner in which they are taught rather than endured as part of the 'craft' of students for the economic value they deliver. It requires not only a blurring of the boundaries between 'academic' and 'vocational' in the formal frameworks of curriculum – as, for example, in some Nordic models of upper secondary education – but a pedagogical transformation which operates across all strands to ensure that young people from all social backgrounds can be exposed to high cognitive demands, but properly supported. This assumes that the top-down pressure for selection which acts through a hierarchy of 'noble' and 'base' streams of higher education is relieved. But does that not also require basic reform, not only of structures, but of processes of teaching and learning in higher education itself?

In the end, the solution to equity lies in *raising demands* on young people, not lowering them through less challenging streams, including vocational options. If this is followed through consistently, there can be no question of retaining structures which allow the socially most advantaged families to exploit the narrowest academic means of preserving status under the guise of achievement – in effect *lowering demands on their children* – while systematically removing challenge and value from the educational experience of the poor.

References

Agulhon, C. (2000). L'enseignement professionnel, entre rénovation et domination. In A. van Zanten (Ed.), *L'école, l'état des savoirs* (pp. 44–53). Paris: La Découverte.

Anweiler, O. (1996). Deutschland. In O. Anweiler, U. Boos-Nünning, G. Brinkmann, et al. (Eds.), *Bildungssysteme in Europa*. Weinheim/Basel: Beltz.

Arbeitsgruppe Bildungsbericht am Max-Planck-Institut für Bildungsforschung. (1994). *Das Bildungswesen in der Bundesrepublik Deutschland*. Reinbek: Rowohlt.

Arbeitslose Jugendliche kommen Deutschland teuer zu stehen. (2010, February 8). *Frankfurter Allgemeiner*.

Baethge, M. (2008). Das berufliche Bildungswesen in Deutschland am Beginn des 21. Jahrhunderts. In K. S. Cortina, J. Baumert, A. Leschinsky, et al. (Eds.), *Das Bildungswesen in der Bundesrepublik Deutschland* (pp. 541–597). Reinbek: Rowohlt.

BREF. (2008, January). *Génération 2004, des jeunes pénalisés par la conjoncture* (Centre d'études et de recherches sur les qualifications No. 248). Marseille: CEREQ.

Carte scolaire: la Cour des comptes dénonce la ghettoïsation de colleges. (2009, November 9). *La Lettre de l'Éducation, 646*.

Delion, A. G. (1973). *L'Éducation en France. Problèmes et perspectives*. Paris: La Documentation française.

Dravenau, D., & Groh-Samberg, O. (2008). Bildungsbenachteiligung als Institutioneneffekt. Zur Verschränkung kultureller und institutioneller Diskriminierung. In P. Berger & H. Kahlert (Eds.), *Institutionalisierte Ungleichheiten. Wie das Bildungswesen Chancen blockiert* (2nd ed., pp. 103–129). Weinheim/München: Juventa.

Dubet, F., & Duru-Bellat, M. (2000). *L'hypocrisie scolaire. Pour un collège enfin démocratique*. Paris: Seuil.

Establet, R. (Ed.). (2005). *Radiographie du peuple lycéen. Pour changer le lycée*. Paris: ESF Editeur.

Feinstein, L., Duckworth, K., & Sabates, R. (2004). *A model of the inter generational transmission of educational success* (Wider Benefits of Learning Research Report No. 10). London: Centre for Research on the Wider Benefits of Learning.

Felouzis, G., Liot, F., & Perroton, J. (2005). *L'apartheid scolaire: enquête*. Paris: Seuil.

Geißler, R. (2008). Die Metamorphose der Arbeitertochter zum Migrantensohn. Zum Wandel der Chancenstruktur im Bildungssystem nach Schicht, Geschlecht, Ethnie und deren Verknüpfungen. In P. Berger, & H. Kahlert (Eds.), *Institutionalisierte Ungleichheiten. Wie das Bildungswesen Chancen blockiert* (2nd ed., pp. 71–100). Weinheim/München: Juventa.

Goux, D., & Nouveau, C. (2007). Expansion scolaire et insertion professionnelle: une évaluation de l'ouverture du lycée depuis le début des années 1980. In D. Cohen (Ed.), *Une jeunesse difficile. Portrait économique et social de la jeunesse française* (pp. 82–106). Paris: Éditions ENS.

Lamb, S. (2008). *Alternative pathways to high school graduation: An international comparison* (Report No. 7, California Dropout Research Project). Santa Barbara, CA: UCSB.

Leschinsky, A. (2008). Die Hauptschule – von der Be – zur Enthauptung. In K. S. Cortina, J. Baumert, A. Leschinsky, et al. (Eds.), *Das Bildungswesen in der Bundesrepublik Deutschland* (pp. 377–406). Reinbek: Rowohlt.

Maaz, K., Baumert, J., & Cortina, K. S. (2008). Soziale und regionale Ungleichheit im deutschen Bildungssystem. In K. S. Cortina, J. Baumert, A. Leschinsky, et al. (Eds.), *Das Bildungswesen in der Bundesrepublik Deutschland* (pp. 205–243). Reinbek: Rowohlt.

Maurin, E. (2007). *La nouvelle question scolaire. Les bénéfices de la démocratisation*. Paris: Seuil.

Mayer, K. U. (2008). Das Hochschulwesen. In K. S. Cortina, J. Baumert, A. Leschinsky, et al. (Eds.), *Das Bildungswesen in der Bundesrepublik Deutschland* (pp. 599–645). Reinbek bei Hamburg: Rowohlt.

Ministère de l'Éducation nationale (MEN). (2007). *Repères et Références Statiques sur les enseignements, la formation et la recherche*. Paris: Ministère de l'Éducation nationale.

Müller, W., & Pollak, R. (2008). Weshalb gibt es so wenige Arbeiterkinder in Deutschlands Universitäten. In R. Becker & W. Lauterbach (Eds.), *Bildung als Privileg* (3rd ed., pp. 307–346). Wiesbaden:VS Verlag für Sozialwissenschaften.

PISA-Konsortium. (2004). *PISA 2003. Der Bildungsstand der Jugendlichen in Deutschland - Ergebnisse des zweiten internationalen Vergleichs*. Münster/New York: Waxmann.

Prost, A. (1992). *Éducation, société et politiques*. Paris: Seuil.

Rault, C. (1994). *La formation professionnelle initiale. Contraste et similitudes en France et en Europe* (Notes et études documentaires, no 4987, pp. 1–146). Paris: La Documentation française.

Renaut, A. (2002). *Que faire des universités?* Paris: Bayard.

Rosner, A. (2006). *Die Erklärung der Reproduktion sozialer Ungleichheit durch das deutsche Bildungssystem mittels der Kapitaltheorie von Pierre Bourdieu*. München: GRIN Verlag.

Shavit, Y., & Müller, W. (2000). Vocational secondary education. *European Societies, 2*(1), 29–50.

Solga, H., & Wagner, S. (2008). Die Zurückgelassenen - die soziale Verarmung der Lernumwelt von Hauptschülerinnen und Hauptschülern. In R. Becker & W. Lauterbach (Eds.), *Bildung als Privileg* (3rd ed., pp. 191–219). Wiesbaden: VS Verlag für Sozialwissenschaften.

Teese, R. (2007). Time and space in the reproduction of educational inequality. In R. Teese, S. Lamb & M. Duru-Bellat (Eds.), *International studies in educational inequality, theory and policy* (Vol. 1, pp. 1–22). Dordrecht: Springer.

Terrail, J-P. (1997). L'essor des scolarités et ses limites. In J-P. Terrail (Ed.), *La scolarisation de la France. Critique de l' état des lieux* (pp. 21–36). Paris: La Dispute.

van Zanten, A. (2001). *L'école de le périphérie. Scolarité et ségrégation en banlieue*. Paris: PUF.

van Zanten, A., & Obin, J-P. (2008). *La carte scolaire*. Paris: PUF.

Chapter 17
Pathways to Completion for School Dropouts

John Polesel, Adrianna Nizińska and Ewa Kurantowicz

Introduction

What opportunities are provided for young people who drop out of school to
re-engage in study and obtain upper secondary qualifications? Mass secondary
schooling has brought about significant change in the kinds of learners entering
upper secondary education. Once primarily focused on university entry, school
systems have had to diversify their curriculum offerings to cater for the needs of a
broader range of learners whose aspirations include vocational training and direct
entry to the labour market, as well as university. These demands have exerted
considerable pressure on schools, on their curricula and on the upper secondary
qualifications that they offer. School systems have had variable success in meeting
these demands and in some countries large numbers of young people still drop out
of school and need to rely on alternative pathways – mostly outside of the school
system – to obtain upper secondary qualifications. These pathways can include
vocational education courses and apprenticeships, equivalent credentials, as well as
the more traditional academic upper secondary qualifications. Sites of provision
include further education colleges, technical and vocational education institutions,
community colleges, adult schools, and, in some countries, even secondary schools
offering 'second chance' or 're-entry' programs for dropouts.

The aim of this chapter is to examine some of the opportunities provided in
different countries for obtaining upper secondary qualifications for young people
who have dropped out of school. This will exclude discussion of the traditional or
school-based pathways to completion such as school-based vocational education
and apprenticeships, even if that activity occurs in designated or separate secondary
schools. Vocational programs in many European systems are located within the
framework of upper secondary schooling, rather than within a framework of adult

J. Polesel (✉)
Melbourne Graduate School of Education, University of Melbourne, Australia

A. Nizińska and E. Kurantowicz
University of Lower Silesia, Poland

S. Lamb et al. (Eds.), *School Dropout and Completion: International Comparative
Studies in Theory and Policy*, DOI 10.1007/978-90-481-9763-7_20,
© Springer Science+Business Media B.V. 2011

357

or further education. Instead, this chapter will focus on the range of activity outside of secondary schools – by and large in adult and community education centres and further education colleges, although not exclusively so – involving education and training leading to upper secondary qualifications for dropouts. To discuss the main forms of provision for dropouts in these alternative settings, the chapter is divided into two main sections: (1) vocational education, and (2) adult and community education.

Vocational Education Pathways

This section focuses on vocational education delivered outside secondary schools in what is described in some systems as the adult or further education sector. The prevalence and strength of this sector varies considerably across countries and this, in turn, affects the capacity for dropouts in some nations to use it as a pathway to gain an upper secondary qualification or equivalent.

In Australia, there is an extensive vocational education and training sector, predominantly comprised of publicly funded Technical and Further Education (TAFE) institutes, though private providers increasingly have become important players. This sector offers the principal pathway for dropouts seeking initial qualifications. Faced with stubbornly low rates of school completion, Australian policy-makers have recently established a range of school completion targets that include recognition of the role of TAFE institutes and other providers in delivery of upper secondary qualifications (whether an upper secondary school certificate or its 'equivalent'). While only a small proportion of school-aged young people in Australia use TAFE in this way – the vast majority of 16- and 17-year-olds who are in full-time education are in schools – quite a large number of school dropouts do, with many entering apprenticeships or traineeships and other forms of vocational education leading to upper secondary-equivalent qualifications (for estimates see Lamb & Mason, 2008; Robinson & Lamb, 2009; Lamb, 2010). Wyn et al. (2004) argue that these programs and settings may be effective pathways for dropouts, although not in all cases. Data from a 2007 school leaver survey in the Australian state of Victoria (Teese et al., 2007) suggest that non-apprenticeship vocational education provides a pathway to completion for a relatively small proportion of dropouts – 12.6% of males and 21.9% of females. If, however, transition to apprenticeships and to traineeships is added, these proportions increase (to 45.2% of males and 22.5% of females).

In England, too, there is a strong post-school vocational education and training system. However, the concept of a recovery mechanism, of education and training programs being available for school dropouts to re-engage in education and obtain upper secondary qualifications, is somewhat more difficult to apply. Post-16, vocational education and training is considered a legitimate pathway for those who fail to achieve the General Certificate of Secondary Education (GCSE) benchmarks of five A* to C grade passes including mathematics and English. The provision of vocational education, for the most part in the Further Education colleges, therefore might be regarded as a school-equivalent pathway. Certainly, in the formulation of national targets for school completion or its equivalent, they are seen to play a major role, with full-time education, work-based learning and part-time education or training all satisfying the requirements for meeting these targets (Sullivan & Unwin, 2010). Some now predominantly cater for a youth market, although most began serving mainly adults and now play an expanded role in dealing with school-aged young people. They are not vocational secondary schools, as might be found in the continental systems, and most young people do not attend these settings to obtain 'A levels' (senior secondary completion qualifications), although some may. However, while Further Education colleges are clearly not schools and have origins firmly rooted in the tradition of adult provision, they have come to represent a pathway for some young people who would be defined as dropouts in other countries. Wong et al. (2006) argue for the efficacy of these programs in giving young people opportunities for success, although Sullivan and Unwin (2010) note that it is the students who want to continue their schooling but fail to reach the GCSE benchmark who enter these programs in Further Education colleges. This in turn results in an intake dominated by disadvantaged students, who are further disadvantaged by the fact that colleges are funded at a lower rate than schools.

In Scotland, where the Youth Guarantee is designed to ensure that all 16- to 17-year-olds not in education or training are entitled to work-based vocational training (Raffe, 2010), vocational education and training provision external to secondary schools also plays a role for this age group. Apprenticeships offer a further pathway but are dependent on supply and subject to variations in quality.

Other nations included as case studies in this book – Iceland, Poland and Finland among them – also include programs for dropouts in their more traditional adult vocational education provision, although, given the strength of school-based vocational education in these nations, such programs do not play the role to the same extent as seen in the English context (Blondal et al., 2010; Mikiewicz, 2010; Rinne & Jarvinen, 2010). There are both public and private institutions which run courses designed to provide young people with vocational skills and qualifications. They include, for example, the Institutions of Professional Training in Poland, which cater for both adult and school-aged students. These deal with a broad range of age groups and consist of education centres for youth and adults at the post-lower secondary level, and training centres offering courses, seminars and workshops and delivering practical vocational skills. They include within their scope the provision of basic skills, vocational qualifications and the upgrading of existing skills and qualifications. These programs may in some cases play a broader role than simply education and training, also delivering services relating to harm prevention and rehabilitation as well as assisting youth at risk of unemployment, and youth requiring special support or mentoring. In Finland, the programs may target both dropouts and those at risk of dropout. They are designed to provide young people with a basic or vocational school certificate as an equivalent to the traditional school leaving certificate and activities include a significant amount of time in workplace learning which is competency-assessed. The programs, which can be costly, are supported financially by the European Union (EU). A similar EU initiative in France also targets early leavers with a program combining vocational education and basic literacy and numeracy, although its reach is limited and it does not deliver certificates or qualifications that can be considered upper secondary equivalent (Blanchard, 2010). Limited reach, lack of funding and lack of continuity characterise similar programs offered at the national and regional level in Spain (Merino et al., 2010).

In other systems, where alternative provision of vocational education has a much lower profile, there are fewer options for dropouts and the opportunities for a pathway to upper secondary completion are negligible. In Norway, for example, vocational programs are offered within the context of secondary schooling only and no other providers deal with this age group. In fact, Markussen et al. (2010) argue that the *Follow-Up Service*, a program designed to assist dropouts re-enter education and training, was hampered by the fact that the only option it had was to advise dropouts to re-enter the same schooling system which they had dropped out of. The authors argue that another option within schools, *competence at a lower level* – a certificate provided to students who do not qualify for university or do not receive a vocational qualification – provides young people at risk of dropping out with a way of recognising their upper secondary participation. They argue that this option is rarely considered as a planned initial strategy, but rather is awarded as a default 'certificate', acting more as a euphemism for failure. The qualification is not equivalent to other upper secondary qualifications because it does not provide access to tertiary study, it is not standards-based in the same way as the mainstream qualifications and it carries very little 'value' in the labour market.

In Germany and Switzerland, school completion is defined broadly, with the Dual System (apprenticeship) pathway included among the mainstream school pathways, as are school-based vocational (non-apprenticeship) pathways. Outside these school-based tracks, there are few opportunities for school dropouts to gain upper secondary qualifications. In Switzerland, an exception is the transitional programs, provided as a pathway for young people who cannot obtain an apprenticeship due to labour market conditions and lack of opportunities provided by employers. Transitional programs are designed to channel young people back into school or into an apprenticeship, a result which is achieved for approximately two thirds to three quarters of the young people in this situation (Pagnossin, 2010). Similarly, in Germany, 'transition system' programs provide a basic preparation for dropouts from school to enable them to enter award-bearing vocational education – but this need not lead to completion.

The United States context is not unlike the United Kingdom or Australia in terms of the role of its tertiary adult sector (mainly comprising community colleges) in delivering vocational education and training. However, in the United States, the community colleges play a negligible role in providing pathways to completion for high school dropouts. This may in part relate to the fact that there is little consistency in skill standards and qualifications across the states (Office for Official Publications of the European Communities [OOPEC], 2002). Exceptions include initiatives such as the *Gateway Program*, which partners a school and a community college in the delivery of the traditional high school diploma (Hyslop, 2007). The inclusion of the school in the partnership is mandated by legislation which disallows community colleges from delivering the high school diploma. However, this type of program is rare and is, moreover, concerned with the mainstream high school diploma rather than an equivalent.

In the American context, while there is little discussion of alternative provision, there is an alternative *certificate* – based on General Educational Development (GED) test results. Murnane et al. (2000) and Bracey (1995) have both found longer term labour market and higher earnings benefits as a result of completing the GED. However, the latter notes that alternative instructional settings might be preferable for young people who fail to achieve a high school diploma in traditional settings. Recovery programs may also be offered in alternative settings and Rumberger (2010) notes that a number of factors are associated with effective programs, including a non-threatening learning environment, caring, committed and responsible staff, positive culture and a low student-teacher ratio. However problems were also identified in the delivery of these programs, including a perception of them as symbolising failure, and uncertain and inconsistent funding.

There has been little comparative evaluation of the relevance and success of vocational education pathways for completion of initial qualifications. Little is known, for example, of the relative success of different programs and the features associated with what works best and why, particularly when viewed from a cross-national perspective. The area is relatively under-researched and under-theorised. There has been a lot of work in each country on the reasons why young people become disengaged and drop out of school and therefore what tertiary education institutions may need to address in attempting to re-engage dropouts, such as the need for imaginative teaching approaches and motivated teachers who enjoy working with young people, effective pastoral care, attention to individual needs, adult settings in which young people are treated with respect, and small class sizes.

Wyn et al. (2004) note that while these features may be vital to successful pathways they are often missing from the existing programs in the adult and further education sector and that a more consistent approach is necessary when addressing the particular needs of school dropouts. Other studies (e.g., Polesel et al., 2004) have also suggested that the range of programs and background and experience of vocational education and training sector staff may not always provide the best experiences for this group. The evidence indicates that while more institutions may become increasingly involved in the provision of programs for dropouts, their role is not a large one, their effectiveness is uneven and they may not be appropriate for the majority of young people in this situation.

Adult and Community Education Pathways

Dropouts in Schools for Adults

In many countries, adult education systems offer opportunities to help re-engage students who have dropped out of school. Generally speaking, it can be said that adult education covers three areas of education: general, vocational and life skills (personal, cultural and social). This section of the chapter concentrates on the general area, that which enables participants, first, to complete an upper secondary qualification, and, second, to access further stages of education. These two 'benefits' are also available to younger students, who for various reasons have dropped out of school and re-commence their learning in the adult education sector. There is, inevitably, some overlap with some of the courses described in the previous section, as many adult learning classes integrate aspects of vocational education in their approaches. As in the previous section, the analysis here is based on relevant data provided in the country chapters and on the authors' own research and experience in this field.

Adult education consists of education organised by various central (national government and ministry of education) organisations, non-governmental educational initiatives (societies, foundations, etc.) and by employers, depending on the country. Financing for these forms of education comes from public funds (government), non-government or private sources (sponsors, employers and students). All of these different forms (in terms of organisation and funding) of adult education appear in the country analyses in this book. In the majority, adult education is also made available to non-traditional students, that is, young people who have dropped out of school.

Most of the education systems presented in this book adopt strategies that involve the inclusion of school dropouts in existing forms of adult education. In Canada, adult sector providers run courses which are available both to adults returning to study and to school leavers aged 16 or older seeking an alternative learning setting. Janosz et al. (2010) note that the adult sector is becoming increasingly attractive to dropouts seeking a less authoritarian learning environment than that provided in schools. However, the authors also note that the less structured style of adult learning may not provide the support and motivation needed by dropouts.

In Scotland, too, school-aged students may enter adult vocational colleges, which, however, are not always equipped to deal with the needs of disaffected youth (Raffe, 2010). In Spain, courses for dropouts are offered in adult institutions originally designed to combat illiteracy and the problems of unemployment in the adult population. Data suggest that 40% of students enrolled in these schools in order to obtain the Secondary Education Certificate are under the age of 20 (Merino & Garcia, 2010).

Two main organisational approaches are adopted in the provision of these kinds of courses. In some cases, evening classes for adults are organised at secondary schools but are delivered in 'senior' classes and departments. For dropouts who participate in these classes, this carries the advantage that it does not force them to leave the school they attended prior to dropping out (e.g., Iceland, Poland). Most of the country analyses, however, describe programs in which school dropouts have access to and participate in programs which were designed around the needs of adult learners (e.g., Canada, United States). Frequently, these institutions offer not only general education (as in *second chance* education leading to an upper secondary qualification or equivalent), but also other forms of vocational education and scope for the development of life skills. Some examples of such institutions are lifelong learning centres in Iceland, and Adult and Community Education providers in Australia. It might also be noted that there are small numbers of adult re-entry schools in some states in Australia which dropouts access, schools which aim to deliver secondary school qualifications (Lamb, 2010). Focusing on dropouts wishing to re-engage in a mainstream senior secondary school certificate, they are often co-located in existing upper secondary schools (Polesel, 2002).

What Happens to Dropouts in Adult Education Settings?

There has been some research examining the suitability of adult education settings for school dropouts. It points to the discord between the needs and backgrounds of dropouts and the outlooks and goals of adult learners, those for whom the sector was originally designed. Dropouts leave school for a range of reasons, many having become disaffected learners with high levels of personal and social support needs. It is not apparent that there are many adult education settings geared to address these particular needs and issues. Adult education theorists sometimes take the view that the processes of adult and non-adult teaching and learning significantly differ from one another and require different skills of teachers. These differences have not only a psychological dimension (needs, motivations, attitudes and the scope of experiences), as defined by Knowles et al. (2005), but also a social and cultural one, which results from the personal and professional context of the everyday life of adult and non-adult students. This means that adult education settings may not always meet the needs of school dropouts, because of the conflicting role that must be served in addressing the needs and dispositions of their more traditional adult users. There is also the issue of the context of learners' age and motivation, with young people, particularly dropouts, often seeking initial qualifications and acquisition of education and training skills that will assist in accessing further study and entry to the labour market, while adults are often looking to achieve life goals in many other areas of life, including social, professional or family ones (Illeris, 2002).

Dropouts bring to the adult setting educational experiences often different from those which are characteristic of adult students. They are frequently burdened with long-term scholastic failure, have become disengaged from learning and suffer from various personal and social issues which contributed to their dropping out of school. They are often educationally neglected, have low self-esteem and lack faith in their own capacities (Nizińska, 2008). These issues require particular support in educational settings if they are to be addressed successfully, meaning that adult education providers have to play a socio- and psycho-therapeutic role for dropouts as well as an educational one. This tendency can alter the focus of adult education.

One of the main reasons dropouts enter adult education is the organisational culture and climate of these settings and programs. The features that are particularly relevant and appreciated by dropouts include: being treated as an adult (which is symbolised by the word 'adult' in the name of the institution), alternative ways of working, freedom, independence and learner responsibility (see Nizińska & Kurantowicz, 2008). In a way, the rituals of adult sector institutions and the philosophy of adult education support the process of recovering school dropouts, offering them a quick 'promotion' to the adult world. Optimistically, this means that in these settings, dropouts gain the chance for recognition in being treated as an adult in their education and, through it, in social and public life. This recognition reduces the sense of social exclusion that dropouts feel due to their failed secondary school experiences.

Conclusion

A key issue for the success of pathways to completing initial qualifications for dropouts is the ability for relevant institutions and programs to meet the needs of this group. This message emerges strongly from the two sections in this chapter. The research evidence on the success in meeting these needs is mixed. Some institutions delivering vocational education question their own track record in meeting the needs of dropouts, while adult schools face the same question when they attempt to cater to the needs of both younger and older students in the same settings.

On the one hand, the pathways for dropouts outside of secondary schools have been shown to offer an important second chance for many dropouts. Vocational education programs delivered in such settings as further education or community colleges may provide more mature learning environments for young people alienated by the discipline and authority structures of schools, not to mention more effective pathways to the labour market. On the other hand, there is evidence that such settings can struggle when confronted with the pastoral care needs of school dropouts.

Similarly, adult education providers, dealing with students scarred by the experience of school, may find themselves having to play a quasi-therapeutic role, re-socialising and re-integrating young people into learning environments leading to recognised qualifications, as well as re-establishing pathways for them into the labour market and lifelong learning. But here too, problems emerge. Adult education is often a system of institutions designed for adult learners and is poorly equipped to meet the substantial needs of young people who have failed to have their needs addressed adequately in the secondary school system. Many school dropouts present with a complex and demanding set of problems and specific needs, such as lack of training and work experience, learning difficulties, lack of family support, difficult social backgrounds, premature parenthood and a general need for counselling and guidance. Programs in the tertiary and adult education sectors can be attractive for this group, as they offer a more adult learning environment and are designed to improve employability by providing market relevant education and training through the attainment of upper secondary qualifications. Several factors should be considered in developing policies to assist school dropouts in the tertiary and adult education sectors. Among the most important considerations are: early action, precise targeting, designing programs relevant to local or national labour market needs, integrating and combining services into a 'comprehensive package', and extensive involvement of all social partners and public authorities (Martin & Grubb, 2001; Quintini et al., 2007).

It may also be important to remember the origins of dropout and why there is a need for recovery at all. It is essential that efforts in all systems focus on prevention, that is, prevention of dropout from school. Te Riele (2006) has suggested that focusing on the attributes and characteristics of dropouts as the source of the problem allows us to deflect attention away from what is wrong with our secondary schools. Privileging alternative approaches to delivery of upper secondary school programs in tertiary or adult education settings may well do the same thing. Building up alternative pathways for dropouts can lead us into the trap of failing to address the deep-seated problems within schools themselves. Moreover, the availability of alternatives in itself is no guarantee of more effective processes of choice. As Lund (2008) argues in the Swedish context there is evidence that increased 'choice' in that country has disadvantaged lower socioeconomic status students.

The evidence from the chapters in this book suggests that pathways to completion for school dropouts provided through adult and further education institutions can play a role in increasing the numbers of young people who gain upper secondary qualifications, though the size and nature of this role varies across countries depending on institutional arrangements and programs. Polesel et al. (2004) suggest that many adult-sector teachers dealing with school-aged students question their own ability to meet the duty of care and pastoral needs of this age group, not to mention their ability to provide the range of programs (both general and vocational) required to cater for the diverse needs of this group. The mixed picture presented in this chapter of the role played by alternative pathways for dropouts indicates that such pathways will continue to offer important opportunities for some dropouts to gain initial qualifications, but will struggle to meet the needs of all.

References

Blanchard, M. (2010). The question of school dropout: A French perspective. In S. Lamb, E. Markussen, R. Teese, N. Sandberg & J. Polesel (Eds.), *School dropout and completion: International comparative studies in theory and policy*. Dordrecht: Springer.

Blondal, K. S., Jonasson, J. T., Tannhauser, A-C. (2010). Dropout in a small society: Is the Icelandic case somehow different? In S. Lamb, E. Markussen, R. Teese, N. Sardberg & J. Polesel (Eds.), *School dropout and completion: International comparative studies in theory and policy*. Dordrecht: Springer.

Bracey, G. (1995). To GED or not to GED. *Phi Delta Kappan, 77*(3), 257.

Hyslop, A. (2007). Flexible learning opportunities to encourage re-entry and completion. *Techniques: Connecting Education and Careers, 82*(3), 33–35.

Illeris, K. (2002). Understanding the conditions of adult learning. *Adults Learning (NIACE)14*(4), 18–20.

Janosz, M. (2010). Educational systems and school dropout in Canada. In S. Lamb, E. Markussen, R. Teese, N. Sandberg & J. Polesel (Eds.), *School dropout and completion: International comparative studies in theory and policy*. Dordrecht: Springer.

Knowles, M., Holton, E., & Swanson, R. (2005). *The adult learner: The definitive classic in adult education and human resource development*. California: Elsevier.

Lamb, S. (2010). School dropout and completion in Australia. In S. Lamb, E. Markussen, R. Teese, N. Sandberg & J. Polesel (Eds.), *School dropout and completion: International comparative studies in theory and policy*. Dordrecht: Springer.

Lamb, S. & Mason, K. (2008). *How young people are faring, 2008*. Melbourne: Foundation for Young Australians. Retrieved from http://www.fya.org.au/downloads/FYA_HYPAFReport_ONLINE_68pp.pdf

Lund, S. (2008). Choice paths in the Swedish upper secondary education – A critical discourse analysis of recent reforms. *Journal of Education Policy, 23*(6), 633–648.

Markussen, E., Frøseth, M. W., Sandberg, N., Lødding, B., & Borgen, J. S. (2010). Early leaving, non-completion and completion in upper secondary education in Norway. In S. Lamb, E. Markussen, R. Teese, N. Sandberg & J. Polesel (Eds.), *School dropout and completion: International comparative studies in theory and policy*. Dordrecht: Springer.

Martin, J. P., & Grubb, W. (2001). What works and for whom: A review of OECD countries' experiences with active labour market policies. *Swedish Economic Policy Review, 8*(2), 9–56.

Merino, R., & Garcia, M. (2010). School dropout and completion in Spain. In S. Lamb, E. Markussen, R. Teese, N. Sandberg & J. Polesel (Eds.), *School dropout and completion: International comparative studies in theory and policy*. Dordrecht: Springer.

Mikiewicz, P. (2010). School dropout in secondary education: The case of Poland. In S. Lamb, E. Markussen, R. Teese, N. Sandberg & J. Polesel (Eds.), *School dropout and completion: International comparative studies in theory and policy*. Dordrecht: Springer.

Murnane, R., Willett, J., & Tyler, J. (2000). Who benefits from obtaining a GED? Evidence from high school and beyond. *Review of Economics & Statistics, 82*(1), 23–37.

Nizińska, A. (2008). *Między nauczaniem a uczeniem się. Edukacyjne swiaty andragogów-praktyków*. Wrocław: Wydawnictwo Naukowe DSW.

Nizińska, A., & Kurantowicz, E. (2008). Najtrudniejsze podróże edukacyjne. Szkoły dla dorosłych w zmieniających się społeczno – kulturowych kontekstach. *Studia Edukacyjne,* 8/2008, 185–200.

Office for Official Publications of the European Communities (OOPEC). (2002). *Agora V: identification, evaluation and recognition of non-formal learning*. Papers from CEDEFOP Conference, Thessaloniki, March 15 & 16, 1999.

Pagnossin, E. (2010). School dropout and completion in Switzerland. In S. Lamb, E. Markussen, R. Teese, N. Sandberg & J. Polesel (Eds.), *School dropout and completion: International comparative studies in theory and policy*. Dordrecht: Springer.

Polesel, J. (2002). Schools for young adults: Senior colleges in Australia. *Australian Journal of Education, 46*(2), 205–221.

Polesel, J., Helme, S., Davies, M., Teese, R., Nicholas, T., & Vickers, M. (2004). *VET in Schools. A post-compulsory education perspective*. Adelaide: NCVER.

Quintini, G., Martin J., & Martin P. (2007). *The changing nature of the school-to-work transition process in OECD countries*. IZA Discussion Paper 2582. Paper presented at the Conference on the European Social Model 'Joining forces for a social Europe', Nuremberg, February 8 & 9, 2007.

Raffe, D. (2010). Participation in post-compulsory learning in Scotland. In S. Lamb, E. Markussen, R. Teese, N. Sandberg & J. Polesel (Eds.), *School dropout and completion: International comparative studies in theory and policy*. Dordrecht: Springer.

Rinne, R., & Jarvinen, T. (2010). Dropout and completion in upper secondary education in Finland. In S. Lamb, E. Markussen, R. Teese, N. Sandberg & J. Polesel (Eds.), *School dropout and completion: International comparative studies in theory and policy*. Dordrecht: Springer.

Robinson, L., & Lamb, S. (2009). *How young people are faring, 2009*. Foundation for Young Australians. Retrieved from http://www.fya.org.au/wpcontent/uploads/2009/05/FYA_HYPAFReportWEB3.pdf

Rumberger, R. (2010). High school dropouts in the United States. In S. Lamb, E. Markussen, R. Teese, N. Sandberg & J. Polesel (Eds.), *School dropout and completion: International comparative studies in theory and policy*. Dordrecht: Springer.

Sullivan, A., & Unwin, L. (2010). Towards compulsory participation in England. In S. Lamb, E. Markussen, R. Teese, N. Sandberg & J. Polesel (Eds.), *School dropout and completion: International comparative studies in theory and policy*. Dordrecht: Springer.

Teese, R., Clarke, K., & Polesel, J. (2007). *The destinations of school leavers in Victoria*. Melbourne: Department of Education and Early Childhood Development.

te Riele, K. (2006). Youth 'at risk': Further marginalizing the marginalized? *Journal of Education Policy, 21*(2), 129–145.

Wong, E., Ngai, E., & Lo, K. (2006). The need of safey-net programme for a mass education. *New Horizon in Education, 54*, 60–78.

Wyn, J., Stokes, H., & Tyler, D. (2004). *Stepping stones: TAFE and ACE program development for early school leavers*. Adelaide: NCVER.

Chapter 18
School Dropout and Inequality

Stephen Lamb

Introduction

Educational inequality is a persistent and common feature of all nations. Levels of educational attainment and academic success vary by family background, race and location in every system suggesting that there are commonalities of process that wealthy nations share. Yet, the extent of inequality and its impact can be stronger or weaker depending on the form and architecture of institutional and program arrangements. This point is made clear in the work of Douglas Willms who has reported in his comparative studies of educational performance that the relationship between home background and school outcomes can be more or less severe: while inequality is quite strong in some nations, others achieve both above-average levels of student achievement and weaker effects of socioeconomic status (SES) on educational success leading to greater equality of educational opportunity (Willms, 2004, 2006; OECD, 2001, Chap 8). In some nations, the social gaps in student performance are weaker and the chances of success for the poor are stronger. To what extent does this apply to dropout and completion rates and what arrangements and features support higher completion rates and weaker social differences?

This chapter explores some of these issues. It draws on the national case studies to examine patterns of inequality in relation to dropout and completion. It begins by looking at research from each country on the patterns of dropout and completion and the factors that influence them. This is used to develop a conceptual model of the commonalities in process. Attention then turns to an examination of the effects of social background and how this varies across nations. The final section develops an explanation for international differences in dropout and completion and in the levels of inequality.

S. Lamb (✉)
Centre for Post-Compulsory Education and Lifelong Learning,
University of Melbourne, Australia

S. Lamb et al. (Eds.), *School Dropout and Completion: International Comparative Studies in Theory and Policy*, DOI 10.1007/978-90-481-9763-7_21,
© Springer Science+Business Media B.V. 2011

Influences on Dropout and Completion

The national case studies presented in this book all highlight similar sets of factors influencing the rates of dropout and completion. Despite international variations in rates, key research studies from each country provide similar profiles of the characteristics of those who complete and those who drop out. Most point to features of family background (such as SES, family structure and parental education), demographic factors (such as gender, race, ethnicity and location), individual attributes (such as disability, health and self esteem), and experiences in school (such as academic achievement, attitudes towards school and grade repetition or retention) as important. They also point to the impact of school context as well as community and economic settings.

Table 18.1 summarises the factors examined in representative research studies from each of the 13 contributing countries. A single key study from each country is listed. Most of the studies base their analyses on data from large-scale cohort studies (mostly longitudinal). They are certainly not exhaustive of the many studies on dropout and completion that have been undertaken in each country. However, they are representative of studies looking at different aspects of the process, often incorporating different groups of variables.

Certain difficulties arise in comparing the studies. Sometimes the outcome – completion or dropout – is defined in different ways. In some studies dropout is defined in terms of young people of an age group (e.g., 20–24 years of age) who are no longer in school and did not attain a post-compulsory school certificate; in other studies, as proportions of commencing secondary school students who did not remain at school to the final year; and for yet other studies, as the numbers of those who did not fulfil the requirements for graduation before leaving school. In some countries the research tends to focus on completion or dropout only at the upper secondary level (such as Markussen et al., 2008, in Norway), while in other countries the research estimates cover dropout in the lower as well as upper secondary years (for example, Janosz et al., 1997, in Canada). A second problem when comparing research studies is that they differ in terms of the methods of analysis used and the format in which the results are presented. For example, Jónasson and Blöndal (2002) in their study of patterns in Iceland provide cohort estimates of the percentages of students with certain background characteristics who completed upper secondary school by the age of 24. Rumberger (1995), examining patterns in the USA, used a multi-level statistical procedure and presented eight models, each including additional variables, so that the apparent effects of background variables (such as ethnicity) were measured as other factors (such as self-esteem and aspirations) were added to the model.

Many of the studies include a fairly comprehensive set of variables in the research design and use some form of multiple regression technique to estimate the relative importance of each variable in explaining the outcome. Some studies are more descriptive and less inferential, focusing more on describing the attributes of completers and dropouts by highlighting rates for different groups of students based on who they are, their backgrounds, their early school careers, and the post-compulsory programs they enter.

Table 18.1 Selected country studies on dropout and completion

Study	Student	Family	School	Peer	Community	State
United Kingdom Payne (2001) Longitudinal data	Academic achievement* Gender* Ethnicity* Truancy* Suspensions* Part-time work* Attitudes to school*	Parent education* Household tenure*	Courses*		Region*	Maintenance allowance*
Canada Janosz et al. (1997) Longitudinal data	Gender* Grade repeating* Academic achievement* Commitment* Beliefs Leisure*	Family structure* Parent education* Supervision Rules* Punishment SES*		Number of friends Interaction* Deviancy		
United States Rumberger (1995) Longitudinal data	Gender* Race* Place of birth Achievement* Repeating* Mobility* Expectations* Attitudes to teachers* Self concept Self efficacy Absenteeism* Homework Engagement Behaviour*	Family structure* Language Parental supervision Expectations* Academic support SES*	SES comp. Grade repeating Race comp.* Sector* Size Student/ teacher ratio Homework Fair discipline*	Interaction* Assist		
Australia Lamb et al. (2004) Longitudinal data	Gender* Disability* Achievement* Education plans* School attitudes* Self concept* Race* Ethnicity* Motivation to learn* Views on teachers* Homework*	SES* Family size* Family structure* Parent aspirations*	SES* Sector* Type Size Teacher skills* Academic climate	Educational plans* Reading habits Attitudes to school Self esteem Hours of TV*	Economy* Region* Race* SES*	State* Income support*
Norway Markussen et al. (2008) Longitudinal data	Gender* Ethnicity* Academic achievement* Disability* Behaviour* Aspirations* Interests* Pastimes*	Work status* Family structure* SES* Parent education* Cultural capital	Program* Classroom Pedagogy		Region*	

(continued)

Table 18.1 (continued)

Study	Student	Family	School	Peer	Community	State
Iceland Jónasson and Blöndal (2002) Longitudinal data	Gender* Ethnicity* Academic achievement* Disability* Educational plans*	Work status* Family structure* SES* Parent education* Views on school	Type of Program* Program structure School type		Region* Economy	
Finland Jarvinen and Vanttaja (2001) Longitudinal data	Gender Academic achievement* Ethnicity* Migrant status* Disability*	SES* Work status* Parent education* Income*	Program*		Region	
Germany Weiss (2002) Longitudinal data	Gender* Ethnicity* Attitudes Achievement*	SES*	School type* Program*		Region*	
Switzerland Eckmann-Saillant et al. (1994)	Gender Ethnicity*	Father's education* Mother's education* Family structure SES* Cultural	Program*		Region Economy*	Canton*
Spain Merino and Garcia (2008)	Gender* Ethnicity*	Parents education* Work status* SES*	Program*		Economy* Region*	
France Blanchard and Sinthon (2010) Longitudinal data	Gender Grade repetition*	Father's occupation* Parent education*	Program*		Region*	
Scotland Howieson (2003)	Gender* Academic achievement*	Father's education* Father's occupation* Attitudes to school* Truancy*	School SES* Location*			
Poland Mikiewicz (2010)	Aspirations Gender	SES	School type		Region	

*Significant at least at the 5% level

Despite these differences, the studies are fairly similar in the factors that they identify as influential. A summary of the studies presented in Table 18.1 shows that 'effects' on the decision to drop out of school may come from a variety of sources. They can be categorised in the following way:

- *Individual student effects*: factors such as gender, race, absenteeism and school attendance, academic performance, health, engagement in academic and school activities, and participation in anti-social behaviour
- *Family effects*: SES, parental education, parenting styles, household composition, and parents' participation in school activities
- *School effects*: quality of teaching and resources, school size, effectiveness and equity of school policies and practices, school type, intake, school climate and engagement of teachers
- *Peer effects*: the role of young people's friends, norms and values, peer culture and behaviour
- *Community effects*: The extent to which young people are affected by the neighbourhoods in which they live, and the broader effects of the social, economic and historical features of their neighbourhoods and communities. An important subset of community factors is the role local labour market conditions play in encouraging or discouraging early exit from school
- *Province/state/nation effects*: populations, institutional arrangements, the organisation of school systems, resource allocation, school management and policies linked to curriculum, qualifications and graduation

Across the studies, the factors have different rankings based on their estimated impact on dropout and completion. The Canadian study by Janosz et al. (1997), for example, combined multiple predictors of dropout relating to families, peers, schools and performance. They ranked grade retention, disrespect of authority and participation in passive activities as the most important predictors of dropout, and concluded that family and school factors were influential though not strong independent predictors. The study by Rumberger (1995) in the USA identified a range of factors across several dimensions (student, family, school and peer) and ranks individual and family context as important, but school as also having large significant effects. The study by Payne (2001) in the United Kingdom ranks social and family factors the highest. The Australian study by Lamb et al. (2004) used a sequence of models to measure the influence of a range of factors linked to student, family, school, peer and community. They show that the different sets of factors have an impact, though family background factors – SES, ethnicity, parental aspirations, family size – are the most influential along with school background and engagement factors such as academic achievement, educational plans and views on school, learning and teachers.

The results of the various studies portray similar processes occurring in each country, though the studies suggest differences in the size of influence exerted by various factors. Differences in national contexts as well as in model specifications and approaches to profiling the characteristics of school completers and dropouts may contribute to some of the different results. Yet, based on the results of these studies, there tends to be greater similarity than difference across nations in the sorts of factors identified as leading to completion or dropout.

Conceptual Model of Dropout and Completion

Taken together, the research on dropout and completion from each country provides a consistent picture of influences or drivers. The studies suggest that dropping out of school is the cumulative result of many factors that reach back a considerable distance into a student's life – predictive factors can emerge very early on in primary school and even before. Recent thinking about the process of disengagement and early leaving points to the process beginning early and involving disengagement over a long period. Some have described understanding the process as needing a 'life course perspective', which moves the focus away from the final decision to drop out and towards the major precursors, such as emerging academic achievement, behaviour and engagement (see Audas & Willms, 2001). They suggest that the very final decision to drop out of school is much less important as a subject to study than the gradual withdrawal from school that most early leavers tend to exhibit long before the actual decision to leave is made. This points to a need to understand the origins and development of low achievement, risk-taking behaviour and disengagement from school that tend to occur at different phases of a child's schooling and are sometimes evident quite early.

Life course theories emphasise the interrelated effects of various levels of influence, including the family, school, system and broader economic and political settings. Figure 18.1 presents a conceptual model of school dropout and completion based on the empirical literature. It shows four separate dimensions related to the process of completion or dropout: (1) *individual attributes*, which relate to the background characteristics of individual students, such as gender, race and health; (2) *institutional context*, which represents the institutional and policy-setting contexts, such as family, peer, community and system, as well as state and nation policy settings that actively and continuously operate to shape and modify the influence of student characteristics and the academic and work dispositions leading to completion or dropout; (3) *dispositions*, which reflect the attitudes, behaviours and achievements of students through particular concepts – school engagement, academic engagement, education and work aspirations and academic achievement; and (4) *outcome*, which is the decision by young people to complete or drop out and the rate at which young people do so.

The model is meant to represent the dropout and completion process as dynamic rather than static. Several theories have been developed in recent years that suggest completion or dropping out of school is but the final stage in a dynamic and cumulative process of engagement or withdrawal that impacts on the dispositions towards school and work (Rumberger, 1995; Janosz et al., 1997; Teese, 2000). Although there are some differences among these theories, they suggest that there are four dimensions that form dispositions: school engagement, academic engagement

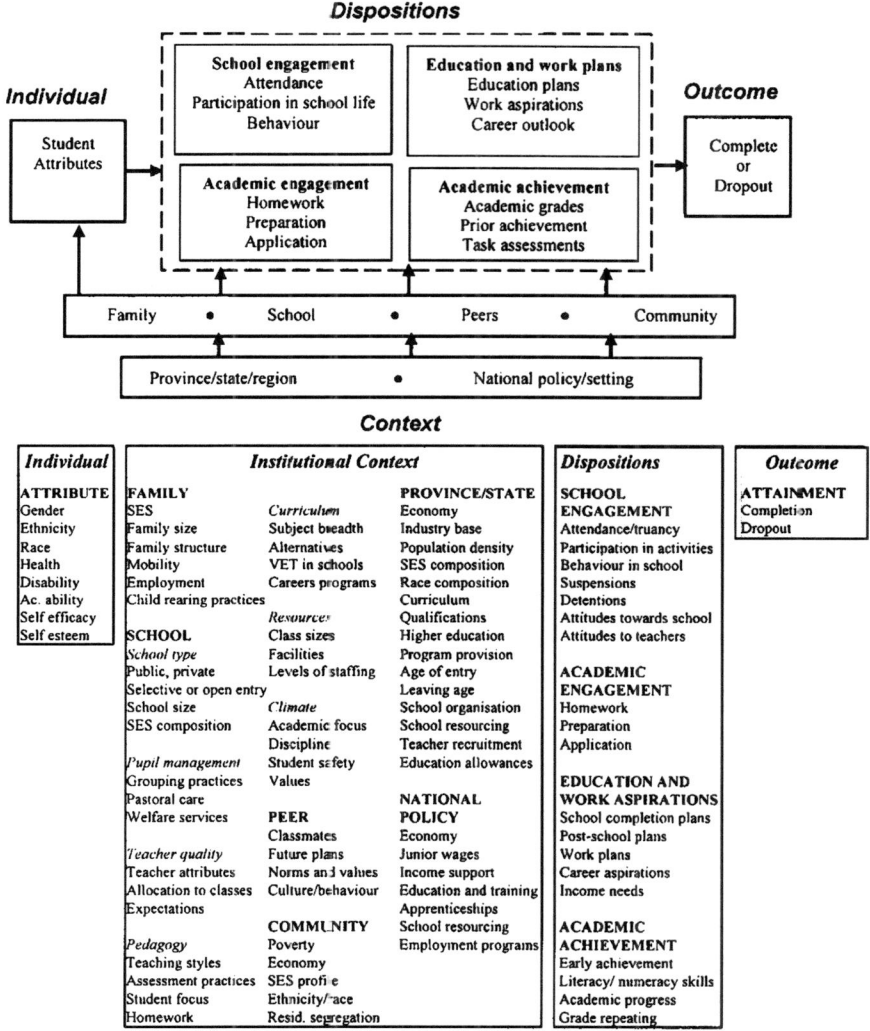

Fig. 18.1 Conceptual model of dropout and completion

in learning, education and work aspirations including career planning and the desire to enter the workforce rather than remain at school, and academic achievement or scholastic success and failure. These dimensions are reflected in students' attitudes and behaviours with respect to both the formal aspects of school (e.g., classrooms and school activities, results, progress and achievement) and the informal ones (e.g., peer and teacher relationships). All of the dimensions related to dispositions can influence the decision to stay or withdraw from school. For example, students may withdraw from school because they lose motivation and no longer apply themselves to their school work (academic engagement), because they do not identify with the goals of school (school engagement), because they want to leave to get a job rather than be at school (work and education aspirations) or because of an established record of scholastic failure (academic achievement).

The framework also suggests that the four dimensions of dispositions are inter-related. For example, students who lose interest in school (school engagement) and learning (academic engagement) are less likely to do well (academic achievement) and develop a stronger desire to obtain employment rather than remain at school (education and work aspirations). Similarly, histories of academic success and reward in school may promote stronger engagement in school activities, positive relationships with teachers, and further education plans promoting completion.

The framework also holds that the dispositions towards school are continuously shaped and influenced by the contexts in which students are located. Different family, peer group, community and school settings work to shape student characteristics and modify the dispositions that young people develop. The settings – viewed as interconnected and overlapping rather than separate and isolated – work to shape the outlooks students bring to school, including their educational aspirations and skills. As young people progress through school, these contexts can modify the impact of individual and demographic patterns of dispositions shaped by state and territory and national educational, economic and social policy frameworks. For example, young people living in remote and isolated communities with limited provision of schools and tertiary education may develop different dispositions toward school and work compared to those located in large urban centres with better provision. Similarly, schools serving largely low SES communities that attempt to address issues of disengagement through provision of a wider range of senior school course options, stronger student-centred approaches and enhanced pastoral care may promote stronger engagement in school and learning and higher rates of completion than schools that retain only a limited range of academic programs and pastoral care services.

This is the sort of model that would be developed based on the processes that research in different countries suggests are important influences on dropout and completion. From a comparative perspective the model reflects both general and local processes that influence student outcomes. It may not be particularly useful for identifying in a single analysis the magnitude of importance of different factors (particularly given the long list of variables grouped under each dimension). Rather, it is more useful in displaying the relationships among the various influences on dropout and completion given different national context and policy frameworks, as portrayed in studies on dropout and completion from different countries.

SES Differences and Inequality Across Nations

While general patterns of inequality evident in rates of dropout and completion may be consistent across countries, the extent of inequality is more likely to vary. This is in part because the challenges each country faces in promoting high levels of completion are different, at least based on the size and diversity of populations.

One measure of the distinctive challenges different countries face can be shown by comparing the educational and occupational profiles of populations.

Figure 18.2 displays the percentages of the 15-year-old population in each country in the bottom and top quintiles of SES according to OECD estimates. The comparison is based on an internationally calibrated scale that uses an equivalent measure of SES composition. The estimates are derived from the Program for International Student Assessment (PISA) index of economic, social and cultural status (ESCS) which was created using several variables: the International Socio-Economic Index of Occupational Status (ISEI); the highest level of education of the student's parents, converted into years of schooling; the PISA index of family wealth; the PISA index of home educational resources; and the PISA index of possessions related to 'classical' culture in the family home. The International Socio-Economic Index of Occupational Status (ISEI) used in the ESCS index was based on the occupational status of the 15-year-old student's mother or father (whichever parent had the higher occupational status), with parental occupation reported by the student. Parental occupations were translated into socioeconomic index scores. For example, whereas a low index score (i.e., between 16 and 34 points) corresponds with a parental occupation requiring a minimal level of education and skill (e g., taxi driver, waiter/waitress), a high index score (i.e., between 71 and 90 points) corresponds with a parental occupation requiring a high level of education and skill

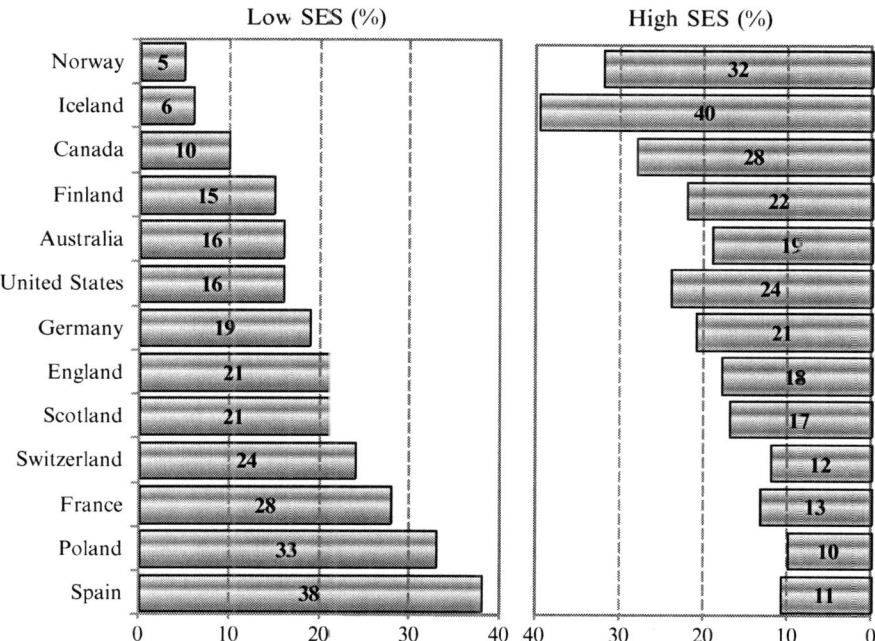

Fig. 18.2 Percentage of the 15-year-old student population in the lowest and highest quintiles of SES, by nation: 2003 (Source: Derived from 2003 PISA data)

(e.g., medical doctor). Similar types of scaling were used for the other components of the ESCS index.

The results show that in 2003, Norway and Iceland had the smallest proportionate shares of low SES students (those in the bottom quintile) – 5%. Both countries also had the largest proportionate shares of high SES students (those in the highest quintile of SES based on the ECSC scale). Conversely, Spain and Poland had the largest shares of student populations with low SES backgrounds – 38% and 33%, respectively. The effects of these sorts of population differences are likely to be marked. Research studies in every country show that the chances of success at school are heavily influenced by circumstances at home and, in particular, by parental education, occupation, economic status and cultural resources. Families in which parents are more highly educated and work in higher status occupations, families that provide supportive material and cultural resources at home such as books, computers, internet access and separate study areas and families that hold positive dispositions towards learning and attainment, provide their children with a major advantage in negotiating the academic demands that schools, teaching and the curriculum place on learning (see Lareau, 2003, for further discussion on this point). The greater gulf between these formal demands placed on learning and the circumstances of poorer families, who are far more dependent on school to deliver success, makes successful school outcomes for their children much less certain. Countries with much higher proportions of families with lower levels of economic, social and cultural resources such as Spain and Poland, therefore, face a much harder task in delivering strong educational outcomes for all. These problems are likely to be compounded if total population sizes are also large.

The importance of the population differences is fairly apparent when examining the relationship between achievement levels of 15-year-olds and social background. Achievement levels are a relevant indicator when thinking about the consequences for dropout and completion because in nearly every country individual student academic performance is frequently reported as the strongest predictor of dropout and completion. This is true for most of the different country studies listed in Table 18.1.

Figure 18.3 shows the relationship between social background and mathematics achievement scores in PISA 2003. The results of 101,259 15-year-olds in 12 case study countries (Australia, Canada, Finland, France, Germany, Great Britain, Iceland, Norway, Poland, Spain, Switzerland and USA) are plotted against OECD PISA index of economic, social and cultural status (ESCS) scores. Despite some scatter, the pattern indicates that as ESCS increases so does mathematics achievement. The slope of the regression line that summarises the relationship is quite steep, indicating that increased social advantage, in general, pays off with a considerable increase in educational performance. The correlation between the ESCS score and mathematics achievement for students across all countries is 0.425, confirming a fairly strong relationship between achievement and the economic, social and cultural backgrounds of students.

The effects of social background can be measured in other ways. When students are grouped into quintiles based on the ESCS index, there is a marked difference in achievement scores. Specifically, on average, students in the top quintile of the ESCS

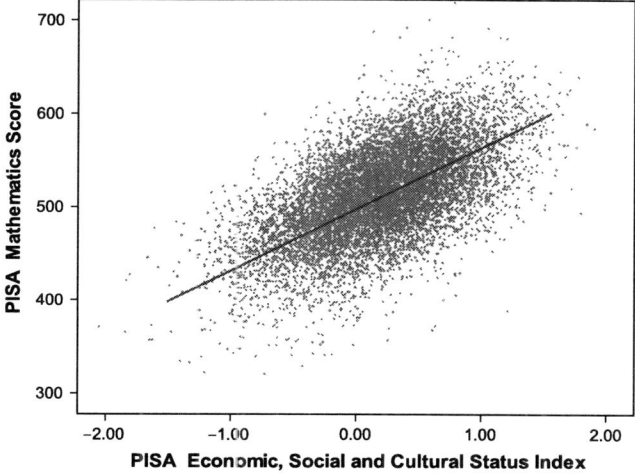

Fig. 18.3 Social background and mathematics performance: 15-year-olds in 12 countries, 2003 (Source: Derived from the 2003 PISA survey of 15-year-olds)

index scored much higher on the PISA mathematics scale than students in the bottom quintile of the index. The gap between top and bottom quintiles was 112 points, equivalent to almost two proficiency skill levels.[1] Average achievement increased by about 28 points with each rise in ESCS quintile. Another way to evaluate the relationship between social background and mathematics achievement is to examine the specific change in score on the mathematics scale in response to a one-standard-deviation increase in the ESCS score. Across selected case study countries, an increase of one standard deviation on the index was associated with an average performance increase of 41.7 score points.

The social patterns in mathematics achievement are consistent with long estab-lished research findings reported in many individual countries. Social background is a key influence on how well young people do in school. However, despite the

---

[1] A difference of 62 points represents one proficiency level on the PISA mathematics scales. According to OECD reports, this can be considered a comparatively large difference in student performance in substantive terms: each rise in level of proficiency represents a major increase in skill requirements for successful completion of tasks (OECD, 2004). For example, Level 1 (bot-tom proficiency level skills) requires rudimentary computational and reasoning skills, while Level 2 requires a capacity to recognise, apply and interpret basic formulas and make use of direct infer-ences. Students proficient at Level 6 can identify and combine multiple pieces of information to solve complex problems in the context of unfamiliar real-world situations. In order to reach a particular proficiency level, a student must have been able to correctly answer a majority of items at that level. Students at each succeeding level are capable of solving mathematical problems of increasing complexity. For a discussion on proficiency skill levels, see OECD (2004, 2005a).

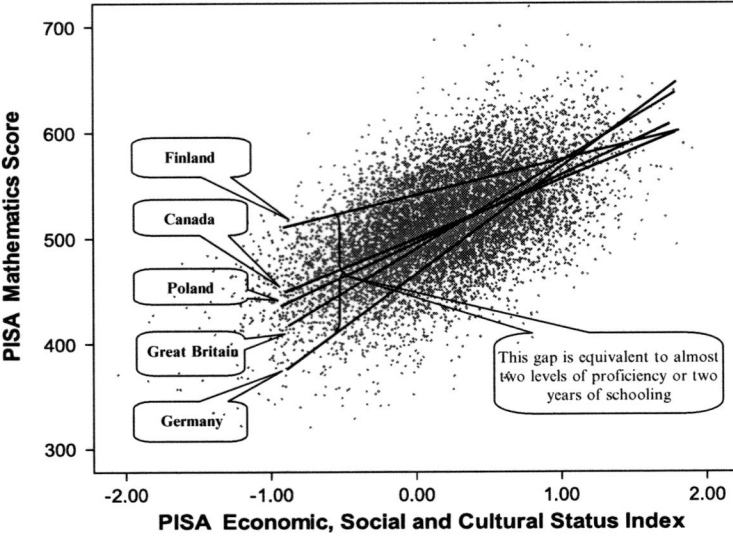

Note: Each dot represents 10 students

Fig. 18.4 Country variations in the relationship between social background and mathematics performance: 15-year-olds in 12 countries, 2003 (Source: Derived from the 2003 PISA survey of 15-year-olds)

strong overall relationship there are important differences in the strength of the relationship across national systems. This is portrayed in Fig. 18.4.

Figure 18.4 reports the same students as in Fig. 18.3; however separate regression slopes are provided for 5 of the 12 countries. Differences in the steepness of the slopes reveal marked differences among countries in the relationship between social background and mathematics achievement. Flatter slopes suggest a weaker relationship, meaning that there is greater equity in achievement across students from different social backgrounds. Steeper slopes suggest the opposite, that there is a higher level of social inequality in achievement, that is, achievement is more dependent on social background. The line for Finland is far less steep than for the other countries. There is less of a rise in mathematics achievement as the ESCS scale increases, implying that there is greater equity in mathematics achievement compared to the other countries. Students in Finland differ in achievement but not in a way that is so substantially related to their social background. The lines for Germany and Great Britain are both much steeper. In both of these countries, achievement in mathematics is much more dependent on students' social background.

Other points are worth noting. The results suggest that, in terms of the gaps in achievement levels for students from poorer backgrounds, how well they do may depend on which country they live in. The differences between the five lines at the lower end of the ESCS scale are substantial. The gap in mathematics achievement between students in the bottom quintile of SES in Finland and equivalent low SES students in Germany represents over 2 years of schooling or almost 2 levels of skill proficiency. Students from the same social background and of the same age have very different skill levels in mathematics depending on the country they live in. Low SES students in Canada, Poland and Great Britain fall between the high levels in Finland and the low levels in Germany.

While students from poorer backgrounds in Germany may not do as well relative to their peers in other countries, on average, high SES students in Germany tend to outperform their counterparts in other countries, accentuating the extent of inequality in that country across students from different social backgrounds. Despite the superior achievement levels of high-status students from Germany, there is less variation in achievement across countries for high-status students. Figure 18.5 presents the mean achievement levels by social status quintile and country. It shows that overall achievement rises by quintile: bottom quintile countries, 442; lower middle, 475; middle, 496; upper middle, 519 and top quintile, 554. But while mean achievement levels increase with each rise in ESCS quintile group, the gaps in achievement across countries tend to narrow. In the bottom quintile, the spread of mean achievement levels is about 83 points. In the top quintile the spread is less than 50 points. Hence, the range of achievement levels across countries narrows as social status increases. What this means is that if you are from a wealthier background, mathematics achievement becomes less dependent on the country you live in – high-status students tend to do well irrespective of country. All national systems tend to support high achievement levels for students from wealthier backgrounds. But, this is not the case if you are poor.

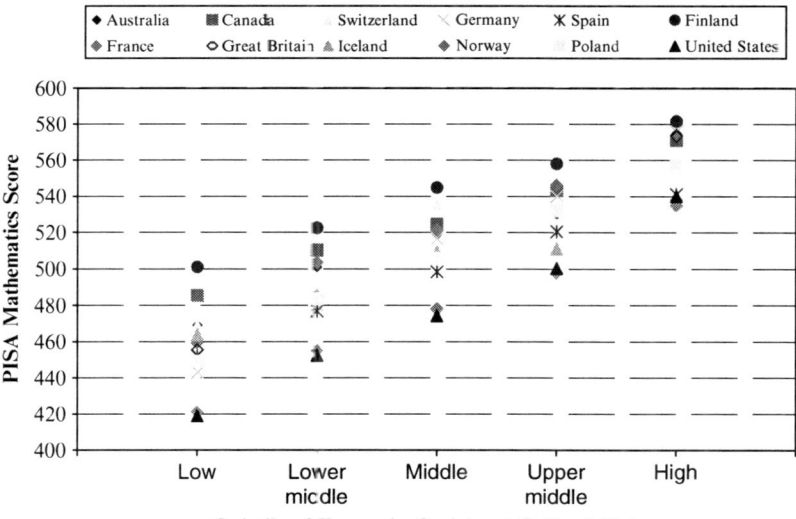

Fig. 18.5 Mean PISA mathematics achievement scores, by quintile of economic, social and cultural status and country: 15-year-olds, 2003 (Source: Derived from the 2003 PISA survey data for 15-year-olds)

Dropout and Completion

Educational inequality linked to achievement is a feature of all systems, but the severity or extent of inequality varies across nations. It is not possible using existing data to undertake the same type of analysis for dropout and completion rates. There is no comparable data that permit analysis of within and between country variations in attainment and relationships with social background. However, as with the achievement data, much research shows that levels of attainment in each country are strongly linked to family background (see the list of studies in Table 18.1). This research also points to achievement as being one of the strongest predictors of completion or dropout. Therefore, it is worth looking at the relationship between achievement and attainment.

Figure 18.6 shows that there is a broad relationship between PISA mathematics achievement levels and upper secondary attainment rates. The attainment rates are based on the OECD reported estimates of 18- to 24-year-olds who had completed an upper secondary qualification (OECD, 2007). The rates are for the year 2004. It is important to note that the rates include alternative qualifications that young people may complete outside of school. For example, the United States rate includes those young people who complete a General Educational Development (GED) qualification. This may involve up to 14% of 18- to 24-year-olds. The Canadian rate also includes GED qualifiers. Similarly, the Australian rate includes young people who complete apprenticeships which are most often undertaken outside the school system. The same is true for the United Kingdom. PISA mathematics

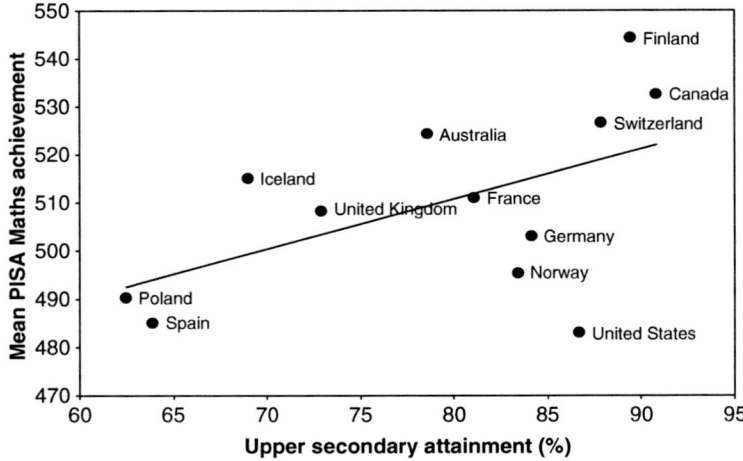

Fig. 18.6 Mean PISA mathematics achievement scores, by upper secondary attainment and country (Sources: PISA figures derived from the 2003 PISA survey data for 15-year-olds. Attainment figures from OECD, 2007)

achievement is the mean country achievement recorded among the 2003 samples of 15-year-olds.

In general, countries that do well on one measure also do well on the other. Canada, for example, has high mean mathematics achievement levels and high attainment levels: the second highest mean achievement score (532) and a 90% attainment rate. Conversely, Poland and Spain have mean mathematics achievement levels well below the OECD average (490 and 485, respectively) and low attainment rates (62% and 64%), together ranking lowest on the attainment indicator and last on achievement. The slope of the line summarising the relationship between achievement and attainment across countries suggests that there is a moderately strong relationship between countries on attainment and achievement. Even so, the association is far from being one to one. The USA, for example, does far better on attainment than on achievement as measured by mathematics in PISA. Norway and Germany, as well, tend to do better on attainment than on achievement. If these three countries were excluded, however, the relationship between achievement and attainment across the other countries would be quite strong.

While it is not possible to examine the levels of internal differentiation associated with social background and attainment in each country, it is possible to look at the general relationships between attainment and social differences in populations across countries. Figure 18.7 displays upper secondary attainment rates for 18- to 24-year-olds against the percentage of the population of 15-year-olds from low SES backgrounds in each country. The SES percentage represents the proportionate share in each country of young people from low SES backgrounds measured using an equivalent scale (as also seen in Fig. 18.2).

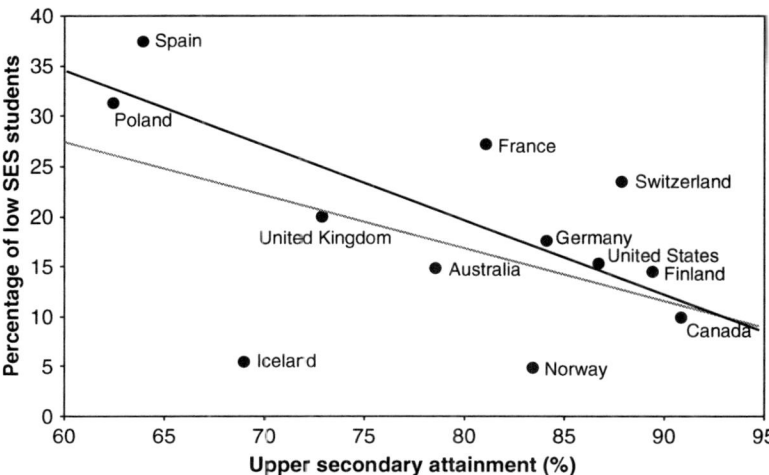

Fig. 18.7 Percentage of students from disadvantaged backgrounds, by upper secondary attainment and country (Sources: SES figures derived from the 2003 PISA survey data for 15-year-olds. Attainment figures from OECD, 2007)

The patterns show that in broad terms as the percentage of low SES students falls, the level of upper secondary attainment rises. Canada, for example, has a high level of attainment and a relatively small proportion of students from low SES backgrounds, while at the other ends of the scales, Poland and Spain have high proportions of low SES students and comparatively low attainment rates. There is some variation from this general pattern. Iceland is the clear example where there are few students from poor backgrounds but relatively low attainment levels. There are two slopes that summarise the relationships, one which includes and one which excludes Iceland. The steeper slope excludes Iceland and reveals a fairly strong relationship between attainment and the shares of students from disadvantaged backgrounds.

If achievement is a guide, the extent of internal differentiation linked to social background is likely to vary across countries when it comes to dropout and completion. Whereas all of the countries have research showing that home background influences children's educational outcomes, cross-national data for achievement suggest that the extent of that influence varies considerably between countries. Inequality exists in all systems, but its size and severity can be influenced by the approaches systems take to the organisation of institutions and the policies that systems adopt.

Explaining International Differences

Cross-national differences in dropout and completion rates and in the levels of inequality are shaped by the institutional arrangements within each system as well as structural features linked to economy, government and population. Figure 18.8 attempts to summarise these elements using a conceptual model of factors shaping national differences in dropout and completion. The proportion of students who move into post-compulsory education and complete an upper secondary qualification varies between nations. Difference in dropout and completion can be attributed to both institutional arrangements and structural influences. The model shows both sets of influences and their interactions.

Existing research indicates that potential system influences on rates of dropout and completion are linked to *institutional arrangements* and include the following:

1. Program provision and accreditation including the availability of academic and vocational options, certification, assessment practices and graduation requirements
2. School organisation such as comprehensive or more selective schools, early or delayed selection, private schooling, stages of schooling, governance, location and size
3. Schooling policies on issues such as age of entry, compulsory leaving ages, grade repetition, teacher training and recruitment
4. Resources including student/staff ratios, class sizes, educational maintenance allowances and facilities

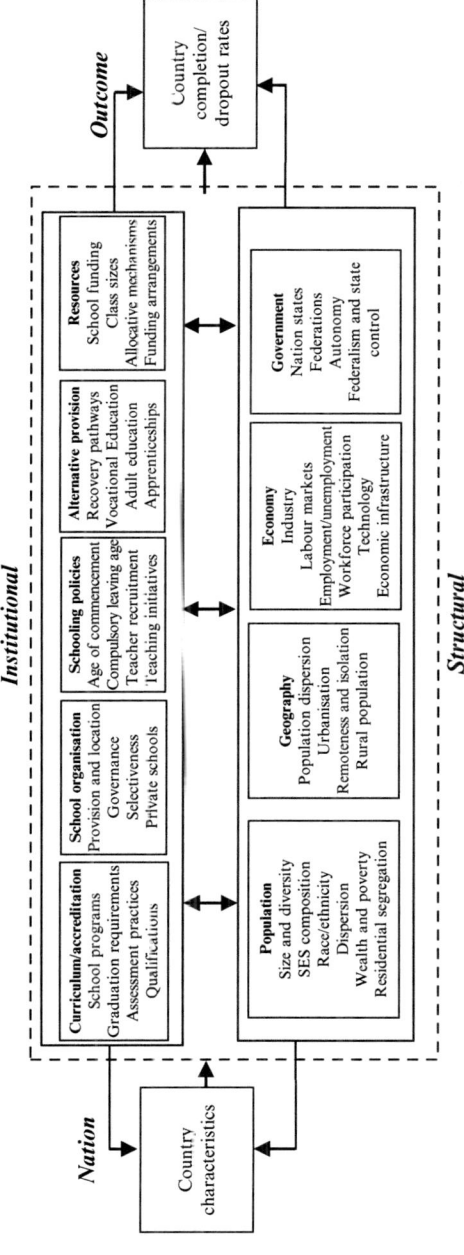

Fig. 18.8 Conceptual model of factors influencing international differences in dropout and completion rates

5. Broad education and training provision including tertiary education policies, pathways between schools and tertiary providers, adult education, post-school vocational education and university selection
6. State and national education policies such as income support for students, target setting, apprenticeship and employment programs

Structural features relate to population differences as well as economic development, geography and government. They include:

1. Population differences related to SES composition, race and ethnic diversity, migration, dispersion of the population, poverty and welfare, and residential segregation
2. Economic differences including those related to industry mix, occupational structure, employment and unemployment levels, workforce participation and labour markets
3. Geography including levels of urbanisation, residential segregation, population dispersion and rurality
4. Government including federalism and state control, centralisation and autonomy

The framework suggests ongoing and dynamic interaction between the sets of institutional and structural factors. For example, policies in curriculum, school organisation, resources and welfare can be developed in response to population needs and economic circumstances. The relationships between factors can change over time – for instance, economic trends and migration can lead to changes in the demand for education and training provision as well as the demand for resources. Together the sets of factors provide a framework for understanding what shapes opportunities and differences in completion rates and levels of attainment.

This general model of structural inequality in school systems can be used to help interpret social differences in systems over time or at one point in time.

Within the model institutional arrangements are key. Secondary school systems portrayed in the national case study chapters reveal a range of different models of practice and organisation. As discussed in Chapter 2 of this book, the organisation and provision of schooling varies across two broad dimensions. The first is the level of *program diversification* or the variety of programs that are offered. This can include differently focused tracks or streams such as academic courses, professional and technical courses and vocational education. Students are offered different types of educational programs, the major distinction being between general and vocational programs. The different programs orient students toward different post-school outcomes. In many countries students who enter and complete academic study qualify more often for university entry, whereas those who undertake and complete vocational education are more likely to enter other forms of tertiary education or go directly into the labour market after secondary education. The programs can be delivered as separate certificates or as separate strands or options within the architecture of a single certificate.

Tied to program diversification is the role of graduation requirements. For academic programs, graduation (sometimes referred to as matriculation, or *'matura'*) in most countries requires successful completion of a minimum number of subjects. In many systems the requirement is to achieve minimum grades in at least five subjects including a set number of compulsory subjects covering different key learning areas (such as mathematics and native language). An overall score, the equivalent of a grade point average derived from a minimum number of subjects, is sometimes used to set a threshold or standard for the successful completion of the award. But the requirements for graduation can vary by program and by country, as well as across jurisdictions within countries. Graduation requirements are usually far more variable in vocational and technical programs and certificates, though this too varies considerably by country, state and region.

The second broad dimension of schooling provision is the extent of *institutional diversification* or the extent to which young people are separated into different schools or streams and tracks on the basis of the programs or qualifications in which they enrol. In some systems, students remain in the same institution irrespective of the program they take since in these countries institutions offer both vocational programs and general programs. However, in other systems, institutions often specialise in a certain type of educational program and therefore differentiation by program separates children by school as well. This may influence the quality and standards of learning, and future chances, based on the workings of school-intake effects reported in the studies of Willms (2006) and the OECD (2005b). In some systems selection into different schools can occur early and extend well back into lower secondary or even primary school. In Germany, for example, it is common at the end of the primary school years for many students to be separated into different schools based on their interests and aptitudes. Alternatively, in other systems, such as in the USA, Canada and Australia, students tend to remain in the same type of school through both the lower and upper secondary years, able to pursue a variety of programs or courses within the one institution.

Associated with institutional differentiation is the role of residential segregation and private schooling. Residential segregation can produce marked divisions in some systems, separating students on the basis of where they live and their racial and social backgrounds. Regional or residential segregation can create sharp differences between schools in terms of intake, separating students almost as effectively as selective schooling. It also has a marked impact on student progress and outcomes, at least according to a range of school performance studies (see, for example, Willms, 2006). Various studies have shown that mean SES intake can have an effect on student achievement, dropout rates and other outcomes thanks to the impact of composition on school climate and performance. In systems that have encouraged decentralisation, parental choice, vouchers, school-based management and other market-based principles of school organisation the effects of residential segregation and stratification can be intensified (see Lamb, 2007). Also, in some systems the effects of residential segregation are modified by the role of private schools. The use of private schools can be a key strategy of the wealthy in some countries in their conversion strategies seeking to translate their material and cultural status into educational success for their children. Through parents buying access to socially selected student populations, thanks to fees, private schools provide high SES enclaves, often highly resourced, which support academic success. Governments in some countries, such as Australia, actively support these endeavours by providing public funding to private schools that can expand the share and size of the private school sector, though not necessarily democratise its intake (Lamb, 2007). In such systems, private schools promote segregation in schooling and contribute to inequality in outcomes.

Institutional segregation and program diversification work together in producing patterns of social stratification. The extent of social differentiation varies across nations depending in part on the stages of selection and the range of alternatives. Countries that leave until much later the point at which students have to choose a particular branch or type of schooling (countries with no or low percentages of students who, in their compulsory years, are enrolled in programs that track to upper secondary vocational courses) tend to encourage more students from a wider range of backgrounds into academic programs leading to higher education. Access to university and careers in the professions is shared more democratically in such systems, though these systems do not necessarily have the highest school completion rates.

Conversely, systems that are more formally selective and group students into different schools and programs at earlier ages can achieve high rates of completion and low dropout rates. Such systems are able to accommodate most of their population through program and institutional diversification even with very early points of selection or differentiation. This is the case with systems such as Germany and Switzerland, where students at the end of primary school can be separated into different schools and programs based on interests, aptitudes and formal selection. While only a minority of students (around 20%) may pursue academic study in a *Gymnasium*, the majority of remaining students pursue and complete technical training or vocational qualifications helping deliver high rates of overall completion (over 85% of young people). High rates of completion are achieved, but this occurs in a context of large social inequalities in program participation and access to university and the professions.

In summary, we have seen that social gaps in dropout and completion can vary across nations depending on the structure of curriculum, programs and qualifications, and the differentiation of schools along social and administrative lines. The result is unequal access to learning and the curriculum within and across nations. Inequality is generated in all secondary school systems even though there are quite different architectures, but the dimensions of that inequality vary depending on how the different school systems work. In some countries, early academic selection contributes to a high level of social inequality in access to upper secondary school, as in the cases of Germany and Switzerland, despite widespread participation (Müller & Pollak, 2008, p. 311). In other countries, selection is delayed and most children undertake a common program of lower secondary education before entering academic or vocational tracks at upper secondary level (as in France, Norway, Finland and Spain). Within either approach, global participation and completion can be achieved, but this does not mean that equality of opportunity is achieved.

References

Audas, R., & Willms, J. (2001). *Engagement and dropping out of school: A life course perspective*. Canada: Human Resources Development. Retrieved from http://www.hrdc-drhc.gc.ca/ sp-ps/arb-dgra/publications

Blanchard, M. (2010). The question of school dropout: A French perspective. In S. Lamb, E. Markussen, R. Teese, N. Sandberg & J. Polesel (Eds.), *School dropout and completion: International comparative studies in theory and policy*. Dordrecht: Springer.

Eckmann-Saillant, M., Bolzman, C., & de Rham, G. (1994). *Jeunes sans qualification: trajectoires, situations et stratégies (Youth without qualifications: The trajectories, situations and strategies)*. Geneva: Institut d'études sociales (IES).

Howieson, C. (2003). *Destinations of early leavers. CES Special Briefing No. 29*. Edinburgh: Centre for Educational Sociology, University of Edinburgh.

Janosz, M., LeBlanc, M., Boulerice, B., & Tremblay, R. (1997). Disentangling the weight of school dropout predictors: A test on two longitudinal samples. *Journal of Youth and Adolescence, 26*(6), 733–762.

Järvinen, T., & Vanttaja, M. (2001). Young people, education and work: Trends and changes in Finland in the 1990s. *Journal of Youth Studies, 4*(2), 195–207.

Jónasson, J. T., & Blöndal, K. S. (2002). *Ungt fólk og framhaldsskólinn. Rannsókn á námsgengi og afstöðu '75 árgangsins til náms* [Young people and the upper secondary school: A study on student progress through education system and attitudes of the '75 cohort to education]. Reykjavík: Félagsvísindastofnun og Háskólaútgáfan.

Lamb, S. (2007). School reform and inequality in urban Australia: A case of residualising the poor. In R. Teese, S. Lamb & M. Duru-Bellat (Eds.), *International studies in educational inequality, theory and policy* (Vol. 3, pp. 1–38). Netherlands: Springer.

Lamb, S., Walstab, A., Teese, R., Vickers, M., & Rumberger, R. (2004). *Staying on at school: Improving student retention in Australia*. Brisbane: Ministerial Council on Employment, Education and Training and the Queensland Department of Education. Retrieved from www. mceetya.edu.au/verve/_resources/studentretention_main_file.pdf

Lareau, A. (2003). *Unequal childhoods: Class, race and family life*. Los Angeles: University of California Press.

Markussen, E., Frøseth, M. W., Lødding, B., & Sandberg, N. (2008). *Bortvalg og kompetanse. Gjennomføring, bortvalg og kompetanseoppnåelse i videregående opplæring blant 9749 ungdommer som gikk ut av grunnskolen på Østlandet våren 2002: hovedfunn, konklusjoner og implikasjoner fem år etter* [Early leaving, non-completion or completion? On completion, dropout and achievement of qualification in upper secondary education among 9749 young people who left lower secondary in the spring of 2002] Report 13, 2008. Oslo: NIFU STEP.

Merino, R., & Garcia, M. (2008). Spain, educational system. *Formazione e Insegnamento, 1/2*, 99–137.

Mikiewicz, P. (2010) School dropout in secondary education: The case of Poland. In S. Lamb, E. Markussen, R. Teese, N. Sandberg & J. Polesel (Eds.), *School dropout and completion: International comparative studies in theory and policy*. Dordrecht: Springer.

Müller, W., & Pollak, R. (2008). *Weshalb gibt es so wenige Arbeiterkinder in Deutschlands Universitäten?* [Why are there so few children of workers in Germany's universities?]. In R. Becker & W. Lauterbach (Eds.), *Bildung als Privileg. Erklärungen und Befunde zu den Ursachen der Bildungsungleichheit* (3rd ed., pp. 307–346). Wiesbaden: VS.

Organisation for Economic Co-operation and Development (OECD). (2001). *Knowledge and skills for life, first results from PISA 2000*. Paris: OECD.

Organisation for Economic Co-operation and Development (OECD). (2004). *Learning for tomorrow's world first results from PISA 2003*. Paris: OECD.

Organisation for Economic Co-operation and Development (OECD). (2005a). *PISA 2003 data analysis manual: SPSS*. Paris: OECD.

Organisation for Economic Co-operation and Development (OECD). (2005b). *School factors related to quality and equity: Results from PISA 2000.* Paris: OECD.

Organisation for Economic Co-operation and Development (OECD). (2007). *Education at a glance 2007: Education indicators.* Paris: OECD.

Payne, J. (2001). *Patterns of participation in full-time education after 16. An analysis of the England and Wales Youth Cohort Study.* Research Report RR307. London: Department for Education and Skills. Retrieved from http://www.dcsf.gov.uk/research/data/uploadfiles/RR307.PDF

Rumberger, R. W. (1995). Dropping out of middle school: A multilevel analysis of students and schools. *American Educational Research Journal, 32,* 583–625.

Teese, R. (2000). *Academic success and social power: Examinations and inequality.* Carlton South: Melbourne University Press.

Weiss, R. (2002). Ausbildungsabbruch – Eine Herausforderung für die betriebliche Berufsausbildung [Dropout – a challenge for occupational training]. In S. Bohlinger & K. Jenewein (Eds.), *Ausbildungsabbrecher – Verlierer der Wissensgesellschaft? Konzepte, Risiken und Chancen aktueller Handlungsansätze aus der Berufsbildungsforschung und –praxis* (pp. 5–16). Bielefeld: Bertelsmann.

Willms, J. D. (2004). What can we say about the quality and equality of educational systems from the first cycle of PISA? *Education Journal, 32*(1), 161–175.

Willms, D. (2006) *Learning divides: Ten policy questions about the performance and equity of schools and schooling systems.* UNESCO Institute for Statistics Working Paper No. 5. Montreal: UIS.

Chapter 19
Policies to Reduce School Dropout and Increase Completion

Eifred Markussen and Nina Sandberg

Introduction

Despite major differences across nations in approaches to the measurement of school dropout and completion, and hence of their dimensions, there is an ongoing struggle, internationally, to reduce dropout and increase completion rates. In each of the country case study chapters in this book, the reported number of students who do not participate in or do not complete upper secondary education is viewed as a serious concern by researchers and by the governments and education agencies in each nation. The issue is treated so seriously in some systems that ambitious goals and targets for improvement have been established. In Switzerland, for example, there is now a target completion rate of 95%, while Australia has established a target of 90% completion to be achieved by 2015. To bring about improvements, some systems have implemented major policy reforms and introduced a range of policy measures, though the scale, nature and effects of these measures vary.

This chapter examines the array of policies that have been used in different countries to reduce dropout and improve school completion. The discussion focuses on the various policies adopted by the 13 OECD countries presented as case studies in this book. National policies to reduce dropout and raise completion are essential parts of each country case study chapter. The case studies include, though to varying degrees, accounts of major policy measures introduced to improve school completion rates and reduce rates of dropout, and their success as measured by evidence-based assessments of impact. The aim in this chapter is to draw on and discuss the material presented in the case studies in order to get a sense of the use and role of policies on dropout and completion in an international comparative context – it provides an opportunity to elucidate and discuss the variety of national policies, and the range of policy effects.

E. Markussen and N. Sandberg (✉)
NIFU Nordic Institute for Studies in Innovation, Research and Education, Norway

S. Lamb et al. (Eds.), *School Dropout and Completion: International Comparative Studies in Theory and Policy*, DOI 10.1007/978-90-481-9763-7_22, © Springer Science+Business Media B.V. 2011

Types of Policies

When discussing and contrasting national differences in policies on dropout and completion, defining concepts is a necessary starting point. For the purposes of this chapter, policy will be taken to mean *a deliberate plan of action to guide decisions and achieve rational outcome(s)*. This can include broad courses or frameworks of action across whole systems designed to guide and/or shape decisions, strategies, programs and behaviours, as well as more specific or localised actions and decisions, devised or implemented in order to reduce dropout and increase completion.

The task of making sense of the diverse policies described in the country chapters requires some way to classify policies. There are different typologies that can be used to classify and examine policies, such as by the theoretical paradigms that influence the types of strategies, or by scale (comprehensive or specific), or by dualistic schemes such as substantive versus procedural, or as distributive, regulatory, self-regulatory or redistributive (Anderson, 1997, p. 12). Whatever way is used, typologies emphasise some aspects and overlook others. In the current case, the need is to compare differences in national policies developed to reduce dropout and raise completion, so as to gain a better understanding of the role and relative value of different policies and policy approaches. Different schemes are used in different case study chapters of this book. Three examples are worth noting here. The chapter on Scotland distinguishes between policies that are framed by rational, cultural and developmental arguments or theories. The chapter on Iceland uses the distinction between preventive (designed to prevent dropout) and remedial (designed to re-engage dropouts) policy initiatives. And the chapter on the United States distinguishes between programmatic, institutional and systemic reform strategies. The reader will find these outlined in more detail in the different country chapters.

For the purposes of this chapter, in deciding on a framework to compare and consider policies, it is assumed that the traditional cycles or stages of policy formation are similar across countries (the policy circle idea), and that, in general, policymakers work in a similar way to form ideas about policy tools, and to decide to whom or what the tools will apply (target group and level), and when they will take effect (Sidney, 2007, p. 79). Policy formation is likely to be shared, or at least similar, as a process, so the focus needs to be on schemes, not process. For this reason, this chapter uses a simple but potentially useful classification scheme: categorisation according to the level – individual, school or system – at which policy on dropout and completion is targeted.

As discussed in the chapter on Scotland, differing theoretical notions or conceptions may guide different policy strategies. Within social sciences in general as well as in the sociology of education, the question of the influence of structure and agency on behaviour is central (see, for instance, Bourdieu, 1977a; Giddens & Sutton, 2009). Attempts to explain and predict behaviour repeatedly centre around either individually or structurally oriented understandings. This will be taken as a starting point and the policies presented in the country chapters in this book will be grouped according to three different levels of targeting policy: the individual level (e.g., students and apprentices), the institutional level (e.g., schools and firms) and the system level (e.g., systems of schools such as secondary schools, whole systems). The national descriptions depict policies attempting to improve completion by targeting individual-level need (strategies that address the needs of those most at risk through case management or mentoring, for example), school-level practice (such as school organisation, the use of mini-schools, teacher allocation) and system-wide reform (such as comprehensive reforms and development of national or state-level upper secondary programs).

As the previous chapters demonstrate, dropout and completion are complex phenomena with multiple and varied causes, calling for a combination of diverse strategies and measures. Further, it is evident that dropout and completion need to be interpreted and understood in the larger social and economic context, because in addition to education systems, labour markets, culture and history contribute to dropout and completion patterns. Thus, there is reason to believe that policies at a system level are necessary to make significant changes affecting the largest numbers of individuals. The focus of the following discussion is therefore mainly on system-level reforms or strategies, after some briefer paragraphs about policies targeting change at an individual and at a school level.

Individual and School-Level Policies

Many of the chapters in this book demonstrate that variation in dropout and completion is often explained using individual background attributes such as social background, indigenous or migrant background, parental education level, gender, grade point average from compulsory education and the individual's (dis)engagement with schooling. These are considered key attributes of individuals that influence the likelihood of dropout or completion. Such findings may lead to a search for strategies to counter these attributes attached to the individual, but, as indicated in the chapter on Spain: 'The fact that working class young people or those who have illiterate mothers have a higher probability of failing in school tells us little about what could be done, for neither their class nor their mothers can be changed'. This may in a sense be true for those who are students at present, but it is no argument against a policy to address differences in need, or against work to diminish social inequalities in society. Even if measures targeting individual need or the needs of groups of individuals may have limited impact on solving the dropout problem, as such, these measures are still of utmost importance to some students. As Raffe argues in the chapter on Scotland:

> Developmentalist strategies focus on the most vulnerable young people and on those who drop out, or are at risk of dropping out, because of specific developmental and social problems. Young people who drop out, and especially those who become NEET, are disproportionately likely to have low self-esteem and self-efficacy, low social, personal and cognitive skills, family problems, and/or a history of offending, alcohol and drug use or teenage pregnancy. Not all these problems are strictly described as 'developmental', but they all invite responses which focus primarily on the individual and his or her problems, rather than on the education system and its cultures and opportunity structures.

The country chapters present and discuss various individual-level measures – efforts that aim to target students or groups of students with particular needs, such as welfare needs. The measures are usually not designed to target all students, but mainly those with specific issues such as those who are low achievers, or from poor backgrounds, migrant or indigenous students, or those with integration needs. The measures, such as mentoring, welfare support, tutoring and targeted assistance for skill development among low achievers, may not work to solve dropout problems across a system, but may work very effectively and be very important for the individuals whom the measures attempt to target. In the following, there is no attempt to go further into the individual-level measures, but instead the reader is referred to the different country chapters.

School-level measures are those implemented by single schools, or by clusters of schools working in cooperation, or even whole systems of schools, in order to solve or reduce dropout and improve completion. The idea behind these reforms, as described in the chapter on the United States, is to reform existing schools on the assumption that they do not perform adequately for their students. To continue with the United States example, one approach is 'whole school reform', which refers to the use of a comprehensive or whole of school program designed to transform all aspects of a school – curriculum, student management, teaching – in an effort to improve the performance of all students leading to reductions in dropout. This approach involves multiple strategies to alter all facets of a school and is built on the premise that unified, coherent and integrated strategies for improvement, knitted together into a comprehensive design, will work better than the same strategies implemented in isolation from each other. Such reforms have been used by schools or groups of schools seeking improvements in student outcomes. Reviews of their success are mixed (see the chapter on the United States for further details).

Examples of school-level measures in other countries are less comprehensive or wholistic in their design, tending instead to target specific aspects or features of school. These include things such as expanding program offerings, introducing programs to counter low achievement, organising teaching and resources to support early intervention, initiatives to improve connections with parents and families, smaller class sizes, using mini-schools to promote better student-teacher relations, and employing team-based approaches to teaching and pastoral care. As with measures targeting need at an individual level, school-level measures are unlikely to produce system-wide improvements, but they have the potential to reduce dropout and increase completion in some of the most affected schools. Such measures may be of great importance to the specific schools and the communities they serve, as well as making a contribution to reducing the overall dropout rate.

System-Level Policies

Some of the country chapters report that systemic or system-wide policies (i.e., policies to reduce dropout and increase completion through implementing change at a system level affecting all schools and students) have not been usual in their country. According to the chapter on France, dropout in that country did not stand out as much of a concern for the authorities until the mid-1990s. Even if large proportions of student cohorts did not complete upper secondary education, this was not seen as a problem as long as the labour market could absorb unskilled labour. The same may be said about Norway, and it was only when entrance into upper secondary education was made a statutory right through a reform in 1994, when attending upper secondary education became the norm and everybody between 16 and 19 was expected to be in upper secondary education, that dropout really stood out as a problem which called for systemic reform. In Finland, dropout has been viewed as a more local, individual issue, and partly as a result of this, system-wide reforms designed specifically to reduce dropout or improve completion have not been evident. In Poland, implemented measures have tended to target individual-level needs rather than systemic reform, partly because the officially reported dropout rates are low.

However, most of the countries discussed in this book have implemented policies directed at dropout and completion issues at a systemic level, even those mentioned above. Several different measures have been presented and discussed in the various case study chapters. This section will focus on only some of the measures, those where it is possible to extract salient features. The themes that will be discussed further are: (1) counselling and career guidance, (2) income support for students, (3) raising the compulsory school leaving age, (4) expanding program offerings to include vocational education, (5) diversifying qualifications and extending schooling, and (6) comprehensive system reforms.

Counselling and Career Guidance

Several countries have focused on better career counselling and planning offered globally in every school. In Iceland, both lower and upper secondary schools are, according to Icelandic law, obliged to provide access to counselling. In some lower secondary schools, career guidance has been introduced as a part of the student's timetable. The idea is that this will help smooth the transition into upper secondary education. A similar concept exists in Norway. As a part of a comprehensive reform of primary, lower and upper secondary education in 2006, two new subjects were introduced, one in lower and one in upper secondary. In both subjects, career guidance is supposed to have a substantial place in the curriculum. The overall intention is that better guidance will help students in making more informed educational and career choices. By lowering the risk of making poorly informed choices, reduced dropout and increased completion are the assumed effects. The same thoughts are presented in the chapter on Finland. The authors note that 'during the past few decades, an attempt has been made to reduce young people dropping out of education as well as interruption of (vocational) schooling, for example by increasing vocational guidance and individual counselling (both in basic and secondary education)'. In Scotland, access to quality guidance is also considered a prerequisite for making more informed choices in relation to further education. As the author of the chapter on Scotland describes it, 'rational decision-making requires good information'. In Australia, pathway planning programs have been introduced. One example is the Managed Individual Pathways program (MIPs) that has been implemented in government secondary schools in the state of Victoria. This program provides all students aged 15 and above with individual assistance to develop education and career pathway plans. It serves as a framework for the development of individual-ised pathway plans and targeted career counselling.

It is clear that some countries have implemented systemic policies related to career guidance and counselling intended to give students a better foundation for their school and program choices, thereby reducing the chances of dropout and increasing the chances of completion. Of reported evidence on impact or effective-ness, the Australian MIPs program has been evaluated with the conclusion that it has helped raise Year 12 completion. For the other countries that have implemented large-scale career guidance and counselling schemes, it is not possible to say how well they work, as no evaluations have been reported.

Income Support

Another policy measure used in some countries is financial or income support to students from poor backgrounds. In Australia, the scheme is titled Youth Allowance. It is a federal government initiative which is family income means-tested and targeted at students 16 years of age or older from poor backgrounds. To receive support, per-sons under 18 must be in full-time education or training. In England and Scotland, young people from low income families can apply for the Education Maintenance Allowance (EMA), worth up to £30 per week. The idea behind this policy is that by addressing financial pressures, the students' economic circumstances will be less likely to prevent them from continuing in education and training. Evaluations in three countries show that there seems to be a positive effect of this kind of income support. In Australia, 'there is some evidence to suggest that this initiative has helped increase school completion'. In Scotland, an 'evaluation of the first pilot EMAs estimated that they increased participation rates by 7 percentage points overall, and by 9 percentage points among young people from low-income families'. In Spain, the conclusion is that the grant policies introduced there have had a greater impact on school enrolment than on school performance.

Raising the Compulsory School-Leaving Age

Possibly the most direct systemic measure targeting dropout is raising the compul-sory school-leaving age, that is, lifting the minimum age at which a person is legally allowed to drop out of school. It may seem obvious that adding another extra compulsory year of schooling will make students more likely to attend during that particular year. But will this bring about lower dropout rates in subsequent, non-compulsory education?

The school-leaving age has been raised in some Australian states. In South Australia the school-leaving age was increased from 15 to 16 in 2003, and further increased to 17 years of age from 2009. Similar changes have been made in Victoria, Western Australia and Tasmania. These changes have been introduced largely in the belief that they will lead to increased school completion and smoother transitions to further education and work.

In the United States, the school-leaving age varies from state to state with most having a leaving age of 17 or 18, but a handful having a leaving age of 16. In some of the states where it is 16 or 17, there have been proposals to raise the compulsory schooling age to 18 years of age. The chapter on the United States refers to a recent review of several studies that examined the relationship between the state compulsory schooling age and dropout or graduation rates, which found that states with higher compulsory schooling ages had lower dropout rates or higher graduation rates (Rumberger & Lim, 2008).

In England it has been decreed that those who started in secondary school in September 2008 will form the first cohort obliged to participate in some form of officially recognised education or training until the day they reach 17 years of age. In 2015 the law will require all young people to participate until their 18th birthday. The intention is to retain students in some form of education and training for longer, and by doing this increase the numbers who obtain upper secondary qualifications.

The new English legislation has been a source of debate. In a critical review of the new legislation, Wolf (2008) argues that it runs counter to the understanding about the relationship between motivation and learning. She also states that this reform will have a negative impact on the youth labour market. Many businesses that employ 16- and 17-year-olds will stop doing so, she writes, because of the requirement to provide them with formal, recognised training. This will, according to Wolf, harm the most disadvantaged and marginalised young people. The counter argument is that now employers will have to provide young people with the necessary vocational education and training to enable them to progress both within and beyond their current employment. This will be good both for the country's economy and for the individual.

Wolf's arguments may be pertinent. It is possible that raising the leaving age will keep a greater proportion of students in school for longer, but it is unlikely that the selection processes that are producing social stratification will change. The different country chapters in this book suggest that the characteristics of dropouts are similar and the same sorts of students are likely to be failures in a system with a raised school-leaving age. The question is, will there be fewer of them? There may be better results if instead of raising the school-leaving age, educational systems invest more in addressing the challenge of creating pedagogy that will make more students want to stay, voluntarily.

Vocational Education as a Program for Reducing Dropout and Increasing Completion

Program reforms have provided one of the main policy tools available to nations to improve completion rates. One of the key program reforms in many systems has been the development or transformation of vocational education.

In Australia, one of the main program developments in recent years that has worked to help raise rates of school completion has been the implementation and expansion of vocational education. In that country, vocational education in schools has been developed as an alternative to traditional academic programs to assist an increasing number of young people, with a wider range of abilities, to participate in upper secondary courses and obtain relevant qualifications. A study which found that Year 9 student who were planning to drop out were ultimately more likely to complete school if they entered vocational education courses rather than academic or general programs (Lamb & Vickers, 2006) indicates that the availability of vocational education courses can improve the likelihood of school completion.

In Scotland, authorities view vocational learning as a way of addressing disengagement and low participation. Policy-makers there, according to the chapter on Scotland, 'see an expansion of vocational learning and an improvement in its status as a means to expand participation in post-compulsory learning as well as to achieve the desired curriculum diversity and cultural change'. This goes for vocational education and training in schools as well as apprenticeships provided in alternative settings.

The chapter on Scotland, however, cautions against this simplistic perception of vocational education as a solution leading to increased participation, reduced dropout and increased completion. The chapter argues that the quality of apprenticeships is uneven, and that even if they tend to be successful under specific sectoral and labour market conditions, they cannot be expanded to any sector or labour market context where these conditions are not satisfied. They are less suitable for the lowest qualified school leavers and cannot be used as the principal means of attracting and motivating young people who would otherwise drop out of learning. It is also argued that 'vocational learning has an important role both as a component of general education and as a principle for organising some learning pathways, but its potential contributions to the problems discussed above are both specific and limited'.

Vocational education is the main alternative in upper secondary education provided in almost all nations. In some countries, such as Switzerland and Germany, it enrols the largest numbers of upper secondary students. This is also true in Norway where, every year, around half of the students entering upper secondary education take a vocational track. The evidence in Chapter 2 suggests that countries that have developed strong systems of vocational education tend to have high completion rates. Countries that do not have these traditions, where vocational education has not really been a strong part of the school system, have recently turned to vocational education as a means of encouraging more young people to remain at school to completion. The evidence from such countries is that there are economic and labour market returns to vocational qualifications compared to not having any qualifications (dropping out). Other evidence, reporting on motivation, learning and disaffected learners, also suggests that vocational education and better vocational options may be an effective way of (re-)engaging at least some groups of disaffected young people prone to dropping out of school (Steedman & Stoney, 2004, cited in the chapter on Scotland).

At the same time, vocational education does not necessarily function as a way to increase completion and reduce dropout. Providing vocational programs is not sufficient to guarantee high completion, and vocational programs may not be the most appropriate way to engage the most disaffected young people. This is suggested by the Norwegian case, where the lowest completion rates are found within vocational education. Currently, around 80% of those doing academic programs complete, while the figure is only 50% for those in the vocational programs. The lower completion rates in vocational than in academic programs could indicate that vocational education is not necessarily the most appropriate solution for young students having problems with completion, though their completion rate may be lower again if these students were to enter the academic track. Those not completing vocational programs in Norway are typically low achievers with high absenteeism and their parents tend to have low levels of education. Thus, they have similar characteristics to dropouts in most other countries. The Norwegian case makes it reasonable to ask whether vocational education in other countries can work to bring such students through to completion. Since vocational education is organised and delivered differently in different countries, it may not play the same role in countries where there is a weak vocational education tradition. It may attract students who otherwise might have dropped out of academic tracks, and help them complete, but this may have little to do with vocational education per se, and simply reflect the fact that it is the main alternative to academic study.

One of the main issues with alternative programs such as vocational education is the tension between the role they can play as a safety net, enhancing students' chances of finding jobs as skilled workers, and the role they play as streams of relegation, orienting students from poorer backgrounds away from higher education and the professions (Shavit & Muller, 2000). If vocational education works to improve school completion it may also contribute effectively to stratification and the reproduction of inequality. There are few examples in the case study chapters of where vocational education provides the same foundations and offers access to the same opportunities beyond school as academic or general education. This remains a critical issue and challenge for systems relying on vocational education to reduce dropout and raise completion rates.

Diversified Qualifications and Extended Schooling

In some countries, schemes have been introduced allowing students to complete equivalent qualifications and, in some cases, qualifications that are not really equivalent to academic upper secondary or vocational qualifications.

In the United States, the *General Education Development* (GED) certificate has been developed as an equivalent qualification to the high school diploma. The numbers of young people now completing a GED are quite large, both in percentage terms and in absolute numbers. Yet there is considerable debate about its equivalence. There is concern about whether or not those who attain a GED have reached or achieved the same standard of skills as those who gain a regular high school diploma. Research suggests that the earnings and employment returns to the GED are significantly less than those to the regular high school diploma though better than for dropouts without any qualifications (see Chapter 1 and the chapter on the United States).

In Norway it is possible to gain recognition of learning or achievement for those who do not complete an academic or vocational qualification through what is termed *competence at a lower level* – a certificate of competence which is awarded after having been a *learning candidate* (such as an apprentice or someone not aiming for the journeyman's exam). This has not been a popular option: less than 1% of all cohorts after 1994 have chosen this option. A new way to achieve competence at a lower level, the *Certificate of Practice*, is being tested in the school years 2007–10. This gives the students the option to go through a 2-year upper secondary education which is mainly based on practical learning in a workplace, finishing with a competence test. Preliminary results from the evaluation of this new scheme are positive, with potential dropouts more likely to remain at school, better able to cope and with more positive attitudes towards school (Markussen et al., 2009). However it is too early to draw any firm conclusions. Even if this program is successful, the benefits of such a certificate in the labour market may well be minimal and therefore the role of the qualification controversial.

In Iceland, a new degree, the *Upper Secondary School Leaving Certificate*, was introduced in 2008. It takes one and a half to two years to complete, and is aimed at students who do not plan to complete further degrees. One of its main purposes is to reduce dropout at the secondary level by offering an alternative course of study for those who are at risk of dropping out. Students who undertake the course can use it as a bridge to other upper secondary courses such as academic qualifications and vocational education, though it does not qualify students for post-school study. Therefore, it is not clear how popular it will be given that it only conveys rights to study at the same level. It may persuade students to complete at least one and a half years instead of the one year which many typically complete before dropping out – but this remains to be seen.

In Australia, a similar qualification has been introduced in the state of Victoria. Known as the *Victorian Certificate of Applied Learning* (VCAL), it was introduced as an option for groups of students who tended to fail or not complete mainstream upper secondary courses. VCAL is a more applied or 'hands-on' option for students at upper secondary level. It provides practical, work-related experience, as well as literacy and numeracy skills and the opportunity to build personal skills focusing on life and work. It is an accredited upper secondary certificate, though it does not provide access to higher education or the main avenues of post-secondary study.

Giving students the possibility of completing upper secondary education with an equivalent qualification, or with a qualification at a lower level than a full vocational qualification, might support higher rates of completion (e.g., Markussen et al., 2009). But research suggests that the alternative qualifications may be less valuable in the labour market (e.g., OECD, 2009, p. 23; Rumberger & Lamb, 2003; Frøseth, 2008).

Linked to the idea of offering alternative qualifications is the notion of offering additional years of school to catch up or as bridging years to other courses. An example is provided by Year 13 courses offered in Australia which aim to work as a bridge between school and further study for students who have completed school but failed to gain a relevant qualification or to reach a satisfactory standard. Another example is the introduction of a voluntary extra year of schooling between compulsory and upper secondary education offered in Finland. In that country there is an option available for young people to have an additional year in basic education before entering upper secondary education. The idea is to prevent dropout immediately after compulsory education and to make it possible for some students to improve their achievements before entering upper secondary education. In 2006, only 2% of the cohort chose this option. However, despite the small numbers it represents an important policy option because it addresses critical issues associated with dropout: it targets students who have reached the end of compulsory education but have fallen behind and are at risk of failure in upper secondary education, and it gives students the opportunity to acquire the skills needed to help them cope with further study.

Systemic Reforms

Some countries have implemented ambitious comprehensive or wide-scale reforms across the whole system with one of the aims (among many others) being to reduce dropout and increase completion.

In Iceland an educational reform of the entire school system is currently being implemented. In this reform the dropout issue was given priority when the legislation was changed (The Preschool Act, No. 90/2008; The Compulsory School Act, No. 91/2008; The Upper Secondary School Act, No. 92/2008). The chapter on Iceland reports that:

> The intention explicit in the reform is that education shall be organised so as to meet the requirements and expectations of students, substantially increase curriculum flexibility, add to the number of educational pathways offered, facilitate the completion of upper secondary programs in 3 rather than the normative 4 years, and create conditions for more students to complete defined study programs. with a view to decreasing school dropout.

In 1994 a comprehensive reform was implemented in upper secondary education in Norway. Reform 94 introduced major changes in both structure and content. Different branches of upper secondary schooling (general, mercantile, vocational) were merged into a single system. Because of capacity constraints within vocational upper secondary education, large numbers of young people were, prior to the reform, forced to be early leavers between compulsory and post-compulsory education, at the age of 15 or 16. One of the main reasons for the reform was to make it possible for everyone who had just left compulsory education to enter upper secondary education. In terms of levels of participation, the reform was a success. As a result of the reform virtually universal entry to upper secondary education was achieved and the completion rate among vocational education students was doubled from 30% in the cohort entering upper secondary in 1991, to 60% in the cohort entering in 1994 (Støren et al., 1998). This suggests that Reform 94 worked because it opened up for almost all the opportunity to enter upper secondary education. But, in spite of this, dropout has remained a problem in Norway, as only two out of three in every cohort completes upper secondary education. When a new comprehensive reform was introduced in 2006, one of the main aims of that reform was to reduce early leaving and improve completion (St.meld. nr. 30, 2003–04).

Some countries have implemented systemic reform of their school systems with the aim of reducing dropout and improving completion. The Norwegian Reform 94 succeeded, even though dropout was not eliminated. It provides a clear example of policy implementation with impacts in the intended direction. Yet there is a need to wait to see if the reforms in Iceland and Norway deliver all of their intended effects.

Reducing Dropout and Raising Completion in All Systems

It is apparent from the case study chapters, and the previous chapter on inequality, that in spite of variations in the rates, by and large the same sorts of factors predict dropout and completion in every nation. This is what might be expected based on educational research and theory on the formation of social differences in education. The sociology of education has long underlined the importance of social structures for individual educational behaviour. There is an extensive literature and well-developed social theories on the mechanisms reproducing social disparities in education (see, for instance, Boudon, 1974; Bourdieu, 1977b; Willis, 1988; Shavit & Blossfeld, 1993). Social background predicts both school achievements and dropout. Across nations, ambitious, high-achieving students from educated, two-parent families are those who in general have the highest likelihood of completing their education.

It is also evident from the country chapters, and through the discussion in this synthesis chapter on policy, that the measures adopted and implemented to prevent dropout and increase completion vary, one might say in spite of the common factors affecting dropout and completion. Further, while noting that far from all of the reported strategies have been evaluated, based on the evaluations and effect studies referred to in the country chapters it is fairly clear that the key policies vary in their impact, with some seeming not to have had much effect on the dropout and completion rates, and others having had considerable impact. However, it is important to note that the systems differ in their starting points and in what they count as completion, and the effects of policies may well vary depending on the amount of 'room for improvement'. It may be that as systems reach similar mass levels cf completion, thanks to reforms and policy efforts and as the result of the effects cf labour market change, they will all report a similar size 'residual' core of dropout that is more difficult to shift. But all systems continue to strive and have implemented recent policies and reforms aimed at increasing completion rates.

Given the various continued efforts in different countries, it would be reasonable to ask two crucial questions. First of all, given where systems are, is it possible to reduce dropout and increase completion further? Second, based on the findings that the main factors accounting for dropout and completion are more or less the same across the 13 countries featured in the national case studies, is it possible to work out some new, perhaps common policies?

The first question may seem easier to answer, keeping in mind that this is a question of possibilities to help bring about better results. Based on the fact that some measures have actually been proven to impact on dropout and completion rates – even at local levels or among groups of schools, such as those in disadvantaged settings (see the chapters on Australia and the United States, for example) – it would be reasonable to conclude that it is possible to reduce dropout and increase completion rates given the right measures. The national case studies give cause to expect that measures targeting individuals and schools (measures defined here as individual-level or institutional-level) can have impact. Schools can be trans-formed and rates of completion for groups of individuals rise. Implemented in the right way, such measures may help to keep individuals in education who otherwise would have left.

Individual and school-level measures may well work effectively in different national contexts given that there are similar predictors of dropout and completion in every country, and similar processes of social differentiation. Of course it is important to recognise differences in national contexts that may affect how well such measures work – differences for instance in how the education system is organised and structured, how the labour market is functioning, and so on. And although the most important predictive variables are found to be more or less the same in nearly all the countries featured in the case studies, when it comes down to individuals and schools, there may be additional context-based variables that are influential.

In the past, as shown in Chapter 1 and in various case study chapters, the most significant reductions in dropout and increases in completion rates at national levels have involved systemic intervention, even if this has been in the context of other influences bringing about change, such as economic shifts and declining youth labour markets. In the period from the middle of last century, different countries have experienced large rises in upper secondary educational attainment across gen-erations. These have been in part influenced by large-scale reforms to schooling and programs. System-level policies linked to school organisation and program provision have been important to producing mass rates of completion. There are some specific examples of system-level reforms that have had a large impact on dropout and completion rates. One is Reform 1994 in Norway where everyone was given the right to 3 years of upper secondary education, alternative options were brought together in single comprehensive schools and vocational programs were strengthened. Following the reform there was a significant reduction in the number of early leavers and a significant improvement in the completion rate within vocational education.

The second question asked is whether it is possible, based on the experiences described in the national case studies, to identify and suggest common policies which might reduce dropout and raise completion. Some systems show that they have already reached mass levels of completion and others are moving towards this situation. The problem for most countries will become how to improve rates further and it may be that the actions needed are rather similar. So despite all the differences in national contexts, and the challenges connected with identifying relevant measures to combat dropout and improve completion, this chapter has discussed some policy measures which have been implemented in different countries: career guidance and counselling, income support for students, raising the compulsory school-leaving age, vocational education and alternative programs as a means to better completion and reduced dropout, and comprehensive institutional and program reforms. The common types of approaches taken suggest that it is possible to share experiences across borders and that effective policies may be relevant cross-nationally. But, this does not imply or prove that these policies have the potential to reduce dropout and improve completion in all countries in the same ways and with the same effects.

If policies are to be effective they need to handle a multitude of reasons for dropout, some of them universal, some of them country or system-specific. Thus, policies need to be based on a combination of a thorough understanding of what leads to dropout, as well as deep appreciation of local conditions. It may be possible for countries to learn from and assist each other since the systems in each country seem to work similarly in generating success and failure and the same sorts of students are affected, regardless of the country. A good starting point for working cooperatively and learning things from each system that may be of benefit for others will be a common commitment to developing better theory in understanding dropout and completion in each country context. Strong policies and interventions will be best developed on the basis of sound and tested theories about the reasons young people complete or drop out, and an understanding of the processes that contribute. Despite the extensive and common ways in which researchers in every country are able to identify the attributes of dropouts and completers, there remains a lack of powerful theories and understanding of the processes involved. There also needs to be a similar commitment to change, and recognition of the concerted effort required to address the complex and various social forces that affect behaviour. As concluded in a recent evaluation of the Norwegian *Plan of Action against Dropout in Upper Secondary Education*, to be successful, policies need to be 'firmly rooted in the educational system on all levels, not as a project, but as an ongoing, ordinary part of the activities of every school' (Buland & Havn, 2007). Thus, the task involves systematic, enduring, goal-oriented hard work across different arenas simultaneously. This conclusion might be valid for most of the countries represented in this book.

Finally, it may be worth repeating the point made by Rumberger in an earlier chapter of this book (on the United States), that in order to reduce dropout and increase completion, it will be necessary to remember that education is only one part of a larger social and economic system in which inequality is a main feature. In his words:

> It is unlikely that [we] will ever eliminate disparities in dropout rates...without eliminating disparities in the resources of families, schools and communities. To the extent that dropping out is a social and not just an educational problem, then effective solutions must address changes in families and communities as well as schools. But the more comprehensive the scope of change, the more difficult change becomes. Ultimately, the ability to 'solve' the dropout problem...may depend more on the country's ability to address widespread inequalities in the larger social and economic system.

References

Anderson, J. E. (1997). *Public policy-making. An introduction*. Boston: Houghton Mifflin.

Boudon, R. (1974). *Education, opportunity and social inequality*. London: John Wiley.

Bourdieu, P. (1977a). *Outline of a theory of practise*. Cambridge: Cambridge University Press.

Bourdieu, P. (1977b). Cultural reproduction and social reproduction. In J. Karabel & A. H. Halsey (Eds.), *Power and ideology in education*. New York: Oxford University Press.

Buland, T., & Havn, V. (2007). *Intet menneske er en øy. Rapport fra evalueringen av tiltak i Satsing mot frafall* [Evaluation of measures against dropout]. Trondheim: SINTEF Teknologi og samfunn. Gruppe for skole-og utdanningsforskning.

Frøseth, M. (2008). *Tre år etter videregående opplæring. Kartlegging av overgangen til videre utdanning og arbeidsliv blant personer som avsluttet videregående opplæring i Østfold våren 2003* [Three years after upper secondary]. Report 46, 2008. Oslo: NIFU STEP.

Giddens, A., & Sutton, P. W. (2009). *Sociology*. Cambridge: Polity.

Lamb, S., & Vickers, M. (2006). *Variations in VET provision across Australian schools and their effects on student outcomes* (LSAY Research Report No. 48). Melbourne: ACER.

Markussen, E., Høst, H., Evensen, E., & Prøitz, T. S. (2009). *Evaluering av forsøk med praksisbrev*. Delrapport 1 [Evaluation of the Certificate of Practice. Report 1]. Report 32, 2009. Oslo: NIFU STEP.

Organisation for Economic Co-operation and Development (OECD). (2009). *Education at a glance. OECD indicators*. Paris: OECD.

Rumberger, R. W., & Lamb, S. (2003). The early employment and further education experiences of high school dropouts: A comparative study of the United States and Australia. *Economics of Education Review, 22*(4), 353–366.

Rumberger, R. W., & Lim, S. A. (2008). *Why students drop out of school: A review of 25 years of research* (Report No. 15, California Dropout Research Project). Santa Barbara, CA: UCSB. Retrieved from http://cdrp.ucsb.edu/dropouts/pubs_reports.htm#15

Shavit, Y., & Blossfeld, H-P. (1993). *Persistent inequality: Changing educational attainment in thirteen countries*. Boulder, CO: Westview Press.

Shavit, Y., & Muller, W. (2000). Vocational secondary education, tracking and social stratification.In M. Hallinan (Ed.), *Handbook of the sociology of education* (pp. 437–452). New York: Springer.

Sidney, M. S. (2007). Policy formulation: Design and tools. In F. Fischer, G. J. Miller & M. S. Sidney (Eds.), *Handbook of public policy analysis. Theory, politics and methods*. Boca Raton, FL: CRC Press.

Steedman, H., & Stoney, S. (2004). *Disengagement 14–16: Context and evidence* (Discussion Paper 654). London: Centre for Economic Performance, London School of Economics.

St.meld. nr. 30. (2003–2004). *Kultur for læring* [Culture for learning]. Oslo: Utdannings-og forskningsdepartementet.

Støren, L. A., Skjersli, S., & Aamodt, P. O. (1998). *I mål? Evaluering av Reform 94: sluttrapport fra NIFUs hovedprosjekt* [Crossing the finish line? Evaluation of Reform 94]. Report 18, 1998. Oslo: NIFU.

The Compulsory School Act No. 91/2008. Retrieved from http://www.nymenntastefna.is/media/frettir//Compulsory_school_Act.pdf

The Preschool Act No. 90/2008. Retrieved from http://www.nymenntastefna.is/media/frettir//Preschool_Act.pdf

The Upper Secondary School Act No. 92/2008. Retrieved from http://www.nymenntastefna.is/media/frettir//Upper_secondary_school_Act.pdf

Willis, P. (1988). *Learning to labour: How working class kids get working class jobs*. London: Saxon House.

Wolf, A. (2008). *Diminished returns. How raising the leaving age will harm young people and the labour market*. London: Policy Exchange.

Index

S. Lamb et al. (Eds.), *School Dropout and Completion: International Comparative Studies in Theory and Policy*, DOI 10.1007/978-90-481-9763-7,
© Springer Science+Business Media B.V. 2011

LaVergne, TN USA
11 March 2011
219686LV00004B/40/P

Hair Highlights And Lowlights

By Amy Miller

An Old Line Publishing Book

Printed in the United States of America

ISBN-13: 978-0-9786948-8-3

ISBN-10: 0-9786948-8-0

Looking for a publisher?

Old Line Publishing is always looking for authors with original manuscripts. We hope that you will contact us and share your thoughts, ideas, stories, and/or already written material with us so that we can help you turn your idea into a timeless treasure and share it with the world.

Old Line Publishing, LLC

P.O. Box 624

Hampstead, MD 21074

Toll-Free Phone: 1-877-866-8820

Email: oldlinepublishing@comcast.net

Website: www.oldlinepublishingllc.com

Dedication

This book is dedicated to my loving husband, Marty. He has taught me the most important life lesson. Do what is right and treat people well. It does not matter if they like you. You will never please everyone so why worry.

Acknowledgements

Thank you to all of my special people! I could have never written this book without so many of you encouraging me to do so. I love you all, and can't thank you enough for your words of inspiration and support. I must first thank my parents for helping me follow my hairstyling dream, my sister, Cindy, for lending me her head so many years ago, and to my best friend Natalie whom has been in my life for almost thirty years. Thanks also to Lisa who helped me make it through hair school. To my loving husband Marty, and my friend Cindy who helped me not only make it through the tough times in this industry, but helped me find the humor in those tough times too. To my inspiring children, Chris, Wyatt, and Kendall, you guys are the reason that I try so hard. To all of my book club friends, clients that have stood by me, and friends both old and new, I give you all credit. I got my material from you guys, so this book is mostly about you, with the exception of some crazy clients. I am glad you enjoy my sarcasm and bathroom humor. Without Cindy, Caroline, Natalie, Carole, Deb, Mike, and Craig, this may not have even happened, so I thank you all from the bottom of my heart. I could go on and on, but I won't.

Table of Contents

In the Beginning. . .

or

My Quest to Become a Hairapist

Let's start from the beginning, shall we? I was born to be a "hair-a-pist." I have always loved harmless gossip, strange people, humor, creativity, and sometimes even a little potty humor. I have always given my hair clients counseling during our hair sessions, free of charge since I am free of psychological training. Given my natural inclinations and a flair for style, a career in hairstyling, or "hairapy," was for me.

Let me break it down for you. To figure out what a career in hairapy actually is we must start with the first part of the word, "hair." I love to style hair. It is my passion. The second part of the word is "a," meaning "one." I am "one." The last part of the word is the "py" part, pronounced "pee," which is the potty humor. So "I" like to style "hair" and "joke around." It is all pretty simple. When you make me mad, I consider myself a "hair-a-pissed."

I am excited to share my hair quest, or my "hair-a-quest," with you. I prefer the word "quest" to "journey," as "journey" sounds way too serious and is, in my opinion, overused. The word journey can also be confused with the 1980s band named Journey, and since I can't sing, "quest" fits better. Now that we are clear on that, let me share my "hair-a-quest" to becoming a "hair-a-pist."

From the time I was a little girl, I knew in my heart of hearts what I wanted to be when I grew up. I knew that I wanted to be a movie star. I have not yet given up on that dream. I am very patient. Other than that, I also wanted to be a hairstylist. Some people say that they know what they want to be when they grow up, but I really knew! Even as a very young girl, I would practice hairstyling on anyone and everyone who would let me. I did not want to be a teacher, marine biologist, or a veterinarian like my friends. Of course I would have *settled* for a television actress, model, or a singer. If I could actually *sing*, I would definitely be a singer! But, mostly I wanted to be a hairstylist.

My life began in the 1970s. My entire future started in my bedroom in Randallstown, Maryland. Let me rephrase that. My hairstyling future started in my bedroom in Randallstown, Maryland. I would sit on the floor, as a child, for hours at a time setting and styling my Farrah Fawcett doll head. I would also deplete my entire stock of hair twists by decorating Barbie's hair. I could have re-named her "Jamaican Barbie" with the amount of beads and hair ties I managed to work into her hair. Or maybe "Alopecia" Barbie for the ones to which I took scissors. "Punk Rock Barbie," ok you get the picture.

I spent hours playing with dolls, all the while perfecting my craft. When I was not spending time styling my dolls' hair, I would often be found in my powder room. I would use the wall mirror and medicine cabinet mirror to check out every single angle of my own hair. I was not in love with myself, or with my hair. In reality, I was being meticulous about my craft. I would comb my hair in hundreds of ways until finally the "wings" or "feathers" as we called them, fell perfectly into place. "I" was my very first hair client. There was some hairbrush singing going on in there too I must admit… sorry, I went back to the singing part. I would lock the cascading hair into place with an extremely flammable substance known as Adorn hair spray. The air was absolutely toxic with the stuff, and that may explain a few things about my personality today.

My dad was quite a trooper back in the day. He was actually not a state trooper, but merely a "good sport." When I say a "good sport," I mean he would let me do whatever I wanted to *his* hair. My dad would sit for hours while I pulled and brushed the hair on his head smooth enough to get the right pigtails placed on the top with no bumps. Then there was the time I cut four inches of hair off of my cousin Kelly's head while spending the night at our grandparents' house. I was only about twelve years old, but confident in my skills. My Aunt Kathy must have really liked me, because I do not remember getting in trouble at all for that caper. I do remember insisting that Kelly should be the one to call her mom and inform her of our hair session instead of me, just in case.

The beauty industry has always been an interest of mine. After all, I *am* beautiful. Well, I *assume* that somewhere, someone thinks I am beautiful. I think my husband might think that…I hope? I took the beauty industry very seriously. At fifteen years old, I moved on from Barbie's hair, to my best friend Natalie's hair. I would cut her hair as if I really knew what I was doing. Needless to say, I did not know what I was doing. We held our own fashion shows with hair freshly cut by me; we put on make-up and changed outfits in hopes of sending our pictures into *Seventeen Magazine* and getting noticed. We never got noticed. We never got noticed, because our pictures never got sent. My mom convinced me that the editors would remove my face and put it on a nude body of someone. Did she not think my body was good enough for that magazine? If they got a hold of these pictures of Natalie and me, this could damage our future careers. "It is just too risky," Mom would say. I really have never known a hairstylist who has had her career damaged because of altered *Seventeen Magazine* photos, but I could have been the first. Then again, it may have actually helped my career. No, I remember what I looked like back then. It would not have helped. That does not matter much at this point. After all, we would not want to sell ourselves short by sending in those pictures. We were much prettier on the inside, and no one would see our insides! I just chose not to be a model. It was my choice.

Natalie and I took a water spray bottle to our armpits in our never-sent or seen photos. We wanted to look like we legitimately got physical. Olivia Newton John was big back in the day, so maybe the magazine would compare us, if my mom had let us send them that is. This experience would prove to help us later on in life when Natalie and I worked in the beauty industry together. We were both all about the beauty, even if it was for our own enjoyment and not for the editors to tamper with. Who cared about a stupid magazine cover anyway?

As time went by, I made the decision to stay in high school full time instead of doing the trade/technological school that was offered within the high school. I wanted to be involved in sports, theatre, and clubs. High school was the place for me. I even attended a Political Science Club meeting at Randallstown High School in my senior year. I wanted to prove how "well-rounded" I was. In reality, my main goal was to attach the club's title to the description next to my name in the yearbook. I thought the Political Science Club made me look intelligent. While I only lasted one meeting, I was still considered a member. I guess even then I cared about how things "looked." Sadly, I did not make it into the Thespian Society for which I thought I was a shoe-in. Trust me when I say, I was, and still am, way more "thespian" than "political." They screwed up on that one. Those missing scenery hours that were not logged in kept me from being a "thespian." I guess being cast as the tomboy character named Anybodies in the school production of *West Side Story* was not "thespian" enough for those prestigious members. Doing hair and make-up for the school productions, in my opinion, *should* have counted toward scenery hours. For sure I am not bitter! Nor am I getting off track. Really?

I did manage to tie with my best friend Natalie for the honored "Best Sense of Humor" award my senior year. How does this relate to a book on hairapy? In many ways humor is "hairaputic." Sometimes humor will save even the most uncomfortable situations in the salon. Natalie and I pretended to trip up the steps as we accepted the award just to prove how funny we were. Just like Laverne and Shirley, we were the funny pair. We have always enjoyed each other's humor and while Natalie may dispute it, we all know who the "Laverne" was! Let me just say I was drinking a milk and Pepsi as I wrote this. You decide who was who. Shirley had the better hair back then. Natalie and I decided to start our own club. We started the "Who Really Cares If You're A Thespian" club. We hold our meetings about once every ten years or so, just about the time that our high school reunions take place. We are the only attending members.

Hair school would come after my most memorable high school years. I have not always made the right decisions in life, but hair school after high school was a perfect fit for me. But, let's not leave the high school years just yet. Here's what I was thinking about my future then. I figured I would just practice my untrained hair cutting skills on my friends, or pretty much anyone who would let me until my high school years had passed. I would learn the techniques later. Until then, I would play softball, go to parties, try out for school plays that apparently were not thespian worthy, spend time with friends, and hang out with my boyfriend, who just happened to *be* a thespian. This all sounded like a good plan at the time! My high school years were truly treasured years. I even did my own hair for the proms I attended. It looked perfect. Well, my hair looked perfect in a 1987 kind of way.

I had orange hair through some of my high school years due to perox-ide and lemon juice experimentations. Not the best look on a brunette. Thankfully Cyndi Lauper was popular. The home perms I had were the best! My *Toni* home perms would last about forty-eight hours, until my thick straight hair reverted back to its natural state. The time finally came when the damage I inflicted on Natalie's poor head called for damage control. Natalie had to get her hair "fixed" at a salon after my experimen-tal cutting. That day at Rosarios' hair salon was quite a memorable one. Fast forward for just a minute. For all the non-hairstylists out there, here is a bit of information for you. When stylists ask you if you cut your own hair, they actually already know the answer to that question.

Do you color your own hair? We know that one too. Natalie was a true friend and did not throw me under the bus when the stylist asked, "Who cut this hair? It's a mess!" All the while I was sitting in the waiting area dying! No, not applying hair color, physically dying! I was also praying that Natalie would love her new Annie Lenox look. This particu-lar look happened to be the only remedy for the botched up creation on top of her head. Thankfully she did love the look, or at least that is what she told me. The look went great for our "physical" photo shoot after all.

While all of my friends went off to college, I stayed home to attend my school. I am proud to say that living at home and receiving my MBA was my greatest accomplishment. It was the start of my career! I got it finished up in only nine months! That is just about the same time some of the girls I knew were having their babies. When I say MBA, I mean Maryland Beauty Academy certificate. Getting that certificate was not as easy as one may think.

Over the past twenty years I have gone from a shampoo girl to salon owner. This book is filled with real life stories too good to be true, yet they are true! None of the boring "how to" stories, but the really funny stories that I have heard from my years in the salon industry.

I have had hair clients and friends stick with me through thick and thin. I have also had clients who have cheated on me and came back and others who have cheated and never came back. It has been fun to see former clients at the market or mall just to watch their reaction. Some former clients seemed inclined to run and hide when they saw me, while others would speak. Before they would even say hi, they would start making excuses as to why they went to someone else for their hair. "I had a gift certificate," or "I went with my friend to her stylist." As long as the reason is not because I screwed up their hair, I am fine with it. I am not, and never have been, the hair police. My hair clients have always inspired me to be as loyal to them as they have been to me.

There are so many things that have happened in the salon that the public had no knowledge of, until now. Other salon owners may find that they are not alone in the situations they have had to deal with after reading these stories. In the text, I have touched on the stylists that I have worked with in the past as well as hair clients from the present. Some of my life experiences I would have never had if I had chosen a different path. This industry has shaped who I am today. I have never been really sure if that is good or bad, but I am in shape. I cannot imagine having such great material to write about if I were in any other field. Don't get me wrong; I am quite sure that accountants have a blast at their jobs, but perhaps in a different way. We all know that most accountants work quietly and alone while crunching numbers. In a lot of ways, I may have more stories to share than these folks. There has always been so much more to this field than cutting hair, and that is what I would like to share with you.

My first inspiration for writing came from the spectacular book entitled *Girlfriends Guide To Pregnancy* by Vicki Iovine. Now this book was what I was looking for! A book about the things "they" don't tell you.

While Shakespeare's, Twain's, or Poe's writings inspire some, Vicki inspired me! Sandi Kahn Shelton's books made me laugh. Let's not forget *30 Rock* writer Tina Fey. Her writing has been truly brilliant and inspirational. Anything with John Candy has always ranked high. I would like to someday be compared to Tina Fey, Rachel Ray, and John Candy, although John Candy is dead, and a man. Of course, I am not dead, or a man. On the flip side, I have never found inspiration from circus clowns. I have always found them uninspiring and creepy instead. I have never been coulrophobic like my friend Mark, but I agree that I have never appreciated the humor or inspiration in them. They always have awful hair anyway, so why should I write about them? Other than that, I am inspired by almost anything, as long as it is not clown related.

You may come to the conclusion that this book, when finished, was a silly, frivolous read written by someone grabbing for attention. You would not be entirely off base. However, written during an economic recession – a recurrent topic among clients in my chair – it was designed to give readers a break from the everyday worries. So, take a break from the worry and the stress, relax, and enjoy some mindless entertainment. This is intended to be a humorous look at the colorful world of the hair business and the fascinating, unique people in it, including myself. It is also a book about finding laughter when things just aren't going your way. If you think there is nothing funny at all about having hard times, you are right. That is why I am not writing about hard times. I have chosen to mask a few of the hard times with humor. It's much funnier that way. When I say mask, I am not referring to a clown or mime mask. Let's instead think of the comedy/tragedy theater type mask.

When I started sharing stories like the one about the hair client who would sit in my chair at 9:00 am and crack open a cold one, people started to listen. No, the client did not go for a "cold one iced coffee," but instead a "cold one beer." At least go for a Bloody Mary or an Irish Coffee, I'd say. The story about the soccer mom who was having an affair and offered to show me a picture of the manly man she was dating has always raised interest. She took her cell phone out of her purse and put it right back when she realized that she only had nudes of him. Do they call that "sexting" if you are over the age of forty, or is that just a high school term? I think I would call it "mid-life crissexting." When I started chatting about the eighty-seven-year-old female client that would tell dirty jokes so raunchy you could not repeat them, people really started to listen up. "Do you want to see the tattoo of my mouse?" the eighty-seven-year-old lady who escaped death just weeks ago would ask everyone in ears shot. I said, "sure." She pointed to her stomach and said, "Where did he go? He's not there anymore, my cat must have eaten him!" Only she did not use the word "cat." WOW! Now there's a joke I was glad she told ten minutes before the youth pastor's wife sat in my chair.

Reality TV has been more popular than ever in recent years because of folks like these. Some people just seem to revel in making real life truly stranger than fiction. People have told me such wild things. In return, I have passed these stories on to you, without naming names or hurting feelings… I hope.

Most of the names in this book have been changed to protect the innocent…or rather the guilty. I will never reveal any secrets that I promised to keep, or reveal any painful details of people's marriages, disturbing facts about their lives, or things that are just too personal or hurtful to share. There are many stories that will never get told. They really aren't funny anyway. On the flip side, sometimes clients speak extra loud so that their story can be heard. Now those are the stories I am sharing! Client retention, as well as client confidentiality, has always been very important to me. Believe me, I would never cut off my nose to spite my face unless it was to smooth out that crooked bump on the top. That being said, I have some funny stories, from some funny clients, that are worth sharing. Since I was never able to be a professional singer, TV actress, or movie star, I will do my best to entertain my readers. Don't worry, this book is not about you anyway; it is safe to read.

I hope to gain the respect for my profession that I and some of my fellow hairstylist friends so richly deserve. The stereotype of a hairstylist is that of someone who is uneducated or flaky. Maybe you think of your stylist as someone that is a little bit quirky, gossipy, gum chewy, and scattered with crazy hair. While I went to hair school with some of these people, and even worked with a few, I assure you that anyone who makes it in this business does not fit those descriptions. Or, maybe we don't fit ALL of those descriptions. To make it in this field you constantly have to find ways of reinventing yourself and tapping into your creative side. You have to be respectful and in a good mood most of the time. Not many depressed hairstylists have ever made a lot of money. Hard work, that positive disposition, and self-motivation will take you far. If you have chronic fatigue, this is not the career for you. This may not be the book for you either. I am sure you are in bed right now and not reading anyway. My intention in writing this is not to offend the sleepy, nor is it to make people mad. I prefer to make people laugh.

Over the years I learned how to "master" the art of hairdressing. I "mastered" how to stay cool in a crisis situation, and how to find humor in the bizarre. That being said, I have my MBA, with a master in communications, and a minor in psychology. It is not an easy field, but it sure beats the circus! As my nurse friend once said to me, "My career is easy, if you mess up someone's hair they will kill you!" This is a true fact. As a non-thespian I say, "Just stay cool buddy boy! Play it cool."

Chapter One
M.B.A.

I have long believed many people have wondered how their hairstylists got their start. Then again, perhaps no one really cares; but hey, you got through the introduction, so here's how I did it.

Some stylists went the high school tech training, some also apprenticed under a salon owner to acquire their license. Then there are the folks that just chose to smoke pot all day and do nothing. Who wants to be mellow and do nothing all of the time? OK, well from the looks of it, a lot of people did, but I was one of the motivated ones! I thought I would try the hair school after high school route. I thought I would learn more that way. I am not totally convinced that I did, but here is how it played out.

When I started off in beauty school I was given some basic rules. You must attend the beauty school. That seemed to be the hardest rule for some to follow. You must attend hair school for 1,500 hours, you must wear a white nurse's uniform, and you must be willing to experiment on the public as well as on each other. In the end, you also had to be able to pass a state board test. You no longer serviced "customers;" these same people were renamed "*clients.*" This just sounded more professional. Sort of like the term sanitation engineer has a more sophisticated ring than trash man, or the media specialist seems more technically polished than the librarian. It's all how you look at it.

Most of all, you learned in hair school the "must nots" of this industry. The topics of conversation that are strictly forbidden were quickly taught to you. Politics were and are never to be discussed, so I guess I wasted that day in high school with the brainy Political Science clubbies. Never discuss religion, but don't be surprised if others do and one day you wind up getting tipped with a Bible. Never ever go on and on about yourself unless it is so entertaining that you make the clients forget entirely about their bad day. Conversation can be used as a distraction tactic so the client is unaware that you just cut four inches off of their head instead of two because you were talking. I have never done that, by the way.

Talking can break that very uncomfortable silence. So can a fart. On the flip side, it is also important to stop talking when the client is not feeling very talky. Coming to your styling chair with a magazine in hand is a red flag that they are not very talky. If a client feels the need to bring you a picture of Halle Berry, be kind and explain that they may not look exactly like Halle Berry when you are finished, but not to worry because they are prettier than she is anyway. Having the client look great when they leave is the most important thing of all. Well, having them at least feel like they look great is the most important thing. I am after all, a beautician, not a magician. Oh my gosh, I hate that phrase!

So what is really important in hair school? Distinguishing dry scalp from head lice is very important, and it is one of the first things discussed in hair school. Is it a nit or dirt? That is a tough call sometimes. If they do have head lice, just get them the heck out before you have to put every-thing you own in a green garbage bag for a week! If you can, try not to embarrass them like I have heard some stylists do. When you say some-thing like, "Oh my gosh, hey Yvette, come look at this. Is this what head lice looks like, gross?!" They tend to take that the wrong way. Just whis-per to them what the situation is and they will be fine.

If the client is set on the outdated "feathering" or "winging" of the hair that meets in the back of the head and looks like a butt crack, give it to them. Let them fly on out with those wings and feathers, but try to up-date them if you can. There is nothing worse than a crying client, so give them what they want, just do not expect any referrals. Or shall I say just don't "accept" any referrals. At some point the style is bound to come back and they will be the first ones to showcase it, even before they know it. At that point their referrals are welcome. Some people are just not up for change as much as you try to make them. That is what makes us all different.

Quickly a stylist learns how important social skills can be. If some-one asks your opinion, you tell him or her honestly what you think while remaining as neutral as you possibly can. Remember how I said politics are never to be discussed? Sometimes, during an election year, clients just can't help themselves. The questions always get back to that same, judgmental and important question, "are you a Republican or Democ-rat?" I always make sure I am the first one to ask it, and my answer to that question back to them is always the same, "me too!" What are they going to do, ask to see my voter's card? I think I'm safe with that answer. I change my mind daily anyway. See that, even in my writings I am still neutral! There are also non-committal words and phrases that come into play such as, "Is that right? Really? No way! How about that? You're joking? Get out of town?" These key words and phrases come in particu-larly handy when the soft talking client is in your chair and your blow dryer is on. You can run into trouble if they ask you a question. Questions do not really fit with "really," "is that right" or "no kidding" repertoire. Whenever I have stumbled on an answer I have usually given them a simple, "Oh I'm sorry, I thought you said something else!", then I side track with a quick, "What was the weather doing when you came in?" After all, we never want the client to feel like we have not been interested or listening to them. Once in a great while, I have just not been feeling that same level of excitement over the fact that a client's two-year-old can say the word "hola" thanks to watching *Diego*, or that they are going to Europe for three weeks to backpack and stay in hostels. Why anyone would want to stay in a "hostel" environment is beyond me anyway.

When a proud dad announces something as ridiculous sounding as, "Hey everybody, Seth David is here," we act like we have never in our lives seen such a child, and we should call the media! Seth David is here for his first haircut! Where is the certificate and camera? Wait, wait, I have stickers and suckers! Bring out that marching band and confetti! Sometimes, on rare occasions, these facts just do not interest us. Most of the time we are tickled about these things, but sometimes our minds are elsewhere. In hair school you learn the art of acting interested! So, now that I can "act" interested, I wonder if I can find a thespian club to enroll in? I think Seth David is about twenty one years old by now. I bet his parents are still proud of him. Maybe they announce his arrival at frat parties these days? I love when the proud new parents come in with the camera crew to document these events. Grandma has the camera, Mom is calming baby Johnny, and Dad has the video rolling. I knew I would get on camera one way or another! I just always thought it would be a little different.

They tell you in school that the art of conversation can be your saving grace. I have heard it said over and over at trade shows that this career is about 20% skill and 80% personality. No one in this industry can dispute

19

the fact that a hairstylist does much more than style hair. Stylists are the sounding board of reason, the person you feel comfortable enough to tell your deepest, most private secrets to, all the while hoping that they do not write a book about you. Ironic, isn't it?

For some clients, we are their only friends. I am a friend to the little old "cat lady" who lives in a shoebox-sized house with her eighty-five cats. I know for a fact that the homeowners association is not her friend! If my Claritin ever stops working, she will not even have me as a friend. You learn quickly that a stylist has a duty to befriend. I am happy to listen, most of the time. I am not happy to cat sit for eighty-five cats though.

We are "hair-a-pists" to many. At times every single stylist has been a "hair-a-pist" to someone. There has never been any formal psychological training whatsoever for stylists who give counsel, and yet we feel more than qualified. Given time, hairstylists gain competence and confidence in their recommendations and consolations. I do not know exactly why, but I have become quite confident in the advice I give! Of course, if I start quoting Dr. Phil or Oprah I *really* gain respect! I told one client that she should try sleeping with another man for a change. The other man I thought she should sleep with was her husband. Her husband, in my opinion, was a better choice than Carlos, her painter. She did not break off her relations with Carlos, well, not until her house was finished being painted at least, but she did send me a gift card in the mail as a thank you for some good, sound advice. I have always tried to always remain honest and true to my clients, even if we kindly disagree. Who am I to judge anyway? My name is not Judy; it's Amy!

Prior to hair school, my experience mainly consisted of experimenting on family and friends. Oh, and sorry about that by the way, I owe you guys! No, actually, I owe nothing, as this same group of experiments would be cashing in on my services after Thanksgiving dinner, cookouts,

Christmas day, or after baby showers. Sometimes I offer before they even ask. Rooty friends and family make me look bad. I can't afford to look bad.

The client selection at hair school ranged from African American clients, Asian clients, Caucasian clients, men, children, and blue haired ladies, to the mentally challenged clients from the group homes behind the school. I can honestly say that because of this experience there is not a head of hair that I cannot tackle. Fred, the thirty-year-old student with a terrible mustache burn from messing around with hair color, cannot say the same. Fred chose to walk home one day instead of mastering the art of Jerri curling. His name was called to do the service and out the door he went. I can just imagine what the folks driving down Reisterstown Road thought when they drove pasted Fred, a 6' 2" Caucasian dude with burgundy hair, an agitated upper lip, and dressed completely in white. Fred had a mannequin head under one arm, a brief case under the other, and was headed for his apartment. I had the fortune to get called after he bolted. It all worked out fine and built my confidence even further. The only Jerri curl I have ever given, was given that very day. I am not sure if "Jerri" liked it, but it was curled!

I brag when I say that I never got called to give the second most dreaded service. Next to the Jerri curl, the pedicure was the worst. I mean think about it. Feet? Even the word is not pretty. My husband reminds me daily about how unattractive my own feet are and he is kind and loving, unless he is talking about my toes. I do have two toes that are longer than my big toe on both of my feet, which by the way is a sign of both intelligence and royalty. I am sure I am not alone. He chooses to call me "Nixon" toes. He claims that my very long toes look like they are giving him the peace sign. He then wiggles his peace fingers and quotes, "I am not a crook." While I like to think I have "dancer's feet," we both can pretty much agree that feet are kind of gross. I don't think Marty, my husband, ever got an offer to be a foot model himself. He really has no room to talk. At least my toenails don't grow straight up! As far as touching feet goes, in school we wore gloves for the Jerri curl application; not the case for pedicures. The Rosewood Group Home pedi did not entail wearing gloves. I escaped the deed of pushing back toe cuticles, scraping off callused heels, peeling out cheese, and cutting toenails so hard you feared scratching your cornea if you did not dodge them right. Most of the pedi's given were on the feet of elderly women with deficiencies evident to us by the pressure we needed to apply to cut through the toenail. The heels alone on these folks were so tough and callused that you could have easily scrubbed your dirty dishpans with them.

Some of the men and women had not been able to reach their feet for many years. A pedi was a true luxury. Let's not mention the very inexpensive hair school prices that they paid. I think they were bordering around, oh, free? "Skip the podiatrist Miss Arleen, just take the van to the beauty school in Owings Mills. The girls there will clean up your feet."

I am almost sure other caregivers were known to say, "No, no, Miss Ruth, you need not worry about that ingrown toenail, the girls at the beauty school can cut it out and just paint the skin." Even when soaked in a bubbly basin, this was a task that would dull any academy starter kit's tools. "They will work lotion in Miss Rose; this will help you out with that nagging psoriasis and get the circulation back into your feet. Just ask for a pedicure today!" The blue feet matched the blue hair at times! You will love the foot massage! It always baffled me why a pedicure was needed for one to acquire a cosmetology license. Doesn't this fall under the "manicure" license? Perhaps I should have gone to barber school? The skill to this day has never come in handy unless you count painting the toes of Kendall, my six-year-old daughter. I guess it does not matter much anymore really. That was twenty years ago. I am sure the students now get to use gloves. I guess when you think about it, the old clients' feet matter very little now. I can pretty much guess our clients from the old days are all, well, let's face it, they are all dead. That or they are all about 105 years old by now. Creepy!

At the time, I also was not sure why I needed to learn finger waves. This technique did come in handy one time for Dana, a bride, years later when she wanted a very romantic old Hollywood look for her wedding. Finger waving sure came in handy then; slippery gooey Jerri curling still has not.

I befriended a girl named Lisa back then; we met in hair school and have been friends ever since. She was the one person that I leaned on in hair school. She was the tall one, so really; she leaned on me I guess. I could write a book just on the experiences we shared alone. As a matter of fact, this book is mostly about Lisa and me. We had gone to the same high school but graduated different years. She was beautiful with her spiked hair and her heavy blue/black eyeliner, and ok, she is just a little bit older than me. She really embraced the late 1980s. Her hair was dark by nature but heavily frosted to a light blond. Her haircut was a perfectly rounded spiky look while still leaving the back very long. Yes, in hindsight it was a mullet, but back then it was edgy and stylish. It was a look that other girls envied, but few had the nerve to wear. Lisa was not the envy when it came to growing out that mullet! I will never forget her long hair in the back, and the hair combs on the sides of her head she placed in an effort to try to disguise the uneven layers growing in. The mullet is never an easy grow out.

Lisa was already twenty-one-years-old and was able to go clubbing on Friday nights when we met. I would sit in our morning theory class and listen to her stories about partying with the local bands. It was funny because, while we were working on styling our mannequin heads, she was talking about hanging out with a group called "Mannequin." Lisa was a fan of a fine establishment called Hammerjacks.

This "Hammerjacks" was the hottest ticket in town back in the day. I was under age, and did not even look eighteen, so my bar hopping days would come much later. I was a bit jealous of her rock and roll ways, and her free spirit. We had hair school classes Tuesdays through Saturdays. On many Saturday mornings Lisa would come into hair school with a flawless face of make-up. She would assure me that it looked even better the night before when she applied it. In time, I would come to visit this club Hammerjacks, but never really loved it like she did. Maybe it was the 1/2-inch of dirty pee water hanging out on the floor of the ladies room in this bar, or the scary bikers with tattoos, leather fringed coats, camel toed jeans, and chains that turned me off. I have never really been a fan of screaming hard rock music. I was more of the bubble gum Debbie Gibson type. Pop music was more my thing. Florescent double-layered socks, with a belted long shirt, and leggings from the store Foxmore where Natalie worked, were not a good Hammerjacks look… my mistake. I remember wondering why I got carded there when others were clearly underage and went right in. I think I know why now. It was my look. Whatever it was about this bar, it was just never my scene. With Lisa's perfect makeup, cool hair, and clubbing, she was the hippest one in this hair school for sure. We were to learn the ropes of hair school together.

Lisa started school with another friend of hers who was not too fond of me. She was probably jealous of my sexy feet. Lisa's friend, Tricia, had a hard life and my perky Rachael Ray personality would drive her insane. I found this out one day… when she told me. Tricia blasted me for being too excited about getting my degree. My MBA was right around the corner and this infuriated her. Could her distaste for me have had something to do with the fact that she was envious that I was way ahead of her in hours, yet we started school the same day? Looking back, I think it had more to do with the extreme morning sickness she had experienced due to her surprise pregnancy. Let's see, a surprise pregnancy? Never mind, that is a whole different book. It might not have been about me at all, but more about my perkiness. Or it could have been the fact that I kept saying, "look how flat my stomach is, I try to gain weight, but I just can't." Like most eighteen-year-olds, I thought for sure it was all about me. Time does change people, and oddly enough, in years to come, Tricia would call me and ask me to do her hair for her wedding. I did it because, truthfully, I am not much of a fighter. I prefer friends to enemies. We are now friends. Her hair looked great for her wedding and thankfully my ass was never kicked.

Every one of us in hair school had one thing in common. We were all humans… or at least most of the students were humans anyway. We were also inexperienced. Maybe inexperience was the only common bond we all shared. We all would learn from our mistakes. "Oops, that wax was just a little too hot this time Miss Sally." In those moments, we were all glad we were still in school. "Try applying some aloe vera gel or ice when you get home. The scabs will only last a day or two." There was the time a student took off of an entire eyebrow in "Waxing 101." "Whoops, oh, that's right, you roll the wax down not up!" "Try picking up an eyebrow pencil from the Rite Aid next door, that will get you by for a while." Then there was the frizzing the hair to oblivion by leaving a perm on too long. "Nope not ready yet, keep processing," Miss Janice would say. "Check it in five more minutes." Miss Janice was one of the African American instructors and was somewhat inexperienced with Caucasian hair in my opinion. She would say to the student when the frizzy perm was complete, "Ok, the hair is a little dry, here is a deep conditioner called cholesterol. Leave it on overnight and cover it with a plastic cap. The cap will insulate the head and add moisture to the hair. Apply it every night for the next three months or so. Rinse it out in the morning. It will repair your hair in no time!" Ok, no it won't Miss Janice!

Time for another Sheena Easton cut! That student happened to be me, and once again, I am so sorry about that Natalie. I really do owe you my friend! I have gotten much better over the years.

In a particularly interesting moment, one girl took the long curly sideburn off of a very religious Jewish client. Hmmm, what do we do next? "Do you want me to take the other curl off to match it up; or would that be an even bigger sin?" she asked. We learned quickly that Hasidic Jews do not wear the hair short around their faces. The sideburns they wear even have a name. They are called "peyos" and they are to always remain long, unless of course a stylist whacks them off by mistake. The stylist assured the young boy's mom that the sideburn hair would grow out by the time his bar mitzvah rolled around. Even tilting his yarmulke a bit could not cover up this mistake. No charge! This one is a freebee. There was no exchanging of "pesos" for cutting off the "peyos." Oi, that was a tough one.

Quickly after such blunders you learned how to communicate. "Do you want the hair cut over the ear?" When the client said over the ear, he meant he wanted hair over top of the ear and covering it. He did not want the hair around the ears cut short. Oops, that one did not have a happy ending. A quick lesson in client communication was learned that day. He was so mean and I believe he started cussing at this stylist. He looked just like Avery Schreiber. You know, the guy from the old Doritos commercial and guest host of the Muppet Show. While Avery, the Doritos guy, did wear his hair long, this guy's fro was now short around the ears. It actually looked much better short around his ears. She did him a favor, but sadly he saw it differently. Sometimes we must give them what they want. Even if it means another free haircut on the house.

I missed hair school one day to fix my sister Cindy's hair. You cannot leave frosting bleach on someone's hair for an hour without paying some sort of a price. The word bleach is as harsh as the product. Another lesson learned. When my friends saw the hair remnants that remained in the frosting cap as I pulled it off of Cindy's head, they magically disappeared. They all vanished into thin air. Even Houdini would have been impressed with this one. The hair party was over friends. This Hell's Kitchen is officially closed! No more kitchen beautician in my house tonight! That would be my first lesson in panic control. I failed my first lesson miserably! The toner toned down what was left of Cindy's hair.

Thankfully, hair does grow back and the tears eventually stopped. Her tears stopped too. Lucky for me, her over-processed hair would make my finger waves fall right into place when it was time to take the state board test. The glass is always half full if you look at it like that. I was not thinking about a glass at that point; unless it was a glass filled with some sort of amnesic liquid I could put in Cindy's drink. I was just trying to get myself together long enough to stop hyperventilating and keep my sister from killing me. My poor mother! Who would she comfort, the victim or the perpetrator? My mom was not in a good spot. Unlike the hair client that would be out of your life forever after these types of accidents, this one was FAMILY! I would feel that wrath for a long time. I would watch Cindy pick through her tangles and I would plead to her, "Please, please, please do not use too much tension, I am afraid the hair may break off!" She would say back in an angry voice, "What hair?"

There are some things that you never get used to in the beauty industry. I, myself, never really get used to lumpy cystic heads, chunky dandruff, and the smell of really dirty greasy hair when it hits a hot curling iron. I have gotten used to moles in the head. Moles do not bother me in the least. I think this is because I have what some have even called a very small "nipple" on the back of my own head. While a "Moley Russell's wart" does not freak me out, catching a "Moley Russell's wart" with my comb unexpectedly does freak me out! It can't feel great for the client either. I have yet to lose one, a mole on the head that is, not a client.

You quickly learn in hair school that some folks are here to learn a trade for a big price tag; others are here to learn the same thing… but for free. What? I am paying money for the same education that some are getting for free? How can this be? How can I get this so called "scholarship" that they speak of? I got good grades in high school. I was involved in after school activities. I was a member of the Political Science Club for gosh sakes! So what if I'm not a thespian! Hair school I found out was a lot different than taking the SAT's, ACT's, or any other standardized test. The letters GED did not even matter much in this school. It appeared that I would be SOL when it came to a free ride. This did not allow me to LOL! Some of these folks could not even pass a drug or paternity test, let alone an entrance exam. They were the ones going to school for free?

Why did I have to pay for the same education? There were no interviews being held for these applicants. Not even a pop quiz given on, "Who's your baby Daddy?" The scholarships for this school had nothing to do with your performance, well not school performance anyway. I guess the hair school scholarship recipients were also the ones that named their new baby boys "Grant." This to me did not seem fair. It did explain some things however. It explained why some people had very little interest in styling hair, yet they were enrolled in hair school. They were not paying for it, so they came if they felt like it. For me, nothing was free. The only thing I was "granted" was a payment book. I came every day eager to learn. For that I am grateful.

In hair school, I learned some quick lessons on how to toughen up. I was not used to being around this diverse group. In high school I do believe that I was the minority. I went to a high school with many African American kids, Jewish kids, and Catholic kids. I was raised Christian, but not Catholic. I befriended all of these different groups of kids and I liked to think I was "friends with everyone." I was no stranger to diversity, right? Wrong! In hair school, with this group, there was nothing stranger than me. I was the outcast for sure. I was the youngest one in hair school, I was small, motivated to learn, and, believe it or not, probably the only one left that was still in love with Rick Springfield. I felt out of my element. I got an education on some things that had nothing to do with styling hair, or birth control. How to "pretend you have been clubbing downtown and eaten at the Buttery." I did not even know what a "Buttery" was, much less had I ever eaten there. I found out it was some sort of restaurant that folks hung out at after the bars closed. I tried to talk the talk, but I do not think I fooled anyone. Honestly, I could not even fool myself. The most important life lesson I learned in hair school was that it is more than ok to use birth control. I also learned that it is ok if people do not like you, or if you don't fit in. After all, I like me. My friends like me. Gosh, I'm a big John Candy fan!

In hair school, I found some of the students to be cliquey. I was not street smart like some of the students. For many students, "street" was the only "smart" they were. One of my teachers, Miss Sheri, helped me through this. The minute I met her, she reminded me of Carol Burnett. Not because she was funny, pulled on her ear, yelled like Tarzan, and wore a curtain rod in her dress, but because she sort of looked like the Carol Burnett cartoon character at the end of the show. That was my image of Miss Sheri. Not a bad thing, she was just very Carol Burnetty. She told me right away that I would do very well in this industry, but that I really needed to toughen up. Do you think she saw my favorite orange teddy bear in my purse? Or was it Natalie's boo boo kitty she saw in my car? I am sure she was clued in by the way I looked. I did not look hard. I also did not smoke during our smoke breaks, or come into school hung over. This made me look a bit child-like. She must have known I was a softie by my appearance. Sure, I wore black eyeliner, just not as heavy as the others. Miss Sheri hardly knew me, yet pegged me right away. This has always been a problem with me, being pegged. I talk a good fight, but I am really quite sensitive. I have gotten maybe a tiny bit better with age. For instance, now I can visit nursing homes without bursting out in tears. Believe me, that was a huge mountain to climb at one point! Emotion can even be strength at times. Sure, it can make you hyper and hateful, but pretty soon after your spazzing is over, the tears of remorse show up. Sensitivity and crying have gotten me out of more than one speeding ticket in my life, so it can't be all that bad. Being sensitive can also help build a successful hair career. I find that compassion is actually much better than being hateful most of the time.

The owner of the beauty school was not seen much. He was a very little man. Only once in a while would he grace our presence. He would show his face once a month if tuition for the paying students was due, or when a new student was enrolling. He was a small, balding man. His name was Lenny. He was nice. He looked like a Lenny. Not like Lenny of Lenny and Squiggy, but maybe more like Larry from the 70s TV show *Threes Company*, only short and stocky. He was always talking larger than life, and acting as if Jose Eber himself had trained him. Lenny fooled no one. He had very little training in this business. His biggest claim to fame was that he went to high school with Barry Levenson and Mama Cass. I was a product of the 1980s so this really meant nothing at all to me at the time. Barry Levenson was just becoming popular and Mama Cass? Well? Maybe he could impress my mom with this news, but I did not really care. He could have easily won my respect if he told me he gave Jon Bon Jovi his first perm, or invented the Flock of Seagulls famous coiffure, but a classmate of Mama Cass? What did this have to do with hair? Maybe if he told me that they shared a "ham sandwich" in the lunchroom, I would have listened closer. You knew that one was coming, didn't you? Lenny was kosher, so I am sure they never shared a ham sandwich or a crab cake for that matter. Did Mama Cass even have good hair? I think it was straight and parted in the middle like Janis Joplin.

How did this relate to hair school? He brought out his Forest Park High School yearbook one time to prove he was a classmate with these stars. Yep, there she was pictured right in the yearbook, Ellen Cohen, a.k.a., Mama Cass Elliott from the Mama's and the Papas. This was Lenny's claim to fame? Knowing someone famous? This was enough to qualify him as a beauty school teacher/owner, I suppose. I am pretty sure that he did quite well for himself by enrolling so many "free" students. My guess was that someone was paying for all of them. I do believe when I filed my taxes that year I figured out that it was me.

When I started hair school I had the written and the practical part of the school day. The written consisted of the morning textbook lecture that would last until lunch and then we moved on to the second half of the day which was the clinic portion. The word "clinic" is about right. The setting reminded me of just that. Whatever comes to mind when you hear the word clinic is just how this place looked.

The public would line up outside the hair school doors in a way that brought to mind cattle waiting to be milked. We would sit at the front of the clinic on slow days and watch some of the "herd" pass by. We would smile and wave to them from the window as we whispered under our voice to each other "...*Keep walking, keep walking, keep walking, please keep walking, who is up next, keep walking...Ahh no, they are coming in.*" We had nothing against these folks personally; it's just that their hair was not really kept up.

Remember I had mentioned earlier about the group homes? I was pretty sure that most of these elderly clients skipped a few weeks of washings most of the time. While they were back at the shampoo bar we would hear comments such as, "Don't even think about getting my back wet; if water gets into my ear canal it could cause an infection!" We would make sure that we cupped our hand around their ear when we shampooed them. We would not want to infect an ear. We did not even look inside an ear either, for obvious reasons. We kept a three pound cotton coil box next to the shampoo bar. This way we could stuff cotton in their ears, or in our ears depending on our mood.

We would get risky sometimes too. While their heads were back in the shampoo bowl, we would see how far down the forehead we could go before the water would squirt into their eyes. This would make a wonderful demarcation line of make-up foundation across the brow, or across the "frontal" bone; that was the term we were to use. Sure, bone structure was part of our education. Even today I hear platform artists use the hair school phrase, "take the section right above the 'occipital' bone…" The anatomy chapter in hair school apparently did pay off. We would look to have fun any way we could, even if it meant getting risky with the hose. It was good training for the real world I suppose. In the end, the nasty clients would go running to Miss Sheri and complain about everything that they were not happy with, in hopes to either get a free service or getting the new stylist in trouble by their tattling. But, given that they were only paying a little more than free for their hair anyway, we were not that concerned.

There were some really sweet clients in hair school as well. One in particular would say the same things week after week. She would say, "I'm eaten lunch today at the Pizzer Hunt, my niece is taking me to the Pizzer Hunt down er on Plastic Highway." This same lady came every week and never once got the teacher's name right. She would call Miss Sheri "Miss Sheraton." Maybe in her younger days she worked in the hotel industry? Who knows? I never minded doing her hair. I knew she would go easy on my rookie self, and I was sure she would not be the one quizzing me on the day's news and current events.

For hair school hair, we used hair school hair products. The products were not the new product lines the industry was launching by any stretch of the imagination. Mint Julep was the shampoo. I am not sure what exactly this was, but I know it came in a gallon bucket and it smelled like chewing gum. This could be made into a couple of gallons of shampoo by simply adding water. The only other choice for shampooing was a cleansing formula called Shimmering Lights. This was the product we used to brighten dull hair. It was a wonderful blue/purple color. It was a nice product to use on the white-haired clients who had yellowed tinges to their hair. You have known the kind of clients that I am referencing. The ones that would smoke like a five alarm fire and speak with the voice of Marge Simpson. Smoking did, and still does, a number on the white hairs. The greatest hazard faced when using Shimmering Lights was that if you did too many shampoos with this formula, you were bound to have a client leave looking like Smurfette. This alone should have been reason enough to break that nasty smoking habit. Then again, half of these women came in wearing those huge black sunglasses that wrapped around their entire face. Their vision was probably not the best, so they probably did not even notice that their hair was purple. Perhaps their hair did not look purple with those huge shades on.

There was also cholesterol as the conditioner. It looked just like it sounds. This too came in a gallon bucket. Additionally, there was the gallon of hair gel that you dipped out with a spatula and put into a Dixie cup. This would make the hair stick to the hair rollers nicely.

For finishing the hair we had a product called lacquer. It was exactly that. I also learned the hard way that a product called oil sheen was not meant for Caucasian hair. While this product would add luster to any African American client's hair, it would simply make a Caucasian client's hair look like they had just shampooed with baby oil. There was one product that resembled cola-colored snot. That was for practicing finger waves on a mannequin head. This school spared no expense, as you can see.

As part of the training, some of the treasured few got to go on a field trip. This was a bonus right before graduation. How exciting! And when I say graduation, I actually mean the day we acquired our mandatory state board hours. There was no measurement for a cap and gown; there were no speeches given or onlookers; there was just a piece of paper to submit to the state board. This was somewhat anticlimactic.

Near the end of my days at this school, Lisa and I were awarded a well-deserved break. We had been the chosen ones picked to go do hair at a nun's convent. Call us the Valedictorian and Salutatorian of hair school if you will. I have to say that while this was hard work, it was quite a rewarding experience. These nuns were clean and very sweet. I had never been to a convent before. I was anxious to see what it was like and it was nothing like I had envisioned. In my mind I had the scene from the movie the *Sound Of Music*. Yet, there were no women dressed in head-to-toe black habits scurrying through the halls chanting and praying and trying to hide out families in the mountains. It was nothing like this. It was not completely as quiet as I had envisioned either. I was disappointed that no one sang "Ado vice," while I was doing her hair, but I got over it.

This was a nursing home type of convent. Villa Julie College was right next to the nun's nursing home. We would drive through this beautiful campus to get to these Sisters. They had a breathtaking view overlooking the college campus and grounds. I still remember how grateful these elderly women were. One nun who was not really with it anymore kept on saying the same thing over and over. She just kept saying, "Seven and Seven and Seven." Lisa was sure that she needed to play the lottery that night. As I looked around at these aging folks that only had a few years left at best, one thought was a constant in my head. No, it had nothing to do with the fact time slips away so fast and that these women were nearing death; instead it had to do with these women nearing death and being virgins. Don't make me feel bad, now. This is a natural thought, right? I am sure some people, at some point, if they were with a bunch of sweet nuns in a nursing home, have had that thought too. At that point I knew I was more than ready to move on. And so I did. School was finished shortly after that field trip and it was time to take my state board test. I would soon have my license and be working in the field I had dreamed of.

The state board test was the finale of hair school. The big guns you could say. You would take the written part first and then you would perform the practical part. The practical portion of the test was the part where you got to show off your skills on a live model of your choice. The testing center was completely silent during this time and very intimidating. The testing instructors would walk around with a clipboard and mark things down while I worked. Because my sister, Cindy, had very little hair left on her head from my frosting disaster, I chose to take her. How traumatic could it be for her, really? I could not possibly screw her hair up more than I already had in the past. The ridiculous tasks we had to perform on our models were more than outdated. We had to do a full head of finger waves, a basic haircut, and a roller set. We had to slice out pin curls, do a manicure, and show how to section and perform a color application. Thank goodness we did not have to demonstrate a pedicure!

The testing instructors would make you do a basic hair cut, making sure you took at least one and a half inches off the hair you cut. I passed every skill with flying colors, except for the haircut portion. There was no way I was cutting Cindy's hair any shorter than I had to. I would rather fail this portion of the test and go back to retake it, than have my sister cry for a couple more weeks thanks to me. We were finally on speaking terms and I did not want to ruin that. I still remember the sight of her hair as I finished. A roller set concluded the test. A roller set on my sister's over-processed short hair was a sight to see. It looked like an old Settee Betty do! June Cleaver would have been so proud! All Cindy needed was a dress, a strand of pearls, and a vacuum, and she could have passed for Mrs. Cleaver hands down. I guess that made me the other "beaver?"

If looks could kill, I surely would have been dead on that day. We left the testing center in downtown Baltimore and headed straight home. Cindy shrunk down in her seat until we pulled into the driveway of our home. She then went straight to the shower to wash out that awful style. I did indeed fail the hair cut part of the test. Since I only had to retake the part of the test that I failed, I chose to take my grandmother back for the haircut re-test. She did not care at all how short I cut her hair. The testing instructors intimidated Gram too. I think that may have been the only time in my life that I remember Gram silent and intimidated! Thankfully I passed the test. My "diploma" came in the mail and I was ready to start looking for a job.

Top 10 Facts About Attending a Hair Academy

10. If a client says, "No, I don't have head lice," that means that they probably do.

9. The word "perm" refers to a permanent wave as well as a permanent relaxer, so be clear.

8. Extra mannequin heads make great April Fools jokes, especially when you drag them from your back bumper.

7. Turn the client away from the mirror while you work. They cannot critique you this way or see you sweat.

6. In hair school the hair you screw up, may just be your own.

5. Do not plan on any hair school class reunions or a class photo.

4. Having a cosmetology license really only guarantees you a spot at the local hair butchery.

3. There is no grade point average to worry about and no measurement for a cap or gown.

2. You will not learn any current styles.

1. No one finishes hair school with virgin hair. Most do not start or finish hair school with virgin anything, unless you were a nun..

Chapter Two

The Cutting Edge of a New Career

The time had come to start job hunting. I was also offered a position as a shampoo girl in a very high-end salon in the Mt. Washington area. I took this job in hopes that it would be the stepping-stone I needed. Besides, the salon was called Stars salon. I had always wanted to be a star, so this seemed like a great place to start. Stars actually brought me back down to "earth!" I only lasted six months there before realizing that they wanted a career shampoo person, not a young stylist eager to learn the trade. My first client there was an elderly woman who had been in a nursing home for a month. This woman needed hair color but they did not tell me that her hair had not been washed in six weeks, until I started applying her color. I started to gag. I could barely get through that one. I am sure that me getting that first client had nothing to do with them not wanting to do her hair. I was probably given her because I was the most qualified.

At one point, the salon sent me to another elderly client's home to shampoo a woman who had just had surgery. I do believe that was the breaking point for me. This "shampoo girl" job title did not include house calls, I thought to myself. I went to this client's home as told, and I knew that this would indeed be the last head I shampooed for the "stars" at Stars. When I got to the door, an elderly woman answered. Her entire face was bandaged. She looked a bit disfigured and I instantly felt a little nauseated and sad for her. Did she have cancer? Was she burned in a fire? Had she been involved in a terrible car accident? At first I was horrified, as well as sick to my stomach. As we started talking, I realized it was nothing more than a facelift and she was thrilled that she had gone through with it. She was also more than thrilled that she had a salon that made house calls. I was not thrilled. I finished her hair and went back to the salon to turn in my shears.

I was still living at home and was nineteen years old by now. My parents assured me that I made the right decision to quit even though I was jobless. I was still in contact with Lisa, my friend from hair school. She told me about a position that was open at the salon she was working in. I had an interview with Roberta and got the job. I had watched some of the stylists at Stars Salon and picked up a few great techniques. I got the job and I was ready and eager to work. This was great news! Lisa and I would have the opportunity to work together. Just like in our hair school days, we connected once again. This salon was perfect for me. This salon was clean, close to home, and I was going to start working on real paying hair clients. It was a very average-sized salon with a great walk-in potential so I could build up my "book." "Book" is hair talk for build-up a following of hair clients. I was very excited to work there. I made enough money in my first year to support myself and buy my first new car. I also figured that I had enough money left over to rent my first apartment. This was the start of the career that I had planned. Things were really working out.

I felt I was really perfecting my craft of hairstyling too. I could wrap an entire spiral perm on interlocking tubes in less than an hour; I could cut a man's hair in twenty minutes even while taking extra caution so that I did not cut off the rat-tail he had spent a year growing; and formal up-dos were becoming my passion. Kids' haircuts were still a bit of a challenge and I may have cut a few ears in my day, but if you let the hair fall the right way, it will clog up a bleeding ear every time. That same hair can also help clog up the slice you took out of your own finger due to the wiggling client. It was a problem when the child was a toe head, a blond-headed kid that is. Sometimes when I would cut a toe-headed kid's hair, I would slash an "artery" in my finger. On many occasions I left a trail of blood that would make their hair look pink.

I had even mastered the art of scrunching hair like a true mall rat in the 1990s, with bangs high up into the air. I still remember "the bigger the bangs, the closer to God" theory. This was a true 1990s trademark. The surfer/skater cut for the boys was big. The Vanilla Ice boxy flat top was a favorite. I stayed in this salon for a little over three years. They were great years.

Christmas parties outside of the salon have always been a blast. When you get so many creative people together in one place celebrating, you will definitely be entertained. Anything can happen. From stylists belting out Delta Dawn with the band, that was not me by the way, to some stylist's boyfriend disrobing, wearing a towel only, and asking his girlfriend to pass the soap. Anything can happen. I have witnessed flashing, dirty dancing, and drunkenness, and that was mostly from the husbands of the stylists. Crazy stylists + open bar with free food = an interesting evening for all. One girlfriend of mine named Dawn even left her own company's Christmas party one year so she could join us at ours. She was convinced that our party was going to be more fun than hers. No question, hairstylists know how to have fun.

I learned some valuable lessons in the salon industry. Like, wait until the wacky clients leave before you start talking about them. Another was, if a client leaves a coat, sunglasses, or a pair of earrings at your station, do yourself a favor and don't wear them. Especially don't wear them to work. I do remember a very pretty pair of earrings being found at a friend's station. No one knew who owned those earrings. The stylist thought she would wear them. They were very different looking earrings. My stylist friend became rather fond of that particular pair and wore them quite a bit, maybe too much. For months and months she wore this beautiful pair of earrings. When the owner of the earrings came in for a haircut and took notice, she said to my friend, "I used to have that same pair of earrings." My friend then took the earrings out of her ears and gave them to the client, assuring her that she was only wearing them in hopes that the owners would claim them. She also added that she was thrilled to find the earrings' owner. She was not thrilled. My friend loved that pair of earrings! Yes, that friend was Lisa.

Top 10 Things I Learned When I Became a New Stylist

10. People will not hire you without experience.

9. You will start your career with very little experience in cutting hair.

8. You will not always be able to tell the difference between a new face-lift and someone that has been in a bar fight. The initial look is the same.

7. Some guys get perms.

6. You can buy great hairstyling equipment, but you cannot buy a personality.

5. You will have to fake your way through the first 6 months of hair cutting.

4. A piggy-back perm does not mean you curl the client's hair while riding on another stylist's shoulders.

3. The product called "brush delete" can delete the hair wrapped around your brush. It can also delete the brush if you leave it in the solution all weekend.

2. Just take it as a compliment if someone compares you to Mary Lou Retton or Jennifer Grey; do not retaliate by saying they remind you of Rocky Dennis.

1. Try to be interested in everyone, or at least act like you are.

Chapter Three

Men: Hair Today, Bald Tomorrow

Servicing client means getting to know many different clients. It does not mean sleeping with them, despite how it sounds. When I say I can "do" you next week, I mean I can do your hair. Don't get me started on how to answer a call for a "cut and blow!" I always enjoy meeting new clients, whether they are male or female. The new cute guy client has always been fun too. In years past, when a new guy client would sit in my chair for a haircut, I would get very nervous. Much like a blind date, you start talking to a complete stranger. In the hair business, you start out touching the clients by shampooing their heads and then moving on to the conversation. From the shampoo to the haircut, you are touching random strangers' heads. With your armpits in their face at the shampoo bowl, stylists are very aware of the hygiene needed. It is amazing how much sweat a body produces when you are nervous. In my career I have had the privilege to cut the hair of some very cute professional ball players, politicians, and local celebrities. I was not only star-struck, but also very nervous and very aware that I needed to apply more deodorant. I have even had the honor of cutting Betty Ford's hair, Kathy Rigby's hair, Michael W. Smith's hair, and have been invited to Jim Baker's house for dinner. Jim Baker's wife is one of my very best friends and has even gone to hair shows with me. I used to cut Michael Jackson's mom and sister's hair before they moved. All of these folks have one thing in common. They are all probably nicer than the "other" celebrities with the same name. We all put our pants on one leg at a time, so what's the big deal?

The biggest star in my book would have to be the man I married. How corny is that? See, this book has romance as well as comedy. You can decipher for yourself which category to put that one under. I can honestly remember very clearly the first time I met my husband. I was not wearing open-toed shoes thank goodness. I started out cutting my sister's boyfriend Charlie's hair. Charlie and I never really got along well. I was surprised that he sent his friend in to see me for a haircut. I remember Marty being tall and skinny and very cute! I have always had a thing for the tall, thin guys and he was just my type.

I was just getting out of a three-year relationship and had no interest at all in dating. I was happy to be single and unattached. He was in a similar situation, only with a woman. So naturally we got together, and we eventually married. But not right away. I did get very nervous cutting his hair. He was much older than I was. He still is as a matter of fact. I was almost twenty-two years old and he was twenty-seven. Wow, an older man! He even had a thick Tom Selleck mannish type mustache. Not the pencil thin kind Jimmy Buffett sings about, or the barely there, almost wax-able young boyish kind, but the thick, grown up, manly kind. He was so tall, fit, smiley, and polite.

I also remember his eyes. They were like two pools! Good one, huh? Ok, now I'm pushing the envelope. They were not like two pools if you compare his eyes to the pools I am used to. That ph/chlorine factor has always been so hard for me to get right. His eyes were a nice color blue. Let's call them "ocean" blue. They were not Ocean City, Maryland, green blue, but "Caribbean Ocean" blue.

I felt clumsy and awkward... because I was clumsy and awkward. I dropped my comb a couple times, as I recall, when I was cutting his hair and was too nervous to ask him if he would like me to trim his mustache. I rushed through his haircut.

Things went very well and he seemed so very pleased with his hair. He then left and never came back for another haircut. Nice! I thought his hair looked great so I had no clue why he never came back in. We met up once again at a party a few months later and surprisingly things progressed into dating. I would tease and torment his friend to get his attention, you know, like a middle schooler. My maturity factor has always been right around the middle school range. I was showing off, as my sister had put it so many times in my life.

In hindsight, I think I may have frightened him. That was probably not the kind of flirting he was used to, and he had no idea that I was even interested in him. I asked him if he hated the haircut I gave him that day. He said no, he loved it! I asked him why he did not come back. He had no clue that hair clients were to remain loyal to their stylists. Cute and smart too I see. What a combo!

This salon thing was all new to him so I forgave him. He was a Cost Cutters/barber shop kind of guy prior to meeting me. As I said, our hanging out eventually turned into dating. Once we started dating, he understood the client loyalty and he never had his hair done by anyone else ever again. Not to mention it is always free when I do it.

The same standard did not hold true for his friend Charlie. I am not even sure if Charlie had standards. Cindy and Charlie did split up. I was happy to lose Charlie as a hair client. Oddly, I think Charlie may even credit himself for our marital bliss. I'm not so sure he feels the same about his own. At least he has helped to make someone happy.

There were other male clients as well. One guy in particular, named Bob, was very loyal to me. He had me cut his hair every four weeks. He would ask for me, and only me. I was a girl in my early twenties so he probably had a big ol' crush on me. Who wouldn't? Or at least I would flatter myself by thinking that. Bob was a man's man. No, not gay, a construction-type man. He would talk about his job in the construction field and in his spare time he was a personal trainer. Bob was built very nicely. He was about 5' 11" with a five o'clock shadow and much body hair. Because he also did some bodybuilding, he would shave off the hair on his arms and legs when he had competitions. I guess I could have called him "Bob the Builder" really! He even had an opportunity to be a contestant on the show *American Gladiators.*

Bob was a man in his early thirties and was trying desperately to get into the police academy to fulfill his life-long dream. I cut Bob's hair for a little over two years before he gave me the news. Bob was accepted to a police academy in Florida. I was so excited for him! You really get to know someone when you do his or her hair for a long period of time. I knew Bob really wanted this position. The last time I saw Bob he came in for one last haircut before he was off to sunny Florida to live. I went to shampoo him and he said to me, "Amy, I have a letter for you but I do not want you to read it until I leave." I said, "I am sorry Bob, what did you say?" He repeated what he had said.

So many things raced through my mind. "Could I wait till he left to see what was in this letter? What kind of letter? Is he sick? Oh my gosh, does he want me to go to Florida with him? That's it! Holy crap, he's in love with me! Yes, yes, he *is* in love with me! I am sure of it! It must have been my spiral perm and my shoulder-padded outfit that was a turn on to him. But I am dating someone. What will I say? Did I give him the wrong signals? I do not want to be with him! I do not want to break this man's heart, but he is really just not my type!" We had gotten to know each other so well, but I was just not interested in him that way!

I remember that very last haircut I gave him could probably go down in the *Guinness Book of World Records* as the fastest haircut in history! I assured him that I would call him later that night after reading his letter. I do not think he was even out the door before I rushed to the back lunch-room to read what was in this sealed envelope. It started something like this:

> *Dear Amy,*
>
> *For the past two years I have always admired you. You are beautiful and I love the way you style your hair. Every time I come here for my haircuts, your makeup is just perfect, as well as your hair, and you have a great personality!*

(I might have added the "great personality" part, but the rest is word for word. Oh my gosh, I knew it! He is in love with me and wants to date me! I just knew it! It was the spiral perm thing! I read on…)

> *We have become such great friends through the years that I really wanted to ask something of you. I have some-thing to ask you that is very hard for me to ask…*

(Ok here it is, here is the part where he is going to ask me to go away with him to Florida! I just knew it! Oh my gosh…. What am I going to tell him? I really do not like him that way! I would keep on reading…)

I wanted to ask you if you could help me. I am going through a tough time in my life and I am really trying to get through this.

(Hah? Does he have cancer? What kind of a hard time? He needs me how? I know he is not dating anyone right now. Advice? What kind of advice? What? I kept on reading... He would then write these words that will forever ring in my mind. He wrote...)

I am a cross dresser and am just coming out of the closet.

(WHAT?????? Did I read that right? Is this a joke? This cannot be true! As I read on I came to believe that he was telling me the truth! He wrote...)

Finding the right pumps and dresses are not a problem for me. The problem is doing my hair and makeup. Your hair and makeup always looks so beautiful and I was hoping you could give me some private lessons on how to apply mine, and how to style my wigs! I am really serious about this. This is not a joke and this is very hard for me to even write. Please call me and let me know if you can help me. I am desperate!

Love, Bob

My guess is that finding the right set of pumps was actually a problem even though he stated that it was not. You can't find cute pumps to fit those size 11 gunboats and not look a little crazy! An even bigger problem than the makeup application, I would think, would be how to hide that gynormous Adams apple, five o'clock shadow, and his man hands. Now I understand why he insisted that I wax that guy brow. He needed much more then his uni-brow waxed to resemble a woman in my opinion. I really was in a big panic.

I thought out loud to myself, "What the heck should I do here?" And I also thought, "I wonder what sandals would look like on those big, gunboat feet?" "Would he paint his toes red?" I was just at a loss. Can we also talk about the part where he did not have a crush on me? That was my first setback. Then to find out he wanted to "use me" for my make-up skills? This was all too much. To think that I was trying to come up with ways to kindly let him down easy and all he really wanted was to borrow my eyeliner.

A crush was the least of my worries at this point really. I mean, what people do in their spare time is their business, but now I was *involved*. He was such a great guy, but I was not trained for this type of request. Then there was my middle school equivalency maturity level. I just figured that I would not call him. Or should I call him? Would he stalk me if I didn't? He is not a stalker, just a guy needing beauty tips.

These thoughts raced through my head. This letter bothered me that entire day and night. I mean Bob was a super nice guy, or part guy, or whatever. I did not want to be rude. The next morning in the salon Bob called. He asked me if I had read his letter. I said yes I did and I thanked him for his compliments on my make-up and hair. I also assured him that I was not comfortable teaching even my best friends how to apply make-up so I would not be able to help him out. He was very upset about this news. I mean in reality, I had no clue how to make a man look like a woman. Maybe pancake stage make-up could help, but whiskers were a bit different than covering up zits! I knew some men that wore "guy liner," but they were not cross-dressers.

We ended the conversation and I wished him a lot of luck. I secretly had hoped that luck was also on my side at this point because I had just accepted a job at Glamour Shots applying make-up. With Bob's love for the police academy, I feared he might do some detective work of his own! If so, I would be caught in my lie. I was praying that Bob would not waste any time catching that plane to Florida.

I have never seen Bob ever again, but I have thought of him often. I wonder if he has ever told anyone else the news of his secret double life. Can you imagine the talk around the precinct if they got wind? Until right now, I could be the only one who knows. I am quite sure he is happier than most of us. I mean, who wouldn't be with such an expanded wardrobe.

I had a note sent to me once by a client. It simply stated how I had just given the best haircut in the world and that I was *so* special. I was such a big part of this person's life. The right haircut gave the client much needed confidence and self-esteem. This person thought about me every single day. I was the best thing that ever came into this client's life and that needed to be shared. She shared it all right, and it *freaked me out*! Maybe she misunderstood. In my heart of hearts I have always been a "thespian," not a "person that likes girls." Maybe she read me wrong? I have always liked guys. I will never know how she got that message.

There was one male client that kept asking me out. He insisted that I looked just like "Baby" from *Dirty Dancing*. Instead of taking that as a compliment, I started seriously considering a nose job. It was a wonderful decision that Jennifer Grey had made after all.

As far as dating and cosmetic surgeries go, men just do not seem to care if their stylists' bodies are "altered." This business is full of change. We are in the beauty business after all. Not many of us are completely procedure free. Between botox, facelifts, lipo, rhinoplasty, tummy tucks, boob jobs, and make-up tattooing, good luck finding a cosmetic virgin in this industry. That list alone is just the procedures I, myself, am interested in. Don't even get me started on spider veins, because after twenty years of standing, my legs are beginning to look like they have been map -blasted.

There are so many stylists who are interested in many more body changing procedures than me. Skip the tattooing and piercing young people, move on to the good stuff! At any rate, I was not a single girl in the dating field for long, with or without cosmetic surgery. Marty seemed to love me the way I was, despite my toes. The procedures would have to wait until I was making the big bucks. When servicing male hair clients, I would quickly demolish any signs of interest. I did remain friendly, though. After all, just because I was dating someone did not mean that I did not have friends that needed a date.

I fixed up my sister a couple times. I found a little side business of my own. I would fix up any nice single clients with other nice single clients. My only request was that I got to do the hair for the wedding. I had one marriage and one engagement under my belt. Call me Cupid if you will. Stupid is more like it. I have fixed up many clients in my day and only have one marriage under my belt. That is actually pretty sad. I did have a client who went out with two of my fix ups, only to find her real love was from her camp counseling days. He found her on Facebook twenty-five years later. Maybe she did not need me after all.

An engagement ended for the one unhappy couple, and I am pretty sure that the guy and girl who married because of my introduction are not the happiest. As a matter of fact, I have heard through the grapevine that the husband still blames me for his life of misery. But hey, I just do the introducing; the rest is up to them. For now I will not quit my hairstyling. Although, when it comes to making matches, I am bound to get better at it. I don't think I could get worse.

Top 10 Ways to Know if a Client Is Interested in Dating You

10. They give you very expensive Christmas gifts.

9. They ask other stylists if you have a boyfriend.

8. They hang out at the salon and get services that they do not need.

7. They leave their phone number at the front desk.

6. They talk about their last break- up to you while you cut their hair.

5. They compliment you.

4. They request you for their next hair appointment.

3. They get very frequent haircuts.

2. They write you letters about your make-up and hair, no wait, he did not want to date me after all; and the other letter was from a girl.

1. You cut their hair once and they never return…well…that happened once and I married him so I guess that counts as wanting to date me.

Chapter Four

Glamour Shots

Lisa and I soon became very driven to make money. We loved to shop and wanted to feed our shopping addiction by making as much money as we could. If nothing else, a side job could allow us to get our merchandise out of "lay away." I figured I could never have too many pairs of leggings or matching scrunch socks. Shopping was our favorite thing next to doing hair. We also had these great new foam shoulder pads that we loved! You could insert them inside any shirt or tee, so shopping was at an all-time high. The linebacker look was really in. After all, it was the 1990s, and we were in the beauty industry. We needed to have a stylish look. I had moved out of my parents' home and now had bills to pay. Lisa was engaged to be married and needed extra money to help out with her wedding. The salon industry was slow in the beginning of the workweek, so we decided to take on a part-time job at Glamour Shots doing hair and make-up. The interview for this position was as simple as answering one question, "When can you work?" We would work Sundays and Mondays, which were our days off from the salon. We could hand out our salon business cards while we worked, so this second job allowed us to build our salon following even more. We were marketing ourselves. I started working there first and soon my friends would follow.

Glamour Shots was located in the local shopping mall. In the early '90s this was a prime place to shop; the mall that is, not Glamour Shots. Long before the carjackings, drug dealing, and murders occurred at local malls, this was the coolest place to be. A job inside a shopping mall was a dream. We were very excited to work at our little side career!

Let me explain what Glamour Shots was all about. It was a place where plain Jane women came in wearing sweaters, and scrunchies, and banana clips in their hair, and left looking and feeling like runway super models. Or hookers? Ok, maybe a cross between the model and hooker was the look we were giving. I spent enough time at the mall as it was; I might as well get paid for it! Glamour Shots was a small storefront with very flashy lights to attract passers-by. They had giant pictures posted everywhere of all of the clients that had modeling potential, or maybe pictures of the patrons who had just spent big money. If you got the jumbo package, you could have your picture posted on the wall of fame for an entire month. In our opinion it was really a wall of shame for those conceited patrons. The "wall o' fame" was nothing more than a wall painted to look like a camera's negative strip with poster sized pictures of the big spenders. For some folks, this was clearly as close as they would get to seeing their face displayed in lights.

We as stylists were to greet these patrons, style their hair, apply make -up, and make sure they bought the big package. Someone from ward-robe would allow the patron to pick from three different outfits to be pho-tographed in. When I say someone from wardrobe, I actually mean one of the high school students who worked there after school. Customers' pictures would be taken, and packages sold. Easy, huh? Not so much!

Keith the manager had his hands full. I am not sure what they were full of, but he seemed to always be very busy. I am not sure how he acquired this managerial position. Perhaps he could work more than just Sundays and Mondays? At any rate, he was the least qualified for this line of work of anyone on staff. That being said, he was the perfect one to run the storefront and manage.

Glamorous is not how I would describe Keith. He was tall, stocky, and resembled Billy Ray Cyrus. The 1980s Billy Ray, not the Hannah Montana Billy Ray with the highlights, but more like the Achy Breaky Billy Ray. My guess is he was working here waiting for his big break. This Glamour Shots job was not his big break. Perhaps he was the only one that answered the ad, which landed him the job. He probably took the job in hopes of having his wife photographed for free. He knew nothing at all about hair, make-up, or photography, but he could work the mall schedule. Naturally he was perfect man for the job.

Keith was sure to hold the early, mandatory Saturday morning meetings about how to answer the phone, stating your name and the glamorous place of business. The main topic of business at these mandatory meetings had to do with all of the pressing questions. For instance, there were the intriguing questions about where the proper place would be to put your fountain coke while you worked. I could have told him a time or two where to stick it. Keith addressed which closet was the best choice to put your coat in when you arrived for your workday. You would not want to see it get mixed up with the costumes, so that topic just had to be addressed. As if this was a problem? I don't remember ever wearing a white, rhinestone studded, pleather jacket into work to get mixed up with theirs, but perhaps others did

The meetings were held at our conference table, the conference table we made by pushing a bunch of tables together in the mall food court. You know the tables I mean, those plastic tables you only found near the

Boardwalk Fries stand and the Talkn' Turkey stand. That was a very professional setting as I recall.

Most importantly, at these mandatory meetings they discussed how important it was to be on time for these mandatory meetings. Lisa had very little patience for these meetings, and both she and I were never on time, so this entire meeting thing was a big problem. Lisa would hem and haw and challenge every word Keith said. The company would also introduce the brand new, colored bow ties that we could purchase to wear with our tuxedo shirt.

As for Keith, I actually liked him despite being meticulous over ridiculous rules and details. After all, he was the "manager!" I remember the meetings being long and drawn-out. I am not sure what their purpose was. No one ever left motivated, unless I am seriously mistaken. I think the average age of the assistant manager's position was about eighteen years old. Keith did not last long at that store. He left this job shortly after starting to become a Culligan man. I guess he could earn more bread with water.

I do credit this job to helping me master the art of schmoozing, or more simply known as BS-ing. When your paycheck is at stake, it is amazing how good looking people become. I have never seen such striking, natural looking women in my life. Model material for sure! Or at least I would tell them that. We were all thankful for the softening filter that would fit the camera lenses when a real winner was being photographed. Even the softening filter could not cover up a woman with lipstick on her teeth, or foundation on her collar. That happened more than once. Time for re-shoot we would think, or maybe she wouldn't even notice.

I got my friend Natalie a job there. So Lisa, Natalie, and I would tell these patrons how beautiful their features were, and how they looked like movie stars. We would sell them the biggest package we could sell so we could make a giant commission. Natalie did not have a cosmetology license or any training in photography, unless you count our Junior High School years of fashion shoots that were held in my basement courtesy of my Le Click camera.

That being said, Natalie had more than enough experience, and was the obvious choice to act as the head photographer. She was also to act as the picture presenter. She was a gem in the sales department! It always amazed me how convincing she was. She would act like she was so excited to show the customer their pictures. Then she would add phrases like, "Wow, I really like this one, look how great you look, you have to get this one for your boyfriend!" This girl could sell milk to a dairy farmer and convince him that her cow was grain fed and the most organic! She would help us all make money, milking the clients for their money.

Once again the two non-thespians used their unappreciated high school theater training to con insecure women into thinking they were centerfold material. We weren't lying; everyone is beautiful in some way or another. I did not say *Playboy* centerfold. We were just helping to build their self-esteem. Everyone left happy; that is the most important thing. We were in no way trained for this position, but we really sold some photos!

Lisa and I would apply the make-up in a prostitute fashion, assuring the customers it was only this heavy because the photography lights would wash out any color, and thankfully the filters would blend the clownish appearance. In reality, we had no clue what we were doing and used every excuse in the book to convince them that this was the only look that would work for the photographs. The owners did not seem to care as long as the appointments were coming in and people were buying.

We would let these patrons rummage through the outfits. It was like a grown-up dress up party. We had categories of outfits. We had the "wraps" or "drapes." They were the sparkly fabric strips we would wrap around the patrons, or sling over their shoulder in a movie star fashion. Sometimes we would wrap the fabric to look like a strapless evening gown or halter. Just like the cover of *Elle,* right? The "sporty" look was a look we pushed. For this we had the white leather Orioles jackets or the football jerseys. "Your husband will love this one," we would tell them. Every man loves a tomboy! Let's add a studded ball cap and slightly tilt it to finish the look!

The "hot trashy," look was popular and was a great sell for those less fortunate folks with a few missing teeth! Natalie would try to make these photographs look the best that she could by introducing a "grin" or "smirk" instead of a big ol' summer teeth smile. Some are teeth; some aren't teeth, so let's go with the closed-mouth pout. "Blow a kiss to the camera, that is sexy," we would say.

We had the studded white pleather and black pleather jackets with the matching pleather biker "bedazzled" hats. Chains and whips were not included. The Michael Jackson red *Thriller* jacket was an option. Here was a great picture to send to any random ex-boyfriend! Add one white glove, and you were golden! And then there was the cream of the crop. What glamorous photo shoot would be complete without a fuzzy pink, red, or black boa? This was the most popular of all. Nothing could beat the sex kitten look of a boa! Women of all ages seemed to love this one, add two white gloves and put one hand under your chin for even more sex appeal. Now that was "hot!"

The sitting fees were usually very inexpensive and we only made money when the packages were sold. When it was slow in the store we would take pictures of ourselves. I must admit the self-portrait time was fun! I still have the photo of my crystal gem studded captain's cap with the red wrap as well as the sporty one with the Oriole jacket and hat. I am pretty sure that I did not buy these pictures, yet for some reason I own them. I am sure it was just the free proof that I have, and nothing else. I am sure I never cropped out the engraved company name at the bottom of the photo, and then reordered prints either.

The big problem came when people did not really come in for the pictures. What they really wanted was a cheap makeover. They got a cheap makeover no matter what, but in addition they wanted it for an evening out on the town. We could quickly spot the women who were not at all interested in spending money at Glamour Shots. Target phrases and questions we would ask would go something like this… "So, do you have plans for tonight?" If they answered "yes" we would know they really just wanted hair and make-up done since they had a free sitting. We would ask them, "Are you doing these pictures to give to someone special?" Just by asking these questions, we could read between the lines and figure out what their purpose was for coming in. We would make an effort to curl the top of their hair nice and tight as well as the sides, while leaving the back straight. We would take a comb and part the hair down the center of the back of the head, or across the "occipital" bone as we call it. Some women instantly had thick hair with this trick. After all, only the front is in the picture. We were under no obligation to style the entire head, especially when they were wasting our time and wanting everything for free. This half-finished look would not do for the bar mitzvah they were going to later in the day or the cocktail party that was planned for later on that night.

I could never understand why some women came into Glamour Shots kicking and screaming. They would say, "My husband is making me do this!" or "My daughter bought me this package." We knew these particular clients were just making excuses for their vanity. They were there to be glamorized and feel beautiful for a day. We were not fooled. There is nothing wrong with feeling beautiful.

It sounds like we did not work hard, but we did. The work was physical, and our patience and ability were put to the test daily. With clients booked every fifteen minutes, it was a real assembly line without a union to pay us hourly.

I was working one day when a "secret shopper" came into the store. I am not sure how we knew, but we knew. Right away we were on to the fact that this woman was asking way too many questions and was not going to be pleased with anything. Maybe it was her clipboard that gave her away. We all whispered to each other that we were sure that she was "the mole" and that we should kiss up to her. That is not my strength, but in this case I put on the charm. She was grouchy, hated her hair and make -up, and did not buy pictures. With the fun job she had, why be hateful? Just before she left, she told us that we were being reviewed. We already knew this. I don't recall Keith the manager caring about our bad report. He "managed" to stay calm.

The Glamour Shots store had a big jar on the front desk. Unfortunately, this jar was not for tips. We would walk out into the mall with this jar at slow times and persuade mall shoppers to put their name and phone number in there. If your name is drawn, you will win a free sitting. News flash, unknown to them, *everyone* was a winner! Later that day we would call those folks back and tell them the good news! "I have never won anything," they would say. "Really? I won? My name was picked?" Yes, you won; your name was picked! There were no losers. Well, there were plenty of losers, but we were the only ones that knew that. They would all think that they won. It sure is fun to think you won, even if it is a ploy to get you back in! I am almost sorry that I am giving that secret away. For that reason, I retract everything I just said. Some folks that put their name in the jar won a free sitting but most did not. There, that's better. Still, anytime I drop a business card into anything and get a call back, I suspect I did not actually "win" a free happy hour. I am on to that ploy now.

The clients ranged from small children to old ladies and everyone in between. The mother-daughter combo was my favorite. You just knew this duo was going to buy! This would be a double sale. It was funny what some people chose to spend their money on. We would be surprised at some of the big spenders. I think some women thought it was worth the money, as these pictures could be their lucky break. With all of the mall shoppers checking them out as they passed, something was going to come out of all this. Fame was right around the corner, with the purchase of the *big* package!

Some of the clients that would come in were not hygienic. We would almost gag at the smell of cigarette smoke clinging to their dirty hair and would wash our hands right away. We did not shampoo the hair in this glamorizing, picture taking industry. More than once, body odor went along with the stinky hair issue. We would dispose of our combs and sanitize all of our equipment as soon as we were through. Hand sanitizer had yet to be invented. We also had to send some costumes out to the dry cleaners. This was one of the things that made this job the most undesirable. The only thing worse was when the odorous patron bought nothing.

The rules, meetings, and politics of this job soon became too much to bear. Lisa, Natalie, and I quit after about eight months and never looked back. The Glamour Shots craze passed shortly after we quit. I really think it was something women did one time only. Surely this business didn't go under because the three of us quit. Whatever the reason, the times were changing and more natural looks were approaching. The whorish look was no longer as popular, and soon the glamour business had run its course. I do believe that all of the Glamour Shots stores closed. That may have been a good thing.

Top 10 Misleading Lines

10. Have you ever thought about doing some modeling?

9. Your husband will love all of this heavy make-up.

8. We work here because we love our job and want you to look beautiful, not to sell pictures and make money.

7. The bigger package is actually the better deal.

6. Because your photographs are so great, we would love to put you on our wall of fame…if that's ok with you.

5. Yes, we have finished many hours of training for this job.

4. That color looks great on you.

3. No, I don't see any foundation on your collar.

2. No, you can't see the lipstick on your teeth either!

1. YOU'VE WON A FREE SITTING!!!!!!

Chapter Five

Locks Of Luck: Don't Let The Door Hit Ya

The salon industry can be brutal. When word gets out that you have found another place of employment, be ready for the salon "throw out." It is something that they do not tell you about in hair school. I have been thrown out of two of the four salons I have worked in. I also have had the displeasure of being on the flipside of that one. Here is the long and the short of it. When you work closely with other stylists and salon owners, you build a relationship of sorts. We stand next to each other, and we share our lives with our clients as well as our co-workers. It usually comes to a break-up at some point. When emotion is involved, there is just no easy way out. The key is to remain friendly but distant at the same time. This is something I struggled with. I am not even sure if that is possible.

When I left Roberta's so many years ago, I did it poorly. Lisa and I used the salon time to have flyers made up and had the information of our new place of employment printed on them. We were both ready for a change and felt that it was time to move on. After all I was twenty-two years old and knew everything, or so I thought. I knew nothing at all about being discrete. Lisa and I had used the printing company in the same shopping center that the salon was in to print out all of our client mail-outs. Yes, indeed, we were idiots. Not the smartest thing to do by any stretch of the imagination. When we both walked up to the printers together, on salon time, we were unaware that we were being followed by the salon owner. We were caught red handed. We were caught red handed by the red headed owner. The flyers were still warm in our hands. "What is that you girls have in your hand?" she asked. "Oh, no, she did-ent?" "Oh yes she did!" While we were prepared to give our two weeks notice, that instead turned into our two seconds notice, and not given by us. We suddenly found ourselves standing in the parking lot with our equipment in a hefty garbage bag looking at each other stunned. We asked each other, "What just happened?" Ah youth, it is truly wasted on the young! What happened was that we were fired! I believe we went straight to Ruby Tuesdays to discuss this over lunch. That too was not the brightest thing to do. While we were grabbing lunch and figuring out why we got canned, the girls at the shop were calling our clients with some "specials" that were being offered that day only if you acted quickly and booked your next hair appointment with a new stylist. We had a tough time contacting our clientele, but our loyal hair clients found us at our new place of employment. In hindsight, I understand why it had to happen that way. I have since made my peace with that salon owner, but it would not come until many years down the road. Not until some-thing somewhat similar happened to me.

The salon we went to was close by. It was a beautiful salon, a full-service salon offering many spa services. We enjoyed our time there. Dan and Luke were partners. Let me be clear, Dan and Luke were business partners. They were crazy and fun and I truly believe it was at this very salon that my real love for Halloween was formed. They would spare no expense in buying, or making, lavish costumes for Halloween. The salon was decorated in a different theme each year. While they were all about the Halloween drama, they did not take kindly to clientele drama. It was their way or the highway, and it was so fun to watch. It was made clear that if you were a client, you would do things their way. Dan in particular had no patience for the irrational client. When a client would go on and on about how they wanted him to change something about their hairstyle, he would simply throw the comb on the station and say in a very calm voice, "I'm done." He would walk away while they were talking and go in the back room to have a smoke. He would not greet them again until their next service, and there was always a next hair service. They always came back! He was busier than anyone there. Perhaps some clients preferred this type of treatment. Maybe he had a way of making them too afraid to go somewhere else. I am not sure.

Luke, on the other hand, was about the nicest guy ever. He had an infectious laugh and was always jolly. His voice was raspy from too many smokes and his hair thick and gray. He and his life partner were very nice people. Luke was a pleasure to work with. I enjoyed my time at that salon and did not get thrown out when the time came to leave. When it was time to part ways, they more than understood, and for that I am still grateful. I even got to finish out my two weeks notice this time. This time I actually got to give it.

The next salon I was to work in would also fire me. Lisa did not follow me to this salon, but we still remained friends. This salon marketed itself as a high-end salon. "High" is the right word when I think about describing that staff. Many of the stylists were high most of the time. I grew very tired of the sexual comments made by one very unattractive male stylist who, in my opinion, was acting as a pervert only to prove he was straight. He even approached one of my hair clients and told her that he loved how nice her underwear looked under her scrubs, and yet another that he enjoyed her tight shirt. Clearly he was proving he was straight through sexual harassment. The atmosphere here was cold, snooty, and unfriendly. I remember the back lunchroom doors being locked so that a drug dealer could come in and sell whatever it was that he was selling. I hated my time in this salon and was worried that I would get caught in some crazy drug deal gone bad. I am not sure why I worked there for a little over two years. Oh yeah, because I needed the money, that's right.

When a stylist picked a fight with Joan, a long time client of mine, I knew it was time to make my exit. This stylist had it out for my very eccentric client. I am not sure what Joan did to this woman, but this stylist, a German woman, and Joan, part Jewish, were not the best mix. One day Joan came in for her weekly hairstyle and the German woman was on the attack. Someone had burned a bagel in the back lunchroom. The German stylist pointed her blow dryer to Joan's back as if it were a gun and yelled out to her, "Is this what it smelled like when they burned the Jews in Germany?"

Joan jumped up, and I literally had to hold her back. The nail girl next to me was as shocked as I was. I still, to this day, cannot believe she said that. Even at nine months pregnant I knew my time here was coming to a fast end. I am surprised I did not go right into labor over this. At least if I peed myself I could say my water broke. This was a crazy situation to be in. That stylist never even felt bad and never apologized to my client. I was so out of there.

Joan's incident was the "push" I needed to get the heck out of Dodge. Just a few months after I "pushed" my baby out, I left. The owners of this salon got wind that I was leaving before I was ready, unfortunately. I found out later that the real estate landlord knew someone who knew someone who told the salon. Once again, I was thrown out of a salon. I left gladly. At twenty-seven years of age I was ready to move on. I was excited to have my new baby, start a new salon, and have a peaceful work place. I had absolutely nothing at all to lose, except a bunch of losers.

Top 10 Signs That it is Time to Leave Your Salon Job

10. You get false promises about a raise in commission.

9. Your equipment has been gathered up for you and placed in a green plastic garbage bag.

8. You're tired of your clients being attacked by a blow dryer.

7. Drug dealers are taking up all the good salon time.

6. The receptionist gladly gives your referrals to other stylists.

5. There's a loss of salon teamwork and lack of enthusiasm in the staff.

4. There's a decline in your income.

3. The clients complain that they are unhappy.

2. There is no praise at all for work well done.

1. You hate getting up and going to work.

Chapter Six

A New Permanent Solution

After I gave birth to my oldest son, Christopher, I just could not see myself back in my old place of employment. Shortly before I got fired, I signed a lease to rent a small storefront. The rent on my space was very inexpensive, so I did not feel that this was a tremendous risk. I sat down with my ideas and turned them into a business plan. I signed the lease and started recruiting stylists. I knew I could carry the business on my own for a short time. This allowed me to be selective in my hiring. I could take my time and hand pick my staff and not be pressured into taking on just anyone. After all, this was a small four-chair salon. I would be working in close quarters with my staff, so I needed to make sure we were all suited for each other. I also made no mention of my new salon to any of the stylists from the salon I had just left. I was looking forward to a "drug free zone." I did not encourage Lisa to come with me because I felt this could do harm to our friendship. I wanted a fresh start with fresh stylists. This all panned out well. My husband is a builder by trade. He is not a cross-dresser, but he is a builder, so all of the labor was taken care of. I could not have done it without him. Now all I needed was a name.

On my honeymoon, I met two girls named Sandy and Cori. Sandy and her husband Doug were from Rhode Island, and Cori and Bob were from Massachusetts. The three of us girls did not know each other prior to our trip to the island of St. Martin, but we all three happened to be hairstylists. If you can imagine three hairstylists meeting for the first time at the resort's happy hour, very few others got a word in edgewise. Everyone's hair looked great! We had an instant bond, like the one you get when you see an old high school friend at a class reunion. We acted as if we had known each other for years and had just gotten reacquainted. The guys seemed to get along too. We started talking about hair and the time got away from us. Doug was hungry, so the friendship almost ended before it even started.

While our new friends were ready to go out, Marty and I persuaded them to wait at the tiki bar for us while we got changed and showered. Doug assumed we were blowing them off since we took so long getting ready. Did I mention that we were on our honeymoon? We then showed up and Doug learned quickly that we actually were interested in joining our new salon owning friends for dinner. Fortunately, Sandy had made him wait. We had not been gone *that* long we thought. We went back to the room and were just busy getting ready, or maybe we were just getting busy, and weren't ready? It was one or the other. I'm sure I was just running late as usual.

Hairstylists always run late. Sometimes things just take longer when you are on your honeymoon. Things really should take longer when you're on your honeymoon. We were glad Sandy convinced Doug to wait. Cori and Bob waited too. The more we talked to our new friends, the more information I got on the background of these stylists and how their businesses ran. Cori's salon was called Positive Images. Sandy named her salon New Image. These girls became great mentors to me. We even went to Rhode Island and Boston to tour their salons. After much thought, I decided I should use the word "Image" somewhere in my salon's name to honor my new friends. We met these hairstyling friends at a happy hour tiki bar singing songs by Inner Circle. This is the "image" I chose to remember. We have now had these friends for a "la la la la, long, a la la la la, long, long, le long long time." Thanks for waiting Doug. Sometimes we all get busy!

Being the jokester that I am, I also batted around a few other names. "Cut One" was one I thought was pretty funny. "Cut It Out," "Do or Dye", or "Hair Ball" were just a few of the others that just did not make the "cut." I have always found myself to be creative in many ways, so I decided to use this word in my salon name. I would call my salon "Creative Image Salon." To this day I still like the name.

Less than six months after opening my salon, I had all of my styling chairs filled. I had built a wonderful relationship with my sales reps and I was launching many new product lines. Sales were up, which added to my income. I had also hired a massage therapist. I enjoyed my salon and everyone in it.

Two years later I gave birth to my second child, a baby boy named Wyatt. Things were starting to change a little bit. I had one stylist named Dinah who gave her two minutes notice twenty-four hours after my son was born. Maternity leave is overrated anyway. Thanks for waiting for the umbilical cord to be cut! I would have hated for her to give her notice in the middle of that. Hey, it's my shop, so what if I have to stop to breastfeed an infant every fifteen minutes. I could go back to work with a one-day-old, Dinah would think. Thankfully, I had a chance to deliver the placenta before she quit.

I am sure that Dinah had her reasons for leaving so quickly. I'll bet she thought this was all in my best interest. I mean, why would I want her hanging out in my salon working all unhappily and what not. That would just make me sad. She was thinking of me. Despite the challenges, Dinah was soon replaced. I have seen Dinah from time to time and I wish her no ill will. She, after all, was only thinking of me.

I took on a make-up artist/esthetician when my massage therapist decided to steer her business in a new direction. Things were very peaceful and very exciting. Every change thus far had ended well, for the most part. We were all driven and making great money. We would go to hair shows in Las Vegas as well as Orlando. We would enter hair competitions and pretty much spend all of our spare time together. I was even labeled the "up-do queen." This field is filled with "queens," so I was happy to add the label "up-do" before it. I think I might be more of an up-do princess, however.

Halloween time in the salon industry can be so much fun. Clients would book their hair service on these days just to see what we would come up with. We had an Austin Powers theme one year, a Pop Star theme, Big Comfy Couch theme, and a Scooby Doo theme. The salon spirit was great. Halloween, Black Friday, and April fool's day rank high with me. I love to tell my clients that they do not have an appointment with me when they show up on April fool's day. I use that one every year. Holidays are the best. I always closed my salon on Black Friday. Who wouldn't?

One time, when the salon was rather slow, I ran some errands with one of the stylists. We were in Target when her name came over the loud speaker. We scurried to the service desk to take the call. This was in the days before cell phones became popular. We were sure that something terrible had happened. Since we both had children, we immediately thought it had to do with them. It had nothing to do with our kids, but it was terrible nonetheless. The phone call was from my shampoo girl in the salon. This stylist that I had gone shopping with had left a client under the heat lamps and the shampoo girl that called Target had noticed. Thankfully the client did not have bleach on her hair or she would have not had hair. Nonetheless, this client was under the heat for about one hour too long. I am not sure why she did not question the length of time she was under the lamps. I know for a fact that my ADHD self would never sit under heat lamps for over fifteen minutes, much less an hour and a half, without asking where everyone had gone.

We darted back and the stylist finished the client's hair. Remarkably the client's hair turned out great. I am not even sure what tale she told this client, but I think it may have had to do with some sort of emergency situation that she dashed out to attend to. If this kind of thing ever happens to a stylist, I assure you it will only happen once. You are forever on your toes after a trauma like that one. Every evening before closing I would check the salon for remaining clients, just in case.

We had so much fun with certain clients. Sometimes their names were just as funny as they were. I am not talking about the made up urban legend names like Oranjello, Lemonjello, Placenta, Femaleee, or Clitoris, but the real funny names. If your last name is Ball, Weiner, Gross, Dick, Dickoff, Johnson, Seamen, Hyman, or Duty, I am sorry, but I am immature and I am going to laugh. There it is again, that middle school maturity thing! We have had people with these real last names frequent my salon. I am sorry if you are reading this and you take offense. I can think of some real nice clients with these terrible last names. I do not fault you.

Some client's names we just made up. There was "Fun Sally" and her fun sister Katie. One friend of mine named a salon client "Titty Cacca" which stood for, "the girl with big boobs that is full of crap." One client named Karen would come in for a bang trim. She liked the front triangular section trimmed around her face. She took kindly to her new name. K-Pie and I still get along just fine. I love K-Pie! My client Liz, who sent me hundreds of new clients, got a new name of her very own. She sent her family to me as well as her church friends. She was now named OCG. This stood for "Original Church Girl." I even once sat down and traced the client referrals that she alone had sent to me. It was in the hundreds. She told a friend about me, they told their friend, and so on, and so on. It is awesome when a fun client refers because their people are always fun! I love all of Liz's friends!

I had the opportunity to help some very nice people. One in particular was a client/friend named Tracy. She was a referral from Elise, who was a referral from my OCG, Liz. Tracey lost her husband to cancer. They were the perfect couple and were truly meant for each other. Her husband died in his early thirties and that left Tracey as a single mom with two beautiful children. Our children were the same ages, so this hit close to home for me. I wanted to help and so did many others in my salon. I used my hair salon for a fund raiser as a way of showing how much we all cared for her and her family. We had a very successful evening filled with many people booking hair and spa appointments. Just knowing that others care for you is a priceless gift. She is a priceless client who has been loyal to me, and I still service her hair to this day.

I helped the family of another stylist who was suffering from breast cancer. Deb, the sister of my friend Sam, passed on and left her husband and three children. She had a salon in her home and I helped out with a cut-a-thon. Even as sick as Deb was, she never gave in. She was even at her own fund-raising event sweeping hair. She was one of the good ones in this industry. Deb passed shortly after, and will always be remembered.

My first chemo patient's haircut was actually on a family member. Over the years I have helped out with many clients undergoing chemotherapy, but my first was the hardest. My Uncle John was in his late thirties and was diagnosed with terminal cancer. I remember the last time I cut John's hair. The hair from a chemo patient literally comes out on contact. When you comb through the client's hair, clumps are left in your comb. It is always quite shocking how much hair comes out. The last time I cut Uncle John's hair was four days before his death. Even in his last days, his thoughts were on the future and positive things. I cut his hair and we chatted about snowboarding and skiing. I do treasure that last haircut. While he died way too young, he touched so many lives in that time. He also left two great boys who will for sure make a difference in others, just as he and his wife did.

Speaking of making a difference, how about all of those brave girls that give their hair to Locks of Love? They bravely cut off a foot of hair to donate to organizations that makes wigs for cancer patients. I love how both children and adults give selflessly so that others can be confident in their looks. If you have ever given your hair for such a thing, you have done a wonderful deed!

On a lighter note, I was meeting so many new people and making so many new friends. I met Cindy at my oldest son Christopher's day care. She was hip, beautiful, and so very fun. Instead of hating her for this, I befriended her. Why is it that all my friends are great looking? I am not even kidding about that. I also am not writing that so that they will sell or buy my book! I just have great looking friends! Maybe the beauty industry breeds beautiful people. It makes me look better to surround myself with the ugly, but it just never works out that way. I was actually looking for someone fun, with a great personality, to answer the phones. Cindy took the job, and worked one night a week and Saturdays. She was fantastic with the clients and was wonderful with customer service. The shampoo girls loved her and so did the stylists. We would all laugh so hard at times that the nail salon owner next door would stop by to see what was so funny.

Kim, the Vietnamese nail girl, would stop by and say in her broken

English, "Oh Amy, I hear you girls laughing all day, you laugh and I hear through the walls; you fun Amy." We loved Kim! I know, it's an odd name for a nail salon owner, but her name really was Kim. You are not going to believe what her husband's name was. This is the honest truth; her husband's name was "Ha." Can you ever be in a bad mood if you are married to a guy named Ha? Ha and Kim were great to work next to. Ha was funny. I am pretty sure that they would hear Cindy's most infectious laugh from next door, not mine. Although many girls have called me their "loudest" friend, Cindy's laugh is much louder.

I looked forward to going to work and was very happy. We held Princess Parties on weekends at the salon. We would do up-do's and make-up at these parties. My salon was small, so it was the perfect spot to host a party. Shoot, any spot can be the perfect spot to host a party, but this one really was great. The kids had fun as well as the stylists. It was great networking with the folks in the community. The salon was really getting busy. Everyone was making great money too.

Things were going so well that Marty and I decided to renew the salon lease for another four years. We also decided that it was time to have another baby. This time we were blessed with a baby girl, Kendall. Things could not have been any better in my life. I had a loving husband and three adorable children; what could be better? Winning the lottery could be better, singing on American Idol would have run a close second, but other than that, things were great. I had a thriving business, a salon that I truly loved, and a wonderful home life. I even had salon employees as my very best friends! My children had bonded with the children of my employees. They were all wonderful playmates. We were all one big happy family; or so I thought.

Top 10 Fun Things About Owning Your Own Salon

10. Picking out salon fixtures.

9. Creating a creative salon name.

8. Making your own hours.

7. Not having a boss.

6. Getting business cards that say owner/stylist.

5. Great friends.

4. Enjoying coming to work every day.

3. The free magazines they send you.

2. Hand picking the product lines you wish to launch.

1. Touching Lives.

Chapter Seven

Knot

Changes indeed were coming. This is the chapter that I really want to write, knot!

Top 10 Reasons for Knot Writing About the Ol' Salon Walk-out.
Why Knot?

10. It's Knot that funny.

9. I would struggle to Knot name names.

8. I got too busy and time got away from me.

7. Murphy, the dog, needed to be bathed.

6. Used my time wisely and watched 30 Rock instead.

5. Had to get the kids off the bus.

4. Bathroom needed cleaning.

3. Toenails needed clipping.

2. That mess is Knot worth sharing.

1. Because you can't make me! I don't make trash I burn it.(Yep, back to Jr. High humor!)

Chapter 8

Oh, What a Tangled Hair We Weave

I might as well face the music. If I am writing a non-fiction book, then let the story be told. I dreaded, no, not Bob Marley dreaded, but dreaded in the "did not want to" kind of dreaded writing this chapter and almost skipped it entirely as you saw. Perhaps some sort of lesson could be learned. I wanted to write a book about funny things, but in this chapter I will struggle to find humor. I will give it a shot. Or take a shot before I start writing. Something good always comes out of something bad, right? For instance, while I was very down on my luck at this point in my life, I learned who my real friends were. There is the good! If you have ever gotten a really terrible hair cut, you are so thankful a month later when it grows in. There's something good. Or how about a real bad case of food poisoning? I felt very slim when the diarrhea and vomiting stopped. I see good! My situation was similar to that one. It was like getting a botched-up haircut while eating bad chicken. You're just glad when a month passes.

While I do tend to live my life at times with rose-colored glasses, I seemed to experience the 1980s version of the "Every Rose Has Its Thorn" theory. After all, Poison was a "hair band" and although that "half-full glass" was not "poisoned," I am pretty sure it was tampered with. Everyone knows that I do not sip or drink after people, so this really pissed me off. Am I losin' ya yet? Let me explain.

I was starting to have some tensions with one particular stylist. I was beginning to feel like The Outkast, only I was not singing "Hey Ya." Some real personality conflicts were beginning to show. For instance, in the past when I came into a room everyone would say "hello," and not leave the room. I was starting to develop a big ol' migraine. It was a headache of the worst kind. I needed to part, not my hair, but ways.

I had no control of my salon and I knew it. No control of my weight loss either. Perhaps the weight loss was a bonus to a stressful end. Lose weight without exercise? No weekly weigh-in fee? Not bad! I was being treated as if I should feel privileged to work in the salon that I had established. I worked so very hard to build my salon, and I was beginning to feel that uneasy, tense feeling you get when a case of irritable bowel is coming on. It's the same feeling you get when you know people are talking about you. No, my zipper was not down and I did not have my shirt on inside out. That kind of thing has happened before, but not this time.

One employee even pulled me aside and told me that I should just "clean house around here." I am still to this day not sure what she meant by that. What did she mean when she said to "clean house?" Go buy a Dyson? That was way too expensive a purchase! Hmm, maybe she was not talking about vacuuming. Was this a threat of some sort? Or maybe this was a warning? I was trying to "clean house" by removing the trash, but I was guessing that was not enough. A strange comment I would think. She was a strange person. A strange comment coming from a strange person, it was almost as if she were talking in code. Without a decoder ring I was screwed. Or shall I say, I was about to get screwed.

My clients would ask me what was wrong and I would just remain quiet. Mainly I remained quiet because nothing had happened yet. Or maybe I was quiet because I felt the entire staff hated me. I had nothing to share. I just had a "gut" feeling. Can you believe that? Me? Quiet? I have always had a "gut" but never have I been "quiet."

I could not gossip about my suspicious employees, especially in my own hair salon. Besides, whom would I gossip to? Myself? I already knew the news! And there was not any real news to know yet. Besides, "everybody knows" there is never gossip in a hair salon, for gosh sakes! Never gossip or drama! Never gossip, drama, backstabbing, or hair on the floor of a salon will you see. You will see hair on my face before I wax it, but not on the salon floor. I can see finding hair on the bedspread of your hotel room, or in your burger at the fast food drive-through, but never will you see hair on the floor of a hair salon.

I must admit, I took a hard look at myself, waxed my facial hair, ate a burger, lost weight, and for a long time wondered why I had let this happen. I mean really. I was good at waxing, and I know how to sweep. I always tend to throw the hotel bedspread in on the floor to avoid hairy situations. Why was I not wise to their ways?

My salon became very uncomfortable. The kind of tension that does not mount overnight was starting to show its nappy head. My anxiety level was at an all-time high. I was experiencing tension, with a little bit of the fear of the unknown. Sort of like that feeling you get when you see that credit card statement in the mail weeks after Christmas, that sort of feeling. I had that same feeling one time when Junior High School report cards came out I remember. Let's just get it over with, I thought. I was aware of the constant whispering when I left the room. I was given the silent treatment by most when I appeared. It was silent, but deadly. It was not a fart. The stylists would hold fake conversations with me as if they were forced to converse. I was not dragging toilet paper from my behind like my friend Staci once did, so I knew the whispering was something else. How does that happen anyway? Not the talking behind my back, but the toilet paper dragging from behind the back? Was I "back" in beauty school? Where is Fred? Is his mustache still red? Is Trisha gonna pop out of the back room and open up a can of whoop ass on me? I was not thinking clearly as you can see.

I also noticed that no one made eye contact with me. I did not have a poppy seed in my teeth like June had pointed out to me once, so I knew it was something more. It was a different kind of no eye contact then the toilet paper dragging, poppy seed kind. They were all building a case against me. They were "builders" all right. As far as I knew, none of my staff were cross-dressers like Bob, but they were for sure case "builders." I speculated that anyway. I was hoping I was wrong, and that maybe they just found men's clothing more comfortable. For now, I just chose to load my teeth up with poppy seeds and wait. Maybe someone would tell me something. If not, I would at least know what they were talking about.

I was dead-on right about the talk behind my back and the building, minus the cross-dressing and poppy seeds. The conspiracy theory was not a theory at all. It was factual. Why had I treated these stylists as if we were the same? We were not the same. For starters, I love girly clothes and I talk to people. On top of that, they were not the ones paying the insurances, rent, or the utilities. They were not the ones doing the hiring or firing. They weren't really doing much of anything in my opinion. We were not the same, yet I had treated every one as if they were my equal. They were not even "splenda" much less my "equal"! They were not "equal," "splenda," or "sweet" but they were definitely "low."

I had broken the cardinal rule. Not the one about sleeping with co-workers, these were all women and I am straight. I broke the other cardinal rule. I befriended my staff, and they all turned against me. They were all artificial and not the "real deal." I was treated with complete disrespect, and I had no one to blame but myself. Don't do it! Do not socialize with your employees or become too friendly. It will not end well. Sleeping with them is usually not a good idea either. Before you know it, you too will be adding fake sweeteners to your coffee and you will start dressing butch. When people are ready to move on, it is way too difficult when you are friendly. When you are ready to ask them to leave your salon, the friendship will always get in the way. Or you could become pregnant.

Ending a work relationship or a friendship can be compared to a marriage break-up or a death. A Hatfield-McCoy situation at its best! Someone has to move out of the hood! Just hope that it is not everyone, but it probably will be. Hope for the best, but prepare for the worst. The decisions that are made in a small salon will affect everyone. I parted on the other side! I should have taken "The Donald's" advice. He always parts way on the other side. I should have stated a quick and easy "you're fired" and been done with it. Maybe I should have pulled an *Uncle Buck* and told them all to just, "turn around, get in your mouse, and get out of here." That, after all, was the way other salon owners had done it to me, minus the *Uncle Buck* mouse car. Instead I took the sucker approach. Call me a tropical fruit dum dum because I was a sucker for sure.

I held heart to heart talks in my attempt to end things peacefully. One stylist alone struck a deal with every one of my staff behind my back. What was the deal with her anyway? Why did she feel she had to give me the silent treatment for such a long period of time? Thankfully, in her silent treatment she did not whistle. Whistlers are very annoying to me! A silent whistler would have been the worst! Maybe she never spoke or whistled because she was a mime. She was complex and very quiet all the time when I came into the room. Mimes are a bit complex I know, and we all know they never utter a sound, not even a whistle. If she was a mime, she certainly could not "tell" me she was stealing my staff, so that would explain a lot. Now that I think about it, she did wear a lot of black!

I do not know what exactly she told those other stylists, but I am sure it had something to do with me closing my shop, and them being out of a job. I cannot imagine it had anything to do with me running out of white gloves and face paint. I am pretty sure that she was not a mime anyway. I think she may have told my staff that they were next on the chopping block. I am sure that they had reasons for leaving that I knew nothing about. They were not big about sharing those reasons with me. Were they mad because I was funnier and prettier? It could not have been that. None of this was true anyway. Well, except the funnier part, and maybe the prettier. I for sure was nicer. I hate clowns, mimes, and whistlers! I am not a fan of lying, moody, back stabbers either.

If that was what she told them, the losing their job part, that was a lie. One stylist said to me that very dark day, "Amy, I am so sorry, please understand that she made me an offer I just could not refuse." What kind of offer? Free white make-up for life and props? I still wonder what kind of offer was made. Then "she" opened her own salon and took them all. I understood what happened. They were all "acting out," those thespians! No one could just be honest. I was not sure why it had to happen like this. Maybe because they were all insecure, psycho bats as my friend Dawn had described. That is just speculation. I do believe that they were psycho, but maybe the word was not bats but witches. Or a word that sounds like the word witches. I do like Halloween. Let's just say that they were mimey, clown-like, psycho bat witches. Just for Halloween's sake.

Another one of those witches, I mean stylists, I actually called right away and confronted. I called her before she had the chance to call me. Who am I fooling? She was never going to call me. She was just going to walk out like everyone else. I was right. She too was leaving me for this new salon. I do not recall her being a big smoker, but all signs pointed to the fact that she was; smoking crack cocaine that is. She would have had to be smoking crack to expect to have the demands met that she expected. She asked me if she could work alone in my shop for a week and gather her clients before she left, since I caught her off guard and all. She told me that she was not completely ready to switch salons, but a week working alone in my shop could prepare her. She informed me that I was supposed to take a vacation from my business while she prepared for her exit. I was told, by her, that if she worked alone it would be easier on me. My babies were all born, their placentas delivered, and I had no more time to wait. I am surprised that she did not ask me for my ATM PIN while she was at it. I had a great idea myself. In light of what I had just gone through, maybe while she was doing all of that calling and organizing, I could borrow some of her Paxil, mix it with her Xanax, and wash it down with a bottle of Luna di Luna? I was ready for a nice long nap anyway after this episode. I could just sleep the days away and feel nothing while she got "organized." That would be the right thing for me to do in her eyes. Instead I went with plan "B." I gave them all the boot and told them to leave. Well, I did not really give them my boot. I really like my shoes! But I did tell them bye byes.

They all hit the road. Everyone left except for two of my part-time shampoo girls, Ruby and Jamie, and my very true friend Cindy. I let the main clown/mime stay six weeks longer than I should have because we were "friends." Rachel would have never done this to Monica! I mean, sure Angelina may have done it to Jennifer, and Richie did it to Heather. Brittany and Kevin did not end well, but never would Rachel and Monica do such a thing. We were not "friends" at all! Forest Gump could have made a more educated decision than I did at this point. Forest, as a matter of fact, was right on one level. My life was like a box of chocolates at that time! It was dark and full of surprises, with a big ol' nut inside.

I called my friend Cindy the Saturday that I was faced with my very own "walk out" and said to her words she would never forget, "Can you learn how to cut hair really quickly?" Now, when I really think about it, I was not so jokey. I said, "Cindy, they left, my stylists all left." This ironically was the very same day that hurricane Isabelle came through. I had just blown through a hurricane of my own. I hate all hurricanes, especially hurricanes with common girl's names. These girls were all common, with common girl's names. I was really not sure what my next step would be. One thing I knew for sure. Even as bad as things were, I was never going to clown school. I had no interest in learning how to juggle either.

Marty took over from there and changed all the locks on my salon doors within hours. Now they could call me "Ha" like the nail tech guy next door. No one was to be trusted at this point. They could call me when they were ready to get their stuff. They did call, and one girl in particular called me quite a few things as I remember. She was a clown, I guess, and not a mime since she spoke. I don't recall clowns using foul language but perhaps they do. My husband let them in my shop to pick up their styling tools. He took over where I just could not. I am forever grateful. They called me cowardly for not being the one to let them in. They even tried to bully me up until the last minute. To that I now say, "Put em up, Put em up, you stupid freakin' mimes." I was just not in the right frame of mind to deal with this anymore, as you have probably noticed. Be gone with your bad selves! For the first time since pregnancy, I was forced to put really, really big girl panties on. They were not thongs. They were not thongs with gems across the top. They were not granny briefs either. They were just big and they were panties. I had them in a bunch. I had my really big girl panties in a bunch and I put them on.

Top 10 Positive Things About Losing Your Staff

10. No pay roll to meet.

9. Weight loss.

8. Less product ordering.

7. You can feel free to be a total jerk because you are probably already being pegged as one. No one is left to see you being jerky anyway.

6. Leaves you plenty of openings for new friends.

5. They can take your staff and income, but they can't take your sense of humor.

4. Lots of working space.

3. Makes a root canal look like fun.

2. Less money spent on a Christmas party or Secret Santa.

1. You learn how wonderful your true friends and family really are.

Chapter Nine

A New Style

After the dust had settled, it was time to take a look at the situation at hand. I decided to rebuild my salon. Why not? There was only up from there. I had about a year and a half left on my lease and did not want to take another devastating hit by paying a lease on an out-of-business salon. I also did not have the money to invest in juggling lessons, but that is neither here nor there.

More disturbing to me than the Stephen King movie *It,* was the realization that girls I had thought of as friends were less than a mile down the road without me and making money. I was fine with the "without me" part but the "making money" part bothered me. It was a very nice picture of them in the local paper mind you. Black shirts, white faces, that sort of thing. You know the kind of article announcing the NEW salon opening. The kind of ad that helps a stylist to gather any of her MIA clients; no, not gather any of *my* clients named Mia, but the missing in action ones. I did contact Mia though, just in case she got confused. It is also a great way to lure Amy's clients, my clients that is, into that new, bigger, coffee bar type salon. Some clients left me for that salon, those Trader Joe's! Who cares anyway? I mean I was already doing a friend weed out. I might as well do some client weeding too. On a happier note, I just love those loyal clients that stayed! They are still with me to this day! And I don't even have to pay them! They pay me! They pay me even without a coffee bar. Glass? Remember? Half full? I remember a few drops being left in that glass. It was filling back up. I was actually thrilled to be in this situation. I was acting, right then, much like a thespian. I was not thrilled, but dealing … and the show must go on. At least no one was left to drink after me or lick the rim of my glass. I hate when that happens!

I was not looking forward to the first time my own returning clients would enter my salon after the walkout and ask, "Where is everybody?" Or "Why is it so quiet in here?" It should have been loud since the mimes were gone, but it wasn't. I wanted to stay professional but needed to explain. I decided to tell my clients that my staff was so jealous of my new haircut that they just could not work for me any longer. They all needed to work somewhere that they were more comfortable. Things change in this industry; sometimes people just follow the "ring leader" of the circus. I would then mention that I was still around, and I was ready to do some hair. I could "juggle" my salon all by myself. I would ask my clients if they had been anywhere fun lately, I would comment on how nice the weather was, and then I would ask them if they could pay double for their hair service for the next year or so. You know, until I got back on my feet. I would also ask them if they knew, oh, three, maybe four seasoned stylists that were looking for work. Suddenly, I had some open chairs.

I would get many phone calls asking for appointments with the stylists who had left me. I would simply say, "They will contact you." I must admit, working alone for that first month did have its advantages. I could wear the same thing every day if I wanted to.

There was one message on my salon phone left by a former stylist. I remember a lot of cussing and tons of mean things being said. That was before I even turned the machine on to take a listen. Marty quickly deleted the sour message. I never even had the chance to finish hearing it. I was mad at him for doing that. I wanted to hear what terrible things she had to say to me. The other salon had the clients and my staff, so why would this stylist feel the need to cuss on my machine? Was she bummed that I did not send them flowers? Maybe she was hoping I would bring them down champagne, or peanuts. They were only a mile down the road. It really was the least I could do. Marty knew what he was doing by deleting that message. I would have just harped on it all day. It looks like I am harping on it right now. I'm not though, because I never heard the entire message. I never heard the message that was left by … let's just say that the stylist's name was Sharon. I said I would not use real names, right? I don't think Taren, or Sharon, or Darren, or whatever we want to call her, liked me that much. That's ok though, I am good with it. I am actually not so crazy about her either.

I came to the realization that I may have been… what's the word? Oh yes, I may have been bummed. Could that be it? Yep, that was it for sure. I was bummed out. Not the word you thought I was going to use, was it? No one has a perfect life. Sometimes we all get bummed out, at least for a minute or two. Things sometimes just happen.

At that time I let my hair grow long, not long like the Polygamist Ranch wives with the puffy bangs, French braids, and prairie dresses, but pretty long. I looked entirely different. I still looked pretty, but different. I did not have anyone to cut my hair, so I grew it. I think my long hair days are over. While I am not willing to give up short skirts, tank tops, or high-heeled espadrilles, I guess I can part with long hair. As I write this, I am closing in on forty and the long hair days are over for me, unless I choose to swirl it up on top of my head in a bun. There's a look for ya! I am happy to look my age, minus the bun.

In the thick of this mess, Marty and I were building our home. I had three little kids in school and day care and I was a bit stressed. Are you feeling sorry for me yet? Well don't, because I had plenty of "me" to feel sorry for "me." Not to worry, it would not last. I have never been one to wallow in grief and self-pity for too long. I was determined to turn things around.

There was one funny thing that happened in the thick of the madness. My middle son, Wyatt, was in kindergarten. We had sold our house and were living with my sister Cindy, her husband Tim, and my nephew Patrick. Wyatt had afternoon kindergarten so I would bring him into work with me. I would then take him to school in the afternoon and he would stay for after school care with his brother, Chris. One day I had noticed that his backpack was abnormally heavy. I looked inside and found a lot of change. I asked Wyatt where he got the money. I immediately feared that my chaotic life had led him to a life of crime and thievery. Was he the schoolyard bully stealing from the other children for attention? I quickly found out that this was not the case. He simply told me that he was selling candy at school and asked me if we could go to Wal-Mart to buy some Yu-gi-oh cards with the money he had made. Whose candy was he selling? Come to find out, while I was doing hair in the mornings at the salon, and he was watching TV in the back room, he was also stuffing his backpack with the haircut treats I had kept my salon stocked with for children. He would take the candy to school and sell it at after school care. Perhaps I could take some business advice from my five year old. Money was particularly tight in those days.

So there I was, the owner of an empty salon, my husband and I were building a house with his income alone due to my situation, and we were living in a small one-bedroom apartment attached to my sister and brother-in-law's house. Are you jealous of me yet? I can imagine that it looked like some sort of immigration situation to an outsider. We had our bed, a portable crib, and two mattresses on the floor of this one bedroom apartment. The stress level was at an all time high. Marty and I had no time for us as a couple, so you can imagine our relations were few. A shadowy seven-year-old son of mine that we never saw apparently over-saw the one opportunity we had to "relate." It was not until the morning when my son asked me why Daddy was "pushing me off of the sofa" that the real alarm went off in my head. I would instantly whisper to myself, "What did he see, WHAT DID HE SEE!?" I would calmly explain to Chris that the sofa was very uncomfortable and we were just trying to find a comfortable spot. That satisfied him for the time, but he would mention this so called "pushing" many more times in the next couple days. At this point I was sure that I would wait at least another year to share the birds and the bees story with him. He was sure to piece together what he had witnessed if I told him too soon. After all, thinking about one's parents "pushing each other off the sofa" could certainly scar a kid for life! We already had so many changes going on in our lives. I did not need this situation. I am still not sure exactly what he saw. Maybe that is best.

I had lost a lot of my income. Even despite the candy sales, we were still coming up short with our bills. In this business, when you are not charming your clients you sometimes see a decline in new referrals. We had many added expenses due to our home building. Then there was los-ing all my staff, losing some of my clients, and my self-esteem was not at an all-time high at this point. Let's not forget the part about us living in a one-bedroom apartment and being "busted" by a seven year old for "relating" to each other. Things were on edge at this time in our lives. There was a pity party in town and I was the guest of honor. I would give myself a year to work up a game plan. I prayed and read self help books and waited. I am not very good at waiting, but I had no choice.

I hired some new stylists and they helped me finish out the year I gave myself. Two of the girls were seasoned stylists and they really helped me out. One was even a distant relative named Linda that I went through hair school with. She was one of the few normal hair school girls. She was great to have around. I also hired some very young stylists. I was not a friend to these girls. I was good to them, but not their friend. I had learned from my mistakes. I would soon grow tired of being a mother to the young, inexperienced girls in my salon. I am still not a fan of tongue piercing, tribal earrings, bodies peppered with tattoos, and belly shirts. I am not sure why. Perhaps, in my opinion, it tends to de-class a person. Maybe I am old and just do not understand these things on young people. One thing is for sure, if that looks bad on the young, it looks even worse on the old! Why is it that you need a boss to tell you not to wear that extra, extra small size to work when you are really a large. If your belly is popping out of your pants like a tin of Jiffy Pop, the shirt is either too tight or the pants are too small. Just because you can squeeze into a size 8, does not mean that you are a size 8!

As a word to the wise, please do your hair if you work in a salon. Put a little bit of make-up on, and do not say the word "form a la." The word is actually "form*u*la." We refer to clients of color as African American clients and clients from Asian countries are Asian client's not "Oriental." Under eye cream also does wonders for covering up dark circles from a hangover. I guess my young staff was unaware of these bits of practical wisdom. I must be getting old.

The year I gave myself to mourn and wallow in self-pity was coming to an end. I was thankful for that! Out of nowhere an opportunity knocked. Did I start going to karaoke and get noticed you asked? No, in-stead I got a call from a girl that was interested in buying my salon. She had walked by it many times when she was getting her nails done next door and inquired of the nail tech how to contact me. Not only was she interested in buying the salon, but also she was interested in taking over the many months left on my lease and wanted to purchase my equipment. A divine intervention was taking place. I was afraid to get too excited. This was the answer I was looking for! Things were going to change. This was a true answer to my prayers! I too had changed. I was embracing life and happiness in a brand new way! I even put away those crazy voodoo dolls and pins.

To this day, I feel as if I am a changed person due to the demise of my hair salon. I now trust no one. I trust no one and I never wear black. I am also quick to hate. See how changed I am? Well, that is actually not true. I do still love black. Most of my wardrobe is black and white. True mime colors.

It is truly the best feeling when things start to turn around. I will get through the tough times in life if I have to. It is more fun to trust people and take chances. Thankfully I am richer than I was in those last days; emotionally and financially. I am much wiser too. I needed that year. I was once again happy and I was looking to the future. I was peaceful in my life.

I remember a client asking me if I felt like a failure because I closed my shop. I told him that, quite the contrary, I felt like a failure because I could not figure out how to load my son's new iPod, or get his videos on YouTube. Not to mention that I have yet to host "SNL;" however, that failure has nothing to do with closing a hair salon. I am way funnier than Michael Phelps, and he got to be a guest host, and I don't smoke anything!

Truthfully, I needed that year's time to get over what had happened to me, and now I had. Everything has its time, and it was my time to move on. I am a better person for my experiences even as hard as the end was.

I have learned so much. I still am able to laugh a lot, and now I can download all kinds of music.

As an added bonus I also received a call from an old boss, a surprise phone call from Roberta. Roberta, my boss from fifteen years prior, looked up my phone number and called me. She had heard that I had closed my salon and she was inquiring about some of my salon equipment. I talked to her briefly about how I now understood what it was like to have been in her shoes so many years ago. I told her that I was sorry for the way I had left her. I wondered to myself if she felt karma had taken place.

Two years after closing my salon door, a former stylist looked up my number just like Roberta had. This stylist told me she was sorry for the way she had left me. She told me that she often felt bad about that. She said she had since left the circus and had moved on to another shop. She was calling me to ask for forgiveness. I assured her that she had already had it long before she called. She was the one person that I always knew felt bad about the way things ended. I thanked her for her call and assured her that she had my friendship. Sometimes timing is important. Her phone call came at a time that I can honestly say was perfect. I was truthfully over this entire experience. I healed much faster than I ever imagined I would. I credit the wonderful support of my family and friends. I could have never done it alone.

These two chapters were much easier to write than I could have ever imagined when I was living this hardship. Time does heal all wounds.

So much time has passed since those troubled Creative Image Salon days. Not too long ago I had a nice long talk with my sons, Christopher and Wyatt, over some very important facts that I have learned along the way. We talked about some of the facts that I have written about in these past two chapters. I plan to share these same facts with Kendall, my youngest, in due time. I will wait until she is old enough to understand.

After all, some of life's situations are meant to be shared with your children. Both of my boys are now aware that their mom and dad were both pushed off the sofa "three" times because we have three kids. At one point, we actually did find a comfortable spot. Two kids down, one kid to go. I will fill in the rest of the blanks as needed.

Top 10 Great Things About Selling a Business

10. The heaviness on your chest is lifted.

9. A chance at a "Do-Over."

8. You tend to laugh harder and longer.

7. Less paper work.

6. You have more time to spend with your family.

5. A feeling of calmness and peace.

4. Make a few bucks with the sale.

3. Bill collectors stop calling.

2. Sleep through the night.

1. You find your sparkle once again.

Chapter Ten

My Next Appointment

With the sale of my salon I was ready for a fresh start. I was elated to turn the page! You probably are too! Enough with the "clowning" around about those "bozos," let's move on to the fun stuff.

Marty built me a salon in our new home's basement. I would service my neighbors, friends, and family there. I would acquire my zoning license, but it was not easy. I had to talk the judge into allowing me to work from home. The heels, cute little dress, and wink may have helped my situation because at one point everyone in the room was being denied their home salon requests. I had much worry, thanks to a backstabbing neighbor who mailed in a letter of concern about more traffic on our rural road. The board advanced me the license despite her negativity. As a thank you gift to my nosey neighbor, I left her a gift on her porch. I don't think anyone saw me run when I dropped off that flaming brown paper bag filled with dog poo, so I think we are good.

I am able to make dinner for some special clients due to my home-based salon situation. Sometimes I even eat it with them. I am never bored working at home because I have constant conversation with different clients coming in and out all day long. I consider myself a hair-a-pist now more than ever. With appointments scheduled one at a time, the conversations can get pretty deep. There are many highlights and lowlights in my workday depending on the hairapy needed.

I have formed some great friendships over the years. My friends Lisa and Marnie keep me updated on what I miss by not working in a salon, and we always attend hair shows together. The only thing I lack in my home salon would be the constant dirty looks from others when I start getting out of hand. At home I can wear khaki if I want, for every day here at home is casual day. I could even get away with bedroom slippers if I felt like it. When I run a few minutes late, as I tend to do, there is no one here at my home to steal my client. This sort of thing is a problem in some salons.

At the end of the nights I do have to remember to "tip" myself out since I am the shampoo girl as well as stylist. It is a great set up for me.

Top 10 Nice Things About Having a Home Based Salon

10. Your dog has company all day long.

9. You can e-mail your friends in between clients.

8. Facebooking.

7. No need to call out for snow days.

6. No conflicts with co-worker.

5. No babysitters needed.

4. Every day is casual Friday.

3. Free parking and no gas money needed.

2. Can get the kids off the bus.

1. You are home with your family.

Chapter 11

Out With A Bang

There are times when it is necessary to send the dreaded "you are not welcome back" letter. Some clients you just need to get out of the salon, and off of your book. I know some stylists that are pretty set on sending out a standard form letter. I have done it over the phone, e-mail, and in person. This is the out with a bang chapter, or how to respond when a client becomes a burden and not a blessing.

I can usually tell when a client is going to become a burden. It only takes about two minutes of conversation before you realize that this client is going to be a "hair whore."

A "hair whore" by definition is someone that hops from salon to salon, stylist to stylist, in hopes to find one that will get her hair right. There is no such stylist because no one will get it right. It has nothing to do with the stylist and everything to do with the client in this case. When a client comes in and says, "No one can seem to do my hair the way I like it," or "The last girl I went to butchered my hair," or "I have been to three other stylists looking for someone that can do my hair," I know right away that this will be our one and only meeting.

I sent a client packing one time before I even did her hair. Sue came into my salon and I was backed up. I told her right away that I was running late and to help herself to some coffee. She did not seem to mind and watched me work frantically while I tried to catch up. When it came time to do Sue's hair she told me all about how she was tired of driving to her last stylist's salon and how she was referred to me. Her last stylist happened to be my friend Lisa. She asked me if I knew how many minutes she had waited. I was unsure. She said she never even waits at the doctor's office this long and that she surely would not wait long for her hair coloring. I told her again that I was sorry for the wait, and not to call me Shirley, I prefer Laverne. She then told me she had waited for twenty-five minutes because she had watched the clock. She was very angry with me. She must have really caught me at a bad time because I clearly remember that I simply told her that she would never have to wait again. Our time was over and there would be no charge for her consultation. I wished her luck. I told her she was free to leave. I walked away and she just sat there. I told my next client, Steve, "I am all caught up now and running on time." Perhaps I was abrasive, but I just was not in the mood to be reprimanded by a client that I did not even know. I was especially not going to be bossed around by a client that had left my friend Lisa. See that Miss Sheri, I am getting tougher! At that point I refused to be disrespected in my own hair salon.

I had a stalker client who would e-mail me, call me, and even got my cell phone number from another stylist and texted me. He was not welcome in my home. I had done his hair fifteen years ago and had not seen him since, but suddenly he was interested in coming back to me. I wondered if it had anything to do with his soon to be ex-wife confiding in me? I think his desire to have me cut his hair started right around the same time he caught his wife in bed with her co-worker.

There have been a few clients whose hair I just could not get right. Every time one particular client named Jill would come in, she would tell me she liked her hair the last time but it was a little too short, not light enough, too light, not layered enough, or did not last. She would grimace in pain as I shampooed her hair and then actual tears would come to her eyes when I combed out the tangles. I would "re do" her hair the next day almost every single time. I would also bring on her migraines, and she would leave feeling sick on most occasions. She would always inform me that her boyfriend did not think her hair was right. She of course loved it she said. I am pretty sure that she was her own worst critic. Jill would swear that she never ever took scissors to her own head either. I was the only one that ever cut her hair. I would bet differently. I would also bet that the rattling in her purse was more than a box of Tic Tacs.

I have also had a situation where a letter was necessary. A client that kept missing her appointments started to become a huge problem. This happened four or five times. Once or twice is no big deal, but when it happens over and over, it is time for a switch. The last time this happened she called me after her appointment time and said she was home from work and too exhausted to come in. There is no filling a slot that has lapsed! Her letter went like this:

Dear Client,

I am unable to give you an appointment at this time. You have missed several appointments and have only called me after your appointment time has lapsed. This hurts my business as well as my pocketbook. I feel you do not respect my time. I think a walk-in based salon may be a better fit for you. As of now I am not able to put you on the books. I hope you understand. Thank you for your time. Oh and there is a salon in town that can service you. Just drive into town and look for the salon underneath the red and white striped circus tent. The clowns in there would be happy to give you an appointment! They even have free coffee! You will love it there, and please make sure you tell them that Amy sent you.

Sincerely, Amy

I really have a tough time with the children that you have to be a contortionist to service. I love children, I even have three, but sometimes there is only so much you can do. Children are still the absolute hardest clients to service. The only good thing here is that they always grow-up, and they always get better. Every stylist would probably agree that it is never a picnic to cut a little one's hair. On top of that, they are charged the least amount of money. How can you charge a lot to cut a kid's hair? You can't. While we do not usually fire these clients, we do let the parents know that their time in our chair is limited. There is only so much we can do. The parents are usually just as troubled over this situation as we are. I even had a friend take her son to a barbershop for two years because she liked me too much to put me through that. I have a better understanding these days for those poor parents who have to endure this painful visit to the salon. After all, I have three kids with soft teeth. The dentist is my own personal children's hair salon hell visit. I feel your pain.

My favorite salon experience in cutting kid's hair comes from a woman that brings her two young girls to me. The five year old has very long hair. Her hair is so tangled and knotted up that it takes a full forty-five minutes just to get a brush through it. She continues to tell me that her daughter does not brush it very well. Really? I actually can see that, and I believe this may have something to do with the fact that she is five! News flash, most five year olds do not brush their teeth, much less brush out tangles!

No one warned me of the dangers associated with children's haircuts. There are many. Sometimes you need to stand at an arm's length to keep from getting vomited on. I have witnessed situations where some children have gotten so worked up that they barf-up their lunches while getting their haircut. One time I was even punched in the stomach. For these clients I have considered wearing my son's protective catchers gear as I cut them. I have been squirted in the face with a squirt bottle more times than I can count. There has also been uncontrollable crying due to frustration. The kids sometimes cry too. I have seen kids ingest entire lollypops that were fur lined. The lollypop/haircut Heimlich has been given more than once. My favorite thing about this entire experience is watching how the parents handle this half hour of giggles and fun. Most of the time, we as parents reward this type of behavior. It makes no sense, but we do. Parents say to their youngster, "Here is a treat for getting your hair cut." Maybe I could add, "Here is a treat for doing a crappy job." Or, "Great job spitting out all that hair that fell into your mouth. Here take two lollypops for that one." Oh yes, next comes peppering my salon with baby powder to calm down that hairy itch. This entire experience only takes about ten minutes. I love that these same little ones scream and cry the minute they lay their eyes on me. That kind of stuff makes an overworked stylist feel great! I have heard parents say to me, "WOW, that was fast." Yes it was! For those children that are just way too tough, we just do what we can, and we do it fast! I do not get mad at them because, after all, they are only kids!

One of my favorite comments during this haircutting experience came from a little boy named Jacob. Jacob may be a future motivational speaker. Every time I cut Jacob's hair, he sits on his dad's lap and chants over and over, "It's OK daddy, it's OK daddy, it's OK daddy." With his cheering squad of cousins by his side, he remains positive. I had no idea when I started out in this business that haircuts could be so traumatic for kids. "It's OK Amy, it's OK Amy!"

Some other problems in the salon occur when payment is due. "I am going out to dinner with friends tonight before we leave for an all-inclusive trip to Jamaica on Monday, but my automatic deposit will be in my account next Thursday, is it a problem to hold this check until then?" Um, yes, this is a problem. It is only fifteen dollars; do you think you could borrow it from your husband?

"Do you think you can get me some hair products at wholesale prices, because even though you do not actually do my hair, and we only know each other from the gym, my friend is in a fight with her sister who is a stylist and gets us hair stuff at cost usually, but now that they are not on speaking terms, we can't get our supplies, can you get them for my friend and me at wholesale?" Um, no actually, I can't. Well, I could, but I won't.

"I know you are finished, and I did not mention this before we started because I forgot, but can I ask you something? Can you hold this check till I get paid? When things are put that way, I guess I have no other choice.

"I am not sure if I can make my high lightening appointment next Tuesday, but I sure am going to try." Well, "I am not sure if I will be able to give you that high lightening appoint without a commitment, but I sure am gonna try."

Top 10 Reasons to Fire a Client

10. They smell funny.

9. They make you wait till they are back from their trip to get paid.

8. They are a spy for another salon.

7. You have to drink heavily when they leave.

6. They're always working you for free services.

5. They are way too negative.

4. They use you for your wholesale product perks.

3. They make offensive or racist comments.

2. They constantly miss their appointments yet they are never sorry.

1. You just can't please them.

Chapter 12

I Am Sure This Is the Wrong Style For You

Maybe I have missed my calling, but I am a self-proclaimed fortune-teller. I pay close attention to detail. As a seasoned stylist, I must share some stories that I knew would come to pass. Conditioning will prevent breakage, as well as keep hair healthy. Some things I just know.

Here is the scenario. A young client came into the salon with his girl-friend. They were both seniors in high school. He was headed to college in California. She was staying here. He sat in my chair and she sat next to him "supervising" my cut. She wanted to be clear that she knew what the best look for him was. He then told me that he was going to a college in California in a couple months and that she was going to come out his second semester to live close by. No she's not. You are going to leave for school in August. You will meet all new friends, and leave your possessive girl behind. She will not come out there because you will have replaced her with some new girl from your English 101 class. Not to worry though because she too will have already replaced you with another boy she can control just minutes after you board the plane. Because while you are there, and she is here, she will not be able to tell you how to get your hair cut, what to wear, or where or what you are going to eat. So she will quickly find some other sucker that she can boss around. Going away to school was the best bet for this couple. I was right. I saw it coming! This very thing happened.

Here is another one. A woman named Heidi came into the salon filled with excitement. She had been in a stale marriage for a long time. Her husband paid her no attention at all, and they had no children. Heidi took on a second job where she met a married male co-worker. This married guy desired to have sex with her all of the time and videotape it. This she found to be very exciting and sneaky and she loved it! He had fallen madly in love with her and wanted to watch them having sex over and over, which is why he wanted to videotape their affair. I told Heidi point blank that, in my opinion, he may not be in love her, he is not leaving his wife, and he is going to kick you to the curb when he gets bored. Either he is going to eventually kick you to the curb or his wife it going to kick your ass. I knew it would be one of these two scenarios. Videotaping never ends well. I was sure there were others. She was not as sure. My fortune-telling instincts told me that this was not going to be a lasting relationship. She was convinced that this guy was the one and only for her. She must have forgotten that she had a husband at home. I don't think her husband would have liked hearing that part. This other man was smitten with her she told me.

Heidi's affair happened over the course of a year. One day she went to his office and was surprised at what she found. Interestingly enough, he was in the restroom having sex with yet another co-worker. Forget for a minute that he was with another woman; let's get back to the "having sex in a restroom" part. Gross! People poop in there! He did not answer the knock on the bathroom door. She then looked frantically for her tape.

She found many tapes of other women but not her own. She left cussing and screaming at him; she also threatened the tramp he was with, and then stalked them both. She called his cell phone thousands of times, e-mailed him constantly, and left him love notes of desperation. I could have told her it was going to end something like this. I think I even did.

A baby will fix our marriage. That is the oldest one in the book! No it won't. A client named Rita came in for a haircut. We started chatting and she began to get upset when I asked her what was new. She suspected that her husband had been cheating on her. Instead of doing some investigative work of her own, she chose to believe him when he said he was not cheating, even though her gut told her otherwise. She then tried to get pregnant and succeeded. They had the baby and suddenly her husband was no longer interested in her. He started working late nights while she was home with their infant. He took a position for a job that he could not commute to. He was forced to get an apartment to live in during the workweek since this commute was so long. He said that he would come home on weekends. No he won't. He got an apartment near his new girl-friend and he was leaving his wife and newborn baby. In less than six months they filed for divorce because he was no longer in love with her. Later down the road I found out he had broken up with that very girl he had left his wife for. Shocker! Did anyone see that coming? I did!

The get-rich-quick scheme: Here is how the pyramid works. Amy, you have to join us they all said. You can make tons of money very quickly! No I won't! My client and some co-workers of mine were to bring a large sum of money to a hotel conference center. By bringing other people in you move your name up the pyramid. This allows you to be next in line to collect five times the money you have brought in. The system was called the "friends helping friends" meeting. Or, if you were on the bottom of the pyramid before it got busted, it was called the "friends screwing friends" meeting. In two weeks you will be through the pyramid and rich. I was not interested in this scheme at all. Waaay too risky! One friend of mine did move quickly up the ladder, got her money, and got out. Two other co-workers were not so lucky and lost the $1,200 that it cost them to join this "club." That was a fun couple of months in the salon. Many services were tacked on to try to make up the difference for these stylists. Hard work will make you money. Everything else is just too risky!

When the marriage ends, who gets the stylist? This has happened several times. I do both the husband's hair as well as the wife's. It makes things interesting I must admit. They both share things about the other one. I pegged one marriage's end before they even walked down the aisle. The husband had not been faithful in the past but a marriage certificate was sure to straighten him out. No it wasn't. It only took two years before he left her for a girl he met online. There have been times where I wanted the "other" one in the relationship as a client. I hate it when I am stuck with the miserable one. Sometimes I keep them both. I just make sure that the appointment times do not overlap.

What is it they say? Is it something like fifty percent of marriages end in divorce? Honestly, that seems about right. I think fifty percent of this world is crazy too. I know I am! People do crazy things when acting on emotion. What is the phrase? Hell hath no fury like a woman scorned. Boy, ain't that the truth!

Another client, Tammy, lied about an illness she had just to keep her husband from leaving. We know which side of the "fifty percent" she was on. She went to desperate measures to save her marriage. She even faked being hospitalized many times to keep her man. He would stay a little longer because of her illness. Once he found out she was fooling him to keep him the marriage was over. I think she would even go as far as to make herself sick for attention. Perhaps she has Munchausen's Syndrome. She even told me that she had incurable cancer. Tammy told me that she only had a year to live at best. I believed her. She said her kidneys were in bad shape due to the cancer, so she had to go twice a week for dialysis treatment. All of her organs were shutting down at one point. She conned me for years. I understand that she is now healthy, cancer free, and divorced. I use the word "healthy" lightly. Fake cancer cannot be healthy.

When the client visits her Yoga instructor at his home for some private lessons, I can tell you that her marriage is pretty much over. Now that is a twisted situation. Namaste.

My client Judy told me that she was being featured in a reality show about her life. Cameras would follow her everywhere she went. I saw no cameras when she was in getting her hair cut. I guess they left her alone for her hair services. Judy said that the party she was hosting at a downtown nightclub was the highlight of this reality show.

I didn't remember seeing a trailer for this. She eventually got bored with the "in your face" camera crew, so she ended the reality show. It can't be easy having people stop you everywhere you go when you are so famous. After all, she was a bathing suit model, or some sort of model. I guess her show never got picked up. Or maybe it never got started. I wonder if she wore her bathing suits throughout the show. I'll bet she didn't. Her show must have aired on a network that we don't carry. I sure hope my kids don't find out which network. It must cost more money to carry those channels, so I think I am good.

Fortune Telling...Top 10 Predictions

10. The kids that are into hard drugs will not stop on their own.

9. A marriage certificate will not save a relationship.

8. There is no free lunch. If you gamble you will lose.

7. Going to college in different states will break up even the best couples.

6. You will not go back to school after taking a year off.

5. He's not leaving his wife for you.

4. She's not leaving her husband for you.

3. A baby will make the marriage harder not easier.

2. Video taping never ends well.

1. Neither does stalking.

Chapter 13

I Doooooooo

Formal hairstyling has always been my passion. I do believe this is my favorite part of hairdressing, and it for sure is what I do best. You have to be confident, creative, and willing to think outside of the box in order to make this a memorable experience for the client being serviced. I always embrace this experience.

Let me start by saying that you can tell a lot about a bridal party by looking at the bride. If the bride is kind, sweet, beautiful, and generous, her bridesmaids are bound to be the same. If a bride is difficult, angry, and demanding, her friends will be the same.

Earthy and Granola, they will wear Birkenstocks instead of Jimmy Choos. Nerdy? You know the drill. Sometimes the nerdy ones are the most fun. The nice thing about the dorky bride is that these girls have no clue that they are dorky. I mean Claymates are people too! After all, Donny Osmond is a "Soldier of Love." What's so dorky about being a soldier? I think this particular bride even made her husband wear purple socks on their wedding day.

The nice thing about the very simple, and maybe slightly dorky, client is that they are completely unaware of their dorkiness. They are usually the most gracious girls. They are carefree and they always let me show my creative side when it comes to up-dos. They even let me sprinkle their hair with baby's breath when I am finished. It is a proven fact that there is someone out there for everyone. I have seen it. This is true. Some girls I thought would never marry; I am pleased to say that they have done just that. You know the type of guy that matches this sweet bride. This is the guy that spends all of his spare time in those weird stores in the mall painting little metal figurines. Once those two are a couple, both of them spend their time painting those figurines. That is fine if you are in high school, but once you hit about twenty-five, this seems odd to me. That is just my opinion. Sometimes these folks have even married more than once. Now that is strange.

I have so learned the hard way what not to say to the Trekkie/Osmond loving bridesmaids. For starters, don't say Star Wars sucks! Remember that the bridesmaids usually mirror the bride.

I made the mistake once in asking the forbidden question. No, not the sex question, but the other forbidden question. I asked the bride how her mom would like to wear her hair on the wedding day. I asked it, and I was clueless. The woman sitting before me was not the bride's mom! I had wondered why the maid of honor had been a no-show. The next thing I knew, the bride's mom was walking in the door and the maid of honor before me was fuming. My fault! Sometimes the maid of honor looks like she could be the mother of the bride, so never assume.

On this same topic, one couple met on an online "War of the Worlds" gaming chat room. Description of this happy couple is not needed. They are a perfect match. WOW!

I have done so many weddings for folks who have met on

Match.com, Jdate, and E-Harmony web sights. If you are forty-five, like to collect antique dolls, enjoy Harry Potter conventions, and basket weaving, this may be your only hope in finding a match. That market is rather narrow. It does work. I'm just sayin'….

One couple got married at the renaissance festival. Their first date was spent at the renaissance festival, so they decided to marry there. The bride was a beautiful wench.

More than once I have seen the jealous single sister of the bride. I can spot the envious maid of honor every time. "Always a bridesmaid, never the bride." They usually are the ones standing behind the bride with a bucket of red paint. Maybe they don't go to that extreme, but for sure they have an attitude problem. I had a bridal party once who thought they were as important as the bride herself. I spent a half hour on one bridesmaid just getting her bangs "right." Another bridesmaid had a picture. When I made her hair look exactly like the picture, she said, "Nah, I don't really like this on me." A few other girls said, "When you're done, can you just fix this one piece?" I came up with this formula. When you have one bridesmaid that had a baby three weeks ago, another eight months pregnant, and one never been married, jealous bridesmaid, you have your work cut out for you. A great idea is and always will be to start with the bride or you may run out of time.

I was asked to do a wedding party in Michigan once. My cousin, Steve, was marrying a girl named Kristin from Michigan. My mom was having radiation treatment to cure her breast cancer, which I am happy to say had a wonderful outcome. That meant that I was to fly my grandmother to Michigan alone for the wedding. I was doing the bride's hair for the wedding anyway, so I decided to take a road trip with my grandmother. When our plane landed in Cleveland, they announced that all connecting flights were canceled. I tried to remain calm but I knew in my heart of hearts that we were in a bad situation. The thought of my grandmother sleeping on a cot in the airport horrified me. The scene from *Planes, Trains, and Automobiles* came to my mind. Gram sleeping on a cot at the airport was just not an option. I called my husband from my cell phone to ask him if he had any ideas. We had to get to Michigan. I was doing everyone's hair! The rain in Cleveland was so heavy that I worried about renting a car. I worried even more about driving a rented car. Just as I hung up my cell phone, a stranger tapped me on my shoulder. He said he overheard my conversation and noticed that I was on his same canceled connecting flight. He also heard me telling my husband that we were heading to a wedding. I guess being everyone's loudest friend worked to my favor for once. This stranger told me that he was an airline pilot named Don, and that he was headed to the same airport we were headed to. He offered to drive us to Michigan since that was his final destination too.

My immediate thought was not that he was a murderer/rapist; I thought that if he can land a 747 in an ice storm, driving to Michigan should be a cinch. Two other girls overheard our conversation and asked if they too could join us. At this point I felt that there was safety in numbers. So this stranger named Don, bathing suit Barbara still wearing her bikini top and coming from Florida, a sweet girl Tina, my grandmother, and I drove through the stormy night. Well, Don drove through the storm, but we rode alongside him. He drove us straight through the night until we arrived in Lansing, Michigan, for the wedding. We hopped out of the car rented by the stranger pilot named Don. Don was far from strange, and we offered him some money for his car rental and gas. He refused our money. We thanked him, and as we got into my aunt and uncle's car, my grandmother said to me, "Amy, we did not even get Don's last name, and we have no idea where he lives." I assured her that it did not matter much. Don was sent to us. I believe an angel touched Gram and me both. That, or we just met a really nice guy that was headed in the same direction. I like the angel idea. We made the wedding, the hair looked beautiful, and everyone had fun!

Three times is a charm — I had the pleasure of doing three different hairstyles for three different weddings. All of which were for the same bride. That was a first, or was it a third?

Ah, the Bridzillas! "You finished our hair too fast; you're done already?" The bride's hair took close to two hours to complete, so I guess they did think I worked too fast. I could have named the bride "pin head" when she was done by the number of showing bobby pins in her bun. I did not do the brides hair; instead I did the hair of the ugly stepsisters. I could not believe it took that other stylist *two hours* to do a crappy looking bun. The bride brought her own hairstylist to create her pincushion hair masterpiece. I was there for the rest of the bridal party. I actually do not fault her stylist; she was under too much pressure for sure. I have great issues with bobby pins showing. I can't explain it, I just do! While the bride was not my worry, I did have the displeasure of doing the bridesmaid's hair.

Now, call me an idiot, but I really think the finished product is more important than the time it takes to do it. Still, as I stated, the fetching, over pinned bride and her harridan entourage's biggest complaint was that I was too fast. My biggest complaint was that they were all spoiled brats who thought they were above being respectful.

Anna, one of the attendants of this nightmare group, came to me a year later for her hair and told me that I was "on trial." She would see if I could get her hair right. I had already been "on trial" with her, for that "memorable" wedding. Guess what, I decided I was not on trial. I was also sure that, with that attitude, there was no way I would get her hair right in her eyes. She probably should have shared this information with me after I was finished her hair, instead of before I started. I actually failed butt kissing in hair school. Had I passed butt kissing, I would have exchanged phone numbers with fellow classmates, but I failed. Remember Lisa was one of my only friends in those days.

Sadly, Anna was unaware that I was not a kiss up. I did not speak to her for the rest of her hair service. That was not easy for a chatty person like me. I remember when she left she said, "Please don't take this personal, I have enjoyed our time together but I am going to try someone else." She left and I have never seen her again. She broke-up with me. Little did she know that I was going to dump her, or maybe she figured that out and beat me to it? I have heard that this client now goes to Dan for her hair. Remember Dan, the guy that I used to work for years ago — Dan, the stylist who had no tolerance for his clientele? WOW! Wait till he pulls the "I'm done" and throws the comb down with her.

It was so funny that she told me before she left that she chose him over me. She did not even know that I knew him. This industry is filled with people who know each other. Be careful! The turnover is huge in this business. The ex-stylist you talk smack about could be a friend of your current stylist.

Some brides have been extremely generous to me. They have invited me to the wedding services and their receptions. To one bride named Michelle, I must apologize! Michelle and Bryan made sure that I made the guest list. I hope they are happy with their decision to invite me. Remember I mentioned that if I could sing I would be a singer. The side note to that one is if the band invites me to sing Madonna, I will sing Madonna. I will and I did. I sang with the band, and it will forever be remembered when they watch their wedding DVD. I know this for a fact. Michelle still mentions it when I do her hair. I should offer up a warning. If you invite me to your wedding after I do your bridal party's hair, not only will I touch-up your hair during the wedding, but I will also sing with your band. I can even bring my friends Mark and Traci to DJ if you like. I mentioned the dorky brides earlier in this chapter, but I forgot to mention the dorky hairstylist. I *am* the dorky stylist.

I once flew to Florida and had my expenses paid to do a wedding for a long time client. I even got to do the hair of a celebrity's child who was an attendant in the wedding. That was fun! I really love brushes with "fame kids."

Sometimes people are more than generous when tipping for special events. Other times, not so much. I am sure every stylist will agree that tips are best when they are cash. While every gesture is appreciated, tipping with "things" can be a bit uncomfortable. Let's just say that it is best to leave the re-gifting for your stylist's Christmas gift. A simple thank you is plenty.

I had one bride who not only had a fantastic bridal party, but an awesome make-up girl. We connected right away; the make-up girl and me. You would have thought that we knew each other for years. She was a fantastic make-up artist, and I look forward to working with her in the future, or maybe shopping with her. She had such a cute outfit on. The bride and her bridesmaids looked fantastic too!

One couple decided to hold their wedding and reception at the Baltimore Zoo. The bride was so excited because they both loved animals. She wanted a "natural" looking hairstyle since her wedding was outdoorsy. They held the ceremony close to the petting zoo. Do you think the guests threw corn instead of rice? I bet they did!

I once did an entire bridal party, including the grandmother. The grandmother was in the way most of the time and quite intrusive, if I remember correctly. She would watch as I styled the bridesmaids' hair and I could see she wanted some serious pampering herself. When I finished the bridal party, she came over to me and said in a nasty voice, "You did not give me enough spray like you did the others, I want more spray!" I no sooner said, "sure," than she grabbed a can off of my station. She coated her entire head with this spray. Much to her surprise, she grabbed the glitter spray I was using on the attendants. To that I said, "fancy." This grandmother had no clue that she was covered with glitter and, believe me, I was not telling!

From time to time a bride will come into the salon without any idea what style they should have for their wedding hair. They sometimes even change the style and color way too close to their event. Most of the time, these indecisive brides come to regret the last minute changes they have made. That is when the reassuring comes in. Rescue 911 was actually a hair phrase before it was a TV show.

Have you ever noticed that stylists have each other's back most of the time? We are especially attentive to each other when a bridal party is in the house. When we close ranks, clients think twice about tattling on one of us to a salon owner or manager if their stylist does not get their hair just like the picture they brought in. Clients who complain loud and long become the clients that we remember in a bad way, and get labeled "difficult." We take note of the "difficult clients." If a stylist has been way out of line, which has certainly been the case at times, it is worth a good squealing, but otherwise don't bother. If a stylist sees another stylist being intimidated, we help out right away. This is an unwritten code. We start off with a simple, "That looks great," and then we move on to, "I love your hair like that!" or "That hairstyle really makes your face look thin!" or "That was the right choice doing half-up-half down with curls. Good thinking!"

Sometimes it works and sometimes it doesn't. I always try it; it can't hurt. Some girls expect the stylist to create something that is just not right for their personality and then they hate it. Stick with what you know. If you are funky and wild with your looks go funky and wild. If you are not, twists and sprouts and wild hair will not please you.

The prom girls are similar to the brides, only far more hormonal. They can leave the salon loving their hair and call fifteen minutes later stating that they hate it and they want a redo. Someone at home is usually responsible for this phone call, or their girlfriends told them that their hair looked bad. I will never understand why some moms and dads say negative things about their daughter's hair just minutes before the prom. If it is not your taste, and you are not wild about it, just lie would ya? Let's not have these young girls putting cold compresses on their eyes minutes before their dates arrive because they are hysterical. Don't say, "I thought you were doing half up half down?" or "Why did you wear it down? You know your hair looks better up, I did not pay all that money for you to wear it down!" Don't do that to your kids, or your stylist. When the hair is finished, make it a point to be kind. All seventeen and eighteen-year-old girls are beautiful. Let's make sure they know it.

One girl told me right off the bat that I would not get her hair right the first try for her prom. I did her hair, and it looked beautiful. She hated it. I took it down and did the exact same thing and she loved it. I even thought it turned out better the first time. Sadly, I could not charge her for two up-dos. She just wanted to feel like she was in control. I think she was out of control. I can just imagine what she will be like on her wedding day. I am sure I will be busy that day flossing my teeth or counting the carpet squares in my basement. She will be a Bridezilla for sure.

Top 10 Wedding and Prom Comments and Questions

10. My fiancée likes my hair down, so we need to do it down.

9. Can you do my hair like this picture?

8. This does not look exactly like it did for the trial.

7. Do you have any glitter hair spray?

6. What time is it?

5. Do you have time to do one more?

4. Can you spray it good?

3. Can you help me with my headpiece?

2. Champagne and orange juice anyone?

1. Will you take a picture for me?

Chapter 14

Same Time Next Week

Clients who come in once a week to have their hair done are called "standings." They are what we call our "bread and butter" in this industry. I sometimes feel the closest to these clients. They become more friends than clients.

I had one client for eighteen years. Miss Ethel was the best. She was funny, sweet, and very loyal. She was in her mid-eighties when she died. She was the first long time client of mine who passed away. She had a stroke and passed quickly. Her family was as beautiful as she was. For eighteen years I was a part of Miss Ethel's life, and she mine. She saw me date, get married, build my home, and have three children. Her birthday was in November, just like mine, so we were both Scorpios. She was always happy and her husband was a delight. He passed a little more than a year after she did. That was a blessing too because they were a match made in heaven. They had a real love for each other. Miss Ethel loved Nicholas Sparks and *The Notebook* was one of her favorite books/

movies. Her husband was lost without her and she would have been lost without him. Very much like *The Notebook*. I remember at Miss Ethel's viewing I got to meet her entire family. I also remembered that they put pink nail polish on her, which she would have never worn. Miss Ethel always wore red polish! Shoot, I should have told them that! She had a great family. Miss Ethel's husband came over to me at the viewing and said "Amy, I wanted to call you, you should have been the one to do Ethel's hair for the viewing!" I also should have told them to go with red polish and not pink! I screwed up. I actually thought about doing her hair when her daughter called me and told me she had passed, but I just did not want to remember her that way. Maybe that is selfish, but open caskets are not my favorite things. I was thinking about what I should say to Miss Ethel's husband about his request when her daughter came over. She said, "Dad, Amy does not do corpses!" Feuuh, Kyle saved the day. I immediately after that went to take a peek at what she looked like and hoped that someone got her hair right. They did a fine job with her hair. About a month after the funereal, I got a package in the mail. I had always commented to Miss Ethel about how much I loved her purses. She had great taste in handbags. I would pretend to hide them, or steal them while she was in the salon having her hair shampooed. She must have shared that with her family because her daughter sent me her favorite red handbag. What a treasure that is.

Carole is another special one. I see her every week and look forward to hearing what she has to say. I feel that I do not even need a therapist because Carol does the job quite well. She pays me on top if it, which is kind of fun. We talk about books, our families, and anything else that has come to pass during the week. She is never grumpy and is always kind and generous. I love standings like these.

Carole's husband, Charles, is adorable too. He always smells great. One time he dropped Carole off to get her hair done and went to the Wal-

Mart to pass some time. He was standing at one of the aisles when some-one came up from behind him, grabbed him around the waist, ruffled his hair and said something like "How the heck are ya?" This was a case of mistaken identity. While she claimed she thought he was someone else, I knew the truth. I am sure it was his scent. It drives the women wild. After I cut his hair, his scent lingers. One client named Karen picked up his scent and wanted to meet this "Mr. Charles." Carole and Charles are a perfect match. Carole better watch her back though, the women are after her man.

There have been many more standings in my twenty years but these two are my favorite. Some clients have switched to other stylists, and I have gained other clients from other stylists. There is just something spe-cial about that weekly client!

Most people today can do their own hair. I am sure that in twenty more years the styles will be so different that standings will probably be obsolete. If that is the case, and I am still doing hair at sixty, I will look back with fond memories of the ones I called my standings. They are very special people.

Top 10 Fun Things About Standings

10. It's a free therapy session every week.

9. They don't care if your make-up is not always perfect.

8. They remember your birthday.

7. They become your friend.

6. They treat you well at Christmas.

5. They provide steady income.

4. They give you their old purses.

3. They bring you expensive black licorice as a treat.

2. They compliment you on your work.

1. They bring their wonderful smelling husband with them.

Chapter 15

I'm Gonna Wash That Mistake Right Out Of My Hair

I really want to end this book on a funny note. I want my readers to feel like they have not only learned something about hairstylists and clients, but have also laughed. I am willing to do this at my own expense. I have saved the best hair blunders and embarrassing moments for last. I have no problem poking fun at myself. Why not, everyone else does. Where to start?

While I have made my share of mistakes just like any stylist, they are usually fixable. That is the beauty of being a stylist. We can change just about anything and then take it back if we don't like it—except for a haircut. They say the difference between a good haircut and a bad haircut is about three weeks. I have even been to hair shows where the platform artist had his own hair so white/blond that he joked that he never had to get his hair cut. His hair just breaks off. It is all well and fine to do that to our own hair, but not a good thing to do to others. Some situations have made me very uncomfortable over the years. I have uncomfortable stories a plenty. Everyone is bound to make a mistake or two at times, or three, or four.

Did you know that some women know that they are pregnant by the color of their vajayjay? I did not know this bit of information. I found this out when I simply asked one new client how she was doing, and if anything was new with her. She told me that what was "new" was that she was sure she was pregnant because her "who-ha" was pink. I wonder what color her "who-ha" was before she got pregnant. I did not ask. I, myself, was not turning pink but a nice bright red shade at that point. Or maybe green? That entire conversation made me a little nauseated. Yes, her name was "Suzie."

I had a client for whom I tried to lighten her hair and ended up at a point where it all looked gray. She had salt and pepper hair for starters. She wanted more salt than pepper. It turns out that when you lighten pepper you cannot get it to salt. You can get it to salt and seasoned salt, but not pure salt. Trust me on this one.

I thought it would be a great advertisement to make up tee shirts with the salon's name on them. I could give them to all of the young prom girls as a special treat for coming in. I thought this was a great idea. Everyone likes freebees! I gave a handful of these tee shirts away before I realized that a big mistake had been made. Let me be clear when I say I do not condone underage drinking. That being said, I wanted my tee shirts to read "salon" not "saloon." I am still using those shirts as dust rags... all one hundred of them!

What is that smell? It smells like something is burning! "Oh my gosh, Ruby, your hair is on fire!" When Ruby leaned over to shampoo a client, her side ponytail caught fire, thanks to the candle on the shampoo bar. Thank goodness she had a hose close by.

I had one client early in my career who wanted to be blond. She was a natural blond as a kid and desired to stay that way. She was a young girl in her 20s. When I went to grab her hair color I grabbed a level "1" by mistake. A level "1" is a lot different than a level "11." I meant to grab an "11"! A level "1" is black, and a level "11" is a white blond. When I started applying the color I noticed it start to turn. Most of the colors I use start out a pearly white color until they oxidize, so there was no way of knowing that I made a mistake until it started to turn. I rinsed it off right away, claiming that I must have a bad tube of color. It *was* a bad color, a bad tube of color for her. While there have been times that a bad tube of color has ruined a formula, this was not the case. I still remember that day in the salon. I was able to strip the color out but not without many hours of work. Not to mention that for all of the time I spent correcting her hair, I could not even charge her a dime. That just would not have been right!

I once had a stylist in my salon that asked me if she could borrow my clippers. She was unaware that I had changed the blade. She never saw me change it and never thought to look. Bad move. The client was a male with thick hair. She zipped off the back and suddenly went into panic mode. I had changed the blade right before she grabbed my clippers. The blade was a 00000 blade. A five 0 would be equivalent to taking a straight Gillette razor blade to someone's head. He was sporting a Montel in the back of his head and she was sporting beads of sweat dripping down her back. She dealt with it beautifully. She gave him a free haircut and one that would last him an extra month at that. Look at the money she saved him. He was not mad, but I do not remember him ever coming back for his next haircut. He is probably still growing it.

One friend did a haircut on a blond haired gentleman. He had almost pure white hair. His hair was baby fine too. It was so white and fine that she could hardly see it on his face. When she went to clean up the back of his hairline, she continued to the front to trim his sideburns, the same sideburns that grew into his beard. So much for growing that full beard for your ski trip Tom! Sorry about that.

I have another client who shares my name. I was doing Amy's high-lights the same way for a while. We were getting bored with it and de-cided to add some warm tones. I used a product new on the market called Color Graphics. The red additive was supposed to add warm red tones; the blue and green additives were to add cool tones. We were thinking warm. Red on hair with heavy highlights, by the way, actually pulls hot pink, not warm tones. I finished Amy's hair and it was close to 9pm. I was the only girl closing the salon. Since the salon was closing, and Amy was "cool," or shall I say "warm," Amy was willing to leave the salon with "beauty school drop out bright pink Frenchie hair." She agreed to come back in the morning to get it fixed. I did fix it the next day, but she had to pick something up at the mall on her way home that night. She told me her kids laughed at her, and poked fun of her the entire night. They would not even ride the escalator with her. I went home and threw-up the entire night. Or I felt like I was going to throw-up the entire night. I am sure I did not sleep a wink in fear that she would have to wear cot-ton candy hair for the next year.

Wrong scissors: I was in the middle of cutting a client's hair when she had mentioned she would like her very thick hair thinned out. I reached for what I thought were my thinning shears. Well, I was wrong. I went into the back of her hair very close to her scalp and thinned her hair. I thinned it out a lot because I grabbed the wrong shears. A very large chunk of hair close to her scalp fell to the floor. I screamed very loudly, "Oh my gosh!" The client jumped up and said, "WHAT?" I then said, "Oh nothing, I'm just kidding!" All of the stylists around me knew exactly what had just happened. Thankfully, I was not cutting her bangs at the time! I then tried to blend the back to make it look like no mistakes were made. If she knew what had happened, she never let on to it. Nei-ther did I! Her hair was very thick, so I do not think she noticed, but I am sure I skipped lunch that day.

A perm wrapped too tightly will cause breakage. That means the rubber band that is across the perm rod will lie directly on the hair. When you mix a chemical solution and apply it to the perm rod the hair can break right off like a pair of shears have cut it. Someone with very thin, fragile hair is a prime candidate for this. While I have only had it happen to me on a small scale, I have seen it happen on a large scale to others. One girl went home after a stylist's mistake with partly curly, partly spiky hair. That was not a good look at all. But it was a "free" look.

I have also witnessed hair coming out right in the foils. I saw one girl forget about a client that was under the heat lamps for too long and her hair broke entirely off. Or I should say it dissolved. She had bald patches where the foils were. Her hair was long, but she was forced to get her hair cut shorter and her stylist was forced to partake of a large quantity of Imodium. "IBS" at its best! The client was given a year's worth of free hair services, although I do not think she cashed in on this lovely parting gift. Thankfully she did not take the stylist to small claims court either.

When you apply perm solution, be sure to change the wet cotton around a client's neck. Early on in this business I skipped this stage. Skipping this stage allowed me to have the client come back sooner. She came back the next week to hand me the bill for the ointment that the doctor gave her for the bad chemical burn on her neck. Sorry about that one! Always change the cotton. It only takes one time not changing cotton for a chemical burn. It's not worth skipping this step.

If you do your hair fire engine red, just keep your eyebrows their natural color. Crazy neon red brows do not look good on anyone, especially on me. I do not like clowns, remember.

My first pregnancy was a great one, except for the fact that for some reason before I even gave birth I would lactate. It seemed to my pregnant body that my blow dryer sounded like a baby crying. I remember this cute blue shorts set I had. I wore it to death because it was so comfortable. When you are pregnant you want to look cute, but comfort becomes most important. I remember blowing dry a client's hair and out of nowhere I started lactating. Both of my breasts were leaking at the same time. I had two huge circles on my shirt and did not even know it. My client knew it of course. When I was through with her hair she whispered to me, "You might want to go put a smock on! Your breasts are leaking." Instead, can I just get in my car and go home because I am mortified at this point and hormonal to the point of a crying break-down. I was unaware that I could breast feed before I had even met my baby. Well, you can apparently. How embarrassing.

"Do you want your bangs cut?" I asked Jamie. She said, "Yes." She meant the front bang area not new, short bangs cut in. I went right in without even giving it a thought and cut bangs in. She had all one-length hair. For a short time after that, she had all one-length hair with bangs thanks to me. She started to tear up and so did I. I still do her hair and she will have to beg, beg, beg me to cut bangs in if she every wants them. It only takes one time to make that mistake and a half of a second to cut in unwanted bangs.

A client came in with her six-year-old daughter for a haircut. It was summertime and the little girl had very long hair. The mom was tired of the tangles, as was the little girl. This little girl was a tomboy. She loved to hang out with boys and play sports. She even told me she wanted to be a boy and hated anything girly. They noticed a family sitting on the salon sofa waiting for their turn to get a haircut. This mom turned to this family in the waiting area and said to them and me, "This is just how I want you to cut little Ella's hair!" The mom sitting on the sofa had a very cute hair cut. Her hair was in a layered bob just above the shoulder. I agreed that this cut would be cute. I cut the little girl's hair and was about to blow it dry when she burst into tears. "This is not at all the way I asked to have my hair cut," the girl yelled. The mom quickly said to her daughter, "Don't worry Ella, we are not leaving here until Amy gets it right!" Yes, a bit offended at the "until Amy gets it right part." The mother then looked around the salon and pointed to the haircut she desired. This was a miscommunication that I cannot take credit for. While I assumed she wanted this cute layered bob, she actually wanted the haircut of the little boy who was sitting on the sofa next to the Mom. I gave her the Elton John haircut she desired when I realized that she truly wanted to look like a boy, and she was happy. In this case less was more. Less hair was what she desired. This girl said she wanting to be a boy, and now she looked like one. I believe her name was Pat.

I am always one to tell someone if they have something in their teeth. But I must be sure. A friend of mine told a client that she had something in her teeth. She kept saying it, and the client either did not hear her, or ignored her. She did not even see my face, as I was shaking my head "No, don't do it." Little did she know that this client just had a rotten tooth. The client acted as if she did not know what my friend was saying. I am sure she knew the black tooth already existed. Ooops. Much like the pregnancy thing, you must be sure before you speak.

We tend to overlook things to spare clients from embarrassment. I once did a guy's hair in my salon. He was a nice looking guy. I would say he was about a size 36. As a matter of fact, I know he was a 36 because he still had the sticker running down the leg of his brand new jeans. I just could not bear to share.

I also have done hair for clients who must have gotten dressed pretty quickly. One girl had one brown shoe and one black shoe on, just like my middle school chorus teacher used to wear. She never noticed. Another elderly lady had her shirt on inside out. While I usually pay attention to detail, I chose to let these people figure that out for themselves. I know for a fact that this type of thing has happened to me.

Never tell the client that they look like a celebrity unless they look like a beautiful celebrity. My friend Lisa had a client that was a dead ringer for Rosanne Barr. Some things are better left unsaid. Unfortunately I said it.

A local TV weatherman came into the salon to make a hair appointment. I recognized him right away because I had seen him on TV for years. I happened to be at the front desk when he asked for an appointment with Mr. Blizzard. I chuckled, and waited for him to say whom he really wanted to have cut his hair. He said nothing so I said, "No really, whom would you like to make your appointment with?" He failed to see the humor. He again said, "Mr. Blizzard!" Little did I know that his hairstylist's last name was actually "Blizzard." He wanted Mr. Blizzard like he had asked! Now who's the dumb stylist? But what are the odds? Really?

If you buzz your son's hair and he puts the entire video of this on YouTube, make sure he labels it right. While he thinks he has had over 1,000 views because he is so popular, I think the title is what caused people to check it out. The YouTube title, "I get buzzed" may have led some to think he was getting more than a haircut. I will not share this information, however. I prefer to let him think that he is very popular.

I applied color to a client's hair, but for some reason the form-a-la was not as thick as I was used to. It was quite runny. I have no idea why I did not try to thicken it up. They make additives to make a color thicker. I was probably in a hurry so I did not bother.

That was real professional! Back to my ADHD problem.—I was already moving on to the next client. I went ahead with my hyperness and applied this very thin solution to the client's re-growth area. The color happened to be almost black, just the way she liked it. I set her timer and walked away. Why she did not feel this drippy formula dripping down her face I will never know, but she did not. She just sat there and read a magazine. When I went into the color room to tell her to get shampooed, I noticed that the color I had applied had run all the way down her face and met itself in the middle of her neck. One of the stylists asked me why my client was wearing a hair bonnet and I had no clue what she meant. At first glance I too thought she was wearing a bonnet, a dark, black, shiny bonnet. I was like, Huh? When I went to shampoo her, I tried to scrub the wayward color off. It would not come off. It was deeply stained around her chin and neck. It even stained the facial hairs on the side of her face. She had no idea that the day she came in for color, she would leave wearing not just her coat, but a hat as well, a shiny black bonnet to be exact. I like to think that in a couple of days it faded off. At least it covered her gray! I'm not sure if she ever came back for a touch up now that I think about it.

Top 10 Uncomfortable Salon Situation

10. Wiping your nose and not knowing that you have color on your glove.

9. Asking someone if they are ready for their lip wax when they are in for a haircut.

8. The bran muffin and coffee kick in while you are wrapping a perm.

7. When the client you love chooses to get a haircut by the girl in the next chair.

6. Grabbing the wrong scissors.

5. Using the travel coffee mug of the person that left it, and them coming back for it.

4. Mistaking food in the teeth, for rotten teeth.

3. Forgetting to remove the size sticker on your new jeans.

2. Grabbing the wrong tube of color.

1. Farting when you laugh too hard.

Conclusion

So these are the highlights and the lowlights of my twenty years in this industry. I have often said that if I did not have to work for money, and was able to work for fun, I would consider taking a job at the gift shop at the airport. Didn't see that coming did ya? At the airport you see people excited for planes to land so that they can meet up with loved ones, you see people embrace as they leave their loved ones, and you see people that are elated to go on that once in a lifetime trip. That too would be fun. But in reality the hairstylist gets all that and more.

I have the opportunity to make people feel good about themselves by creating that perfect look. I also personally get to hear stories about people's lives, and I have built wonderful friendships. I have learned from my mistakes, and the mistakes of others, and I have gotten a wonderful education on humanity. I have laughed with clients, cried with clients, and have had my own life touched by clients. As a young girl I knew what I wanted to do. I wanted to be an actress/singer/airport gift shop worker. Secondly though, I wanted to be a hairstylist. The first is over-rated, so I am happy to work on my second favorite career. Oh, and I always said that one day I would like to write a book! Two out of three ain't bad! In the future, I look forward to servicing you. For now, I gotta roll. My next client is at the door.

The Funny Comments and Questions Clients Say Over and Over Again

10. If I cut it, will it grow faster?

9. Can you come to my house every morning and do my hair?

8. I want something different, but I don't want to get rid of any length. I do not want layers, and please do not cut in bangs. I want something different though.

7. I need you to do me. When can you do me?

6. I want the gray covered, but I don't want to see roots when it grows in.

5. It never looks the same after I leave.

4. I need a cut and a blow.

3. I don't want a haircut, I want a trim.

2. Can you cut it and see if it's short enough, then cut it again when we're done if I want it shorter?

1. Amy, you changed your hair again?

About the Author

Amy Miller lives in a small rural town in Carroll County, Maryland. She lives in a beautiful home that her husband, Marty, built. They have three children, Chris, Wyatt, and Kendall. Amy spends her days doing hair, and running her kids to dance classes, gymnastics, and baseball games. She spends her nights pounding away on the keyboard of her computer, sending out funny e-mails, and painting the bathroom as her family sleeps. She has a reputation for showing up for baseball games dressed as Vanna White so she can be the one picked to turn the inning scoreboard numbers for the game. She always dresses up as characters for her book club meetings. Yes, she is a bit of an attention seeker. Amy's children have learned not to utter the phrase, "Mom, you are so embarrassing," as it comes with a price. She enjoys comedy, and has been a lifelong fan of Saturday *Night Live*, even when it goes through transitional phases. She continues to stand behind the chair cutting hair, teaching, and entertaining. This is her first book and she has thoroughly enjoyed putting these stories together for you. If you would like to contact Amy please feel free to email her at hairapywithamy5@aol.com.

"There is nothing more rewarding than making people laugh, I hope I have accomplished just that!"

~Amy Miller

THE END

Artwork by Natasha MacNichol